THE INQUISITION IN NEW SPAIN,

1536–1820

The Inquisition in New Spain,

1536–1820

A Documentary History

Edited and Translated by

JOHN F. CHUCHIAK IV

The Johns Hopkins University Press   *Baltimore*

This book was brought to publication with the generous assistance of the College of Humanities and Public Affairs, the History Department, and the Latin American, Caribbean, and Hispanic Studies Program of Missouri State University.

The Johns Hopkins University Press
2715 North Charles Street
Baltimore, Maryland 21218-4363
www.press.jhu.edu

Library of Congress Cataloging-in-Publication Data

The Inquisition in New Spain, 1536–1820 : a documentary history / edited and translated by John F. Chuchiak IV.
p. cm.
Includes bibliographical references and index.
ISBN-13: 978-1-4214-0385-4 (hardcover : alk. paper)
ISBN-13: 978-1-4214-0386-1 (pbk. : alk. paper)
ISBN-10: 1-4214-0385-4 (hardcover : alk. paper)
ISBN-10: 1-4214-0386-2 (pbk. : alk. paper)
1. Inquisition—New Spain—History—Sources. 2. New Spain—Church history—Sources. I. Chuchiak, John F.
BX1740.N49I57 2012
272'.20972—dc23   2011022947

A catalog record for this book is available from the British Library.

Special discounts are available for bulk purchases of this book. For more information, please contact Special Sales at 410-516-6936 or specialsales@ press.jhu.edu.

The Johns Hopkins University Press uses environmentally friendly book materials, including recycled text paper that is composed of at least 30 percent post-consumer waste, whenever possible.

In Memory Of Richard E. Greenleaf (1930–2011)
An Inquisition scholar
A mentor
A friend

CONTENTS

List of Documents   ix
Foreword, *by Asunción Lavrin*   xiii
Preface   xvii
Acknowledgments   xxi
Editor's Note   xxiii

The Holy Office of the Inquisition in New Spain (Mexico): An Introductory
    Study   1

I. **Laws, Regulations, and Instructions concerning the Holy Office**
Regulations concerning the Tribunals of the Holy Office of the Inquisition   57

II. **Documents concerning the Operations and Procedures of the Inquisition in New Spain**
Edicts of Faith of the Inquisition in New Spain   107
Inquisition Prisons and Life in the Cells   122
Administration of Torture in Inquisition Trials   132
Autos-da-fé in New Spain   150
Finances and Assets of the Inquisition in New Spain   186

III. **Selections of Trials and *Procesos de Fe* of the Inquisition in New Spain, 1536–1820**
Blasphemy Trials   205
Bigamy, Polygamy, and Crimes against the Sacrament of Matrimony   218
Trials and Testimonies against Jewish and Crypto-Jewish Practices   235
Trials and Testimonies against Lutherans, Calvinists, and Other Protestants   257
Trials and Testimonies against *Alumbrados* (Illuminati) and Others for Heretical Acts
    and False Revelations   274
Trials and Testimonies against Superstitions, Sorcery, and Magical Practices   292
Trials and Testimonies against the Use of Peyote and Other Herbs and Plants
    for Divination   308
Trials and Testimonies Related to Prohibited Books   318

Glossary   343
Notes   357
Selected Bibliography   395
Index   415

Figures appear following page 202.

DOCUMENTS

1. Instructions of the Holy Office of the Inquisition Compiled by Order of the Illustrious and Reverend Lord Don Fernando de Valdés, Archbishop of Seville and Apostolic Inquisitor (Toledo, 1561)   59

2. Royal Order Issued by King Philip II Establishing the Foundation of the Holy Office of the Inquisition in the Indies (Madrid, 1569)   81

3. Instructions of the Illustrious Lord Cardinal Don Diego de Espinosa, Inquisitor General, for the Establishment of the Inquisition in New Spain (Madrid, 1570)   82

4. Instructions and the Order That Should Be Maintained and Followed by Commissaries of the Holy Office of the Inquisition in New Spain (Madrid, 1667)   91

5. General Rules and Orders Taken from the New Index of Prohibited and Purged Books for the Spanish Catholic Kingdoms of King Philip IV Written by Don Antonio Zapata, Inquisitor General (Seville, 1632)   98

6. Edict of Faith Issued by Inquisitor Dr. Pedro Moya de Contreras (Mexico City, 1576)   108

7. Edict of Faith That Requires All to Denounce the Practitioners of Astrology, Necromancy, Geomancy, Hydromancy, Pyromancy, and Chiromancy, as well as Anyone Who Possesses Books on These Themes (Mexico City, 1616)   110

8. Edict of Faith concerning the Illicit Use of Peyote (Mexico City, 1620)   113

9. Edict of Faith against Prohibited Books (Mexico City, 1621)   114

10. Edict of Faith concerning the Extirpation of the Abuses Committed by Priest Confessors against the Honesty and Purity of the Sacrament of Confession (Mexico City, 1783)   116

11. The Inquisition's Edict of Denunciation against the Priest Miguel Hidalgo y Costilla (Mexico City, 1810)   118

12. Register and Account of the Pesos Spent by Order of Their Lordships in Order to Pay for Extraordinary Rations to the Following Prisoners (Mexico City, 1601)   124

13. Register of Rations Given to Prisoners in the Prisons of This Inquisition, Order for Payment, and Receipt during Part of the Year (Mexico City, 1615)   125

14. Letter from Inquisitor Pedro Medina Rico, concerning the Plan and Layout of the Palace of the Tribunal of the Inquisition of Mexico (Mexico City, 1661)   128

15. Letter and Description of the Interior of the Palace of the Extinct Tribunal of the
    Holy Office of the Inquisition of New Spain (Mexico City, 1820)   129

16. Instructions for Administering Questioning under Torture using the Rack (Madrid,
    Sixteenth Century)   135

17. Inquisition Trial against Michael Morgan, Englishman and One of Those Who Came
    with the Armada of John Hawkins (Mexico City, 1572–1574)   138

18. Extract of the Sentence and Torture Session, Taken from the Proceedings of the
    Tribunal of the Holy Office against Rodrígo Franco Taváres, Native of Fondón, a
    Neighborhood of the Village of Cubillana, in Portugal, an Ambulant Merchant, for
    the Suspected Heresy of Being a Judaizer (Mexico City, 1601)   144

19. Brief Relation of the Auto-da-fé (Mexico City, 1574)   154

20. Relation of the Order That Has Been Observed in the Holy Office of the Inquisition
    of New Spain since Its Founding on November 4, 1571, concerning the Celebrations
    of the Public Autos-da-fé (Mexico City, 1594)   155

21. Relation of the Auto-da-fé That Was Celebrated in the City of Mexico in the Major
    Plaza on the Second Sunday of Advent (Mexico City, 1596)   165

22. Relation of the Preliminary Preparations for the Small Public Particular Auto-da-fé
    Celebrated with Thirteen Prisoners in the Church and Convent of Santo Domingo
    on June 1, 1783 (Mexico City, 1783)   177

23. Register and Account of the Pesos that I, Juan de León Plaza, Alcaide of the
    Secret Prisons of this Holy Office, Have Paid for Necessary Things for the
    Operation of the Prisons by Order of Your Lordships from the 17th of July 1599
    When I Was Received as the Said Jailer until the End of July 1600 (Mexico City,
    1599–1600)   187

24. Relation of What Has Been Spent since the 8th of January 1616 in the Purchase of
    Pens, Ink, String, Wafers, Canvas, and Other Miscellaneous Items for Use in the
    Chamber of the Secret of This Holy Office (Mexico City, 1616–1617)   192

25. Documents Relating to the Making of an Inventory of the Assets, Goods, and Estate
    of the Palace of the Extinguished Tribunal of the Holy Office of the Inquisition of
    New Spain (Mexico City, 1814)   194

26. Documents of the Minister of Finance of the Intendancy of Mexico concerning the
    List of the Employees of the Extinguished Tribunal of the Inquisition (Mexico City,
    1823)   198

27. Inquisition Trial and Proceedings against Juan de Pórras, for Gambling and
    Blasphemy (Mexico City, 1536)   206

28. Inquisition Trial and Proceedings against the Tailor Juan de Villate for Blasphemy
    and Heretical Propositions (Mexico City, 1539)   209

29. Self-Denunciation and Sentence against Alonso Bueno for the Crime of Blasphemy
    (Mexico City, 1541)   213

30. Inquisition Testimony against Pascuala, a Mulatta Slave on the Sugar Plantation of
    Tlacomulco in the Region of Cuernavaca, for the Crime of Blasphemy (Tlacomulco,
    Cuernavaca, 1710)   214

31. Inquisition Trial against María de Sotomayor, for the Crime of Polygamy (Mexico
    City, 1538–1540)   219

32. Proceedings before the Holy Office of the Inquisition against Nuño Méndez for the Crime of Incestuous Liaisons (Mexico City, 1537–1538) 227

33. Documents and Accusations Presented to the Commissariat of the Inquisition in the Province of Yucatan by the Maya Villagers of the Town of Hocaba against Their Parish Priest, Padre Cristóbal de Valencia, for the Crime of Solicitation, Fornication, and Other Nefarious Acts against Nature (Merida, Yucatan, 1609) 230

34. Proceedings before the Holy Office of the Inquisition against the Barber Juan de Salamanca for the Crime of Judaism, or Jewish Practices (Mexico City, 1539) 237

35. Selected Autos and Proceedings of the Second Trial against Luis de Carvajal the Younger, Reconciled by This Holy Office as a Judaizer, a Relapsed Practitioner of Judaism, and a Formal Heretic (Mexico City, 1594–1596) 240

36. Relation of the Prisoners of This Holy Office of the Inquisition in Mexico Who Have Been Penanced and Have Been Punished in Two Autos-da-fé That Have Been Celebrated Along with Others for Their Observance of the Laws of Moses and Subsequently Exiled Permanently from These Kingdoms and Provinces of New Spain and Peru (Mexico City, 1647) 245

37. Summary Report on the Visitation and Examination of the Proceedings of the Holy Office of the Inquisition in New Spain, by Don Pedro de Medina Rico, Citing the Inconsistencies, Negligence, and Violations of Inquisitorial Procedures in the Trials of Faith Pursued by the Said Inquisition against Various Persons and Prisoners in the Secret Jails of the Holy Office (Mexico City, 1656) 249

38. Inquisition Trial against Cristóbal Miguel, the Official Who Separates Out the Gold from the Silver, Reconciled by This Holy Office for Believing in the Sect of Calvin and Who Continues to Ride on Horseback and Wear Silk and Carry Arms, Things Forbidden to Those Who Have Received Penance from the Holy Office (Mexico City, 1604) 259

39. Documents Pertaining to the Reconciliation to Our Holy Catholic Faith of Joshua Morton, Native of England and Protestant Heretic Who Has Followed the Rites of the Anglican Church (Mexico City, 1720) 264

40. Documents Pertaining to the Reconciliation to Our Holy Catholic Faith of Jacob Fors, Native of Sweden and a Lutheran Heretic (Mexico City, 1720) 267

41. Spontaneous Denunciation Made against Himself by Edward Rivet, Native of England, for Having Been Raised and Lived in the Sect of the Quakers, or Tremblers, Seeking to Be Reincorporated to the Fold of Our Holy Catholic Faith (Mexico City, 1719) 270

42. Inquisition Proceedings against Padre Fray Juan de Santa Ana, a Religious Carmelite Friar, for Dreams, Revelations, and Other Disparate Prophesies (Mexico City, 1690–1691) 275

43. Inquisition Trial Proceedings against Tomasa González, Who Wears the Habit of a *Beata,* for Suspicions of Being an *Alumbrada* (Aguascalientes, 1692–1695) 284

44. Trial Proceedings against María de Armenta, for the Crimes of Sorcery and Witchcraft Involving a Demonic Pact (Mexico City, 1536–1537) 293

45. Trial Proceedings against Br. Pedro Ruiz Calderón, Clergyman, for Superstitions, Witchcraft, and Practicing the Black Arts of Necromancy (Mexico City, 1540) 299

46. Denunciation against María de Bárcena, the Wife of Medina the Tailor, for Suspected Sorcery and Sexual Magic (Mexico City, 1570–1572)   302

47. Denunciation against Several Acts of Supposed Sorcery and Witchcraft Presented by Doña Juana Rosado (Merida, Yucatan, 1672)   303

48. Denunciation against Several Acts of Supposed Sorcery and Sexual Magic Presented by Lorenza Márquez (Merida, Yucatan, 1672)   305

49. Denunciation and Inquisition Investigations and Documents concerning the Prohibited Herb and Hallucinogen Pipiltzintzintli, Which Was Discovered in the Village of Tepepan and Xochilmilco, Valley of Mexico (Tepepan, Xochimilco, 1698)   309

50. Inquisition Trial against a Mulatta Named María, for the Use of the Herb Pipiltzintzintli and Other Diverse Charges (Texcoco, 1704)   313

51. Correspondence of the Commissary of the Holy Office of the Inquisition in the Province of Yucatan with the Inquisitors in the City of Mexico concerning Prohibited Books, (Merida, Yucatan, 1574–1587)   320

52. Order and Information Given to the Commissaries of the Inquisition concerning Prohibited Books in the Kingdom of New Spain (Mexico City, 1587)   322

53. Documents Pertaining to Licenciado Don Manuel Abad Queipo's Petition to Request a License to Read Prohibited Books (Valladolid [now Morelia], Michoacan, 1796)   323

54. Documents and Papers concerning Several Printed Cloths or Handkerchiefs Remitted to this Holy Office by the Chief Constable of the City of Veracruz Which Contain Inscriptions in the English Language (Veracruz, 1775)   325

55. Documents Relating to the Petition of the Surgeon and Doctor Don Anacleto Rodríguez Requesting Permission to Read Prohibited Books (Veracruz, 1799)   333

56. License to Read Prohibited Books Issued to Don Josef García Armenteros, Consul of the Royal Merchant Guild of the Philippines and Royal Historian, so That He May Acquire, Have, and Read All Books concerning Political and Natural History Forbidden by the Holy Office (Madrid, 1799)   336

57. Self-Denunciation of Don José Ignacio Sánchez concerning His Support for the Miguel Hidalgo Revolt (Mexico City, 1811)   337

FOREWORD

Throughout time, historians of all beliefs have approached the Inquisition with much concern about ever being able to write an unbiased or complete history of this enigmatic and challenging institution. After slowly spreading across Catholic Europe, it eventually reached the "new" worlds annexed to European religion by means of conquest and expansion in the sixteenth century. The Spanish Inquisition re-created itself in the Americas in only three locations, but its influence in shaping the religious culture of Spanish America belied the small number of offices in such a vast territory. Colonial Mexico (the Viceroyalty of New Spain) was the most important and remains the best documented of the three inquisitorial offices.

In the past four decades, historians in several countries have reapproached the Inquisition armed with new questions and new methodologies in search of social, political, and economic meanings hidden in the apparent uniformity of inquisitorial procedures. Research remains open-ended and promises further understanding of viceregal society and the lives of those people directly or indirectly affected by the institution. For students of history at all levels who wish to learn how to read and understand the records of the institution, Chuchiak's *The Inquisition in New Spain, 1536–1820: A Documentary History* provides a guide into the intricacies of the data created by the Holy Office.

For centuries, as Chuchiak states, the Inquisition has been feared and hated. It is the type of institution about which most people have strong feelings but relatively little sound knowledge. This was not an institution to be loved but to be in awe of. Looking at itself, the Inquisition aspired to be feared but not hated and advised its members to act with temperance and gentility. Reaching such a sanguine outlook was, in itself, an indication of the climate of the times. Late medieval and early modern societies relied on a sufficient level of force to maintain social order and respect for the authority of the rulers, and most people accepted those premises. As Catholic Christianity gained the upper hand in the Spanish peninsula and expanded into the New World in times of religious crisis in Europe, the spirit of the law applicable to transgressors was understood as necessarily intolerant for the benefit of higher ends: the salvation of Christian souls. Respect for the "right" faith was compulsory and not negotiable. Unsurprisingly, the inquisitors could see a great deal of good about themselves and their institution.

Reading and analyzing the texts produced by the Inquisition is essential for understanding it. With this anthology in hand, readers will have a trustworthy basis on which to
learn about this institution and make informed judgments about its goals, its methods,
and its accomplishments. Understanding the documents produced by the Inquisition is no
easy task given the subtle forms of encodement in the language, the procedures peculiar to
the age, and, above all, the mentality guiding those who enforced the laws that aimed at
safeguarding the faith. To guide and kindle the interest of a personal search into the practices of the Mexican Inquisition, John Chuchiak has arranged a selection of representative
documents that reflect some of its concerns, goals, and procedures. The Inquisition's internal laws and regulations shed light on the nature of civil and criminal legislation that
was at the base of the inquisitorial processes. These rules formed a body of nuanced complexity. The Inquisition was a tribunal of justice and, as such, required a firm legal foundation, clearly spelled procedural rules, and a notion of certainty about the expected outcome
of any transgression to its own body of laws. The predictability of the process guaranteed
the respect and fear it commanded among the population. Indeed, the stated objective
of the instructions to inquisitors was to raise such feelings about the institution: it re-
flected the set of checks that made its members aware of the need for collegiality in their
activities and of the need to observe the procedural requirements applicable to each and
every case put under their jurisdiction.

The ideological and theological bases of the Inquisition are contained in the edicts of
faith. The exclusionary nature of the edicts provides a map to the institution's standing
against any person or idea that appeared to depart from the straight line of Catholic canonical beliefs. Their misuse or misinterpretation would bring condemnation. The as-
sumption that words or practices contrary to the established faith could only be the product of evil forces explains them as punishable crimes. The spectrum of such actions was
wide, covering popular divination practices, substance abuse, and sexual misconduct.
Members of the church were subject to inquisitorial inquiry. Nobody was exempt from the
duty to respect the established forms of belief and appropriate behavior. Unfortunately,
dissent against the faith brought about the worst features of the rigid system. Transgression, real or perceived, led to the dismal inquisitorial jails and the prospects of torture that
appall contemporary readers but reflect practices with deep roots in Western history. The
legal and recorded implementation of torture helped the Inquisition earn its lugubrious
reputation. Several hundred years had to pass before condemnation of such practices became part of progressive legal systems.

The documents on dissenters focus on the most important targets of the Inquisition,
and en masse they allow the reader to be as close as one can be to their words, explanations, and sometimes defiant posturing. Among them were those who denied Catholicism, such as Jews and Protestants, or those who blasphemed, such as slaves, women, and
casta members. The strong animosity created in Spain against religious dissenters within
its own borders, and even more so in the rest of Europe, explains the conduct of the trials
carried against them in the New World. Among those dissenters, the weaker elements of
colonial society were more liable to feel the rod of punishment on their own flesh because
their lack of knowledge about the legal system made them more vulnerable. They were
also charged more frequently with violations of morality than of the faith, which suggests

lapses in personal behavior that civil and ecclesiastic authorities deemed inappropriate and subversive, such as the use of hallucinogenic substances and sexual sorcery. Of course, because individuals and communities could use the institution for their own means by raising false accusations on targeted persons, inquisitorial inquiries could be a double-edged tool.

The public spectacles or autos-da-fé were not as important as the daily routine and the surveillance of the mind, but they still capture the imagination of posterity because, unlike the macabre reality of torture, which was private, the public spectacle embodied a powerful message and involved mass participation. The reader should not conclude that the Inquisition was a daily concern of most colonial subjects. The majority of them lived their lives without personal or public encounters with the institution. Transgressors escaped surveillance due to distance or cunning personal evasion of any outward sign of dissent, and in the course of time the institution itself refocused its attention on matters of a political and intellectual nature. It is undeniable that this pillar of colonial society exercised strong cultural and religious influence for nearly three hundred years. Even after its dissolution, it continues to mesmerize us and challenge us to understand its logic and its behavior. This work will enable us to engage in that process.

ASUNCIÓN LAVRIN
Professor Emeritus of History
Arizona State University

PREFACE

Oh, the Holy Office is so terrible, that if it did not exist in this Kingdom, I could count the Christians on these fingers.

Luis de Carvajal "El Mozo," 1596 (perished in the auto-da-fé of December 8, 1596)

The Inquisition. Just the word itself evokes, to the modern reader, endless images of torment, violence, corruption, and intolerance. In short, the Inquisition is something that we may believe we know very well. But what do we actually know about the Inquisition, its ministers, its procedures? Few scholars, or even polemicists, have attempted to step back and examine the Holy Office of the Inquisition and analyze what it was, what it hoped to do, and how it actually functioned. The Inquisition scholar Henry Charles Lea, himself one of the founders of Inquisition studies, echoed the words of one of his major sources, Juan Antonio de Llorente, when he wrote concerning his own study of the Holy Office:

> There can be no finality in a history resting on so vast a mass of unedited documents and I do not flatter myself that I have accomplished such a result, but I am not without hope that what I have drawn from them and from the labors of previous scholars has enabled me to present a fairly accurate survey of one of the most remarkable organizations recorded in human annals.[1]

Long before Henry Charles Lea, Llorente, who had been an Inquisition commissary and the general secretary of the Suprema in Madrid before he wrote his own history of the Holy Office, had proclaimed, "No one could write a complete and authentic history of the Inquisition who was not either an Inquisitor or secretary of the Holy Office."[2] Llorente knew this well, because he had technically been both, and although his own work remained polemical and filled with his own acquired biases against the tribunal, he had access to a vast amount of archival information and knew that as long as most remained unedited, his history would be incomplete.[3] With this notion in mind, and with a desire to give the modern English-language student of the Inquisition access to a larger corpus of primary sources and a better perspective on the types of documents and Inquisition materials available for the study of the region of New Spain, we present this documentary history and selections of translated Inquisition documents.

The Purpose of This Book

In this volume, I offer a collection of translated primary-source documents written by and about the people who made up the diverse multiethnic society of colonial Mexico, or New Spain. The documents published here reveal the views of their authors, both the inquisitors and those they arrested and tried for heresy, as well as the historical context in which they were written and the major religious and cultural developments and controversies of their time. Reading these documents allows the student to gain a depth and breadth of understanding of the events, ideas, and experiences of those colonists of Mexico who found themselves involved in religious and politically contentious conflicts with the Catholic Church in New Spain.

Although designed for undergraduate and graduate students of the Inquisition and colonial Latin American history, this collection of documents will also be of interest to the general reader who wishes to learn more about the Inquisition in New Spain, a territory that stretched from the southwestern portion of the present-day United States into Florida (and later Louisiana) and all the way into Central America to the borders of modern Panama.

The initial idea for this volume came out of a senior seminar I taught in 1999. In order to give my students access to primary sources in English, I translated a large number of these New World documents. Since that time, each semester that I taught a course on the Inquisition or colonial Mexican history I realized the need for a corpus of translated documents for the study of the Inquisition. In 2006 Lu Ann Homza published her excellent book *The Spanish Inquisition, 1478–1614: An Anthology of Sources,* which provided a significant collection of translated documents for the early foundational period of the Spanish Inquisition. My hope is that the present book not only fills a similar gap for the New World but also illustrates the cultural and religious attitudes of the Spanish, indigenous, African, and mestizo peoples of colonial Mexico.

Source Survival

In the New World, the Spanish crown established three separate tribunals of the Inquisition: the Inquisition in New Spain, with its headquarters in Mexico City, which controlled the entire territory of Spanish North America south to Panama; and two other tribunals that controlled Spanish South America: one in Lima, Peru, and another in Cartagena, Colombia. With the official decree in the early nineteenth century to abolish the Inquisition, the various palaces and buildings that held these tribunals were looted, sacked, and destroyed. Although the archives of the Inquisition in New Spain and Peru survived for the most part, the tribunal of Cartagena de Indias was completely destroyed, leaving only a small collection of documents concerning this tribunal extant in those copies of the trial transcripts and documents remitted back to Spain and now held in the Archivo Histórico Nacional in Madrid, Spain.

The fifty-seven documents selected, edited, and translated here are ordered chronologically by theme. The documents come mostly from the surviving archives of the Inquisition in New Spain currently housed in the Archivo General de la Nación in Mexico City. As one of these three special tribunals of the Inquisition established in the Spanish New

World, the archive of the Inquisition of New Spain has been, for the most part, remarkably well conserved.[4] The archive consists of more than 1,555 bound volumes (called *legajos*) containing documents dating from 1522 to 1820, including those from the primitive monastic and episcopal inquisitions that operated until the arrival of a formal Inquisition Tribunal in 1571.[5] Contained in this collection are all of the surviving documents, trials, and account books of the inquisitors, prosecuting attorneys, notaries, constables, jailers, and accountants of the Inquisition in New Spain. Five additional volumes of Inquisition edicts of faith covering the period from 1603 to 1820 also exist, along with 147 volumes of account books and financial records of the fiscal office.[6] According to the Spanish Inquisition scholar Virgilio Pinto Crespo, this archive of the Inquisition of New Spain contains "the largest and most important collection of Inquisition documents outside of Spain."[7] The archive in Mexico City is exceptionally well organized and easy to consult with detailed online guides and other published indexes to the collection. The Inquisition archive in Lima, Peru, has also survived but is not as large or inclusive.

Selection of the Documents

The selected sources published here offer a surprisingly diverse panorama of actors, events, and ideas that came into contact and conflict in the central arena of religious faith controlled by the Inquisition in New Spain. The chosen documents were selected for their representative character and for their geographical and temporal diversity because they cover the entire period of inquisitorial proceedings in New Spain. The documents themselves offer a varied collection of royal orders, inquisition manuals, instructions, edicts of faith, and documents concerning the autos-da-fé, along with sources dealing with inquisition finances and a representative selection of denunciations, investigations, and trials. The documents are published for the most part unabridged with a few noted exceptions. The limitations of space made it necessary to choose documents that were brief but fairly complete and representative of a typical type or genre. The final documents selected illustrate the various types of sources produced by the Inquisition in New Spain and the types of cases that the tribunal most routinely conducted.

Similarly, most of the documents in this volume are published for the first time in any language. Only five have appeared in print before, and all are in rare and hard-to-find Spanish-language publications from Mexico City. With the exception of abridged selections of Fernando de Valdes's 1561 *Instructions* previously translated and published by Lu Ann Homza in her 2006 anthology, the documents contained herein have not been translated or published before in English. All of the translations in this volume of edited primary sources are my own. In most cases, I attempted to work with the original documents whenever possible. Thus, a majority of the documents were transcribed and then translated into English, working from the original primary sources. Only a few of the documents were translated from several early Spanish transcriptions of the originals belonging to the Richard E. Greenleaf collection or from the author's own private collection.

In terms of introducing the documents, I opted for brevity. It is my intention to avoid introducing the various translated documents with more than a brief contextual introduction so as not to dissuade students from interpreting and analyzing the individual documents on their own. Unfamiliar terms, concepts, and ideas are often explained in an accompanying note or in the glossary at the end of the volume. It is also my intention to let the voices of the people who found themselves swept up into the repressive apparatus of the Inquisition in New Spain speak for themselves. In most cases, in my translations I attempt to preserve as much of the flavor of the original documents as possible without editing or abbreviating them excessively, except for an eye toward general intelligibility and coherence in terms of the flow of sentences and the breakup of paragraphs that in their original manuscript source do not have either standardized punctuation or spellings. As the reader will see, the documents selected for this volume give us rare glimpses into the daily lives, thoughts, beliefs, and fears of the Spanish, indigenous, African, and mestizo people of the region of New Spain.

Division of the Volume

A selection of the most important laws, manuals, and regulations concerning the Inquisition, including the special instructions issued by the inquisitor general for the establishment of the Inquisition in New Spain, appears in the first part. This section also contains instructions issued by the Inquisition to its many commissary judges who operated in distant outlying regions, far from the seat of the tribunal in Mexico City.

In the second part, a representative selection of primary sources includes several important edicts of faith, materials concerning the Inquisition's prisons that illustrate the life of the prisoners in the cells, and documents related to the administration of torture during the proceedings and other selections related to the sentencing and public punishments handed out at the many autos-da-fé held in New Spain.

The third and final section contains documents representing the trials, denunciations, and investigations that were initiated in response to suspected heresy and other crimes against the faith. It covers trials and documents as varied as those concerning bigamy, blasphemy, and other minor crimes, as well as more serious allegations and proceedings against suspected Protestants and Judaizers. The actors and perspectives contained in this selection of documents reveal not only the complexity of the cultural mosaic in New Spain from the sixteenth to the nineteenth centuries but also the diversity of ethnic responses to both religious instruction and coercion.

ACKNOWLEDGMENTS

In the writing of this book I owe acknowledgments to a countless number of people, without whom the volume would never have seen the light of day. First and foremost I must acknowledge the debt, both scholarly and personally, that I owe the late Richard E. Greenleaf, the France V. Scholes Chair of Colonial Latin American History emeritus at Tulane University. Not only his passion for studying the Inquisition but also his sense of humor and mentorship have served me well in choosing the path that I have followed. I also owe a personal and academic debt to Victoria R. Bricker, Guillermo Nánez-Falcón, Gene S. Yeager, Judy Maxwell, the late Munro Edmonson, and many others at Tulane University who over the years have helped to keep my enthusiasm for colonial history going strong.

Nevertheless, I first started my serious study of colonial Mexican history when I was an undergraduate at Virginia Tech, and I benefited greatly from my early mentor there, Linda Arnold. Without her encouragement, unstinting generosity with her time, and her willingness to share her expertise on all things related to the Mexican archives, I do not think that I would have chosen this career. Now, it is thanks to her that I can't see myself doing anything else.

I want to thank several of my fellow graduate students and friends who studied with me at Tulane University and encouraged me along the way, especially Thomas M. Edsall, Linda Curcio-Nagy, Servando Hinojosa, Jimmy Huck, Michael Polushin, Daniel Dwyer, Daniel Castro, Karen Racine, Douglas Keberlein, William Connell, and Juan Manuel de la Serna for their support, early advice, and encouragement throughout the years.

I owe a personal and scholarly debt to many of my colleagues and friends in the field. I especially want to thank Asunción Lavrin, Stafford Poole, Matthew Restall, Kevin Gosner, John F. Schwaller, Kevin Terraciano, Kris Lane, Ben Vinson, and Michael Francis. In particular I must also recognize my fellow scholars of the Inquisition, including Solange Alberro, Stanley Hordes, Javier Villa-Flores, Martin Nesvig, Martha Few, and Bob Ferry, for their inspiration and support over the years. In Mexico City, I owe a special debt to Michel Oudijk and Maria Castañeda de la Paz, who have not only shared their friendship but also generously shared their home and their research experience. In Spain, special thanks are also due to Manuela Cristina García Bernal and Julián Ruiz Rivera. In Merida, Yucatan, I owe a special debt of gratitude to Michel Antochiw, Sergio Quezada, Ines Oríz Yam, Ruth Gubler, Roque Pech, Ema Dolores Uhu de Pech, and many others for their invaluable support. I also want to express my gratitude to several of my younger colleagues who have helped to shape and influence both this book and my own present research, including Mark Lentz, Ryan Kashanipour, Richard Conway, Robert Schwaller, and Mark Christensen, and many other countless friends and supporters. Without the support and encouragement of all of these people, I would not have completed this book.

Several institutions provided financial and research support for the publication of this book, including Missouri State University's Department of History and the College of Humanities and Public Affairs, as well as the Honors College. I also wish to thank the staffs and directors of the Archivo General de la Nación in Mexico City, the Archivo General de las Indias in Seville (especially Pilar Lázaro de la Escosura), and the Archivo Histórico Nacional in Madrid for their aid and their support in conducting the research for this book.

I am especially thankful for the hard work, encouragement, and endless labors of Robin Gold, at Forbes Mill Press, for her tireless efforts in the early shaping of this manuscript. Without her constant prodding, her artistic flair, and her generally awesome disposition, I am sure I would never have finished this project that began so long ago.

The late Henry Y. K. Tom, as executive editor of the Johns Hopkins University Press, offered his support, encouragement, and editorial advice throughout the earlier stages of the life of this manuscript, and I am very grateful and lucky to have had the support. Thanks to our correspondence, and the helpful comments of the external reviewers, this book has improved and developed along the way. News of his untimely death saddened me, and I am sure that I am not the only one to say that he will be sorely missed.

Similarly, Suzanne Flinchbaugh at the Johns Hopkins University Press helped guide this manuscript through the publication process. I must acknowledge her personal advice and other correspondence, which helped me through some difficult times in the past year. I also owe thanks to the other important editors and staff at JHU Press, such as Juliana McCarthy, Deborah Bors, and others who helped in the production of this book. A special note of thanks is also due to Brian MacDonald for his invaluable work as copyeditor on this manuscript. His detailed review and meticulous copyediting have made the finished product a much better book.

I also want to thank my parents, John Chuchiak III and Patricia Chuchiak, for their long years of support for me and my chosen career as an "academic." Without them I am sure I would not be who I am today.

And finally, to my wife, Argelia Segovia Liga. I am deeply indebted to her for contributing much of the artwork and illustrations for this book. She accepted many sleepless nights and time spent away from her because of the demands of this book. For me, no words can express the debt that I owe to her.

No doubt the reader may yet find errors, omissions, and oversimplifications, for which I take absolute responsibility, as is customary, while still hoping that the material published here will be enough to stimulate further interest and future study of the history of the Mexican Inquisition.

EDITOR'S NOTE

All foreign terms other than proper nouns are italicized, and some are annotated with glosses and definitions where appropriate. A separate glossary of terms used in Inquisition documents is provided as an appendix. In an attempt to make it easier for the modern reader, I have modernized most spelling conventions from the original documents, and I have translated and resolved all abbreviations and scribal errors. In the translations of the original documents, I have also chosen to divide the text into paragraphs and break up longer sentences, adding punctuation that was often missing in the original documents. Occasional notes or brief explanations in the documents themselves are added in brackets. Any errors of paleographical transcription or translation are entirely my own.

THE INQUISITION IN NEW SPAIN,

1536–1820

The Holy Office of the Inquisition
in New Spain (Mexico)
An Introductory Study

What Was the Inquisition?

The term *inquisition* comes from the Latin word *inquisitio*, meaning inquiry or investigation.[1] Technically speaking, an inquisition was a formal judicial trial or procedure used by medieval and early modern courts throughout Europe. This trial process derived from pre-Christian Roman law and procedures,[2] evolved during the Middle Ages, and emerged out of a central conflict between two opposing theories of criminal law: the accusatorial (or adversarial) method of legal procedures and the inquisitorial trial method. In the accusatorial or adversarial method of trial procedure, the judge served as an impartial arbiter between the accuser and the accused in a criminal case.[3] The burden of proof rested on the state, and the judges conducted the entire trial process publicly. To start the process of an accusatorial trial, someone had to make a formal accusation against someone else. During the Middle Ages, this type of trial procedure required the accuser to prove the validity of his or her accusation, and the courts severely punished those who made false or unsubstantiated accusations. The court considered the accused, in these cases, innocent until proven guilty.

In contrast, in the inquisitorial system there was no accuser, and the judge, instead of remaining impartial, investigated and prosecuted the crimes of the suspect. The church courts or "inquisitions" that later formed to investigate and punish heresy against the church's established beliefs operated under this system of trial procedure. The inquisitorial method of trial procedure gave a great amount of power and independence to the investigating judge. As Richard Kagan and Abigail Dyer note, this inquisitorial procedure "empowered the presiding judge or judges to order arrests, gather evidence, interrogate witnesses, and render judgment, that is to direct the entire court proceeding."[4] The judge in these inquisitorial proceedings became both the investigator and the prosecutor of the suspected heretic, who was considered at the outset guilty and whose innocence he himself had to prove to the investigating judge. In these inquisitorial trials, the proceedings were not public but rather were held and conducted in secrecy. Similarly, those who reported or denounced heretical acts to the inquisitorial judge served more as "witnesses" than as formal accusers, and as witnesses in these secret inquisitorial trials, they were given anonymity, which protected them from revenge or retribution from the suspected heretic. Withholding the names of the witnesses, however, often hampered the suspected heretics' ability to successfully defend themselves and prove their innocence. At the same time, the secrecy involved in withholding the names of witnesses from the accused heretic often led to many abuses, such as allowing witnesses with personal enmity and animosity against the accused to successfully pursue personal revenge against the suspect without the fear of their identity being revealed.[5]

Regardless of the apparent injustices in inquisitorial trial procedures, by the later Middle Ages this method of trial proceedings had become the dominant form of judicial procedures in ecclesiastical and heresy cases. Pope Gregory IX established the first formal ecclesiastical Inquisition in 1231 as a tribunal to combat several heretical movements of the later Middle Ages. Before that time, the job of punishing crimes against the faith using this inquisitorial method of trial procedure belonged to the bishops in their ordinary episcopal courts. Edward Peters successfully argued that, "in some respects, it was the failure of the ordinary episcopal tribunals that . . . led to the creation of the professional inquisitor."[6] Pope Gregory IX, seeing the bishops burdened by their pastoral duties, created tribunals throughout France, Germany, and Italy. Spain, busy in its wars of reconquest against the Moors, had no formal inquisition during the medieval period.[7] Later, however, Pope Sixtus IV, at the request of King Ferdinand of Aragon and Queen Isabella of Castile, established an independent Spanish Inquisition in 1478 that served as the model for the Inquisition in the Americas.[8]

From its initial founding, a unique aspect of the Spanish Inquisition was its virtual independence from papal control. The pope conceded to the Catholic monarchs the privilege of royal patronage (*patronato*) in 1508, giving them control over the nomination of the Inquisition's personnel in Spain and the Americas.[9] Although in theory the Inquisition was an ecclesiastical institution, the appointment of inquisitors and other functionaries became the privilege of the secular monarch.

In Europe, the Inquisition had undergone a great amount of change from its inception in the thirteenth century to its establishment in Spain. Once transplanted in the New World, the Inquisition again experienced change as it faced the problems of religious heterodoxy in a new environment.

The Inquisition and Heresy

God was the first inquisitor.

Ludovicus de Paramo, *De Origine et Progressu Officii Sanctae Inquisitionis*, 1598

In its formal Roman Catholic and theological definition, *heresy* refers to a sin committed by one who, having been baptized a Christian, continues to deny or doubt any of the truths or beliefs that one is under obligation under divine and Catholic faith to believe.[10] The word itself is derived from the Greek word *haeresis*, a term that means to make a choice or "to select," and the term *heretic* came to be employed to describe those persons who chose to sustain opinions or beliefs contrary to the Christian faith and the Catholic Church's teachings.[11]

The idea of heresy as an evil or a sin emerged in the struggles against a number of major heresies that the early Christian Church fought during the fourth through the eighth century, which resulted in a series of church councils that condemned various false doctrines and formulated fundamental aspects of traditional Christian orthodoxy.[12] For the Catholic Church and the Inquisition, a heretic was a baptized professing Catholic who chose to set aside the truth of the divinely inspired teachings of the Catholic Church and believe in certain false beliefs or erroneous religious propositions. The jurisdiction of the Inquisition over heresy was always confined to baptized Catholics because the unbaptized remained outside of the church.[13]

In the conception of the Catholic clergy and the inquisitors themselves, the teachings, dogmas, and precepts of Catholicism were the direct expressions of God's divine will as it was revealed to humankind.[14] They believed that Jesus Christ himself transmitted this divine revelation to humankind. By this means, the Catholic Church and the inquisitors believed that the basic beliefs of Catholicism remained the only true religion and its teachings the only truth as divinely revealed by God through his son made incarnate in the form of Christ. To deny these central teachings, in the opinion of the inquisitors, was to deny Christ himself.[15]

The Catholic Church and the Inquisition did not categorize unbaptized persons, non-Christians, or even non-Catholic Christians (i.e., Protestants) as guilty of formal heresy. Inquisitorial tribunals had no jurisdictions over people who had not entered into the fold of the Catholic Church through the sacrament of baptism. Rather, a heretic was a deviant "insider" who had become a member of the Catholic Church through baptism and religious instruction but who chose to rebel against these teachings, either implicitly or explicitly.[16] The problem of heresy, for the Inquisition and the Catholic Church, was "essentially a problem of authority."[17]

Heresy was dangerous to the authority of the church, but because it divided and disrupted the social order, it was also a major concern of the state. As a result, both early Christian rulers and the secular authorities supported and defended the Christian faith. By the early part of the fourth century, heresy was defined as a sin and a crime. Both civil and religious authorities came to view heresy as a crime *lesa majestad,* not only a crime against the majesty of God, the church, and its Catholic dogmas, but also a crime against the dignity of the sovereign or state. By the fifteenth century in Europe, heresy represented a serious challenge to church and state and a threat against the public peace. As Lu Ann Homza remarked in her study of the Spanish Inquisition, after the Roman Empire formally adopted Christianity as the only legal state religion, "enemies of religion became enemies of the state," and "heretics were judged guilty of treason and were liable to the same penalties— for example, fines, confiscation of goods, exclusion from inheritance, exile and death."[18] Heresy and the existence of heretics had widespread religious, social, and political consequences.

Many of the theologians and scholastic writers of the later medieval period described and viewed the Catholic Christian community using the metaphor of an organic body. According to these medieval doctrines, heresy was a disease that could bring the plague of false belief upon the pure body of the Catholic state.[19] Just as medical doctors were needed to cure a human body of diseases and other maladies, so too the spiritual body of the church needed a spiritual physician, or the inquisitor, to protect it from the disease of heresy. Similar to the medieval physician who used bloodletting and surgery to purge the body and cut out the sickness, "the inquisitor used the rack and the stake to rid the body politic of bad believers."[20]

Heresy in Spain and New Spain

You should not permit heresies to enter into your kingdoms, to avoid this you should favor the Holy Inquisition.

Instructions given by King Charles V of Spain to his son Philip II, 1543

Spain of the fifteenth and sixteenth centuries faced a pivotal time of change. Having finally conquered the last Muslim kingdom of Granada and expelled all of the Jews from Spain in 1492, the Spanish Catholic monarchy for the first time faced the possibility of creating what it believed to be a pure Christian society free from the influences of supposed false religions. However, this same period also witnessed unparalleled attacks against the Catholic Church and the division of Europe along religious lines. With the advent of Martin Luther's Protestant Reformation in the early sixteenth century, and with international political struggles with newly created Protestant nations, Spain as the self-proclaimed champion of the Catholic Church and its orthodoxy became embroiled in numerous wars of religion. The new historical circumstances that occurred at the beginning of the sixteenth century made it imperative that the Spanish monarchy help preserve the Catholic Church because Catholicism had become the central unifying principal in the creation of the modern Spanish state. It is no wonder that the later Spanish Hapsburg monarchs took Charles V's advice to his son Philip to heart. The Inquisition and its defense of Catholic orthodoxy remained essential for the survival of Spain and its worldwide empire, both at home and abroad. The blurring of the separation of church and state in the Spanish empire during this period led to the Spanish Inquisition's and its New World tribunals' continued association of heretics as religious and civil criminals.

In Spain, heresy was carefully defined by church scholars and theologians, and the Inquisition's obligations to punish heresy depended on the extent and gradation of a suspected heretic's false belief.[21] Unlike in our modern judicial system where "ignorance of the law is no excuse," for the Inquisition ignorance was an excuse. A baptized Christian who committed a heretical error arising from ignorance was not considered worthy of serious punishment. For many of the Inquisition's theologians and jurists, ordinary people could be held responsible not for all beliefs but only for the most basic "articles of faith."[22] Nevertheless, some of these same scholars, such as the Spanish jurist Francisco Peña, believed that the educated could not feign ignorance as an excuse for their heresy, for they argued that "those who should know and must be presumed to understand the details of the articles must be considered heretics when erring in the faith."[23]

True formal heresy in Spain was considered a voluntary and pertinacious error, deserving of punishment. Formal heresy, in the minds of the inquisitors in Spain, manifested itself in several distinguishable forms: mental (or internal) heresies and external heresies. The nature of assessing internal belief versus external actions made an accusation of formal heretical beliefs at inquisitorial trials and proceedings a difficult charge to prove. According to the inquisitors themselves, internal or mental heresy (the *most* difficult type to prove) focused on heresy that was believed in secretly and not manifested in any pronounced word or deed.[24] External heresy, the easiest type to prove, was also subdivided by Spanish theologians into hidden and public. It was hidden if the heresy was manifested in words, symbols, or signs that a suspected heretic uttered either in secret or in the presence of only a couple of people; and public (considered the most dangerous type of heresy for the body of the church) if manifested publicly in the presence of more than two people.

The Inquisition and the civil state also recognized heresy as both a crime and a sin. Unlike the act of confession to a priest, where one's minor sins could be absolved by the priest, a formal act of heresy required not only a full confession as a sin but also some type of penalty or punishment as a crime. Even if a convicted heretic confessed and eventually repented and received absolution, he would remain subject to the imposition of a series of corrective punishments ranging from minor monetary fines to a possible sentence of death.

The nature of heresy in colonial Mexico and throughout the Spanish New World became complicated even more by the diversity of its peoples and cultures. Just as the Spanish Inquisition in the peninsula had gradually taken on more powers and jurisdiction over other crimes, so too did the Mexican Inquisition increase its own power. By acquiring control over a wider range of crimes against the faith, the Inquisition broadened the definition of what could be considered heresy or a heretical practice.

In Spain, formal religious heresy was the prime motivating factor in the Inquisition's existence and its activities. From its inception in 1478, the Inquisition received jurisdiction over all of the existing heresies. With the passage of time, however, the Spanish Inquisition began to expand its power and control over crimes that contained only a hint of heresy. By the sixteenth century, the Inquisition's jurisdiction included the lesser crimes of bigamy, blasphemy, and superstitious practices such as witchcraft and magic. To support their expanding jurisdiction, the inquisitors argued that in these lesser infractions the culprits might hold heretical intentions or reject God's commandments and the precepts of the church.[25]

Gradually, the Spanish Inquisition came to have jurisdiction over a host of crimes and lesser infractions that had previously fallen under the control of the royal courts or other ecclesiastical tribunals. Henry Kamen has argued that "in this way a tribunal that had easily had its powers limited became in reality an all powerful institution, because its authority and jurisdiction eventually came to control all aspects of the daily life of Spaniards."[26] Adding to the expanding powers of the Inquisition was the fact that all the supposed crimes of the faith under its jurisdiction could not be pardoned by any priest or ecclesiastical official—not even through the sacrament of confession.[27] Table 1 lists the sins under the jurisdiction of the Inquisition in New Spain, ordered according to the gravity of the sin and seriousness of offense.[28]

The power of the Spanish Inquisition was based on its direct control by the Spanish crown. King Ferdinand had managed to wrest away complete control from the popes in Rome, an achievement that was unique among all of the medieval and early modern inquisitions.[29] With the passage of time and out of necessity, subsequent Spanish monarchs delegated the direction of the institution to special inquisitors general and their Supreme

TABLE 1
Jurisdiction of the Inquisition in New Spain over Crimes against the Faith, 1536–1820

Type of Heresy/Crime	Category of Crime	Specific Type of Crime Punished by the Inquisition
Crimes against the faith	Apostasy	Judaizing
		Mohammedanism
		Protestantism
		False mysticism
	Heretical propositions	Heretical propositions
		Schismatic propositions
		Impious propositions
		Imprudent propositions
		Injurious propositions
		Blasphemous propositions
Crimes against Christian morality	Blasphemy	Heretical blasphemy
		Simple blasphemy
	Bigamy	Bigamy
		Polygamy
	Nefarious sins	Sodomy
		Homosexuality
		Bestiality
		Incest
		Sexuality immorality
		Masturbation
	Superstitions	Magic and witchcraft
		Divination and sortilege
		Idolatry
	Crimes of the clergy	Solicitation of sex in the confessional
		False celebration of the mass
		Marriage of the clergy
	Crimes against the Inquisition	Impeding the actions of the tribunal
		Offending the tribunal
		Bearing false witness
		Violating ecclesiastical sanctions
		Failing to comply with imposed sentences

Council of the Inquisition. All of the Inquisition tribunals founded later remained under the sole direct control of these inquisitors general and their Supreme Council, or the Suprema. This chain of command enabled the local tribunals such as the one in New Spain to act with greater independence than even those tribunals in the Iberian Peninsula. For one thing, the administrative distance between the Suprema in Madrid and the tribunal in Mexico made it impossible for the Suprema to effectively control the activities of the Mexican Inquisition. Because communication remained slow and irregular, the Inquisition in New Spain by necessity enjoyed greater independence than that given to the provincial inquisitions in Spain.[30] Even Inquisitor General Diego de Espinosa's initial instructions to the first inquisitors of New Spain in 1571 emphasized this greater freedom.[31] The Inquisition in New Spain similarly remained free from any dependence on the local royal or ecclesiastical authorities. Royal orders forbade the civil and religious authorities in New Spain from intervening in cases under the jurisdiction of the Inquisition or inhibiting the Inquisition from conducting its business. They were not to thwart, hamper, or delay the inquisitors in their duties.[32]

In New Spain, however, real doctrinal heresy took a second place to the need for social control and the quest for religious uniformity in a multiethnic and multiracial society where the majority of the population (the indigenous people) lay beyond the Inquisition's jurisdictional control.[33] It is notable that in contrast to the activities of the Inquisition's tribunals in Spain, less than a third (27.5%) of the Mexican tribunal's proceedings dealt with real issues of heresy and heretical propositions (table 2). Most of the Mexican tribunal's documentation focused on the lesser crimes of superstition, witchcraft, blasphemy, moral and sexual offenses, issues concerning ecclesiastical immunities, documents concerning the prerogatives and privileges of Inquisition officials, accusations and correspondence concerning jurisdictional conflicts with the region's episcopal courts, and materials related to the inquisitors' concerns over the reading of prohibited books.

TABLE 2

Distribution of Inquisition Trials for Specific Crimes in Spain and New Spain, 1571–1700

	Spain	New Spain
Formal heresy	17,738 (42.0%)	525 (27.5%)
Minor religious crimes	15,545 (34.4%)	568 (29.7%)
Magical practices / witchcraft	3,356 (7.9%)	138 (7.2%)
Sexual crimes	2,374 (5.6%)	462 (24.1%)
Solicitation	1,094 (2.6%)	157 (8.2%)
Civil crimes	—	52 (2.7%)
Idolatry	—	13 (1.0%)
Total number of trials	38,249	1,913

Source: See Alberro, *Inquisición y sociedad*, chart III, p. 207, as well as Gustav Henningsen, "El Banco de datos del Santo Oficio," *Boletín de la Real Academia de la Historia* 174 (1977): 547–70; and Archivo General de la Nación, Ramo de Inquisición, Lote Riva Palacio, vol. 49.

The Origins and Early History of the Inquisition in New Spain

The King, Our Lord, has established the Holy Tribunal in this Kingdom [of New Spain] not only for the defense and conservation of the Catholic Faith but also for the security of his dominion and monarchy.

Antonio Sebastián de Toledo Molina y Salazar, viceroy of New Spain, 1666

The Inquisition in New Spain was created as a special ecclesiastical and political institution that used the inquisitorial method of trial procedures to combat or suppress heresy and other crimes against the colonial church and the Spanish viceroyalty. As it evolved in Mexico from its early European origins, it developed a complex bureaucracy and system of procedures. Through its use of coercive power to enforce religious and political orthodoxy in New Spain, the Inquisition endeavored to maintain social, religious, and political order. Although its religious and philosophical influence on various aspects of colonial Mexican life has been abundantly researched, the institutional structure, functioning, and jurisdictional conflicts of the Holy Office in Mexico have received little attention.[34]

Roughly divided into three periods of development, the Inquisition in New Spain was not formally established until King Philip II mandated the creation of the Tribunal of the Holy Office in a royal decree of 1569 (document 2). Before the foundation of this tribunal, the early bishops, prelates, and apostolic commissaries conducted the inquisitorial trials, modeling their investigations on what they had inherited from the medieval tradition. In New Spain, two periods preceded the formal establishment of the Inquisition. The first period (1522–62) was dominated by inquisitions carried out by the local provincials or leaders of the monastic religious orders. This period began with the initial spiritual conquest of New Spain and ended with the controversial actions of the Franciscan provincial of Yucatan, Fray Diego de Landa, who in 1562 launched a cruel and repressive campaign against Maya idolatry in Yucatan.[35] Partly in reaction to Landa's brutality and similar harsh measures by the other religious orders, the crown decided to establish bishoprics in all of the regions of New Spain. With the arrival of the first bishops, the second period (1536–69) saw the brief transcendence of the episcopal inquisition, in which the early bishops and archbishops of Mexico served as inquisitors in cases of heresy and superstition involving Mexico's indigenous peoples, Spaniards, and mixed castes.[36] The difficulty of the bishops' successfully defending the faith with such a large number of Indian cases to handle led to the crown's decision to create an official Tribunal of the Inquisition. This third period (1571–1820) saw the official establishment of the Holy Office of the Inquisition in New Spain and the removal of the bishop from the jurisdiction over cases of heresy and superstition among Spaniards, Africans, and mixed castes. Strangely enough, the jurisdiction over the heretical beliefs and heterodox practices of the indigenous peoples of New Spain would remain under the power of the bishop's episcopal courts.[37]

The Early Monastic Inquisitions in New Spain (1522–1562)

During the earliest period, the monastic orders assumed apostolic powers as inquisitors. Many, however, argued that this was not enough. As early as 1516, figures such as the chief defender of the Indians, Fray Bartolomé de las Casas, petitioned the king in Spain to establish the Inquisition in the New World. In a letter to Cardinal Francisco Jiménez de Cisneros, las Casas requested that Cisneros "send the Holy Inquisition to those islands of the Indies, of which I believe there is a very great need, because where the faith has newly been planted, as it has in those lands, perhaps there will be no one who causes the horrible trouble of heresy, but already there they have found and have burned two heretics, and by fortune they kept more than fourteen from entering into these lands."[38] Although the Holy Office of the Inquisition did not set up an official body in the Americas at this time, it did designate further inquisitorial powers to some friars and bishops shortly before 1520. This standard of regular, or occasionally secular, clergy holding authority over the Inquisition became normal from the late 1510s until 1568.

These early officers of the Inquisition focused on a resurgence of idolatry among the indigenous population, as well as the common problem of blasphemy and the graver concerns regarding peninsular Spaniards committing formal acts of heresy. These monastic inquisitions attempted both to correct the spiritual crimes of the early conquerors and to reprimand erring Indian converts. Basing their powers on a papal bull of concession, called *Omnimoda,* the leaders of the religious orders conducted primitive inquisitions.[39]

The first friar given inquisitorial powers was the leader of the first Franciscan missionaries, Fray Martín de Valencia. Arriving in 1524, Valencia exercised the office of inquisitor. Little is known of his inquisitorial activities, and few documents have survived.[40] His term expired in 1526 when the head of the Dominican order, Fray Domingo de Betanzos, became commissary of the Inquisition in New Spain. During his brief period as inquisitor, Betanzos tried nineteen cases of blasphemy against Spanish colonists.[41] The Dominican order controlled the monastic inquisition until the arrival of the new bishop, Fray Juan de Zumárraga, in 1536. From 1526 to 1536, the Dominican inquisition punished nine more cases, at least two of which ended in burnings at the stake (table 3).[42]

TABLE 3

Early Monastic Inquisition Cases Investigated or
Tried by Fray Domingo de Betanzos and Dominican
Inquisitors, 1526–1536

Type of Case	Number of Trials
Blasphemy	22
Idolatry and sacrifices	12
Jewish practices (*Judaizantes*)	5
Crimes of the clergy	5
Bigamy	5
Superstitions	4
Heretical propositions	2
Total cases tried	55

Source: Archivo General de la Nación, Ramo de Inquisición, vol. 1, exp. 9, 9a, 9b, 9c, 9d, 9e, 10, 10a, 10b, 10c, 10d, 10e, 10f, 11, 12, 13, 14, 15; vol. 1a, exp. 2, 10, 12, 13, 14, 15, 16, 17; vol. 14, exp. 1, 2, 4, 5, 6, 7, 8, 9, 10.

Monastic inquisitions in central Mexico ended with the bishop's 1536 arrival, but the provincials of the outlying provinces continued to hold monastic inquisitions. In 1560 the Dominican friars in Oaxaca conducted a monastic inquisition in which they engaged in the torture of the Indians of the village of Teitipac and conducted an *auto-da-fé* (a public ceremony of the execution of Inquisition sentences).[43] Dominicans, Augustinians, and Franciscans throughout the rest of New Spain also engaged in cruel monastic inquisitions. The final and most brutal monastic inquisition culminated in Fray Diego de Landa's widespread use of torture during his rigorous campaign against Mayan idolatry in 1562.[44] His sentences were harsh, and many Maya committed suicide to escape the torture. So great was the scandal over the Landa affair that the crown quickly repealed the monastic orders' right to conduct inquisitions.[45] With the arrival of a bishop in the province of Yucatan in 1563 to replace Landa, the monastic inquisitions in New Spain officially ended.

The Episcopal Inquisition (1536–1569)

When Fray Juan de Zumárraga became the first bishop of Mexico, the first episcopal inquisition was established in New Spain. On the basis of powers inherent in his own office as bishop and reinforced by a commission as apostolic inquisitor, Zumárraga began a systematized episcopal inquisition that conducted all cases of heresy. He was given power as bishop to hold trials, hand out penitence, issue arrest orders, and relax the condemned to the secular arm. During the period of Zumárraga's episcopal inquisition, he tried and oversaw 156 cases against Indians, Spaniards, and mixed castes (table 4).

Most of Zumárraga's trials against indigenous superstitions, idolatry, and polygamy occurred from 1536 to 1540. In 1536 Zumárraga conducted the first of a series of idolatry trials and harshly punished two native Otomi priests from the town of Tanacopán.[46] Three years later, in June 1539, Zumárraga began the infamous trial against the cacique of Texcoco,

TABLE 4

Episcopal Inquisition Cases Tried by Bishop Fray Juan de
Zumárraga, 1536–1546

Type of Case	Number of Trials
Blasphemy	56
Superstitions	23
Bigamy	20
Jewish practices (*Judaizantes*)	19
Idolatry and sacrifices	14
Crimes of the clergy	11
Heretical propositions	8
Lutheranism	5
Total cases tried	156

Source: Archivo General de la Nación, Ramo de Inquisición, vol. 1, exp. 9, 9a, 9b, 9c, 9d, 9e, 10, 10a, 10b, 10c, 10d, 10e, 10f, 11, 12, 13, 14, 15; vol. 1a, exp. 2, 10, 12, 13, 14, 15, 16, 17; vol. 14, exp. 1, 2, 4, 5, 6, 7, 8, 9, 10.

Don Carlos Ometochtzin, whom he had burned at the stake.[47] So cruel was this punishment that the crown rebuked the bishop for his harsh treatment of the Indians.[48] Bishop Zumárraga relented and eventually relinquished the title of apostolic inquisitor in 1546. Succeeding bishops conducted more lenient episcopal inquisitions.

Monastic provincials and the first bishops were zealous inquisitors in cases against Mexico's indigenous peoples, but many abuses occurred because their inquisitions lacked any central direction or adequate training in inquisition procedure.[49] Various provincials of the religious orders and early bishops committed excesses and illegalities in their procedures. Increasingly, colonists requested that the crown formally establish a permanent Tribunal of the Holy Office, and eventually King Philip II consented.

The Tribunal of the Inquisition in New Spain (1571–1820)

King Philip II did not officially create the Tribunal of the Inquisition in New Spain until his signing of a royal decree on January 25, 1569 (document 2). Another royal order dated August 16, 1570, removed the indigenous peoples from the tribunal of Mexico's jurisdiction, which covered all of New Spain, including the Philippines, Guatemala, and the bishopric of Nicaragua.[50] In terms of the indigenous peoples of New Spain, as the process of evangelization and conversion of the natives progressed, control over religious heterodoxy evolved through various stages, and, as it did, the Inquisition's effect on indigenous cultures also changed. The earliest phases before the establishment of the formal tribunal saw the greatest number of cases carried out against indigenous peoples. As the Inquisition evolved into a more formal tribunal, Indians were removed from its jurisdiction. By that time, the racial climate of the colony had changed, and racial mixture and population decline among the native populations of Mesoamerica forced the tribunal to exercise its jurisdiction over an increasing number of mixed castes, or mestizos. Fearing contamination of indigenous elements of superstition and religious beliefs, the Holy Office investigated cases of Indian superstition and idolatry not to punish the Indians (who were legally removed from its jurisdiction) but rather to gain evidence and information against Africans, mestizos, creoles, and Spaniards who were guilty of practicing superstition.[51]

Although the Inquisition continued to develop cases against the heterodoxy of Mexico's indigenous peoples, it did not proceed in any formal legal trials of indigenous peoples after 1571.[52] Of the 38,802 documents and denunciations remaining in the archive, only 549 pertain to cases involving investigations against indigenous peoples.[53] Indians did continue to be punished for their heterodoxy but not by the Inquisition. After 1571, the jurisdiction over Indian cases and the examination of their alleged superstitions and other crimes against the faith reverted to the episcopal courts and their institution of the *Provisorato de Indios*.[54]

As a formal tribunal with a wide range of powers, the Inquisition in New Spain functioned from 1570 until its final abolition in 1820 when Mexico gained independence from Spain, changing over time in its focus and primary functions. The new tribunal of the Inquisition served as a policing agency of the church and government through attempts to enforce both political and religious orthodoxy in New Spain. With the official founding of the tribunal in Mexico, the Inquisition was designed to serve as the colonial government's main means of social, religious, and political control over what it saw as seditious ideas and heretical propositions spread by foreigners and other dissenters in the colonial milieu, as well as to serve as a check against rising clerical immorality. The final phase of the Inquisition saw the tribunal's increasing use as a political tool during the Bourbon period, culminating in the famous trials of some of the major leaders of Mexican independence.[55]

The new Inquisition tribunal's official functions included the prosecution and punishment of all acts contrary to the Catholic faith, including apostasy, heresy, and the continued practice of the Jewish religion by previously converted Jews (called *conversos*). Although functioning mainly as a safeguard for the orthodoxy of the Catholic faith since its early founding in Mexico, the Inquisition also served as an important tool for social and political control. Its use as a political tool is especially evident during the final period in the punishment of all dissidents with respect to Catholic dogma and teaching (including Lutherans and other Protestant sects) as well as those who held or stated propositions contrary to the faith or the king.

Officials of the Inquisition in New Spain (1571–1820)

As to the Inquisition, my will is that it be enforced by the Inquisitors as of old, and as is required by all law, human and divine. This lies very near my heart, and I require you to carry out my orders. Let all prisoners be put to death, and suffer them no longer to escape through the neglect, weakness, and bad faith of the judges. If any are too timid to execute the edicts, I will replace them by men who have more heart and zeal.

King Philip II of Spain, in a letter concerning the Inquisition, October 1565

The highest official of the Inquisition was the inquisitor general in Spain, who was nominated by the crown and confirmed by the pope. This official created regional tribunals and named their inquisitors and the other officials of the local courts. Later, a special Castilian state council, the Consejo de la suprema y general Inquisición (Council of the Supreme and General Inquisition), was created to assist the inquisitor general in matters of administration.[56] Ordinarily there were at least five councilors appointed by the inquisitor general, and the council, together with the inquisitor general, appointed, transferred, and removed regional officials from office and had the ability to visit and inspect all of the local and regional tribunals. All Spaniards and others who were baptized Catholics were subject to the jurisdiction of the inquisitorial tribunals, including technically the king himself. To ensure that all suspected heretics were denied access to the colonies, the Suprema examined the backgrounds of all who wished to immigrate.[57] After the failure of this policy, however, the Suprema and the crown by the middle of the sixteenth century accepted the need for new tribunals of the Holy Office in the New World.

The tribunal in Mexico (along with two others founded by Philip II in Lima and Cartagena de Indias), consisted of two to three inquisitors who were the superior ecclesiastical judges of the Inquisition in their district. These inquisitors were aided by a *fiscal*, or prosecutor, who brought the initial accusation of the prisoners before the tribunal, and a *secretario*, or secretary, who authorized all of the documents, edicts, and dispatches of the Holy Office. Two *notarios del secreto*, or notaries of the secret, certified the declarations and testimony of witnesses before the tribunal and cared for the archive of the Inquisition.

The inquisitors relied on the help of at least six *consultores,* or councilors, who gave them legal advice. These councilors included two theologians and four doctors in canon law. Along with these councilors were eight *calificadores,* or qualifiers (all doctors in theology or canon and civil law), who weighed the evidence presented in each case to decide if there was sufficient cause to proceed in a formal trial.

Twelve *alguaciles,* or constables, oversaw the apprehension of the prisoners. Officials called *alcaides* served as jailers at the various jails used by the Inquisition, including the *cárcel secreta* (for incarceration during the trial until sentencing), the *cárcel de penitencia* (for short prison sentences), and the *cárcel perpetua* (for those condemned to life in prison). There were also several *proveedores,* who were entrusted with the proper alimentation of the prisoners. The other lesser officials of the tribunal in Mexico included many doormen, several surgeons, physicians required by law to be present during the interrogation and torture of prisoners, and even a barber for the prisoners.

Most of the men who occupied positions in the Tribunal of the Holy Office in New Spain shared a similar background. As the Mexican scholar Solange Alberro stated in her monumental study of the Inquisition in Mexico, "The majority of those who occupied positions in the Holy Office of New Spain shared the same profile: they had university studies, perhaps at the Great University of Salamanca, and other times in one of the six prestigious major colleges (*colegios mayores*) in Osuna, Sevilla, Cordoba, Granada, and most often in Lima and Mexico City. . . . most of them had the terminal degree of Doctor or Licenciate."[58] To understand the workings of the tribunal in New Spain, and its functionaries, it is necessary to examine in greater detail the officers and their duties, privileges, and responsibilities.

Salaried Officials of the Holy Office

According to the official instructions, the Inquisition tribunal in New Spain consisted of a series of salaried officials and other supporting staff. The salaried officials included two inquisitors and a prosecutor (*fiscal*), all three appointed by the inquisitor general in Madrid, as well as twelve other ministers who were named and appointed in New Spain by the local inquisitors. After the formal establishment of the tribunal, a larger number of officials existed, and several new positions were created. Still, the economic problems and lack of resources until the middle of the seventeenth century made it impossible on occasion to appoint or keep officials in the offices. On other occasions, many of the tribunal's ministers served in offices without receiving their apportioned salaries for long periods of time.[59]

At the same time, the officials of the Inquisition enjoyed many benefits and privileges. All of the officials of the Holy Office (both salaried and nonsalaried) enjoyed legal immunity from criminal and civil prosecution in the royal and ecclesiastical courts. Their cases were reserved for the jurisdiction of the Inquisition, which more often than not judged its own officials with leniency. Several of the more important ministers also received more tangible benefits. For example, the tribunal's inquisitors, the prosecutor, the chief secretary, the receiver, one messenger, and the jailer of the secret prison all received an exemption from taxation, and the royal officials in New Spain were ordered under the penalty of a fine of 1,000 ducats to observe this exemption and protect all of their honors, immunities, and privileges.[60]

THE INQUISITORS (*INQUISIDORES*)

The regional tribunals of the Inquisition were directed and controlled by their respective inquisitors. Each tribunal held jurisdiction and exercised complete control over a certain territory. The three major tribunals were seated in the principal capital cities of the viceroyalties: Mexico City in the Viceroyalty of New Spain, Lima in the Viceroyalty of Peru, and Cartagena de Indias in the Kingdom of New Granada. A host of lesser officials served under the inquisitors in their jurisdiction.[61]

Only the inquisitors and the local prosecutor were named directly by the inquisitor general in Spain in consultation with the Supreme Council of the Inquisition. Generally at least three inquisitors served in each tribunal. The local inquisitors received the powers, according to their original instructions, to name and appoint all of the other lesser ministers and officials of the tribunal.[62] The instructions charged them with the selection of those candidates who appeared most qualified for the position. Similarly, the minimum age for an inquisitor was set at thirty-five, and all those appointed had to exhibit the qualities of "prudent and suitable men of good repute and sound conscience and be zealous for the Catholic faith."[63]

The minimum number of inquisitors required for the operation of a tribunal, however, was two, one who was supposed to be a theologian and the other a jurist or lawyer. If neither one of the inquisitors had received training as a theologian, they had to count on the aid of local theologians for the exercise of their office.[64] The prominent Spanish jurist Francisco Peña in his commentaries on Nicolas Eimeric's popular Inquisition manual, the *Directorium Inquisitorum*, maintained that in distant tribunals, such as the one in New Spain, if the tribunal had only two inquisitors, "one must be a highly proven and extremely learned theologian, and the other should be a most expert canon law jurist, given the great magnitude and gravity of the subject of the faith."[65] Although this goal existed in theory, the Inquisition of New Spain violated this directive in practice. During the first sixty years of the tribunal's history (1573–1631), it ignored Peña's recommendation and remained exclusively run by jurists and professional lawyers.[66] Later, in 1608, King Philip III mandated a preference for certified lawyers and made it a prerequisite that all those appointed as an inquisitor or a prosecutor had to have formal legal training.[67]

The most important duties of the inquisitors included serving as judges in the determination of the trials and cases that pertained to the Holy Office. The head or senior inquisitor usually controlled the administrative aspects of the tribunal. Throughout the sixteenth century, secular clergymen predominately served as inquisitors rather than appointees, who belonged to the various religious orders.[68] The Suprema began to appoint more members of the Cathedral chapters who had training in jurisprudence and canon law, most notably men who had held the position of canons[69] in the various regional cathedral chapters throughout the New World.[70]

For ecclesiastics to attain the position of inquisitor, they were often required to serve as a lesser official of a local tribunal or as a consultant, qualifier, or other official of a tribunal elsewhere in the greater Spanish world. Usually, dutiful service in a lesser regional tribunal would earn an official a later appointment as an inquisitor in a tribunal of greater prestige.[71] Throughout the sixteenth and seventeenth centuries, in a majority of cases peninsular Spaniards predominated among those men appointed as inquisitors in New Spain; only a scant few creole ecclesiastics who had been born in the New World ever attained the position of inquisitor. In fact, of the men who served as inquisitors in the tribunal of Mexico from 1572 to 1820, only four of them were creoles born in the New World.[72] Even then, a creole appointee could not serve in his own native district or region.[73] This restriction attempted to limit corruption and nepotism in the exercise of the office by local creoles.[74] In one specific case in New Spain, Inquisitor Juan Gómez de Mier felt strongly enough about apparent conflicts of interest in naming a local Mexican-born creole as prosecutor that he wrote to the Suprema to protest the appointment of Dr. Francisco de Deza y Ulloa because "he was born and raised in this city and he has a great familiarity of all types of people here," which de Mier argued precluded de Deza's ability to act impartially in prosecuting the tribunal's cases.[75] Although the Suprema did not allow the Mexican Inquisition to have direct relatives concurrently serving as ministers in the tribunal, it was common in the Mexican tribunal for various members of a single family to succeed their relatives in the holding of their offices.[76]

The inquisitors in New Spain held practically unlimited power over the nonindigenous inhabitants of their region. They could arrest and imprison anyone within their district at will, and their edicts of excommunication could bring down even the highest secular official.[77] The position brought with it an established salary of 3,000 pesos per year and added privileges and other honors. Similarly, service as an inquisitor in New Spain often led to later appointments to higher, more prestigious positions within the colonial church or the royal bureaucracy, most commonly promotion to a bishopric.[78]

THE PROSECUTING ATTORNEY (*FISCAL*)

The tribunal entrusted the *fiscal*, or prosecutor, with the prosecution of the case, from the initial accusation until the inquisitors passed their definitive sentence. His job was to present the official accusations against the accused, which were formulated according to the instructions from the Holy Office.[79] The *fiscal* accused the suspect in general terms of being a heretic and then in particular terms according to what was discovered in the initial investigation. In many of the larger tribunals, such as that of New Spain, the *fiscal* had several assistants.

The post of *fiscal* was the most important position after that of inquisitor. If there were more than two inquisitors presiding on the tribunal, one of them would occupy this position and use the title *inquisidor fiscal*. In many cases, service in the position of *fiscal* often led to an eventual promotion to inquisitor. A review of the established salaries for the officials of the Holy Office shows that the prosecutor received the same salary as the other inquisitors (see table 8). His responsibilities included the keeping of the keys to the chamber of the secret (*cámara del secreto*), which was where all of the documents of the trials were kept. The Instructions of 1561 listed among the prosecutor's duties the maintenance of the chamber of the secret and the arrangement and archiving of all of the documents.[80] The later instructions of 1632 dictated that the prosecutor also had to submit a monthly report to the Suprema describing every pending case with a summary of the proceedings.[81]

The prosecutor also received the charge of elaborating all of the accusations against accused heretics and served as the chief minister who interrogated the accused and brought formal charges against them. Because of his role as a prosecutor, the *fiscal* did not have the right to vote at the final moment before the definitive sentence was dictated.[82] In general, in New Spain few officials occupied the post of prosecutor very long. The first three prosecutors of the Inquisition of New Spain together served for less than ten years. For instance, Licenciado Alonso Granero Dávalos served as prosecutor from 1573 to 1574, and his successor, Licenciado Santos García, served from only 1575 to 1580.[83] During extended periods when the position of prosecutor remained vacant for lack of an appointee, a situation that occurred frequently in the Inquisition in New Spain, one of the inquisitors executed the functions and duties of the prosecutor. The inquisitor who acted as the prosecutor lost his right to sit and dictate the final sentence at the end of the trial.[84] In only three separate occasions did an appointee to the position of prosecutor hold the position for more than ten years.[85]

SECRETARIES AND NOTARIES OF THE SECRET (*SECRETARIOS* AND *NOTARIOS DEL SECRETO*)

The notary or secretary of the secret was in charge of recording and writing all of the official documents of the tribunal.[86] He was entrusted with keeping all the papers and correspondence of the Holy Office in order, as well as maintaining a proper count of the official papers.[87] The notary also took part in and recorded all of the official audiences and actions of the tribunal, both inside and outside of the audience chamber. From the outset, these notaries were forbidden to employ assistants or clerks and instead were required to write down everything in their own hand.[88] There were usually two or three of these notaries in every tribunal. They also had the responsibility of maintaining the *cámara del secreto* in conjunction with the prosecutor. All correspondence between the Holy Office and other officials was signed and testified to before these notaries.

SECRETARY OF THE SEQUESTERED GOODS

Another official was the secretary of the sequestered goods, who kept the detailed accounts of goods confiscated from the suspected heretics. Required to be present when arrests and sequestrations occurred, these secretaries drew up the documents dealing with the sequestering of goods in Inquisition trials and kept the accounts of the expenses of each prisoner, which they deducted from the goods belonging to his or her estate.[89]

CHIEF CONSTABLE (*ALGUACIL MAYOR*)

The *alguacil mayor,* or chief constable, of the Holy Office had the duty and obligation of arresting those suspects formally accused by the inquisitors and the *fiscal.* The *alguacil mayor* enforced the arrest warrants in the company of the receptor, the secretary of the sequestered goods, and the familiars of the Inquisition.[90] In most tribunals, several assistant constables were also employed.

The *alguacil mayor* had the authority to request the aid of other secular authorities for the arrest of the accused. Also, the chief constables were entrusted with the security and safety of the prisoners detained until they reached the Inquisition's jails. During their transportation to the Inquisition's prisons, the *alguacil* ensured that the prisoner had no contact with persons who were not authorized by the inquisitors.

Among the salaried officials of the Holy Office, these *alguaciles* occupied one of the most important posts, along with the notary of the secret. The chief constable executed all seizures of goods and was also entitled to receive fees for his services.[91] Because of the low number of arrests and lack of other duties, in New Spain the position of chief constable seems to have become more of a decorative or honorific post.[92] The inquisitors themselves used appointment to this post as a means of bestowing honor and prestige upon prominent citizens and especially those who could benefit the tribunal through their connections. An example of this occurred in 1607 when the inquisitors of New Spain requested that the Suprema confirm their appointment of Don Juan de Altamirano to this position. Inquisitor Alonso de Peralta wrote that they had selected Altamirano because "he was an honorable man who had sufficient financial means, and he was the son-in-law of the Viceroy."[93]

CHIEF JAILER (*ALCAIDE MAYOR*)

The *alcaide mayor,* or chief jailer, was the official in charge of maintaining control and order in the Inquisition's prisons. He supervised the other guards and their mission to care for and watch over the prisoners. The *alcaide* received the prisoners when the *alguacil mayor* brought them to the prison for the first time. The *alcaide* kept and maintained a count of all of the prisoners and had a book that recorded the particulars of their stay in the prison.[94]

The *alcaide* had the responsibility of taking an inventory and noting all the clothing and personal belongings that each prisoner brought into the jail. The *alcaide* was also in charge of the maintenance and feeding of the prisoners. The instructions obligated him to ensure that the prisoners remained isolated and that they had no communication with anyone, not even their fellow prisoners.[95] The *alcaide* also accompanied the prisoners to and from their audiences with the inquisitors. In the preparations for the auto-da-fé, the *alcaide* played a major role (see documents 1, 3, and 20).

This office was continually occupied in the Inquisition of New Spain, and the jailer in Mexico also counted on the aid of a salaried assistant. The officeholder often used his own African slaves to assist in the labor of maintaining the Inquisition's jails.[96]

RECEIVER (*RECEPTOR*)

The *receptor,* or receiver, managed the fiscal and financial accounts of the Holy Office. Named by the king, the *receptor* depended directly on the local inquisitors. Without the signatures of the inquisitors, the *receptor* could not conduct any action. All expenses and all proceeds gained by pecuniary fines and other seizures had to be accounted for in minute detail. This official was entrusted with the sequestered goods along with the *alguacil* and the secretary or notary of sequestered goods.[97] The *receptor* also acted as the crown's representative in all dealings that touched on the confiscated goods of the suspects.

The post of receiver held a great amount of fiscal responsibility, so the crown and Inquisition required that those appointed to this position be bonded and put up a substantial amount of money as a guarantee before the Suprema could give them formal title to the position.[98] The first receiver of the Inquisition in New Spain, Don Pedro de Arriarán, paid a bond of 30,000 ducats to occupy his post.[99] Because the required bond became such a burden that few applicants applied for the post, the crown reduced the required bond to 12,000 pesos. Even with this lowered amount, the Mexican Inquisition found it difficult to fill the position. As a result, most of the occupants of this post in New Spain served provisionally as interim officials.[100] The moneys confiscated by the Inquisition and held by the receiver were required to be deposited into armored chests and strong boxes secured by three separate keys. However, the receivers in New Spain failed to deposit the funds many times, and shortfalls and embezzlements occurred. Many of the later visiting judges sanctioned various receivers for mismanagement of the funds. In 1672, for instance, the Mexican inquisitors complained in a letter to the Suprema that at his death that year receiver Francisco López Sanz owed the Inquisition more than 25,000 pesos.[101]

ACCOUNTANT (*CONTADOR*)

The Inquisition in New Spain also counted on the service of an accountant who had the duty of periodically balancing the account books of the tribunal.[102] The accountant reviewed the books and registers of the receiver in which all of the fines, confiscations, and other fees were recorded. The accountant also had the responsibility of administering the rents and managing the monetary investments that the tribunal often held.[103] Together with the receiver and the notary of sequesters, the accountant submitted routine certified accounts to the prosecutor who annually sent a report to the Suprema in Spain.[104]

Lesser Salaried Officials and Ministers of the Holy Office

The inquisitors and other major salaried officials were assisted in their duties by a host of lesser officials, who also received a small salary attached to their positions. The qualifications for holding one of these lesser offices included the meeting of a minimum age requirement and the proof of one's *limpieza,* or purity of blood from any admixture of Jewish or Moorish heritage, as well as proof that none of one's ancestors had been proceeded against by the Inquisition.[105] The tribunal also required each applicant or appointee to prove the legitimacy of both himself and his wife if he was married, although dispensations could be given in cases of illegitimate birth.[106] A later order from the Suprema, or *carta acordada,* mandated that all of those ministers who were unmarried could not marry without the permission of the Suprema and without furnishing proof that the prospective bride was not a foreigner or the daughter or granddaughter of foreigners.[107]

DEFENSE ATTORNEY (*ABOGADO DEFENSOR*)

In the tribunals of the Inquisition in Spanish America, the new position of a court-appointed *abogado defensor,* or defense attorney, was created to protect the rights of the accused heretics. To offer the accused suspect at least the pretense of a fair trial, the inquisitors would appoint one of their official lawyers to serve as the suspect's defense attorney. However, the *Instructions of the Holy Office* limited the lawyer's position to a minimum series of highly regulated and controlled meetings with the accused before the presence of the inquisitors and the notaries of the tribunal (document 1). These lawyers were not allowed to divulge many of the facts of the case, including even the reasons for a suspect's arrest, so that the prisoners often went days and sometimes even months without knowing why they were arrested.[108] Even after release of the official accusation, the defense attorneys were permitted only to review the accusation with the accused and to help the suspect formulate a rapid response to the charges in a point-by-point confession.

Messenger (*Nuncio*)

The *nuncio,* or messenger, of the Holy Office was the officer entrusted with personally delivering the communications and correspondence of the inquisitors within their jurisdiction and occasionally outside of the district. The messenger also had other special tasks associated with the administration of the auto-da-fé and was kept busy in most cases as a courier, carrying writs and orders from the inquisitors secretly to other people in the city.[109] Although on rare occasions, these messengers could be sent outside of the capital city of the tribunal, they most often served as urban messengers and assistants in the day-to-day operation of the tribunal.

Doorman (*Portero*)

The *portero,* or doorman, of the Inquisition served as the chief guard of the Inquisition's prisons. This official was entrusted with all the duties and responsibilities for incarcerating a suspect. He was also charged with maintaining the vigilance and control necessary to ensure that the prisoners did not escape. He also kept a registry of all visitors entering and leaving the Inquisition's jail.

Although the positions of messenger and doorman remained separate in most Inquisition tribunals, including in New Spain during the initial period from 1571 to 1579, from 1579 on in New Spain a single individual occupied both positions and received one small salary.[110]

Chief Dispenser or Steward of the Prisoners (*Dispensero de los Presos*)

The *dispensero de los presos,* or chief dispenser or steward of the prisoners, had the duty of maintaining the provisions and food supplies given to the prisoners. He received from the *alguacil* and the secretary of the sequestered goods all of the moneys necessary to support each prisoner from the proceeds of their individual sequestered estate. In the Inquisition in New Spain, this position of chief dispenser existed only during the tribunal's first decade and then only briefly during the middle of the seventeenth century, from 1640 to 1670, when the Mexican tribunal's prisons became more frequently occupied.[111] From then until the extinction of the tribunal, this position remained vacant. During periods when this position did not exist, the chief jailor and his assistant received the charge to take over these duties.

Medic, Surgeon, Pharmacist, and Barber

The tribunal of Mexico also variably counted on a number of specialists to tend to the prisoners in the perpetual prison and the accused heretics who awaited the completion of their trials. Because these positions played an important part in the proceedings of the Inquisition, in New Spain these posts were constantly occupied. Both the medic and the surgeon received a salary that varied from seventy-five to one hundred pesos per year. In the decade of the 1640s, with the influx of prisoners, the barber received as much as three hundred pesos a year for his increased workload.[112]

Nonsalaried Officials of the Tribunal

A host of other lesser, nonsalaried officials also served the tribunal of New Spain in its daily operations, both in the seat of the tribunal and in the local commissariats, or regional courts. These nonsalaried officials served as part-time consultants whom the tribunal called to serve on special occasions.[113] According to the Inquisition scholar Henry Charles Lea, there was no difficulty in finding men ready to serve without pay because the honor of being connected to the Inquisition and the privilege of its *fuero* and the many special considerations and exemptions from civil and criminal prosecution offered to its consultants more than made up for the lack of salary.[114] These unsalaried officials of the tribunal consisted of advisers and consultants who aided the inquisitors in the processing of cases against suspected heretics.

Advisory Officials and Other Ministers

The jurist Francisco Peña realized that in many cases the inquisitors themselves may have lacked training and experience in either theology or law, so he argued that the inquisitors should consult advisory officials and consultants in making their deliberations in heresy cases. In order to rectify this imbalance, inquisitorial law mandated the use of experts in both law and theology to assist the inquisitors in rendering a fair verdict in an inquisitorial trial.[115]

THEOLOGICAL QUALIFIERS (*CALIFICADORES*)

Officials known as *calificadores*, qualifiers or censors, served as theological assistants who helped the inquisitors determine the theological validity or guilt involved in the accusations of heresy. Inquisitor General Valdés's *Instructions* of 1561 (see document 1) mandated that the inquisitors had to consult with these theological advisers to examine the qualification of any heretical propositions. Once the initial evidence against an accused heretic was collected, the *calificadores* examined all of the statements, declarations, and writings of the accused to decide if an act of heresy or crime against the faith had been committed. Usually the inquisitors submitted the initial evidence gathered against a suspect to three or four qualifiers, who together decided whether the actions or words stated by the witnesses amounted to heresy or a suspicion of heresy.[116] The *calificadores* also qualified the crimes and stated whether they were "light" crimes or more serious offenses. If the qualifiers believed that an act of heresy had occurred, then the inquisitors could proceed with an arrest warrant, and a trial followed. If these qualifiers decided that the incident or case did not concern the Inquisition or contain any suspicion of heresy, the tribunal usually dropped the case.

Similarly, these qualifiers also served as an official consulting board for the censorship of books and other publications. In addition, the inquisitors submitted any suspected works, published prayers, broadsides, or even printed textiles (such as the one contained in document 54) to these qualifiers or censors, and according to their decision, suspected publications or prints could be either approved, expurgated, or suppressed.[117]

These qualifiers were designated from among the members of the clergy who, besides being theologians, belonged to the highest levels of the hierarchies of their respective religious orders.[118] Because of the importance of their positions in the trial proceedings, the *calificadores* of the tribunal of the Inquisition enjoyed a great social prestige.

Legal Consultants (*Consultores*)

The *consultores* (consultants) were nonsalaried specialists who participated with the inquisitors in examining crimes against the faith. These *consultores* were by definition jurists who acted as advisers to the inquisitors "on matters of law."[119] The *consultores* had the right to vote on whether to issue an arrest order, on when to submit a suspect to questioning under torture, and on the decision of the final sentence. If the inquisitors and the ordinary (the representative of the local bishop) were in agreement, but the *consultores* disagreed, the decision of the inquisitors was to be enforced. The selection of these legal consultants depended on the types of judicial officers available in a region. In areas where a viceregal *audiencia* was present, these officials were usually selected from among the local judges of this high court. Others were chosen from among the chief clergymen of the area. The only requirement was that they should have a university degree in law.

The Ordinary (*Ordinario*)

The *ordinario* was usually a chief ecclesiastical judge who represented the local bishop of a diocese in Inquisition proceedings. The bishop's representative had a decisive and important vote in cases of crimes against the faith. For example, during the voting that approved final sentences in these cases, the ordinary voted after the legal consultants and before the inquisitors. The ordinary also had to vote on all requests for the administration of questioning under torment. As the theoretical and actual ecclesiastical official who had control over all members of their bishopric, the ordinary had a deep interest in observing the proceedings in cases when votes of torture existed. The ordinary also had the responsibility of being present while the suspect underwent torture, to safeguard against abuses. The participation of the ordinary signified the consolidation and cooperation of the secular diocesan church in the inquisitorial activities of the tribunals of the Holy Office.[120]

Familiars of the Inquisition (*Familiares*)

A separate system of secular or laypersons called *familiares* formed an elite group of constables that made up an inquisitorial militia. The familiars of the Inquisition, or *familiares*, served as a permanent force of assistants, constables, and informers for the Holy Office. In addition to aiding the officials of the Inquisition in the discovery, apprehension, and arrest of suspects, they were required to:

- Attend to the various tasks given to them by the inquisitors
- Denounce all suspects to the Inquisition
- Serve as bodyguards or protectors of the inquisitors
- Aid in bringing suspects to the Inquisition's prisons

All those nominated had their family histories investigated to ensure that they were "Old Christians of good faith and customs."[121] Once in office, their privileged positions exempted them from prosecution in civil and criminal cases. The numbers of these familiars varied, but by law at least twelve familiars served in Mexico City, four familiars in the seat of each bishopric, and at least one familiar in each Spanish town throughout New Spain.[122]

Local Provincial Officials of the Inquisition in New Spain

Since the district is so large that it is not possible to visit all of the regions of it by your-selves, you, the said Inquisitors, should send out commissaries to the parts and places where you cannot comfortably go and visit yourselves.

Don Diego de Espinosa, Inquisitor General, 1570

The territory that made up the tribunal of Mexico's geographic district was vast indeed, stretching from the unknown lands to the north of Mexico, deep into Central America as far south as Nicaragua, to the east as far as the island of Cuba, and in the west across the Pacific to include the Spanish territory of the Philippines.[123] This single inquisi-torial tribunal had as its jurisdiction a massive extent of territory that spread over more than 3 million square kilometers and which contained approximately 450,000 people un-der its control (excluding the large numbers of the region's indigenous people, who were removed from its jurisdiction).[124] Within this vast district of the tribunal, territories were divided into local commissariats that coincided with the territorial divisions of ecclesiasti-cal bishoprics (see map 1).

Territorially, the Inquisition of New Spain eventually came to include a local depu-tized inquisitorial court, or commissariat of the Inquisition, in each of the bishoprics throughout the kingdom of New Spain.[125] The inquisitors who sat in the seat of the tribu-nal in Mexico City directly controlled these subordinate regional courts by naming subdel-egated regional commissaries or commissioners. Each commissary general or Inquisition commissioner presided over the commissariat of the Inquisition in his region. In effect, these local courts of the Inquisition saw most of the routine denunciations against people for crimes against the faith.[126] The commissary would then forward the initial case after investigating it to the seat of the tribunal that had jurisdiction over his district.

The creation of local commissariats of the Holy Office occurred gradually, first in the regions with the largest Spanish presence; later, other commissariats formed as needed with the expansion of the Spanish and mixed-caste population beyond the major urban areas. After sending its ministers throughout the kingdom, the tribunal subsequently cre-ated numerous local inquisitorial commissariats in outlying districts.[127] As the Spanish and mixed-caste populations increased in some regions, the inquisitors forcibly subdivided earlier commissariats into smaller regions, with lieutenant commissaries in each major town within a bishopric or region in order to achieve greater vigilance over the newcomers. Generally, as time went on, the Inquisition licensed an increasing number of commissar-ies in outlying regions and distant mining or other agricultural centers where the non-Indian populations increased (table 5).

The dates of the foundation and subdivision of inquisitorial commissariats serve as a useful indicator in understanding the gradual growth of the nonindigenous population of New Spain. The inquisitors believed that the closer the Spaniards, Africans, mulattoes, and mestizos came in proximity to the indigenous peoples, the more contaminated their re-ligion and morals would become. This increasing fear of the contamination of indigenous

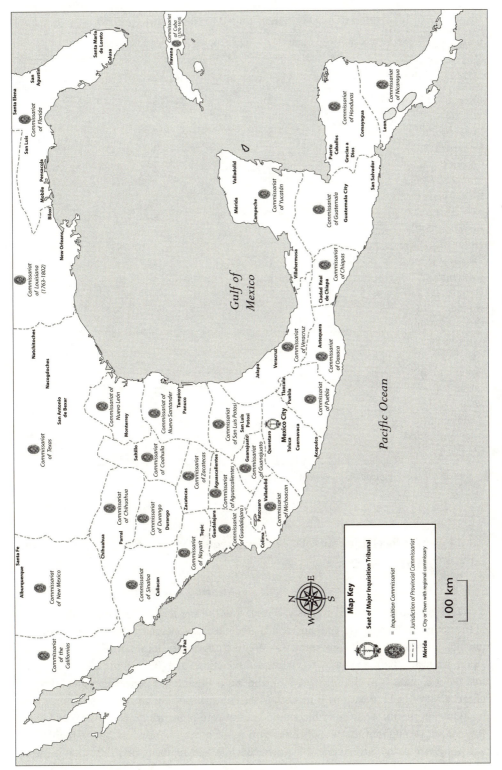

MAP 1. Territorial Jurisdiction of the Inquisition in New Spain, 1571–1820

Map Key

 = Seat of Major Inquisition Tribunal

= Inquisition Commissariat

- - - = Jurisdiction of Provincial Commissariat

Mérida = City or Town with regional commissary

Commissariat of the Californias

Commissariat of New Mexico — Alburquerque, Santa Fe

Commissariat of Texas — San Antonio de Bexar

Commissariat of Sinaloa — Culiacan

Commissariat of Chihuahua — Chihuahua, Parral

Commissariat of Durango — Durango

Commissariat of Nuevo León — Monterrey

Commissariat of Coahuila — Saltillo

Commissariat of Nuevo Santander — Tampico, Panuco

Commissariat of Zacatecas — Zacatecas

Commissariat of Aguascalientes — Aguascalientes

Commissariat of Nayarit — Tepic

Commissariat of Guadalajara — Guadalajara

Commissariat of Guanajuato — Guanajuato, Queretaro

Commissariat of San Luis Potosí — San Luis Potosi

Commissariat of Michoacan — Valladolid, Pazcuaro, Colima

Mexico City — Toluca, Cuernavaca, Tlaxcala, Acapulco

Commissariat of Puebla — Puebla

Commissariat of Veracruz — Veracruz, Jalapa

Commissariat of Oaxaca — Antequera

Commissariat of Chiapa — Ciudad Real de Chiapa, Villahermosa

Commissariat of Yucatán — Mérida, Campeche, Valladolid

Commissariat of Guatemala — Guatemala City, San Salvador

Commissariat of Honduras — Puerto Caballos, Gracias a Dios, Comayagua

Commissariat of Nicaragua — Leon

Commissariat of Louisiana (1763–1802) — Natchitoches, Nacogdoches, New Orleans

Commissariat of Florida — San Luis, San Agustin, Santa Elena, Calusa, Santa Maria de Loreto, Pensacola, Mobile, Biloxi

Commissariat of Cuba (1570–1610) — Havana

Gulf of Mexico

Pacific Ocean

La Paz

100 km

N W E S

TABLE 5
Inquisition Commissariats Founded in New Spain, 1571–1700

Regional Inquisition Commissariat (Year Founded)	Towns with Commissaries		
	1571–1600	1600–1650	1650–1700
Bishopric of Mexico (1571)	2	5	14
Yucatan (1571)	1	4	6
Puebla (1571)	1	3	5
Veracruz (1572)	1	3	10
Oaxaca (1572)	1	7	12
Michoacán (1572)	1	3	5
Guadalajara (1572)	1	2	3
Nicaragua (1579)	1	2	2
Acapulco (1581)	1	1	3
Philippines (1587)	1	4	6
Zacatecas (1594)	1	1	2
Guatemala (1596)	1	2	4
Durango (1608)	0	3	5
Honduras (1612)	0	1	3
Chiapas (1619)	0	1	2
San Luis Potosi (1621)	0	2	3
New Mexico (1623)	0	1	2
Colima (1635)	0	1	2
Coahuila (1645)	0	1	3
Sinaloa (1645)	0	1	1
Tampico (1646)	0	1	2
Guanajuato (1653)	0	0	2
Total	13	49	97

Source: Alberro, *Inquisición y sociedad*, appendix 2, 85–96.

culture on the religious practices of the colony witnessed the increasing subdivision of the early commissariat regions.

INQUISITION COMMISSARIES GENERAL AND LOCAL COMMISSARIES

The commissary general exercised control over the territory entrusted to him. Because of the nature of the position, the candidate had to hold an ecclesiastical post and have social prestige. In practice, these commissaries were in charge of the local familiars of the Inquisition. They also participated by receiving denunciations, making the initial investigation into reports, publishing the edicts of faith, and inquiring into the genealogies and lifestyles of those who sought to become ministers of the tribunal (see document 4).[128]

Outside the major seats of bishoprics, there were other minor commissaries of the Inquisition throughout the rest of the provinces who were nominated by the inquisitors and approved by the viceroy and the crown. Each large city, town, or village that came to have a sizable Spanish and mixed-caste population would usually have a local commissary (*comisario*) who operated a minor tribunal of the Holy Office, investigating crimes against the faith and then conducting the initial investigation and arrest of the accused in certain cases. These commissariats employed at least one notary and a constable. In some cases, they could even pass preliminary sentences but not the definitive sentences unless ordered to do so by the tribunal in Mexico.

In more outlying commissariats and provinces, members of the various religious orders almost exclusively held the posts of commissaries of the Holy Office, whereas in major urban regions and more populated provinces, members of the secular clergy or, in a few isolate cases, an occasional Jesuit wherever there existed a major Jesuit college or mission held the post of commissary more often.[129]

The commissaries of the Holy Office in local regions had as their central duties the reading and proclaiming of the Inquisition's edicts of faith, the taking of periodic visitations of their district to inquire or make "inquisitions" into crimes against the faith, and the reception of denunciations and testimonies against people of suspected inquisitorial crimes.[130]

The quality and character of the various commissaries of the Inquisition differed, and generalities are difficult to make concerning their activities. Many commissaries of the Inquisition in outlying regions were indeed zealous men who exercised the office of commissary with a desire to root out crimes against the faith. For instance, Fray Diego Muñoz, who served as the commissary of the Holy Office in the region of Michoacan from 1615 to 1620, scoured his region actively seeking out denunciations and other testimonies, which he subsequently forwarded to the inquisitors of the tribunal in Mexico.[131] Other commissaries, however, were not always so zealous or even good Christians themselves. For instance, in Zacatecas during the 1620s, Diego de Herrera y Arteaga, rather than exhibiting zeal and desire for denouncing crimes against the faith, was himself a paragon of vices and defects.[132] Apparently, according to testimonies against him, Herrera was a "blasphemous, irreligious, and sacrilegious man, who sought to sow discord with gossip, and anonymous denunciations, which even instigated violence—and on several occasions he even hit several women."[133] Other commissaries, though not as scandalous in their actions, committed crimes against the faith. In one instance, Diego Ortiz de Saavedra, commissary of the region of Lagos in the 1640s, lived openly with his lover, a mulatta woman, and even had children with her.[134]

NOTARIES (IN LOCAL INQUISITION COMMISSARIATS)

The local *notarios,* or notaries of the Holy Office, served the functions of both the notary of the secret and the secretary of the sequestered goods in remote outlying regions distant from the seat of the tribunal. They also drew up and wrote all of the documents of the local inquisitorial courts and maintained the register of all the documents and cases pending investigation by the local commissariat of the Inquisition.[135]

CHIEF CONSTABLE (*ALGUACIL MAYOR*) OF THE LOCAL INQUISITION COMMISSARIATS

Along with the commissary and an appointed notary, each major seat of a regional commissariat often had another appointed official, the *alguacil mayor del partido,* or local

TABLE 6

Familiars in the Territory of New Spain, 1571–1636

City	Number of Familiars
Mexico City	144
Puebla de los Angeles	19
Zacatecas	16
Guatemala City	13
Mérida	10
Campeche	6
Total	208

Source: Alberro, *Inquisición y sociedad*, 97–102.

chief constable. In larger cities and in all of the colonial ports, these *alguaciles mayores* enabled and aided the local commissaries to conduct their business, including visitations of ships, arrests, and sequestering, without the need to involve the local civil authorities and, thus, to reveal the secret of the proceedings.

LOCAL FAMILIARS OF THE INQUISITION (*FAMILIARES*)

Just as those in the seat of the tribunal, other local commissariats of the Inquisition relied on a varying number of familiars to conduct the major business of the Holy Office in their regions (table 6). According to figures from 1571 to 1646 collected by Mexican Inquisition scholar Solange Alberro, more than 314 familiars existed in the territory of the tribunal of New Spain, including 20 familiars throughout Central America, and 24 familiars residing in the Philippines. These 314 familiars were spread out among sixty-four of the largest towns in the region that contained significant proportions of Spanish residents. Together with the *alguacil mayor* in each regional commissariat, these local familiars aided the commissaries in their initial questioning and arrest of suspected heretics for later processing in the tribunal in Mexico City.

Finances of the Holy Office

If a remedy is not soon found [for the lack of funds], this Tribunal could easily find itself closed within a few days, because it has nothing left . . . neither can it feed its prisoners nor pay its officials, and these cannot be expected to serve in vain.

Official Report of Don Martín Carrillo y Alderete, Visiting Royal Judge in New Spain, 1625

Although the Suprema and Spanish crown expected the Inquisition tribunal of New Spain to become financially self-supporting, paying for its expenses out of the confiscations, fines, and pecuniary penances it imposed, during the first decades of the Mexican Inquisition's operation they provided a royal subvention of 10,000 pesos a year, including 3,000 pesos for each of the two inquisitors and the prosecutor, and 1,000 pesos for the notary or secretary.[136] Although the crown set aside specific funds for the salaries of the tribunal's major officials, it gave no funding for the payment of the salaries of the tribunal's minor officials. In 1583 several local inquisitors in New Spain, facing a lack of necessary funds, even petitioned for the abolition of several of the lesser offices without other funding from the crown. Inquisitors Francisco Santos García and Alonso Fernández de Bonilla argued that these lesser offices should be abolished because their salaries relied on the hope of confiscations that never came. The situation was so bad, they reported, that the holders of these lesser positions resigned one after another, "leaving only the *alcaide* and *portero*, who are so poor that they would also have gone if they saw other means of escaping their creditors."[137] Continued complaints from the inquisitors of New Spain concerning the poverty of the tribunal continued until later in the sixteenth century when confiscations increased the Mexican Inquisition's access to funding.

Royal Fiscal Office of the Inquisition (*Real Fisco de la Santa Inquisición*)

The Inquisition in New Spain managed its finances independently of either royal or ecclesiastical control. A subsidiary institution controlled by the tribunal of Mexico, the *Real Fisco*, or the Royal Fiscal Office of the Inquisition, became entrusted with the management of the confiscated property and goods of those convicted by the Inquisition.[138] This branch of the Holy Office had the power and duty to oversee the finances and pay for salaries and various fees that the Inquisition incurred during its proceedings. The Real Fisco counted on the services of a *contador* (accountant), several lawyers, and two *notarios del secuestro*, who testified to everything relative to the confiscation of goods.

Although Philip II gave each of the tribunals in the New World a subvention of 10,000 pesos per year to cover the salaries of the major officials of each tribunal,[139] the king intended that the tribunals would eventually become self-supporting, from confiscations, fines, and pecuniary penances, but this would require time.[140]

Inquisition Finances and Corruption

Previous interpretations of the Inquisition as a corrupt institution bent on the confiscation of as much property as possible emerged from the study of the finances of the Inquisition.[141] Although this extreme interpretation has been disproved, the payment of the officials' salaries almost exclusively from the sequestered goods of the accused lent itself to corruption.

Previous Inquisition scholars such as Henry Lea and Helen Phipps both described the Mexican Inquisition as an institution "hungry for new sources of revenue and eager to seize upon any opportunity to enlarge its power and authority."[142] Nevertheless, according to the surviving sources, the Inquisition in New Spain apparently suffered from a lack of adequate income from its inception to the early seventeenth century, earning only about 15,000 pesos in confiscations from 1614 to 1637.[143] Things began to change, however, once the Mexican Inquisition began to focus on prosecuting a larger number of Portuguese New Christians and crypto-Jews who had migrated to New Spain during the later part of the sixteenth century (table 7).

Unfortunately for the large number of Portuguese New Christians, a 1640 revolt against the king of Spain, led by the Portuguese Duque de Braganza, combined with an unstable political climate in New Spain, led to the Inquisition's renewed persecution of crypto-Jews. By 1642 the Mexican Inquisition began to arrest large numbers of Portuguese

TABLE 7

Quantities of Money Confiscated by the Tribunal
in New Spain, 1640–1650

Year	Pesos Confiscated by Tribunal
1646	38,732
1647	148,562
1648	234,000
1649	3,000,000
Total	3,421,294

Source: Lea, *Inquisition in the Spanish Dependencies*, 219.

residents in Mexico, suspecting them of treason by the virtue of their Portuguese origins. As the scholar Stanley Hordes described earlier, "The bulk of the Mexican crypto-Jews in 1642 traced their roots back to Portugal."[144]

Although confiscations primarily from Portuguese New Christians would net the tribunal massive wealth after 1642, moneys procured from confiscations were not enough to cover the salaries of the tribunal's officials during the first fifty years of its operations. Evidence of fiscal corruption began early in the Mexican Inquisition's history. For instance, although only one inquisitor existed in the early years, the local tribunal's receiver and treasurer collected the salary for two inquisitors.[145] When called to account for the sum of money, he claimed that he had spent it on the maintenance of poor prisoners.

To ensure a more secure source of revenue and eliminate corruption, in 1627 Pope Urban VIII ordered that in each cathedral seat of the Inquisition one of the prebends or canonries paid for by tithe revenues was to be suppressed and its rents applied to the payment of the Inquisition salaries. But many scholars, including Henry Lea, argue that the finances of the Inquisition in Mexico remained precarious, as the Holy Office continued to clash with the king and treasury officials concerning salaries.[146] Even when the coffers of the tribunal began to fill with large confiscations, the officials still managed to collect the royal subvention of 10,000 pesos per year, though they often were met with royal resistance, which caused increasing controversy throughout the seventeenth century.[147]

Despite the increase in confiscations and the new funds received from a portion of tithe revenues, the officials of the tribunal in Mexico continued to send numerous requests for increases in their salaries throughout the years. Apparently, however, their salaries remained relatively unchanged from 1572 until the end of the colonial period as can be seen in table 8. What the figures also appear to show is that, when shortfalls occurred, the officials often suffered by receiving lower salaries.

Regardless of its lack of income before 1630, the tribunal of Mexico soon came to acquire a vast amount of wealth (document 25).[148] As early as 1579, the tribunal requested the appointment of a receptor to receive and administer its assets, which amounted in that year to only 4,283 pesos.[149] Shortly afterward, the tribunal began to collect larger sums of moneys from confiscations and from properties that it began to hold. By the end of the colonial period, the Holy Office became one of the wealthier institutions in New Spain, with reve-

TABLE 8

Salaries of the Officials of the Inquisition Tribunal of New Spain, 1572–1820

Official	Established Legal Salary in Pesos/Year	Salaries Paid in 1711
Inquisitors (at least 2)	3,000	2,940
Prosecuting attorney	3,000	2,940
Secretary of the secret	1,600	1,375
Receiver	1,500	825
Accountant	1,000	550
Secretary of sequesters	750	550
Chief constable	750	550
Jailer	750	668
Lieutenant jailor	350	—
Messenger[a]	600	551
Doorman	200	—
Procurator of the fiscal office	200	150
Medic	100	60
Surgeon	100	30
Barber	50	—
Total	16,750	11,189

Source: Archivo Histórico Nacional, Sección de Inquisición, leg. 4814, caja 1; Archivo General de la Nación, Ramo de Inquisición, vol. 84, exp. 32 (1578); vol. 289, exp. 9 (1593); vol. 446, exp. 3 (1659); vol. 468, exp.1 (1600–1640); Lea, The Inquisition in the Spanish Dependencies, 212–20, 289.

[a] In 1711, the same official occupied the positions of messenger and doorman.

nue that was twice as much as expenses.[150] In fact, the tribunal's total assets in 1814 when the crown suppressed the Holy Office amounted to more than 1,775,676 pesos.[151]

The Inquisitorial Process in New Spain

Throughout the territory of the Tribunal, the Inquisitors should act with all temperance and gentleness and with much consideration, because it is convenient that they do everything in this way so that the Inquisition can be much feared and respected and they should not give any occasion or reason for the people to have hatred for [the Inquisition].

Instructions from the Inquisitor General Don Diego de Espinosa for the Tribunal of New Spain, 1571

Rather than detail all of the institutional peculiarities and procedures used by the Inquisition in New Spain, this section provides a brief sketch of inquisitorial procedure as it typically unfolded in the Mexican Inquisition, with examples from actual cases from New Spain and comparisons with similar procedural issues in Spain. An outline of each of the steps in the complex series of events that occurred during an Inquisition trial accompanies the descriptions of procedures.

In strictly legal terms, the Inquisition and its inquisitors pursued the prosecution of heretics, blasphemers, bigamists, and those guilty of other acts of immorality in the same manner and with the same procedures that all civil and criminal judges and tribunals of the same period pursued cases against traitors, murderers, thieves, and other lesser criminals. In the unique case of Inquisition trials, however, the judge who would pass sentence was one of the officials who had initially gathered the evidence used to inculpate the accused. Thus, the impartiality of the judge in any Inquisition trial was unlikely. The entire structure of an inquisitorial trial and its proceedings placed the accused heretic in an inferior position without many options or tools for an effective defense.[152]

The inquisitor led the entire trial process from beginning to end, investigating the facts, leading the official inquiry or inquest into the suspected act of heresy, and accumulating evidence against the accused.[153] Inquisition procedures did not require an initial accusation or indictment. Instead, the inquisitor himself could inquire, investigate, and take evidence about a suspected act of heresy. The primary objective was to discover the act of heresy, apprehend the suspected heretic, gain his confession, eventually pass judgment, and sentence the accused heretic to corrective punishments and penance in order to readmit him into the fold of the church. As Richard Kagan and Abigail Dyer noted, unlike royal and criminal courts, "which understood their sentences as retributive for injuries done to the accuser, the Inquisition framed its punishments as atonement, a penance that had to be done in order to make amends for the defendant's injury to God, the Church, and the sacraments."[154]

The Importance of the Oath of Secrecy for Inquisition Proceedings

¡Con el Rey y la Inquisición, Chitón! (Concerning the King and the Inquisition, Hush! Be Silent!)

Common sixteenth-century Spanish refrain

The very nature of the Inquisition's proceedings and the secrecy with which much of the testimony and evidence against the accused heretic was gathered in itself prejudiced the prisoner's effective defense. The single-most prejudicial aspect involved the secrecy required of witnesses, which helped to encourage anonymous denunciations and accusations of a person's enemies without a deponent having fear of ultimately having his or her identity revealed to the accused.[155] In addition, the nature of the secrecy surrounding the actual contents of the official accusation itself and the successive formal interrogations of the isolated prisoner, which often led to self-incrimination of other crimes that might not have been included in the original accusation, further hampered the effective defense of the accused heretic.[156] Similarly, the accused heretic's sequestration and imprisonment in the secret prisons of the Inquisition and his prevention from having contact with the outside world also limited his ability to summon witnesses and challenge incriminating testimony.[157]

The procedure of the Inquisition was held in such secrecy that in 1573 the Venetian ambassador to Spain, Leonardo Donato, could report that "nothing was known of its victims and their cases until their sentences were published in the autos-da-fé, but the fear entertained of it was so universal that little was said concerning it through dread of arousing suspicion."[158] Even when they were printed, the Inquisition's instructions and manuals remained strictly for the use and possession of the Inquisition's officials and ministers.[159]

The Inquisition and its ministers viewed the oath of secrecy as a solemn "seal" that ensured the proper functioning of the tribunal. In 1595 King Philip II in his instructions to the inquisitor general Alonso Manrique de Lara remarked that, without the seal of the oath of secrecy, "the Holy Office could not preserve the exercise of its functions."[160] Shortly after receiving these instructions from the crown, Manrique issued a harsh letter of reprimand to the inquisitors in New Spain for not having maintained secrecy in their proceedings. In his rebuke, the inquisitor general warned the inquisitors that future infractions would be rigorously punished.[161] The king's demand that officials violating the oath of secrecy be punished with the utmost rigor resulted in any such infraction being considered a formal act of perjury.[162] As the Suprema warned the inquisitors in New Spain in a later *carta acordada* issued on February 26, 1607, only a single witness could provide the necessary proof of an official's breach of the vow of secrecy, and a first offense earned the offending minister a year's suspension from office and a fine of fifty ducats.[163]

The oath of secrecy also covered all votes, orders, dispatches, and letters issued by or to the tribunal and all other documents and procedures that its ministers created.[164] The Mexican Inquisition's officials did not remain immune from censure if they violated this oath of secrecy. For instance, on September 10, 1590, the Suprema rebuked the Inquisition in New Spain for having printed and allowed public access to copies of several instructions and other documents pertaining to the abjurations of convicted heretics.[165] The Suprema warned the inquisitors not to publicly print any such documents because it broke the veil of secrecy under which the Inquisition should operate.

At every step in an inquisitorial trial, the Inquisition's ministers took thorough precautions to ensure absolute secrecy. Not only the Inquisition's officials and ministers but also the accused, any accusers, and all of the witnesses for both the defense and the prosecution swore an oath of secrecy.[166] The suspected heretic at the very first audience with the inquisitors vowed to tell the truth and to remain silent and keep secret not only his own case but also everything that he might see or hear while in the tribunal.[167] Even when freed from the Inquisition's prisons, a convicted or acquitted suspect made a formal oath of secrecy that prohibited him from speaking about his case or what occurred in the tribunal, and any violations of this oath of secrecy earned the suspect one hundred or two hundred lashes.[168] Moreover, in the public edicts of faith, the Inquisition required all people to denounce any violation of these oaths and to report anyone who printed, possessed, or wrote anything concerning the Inquisition and its procedures. Even the published instructions given to local commissaries of the Inquisition warned them that the preservation of the Inquisition depended on absolute secrecy being observed in its proceedings (document 4).

Inquisitorial Trials and Procedures

In considering the judicial functions of the Inquisition, we shall meet with much that is abhorrent to our conceptions of justice. We shall see that the accused was assumed to be guilty and that the object of the tribunal was to induce or coerce him to confess his guilt; that, for this purpose, he was substantially deprived of facilities for defense and that the result, for the most part, depended on his powers of endurance which the judges, at discretion, could test to the utmost.

Henry Charles Lea, *A History of the Inquisition in Spain*, 1907

Regardless of the veil of secrecy under which the Inquisition functioned, inquisitorial courts remained governed by strict rules and regulations. According to civil and canon law, all Inquisition trials had to follow a standard procedure established at the founding of the Inquisition in Spain by the publication of Tomás de Torquemada's *Instrucciones* in 1484.[169] Over the years, the work was reissued repeatedly and adapted for changing circumstances. The most popular copy of the *Instrucciones* used in New Spain was the 1561 version by Don Fernando de Valdés, who was inquisitor general in that year. The volume was reprinted in 1576 and again in 1592,[170] when the Suprema sent copies to the Inquisition in New Spain after reports that the inquisitors there had violated the established rules and regulations.[171]

Similarly, special Inquisition manuals also existed, such as one written by the Aragonese Dominican Fray Nicolas Eimeric and later published with annotations from the sixteenth-century Spanish jurist and commentator Francisco Peña.[172] Written as early as the 1370s, Nicolas Eimeric's *Directorium Inquisitorum* served as one of the most influential and commonly used Inquisition manuals among Spanish and Mexican authorities.[173] After its initial publication in 1578,[174] many subsequent inquisitors, including those of New Spain, looked to Peña's work as an authoritative source of inquisitorial law.[175] It was so influential that many libraries and booksellers throughout New Spain owned copies of the manual by the early seventeenth century.[176]

There were also rigidly defined protocols and protections included in these procedures for the defense of the accused heretic. The Inquisition's notaries had to maintain detailed records of evidence, witness testimony, judgments, penalties, and other judicial documents.[177]

The Crucial Importance of Full Proof and Confession in Inquisition Trials

> A prisoner in the Inquisition is never allowed to see the face of his accuser, or the witnesses against him, but every method is taken by threats and tortures, to oblige him to confess and accuse himself, and by that means corroborate their evidence.
>
> John Foxe, *Book of Martyrs*, 1583

Because a heretic was both a criminal and a sinner, the Inquisition had two major goals in its proceedings: to uncover and punish a crime against the faith and to save the soul of the heretic. In terms of legal procedures, the most basic premise of the inquisitorial courts focused on the belief that no accused heretic could be convicted without full proof of his heresy. This necessity was rare in the criminal and civil court systems of the period. Even the modern courts of law in the United States require only proof "beyond a shadow of a doubt" to convict someone accused of a crime, which can allow the courts and juries to make mistaken convictions. Thus, the burden of proof required today in our own criminal court system falls far short of the necessary full proof required by the Inquisition to convict an accused heretic. In the minds of the inquisitors, anything short of full proof was not enough evidence to convict a defendant.[178]

For inquisitorial trials, only two forms of "full proof" could lead to a conviction. The first and most important, of course, was a confession to the crime. The second, more common means of full proof was the independent testimony of eyewitnesses. In the inquisitorial courts, other indications or circumstantial evidence could never add up to full proof.[179]

The defendant could not be convicted on partial proofs or other circumstantial evidence as long as he refused to confess and there was no eyewitness testimony against him. Without one of these two types of full proof, the inquisitors faced a difficult decision. Either they could acquit the defendant for lack of evidence and release him, which did occur on occasions, or they might decide to force the defendant to make a full confession through the controlled and regulated use of physical pain by means of torture.[180] The inquisitors did not consider a confession given under torture valid, or full proof, unless the prisoner later repeated and ratified the confession freely without the pressure of continued torment.[181]

Although our modern sensibilities view the use of torture as abhorrent and contrary to just due legal process, in the minds of the inquisitors (and most other contemporary criminal courts of the period), the use of torture in trial proceedings was justified in order to achieve full proof of the crime. The Inquisition's use of juridical torture remained quite moderate in comparison with the civil courts of the time. Torture techniques used in this same period were far harsher, persistent, and lawless in parts of western Europe, including Germany and England, than in Spain and Latin America.[182]

In this light, it is understandable how important and crucial a full confession by the accused heretic was in the ability of the inquisitors to conclude an Inquisition case. Convicting a suspected heretic without full proof would have violated the norms of due legal process even for the Inquisition. This rigid hierarchy of proofs demanded in inquisitorial proceedings and the central importance of a defendant's confession often hampered the Inquisition's ability to convict suspected heretics.[183] Inquisitorial courts often found it difficult to secure the eyewitness testimony of two or more witnesses or the spontaneous confession of the accused in order to seek a conviction. Similarly, the testimony of unique or single witnesses remained a serious obstacle in the prosecution.[184] As late as 1630, the Suprema issued orders that no tribunal should order the arrest of a suspect on the testimony of a single witness.[185] In cases where an apparent death penalty or relaxation to the secular arm for execution was sought, the burden of proof was higher. In these cases, the inquisitors could not convict the accused unless they had accumulated five eyewitness testimonies or acquired the defendant's full confession.[186] Even then, the local district courts of the Inquisition were required to remit their final sentences and request for relaxation to the Suprema in Madrid for its final ruling in the case.[187] Although many modern readers may find it difficult to believe, in this way the Inquisition's courts had many more protections for the rights of the accused than any civil or royal court of the same period.[188]

The Various Stages and Procedures in a Typical Inquisition Trial

We must remember that the main purpose of the trial and execution is not to save the soul of the accused but to achieve the public good and put fear into others.

Francisco Peña in his commentary to Eimeric's *Directorium Inquisitorum*, 1578

All inquisitorial trials occurred in two distinct stages, in which a preliminary investigative stage preceded a formal judicial or trial stage.[189] During the first stage, the investigation occurred in secrecy, and often the suspects were unaware that the court was compiling evidence against them. As a result, the suspected defendant was unable to prepare any defense. The Inquisition's prosecuting attorney did not even reveal the actual charges or alleged heretical crimes to the defendant until the opening of the formal trial.[190] In the trial phase, the inquisitor officially became an acting judge between two parties, the prosecuting attorney and the defendant. A defense lawyer, most often himself a salaried member of the court, assisted the defendant.

To better understand the process of inquisitorial proceedings and illuminate the types of documents compiled by the Inquisition and its officials, it is necessary to understand the formal judicial process that occurred in a typical Inquisition trial. No matter what the charge or allegation against the accused, Inquisition proceedings from the denunciation to the initial investigation, arrest, and subsequent trial all followed the same standard procedure.

Phase 1: The Pretrial or Investigative Stage of Inquisition Proceedings

Any who have seen, heard of, or witnessed acts of heresy should come and appear personally before us [the inquisitors] in our Audience chamber to declare and manifest anything that they may know or have done or seen done or said, touching upon Our Holy Catholic Faith and this Holy Office.

Standard form and order of an inquisitorial edict in New Spain, 1571

The procedures usually began uniformly with the issuing of an edict of faith (*edicto de fe*), or a proclamation requiring, under pain of excommunication, the denunciation of all offenses against the faith.[191] When the Inquisition periodically issued these edicts, it ordered them placed or read in all parish churches. A public reading often began the process by urging people to denounce themselves or others of crimes committed against the faith (see documents 6–11). After the edict's initial publication, the faithful received periodic warnings to denounce what they knew about crimes against the faith or else be liable for being considered an accomplice to those same crimes.

Discovery and Initial Investigation

Induced by the warnings of the *edicto de fe*, many people came forward denouncing themselves or giving testimony of crimes committed against the faith by their neighbors. An Inquisition judge could discover an act of heresy in one of only three ways: by either a formal accusation, a denunciation, or an inquest or inquisition into a suspected act of heresy.

An Inquisition trial based on an accusation began when one person formally accused another person of an act of heresy in the presence of the inquisitor. Unlike a simple denunciation of heresy, in a *formal accusation* the accuser became a party to the legal proceedings, and therefore the burden of proof of the crime fell upon the accuser. The Inquisition actively tried those discovered giving false testimony for perjury (*testigo falso*).[192]

Most frequently, a trial began with a *simple denunciation* by a third party. In these cases, the person simply brought the existence of suspected crimes against the faith to the notice of the inquisitors so that they could investigate the matter. The person making the denunciation did not become a formal party to the trial proceedings, and by this means the deponent did not have to present any proof of the crimes. Although a denunciation marked the preliminary stage in the identification of a heretic, not every denunciation automatically led to the subsequent arrest and trial of an accused heretic.[193] Nevertheless, scholars have harshly criticized the Inquisition for its reliance on and admission of denunciations by all classes of people. For instance, the Enlightenment French philosopher Voltaire joined his contemporaries in criticizing the Spanish Inquisition's stance on accepting dubious witness testimony:

> Their form of proceeding is an infallible way to destroy whomsoever the inquisitors wish. The prisoners are not confronted with the accuser or informer. Nor is there any informer or witness who is not listened to. A public convict, a notorious malefactor, an infamous person, a common prostitute, a child, are in the holy office, though nowhere else, credible accusers and witnesses. Even the son may depose against his father, the wife against her husband.[194]

Although Voltaire and others exaggerated the Inquisition's abuses, the modern scholar Edward Peters noted that the Inquisition did admit the testimony of otherwise doubtful witnesses, such as obviously biased parties and those declared infamous or already convicted of perjury.[195] The Inquisition permitted virtually anyone to denounce a suspected act of heresy, and this denunciation could be made either verbally or in writing in the presence of the notary of the Inquisition as long as the denouncers identified themselves by name and included all of the pertinent allegations.[196] Although the Inquisition did allow many people of dubious character and repute to denounce and testify against suspected acts of heresy, it did not usually accept anonymous denunciations.

Furthermore, all denunciations had to occur under oath before the notary of the tribunal and in the presence of two witnesses, all of whom had previously sworn an oath of secrecy.[197] During the denunciation, the inquisitors asked if the person making the denunciation knew of the existence of other persons or witnesses who might have seen or knew about the same crimes. If he or she responded in the affirmative, the Inquisition would summon the people named for later interrogation. During the subsequent interrogations of possible witnesses, those summoned were asked generally if they had anything to declare concerning crimes against the faith.[198] In many cases, these cited witnesses, not knowing what to respond, often implicated themselves in other crimes of the faith. In order to continue, the inquisitors needed to compile the clear and credible testimony of at least three witnesses.[199] Once the denouncer or the cited witnesses completed their denunciations and testimonies, they were sworn to secrecy.

A third commonly used scenario in the medieval Inquisition, but less frequently used in New Spain, focused on a formal *inquisition* (*inquisitio*). This meant that the Inquisition, or the local Inquisition commissary, began the investigation into crimes against the faith. The inquisitors, or their commissary judges, conducted this scenario *de oficio*, on the powers inherent in their offices, without needing a third party to denounce a suspect. Although most inquisitors had the ability to conduct these inquisitions *de oficio*, they rarely did so because of the huge cost involved in a special visitation of the region. As René Millar noted for the tribunal of the Inquisition in Peru, the inquisitors almost exclusively initiated their cases on the basis of denunciations of third parties.[200] Most of the cases initiated by the Mexican tribunal's inquisitors, and formally presented by the prosecutor, apparently also dealt with third-party denunciations of suspected heretics.

The case was different, however, in the outlying provinces in New Spain. In many instances, local commissaries, hearing rumors of some crime against the faith, would begin an investigation *de oficio,* summoning witnesses and taking testimony that they would then remit to the tribunal in Mexico City. Although they had no power to begin the trial phase of inquisitorial proceedings, commissaries remained the primary agents in taking denunciations and creating the initial summary phase of inquisitorial proceedings.[201]

Depending on the contents of the denunciation, the inquisitor (or local commissary) could summon other witnesses to testify whom the deponent named in the initial denunciation or accused during the subsequent inquest. This collection of testimony occurred in the utmost secrecy. The inquisitor or commissary then compiled the denunciations and testimonies of witnesses and collected them along with their own initial findings into a document called an official summary (*sumaria*).[202]

At this stage, no formal accusations or allegations existed, and nothing had yet been proved against the suspect. Often the accused or suspected heretic at this point had no idea that he had been denounced or that the Inquisition had begun conducting an investigation against him.

Qualification and Decision to Proceed in the Case

No actions were taken against the suspect or his property until the formal review of the *sumaria* by the tribunal's inquisitors and its qualifiers (*calificadores*). Before any arrest could occur, the inquisitors had to hand over the compiled evidence and summary to the qualifiers. As one of the checks and balances on the proper procedural order of inquisitorial trials, these qualifiers served as censors to determine if the collected evidence and the charges constituted a formal act of heresy.[203]

If the qualifiers, most often theologians or experts in canon law, decided that the denounced actions did not constitute a formal act of heresy, the inquisitors then weighed their decision with the evidence and testimonies compiled by the Inquisition's prosecuting attorney. If they concurred that sufficient evidence did not exist to proceed to the formal trial stage and gain a conviction, the inquisitors could archive the collected information and wait for subsequent denunciations or testimony to be gathered so they could proceed with the case at a later time.

PHASE 2: THE SUSPECT'S ARREST AND THE SEQUESTRATION OF HIS GOODS AND BELONGINGS

If there appeared to be enough evidence and proof of a formal act of heresy, the Inquisition's prosecuting attorney could issue a citation ordering the suspect to appear before the tribunal, or with the inquisitors he could draw up a formal arrest warrant and order the immediate detention of the accused.[204]

Arrest and Detention of the Accused Heretic

Once the accused is imprisoned, the constable should place him where no one else can see him, talk to him, or give him any news either in writing or in word of mouth . . . and he should not let prisoners communicate with one another except when the inquisitors have advised him that the communication between them should not result in any inconveniences.[205]

"On Prisoners," in the Compilation of the Instructions of the Holy Office, 1561

In issuing a formal citation to appear before the tribunal, the Inquisition intended to make the suspect appear before the inquisitors, answer their queries, and dispel any doubts about his good Christian conduct. The inquisitors did not issue these citations with the goal of arresting the suspect, but an ultimate arrest could follow depending on the initial interview with the suspect. The prosecuting attorney issued a request for a formal arrest warrant only in cases that implicated the suspect of having committed serious crimes against the faith.[206]

The inquisitors could call for the arrest of a suspected heretic only when the evidence or proof of the crime came from the declarations or testimony of at least five witnesses.[207] In these cases, the inquisitors ordered the tribunal's chief constable (*alguacil*) to detain the suspect.

Once brought into custody, the constable handed the suspect over to the tribunal's jailer (*alcaide*), who imprisoned the suspected heretic in the secret jails of the Inquisition, where the prisoner would remain isolated and incommunicado for the duration of the proceedings.[208] More disconcerting for the prisoner was the fact that he did not receive any information concerning the charges against him or any information about his accuser. In most cases, the prisoner had no idea why he had been arrested.

Confiscation and Sequestering of Goods

Either during or shortly after the arrest and detention of the accused heretic, his goods were confiscated and sequestered in order to pay for the costs of the trial and the expenses of maintaining the accused in the secret prisons (see documents 12 and 13 for examples of the expenses paid by Inquisition prisoners).[209] The Royal Fiscal Office inventoried the prisoner's estate and embargoed his goods, including all personal effects, for the duration of the trial. The accused paid the cost of imprisonment from the revenues of his estate; or, if he was poor, the Inquisition provided for his sustenance.

PHASE 3: THE FORMAL INVESTIGATIVE OR INQUEST STAGE OF THE PROCEEDINGS

With the arrest of the suspected heretic and the confiscation of his property and estate, the formal inquest or investigation stage of the trial began. During this first investigatory stage of the trial, the inquisitors continued to investigate the suspected crime and compiled evidence and proof against the accused. Again, the inquisitors conducted this stage of the inquisitorial trial under the strictest of secrecy. At this point the accused, now in prison, still did not know the charges against him and had no means of any defense until the opening of the formal judicial or trial stage. The inquisitors throughout this investigatory stage continued to compile testimonies and evidence against the accused, which further tended to lead to a firm presumption of the prisoner's guilt.

The Initial Hearing and Interrogation

And he was asked for an account of his life, asked to declare where he was born, raised and where he had lived and resided, and with whom he treated and had common communication, all of this he was asked to give in great detail with particular care.

The inquisitor's initial questions to an accused heretic who appeared at the first Interrogation, Instruction 13 in the Compilation of Instructions of the Holy Office, 1561

The prisoner usually appeared before the inquisitors for an initial hearing within eight days of the arrest, but the tribunal seldom informed the defendant about the nature of the alleged crimes at this time. The tribunal instead told the accused to "examine" his conscience and make a declaration of anything that he found to be "contrary to the faith."

The initial interrogation had a well-defined structure (fig. 1). During this first audience, the prisoner provided a life history, and oftentimes the accused perjured himself, lying or misrepresenting his own background or denying that his family members had been tried by the Inquisition.[210] The inquisitors then questioned the accused about his life and religious instruction.[211] The inquisitors also specifically incorporated an examination of the prisoner's knowledge of the basic Catholic prayers and doctrines during this first interview. From 1565 onward, the Inquisition required its prisoners to recite the four basic Christian prayers (Our Father, Ave Maria, The Creed, and the Holy Rosary) and make the sign of the cross.[212] If the accused did not know these basic prayers, the inquisitors' suspicions of his guilt increased.[213]

At this point in the interrogation, the inquisitors asked if the accused knew about the reasons for his arrest. If the prisoner responded negatively, the inquisitors informed him that there existed indications and evidence that the prisoner had engaged in conduct against the Catholic faith.[214] On the basis of the prisoner's answers, the inquisitors further interrogated the suspect concerning the details of any apparent crimes against the church or the Catholic religion. The inquisitors also informed the accused at this point that if he confessed his guilt freely, the tribunal would proceed with mercy.[215] They also warned the prisoner that if he did not confess and freely declare the truth, they would proceed against him with rigor.

As most Inquisition documents in both Spain and Mexico attest, more often than not the accused did not confess at this stage of the proceedings to any deeds or acts against the faith. Rather, the prisoner attempted to give the inquisitors the impression that he was a good Christian. In subsequent audiences and interrogations, however, the accused gradually began to tell half-truths and give away small incriminating details. All the while, in each session the inquisitors continued to pressure the accused in subsequent interrogations in order to gain the suspect's complete confession, which was indispensable as a full proof for conviction and also necessary to give the accused heretic ultimate forgiveness for his sins and crimes against the faith.

If the prisoner confessed completely at this stage, the inquisitorial proceedings could be abbreviated and concluded quickly.[216] If this occurred, the prosecuting attorney verified the confession and presented his concluding evidence.[217] At the same time, the Inquisition's legal and theological consultants would review the case and ensure that the proper procedures and legal forms had been followed. At that point, the inquisitor would dictate the final sentence in the case, which, depending on the prisoner's apparent attitude of repentance, could often be quite merciful.

On the other hand, if the accused heretic continued to maintain his innocence and refused to confess his guilt fully, the inquisitors gave the prisoner two more formal warnings during subsequent audiences.[218] If the accused continued to refuse to confess, the proceedings advanced to the next stage of the presentation of charges and the prosecuting attorney's formal accusation of heresy, which began the start of a formal judicial trial.[219]

The Prosecuting Attorney's Accusation and Formal Charges of Heresy

The formal judicial or criminal trial phase of inquisitorial proceedings began with the Inquisition's prosecuting attorney formally accusing the prisoner of having abandoned the Catholic Church and committed formal heresy. The prosecutor's formal accusation contained a detailed list of charges that omitted only the names of the eyewitnesses and any other circumstances or apparent evidence that the accused might be able to use to identify the prosecution's witnesses.[220] Regardless of the initial charges or the gravity of the supposed offense, the prosecutor usually added harsh language in the accusation that called for the inquisitors to impose upon the accused very severe penalties, including even the death penalty and total confiscation of the prisoner's goods. Most often, this harsh wording served to inspire fear and hopeful repentance in the accused as he listened to the formal reading of the charges.

Immediately after the formal reading of the charges in the presence of the prisoner, the inquisitors forced the accused to take an oath, and another interrogation followed. In this interrogation, the inquisitors had the prosecutor read the accused each of the charges one by one in detail. The inquisitors then expected the prisoner to respond to each charge. The prisoner was required to answer each charge there on the spot without the benefit of a defense attorney.[221] If the prisoner decided to begin to answer the charges, each one of the prisoner's answers to the charges was then recorded by the notary. The prisoner's responses often took more than one interrogation session. In most cases, however, the accused denied the charges and refused to accept them.

The defendant received a formal written version of the accusation without the identities of the prosecution's eyewitnesses revealed. Then the inquisitors ordered the accused taken back to his prison cell where he could read the accusation and any of his comments or responses in detail.[222] At this point in the trial, the prisoner's formal defense began.

Assigning of a Defense Attorney for the Accused

Though the Inquisitor might give him an advocate, he would give him no one good but a fellow who would do only what the inquisitor wanted, and if by chance he asked for an advocate or solicitor not of the Inquisition, they would not serve, for if they went contrary to the inquisitor's wishes, he would get up some charge of false belief or want of respect and cast them into the prison.

Reportedly said by an Inquisition prisoner in Valencia to his cell mate, 1559[223]

Although many previous scholars have criticized the Inquisition's procedures for a lack of any real defense for the accused, formal defense strategies did exist. Each of the prisoners was permitted to count on the legal aid of a lawyer in order to draft a response to the charges, gather evidence in support of the innocence of the accused, or attempt to strike, *tachar,* or invalidate some of the prosecution's witnesses and their testimonies.[224]

In most documented inquisition cases, the inquisitors did not deny the accused the right to name his own defenders. Even when a defendant repeatedly denied the need or the desire to have a defense lawyer, the inquisitors would name one for the accused on his behalf. In Spain, although prisoners early on named their own defense lawyers, by the middle of the sixteenth century the defense attorney for accused prisoners was already considered an official of the Holy Office.[225] In New Spain, though, the position of defense lawyer was always a salaried official of the tribunal who was paid out of the sequestered goods of the defendant's estate.[226]

Once a defense lawyer was appointed for the accused, he often waited a few days before contacting the prisoner in order to allow him the chance to consider the charges and perhaps confess freely to his guilt, thus avoiding the necessity of further judicial proceedings.[227] If the prisoner continued to deny the charges, then the defense lawyer intervened in the case and began to help the accused compile his defense strategy. One of the most often criticized parts of a defendant's ability to defend himself in Inquisition trials was the lack of a right to private counsel between the accused and the defense lawyer.[228] Defense lawyers could meet with the accused in order to help him with his defense, but each one of their meetings had to occur in the presence of the inquisitors.[229] This requirement no doubt often hampered the creation of a successful defense strategy.

The Inquisition's procedures also placed two specific limits on the defense attorney's actions. First, it forbade the attorney from trying to utilize formal tactics of delay in order to prolong the proceedings. Second, the Inquisition also mandated that if at any time during the trial the defense attorney should discover that the defendant was guilty, he had to inform the inquisitors of this fact and desist from representing the defense of the accused.

The First Defense against the Formal Accusation

Once the accused was given a defense attorney to represent him, the inquisitors again had the accusation and charges read to the prisoner, this time in the presence of the defense attorney. After this formal reading of the charges in the presence of the defense lawyer occurred, the inquisitors usually granted the accused at least nine days to prepare a formal written response to the charges with the aid of the defense attorney.

At this point, the accused prisoner usually continued to deny the charges against him and requested formally with the defense lawyer that he be set free and that his goods and properties be released. At this point, the prosecuting attorney, seeing that the accused denied the charges, requested that the inquisitors begin the formal trial and open the case up for the gathering of proof and presentation of evidence and witness testimonies in the case.[230]

PHASE 4: THE JUDICIAL OR FORMAL TRIAL PHASE

Inquisitors opened the judicial phase of the trial by allowing a period of nine days for both the prosecuting attorney and the defense lawyer to present their evidence and witness testimony.[231]

The Proof Stage of the Trial and the Gathering of Evidence

On the basis of the nature and extent of the formal charges against the accused, the prosecuting attorney now presented the evidence and proof of the prosecution's eye-witness testimonies. The prosecution's witness testimonies were taken individually in private under the oath that witnesses swore to tell the truth and keep the proceedings secret. The inquisitors kept the witnesses' identities secret from the accused and the defense attorney in order to avoid any attempts at future retribution.[232] During the taking of the prosecution witnesses' testimony, only the inquisitors, the notary, and other necessary officials of the Inquisition were allowed to be present.

The interrogation of the witnesses was based on a series of questionnaires concerning the details of the formal charges against the accused. Once the testimony had been taken, the prosecution's witnesses were required to have it read back to them, and then they were expected to affirm to the truth of all they declared in their sworn testimony.[233] The witnesses were also required under oath to swear that they did not accuse or give testimony against the prisoner out of hatred or animosity. Often the inquisitors, as an extra measure of validity, later summoned the witnesses to have them ratify and reaffirm the truth of their previous declarations. This ratification of the witnesses' testimony and their formal affirmation under oath was necessary, especially in cases where the accused did not confess, because any future conviction would have to be based on the validity of a significant number of these sworn affidavits.[234]

During subsequent sessions in the tribunal in the presence of the accused and the defense attorney, the prosecuting attorney would read and cite the accusations and details of the prosecution witnesses' testimony without revealing the names of the witnesses. The inquisitors expected the accused to respond point by point to all of the testimony given against him.

Formal Defense Strategies of the Accused during the Stage of Proof
and Presentation of Evidence

It is most true that our Holy Mother Church is a fount overflowing with mercy and pity. . . . As for Juan Ingles . . . if the inquisitors show mercy in imposing penance, when he returns to his native land and tells about it, it may be the means of converting others of his countrymen in England from their evil ways.

Statement of Antonio Ponce, defense attorney appointed by the Mexican Inquisition in the trial against the English sailor Juan Ingles for Protestant practices, May 7, 1560

At this stage the defendant launched his formal defense against the charges. The main goal of an accused heretic's defense focused on countering or refuting the testimonies of the prosecution's witnesses. With the help of the defense attorney, an accused heretic had several options in terms of presenting evidence in his favor or refuting the validity of the prosecution witnesses' testimony.[235]

The defendant and the defense attorney could present a petition detailing any mitigating circumstances, such as drunkenness, nervous disorders, or other mental problems, including undue stress or even mental insanity.[236] The defense attorney and the defendant used this tactic in order to attempt to prove that the so-called act of heresy (especially in cases of heretical propositions or simple blasphemies) may have been caused by a momentary lapse of judgment or in the heat of an alcoholic stupor.[237] The goal of this defense strategy was to show that the supposed heretical action or statement was apparently only an aberration and not the typical good Christian behavior that the defendant observed the rest of the time.

In conjunction with this type of petition, the defendant and the defense attorney submitted sworn affidavits from character witnesses (called *testigos de abono*), who appeared and testified on behalf of the defendant concerning his good Christian character.[238] The secrecy in which all of the prosecution's witnesses were held, however, made it difficult for the defendant and the defense attorney to choose the proper character witnesses who might be able to refute the charges or corroborate the good character of the accused. The inquisition's instructions also severely limited whom the accused could call upon to serve as his defense witnesses. For instance, any witness called could be neither a relative nor servant of the prisoner.[239] Similarly, without the defendant's ability to know who his accusers were, it was difficult to mount a proper defense and to know just which character witnesses to call in order to refute the validity of the general charges or to challenge the accuracy or falsehood of any specific single charge.[240]

The most effective defense strategy, but also the most difficult one to use effectively, was the formal repudiation for bias or animus (called *proceso de tachas*) of the prosecution's witnesses and their testimonies.[241] In this legal tactic, the defendant and the defense attorney attempted to disqualify the prosecution's witnesses by identifying them on the basis of the content of their denunciations. Again, without knowing the exact identity of the prosecution's witnesses, this tactic was difficult to utilize effectively. The defendant had to prove that the prosecution's witnesses presented against him had made their declarations not out of truth but rather out of animosity toward the accused.

The defendant, with the aid of the defense attorney, was able to present a petition and list with the names and other particulars of all of the people who he believed may have testified against him out of personal animosity or hatred.[242] This petition with the *tachas*, or identities of the defendant's sworn enemies, was the single-most effective strategy for the defense in an inquisition trial because any witness whose identity was mentioned on this list would have his or her testimony stricken from the trial proceedings.[243] If the defendant could demonstrate that these witnesses had deposed against him out of animosity and not a desire to tell the truth, the inquisitors would most often disqualify the witness. The goal was to disqualify all of the prosecution's witnesses, forcing the inquisitors to strike all of their testimonies from the trial proceedings. If successful, the inquisitors might declare that the prosecution's witnesses had acted out of their own personal animosity toward the accused and suspend or cease the trial for lack of viable evidence against the defendant. Because most of the witness testimony routinely came from members of the defendant's own family, friends, or close acquaintances, this defense tactic often was not enough to disqualify the serious allegations against the accused.

There was even one last legal tactic in the inquisition's proceedings that allowed an accused heretic to attempt to force the disqualification of an inquisitor from hearing the case because of bias or partiality.[244] Inquisitor General Fernando de Valdés's *Instructions* of 1561 required that, in the case of a recusation or disqualification of an inquisitor, he had to leave the case to his colleague, and if no other inquisitor was available, the issue had to be remitted to the Suprema for its decision in the case.[245] Although a possible tactic permitted by inquisitorial proceedings, in practice employing this technique remained an almost impossible task for the defense. In the end, in a typical inquisition trial the extent to which most defense attorneys went in defending the accused heretic was no more than presenting a simple petition stating that there were mitigating circumstances concerning the heretical statements or actions allegedly said or done by the defendant.

After the defendant presented his own character witnesses and attempted to disqualify the prosecution's witnesses, and after the prosecution's witnesses ratified their previous declarations, the proof or evidentiary stage of a formal inquisition trial ended. If the evidence and proof compiled against the accused continued to weigh toward guilt and the inquisitors did not disqualify the prosecution's witnesses, the final stage of evidence required the defendant to admit guilt or give a full confession to serve as definitive proof in order to conclude the case and take it to the stage of sentencing. It was at this stage and only at this stage that the inquisitors considered the use of juridical torture to force the defendant to make a full confession.

The Objective of the Final Proof Stage: The "Queen of All Proofs" or the Confession of Guilt

The compassion of this tribunal is ever merciful and kind to those who speak the truth.

Inquisitor's words to John Coustos upon his first audience, 1743

As we have shown earlier, the Inquisition could not condemn the accused on any allegations or charges that were not well proved or sustained by the weight of full evidence. As later medieval jurists and other inquisitors earlier stated, a full confession of guilt was the only "Queen of all proofs."[246] Because a confession served as the only full proof of an act of heresy, the inquisitor's ultimate goal was always to obtain a full confession from the defendant. At this final evidentiary stage of an inquisitorial trial, if there was not enough proof from a credible number of eyewitnesses, and the defendant had not freely offered a full confession, the inquisitors had one final means of extracting a full confession forcibly from the accused: they could question the defendant under torture.[247]

Questioning under Torment

Having examined the case, evidence, and merits against the Frenchman Guillermo de Siles, we are all in conformity and of one opinion and vote that the said Guillermo de Siles should be questioned under torment *in capite propio y alienum* [in his own case and for information against others] because of the strong suspicions and indications of heresy that have resulted in the case, and once this questioning under torment has been conducted, the case will be reviewed again.

Vote and sentence for the administration of torture in the Mexican Inquisition case against the French sailor Guillermo de Siles, October 21, 1573

Inquisitors were required to use every means possible to uncover the truth before they resorted to the use of questioning the defendant with the application of torture (fig. 2).[248]

The Inquisition applied the use of torture far less frequently and less severely than popular myths suggest.[249] Most prisoners either confessed without torture or were convicted on the basis of numerous eyewitness testimonies and other direct evidence. According to the Inquisition scholar Helen Rawlings, the results of modern research suggest that around 25 percent of those charged with major heresy in the Spanish Inquisition were subject to torture and a much lower ratio of 5 percent or less of those charged with minor heresies were questioned under torture.[250] Apparently, according to similar statistics for the Inquisition in New Spain, far fewer prisoners were questioned under torture, with only about 5 percent of all of those charged with major heresy having been tortured and less than 3 percent of those accused of minor heresies.[251]

The Inquisition's procedures limited the administration of torture itself by a series of official protocols and regulations. Any method of torture used could not cause death or permanent injury, and in the case of inquisitorial tortures, further limitations forbid the executioner to use any torture that might shed the blood of the prisoner. When the inquisitors sought to use torture to force a confession from the accused defendant, they stated that they did so *ad eruendam veritatem* (in order to uncover the truth). The purpose of the administration of torture was the ultimate confession of the accused.[252]

The Inquisition used torture only as its last means of obtaining full proof of an act of heresy (i.e., the defendant's full confession). The Inquisition did not use torture systematically or indiscriminately throughout the investigative stage of its proceedings.[253] Questioning under torture could occur only in cases in which the defendant had apparently conducted an act of formal heresy and not in cases where the alleged crime was only a minor infraction.[254]

Unlike in most secular courts, which allowed certain privileges of gender, class, and rank to exempt noblemen, children, or many women from the administration of torture, in Inquisition trials, with the exception of the king and the pope, all people regardless of gender and class could face questioning under torture. Although the Inquisition did not recognize a formal age limit in terms of administering torture to its prisoners, it was not common to torture either very young prisoners or those of advanced age. In the cases of older prisoners, the Inquisition often ordered that elderly prisoners be taken into the torture chambers and shown the instruments of torture (*in conspectu tormentorum*) to inspire fear in these older defendants and force them to confess. Only on rare occasions did the Inquisition force older prisoners to face questioning under torture.[255]

Even when a prisoner confessed, any confession under torture remained invalid unless the prisoner ratified and repeated the confession no later than two days after the torture session.[256] If the prisoner refused to ratify his confession or denied the charges again, the inquisitors could subject the defendant to torture again.[257] However, if the prisoner ratified his testimony and agreed to his previous confession under torment, the prosecutor and the inquisitors considered the trial ready for the final stage of sentencing.[258] In the rare occasions when the prisoner had resisted the administration of torture and continued to maintain his innocence, the inquisitors had to consider the weight of the evidence and eyewitness testimony against the accused in the subsequent sentencing phase.

Phase 5: Verdict and Sentencing

Judicial Review of the Case by the Inquisition's Consultants

Either with or without a confession during a torture session, the proof or evidentiary stage of the trial ended. The inquisitors then submitted the trial transcripts for judicial review by the tribunal's consultants and their legal and theological advisers.[259]

At the meeting of these advisers, the chosen consultants reviewed the entire case and the evidence collected against the accused to determine if the inquisitors and the other officials had proceeded correctly in the processing of the case. The jury or body of consultants and advisers consisted of both religious and secular officials, specialists in theology and both canon and civil law. The number of consultants varied from tribunal to tribunal, but in New Spain the Inquisition counted on from six to ten consultants for the judicial review and sentencing in their cases.[260]

Once the consultants completed the judicial review and approved the inquisitors' proceedings in the case, the inquisitors turned to a jury of advisers to help them determine the verdict in the case. The official deliberations of this type of jury, called a *consulta de fe*, included the opinions of the inquisitors, a representative of the local bishop (called the ordinary), and several legal or theological advisers (the *consultores*), who together decided upon the guilt of the accused heretic and jointly decided on the sentence to impose.[261] These advisers then made a formal decision of innocence or guilt in the case of the accused heretic, and without this decision, the inquisitors could not issue a sentence in the case.

Limitations in sentencing did exist, especially in cases of formal heresy that merited a death sentence. In cases where the prisoner might be condemned to death, the final decision and definitive sentence had to be unanimous on the part of the inquisitors and their advisers and consultants.[262] If only one of the Inquisition's advisers voted against it, the accused could not receive a sentence of death. This is one of the reasons that help to explain the gradual reduction in the numbers of those condemned to death after the application of these regulations. However, in terms of sentences that did not include a death sentence, a simple majority among the inquisitors and the advisers and consultants decided the final verdict.[263]

The Final Verdict and Formal Sentencing in the Case

All inquisitorial trials, if they passed through the stages of proof and testimony to their definitive sentencing, ended with one of a number of verdicts that were possible in heresy cases. *The Inquisitor's Manual* written by Eimeric and later annotated by Francisco Peña describes the most common types of verdicts in inquisitorial trials.[264] In general, only four possible types of sentences existed: absolution, penance, reconciliation, and relaxation.[265]

Verdict of Innocence: An Acquittal

Sometimes also, after they have imprisoned men in such a miserable state for a year or two, and can extort nothing out of them by their torments, nor prove anything against them by witness, so that they must necessarily dismiss them, they then call them into the Court, begin to flatter them, and tell them what a good opinion they have of them; and that they are resolved to send them home, for which fatherly favor extended toward them in saving their Lives and Goods, they are to account themselves much beholding to their Lordships.

Richard Dugdale, *Narrative of Unheard of Popish Cruelties towards Protestants beyond Seas,* 1680[266]

In an acquittal, the inquisitors declared the prisoner innocent of the charges and either absolved him or suspended the case because of insufficient evidence.[267] The inquisitors could issue a sentence of absolution, which formally admitted that the prosecuting attorney had not proved the accusations against the defendant and that the accused remained free to leave once he had sworn to maintain secrecy concerning all that had occurred during his imprisonment and trial.[268] But if the inquisitors believed that there were at least some suspicions of guilt based on the defendant's public reputation, they could issue another type of acquittal under a verdict called canonical compurgation.[269] In the Inquisition in New Spain, however, the verdict of a total acquittal remained quite rare, occurring in only 3.6 percent of the cases sentenced from 1571 to 1700.[270]

A Verdict of Partial Innocence: Canonical Compurgation

The inquisitors issued a verdict of canonical compurgation when a suspect or prisoner appeared to have a public reputation for having been a heretic, but the trial and its evidence were unable to prove or materialize any apparent guilt of heresy. This verdict allowed the trial to remain technically open for new evidence but also permitted a type of partial absolution by having a specified number of "Christian character witnesses" swear that the accused was not a heretic.[271] However, if the accused later was denounced for suspicions of heresy, on the basis of this "compurgation" the inquisitors would proceed against the suspect as a relapsed heretic and thus could sentence him more harshly by relaxing him to the secular arm.

In other cases with similar lack of proof, the Inquisition decided more often than not to suspend the case instead of admitting that the accusations had been unproved or requiring a formal compurgation.[272] By this means, the released prisoner remained under the threat of having his case reopened with new evidence. A sentence of innocence or absolution remained a rare occurrence in Inquisition proceedings. In New Spain, for instance, of all the cases tried and sentenced by the Mexican Inquisition from 1571 to 1700, only 2.7 percent ended in an acquittal or absolution.[273]

Possible Guilty Verdicts in Inquisitorial Cases for Heresy

Because most of the defendants remained under some suspicion of guilt, a guilty verdict usually meant that the prosecuting attorney's proof and evidence warranted the sentencing and punishment of the prisoner. Depending on the weight of the evidence, the repentance of the prisoner, and his acceptance of the charges or obstinate denial of the allegations, a guilty verdict placed a defendant in one of three major categories of convicted heresy: penance, reconciliation, or relaxation. According to the degree of apparent guilt, the level of repentance, and the conciliatory attitude of the prisoner, the categories each held their own established penances, punishments, and procedures in terms of the final sentencing.[274]

1. By a sentence of penance, the convicted heretic was considered to have been "penanced" by the Inquisition.[275] The inquisitors believed that the prisoner was guilty of heresy, but he continued to deny the allegations against him and insufficient evidence existed of his guilt. Although no firm proof or confession supported this guilty verdict, the weight of circumstantial evidence led the inquisitors to insist that the convicted heretic should make a retraction or abjuration, which was a formal public act of contrition that included a denial or renunciation under oath of suspected heresy.[276] Depending on the types of partial proofs or evidence compiled against the heretic, the inquisitors could insist that the prisoner make one of three separate types of public retractions or abjurations (fig. 3). All three of these acts consisted of the penitent's publicly swearing an oath never to separate himself from the Catholic faith and to publicly detest all types of heresy.

a. Abjuration *de levi* was required of a convicted heretic whom the inquisitors only slightly suspected of heresy. It was usually given to someone suspected of being guilty of lesser infractions such as blasphemy, bigamy, and other minor religious crimes.[277] This sentence signified that the suspect's trial contained the lowest level of proof that still permitted a conviction. A penanced heretic sentenced to make a public abjuration *de levi* usually did so by appearing in a spectacle known as an auto-da-fé where he would have his sentence and crime announced and receive subsequent minor punishments, such as small monetary fines, temporary exile, and occasionally flogging.[278] In many cases, these penanced suspected heretics had to wear a simple frock or garment of shame called a *sanbenito*. At the auto-da-fé, the inquisitors also warned the penanced heretic who made a public abjuration *de levi* that if he repeated his offense or was tried again for heresy and found guilty, he would be declared an impenitent heretic and face much harsher punishments.[279]

b. Abjuration *de vehementi* was required of a penanced heretic when the inquisitors seriously suspected the defendant to be guilty of heresy; however, despite the evidence produced against him, he refused to confess. Inquisitors also required an abjuration *de vehementi* from those suspected of heresy though no more than two witnesses testified against them and there were other indicators of guilt.[280]

A penanced heretic forced to make an abjuration *de vehementi* usually also appeared in an auto-da-fé wearing a *sanbenito,* but his garment of shame was not plain but instead was adorned with one-half of a Saint Andrew's cross.[281] The Inquisition usually required a heretic who made this type of abjuration to wear this garment of shame for one or more years and to remain imprisoned for as long as a year. He also faced a monetary fine and the loss of half of his confiscated goods as well as exile from the region for a period of no more than six years.[282] Depending on the nature and gravity of his suspected crimes, the heretic could also be sentenced to public flogging with punitive sentences of up to two hundred lashes for men and one hundred lashes for women.

At the auto-da-fé, the inquisitors also warned a heretic who made a public abjuration *de vehementi* that if he should fall back into heresy and once again face a trial, he would be considered relapsed or a repeat offender. If found subsequently guilty, the heretic could receive the death penalty and be relaxed to the secular authorities for the execution of his sentence.[283] Throughout the entire history of the Inquisition in both Spain and New Spain, however, most heretics made abjurations *de levi* rather than the more serious abjuration *de vehementi*. In the particular case of New Spain from 1571 to 1700, only 5.1 percent of all the cases required the accused heretic to make an abjuration *de vehementi*.[284]

c. Abjuration *de formali* was issued when the proof and evidence convicted the prisoner of heresy, but the prisoner was penitent and not a relapsed heretic.[285] It was required of a penanced heretic who was known to be guilty and who had freely confessed of his crime. A heretic sentenced to make a public abjuration *de formali* also appeared at an auto-da-fé dressed in a *sanbenito,* but his garment of shame had a full Saint Andrew's cross emblazoned on its front. Those who made an abjuration *de formali* usually had to wear their *sanbenito* for life. Moreover, if the *sanbenito* should wear out, the Inquisition ordered another one made.

Both abjurations *de vehementi* and *de formali* shared the further characteristic that, in the event of a second repeated offense, the penanced heretic would be considered a relapsed heretic and would most likely face a death penalty.[286]

2. A sentence of reconciliation occurred in cases where the Inquisition had sufficient full proof of heresy.[287] Because this sentence formally declared that the suspect was a heretic, the inquisitors demanded more serious penances and exemplar punishments as a warning to the rest of society to avoid the sin and crime of heresy.

Whereas in Spain more than 70 percent of all of those convicted of heresy received sentences of reconciliation,[288] in New Spain this sentence was issued more sparingly, with the number of reconciliations from 1571 to 1700 accounting for no more than 18.3 percent of all sentences.[289] A reconciled heretic was spared the death penalty, but if he repeated the offense, he could be sentenced to relaxation and the death penalty.

For the most part, a suspect sentenced to reconciliation also had to make a formal abjuration of his heresy. The Inquisition also forced him to appear in a public auto-da-fé to receive his sentences dressed in a penitential *sanbenito* decorated with a full Saint Andrew's cross (as a repentant formally accused heretic).[290] A second symbol of shame for a reconciled heretic was a conical miter, resembling a fool's or dunce's cap, called a *coroza*.

A reconciled heretic also received harsher sentences, such as imprisonment for up to three years, in combination with the loss of all of his goods and exile from the region as well as public flogging (again, two hundred lashes for men and one hundred lashes for women). As a more serious offense, a reconciled heretic could also receive a sentence of forced servitude on a public works project in a church or convent, or a specified period of forced service as a rower in the royal galleys or as a laborer in the royal mines.[291]

3. A sentence of relaxation, or the so-called relaxation to the secular arm, remained the most severe sentence possible.[292] It meant the imposition of the death penalty. The inquisitors issued a sentence of relaxation for a very serious case of public heresy, for a repeat offender, or someone whom the inquisitors considered a relapsed heretic (i.e., someone who had fallen back into the errors of heresy after receiving a lighter sentence earlier).[293] A sentence of relaxation could also occur in cases where the requisite number of eyewitness testimonies proved the suspect's guilt completely or where the suspect confessed to formal

TABLE 9
Distribution of Inquisition Cases Sentenced by the
Tribunal of New Spain, 1571–1700

Types of Sentences	Percentage of Total Cases Sentenced
Abjuration *de levi*	67.7
Reconciliation	18.3
Abjuration *de vehementi*	5.3
Relaxation in effigy	3.4
Absolution	2.7
Suspended sentences	1.6
Relaxation in person	1.0

Source: See *Abecedario de los relaxados, reconciliados y
penitenciados*, Huntington Library Manuscript, San Marino,
California; also see Alberro, *Inquicisión y Sociedad*, 208.

external heresy. If the weight of the evidence against the suspect proved the case but the suspect did not formally confess to the heresy, the inquisitors considered the convicted heretic an impenitent.[294] Repeat offenders most often received this harsh sentence of relaxation.

In Spain, according to modern scholars, the Inquisition's use of the sentence of relaxation varied with time. From 1478 to 1540, scholars estimate that as many as 25 percent of all heretics received a sentence of relaxation.[295] The period from 1540 to 1700 saw a decrease in this number, with no more than 3 percent of all cases receiving a sentence of relaxation. In New Spain, in contrast, from 1571 to 1700 the tribunal issued sentences of relaxation in person in no more than 1 percent of its total number of cases (table 9).[296]

Penalties and Punishments Imposed on Convicted Heretics

Such as are not condemned to die, are carried back, and the next day they are brought up to be whipped; after which some of them are sent to the Galleys; others kept in Prison all their lifetime. But all have this special charge given them, that they never speak of anything that they have heard, seen, or felt, during their imprisonment in the Inquisition; for if the contrary be ever proved against them, and that they utter any of their secrets, they shall be taken for persons relapsed, and be punished with greatest severity; their Judgment being Death without Redemption.

Richard Dugdale, *Narrative of Unheard of Popish Cruelties towards Protestants beyond Seas*, 1680[297]

The Inquisition in Spain and New Spain differed greatly from the civil and secular courts in the imposition of fines and punishments. In Spanish law, the privileges of the nobility and members of the upper classes dictated that for many crimes the penalties assigned to the rich and wealthy were much milder than were those inflicted upon the common people.[298] The Inquisition, however, believed that nobles and prominent people found guilty in cases of heresy deserved a harsher punishment than that given to common people.

Penalties and punishments of reconciled heretics varied considerably. Invariably, a reconciled heretic received a combination of confiscation of his goods, monetary fines, and other public and corporal punishments. One long-term impact of conviction was that the Inquisition declared all those reconciled as unfit to hold public or ecclesiastical offices.[299] Furthermore, a convicted reconciled heretic could not exercise certain professions, including those of doctor, surgeon, public clerk, or bureaucrat. These injunctions and punitive sanctions applied not only to the convicted heretic but also to his children and grandchildren. Because the inquisitions in Spain and New Spain were often in need of revenue, they frequently allowed heretics to pay a fine or fee known as a composition (*composición*) in place of these bans and prohibitions.[300] As table 10 indicates, the most common types of punishments decreed by the Mexican tribunal focused on exile, public flogging, public shame, and imprisonment.

Strangely enough, the Mexican Inquisition apparently did not consider spiritual penances worthy of much consideration in their sentencing because they issued them as a punishment in only 1.3 percent of all cases sentenced from 1571 to 1700. Formal prison sentences also appear to have been rare, occurring in only 1 percent of all cases during this period.

TABLE 10

Distribution of Punishments in Inquisition Cases Sentenced by
the Tribunal of New Spain, 1571–1700

Types of Punishments in Sentenced Cases	Percent Distribution
Public flogging	14.3
Exile	13.8
Public shame	6.8
Reclusion in convent/monastery	6.3
Galley service	5.7
Pecuniary fine	5.3
Public reprehension	4.6
Suspension from office	3.5
Service in church/convent	2.7
Spiritual penance	1.3
Private penance	1.0
Imprisonment	1.0
Other sentences	33.7
	100%

Source: See *Abecedario de los relaxados, reconciliados y penitenciados*, Huntington Library Manuscript, San Marino, California; also see Alberro, *Inquicisión y sociedad*, 208.

Public Humiliation: The *Sanbenito* or Garment of Shame

We were brought into the Church, every one with a *San Benito* upon his back, which is half a yard of yellow cloth with a hole to put in a man's head in the middle and cast over a man's head both flaps hang one before and another behind, and in the middle of every flap a St Andrew's cross made of red cloth sowed on upon the same and that is called *San Benito.* The common people before they saw the penitents come into the Church were given to understand that we were heretics, infidels, and people that did despise God and his works and that we had been more like devils than men.

Robert Tomson, Englishman penanced by the Inquisition in New Spain, 1560[301]

One of the most common sanctions that all convicted heretics commonly received remained the forced use of a garment of shame, called a *sanbenito,* or *saco bendito* (blessed smock). *Sanbenitos* consisted of a type of rough linen cloth tunic or smock that could be white, yellow, or black depending on the region and particular traditions of the regional tribunal.[302] Depending on the gravity of the crime of the convicted heretic, the garment had different adornments on it to symbolize the heretic's crime and penance.[303] The most common type of adornment consisted of a red or black Saint Andrew's cross emblazoned on the front and back of the garment. A reconciled heretic's garment could also hold images of flames and demons or devils to inspire terror or fear. Those convicted of strong suspicions of heresy wore a *sanbenito* with a full Saint Andrew's cross, sometimes accompanied by a high conical hat of shame made out of stiff fabric or pressed paper called a *coroza* (see figs. 4 and 5).[304]

The *sanbenito* was usually worn over the clothes of a convicted heretic. The garment that resembled a type of apron or tunic when worn usually came down to the person's knees and opened on the side. As a punitive sentence, a convicted heretic could be forced to wear this garment of shame for periods ranging from one year to life. Once the period of the sentence ended, the Inquisition ordered the convicted heretic's *sanbenito* with the convict's name and the particulars of his crime hung on the walls or ceilings of his local parish church. The permanent display of this garment of shame with the heretic's family name and his accused crime against the faith served as a perpetual reminder of his act of heresy for the entire parish.

By means of this public humiliation, the Inquisition attempted to make the infamy of the heretic's shame a burden shared by his whole family. Periodically the inquisitors or their agents also conducted visitations of the parish churches in their district with the goal of ensuring that all of these publicly displayed *sanbenitos* remained in place. Whenever the garments disappeared or appeared damaged, or deteriorated, the Inquisition ordered them replaced.

The Auto-da-Fé and the Executions of Sentences

At the end of seven months we were both carried to the high Church of Mexico to do open penance upon a high scaffold made before the high Altar upon Sunday in the presence of a very great number of people who were at the least five or six thousand. For there were some that came one hundred miles off to see the said Auto (as they call it) for that there were never none before that had done the like in the said Country nor could not tell what Lutherans were nor what it meant, for they had never heard of any such thing before.

Robert Tomson, Englishman who appeared at the Auto de Fe of 1560, Mexico City

The Inquisition and the secular authorities administered all definitive sentences at a formal function called an *auto-da-fé,* most often held on a particular Sunday. The auto-da-fé served as a public spectacle undertaken at great cost and attended by all major functionaries of the ecclesiastical and civil governments of New Spain (see documents 19–22). The Inquisition intended such spectacles to serve as a major didactic tool and a deterrent to religious heterodoxy. The auto-da-fé's display and humiliation of those condemned served as the Inquisition's cruelest and most degrading weapon against those guilty of what it considered public immorality and formal heresy.

Those condemned to death were executed not at the actual auto-da-fé but at another site, generally the following Monday morning. In New Spain, the public executions of the sentences of those handed over to the royal justices occurred in a public plaza called the *Alameda* where the civil authorities routinely placed the stakes and pyres for those sentenced to death by fire.[305] After the relaxed heretics had their sentences "read out, a detachment of police took charge of the condemned and escorted them to the place of execution."[306]

The civil authorities controlled the events surrounding the execution of the death sentences. One of the Inquisition's secretaries along with several other minor officials served as witnesses to the executions. The other punishments and sanctions imposed on the reconciled and penanced heretics occurred afterward.[307]

The Study of the Inquisition and Inquisition Documents

From its very inception, the Inquisition in Spain provoked a war of words. Its opponents through the ages contributed to building up a powerful legend about its intentions and malign achievements. Their propaganda was so successful that even today it is difficult to separate fact from fiction.

Henry Kamen, *The Spanish Inquisition*

Henry Kamen's assessment of the legacy of the myths surrounding the history of the Inquisition still rings true today. Modern revisionist studies, however, are now beginning to examine the Inquisition and the documents that it produced, not in the salutary nor condemnatory light characteristic of past scholarship but rather with an eye toward better understanding the significant role that the Inquisition played in the formation of the society of New Spain.[308] Recent scholarship illuminates how the documentation produced by the complex bureaucracy of the Inquisition serves as an important source in the modern historian's attempt to reconstruct what might be known about the sexual, moral, ethical, and religious life of colonial Mexico.[309]

Still, the study of history is not simply the study of what happened in the past but rather the study of past people, events, and institutions. The recoverable documents that these people have left behind can be used to understand the historical reality of both past and present societies. These few snippets of the past that remain, known as primary sources by historians, are records or artifacts created by the participants themselves or their observers. Without the evidence from primary sources, there is a past but there can be no history because history itself is a creative exercise in which the historian or student of history interprets the events and people of the past by critically examining the remaining primary sources. Clearly, even when sufficient primary sources are available, the process of reconstructing or interpreting history is problematic at best. In the case of the polemical institution of the Inquisition, the modern historian or student of history is left with a massive collection of primary sources at his or her disposal. As Henry Kamen noted, "Because the Inquisition was a conflictive institution its history has always been polemical."[310]

Even the surviving documents of the Inquisition do not offer us a completely unbiased representation of the religious and cultural lives of people in the past.[311] The student of the history of the Inquisition should take to heart Henry Kamen's warning that "the Inquisition, like any other policing body, needs to be studied within the broader context that it occupied in history: its significance can be grossly distorted if we rely only on its own documentation for information."[312]

The historian should keep in mind that the Inquisition's documents were created by the notaries, inquisitors, and other officials of the Inquisition and that they remained unpublished and were meant only for internal review. As such, the documents generated by the Inquisition came out of an encounter between a judge and a suspected heretic that was coercive, confrontational, and disconcerting to the accused. The entire process of an Inquisition investigation and trial was conducted in secret and under strict rules of procedure. The inquisitors asked only certain questions, and the notaries recorded the suspect's specific answers to these questions. The inquisitors also permitted the accused and his or her defense attorney to use only limited and specific types of defense, making the entire proceedings structured and the testimony forced. As Andrew Keitt states, both witnesses and the accused "said what they thought the inquisitors wanted to hear, and the inquisitors in turn framed their questions in such a way as to elicit the kinds of answers they wanted to receive."[313] On the basis of these considerations, the student of history should remember that, as Lu Ann Homza has noted, there is "no transparency of representation here but rather the working out, in cat-and-mouse fashion, of legal phenomena such as capital enmity, recusation, the presentation of character witnesses, and the substantiation of public representation."[314]

We also cannot forget that the Inquisition created its documents in the context of forced secrecy, using open and veiled threats, leading questions, and sometimes torture. Still, Inquisition sources, as Jean Pierre Dedieu has noted, are a "magnificent source from which specialists in various disciplines can glean valuable information," but the student should also remember that Inquisition documents may be tainted as documentary records.[315] As Dedieu points out, "The Holy Office was an ideological tribunal; even though the legend that it fabricated accusations has long since been laid to rest, it is nonetheless true that the material which it offers may well have been heavily biased. I think that the problem is real and that a good share of our information has been re-thought and re-shaped according to the preoccupations and mental 'filters' of the judges."[316] Nevertheless, he and others concluded that, "with certain precautions, when we are in possession of the best classes of documents, the Holy Office papers are an extremely reliable source, and they are far richer than most."[317]

Even so, the historian and student should keep in mind the adversarial nature of any judicial document, as well as the possibility of erroneous information based on false denunciations or forced confessions under torture. Even so, as John Edwards has concluded, "Scholars have increasingly come to regard inquisitorial records as worthwhile historical sources, as often as not, for what they can say about personal and social beliefs and practices, hopes and fears, social conflicts and economic difficulties."[318]

In the final analysis, regardless of the dangers of interpretation that Inquisition documents pose to the modern researcher, as a primary source these documents offer the historian a very rare glimpse at many aspects of daily life in the past. However flawed they maybe, Inquisition documents such as those from New Spain translated in the present volume remain an extremely valuable source of information for the reconstruction and interpretation of past events and should bring students closer to the people and subjects that these documents represent.

PART I

Laws, Regulations, and Instructions
concerning the Holy Office

Regulations concerning the Tribunals
of the Holy Office of the Inquisition

Inquisitorial courts were governed by strict rules and regulations. According to civil and canon law, all Inquisition trials had to follow a standard procedure established at the founding of the Inquisition in Spain by the publication of Tomás de Torquemada's *Instrucciones* in 1484.[1] Reissued repeatedly and adapted for changing circumstances, the most popular copy of the *Instrucciones* used in New Spain was the 1561 version included here by Don Fernando de Valdés, who was inquisitor general in that year; this version was reprinted in 1576.

Similarly, the realities of creating inquisitorial tribunals in the New World necessitated several adaptations in Spanish inquisitorial procedures, especially concerning the nature of the appeal process. Realizing the complexity of founding an inquisitorial tribunal in New Spain, Don Diego de Espinosa, inquisitor general in 1570, issued special instructions for its establishment (see document 3). Along with copies of the *Instrucciones* of 1561 and a separate manual for the procedures to be followed by the commissaries of the Holy Office (see document 4), the inquisitor general issued these special orders to allow the tribunal of Mexico to exercise more power than tribunals in Spain, especially in the case of using torture in questioning suspected heretics and in matters of appeal in inquisition cases.

The other rules and regulations that guided inquisitorial procedures in both Spain and the New World included papal bulls and briefs that dealt with the process, punishments, and procedures in inquisitorial cases.[2] These papal bulls had been instrumental from the beginning of the medieval Inquisition in delineating and creating an institutional structure for the various tribunals in Spain. After 1478, added to the general collection of papal bulls and briefs were royal orders and laws, called *cédulas reales*, which the Spanish kings issued concerning the Holy Office and its operations. These royal orders were usually directed toward a particular tribunal, and later a collection of the most important *cédulas* concerning the Holy Office in the New World was contained in the famous compilation of laws known as the *Leyes de Indias*.[3] Finally, the inquisitors and other officials of the Holy Office also counted on specialized inquisitorial manuals that contained the specific regulations on proper juridical procedures in inquisitorial cases. Of all of the many inquisitorial manuals that were printed, the one that was most often used in the New World was the *Directorium Inquisitorium* written by Nicolas Eimeric, the inquisitor general of Aragon in 1376 and republished and annotated by Francisco Peña in 1578.[4]

Along with the royal cedula issued for the creation of the Holy Office in New Spain (document 2), the president of the Supreme Council of the Inquisition, Diego de Espinosa, also issued another series of orders in 1570 with complimentary instructions for the tribunal in Mexico (document 3). In these instructions, the president of the Supreme Council, without modifying any of the other instructions and orders for the inquisitors, issued his own special instructions so that the tribunal in Mexico could adapt itself to the unique conditions in the colony.[5]

Because of the administrative distance between Mexico and the Supreme Council in Spain, Espinosa's 1570 instructions introduced several changes to standard inquisitorial procedure that provided the inquisitors and other tribunal officials in New Spain with more power than their counterparts in Spain enjoyed. For example, in cases involving the use of torment or torture during questioning, the local tribunal could make the decision without the need to recur to the Supreme Council. Similarly, because the vast territory given to the tribunal of Mexico made it impossible for two inquisitors to cover the entire region, Espinosa's 1570 instructions permitted them to visit only the largest possible region near the seat of their tribunal and leave the reception of testimonies in the outlying regions to the local commissaries of the Inquisition, who would then remit such testimonies to the capital and seat of the tribunal for further investigation.

In terms of conflicts of jurisdiction, Espinosa's instructions ordered that the viceroy should settle all disputes between the inquisitors, their tribunal, and secular justices and other civil officials. They also reiterated the king's 1569 order, to exempt the Indians from inquisitorial justice until instructed otherwise. The instructions closed with the admonition that the tribunal should act "with a temperate and gentle nature and with much consideration, because that is what is most convenient, so that the Inquisition would be feared and respected, and give no occasion or reason so that it should be hated."[6]

All of the inquisitors named and appointed to the tribunal of New Spain received a package of documents and orders that resembled the documents compiled here. It included several important publications, laws, orders, and regulations concerning the tribunal and its proper order, functions, officials, and operations. Specific reference is made in both the *Compilación* and in Espinosa's special instructions concerning the sending of sample commissions, titles, and other documents for the inquisitors to use as models. Where appropriate the same types of documents are included here to illustrate the guidelines and models that may have been at the disposal of newly arrived inquisitors in New Spain.

DOCUMENT 1

Instructions of the Holy Office of the Inquisition Compiled by Order of the Illustrious and Reverend Lord Don Fernando de Valdés, Archbishop of Seville and Apostolic Inquisitor

Toledo, 1561

SOURCE: Archivo General de la Nación, Ramo de Inquisición, vol. 1480, exp. 1, folios 1r–12v, Lote Riva Palacio, vol. 4, no. 1.

NOTE: Don Fernando de Valdés (1483–1568), the archbishop of Seville, was commissioned as inquisitor general of Spain on January 20, 1547, and took possession of the office on February 19, 1547. As inquisitor general, he worked to centralize and standardize the operations and procedures of the Inquisition throughout Spain and its territories. Nevertheless, no formal Inquisition existed in the New World during his tenure as inquisitor general. He resigned his position due to illness in 1566 and died on December 9, 1568. This *compilación* of the Instructions of the Holy Office published in 1561 was based on Valdés's refinement of the previous instructions issued by the first inquisitor general, Fray Tomás de Torquemada (r. 1483–98), and later amended and refined by the inquisitor general Alonso Manrique (r. 1523–38).

Don Fernando de Valdés, by divine mercy the Archbishop of Seville, and Apostolic Inquisitor General against Heretical depravity and apostasy in all of these kingdoms and realms of His Majesty & etc: We order it be known to you, the reverend apostolic inquisitors against heretical depravity and apostasy in all of the said kingdoms and realms, that we are informed that, even though it has been ordered and proclaimed by the instructions of the Holy Office of the Inquisition, all of the Inquisitions should guard and have the same style of procedures and by this means be in conformity. In several of the Inquisitions, these procedures have not been followed or guarded as they should be. In order to ensure that from here onward there are no discrepancies in the said order of procedure, the Council of the General Inquisition[7] decided and is in accord that all of the Inquisitions should observe the following orders:

Examination and Qualification of Propositions

1. When the Inquisitors come together to see the testimonies that result from some visitation or by other means, or by any other cause that they may have received, or having present some persons testifying on something whose knowledge belongs to the Holy Office of the Inquisition, if such cause should need qualification, they should consult with theologians of letters and conscience who have the concurrent qualities that are needed for this qualification. These said consultants should give their opinion and sign it with their names.

Denunciation

2. When the Inquisitors are satisfied that the material concerns the Faith according to the opinion of the Theologians, or is based on a known ceremony of Jewish or Moorish

nature, or heresy, or the complicity of an abettor, and when they cannot doubt it, the Prosecutor [*Fiscal*] should make his denunciation against the said person or persons, requesting that they be arrested and presenting the said testimony and the qualification of the case.

Agreement of Imprisonment

3. When the Inquisitors have seen and reviewed the information together (and not one without the other), if both are present they may agree upon imprisonment. It also appears justified that they should communicate this agreement to the consultants of that Inquisition (that is, if it can be done well and seems convenient and necessary to the Inquisitors). They should place their agreement in a formal juridical act [*auto*] or decree.

No One Should Be Called or Examined If There Is Insufficient Testimony

4. In case someone is testified against concerning the crime of heresy, if the testimony is not sufficient to warrant imprisonment, the accused should not be called nor examined, nor should any other proceedings be made. This is because it is known from experience that the accused would not confess that he is a heretic if he is set free and in his liberty. Similar examinations based on insufficient testimony serve more to warn the accused than for any other good effect. Thus, it is necessary to wait until new proof or new indictments come forth.

Remission to the Council in Discord When the Matter Is Qualified

5. If the Inquisitors should be in agreement with imprisonment, they should order it done as they agreed. In the case that the matter should be qualified because it deals with persons of quality or for other respects, they should consult with the council before they execute their opinion. And if there is a discrepancy in their votes, they should remit it to the Council so that it can order what seems most convenient.

Arrest Order and the Secret

6. The arrest order should be signed by the Inquisitors, and it should be given to the Constable of the Holy Office and to no other person so long as he is not otherwise legitimately occupied. The imprisonment should be done with the sequestering of goods according to what conforms to the law and Instructions of the Holy Office. In an arrest warrant, no more than one person should be cited because it may be necessary to communicate some capture to a person outside of the Holy Office. Any other [imprisonments] should remain secret so that each legal process or trial should have its own arrest order. The sequestering of goods should be done only when the imprisonment is for formal heresy and not in any other Inquisition cases. In the said sequestering, they can take only those goods which are found in the possession of the person whose arrest was ordered and not those which are in the possession of a third person. They should place within the trial transcripts the decree and act in which the prisoner was ordered arrested, the day on which the order was issued, and to whom the prisoner was turned over.

Who Should Assist in the Arrests?

7. In the imprisonments that the Inquisition should make, the Receptor of the Inquisition or his lieutenant (if he is occupied in other matters of his office) should assist the constable [*alguacil*], along with the Notary of Sequesters, so that the said Receptor will be in conformity with the person the constable selects to sequester the goods. And if he is not in conformity with the chosen person who will sequester the goods, he may name another one that is sufficiently bonded.[8]

How the Sequestering Should Take Place

8. The Notary of the Sequesters should take a minute and particular inventory of all of the goods to be sequestered so that when the goods are turned over to the Receptor, or when the sequestering should be lifted, they can make a good and true account of everything. They should place at the head [of the inventory], the day, month, and year and the name of the person or persons who sequestered the goods. They should then sign at the bottom of the inventory along with the constable, before witnesses and with the person who sequestered the goods making an oath of obligation.[9] The notary or scribe should make a simple copy for the sequesterer free of cost because this belongs to his office and is within his charge. If any other person who is not the receptor should ask for a copy, he is not obligated to give one unless they pay him his fee.

Which of the Sequestered Goods the Constable Should Receive

9. The Constable [*Alguacil*] should take from the sequestered goods the moneys that appear necessary to take the prisoner to the jail along with six or eight ducats more in order to sustain the prisoner.[10] And they should not charge the prisoner for more than what he eats and what he spends to acquire beasts to take the prisoner and his bed and clothing. If there are no moneys in the sequestered goods, then they should sell them at the least prejudicial price until the required quantity is obtained. Whatever they should receive should be signed for at the bottom of the inventory. Whatever is left over should be turned over to the dispenser of the prisoners before the Notary of the Sequesters who will add this to the said inventory. And all of this should be presented to the Inquisitors, and what is to be given to the Dispenser should be given by the Constable in the presence of the Inquisitors.

The Order That the Constable Should Keep Concerning Prisoners

10. Once the accused is imprisoned, the Constable should keep him in a place where no one else can see him, talk to him, or give him any news either in writing or by word of mouth. The same should be done if he apprehends many prisoners, and he should not let them communicate with one another except when the Inquisitors have advised him that the communication between them should not result in any inconveniences, and in all of this he should guard and keep the orders of the Inquisitors. He should not leave in their possession arms, money, writing implements, paper, or any jewels, gold, or silver. Under these circumstances, prisoners are taken to the jails of the Holy Office. He should hand the prisoner over to the Jailer who should sign for the receipt of the prisoner at the bottom of the original arrest warrant, adding the day and hour (for the account of the dispensation).

The said arrest warrant should then be placed, signed, in the trial transcripts. Later the Constable will give an account to the Inquisitors of the execution of his warrants. The same will be done by the Jailer with every prisoner who comes into the jail, examining the prisoner's clothes in the presence of the notaries of the Holy Office, so that he does not bring into the jail any of the above-mentioned things or any other dangerous things. And whatever is found in the possession of the prisoner should be placed among the sequestered goods, and notice should be given to the Inquisitors so that they can deposit them in some person.

The Order That the Jailer Should Keep

11. The Jailer should not bring the prisoners together nor let them communicate with one another without explicit orders to do so from the Inquisitors, which he should obey faithfully.

Also

12. Similarly, the Jailer should have a book in the jail in which he notes the clothing, bedding, and other things that the prisoners brought with them, and this should be signed by the Notary of Sequesters. And the same should be done with all of the other things received by the prisoner during his imprisonment. All of which he should bring to the notice of both the Notary and the Inquisitors before receiving the things, even though they are things to eat or other things. With their license and after examining and testing them so that they do not contain any hidden messages, they should receive them and then give them to the prisoner if they contain necessary things and not anything else.

The First Audience and Hearing and the Questions That the Inquisitors Have to Ask

13. After having placed the prisoner in jail, whenever the Inquisitors believe it is time, they should bring the prisoner before them. Before a Notary of the Secret, they should question him according to oath asking him his name, office, and residency, and how long has it been since he came as a prisoner. And the Inquisitors should treat the prisoners humanely, according to the quality of their persons, reserving for themselves the appropriate authority without going too far. Usually, the prisoners should be seated on a bench or a low chair because in this way they can pay more attention to their cases, even though at the time when they are to hear their accusation they are to remain standing.

Also

14. Later, consecutively they should order that the prisoner declare his genealogy to the greatest extent that he can, beginning with his parents and grandparents with all of the other collateral relatives of which he has memory, declaring their offices, residences that they had and with whom they were married, and if they are alive or dead, and the names of the children that the said descendants and collateral relatives left behind. They should also make him declare to whom the prisoner is or was married, and how many times he was married, and the children that he has had and has, and also what is his age. And the notary should write down the genealogy in the trial transcripts, placing each per-

son at the beginning of the line. He should also declare if any of his relatives or his lineage may have been prisoners or penitents of the Inquisition.

Admonitions That Should Be Made to the Prisoner

15. After this has been done, they should ask the prisoner where he was raised and with which persons, and if he has studied in some university, and if he has traveled outside of these kingdoms and if so, in whose company. And having declared all of these things, he should be generally questioned to learn if he knows the reason for his imprisonment. On the basis of his answer, they should make him answer the other questions that correspond to the case. And they should admonish him to say and confess the truth according to the style and instructions of the Holy Office. They should make three different admonitions on separate days, with several days in between. The notary should write everything that transpires into the trial transcripts in case he should confess anything, and he should record all that transpires in the audiences. Similarly, he should be asked to say the prayers of the Christian Doctrine,[11] as well asking him where and when he has confessed and who are his confessors. And the Inquisitors should be advised that they should not be importune or excessive in their questioning of the prisoners, nor should they be remiss forgetting to ask something substantial. They should also not question the prisoner about things that are not indicated or related to the case or to things that the prisoner may mention offhand in his confession. And if the prisoner is confessing, they should leave him to freely confess without attacking him as long as the things that he is saying are not impertinent things to say.

Advice to the Inquisitors

16. In order for the Inquisitors to be able to do this and justly judge, they should always be suspicious that they are being tricked, either in the testimony against the prisoner or in the confessions. With this care and zeal they should look at and determine the case according to the truth and justice, because if either party is determined, the Inquisitors may be easily tricked.

The Inquisitors Should Not Deal with the Prisoners Outside of the Trial

17. The inquisitors should not deal with or speak to the prisoners outside of the hearings and proceedings except for things touching upon the case. The notary of the case should write down all that is said between the Inquisitors and the prisoner's response. When finished, the Inquisitors should order the notary to read what is written so that the prisoner can correct, amend, or add something without erasing anything written before.

The Accusation of the Prosecutor [*Fiscal*]

18. The Prosecutor should be careful to put the accusations against the prisoners within the time limits that the instructions order, accusing them generally as being heretic and particularly of all that is indicated in the testimony and the crimes that they admitted or confessed to committing. And even though the Inquisitors have no jurisdiction over crimes that do not touch on heresy, when the prisoner is accused of crimes of another quality, the Prosecutor should accuse him of them, not so that the Inquisitors should punish

them by themselves, but rather as further proof of the crimes of heresy of which he was accused, so that they testify to his bad Christianity or way of life, and from these things take that which touches upon and deals with the faith.

A Confessant Should Still Be Formally Accused to Proceed with the Case

19. Even though the prisoner has confessed entirely according to the testimony that he has made, the Prosecutor should still accuse him in due form, because the case should proceed at his instance just as it began with his formal denunciation. This is done so that the judges have more liberty in deliberating on the punishment or penance that they should impose after having followed the case at the insistence of third parties. Doing anything to the contrary would result in inconveniences.

The Prisoner Should Always Declare under the Oath That He Took

20. Because the prisoner had made an oath to tell the truth since the beginning of the case, every time he should appear in audience he should be reminded of his oath, telling him that he should tell the truth under the oath that he had taken (which has a great effect when he speaks or declares about other persons) because the oath always precedes the deposition.

The Prosecutor Should Always Request That the Prisoner Be Questioned under Torment

21. At the end of his accusation, it appears that it is convenient that for the effects of the trial the Prosecutor should request that, in case the prisoner's intentions are not well proven, then there is a necessity that the prisoner should be questioned under torment. Because the prisoner should not be tormented without the Prosecutor's request and the subsequent notification of the prisoner, it is done so at this point because it is not possible to use torment in any other part of the trial because it would give the prisoner the occasion to prepare against the use of torture or to alter his testimony.

Admonition of the Prisoner and the Naming of a Defense Lawyer

22. The Prosecutor should present the accusation before the Inquisitors and the notary in the presence of the prisoner, and he should read it all and take the oath according to law, and afterward he should leave the Audience chamber. The prisoner should respond point by point to the accusation before the Inquisitor or Inquisitors who received the accusation. And thus his responses should be recorded, even if they are all negative responses to the charges. Because by doing it any other way there results a great deal of confusion and little clarity in the business at hand.

Sentencing to the Stage of Proof without a Set Limit of Time

23. The Inquisitor or Inquisitors should advise the prisoner on how important it is to tell the truth. And once this is done, they should name a lawyer or lawyers of the Holy Office who are deputized to defend prisoners. And in the presence of the Inquisitors, the prisoner should communicate with his lawyer, and with his opinion in writing or in word he should respond to the accusation. And the lawyer, before he should be entrusted with

the defense of the prisoner, should take the oath to faithfully defend him and to maintain the secrecy of all that he would see or know about the case even though he may have sworn an oath before when the Holy Office received him as a lawyer. He is obligated as a Christian to admonish him to confess the truth and, if he is guilty for this, that he should ask for penance. When the response is given, the Prosecutor should be notified. In the presence of the lawyer and the two parties, the case is closed and sent and sentenced to the stage of receiving proof. In this sentence there is no custom of signaling a certain deadline, nor do both parties make a date to hear the testimony of witnesses, because neither the prisoner nor his agents are permitted to be present during the taking of testimony.

Testimony Should Be Read to the Prisoner's Lawyer

24. So that the lawyer may better know how to counsel the prisoner and to better defend him, he should read him the confessions that were made in the case and in his presence read the testimony of third persons. But if the prisoner wishes to continue with his confession, then his lawyer should leave, because he should not be present.

25. If the prisoner is a minor, younger than twenty-five years old, a guardian or trustee [curador][12] should be appointed to respond for him to the accusation, and with his authority, the confessions that were made should be ratified, and he will serve as a guardian throughout the whole trial. The guardian cannot be an official of the Holy Office. He can be the lawyer or another person of quality, confidence, and good conscience.

The Office of the Prosecutor after the Sentencing to the Stage of Proof

26. Later, the Prosecutor in the presence of the prisoner should reproduce and present the witnesses and evidence against the prisoner. This should be done in the trial as well as in the registers and documents of the Holy Office, and he should request that they examine the witnesses and ratify their testimony according to law. When this is done, they should publish the witnesses. And if the prisoner or his lawyer wishes to say something else about this, they should place it in the trial proceedings.

Accuse the Prisoner of Any New Evidence

27. If after having received the parties who gave evidence, if in any part of their testimony or the proceedings any new evidence should arise, or should the prisoner commit any new crime, the Prosecutor should issue a new accusation to which the prisoner should respond in the said form. And according to the said article the case should proceed. Even though the evidence that arises concerns the same crime of which he had been accused, it appears sufficient to tell the prisoner that even more evidence has been found against him.

Give the Prisoner All of the Audiences or Hearings That He Requests

28. Because from the sentencing for evidence until the publication of the witnesses there can be some delay, whenever the prisoner should request an audience or hearing or send for one with the Jailer (which often occurs), they should grant him an audience. This is because it is consoling to the prisoners to be heard, and also because many times it happens that a prisoner has set a day on which to confess or say something else that may lead

to the search for justice, and with the delay in granting a hearing many new thoughts and determinations may come to mind.

Ratification of the Witnesses and Further Proceedings

29. Later the Inquisitors should place care in ratifying the witnesses and in all other things that the Prosecutor has requested for the investigation of the crime, without leaving behind anything that might correspond to discovering the truth.

The Form of the Ratifications

30. After the parties have received the evidence from the witnesses, they should be ratified in the form according to law before two honest persons who are ecclesiastics who have the required qualities and are old Christians who have sworn the secret, and of whom there is a common knowledge of their good life and customs, and they will be presented by the Prosecutor as witnesses. The witnesses will then be questioned if they remember having said anything before a judge concerning things touching upon the Faith and, if they did, they should be asked that they repeat the substance of their deposition; and if they do not remember, they should give testimony to the general questions of the case so that they can remember what they said. And if they request that they be read their testimony, it should be done. All of which they understand, regardless of whether they are witnesses in jail or out of jail. The notary will write all that transpires in the disposition of the witness, if he is imprisoned and what for, and if he is ill, and if he is in the audience chamber, or in the jail in his cell, as well as the reason for which they do not bring him before the hearing. And all of this should be taken from the trial proceedings of the person against whom the witness is summoned to testify, so that he will confirm it all.

Publication of the Witness Testimony

31. After the witnesses ratify their testimony as has been said, it should be taken out and published word for word according to the testimony that touches upon the crime, taking away from this only that which may reveal the witnesses (according to the Instruction's orders). And if the testimony of the witness is very long and demands division, it should be divided into articles, so that the prisoner can understand it so that he can better respond to particular articles. To each one of these articles he should respond under oath, point by point. He should not read all of the witnesses' testimony together, or all of the deposition of each witness when a witness deposed according to articles: but rather he should go in order, responding point by point. The Inquisitors should proceed to give the publication of testimony with brevity, and they should not hold the prisoner in suspense for very long, telling him and making him understand that they had testified to many other things more than that which the prisoner had confessed, and even though the witnesses responded negatively to the articles, they should not let the prisoner do the same.

The Inquisitors Should Make the Publications and Sign with Their Signatures

32. All of the Inquisitors or any one of them should make the publication, reading to the notary what he should write or writing it out by hand, and sign it with his signature

according to the instructions. And because it would be very prejudicial, they cannot entrust it to anyone else. In these they should put the month and year in which the witness gave his deposition: because if it is inconvenient to place the day, it should not be placed, for it is sufficient to give the month and year (this is what often happens with witnesses who are in jail). Also, the publication should include the date and time in which the crime was committed because this touches upon the prisoner's defense, but the inquisitors should not name the place where it took place. They should also include as much of the witness's statement as possible, not relying on a summary of the statement. And also it must be advised that, even though the witness makes his deposition in the first person, in the publication of the testimony it should be written in the third person, saying that such and such said or heard that the prisoner dealt with certain persons.

Advice concerning the Testimonies which Touch upon Accomplices

33. Also, it is necessary to advise that when during the course of his trial a prisoner should mention the names of many persons and afterward he wishes to recant them under the pretense of forgetfulness, such testimony should not be placed into the publication, because the prisoner can easily trick them by not testifying to anything more than that which was declared. In order to avoid such difficulties, each time that such a thing occurs the Inquisitor should ensure that the prisoner should make his declaration in great detail, describing as much as possible and naming all of the persons involved, not letting him simply say "the above mentioned" or "those that I have mentioned in other declarations."

Give the Publication Even Though the Prisoner Has Confessed

34. The publication of the witnesses should be given to the prisoner even if he is consenting so that they can be certified that they were prisoners before the proceedings (because by any other means the imprisonment would not be justified), so that it can be said that the prisoner was convicted and confessed. A sentence can be pronounced against such a prisoner which enables the judges to pass judgment because they cannot place charges based on unpublished testimony.

The Prisoner's Lawyer Should See the Publication in the Presence of the Inquisitors

35. After the prisoner has replied to this, the publication will be communicated to his lawyer, and he will be given a place to hear the communication of the accusation with the prisoner because never should it be permitted that the prisoner meet with his lawyer or anyone else except in the presence of the Inquisitors and the notary who testifies to all that transpires. The Inquisitors should also be warned that they should not allow servants, friends, or any other persons to speak with the prisoner, even though they may try to make them confess their crimes, except when by necessity they may permit several wise religious persons to speak with him for this effect, but always in the presence of the Inquisitors and the notary: because not even the same Inquisitors or any other official is permitted to talk to the prisoner alone or enter into the cell unless he is the jailer. Even though the instructions state that they should give the prisoner a procurator,[13] they should not do so, because experience has shown that many inconvenient things result from this.

And because of the little utility gained from this practice, it should not be the custom to assign a Procurator to the prisoner, even though sometimes when there is a great necessity they can give the power to the lawyer who defends him.

How They Should Give Paper to the Prisoner

36. If the prisoner should request paper on which to write things touching upon his defense, they should give him certain counted sheets signed and sealed by the notary, and these sheets should later be placed into the trial transcripts. When he returns them, the sheets should be counted so that no paper should remain with the prisoner, and he should be given something with which to write with when he requests that his lawyer come to him. And they should hand over to him only the papers upon which are written things dealing with his defense and no other things or papers. And when it should be ordered, the prisoner will come to the audience in the company of his lawyer and present the papers. Also they should order that, when the prisoner wishes to prove the articles contained in his interrogatory, he should call up a great number of witnesses so that only the most competent and sufficient of these should be examined according to the interrogatory. He should also be warned that he cannot summon his servants or debtors as his witnesses and that all witnesses should be old Christians, except for the cases in which the questions are such that only other types of people can verify and prove the truth.

And if the prisoner wishes to see the defense documents before his lawyer presents them, he should be able to in a specified place. It is also warned that the Inquisitors should ensure that the lawyers and any other persons should not have any other dealings with the prisoner except for matters concerning his defense, nor should he or they bring him any news from outside of the jail, because from this no good can result, and many times this news results in damages to the persons or the case of the prisoners. The lawyers should also not retain any copies of the accusations, the publications of the witnesses, or any other documents, but rather he should return them all to the Inquisitors.

The Prosecutor Should See the Case Transcripts after the Audiences

37. In whatever part of the trial that occurs, the Prosecutor should pay special attention to ensure that after the prisoner has left the audience chamber that he should look over the case transcripts to see what has occurred. And if he should see that the prisoner has confessed, he should accept the prisoner's confessions that are in his favor, and he should make annotations in the margins of the confessions made by him and all of the other witnesses that help to maintain clarity in the matter at hand, and this acceptance of the transcripts should be done juridically.

Diligences Dealing with the Defense of the Prisoner

38. Later, the Inquisitors should occupy themselves diligently in taking the testimony of the defense witnesses that the prisoner has requested and are relevant, receiving and examining the witnesses by means of the direct questions and indirect questions, as well as those who he presents in order to refute the witnesses who testified against the prisoner. And they should do everything in their power to ascertain his innocence with as much rigor as they used to investigate his crime all the while having consideration that as a

prisoner, the accused is unable to do everything necessary that he could do if he was at liberty to pursue his own case.

Admonition of the Prisoner before the Conclusion of the Testimonies

39. After they have received the important defense testimonies, the Inquisitors should order that the prisoner appear before them together with his lawyer and that they certify that they have collected the requested defense testimony, such that, if he wished to conclude his defense, he could do so, and if there is any other thing that he should wish, he should say it. If he does not desire to request anything else, the acceptance of defense testimony and evidence in the case should be concluded even though it is certain that the Prosecutor will not conclude the case, because he is not required to do so, and so that with greater ease he may request whatever other new diligence that is necessary. If the prisoner requests a certified copy and publication of his defense testimony, he should not receive it, because by means of these documents he might be able to ascertain or gain knowledge of the witnesses who have submitted depositions against him.

Review of the Trial Proceedings and the Order of Voting

40. After the case has reached this state, the Inquisitors should bring together the ordinary [representative of the local bishop] and the consultants of the Holy Office, to all of whom they should share all of the proceedings of the case without leaving out any substantial detail. After all have reviewed the case, they should vote, each one of them giving his opinion as his conscience dictates: voting in order, first the consultants, after them the Ordinary, and after them the Inquisitors who should vote in the presence of the consultants and the Ordinary so that everyone may know their motives. If they should have a different opinion, the consultants should be satisfied to know that the Inquisitors moved in conformity to the law and not of their own free will. The notary should write down the votes of each party, particularly in the registry of votes, and from there it will be placed into the trial proceedings. The Inquisitors should allow the consultants to vote with total liberty, and they should not consent to allow anyone to dare speak out of place.

The Prosecutor Should Be Present during the Review, but He Should Leave before the Voting Begins

And because in the Office of the Inquisition there is no *relator* [court reporter], the oldest Inquisitor should submit the case without expressing his vote, and later the notary should read it. The Prosecutor should be present during the review, and he should sit below the consultants, but he should leave the chambers before the voting begins.

Prisoners Who Confess Should Be Reconciled

41. If the Prisoner has been agreeable and consenting, and his confession is of the quality required by law, the Inquisitors, Ordinary, and the consultants should receive him in a state of reconciliation, with the confiscation of his goods in the form dictated by law. He should be given a penitential habit, which is a *sanbenito* made out of linen or yellow cloth with two cross-shaped red lines emblazoned upon it, and they should imprison him in the prison called the Perpetual Prison or the Prison of Mercy. However, concerning the

confiscation of goods and the colors of the habits, in several places in the kingdom of Aragon there are particular rules and regulations concerning these things. At this point, [the Inquisitors] can give the terms of the sentence and the length of time to wear the habit or imprisonment according to what resulted in the conclusion of the case. And for whatever reason, if they might decide that the habit should be voluntary, they should allow this only by consultation with the Inquisitor General at the time in order to decide upon this, because this should not be left up to the will of the Inquisitors.

Prisoners Who Have Relapsed Truly or Are Believed to Have Relapsed Should Be Relaxed

All of this pertains to those who have not relapsed because this is expedited by law, because if they are convinced and in agreement that the prisoner has relapsed, then he should be relaxed [to the secular arm], and in this case the Inquisitors cannot reconcile him, even if he is not truly relapsed, but rather is only previously convicted by Abjuration *de vehementi*, which may have been done previously.

Abjuration

42. Any abjuration that the prisoner should make should be placed at the bottom of the sentence and the document that certifies its pronouncement, referring to the Instructions according to the instruction under which they abjured. If the prisoner knows how to sign, he should sign it with his name, and if he does not know how to sign, one of the Inquisitors or the Notary should sign for him. This should be done because when a public act is made, no one can sign there; instead, he should sign it on the following day in the audience chamber without further delay.

Denial or Rejection of Guilt

43. When the prisoner denies his guilt when the crime of heresy of which he has been accused has already been legitimately proved, or if he should stubbornly persist in his heresy, it is a necessary thing by law that nothing else can be done but to relax him to the custody of the secular arm. But in such a case the Inquisitors should seek with great effort for ensure his conversion so that at least he can die with the knowledge of God. The Inquisitors should do everything Christianly possible in order to secure his conversion.

Advice concerning Those Who Confess at the Scaffold

44. Many times the Inquisitors are forced to sentence to the scaffold stubborn prisoners who deny their guilt, and at the scaffold, before the administering of the sentence, they convert and admit to their guilt and sins and receive reconciliation and cease the execution of their case. This appears to be very dangerous and suspicious, and one should suspect that they do so more out of fear of death than out of true repentance. Thus, these confessions and conversions on the scaffold should be permitted only rarely and only in very particular cases. And if someone notifies that the night before the public auto-da-fé the prisoner confessed because he was about to die and he should judicially confess his crimes completely or in part such that it appears convenient to postpone the execution of the sentence that was given to him, they should not take him out to the scaffold because his case should not be completed

[but depends upon further investigation]. Because if he goes out to the scaffold and has had accomplices in his crimes, many great inconveniences may result because he will hear the sentences of the others and see which were condemned and which were reconciled, and he will have time to compose his own confession at will. And for similar such prisoners, little faith should be placed in what they say against third persons, and much should be doubted about their own confession because of the grave fear of death that they have.

Those Who Deny the Charges Will Be Questioned under Torment
in caput alienum

45. If the prisoner denies the charges that he is accused of and shares with other accomplices, and is involved in a case in which he should be relaxed to the secular arm, he should be questioned under torment *in caput alienum*.[14] In case he defeats the torment, because he is not given torture in order to confess his own guilt, which is legitimately proved, he will not be relieved of the relaxation to the secular arm without confessing and asking for mercy. If he should ask for mercy, then they should follow what is required by law. The Inquisitors should consider closely when they should administer the said torture. And the sentence pronounced should declare in it the reason for administering the torture in such a manner that the prisoner understands that in this case he is tormented as a witness and not as the accused.

When There Is Insufficient Proof They Should Impose
Pecuniary Fines and Abjuration

46. When the case only partially proves the crime, or when there are certain indications of the crime so that the prisoner cannot be absolved at this instance, in these cases there are different remedies that the law provides, such as Abjuration *de vehementi* or *de levi*, which appears to be the best remedy to better inspire fear in the prisoner in the future rather than punish what he has done in the past. And for this punishment, they should place pecuniary fines on those who abjure, and along with this they should warn them of the danger that they might incur by any supposed relapse if they should appear once again guilty of the crime of heresy. And for this reason those who Abjure *de vehementi* should sign their names in their abjurations (even though until now these have not been very often used), and they should do to them the same that they do in the cases of those who are reconciled.

Compurgation or Vindication

47. A second remedy is that of compurgation or vindication, which should be done according to the form given in the instructions with the number of persons that the Inquisitors, consultants, and the Ordinary deem necessary, to whose free will they are remitted. In all of this it must be advised that do to the evil of men in these times, this is a dangerous remedy, and it is not in common use and one should use it only sparingly.

Torture

48. The third remedy is that of torture.[15] This remedy due to the diversity of corporal strength and tenacity of men's souls the law reputes as a fragile and dangerous remedy and concerning which no set rule may be given more than to say that it should be up to the

conscience and discretion of the judges who are regulated by law, their reason, and good conscience. In the pronouncing of a sentence of torment or torture and in its execution all of the Inquisitors, the ordinary and the consultants should be present. In cases that may result in the use of torture, it is necessary that they all give their vote and opinions. Nevertheless, in the Instructions given in Seville in the year 1484, it is permitted that the execution of the torment may be subdelegated because that which is ordered here appears to be convenient when one of the judges does not excuse himself due to a grave illness.

Admonition of the Prisoner before He Is Subjected to Torture

49. At the time when the sentence of torture is pronounced, the prisoner should be advised particularly concerning the reasons why questioning by torture will be administered, but after pronouncing the sentence the Inquisitors should not give any more particulars about the case or name any of the other persons who appear guilty or accused in his case. This is because experience has taught that prisoners who are in agony say whatever thing is asked of them or speak names told to them, from which occurs testimony prejudicial to third persons, and this gives occasion for them to revoke their confessions and other inconvenient things.

Appellation of a Torture Sentence

50. The Inquisitors should make sure that a sentence of torture is justified and preceded by legitimate evidence. And in the case that they should doubt the evidence, they should investigate it because any prejudice done is irreparable. Thus, in cases of heresy, there is a place for appealing of the interlocutory, and these appeals should be granted. But in the case that the Inquisitors are satisfied with the veracity of the evidence and indications of a crime that resulted from the proceedings of the trial, the sentence of torture is justified. In such a case, the appeal should be considered frivolous, and the Inquisitors should proceed with the administering of torture without further delay.

A Sentence of Torture Should Not Occur before
the Conclusion of the Case

And they are warned that, if there is any doubt, they should authorize the appeal, and similarly they should not proceed with the sentence of torture or execute the sentence until the case is concluded, and they have received the testimony comprising the prisoner's defense.

When They Should Authorize an Appeal in Criminal Cases

51. And if in some case it appears to the Inquisitors that they should authorize an appeal in criminal cases against prisoners who are imprisoned, they should send the trial proceedings to the Council of the Inquisition without giving notice to any of the parties, and without any other person outside of the jail knowing, because if the Council should decide that something else should be done, it will decide upon the case.

Order That Should Be Followed If One of the Inquisitors Should Be Recused from the Case

52. If one of the Inquisitors should be recused from the case by a prisoner, if he should have a colleague and he is present, he should abstain from proceeding in that case, and he should advise the Council of this, and his colleague should proceed in the case. If he too should be forced to do the same, then the Council should be notified, and he too should not proceed in the case until the Council has seen the proceedings and decides upon the matter. The same should be done when all of the inquisitors should be recused from the case.

Ratification of Testimony Made under Torture

53. After twenty-four hours have passed since the administering of torture, the prisoner should ratify his confessions. And in the case that he revokes what he confessed, they should use the remedies dictated by law. At the time of administering the torture, the notary should note the time as well as note the time when the confession is ratified, because if it is done the following day, then there can be no doubt that it is twenty-four hours after the torture. When the prisoner has ratified his testimony and satisfied the Inquisitors of his good confession and conversion, they can admit him to reconciliation, without regard that he has confessed under torment. It is understood that in the Instructions of Seville in the year 1484 in chapter 15 that if one confesses under torment, he shall be taken as convicted and his punishment should be relaxation. But what is given here is more in the style of the times. Even now the Inquisitors should be much advised as to how they receive similar heretics who have confessed, and they should inquire if they have learned from others, or if they have taught others out of the danger that similar things can result.

What Should Be Done If the Prisoner Defeats the Torture

54. If the prisoner should withstand or defeat the torture, the Inquisitors should weigh the quality of the evidence and indications of the crime, and the quantity and form of torture, and the disposition and age of the prisoner tortured. When everything is considered and it appears that they have sufficiently purged the indications of the crime, they should absolve him at that instance, but when for some reason it appears to them that the torture was not administered with the required rigor (considering the said qualities), they may impose upon the prisoner Abjuration *de levi* or *de vehementi* or some other pecuniary fine, even though this should not be done without great consideration and be done only when the indications are insufficiently purged. The Inquisitors are advised that when some prisoner is voted to receive torment, they should not vote on what they should decide after the determination of the case by confessing or denying the charges, but rather they should return again and review what had transpired during the administration of torture.

Who Should Be Present during the Torture and the Care to Be Shown to the Prisoner after the Torture

55. During the administration of torture, no person should be present except for the judges and the notary and those who administer the torture. When the torment is over, the Inquisitors should show great care in curing the tortured prisoner if he received any lesions

in his person. They should also be careful to watch into whose care they place the prisoner until he has ratified his testimony.

The Jailer Should Not Deal with the Prisoner nor Serve as His Procurator, Defender, or Substitute for the Prosecutor

56. The Inquisitors should be careful to order that the Jailer at no time should speak with or counsel the prisoners in things concerning their case, but rather that they freely do their own will without the persuasion of anyone. And if they should discover that he has done otherwise, they should punish him. And so that all of the occasions for suspicion should cease, they should not permit the Jailer to serve as a guardian or defender of any minor. Nor should he substitute for the Prosecutor or exercise his office in his absence. They should give only the Jailer a license and order him that if any prisoner does not know how to write, he should write their defense testimony for them, writing it down in the same way that the prisoner says it without adding or saying anything from his own head.

Review of the Trial Proceedings after the Torture

57. Once the proceedings have reached this stage, the Inquisitors should gather the ordinary and the consultants and once again review the case and determine what is required by justice, being sure to maintain the said order. And the review of the case should be conducted in the presence of the Prosecutor so that he can note the points that pertain to him, and again he should leave before the voting should commence, as has been said above.

Those Who Should Leave Jail and Are Not Relaxed Should Be Questioned as to Their Communications and Contacts with Others Outside of the Jail

58. Whenever the Inquisitors should remove some prisoner from jail in order to send him away by any means other than by relaxation, they should question him under oath about the things he learned in jail, if he had seen or understood anything or received any communications from other prisoners while he was in jail or from other persons outside of jail. They should also question him as to how the Jailer used his office and if he had any news about any other prisoner. And if he had discovered something of importance, he should tell them under the pain of grave punishments, and he should swear the secret that he will not say anything about that which he saw while in jail. And this final diligence should be placed in writing in the trial proceedings, and it should be accepted as the prisoner consents and signs, if he knows how to sign his name, so that he will be fearful of breaking his oath.

If the Prisoner Should Die, the Case Should Proceed against His Heirs

59. If a prisoner should die in the jail without having his case concluded, even though the prisoner had confessed, if his confession is not sufficient to testify to the matter in order to receive him in reconciliation, they should notify his children or heirs or persons who belong to his defense. And if they should come forth to defend the dead person, then they should receive a copy of the accusation and the testimonies, and they should be admitted in the alleged legitimate defense of the prisoner.

Assign a Caretaker or Trustee for Those Prisoners Who Have Lost Their Reason or Sanity

60. If some prisoner has his case at the said stage and, out of madness, should lose his sanity or good judgment, they should provide a caretaker or Defender for him. But if he is of sound mind and good reason and his children or heirs wish to say something in his defense, they should not allow them to represent him as their party for the law forbids this. But the Inquisitors should take their testimony outside of the case and make an investigation into the truth of the matter as it pertains to the case, without giving any notice either to the prisoner or to anyone who represents him.

The Order in Which to Proceed against the Memory and Fame of a Deceased Prisoner

61. Whenever the Inquisitors should proceed against the memory and fame of a deceased person, when they have acquired sufficient evidence required by the Instructions, they should order that the Prosecutor's accusation be made known to the children and heirs of the deceased and to any other interested persons. In order to do this the Inquisitors should make all necessary investigations into the descendants of the deceased so that they can be cited in person. And after this (so that no one can pretend ignorance), they shall be cited and summoned by public edict with a legitimate time limit. When this passes, if no one comes to the defense of the deceased person, the Inquisitors will provide a defender in the case and make a legitimate just case against the deceased. If any person should appear, they should be received in the defense of the deceased, and the case shall proceed with them, regardless of the chance that the said defender may be noted for the crime of heresy in the registries of the Holy Office of the Inquisition because, having appeared for the defense, it would be a grave injury not to admit them. He should also not be excluded even if he is a prisoner in the same jail. And in similar cases, even when the evidence against the deceased is sufficient and evident, they should not conduct a sequestering of his goods because they are in the hands of a third person. These persons should not be dispossessed until the deceased is officially declared a heretic.

The Definitive Sentence Should Be Read at a Public Auto-da-fé

62. When the Defender of the memory and fame of some deceased should defend the case legitimately and the Inquisitors should absolve him of the instance, his sentence should be read in a public auto since the edicts had been publicly pronounced against him. However, they should not take out his statue in the public auto, nor should they relate the particular errors of which he was accused since they were not proved. And the same should be done to those who were personally prisoners and accused and are absolved of the instance if it is requested on their part.

Without the Appearance of a Defender, One Should Be Appointed

63. When no person should appear to defend the deceased, the Inquisitors should provide for a Defender, an able person who is not an official of the Holy Office of the Inquisition who should be given the orders how he should maintain the secrecy of the

proceedings, notifying him of the accusations and testimonies by means of the lawyers of the Holy Office and by no other persons without the explicit license of the Inquisitors.

Obey the Instructions concerning Proceedings against Absent Prisoners

64. In the proceedings that the Inquisitors should enact against someone who is absent, they should obey what the instructions order. Especially, they should be advised concerning the time limits of the edict if they are to be long or short, according to what may be learned about the absent prisoner, paying close attention that he be called for during three distinct time limits at the end of each of which the Prosecutor should accuse the absent prisoner of disobedience so that the proceedings can continue in good measure.

They Should Not Impose Corporal Punishments in Place of Pecuniary Fines

65. Many times the Inquisitors proceed against those apparently guilty of things against the faith, and because of the quality of the crime and the person, he is not judged as a heretic, such as those who contract matrimonies, or qualified blasphemers, or those who say other ill-sounding words, for these crimes they should impose various punishments and penances according to the quality of the crimes, according to law and their legitimate judgment. In these cases, they should not impose penance or pecuniary fines or personal punishments such as lashings, galley service, or other shameful penitence in lieu of not paying the quantity of money that they were condemned to pay, because this would sound very bad and appears to be a grievous extortion on the part of the debtors. And in order to avoid this, the Inquisitors should pronounce their sentences simply without conditions or any other alternative.

Remission to the Council in Case of Discord among the Inquisitors, or the Ordinary, but Not in Case of Discord among Consultants

66. In all of the cases in which there may be a discrepancy of votes between the Inquisitors and the Ordinary or in cases in which any one of them disagrees in the definition of the case or with any part of the proceedings or sentencing, they should remit the case to the Council. But in cases where they are in conformity, but the consultants have a discrepancy, even if they are in a greater number, the decision and vote of the Inquisitors should be executed. In the case of very grave crimes, they should not execute the vote of the Inquisitors, the ordinary, or the consultants, even if they are in agreement without consulting with the Council as is the custom.

The Notary Should Remove the Testimonies from the Proceedings of the Prisoners

67. The notaries of the Secret should exercise great caution in removing from the proceedings of each of the prisoners all of the testimonies that appear in the registers, and they should not place them or refer to them by remitting to them in the register, because this causes great confusion during the review of the case. And this should be done and ordered, even though it is the job of the notaries.

They Should Make the Investigations into the Communications That the Prisoners Had and Include These in the Proceedings

68. If they should discover or understand that some prisoners have maintained communication with each other while in prison, the Inquisitors should investigate who they are and if they are accomplices in the same crime and what were the things that they discussed. All of this should be placed within the trial proceedings of each one. And they should provide a remedy for this so as to stop all illicit communications among prisoners, because when prisoners have communicated among one another in jail, all that they testify to and say against other people and even against themselves is held suspect.

Everything concerning the Prisoner Should Be Accumulated in the Trial Proceedings

69. Whenever there is a trial against some determined person or undetermined person, even if it does not concern formal heresy, if something is discovered concerning new evidence against a prisoner or person concerning new crimes, these should be accumulated with the old trial material and made into a new trial proceeding to aggravate the guilty suspect's crimes. The Prosecutor should make mention of this in his accusation.

No One Should Be Removed from His Cell in Jail Unless All Are Moved

70. Once they are placed in a cell, prisoners should not be moved from one cell to another cell all together. This method avoids any communications that the prisoners may have with one another, because by moving them in the company of one another they can give each other notice of all that occurs.

The Sick Should Be Cured, and They Should Be Given a Confessor If They Request One

71. If a prisoner takes ill while in jail, the Inquisitors are required to order him to be cured with no delay, and they should provide that he had all that is necessary to ensure his health, such as the opinions of a doctor or doctors who can cure him, and if he requests a confessor, he should be given one who is a person of quality and confidence who will have to swear the secret. And if the penitent should say anything in his confession that touches upon the jail or deals with the case, he should reveal it to the Inquisitors who will notify him of the form in which he should act with the penitent, notifying him that he is a prisoner accused of heresy and that if he does not judicially manifest his heresy if he is guilty, he cannot be absolved.[16] Everything else should be remitted to the conscience of the Confessor, who should be wise enough to know what to do in such cases. But if the prisoner is healthy and asks for a Confessor, he should not be given one, except in cases where he had already judicially confessed and satisfied the case, and in such a case it appears convenient to give him a confessor to console and fortify him. But the confessor cannot absolve him of his heresy until he has been reconciled to the fold of the Church, such that the confession will not have total effect except if the accused should be on his deathbed, or if the prisoner is a pregnant woman who is close to giving birth, and with these cases they should obey what the law says in such cases. When the prisoner does not request a confessor and the

doctor or medic is suspicious of his health, he should persuade by all means that he confesses himself. And when the judicial confession should satisfy the accusations before the prisoner should die, he should be reconciled in due form with the abjuration required. And once judicially absolved the Confessor can sacramentally absolve him. If it is not inconvenient, they should give the prisoner an ecclesiastical burial in the greatest of secrecy.

Do Not Reveal the Witnesses to the Prisoner

72. Even though in other trials judges have the custom of presenting the witnesses to the prisoner in order to verify the crimes, in Inquisition trials this should not be done because not only does it reveal the secret that is required of witnesses in these cases but experience has shown that from this comes many inconveniences.

No Captures or Arrests Should Be Authorized during the Visitations without First Consulting the Inquisitor's Colleagues and the Consultants

73. Because cases involving the Holy Office of the Inquisition should be treated with the necessary silence and authority, when the Inquisitors are visiting an area, and they are offered testimony of sufficient form against someone for a crime committed that deserved imprisonment, they should not execute the imprisonment without consulting with their colleagues and the consultants who reside in the principal town of the region, unless in the case of the accused there is a suspicion of flight. Then, out of necessity and because of the danger of flight (with good accord), the Inquisitor before whom this occurred can order the imprisonment. And with all necessary brevity, he should remit the prisoner and the testimonies to the Inquisition's prison where the case should be tried. But this is not to be done in lighter cases that can be determined without the necessity of imprisonment, such as poorly qualified heretical blasphemy, which he can determine (as he should do) having the power as an ordinary. But under no circumstances should the Inquisitor on his visitation create a jail in order to begin a formal trial for heresy, since he lacks the officials and the disposition of the secret jail that is required of an inquisition trial.

How They Should Make a Declaration concerning the Length of Time since the Prisoner Had Begun to Be a Heretic

74. At the time when they saw the cases of those who will be declared as heretics with the subsequent confiscation of goods, the Inquisitors, the ordinary, and consultants should make a declaration concerning the time when the accused began to commit the crimes of heresy for which he is declared a heretic. This is so that, if the Receptor requests it, he may present it in some civil trial. And the Inquisitors should specify if they know it from a confession of the accused or by testimony placed against him.

Rations That Should Be Given to the Prisoners

75. The maintenance that should be given to prisoners of the Inquisition should be charged for according to the length of time of imprisonment and with consideration of the scarcity of foodstuffs. But if some person of quality who has goods in abundance should be imprisoned and he wishes to eat and spend more than the ordinary ration, they should

give him all that he desires and which appears honest for his person and his servants, if he had any with him in jail, such that the Jailer and the Dispenser should not take advantage of anything that he may have given them, but rather give it to the poor.

What They Should Give to the Wife and Children of the Prisoner

76. Because all of the prisoner's goods are sequestered by the Inquisition, if the said prisoner has a wife or children and they should request food, they should inform the prisoner and request what he wishes to do concerning this. After he is returned to his cell, the Inquisitors should call for the Receptor and the Notary of the Sequesters, and according to the quantity of the goods and the quality of the persons involved, they should be charged. But if the children are of age to earn their own living, they should not be given any food, but if they are old, children, or young women or because they cannot gain any other honest means of living, they should be given the necessary food to sustain themselves, assigning to each person a certain quantity of money and not bread, and the quantity should be moderate.

When They Have Come to an Agreement concerning the Date of the Auto-da-fé, They Should Notify the Secular and the Ecclesiastical Councils [*Cabildos*]

77. When the trials of the prisoners are voted on and sentenced, the Inquisitors should decide upon a festival day in which to conduct the auto-da-fé, and they should notify both the City's Town Council and the Cathedral Chapter of the date, and where there is an Audiencia,[17] the president and judges [*oidores*][18] should be invited to accompany them according to the custom of each place. And they should proceed to ensure that the execution of those relaxed to the secular arm occurs during the day and not at night to avoid any inconveniences.

Who Should Enter at Night before the Auto-da-fé

78. And because people entering into the jails the night before an auto-da-fé cause great inconveniences, the Inquisitors should ensure that no one enters the jail except for the Confessors and, at the necessary time, the Familiars who will take charge of the prisoners in writing before one of the Notaries of the Holy Office so that they can return and give an account of them, except in the cases of those to be relaxed and handed over to the secular arm of justice. And along the route of the solemn procession and on the scaffold, they should not permit any person to speak to them or to give them any news of what is happening.

They Should Tell Those to Be Reconciled What They Have to Do and Then Hand Them over to the Jailer of the Perpetual Jail

79. On the following day, the Inquisitors should order that all of the said prisoners who are reconciled should be taken out of the prison, and they should declare what they have to do according to their sentences and advise them of the punishments that they will incur if they are not good penitents. And after having examined them concerning their time in jail, they should hand them over to the Jailer of the Perpetual Jail, ordering him

to take good care of them and ensure that they comply with their penance and that he should advise them of any carelessness that he observed in them. He should also provide for and help them in their necessities, by helping them make things according to their offices and trades that they may know and which can help them sustain themselves and pass through their misery.

Visitation of the Perpetual Jail

80. The Inquisitors should visit the perpetual jail several times a year in order to see how the prisoners are treated and how they live their lives. This is necessary because in many Inquisitions there are no perpetual jails (which are necessary things), and they should order that they buy houses to serve as these jails. Without the jail they cannot know how the penitents comply with their reconciliation, nor can they guard those who should be guarded.

Where and How They Should Renew the *Sanbenitos*

81. It is a manifestly necessary thing that all of the *sanbenitos*[19] of the condemned, both alive and dead, present and absent, should be placed in the churches where they were once residents and parishioners at the time of their imprisonment, or their death, or flight. The same should be done with the *sanbenitos* of those reconciled after they have complied with their penance and they have been removed, even though they may not have worn them longer than the time in which they were placed upon the scaffold when they were read their sentences. All of these *sanbenitos* should be placed and guarded inviolably and no one has the commission to remove them. The Inquisitors are always charged with their renewal and their visitation so that always there will be the memory of the infamy of the heretics and their descendants. On these *sanbenitos* they should place the time of their condemnation, and if they were Jews, Moors, or one of the new heresies of Martin Luther and his henchmen. However, they should not place the *sanbenitos* of those reconciled during the time of grace because as a point of the said grace period they should not put them in *sanbenitos* because they did not have them at the time of their reconciliation so that they should not place them in the churches because it would be contrary to the mercy that was shown them at the outset.

All of the said articles and each and every one of them I entrust you and order you to obey and follow in the business offered before the Inquisitions regardless of whether or not there existed contrary customs before, because this is in accord with the Service of God, Our Lord and in the better administration of Justice. In testimony of this we order that it be given, and we give the present signed by our name and sealed with our seal and certified by our Secretary General of the Inquisition.

Given in Madrid, the second day of the month of September in the year of our
Lord and Savior Jesus Christ one thousand five hundred and sixty-one.
Fernando Hispalenses
By order of His Illustrious Lordship
Juan Martínez de Lassao

Form of the Oath of Office That All of the Ministers, Officials, Commissaries, and Familiars of the Holy Office of the Inquisition Should Present in the Presence of the Inquisitors When They Are Admitted to the Jurisdiction of the Inquisition

I, ————, swear to God and to this Holy Cross that I will be a good and faithful minister of the Holy Office and that I will always reveal to this Holy Tribunal all of the types of heresies that come to my attention and serve and do everything that is required or requested by its Authority. And with my person and my belongings I will help to discover and proceed against all of those delinquents, accomplices, and their co-conspirators.

- Also, I will inviolably maintain the secret of all of that which as a Minister of the Holy Office should be entrusted to me or ordered done.
- Also, I will obey the Lord Inquisitors as my legitimate superiors and judges.
- Also, that I will obey and comply with all of the instructions, privileges, and exemptions, both Royal and Apostolic, and any other immunities granted to this Holy Office.
- Also, I will maintain a good correspondence with all of the ecclesiastical and temporal justices and their ministers, and I will respect them and revere them with all due reason.

All of which I will comply with the help of God, and if I do not do so, May he make a claim against me, Amen!

DOCUMENT 2
Royal Order Issued by King Philip II Establishing the Foundation of the Holy Office of the Inquisition in the Indies

Madrid, January 25, 1569

SOURCE: *Recopilación de leyes de los reynos de las Indias: mandadas imprimir y publicar por la Majestad Católica del rey Don Carlos II, nuestro señor,* titulo XIX, "De los Tribunales del Santo Oficio de la Inquisición y Sus Ministros," ley 1, folio 91, Madrid: Imprenta de Julian de Paredes, 1681.

Our glorious ancestors, faithful and Catholic children of the Holy Roman Catholic Church, considering what touches upon our royal dignity and Catholic zeal, strove through all measures possible that our Holy Faith be expanded and exalted throughout all the world, founded in these our kingdoms the Holy Office of the Inquisition so that the Faith be conserved in all the purity and completeness necessary. And having discovered and incorporated in our Royal Crown, by providence and the grace of God our Lord, the kingdoms and provinces of the Western Indies, Islands, and *Tierra Firme*[20] of the Ocean Sea, and other parts, they put their great care in giving them the knowledge of the true God, and to strive to enlarge his Holy Evangelical law, and to conserve, free from errors and false and suspicious doctrines, and in their discoverers, settlers, children, and descendants of our vassals, the devotion, good name, reputation, fame, and the strength of care and fatigue they strove to enlarge and exalt. And because those who are outside the obedience and devotion of the Holy Roman Catholic Church, obstinate in errors and heresies, always strive to pervert and to separate from our Holy Catholic Faith, the faithful and devoted Christians, and with their malice and passion work with all effort to attract them to their wicked beliefs, communicating their false opinions and heresies, popularizing and spreading diverse condemned and heretical books; and the true remedy consists in turning aside and excluding all communication by the heretics and suspicious persons, castigating and extirpating their errors, shunning and obstructing what causes great offense to the holy faith and Catholic religion in those parts; and the natives there are perverted with the new, false, and reprobate doctrines and errors: the apostolic inquisitor general in our kingdoms and realms with the agreement of those of our Council of the General Inquisition and, consulting with us, ordered and decided that the Holy Office of the Inquisition will be established and seated in those provinces, and for the discharge of our royal conscience, and for the deputizing and naming of apostolic inquisitors against heretical depravity and apostasy, and the necessary officials and ministers for the use and exercise of the Holy Office.

And because it is proper, we order them to be given the favor of our royal arm [of justice]. And as a Catholic prince zealous of the honor of God, and benefit of the Christian republic, we wish the Holy Office to operate freely: We command our Viceroys, Presidents, Judges, and *alcaldes*,[21] and all other governors, *corregidores*,[22] and *alcaldes mayores*,[23] and all other justices of all cities, towns, and places in the Indies, both Spaniards as well as the native Indians, that from the present time onward from this time forth, that each and every time that the apostolic inquisitors operate in whichever part of the said provinces exercising the Holy Office of the Inquisition, that its ministers, officials, and persons be received with due and decent reverence and respect, having consideration of the Holy Ministry that they will practice, and they should be housed and left to freely exercise their Holy Office, and being ordered by the Inquisitors, all should take the canonical oath, which is usually done, and all should give aid to the Holy Office whenever it is requested, and they should be given all aid of our secular arm of government in order to arrest whatever heretics or suspects in the faith they may find, and aid in whatever may touch upon or concern the free exercise of the Holy Office, which has been decreed by Canonical law, style, and custom and is based on the instructions that have been previously given.

I the King,
Royal Secretary

DOCUMENT 3

Instructions of the Illustrious Lord Cardinal Don Diego de Espinosa, Inquisitor General, for the Establishment of the Inquisition in New Spain

Madrid, 1570

SOURCE: Archivo General de la Nación, Ramo de Inquisición, vol. 1519, exp. 2, Lote Riva Palacio, vol. 44, no. 2, folios 41r–47r.

NOTE: Don Diego de Espinosa y Arévalo (1502–1572)[24] was a cardinal and bishop of Sigüenza who succeeded Fernando de Valdés as inquisitor general of Spain and president of the Supreme Council of the Inquisition. He was commissioned on September 8, 1566, and took possession of the office on December 4, 1566, serving until his death on September 15, 1572. Espinosa played a foundational role in the creation of the Inquisition in New Spain, and the following document reveals his preoccupations and his ultimate decisions in terms of delineating the powers of the new Inquisition tribunal of New Spain.

Don Diego de Espinosa, by divine mercy, Cardinal of the Holy Church of Rome, priest of the basilica of Saint Stephen *in coelio monte,* Bishop and Lord of Sigüenza, president of the Royal Council of His Majesty, and Apostolic Inquisitor General against heretical depravity and apostasy in these kingdoms and Lordships & etc. We make it know to You, the reverend Apostolic Inquisitors against the said heretical depravity and apostasy, in the great city of Temistitán-México,[25] and in all other provinces of New Spain, which are the districts of the *audiencias* of Mexico, Guatemala, and New Galicia, in which resides the Archbishopric of Mexico, and the bishoprics of Oaxaca, New Galicia, Michoacan, Tlaxcala, Yucatan, Guatemala, Chiapas, Verapaz, Honduras, Nicaragua, and their environs, and in all other kingdoms and estates of the said New Spain and its district and jurisdiction (where in consultation with His Majesty), we have ordered the establishment and deputation of the Holy Office of the Inquisition against the said heretical depravity and apostasy, and concerning the cases and causes that pertain to the said Holy Office, and that you and whoever you should select should concern yourselves, besides that which has been ordered by common law and the sacred cannons, you should also be careful to guard and to observe in all ways the following instructions:

1. First, in establishing and placing the said Holy Office newly in the said provinces, you, the deputized Inquisitors in the province of New Spain, once you have arrived in the great city of Temistitán-México, you should make it known to the Viceroy, so that according to the order of His Majesty that you should possess, he should assign to you a house or other competent place where you should establish the audience chambers and jails of the Holy Office. There should be an audience chamber with two separate rooms, and a chamber of the secret, where the papers and other documents should be housed with much care, and there should be living quarters for you, the said Inquisitors, or at least for one of you, and also for the Jailer (*alcaide*), and that the secret jails of the Inquisition should be set apart so that there can be no communication between the prisoners. Once this should be done, the day on which you should come to an accord with the Viceroy, having first given an order in conformity to the ancient instructions of the Holy Office, you should order that the entire population should be brought together, both the ecclesiastical and secular officials, in the Cathedral Church of the said city, and there you should order that your titles and powers that you brought with you should be read and published. Then the Viceroy and Royal judges of the Audiencia, along with the magistrates and other secular officials of His Majesty and all other ecclesiastical and secular personages should be congregated there and they should make the oath of solemn obedience according to law and the instructions of the Holy Office of the Inquisition, as it should be and is accustomed to be done. For all of this you will take royal orders from his Majesty, which you shall use, notifying in particular

the Viceroy and the Audiencia, and ordering them to read them publicly when they should make the solemn oath, and the said Viceroy and Audiencia and other Royal Officials, shall do this, swearing by touching a cross and the holy Gospels. And all the other people who are congregated there should be ordered to raise their right hands and swear, as it is accustomed to do during the public auto-da-fé. Once this diligence is done, the General Edict of Faith should be read, conforming to the copy of which should be handed over to you together with these instructions, and it will not be necessary that you shall have to publish the Edict of Grace at this time.

2. Also, in order to begin to proceed in the cases and crimes that belong to your jurisdiction, you should order and create the following books:

3. A *Registry Book* in which you shall place at the beginning the titles, licenses, and powers that you should bring from us, and all of the Royal orders and provisions of his Majesty, and the documents and other acts that were done on the day that you received your offices, and the order in which each was published and announced, and the oaths that you and the other officials of the Holy Office should have made to exercise your offices honestly and faithfully. Then afterward you should place in this book all of the other titles and commissions that we have given to the other officials of the said Inquisition, no matter when they should be given, and also there you should place all of the other *cedulas* and provisions of his Majesty that may be issued to you. This registry book should have the title *FIRST BOOK OF PROVISIONS*, and once it is finished or full, you should create the second, and then the other consecutive books, each having their own number.

4. Also, there should be another book in which you should place an alphabetical list of the commissaries and familiars that should exist in the district, and the designation of the companions that they are given, with the day, month, and year, and the Inquisitors who provided them with their titles and commissions. In this book, at the head of it, they should place the names of the places that exist in the district, placing them in the order of their distance from the capital and they should be placed in the order in which they can be visited, declaring and labeling those that are the heads of provinces, bishoprics, or convent regions, adding or moving them according to what should be the needs at the time.

5. Also, in another registry book you should place the testimonies that are given against the prisoners, placing at the beginning of the book an alphabetical list according to the style of the Holy Office. Whenever they should proceed against someone, according to the testimonies, they should make copies on separate sheets of paper and turn these over to the Prosecutor, so that at his insistence you may provide what is necessary for justice. This book should be entitled *FIRST BOOK OF TESTIMONIES*, and once this book is completed or filled, consecutively you should make a second, third, etc.

6. Also, another book should be made in which you should record the votes and consultations for imprisonment and the sentences for the administration of torture and definitive sentences, and all other acts and documents that should have the votes of the Inquisitors and their consultants, with the place, day, month and year noted, and at the foot of the votes, they should place their signatures, or at least their signs and marks.

7. Also, there should be a bound bundle [*legajo*][26] in which to place all of the letters that we ourselves and our Commissaries of the General Inquisition should write to you.

8. Also, there should be another book in which you should make a registry of the letters that you should write to us, as well as those to the Commissary.

9. Also, there should be another book in which you should record the visitations of the prisoners in the jails, according to the Instructions of the Holy Office, which you should make every fifteen days, and record that which occurs on the visitation and all that you should provide for during the visitations.

10. Also, there should be another book in which the orders for payments that you may make should be given so that the Receiver should pay the maravedis[27] that may be necessary for things concerning the Holy Office. All of these orders for payments should be registered before they are handed over to the said Receiver (*receptor*) and there should be much caution in this, according to the censure that the Holy Office has concerning this.

11. Also, another book should exist in which you should place the punishments and pecuniary fines that you should make, for which an account should be made by the Receptor, giving him a relation of them after they have been placed in the book, so that he should collect them.

12. Also, there should be another book in which you should place the documents concerning the auto-da-fé that you should make, where you should place in particular the persons who were marched in procession, with a clear relation of the crimes for which they were processed, and the punishments and penance that they were condemned to receive. You should place those that you have given penance to outside of an auto in another book apart from this one.

13. The Jailer should also have another book in which by means of one of the Notaries of the Secret, he should record all of the prisoners who entered into the prisons, with the day, month, and year, with the list of their clothing, bed, and other vestments that they bring in great detail. There they should record the day in which the said prisoner was released. If the said prisoner was relaxed to the secular arm, or reconciled, the goods that he left behind in the prison should be entrusted to the receptor. Once this book is completed it should be kept guarded in the Secret Chamber, and the Jailer will be given another one; and this book should be entitled *FIRST BOOK OF THE ALCAIDE (JAILER)*, and the others labeled consecutively.

14. Also, the Dispenser and the Provider for the Prisoners should have another book, where the Notary of the Secret, on the day that the prisoner enters into the jail or at the latest the next day, in front of the Inquisitors in the audience chamber, records the name of each and every one of the prisoners in the Secret Jails, and places the date in which they entered, and the moneys that they brought for their food and maintenance, and the rations that are ordered to be given to them. If they should be poor, they should record the manner in which the Fiscal office should pay for their food, giving them the poor person's rations,[28] declaring the quantity.

15. Also, you should order that the Notary of Secrets should have a book, where he should record the goods that have been sequestered from the accused, and the moneys and clothing that are given for their food and maintenance, and another book in which he

should record at the end of each month, in front of one of the Inquisitors, an account made in conjunction with the Dispenser of what had been spent in the maintenance of poor prisoners, because from this book the Receptor should take the sums needed.

16. Also, the Judge of Confiscated Goods, should have another book in which are recorded the sentences given against the Fiscal Office of the Inquisition, or in its favor, with the day, month, and year. The Notary of the Court should also have another book so that when the Receptor gives his account, the reasons for it all should be clear, and from that book they should make the charges or discharges of the sums.

17. Also, You should order that the Receptor should have his book in which he records what it is his charge to take from or give back to the confiscated goods which proceeded from the sequestering, and the maravedis of the punishments and penance given, and the documents and expenditures concerning these that are made, advising him that in order for him to receive and pass on to the account that which he spends, he should do so only by Our direct order, or by an order from the Council of the General Inquisition, or by an order from you, the Inquisitors, in the cases given to your cognizance in the Instructions.

18. Also, another alphabetically organized book should exist in which are recorded the relaxed, reconciled, and those who have received penance, which should correspond to the books of the acts and documents that were made in the Trials of Faith. It should be ordered so that the names of all of the relaxed should be placed in one part, and in another those reconciled, and in another those who received penance, in a manner so that the said book should have three types of alphabetical lists, so that by this means one can easily know the names of those who have been relaxed, reconciled, and those who received penance.

19. Also, the Chamber of the Secret, where all of the trials and registers of the Holy Office should be placed, should have four separate rooms or sections, including one in which they should place the pending trials, and in another one those trials that are suspended, and in another one those trials that are completed. In the section pertaining to the finished trials, they should archive in the first space the trials of those relaxed, and then those who were reconciled and after that those who received penance. In the fourth room or section they should place trials relating to commissaries and familiars and the information collected and received concerning their purity of blood[29] and the qualities of the said commissaries and familiars, and it is the responsibility of the Prosecutor to have all of the papers and books of the secret well placed, sown together and bound, with headings and title pages in the manner in which they could be easily found.

20. Once these books are arranged and placed in good order, You should guard and maintain yourselves in the procedures and cognizance of the cases and crimes and the order and form of proceeding in them that was given in the ancient and modern instructions of the Holy Office of the Inquisition, which you should bring with you, placing great care in the observance of them, ordering that the said ancient and modern instructions should be read at least two times each year, once at the beginning of the year during the first days of January, so that they can be read by the first day of the hearings for the new year, which is the first day after the Festival of the Three Kings,[30]

and another time that they should be read is the week before the Sunday of Cua-simodo;[31] and all of the officials should be present, and they should read to each one of them that which touches on their office according to the said instructions, so that they should know what to guard and maintain.

21. And in the form of ordering the trials, you should guard and maintain the order of procedures that is given in the book printed by our order, and that is the book that is followed in the Inquisitions in these kingdoms.[32]

22. It is most convenient that during the days of audience the Inquisitors and officials should come together in the morning in the audience chamber where they should have a mass prayed. We order that the said Inquisitors and officials should be present every day at the mass that should be made in the said chamber before beginning the audiences, and those who should not comply with this you should order to pay a fine that you find appropriate.

23. And because the cases dealing with heresy should be determined with the assistance of the ordinary,[33] if the same prelate cannot assist in the determination of the said cases and instead should send another in his place, you should not admit him until you have first been informed *in scripti* [in writing] concerning his purity of blood in the best means possible. The same should be done in the cases of all other people who should serve as consultants whom you call upon in order to determine the said cases, who should be the judges of the Royal Audiencia, for all of which you shall bring a Royal cedula from His Majesty.

24. *What should be done in case of an inconformity in the votes*

In the said ancient and modern instructions, it is ordered that whenever you the said Inquisitors and the Ordinary should not be in conformity concerning the votes in the determination of the cases, all of the trials in which there is a discord should be sent to the Council of the General Inquisition, so that there they should be determined. But because if this should be followed in the said province of New Spain, there would ensue much damage to the prisoners for the delay that may occur in determining their cases, we order that in all cases in which it appears that there might be questioning under torment or an arbitrary punishment, or reconciliation, and in all other cases where there might be a relaxation to the Justice and Secular Arm; being present both you the Inquisitors and the Ordinary and in the consultation of the said business if the Ordinary and one of you are in agreement, the vote of those two should be executed, without the necessity of having to send the case to the Council. And if the votes are split, the opinion that receives the most votes from the consultants should be executed, without making a remission of the case to the Council. But if the discord should concern whether a prisoner should be relaxed or not, in this case, the said trial should be remitted to the Council of the General Inquisition.

25. *Appeals and Appellations*

Also, because it is stated in law that, in cases within the cognizance of the Holy Office in which the ordinary punishment of reconciliation or relaxation is not given, the accused can appeal the extraordinary punishment and the sentence of torment, and the approval of an appeal suspends the execution, we order that when the accused is to be considered injured by the extraordinary punishment, or the sentence of torment, and appeals before us, in such a case you should order that he allege his injuries before you, and once the Prosecutor has heard them by means of a written copy, you should return and meet again concerning the matter with the Ordinary and the consultants, and whatever is accorded in the case, according to the manner of voting in the previous instruction (24), should be executed. Once the sentence is executed, and the said person wishes to appear before us at the Council, you should send along his trial, so that, once it is seen, justice can be provided for in the case.

26. Also, You should have much care and warning to write to us and the Council at least two times each year, giving us a particular relation of the state of the cases that might have occurred in that Holy Office and concerning the cases determined as well as those pending, sending along a relation of those who were marched in procession in an auto-da-fé and those who were determined outside of an auto, and the punishments and penances that were imposed and the crimes for which they were given penance, and if they were convicted of the said crimes by the witnesses or by their confession, relating all in very particular detail, so that the state of the said business can be known as well as the order in which you have proceeded in them.

27. Also, in all of the cases in which you consult directly with us or with the Council, concerning trials and cases in which you have doubts, and request to be advised by us concerning what it is you should do, you should send us your opinions, and that of the Ordinary and the Consultants, whenever the case should be consulted with them, so that examining all of them we can better advise you what you should do.

28. Also, because according to law you should have cognizance over cases of heretical blasphemy, and not of any other type, you should be advised that if the accused should come before you and, of his own free will, confess the said blasphemies, you should question him if he had been denounced concerning them before the secular justices; and if you prove this from his confessions, or from some other means, you should not proceed in inhibiting the Royal Justices who intervened. You should do the same thing in all other cases of mixed jurisdiction, such as those who are married two times, or those accused of witchcraft or enchantments with the use of Holy relics.

29. Also, once the audience and other things of the Inquisition are attended to, one of the said Inquisitors should go out and visit the part of the district given to you both. Then after, with the Viceroy, you should appear with the power of the Ordinary, if he gives it to you, and if not with testimony of how you requested it, and in this visitation you should publish the edicts of Faith and take cognizance of the crimes included in the Instructions. And if there exists several papers, documents, or testimonies in the archive of the Secret, which touch upon the parish or region where you might go and visit, you should take them with you. During the said visitation, you should take one of the Notaries of the Secret and a familiar with a staff of office and one of the porters, and you should not determine the case unless it is a light case, because the most serious cases you should remit to the Tribunal, so that there with more consideration the case can be determined. Once the said visitation is made, when you write to us and the Council, you should send us a relation of all that may have been done.

30. Also, since the district is so large that it is not possible to visit all of the regions of it by yourselves, you, the said Inquisitors, should send out commissaries to the parts and

places where you cannot comfortably go and visit yourselves. You should send the Commissaries of the said places the edicts of faith, so that they can have them proclaimed in the churches of the region under their charge, and so that they can receive the testimonies of those who respond to the said edicts before faithful notaries and legal old Christians. Once received, without proceeding to the capture or of the making of any other diligence, they should send before you the said testimonies, so that once you have seen them, you can provide for what they concern, seeing to the completion of justice.

31. Also, you should be cautious not to proceed against nor claim cognizance over cases whose jurisdiction, according to law and the instructions of the Holy Office, does not belong to you.

32. Also, because one of the said instructions orders that the Receptor of the Inquisition pay for your orders for payment whatever is necessary for the expenses of the Holy Office, you should look to it that nothing should be ordered to be paid that is not very necessary, so that during the time in which they make accounts, all that which does not appear to be necessary will be forcibly ordered to be placed against the account of your salaries. Thus, whenever you have a doubt concerning making some extraordinary request in great expense, you should consult us and the Council, so that we can advise you concerning what you should do.

33. Also, You should procure to conserve yourselves in all good correspondence and friendship with the prelates of your district, giving them notice of your arrival and offering them from your own part, all good will, and requesting that they name persons in the said city who can assist in the business that touches upon their offices as Ordinaries, and advising them that those whom they name should have the qualities of blood purity and all of the other things required, and also with the secular justices, you should procure to have all good correspondence.

34. *Indians are not to be proceeded against in the Inquisition*[34]

    Also, we advise you that by virtue of our powers you cannot proceed against the Indians of your district, because for now and until something else is ordered, it is our will that you should only use your powers against old Christians and their descendants, and against other people against whom cases are made in these kingdoms of Spain. In the cases that you do have jurisdiction over, you should proceed with all temperance and mercy, and with much consideration, because it is necessary to do this, in such a way so that the Inquisition is much feared and respected, and so that on no occasion should there be any reason for people to hate [the Inquisition].

35. Also, you should have much caution in publishing censure against the bibles and enforce the catalogue of prohibited books that has been entrusted to you, and you should collect all of the books contained in it, providing that, in all of the ports of the sea, the commissaries there have great care in looking at and examining all of the books that enter into these provinces, in the manner that none of the prohibited books should be permitted to enter. You should order that the said Commissaries advise you often about their diligence concerning this that they have done, because this business is important, and it will be very necessary, so that by means of this way no bad doctrine may enter into those kingdoms. You should proceed with rigor and censure against those who are found to be guilty of this.

36. *Familiars*

Also, in the creation of the familiars of the Inquisition, you should guard the form and following order: In the great city of Temistitán-México, where the Inquisition tribunal shall reside, there should be twelve familiars, and in the cities that are the heads of bishoprics, there should be four familiars, and in the places where Spaniards reside, in each of them, one familiar. As for those who are to be named as familiars, both they and their wives should be old Christians, clean of all race of new Christians, and they should not have been given penance by the Holy Office of the Inquisition, and [they should be] peaceful, tranquil, of good customs, married, and have their continued residence in the places where they should be named as familiars, all of which should be conducted by written information *in scriptis* and be seen and approved by you. They should be given an official license of their familiar status, in the same manner as that in the copy that you bring with you along with this Instruction. All of them will enjoy the privileges that are enjoyed by the Familiars of the kingdoms of Castile, obeying in all things the orders of His Majesty, procuring to excuse all manners of conflicts of jurisdiction with the secular justices concerning the said familiars. And when it may be necessary, you should communicate with the Viceroy so that he can order [any conflicts] to cease and that what has been accorded can be enforced.

37. Also, in the cities that are the heads of bishoprics, and in the places of the seaports, you should have in each one of them an ecclesiastical commissary, of good life and customs, learned, if they exist, to whom you should give your commission according to the copy that you bring with you with these orders, advising the said commissaries that they should not engage in the cognizance of anything else, nor engage in conflicts of jurisdiction with the ecclesiastical and secular justices, and that they should only execute your orders and commissions, and receive the information concerning things of the faith which occur before them, and to then remit them so that you can see them and provide for whatever is to be according to justice. They should not order the arrest nor conduct any other ordinary trial without your particular commission. Before you should provide for the said commissaries, you should make an information *in scriptis* concerning their blood purity, life, and customs, and once seen and approved by you, you may give them the commission, and in no other way should they be commissioned. In the places where the said commissaries exist, one of the familiars will serve as notary, procuring that he should be a legal expert to whom the business and secret of the Holy Office can be entrusted.

38. *Ministers who serve the Holy Office*

Also, we inform you that the persons who should be most convenient to have in your district for the offices for which we have not provided shall be the Constable (*Alguacil*), an Accountant (*Contador*), a Receiver (*Receptor*), a Notary of the Sequesters and of the Court of the Confiscated Goods, a lawyer for the Fiscal office, a lawyer for the prisoners, a Jailer (*Alcaide*) of the secret jails, a Dispenser of the Prisoners, a Messenger (*Nuncio*), a Doorman (*Portero*), a medic, surgeon, and a barber. You should communicate this for the first time with the Viceroy, so that you may be best advised and not receive any tricks in the nomination. You should make nominations for those who appear to you to be the most convenient and best suited for the service in the said offices, having first made an information *in scriptis* on their blood purity and customs, and send us relations of those you might have named, where they come from, as well as their qualities, so that we can send the titles to them or to those whom you believe to be best; and, until then, they shall serve as you have nominated them. Also, you should communicate to the said Viceroy the salary that you believe should be given to each one of the said officials, and you should send us in this way a relation of what your opinion is, so that we can, from here, order their payment from the date that they begin their service.

39. Also, once the Holy Office is established, and you have recognized the quality and disposition of the land, you should talk among each other about what should be best for the expenses of the Holy Office, as well as for the payment of salaries and the expenses spent on administering justice, and other extraordinary expenses and concerning how and where the expenses should be placed or paid for, so that the Holy Office can be best endowed with the rent that is necessary. You should pay close attention for this effect to the application of fines and confiscations that can be used to pay for the pending trials in the audiences and, likewise, to *repartamientos* and tithes, in order to understand if from these sources funds may be procured for this purpose. Having communicated with the Viceroy, you should send us a particular relation with his opinion and your own, so that what is most convenient can be provided.

40. For the good administration of justice and the just exercise of the Holy Office, it is convenient that all that is contained in this Instruction be complied with. Thus, we order that you should see the said chapters and guard, comply with, execute, and make all others comply with what is contained herein. In testimony of which we order and give the present, signed by our name, sealed with our seal and ratified by the Secretary of the General Inquisition.

Given in Madrid, August 18, 1570
D. Cardinalis Sigüenza (Signature)
By order of His Illustrious Lordship
Mateo Vázquez (Secretary)
[seal]

DOCUMENT 4
Instructions and the Order That Should Be Maintained and Followed by Commissaries of the Holy Office of the Inquisition in New Spain

Madrid, 1667

SOURCE: Archivo General de la Nación, Ramo de Inquisición, vol. 1479, exp. 2, folios 51r–57v, Lote Riva Palacio, vol. 3, no. 2.

NOTE: Due to the geographic extent of the territory that fell under the control of the Inquisition tribunal of New Spain, the inquisitor general Espinosa realized that the first inquisitors sent to Mexico would need to rely heavily on the aid of local clerics to serve as commissaries of the Inquisition. These instructions, printed in Madrid 1667 in order to guide the inquisitors in their selection of local commissaries of the Holy Office, strictly delineated the powers, functions, and limitations of the position of local Inquisition commissary. Copies of these instructions would be given to each subdelegated commissary in order to guide him in the proper exercise of his office.

1. First, the Commissary should receive all of the testimonies of the said witnesses that appear before him to give their testimony against someone before the notary who is appointed, making the necessary questions of the witnesses, in the manner that they give the reason for their statements and declarations, listing where, when, and in the presence of what persons passed all that they stated and who knew it, or could have known it, placing also the age of the witness. After having made their statement, he should ask them if they made it out of hatred or animosity or for any other reason, ordering the said witness to guard the secret of their statement under the punishment of Major Excommunication. The commissary should sign after every statement and the notary as well, and the said witness if they know how to sign.

2. The people who are named as witnesses should then be ordered to appear in order to examine them, and at the time when they are examined they should be asked if they know or presume the reason why they have been called, and if they do, then they should state yes, and then respond to the business at hand. If he should presume to know why he has been called, he should declare what he knows, ordering him to state and declare all that he knows clearly and openly according to what had been stated in the testimony. And if he replied that he did not know why, he should be asked if he has known, seen, or heard that any person may have done or said something that was or appears to have been against Our Holy Catholic Faith; or against something that the Holy Mother Church of Rome teaches, holds, or believes; or anything against the free and true use and exercise of the Holy Office. And if he should still respond no, then he should be asked particularly if he knows *fulano* [so and so] and if he knows that in such and such a part he did or said such and such a thing, but in no means should the name of the witness be revealed, and all of these investigations and documents should be sent originally, signed, to this Holy Office without making any copy whatsoever.

3. Also, in some cases, many of the witnesses may not name those accused because they do not know their names, or for other causes, or respects, and by means of this in the prosecution of the case there results many inconveniences; then, the commissary should take into account that the said witnesses should inform themselves of the names of the said people against whom they are testifying and that they should declare it in their statements, naming them by their names. They should make the witnesses recognize the accused by placing before them the accused so that the witness can see them without the accused being able to see them, and being present at least two witnesses the notary should set down the said recognition and give faith to the fact that the witnesses named or recognized the accused, and by this means many expenses and much work are excused.

4. Even though many witnesses state the same thing, they should not be examined together, but instead apart, one by one, making them the necessary questions, and entrusting them greatly to hold the secret under the pains of punishment and censure.

5. If it appears to be necessary to give some order against some scribe or some other person, so that they should exhibit some trial or some other business concerning the Holy Office, it should be done with justification and within a competent period, or at least within three days.

6. Commissaries should not examine or call any accused even though there may be a large amount of information against them, except in cases where the accused spontaneously appears of his own will in order to accuse himself and then, in that case, the commissary can receive his confession according to the manner in which he should make it without asking or inquiring anything else more than what he wants to state, and without letting the said accused understand what has been testified against him. All of this should be sent sealed, signed, and delivered to the Holy Office in the original form.

7. Even though there may be sufficient information against someone who may have done or said something against Our Holy Catholic faith, he should not be arrested without an explicit license and orders from their Lordships the Inquisitors, except for the case in which the said accused is a fugitive and that it is suspected that he wishes to escape. In such cases the commissary can arrest him. If it concerns a serious accusation, then the commissary should sequester his goods and record them before the notary and in no other manner, even if the accused is suspected of trying to run away. If the case belongs to the cognizance of the Holy Office, such as a case against someone married two times, it is usual to inventory his goods before the notary and then place them in the power of a person named by the suspect, so that a better account and inventory can be kept of them.

8. The Commissary should be advised that whatever manner in which the goods are sequestered, the inventory should be done before the notary in order to maintain a better record of it. And in cases where the Commissary has doubts whether to sequester the goods, or to prevent transporting and usurping them, he should always make an inventory and a relation of them before the notary and place them in the power of someone who is not an official of the Holy Office, someone faithful and bona fide, and he should not retain them himself, nor should any other officials do so because of the many inconveniences which could result. Sequestering goods should not be easily done, but rather it should be reserved for only the gravest of cases that occur and in no others, and it should be done with much consideration in cases where there is any doubt as whether to sequester the suspect's goods or not.

9. The Commissary should also be advised not to receive information and testimonies except in those cases that pertain to the jurisdiction of the Holy Office, and thus he and the notary, constable, and the other ministers of the Holy Office should deal with all such cases keeping the secret, without giving occasion to any scandal, or discord, nor should anyone be harmed, because this is most convenient for the authority of the Holy Office. And all of the things entrusted or requested by the Inquisitors should be done with all brevity and diligence, advising them continually of all that occurs concerning what should be consulted upon, sending the original dispatches enclosed and sealed with a person of confidence.

10. Whenever the Commissary should send for witnesses so that the witnesses should ratify their statements, the commissary should call each witness before the notary

who had served in the case concerning the business of the Holy Office, and this should be done in the presence of two honest people who should be clerics and Old Christians, who take the oath of the secret, and the witness should reswear their oath. He should then be admonished to tell the truth, and after he has made the oath and promised to tell the truth, he should be questioned if he remembers having deposed something before a judge against another person concerning things touching on the Faith, and when he says yes, before the Judge he should be referred to what he said and against whom he had stated it, and the Commissary should make it known to him that the Prosecuting Attorney of the Holy Office will present him as a witness against the said person. Then his testimony should be read back to him, and if he should wish to add to or change anything in his testimony he should do so in the manner that in everything he should tell the truth and he should affirm and ratify his statement, and so that whatever else he said may not cause prejudice against the said accused, he should have his statement read back to him again *ad verbum*,[35] and in the end he should affirm, and state that what is written is his word under oath and that he does not have anything else to add or amend, and if it should be necessary he swears that he will say it all again, and that he does not state his testimony out of hatred for the said person, but for the discharge of his conscience, after which he will be entrusted with the secret, and he will sign it with the notary.

11. And in the case that the said witness does not identify the accused by his name in his first testimony as stated above, he should be warned at the time of the ratification that he should recognize the accused in the presence of the notary and the same honest persons, putting him in a place where, while not being seen, he can see the accused and recognize him, and all of this should be placed in the form already stated.

12. *Visitation of Ships* (Navios)

Concerning what touches upon the modes in which the commissary should conduct visitations of ships, the commissary should exercise much vigilance and is advised to go and visit the ships in person along with the notary and the selected familiars once a ship has arrived at the bay or port. The Commissary should make the visitation before anyone on the ship should go on land, or before anyone on land should go onboard the ship, and the said visitation should be conducted with an eye particularly for all things that came onboard the said ship, especially if there are prohibited books, and all of the books should be read if possible, and if not then all of the chests, boxes, crates, and other luggage should be sealed so that no one can take anything out of them until the Commissary, or another Learned person who he believes competent to do so, should read and revise all of the books. Any suspected persons believed to have or bring prohibited books should be handled with care and notice should be given to the Inquisitors so that they should send orders on what it is most convenient to do in that case.

13. All of the said books and papers which are found on the ship should be recorded by the notary, where and in whose possession they were found; anything being suspicious will be processed as said above, by sealing the crates, boxes, and other containers in which the books or papers came, and in this way, if it is later determined that someone is a suspect, it should all be attested to in the notaries' inventory and by the witnesses who were there at the sealing. In this way it can be discovered who owned

the sealed boxes and crates in which the prohibited books arrived, and all of this, along with the inventory should be sent to the Inquisitors.

14. The Commissary should also look very particularly throughout all parts and places on the ship, record what arrived and was found in each part, and compare this with the papers that are presented to them from the Masters and Officials of the Ship, because it is always possible to bring things hidden in various places.

15. In this manner, the Commissary should also take the oath of the Master and other sailors on board the ship, asking them to describe what merchandise or books they are bringing, and to where they are taking them. More than that, they should make all of the other merchants and passengers on board of the ship take the oath, and they should be questioned about the particulars concerning if they know of or have seen or understood that onboard the ship some person had done something or said something against Our Holy Catholic faith, and if there are no passengers, they can ask two other people who came on board the ship for their opinion, and if someone should allege something, then the commissary should investigate the truth of the matter by following the above mentioned procedures.

16. The Commissary should also advise the Master or Captain of the ship at the time of the unloading of the ship that he should open up all of the storage containers and openings on board the ship that were not able to be seen, in order to see what may be inside of them, and the commissary or, in his impediment, the notary should be present during this final search in order to see if something came hidden in these places concerning or touching on the Holy Office.

17. And if it should result from the said investigation or visitation of the ship that some person who came on the ship is a suspect in things against our Holy Faith, or if someone should possess prohibited or suspicious books, or if there exists information that someone may have done something that appears contrary to Our Holy Catholic Faith, if it appears that it is a serious business, the commissary may arrest the suspect. If it is a serious allegation, or if he fears the suspect's flight, in this case he can arrest him and sequester his goods, placing them in an inventory and in the power of a person as stated above, until the Lord Inquisitors should review the information and the quality of the alleged case and then provide for what should be done.

18. It should not be permitted that the Commissary should by any means eat or drink or partake of anything onboard the ship, nor should any other official of the Holy Office do so, nor should he try to deal, negotiate, buy, or sell anything that belongs to the goods that came on the ship, nor should he attempt to stop them from selling, nor advise anyone else either directly or indirectly concerning merchandise on board. He should assist in nothing more than those things which touch upon the jurisdiction of the Holy Office, whose authority and upright procedures should be maintained at all time. And in all things the commissary should maintain himself modestly, prudently, and temperately as required so that in this manner no one can claim in a just manner to have been damaged by him. When it is necessary to use rigor, he may then do so with discretion, and if anyone should show negligence in these visitations of the ships, they should be corrected by the Commissary sending information against him to the Lord Inquisitors so that they can remedy these things.

These are the instructions that should be given to all commissaries of the Holy Office of the Inquisition.

Sample Title and Commission as Commissary of the Holy Office

We, the Inquisitors & Etc., because in the town of ———— and the places of its district there occur several things touching upon and belonging to the jurisdiction of this Holy Office, and for its just exercise it is convenient that there exists there a deputized person so that in his name he should conduct the business and take and receive the information and testimonies concerning the things that may occur touching upon Our Holy Catholic Faith, and out of our confidence in You, reverend ————, cleric and Priest, and in your learned good conscious, we believe that you will faithfully and dutifully do the above-mentioned and all other things that you should be entrusted by us, and we have had information that in your person exists the conduct and qualities that are required, by means of the present commission we create, name, and deputize you as Our Commissary Judge for all things touching upon the Holy Office in the said town of ———— and its district so that as a Commissary Judge, and before the notary that you should nominate, you can make and should make all of the information and testimonies that should be necessary, such as those made by witnesses and those made in all other manners, and you should inquire into and investigate all of the business and cases touching upon the Holy Office against every type of person of all types of classes and states and conditions whatsoever, both residents of the said town and its district, as well as all other people whom you find present. You may examine all other witnesses who are alleged in these testimonies, and in order to do this you can order, compel, and force them to come and appear before You by issuing your orders under penalties that you should place, and you should conduct all of the other diligences and things according to the Instruction that You should be given which will be signed by our secretary. In order to do all of this and all things annexed to this and dependent on this, we give you full power on all occasions and entrust you with all of our powers, and we order that all judges, judicial officials, both ecclesiastical and secular, and all other particular people of all stations within the said town and its district, should have you and hold you as our said Commissary Judge of the Holy Office, and they should allow you to freely use and exercise the said office, and for that effect they should show you all favor and aid necessary under the penalty of a punishment that you should decide. They should have and hold you and help you enjoy all of the general privileges, exemptions, liberties, and prerogatives that, by reason of the said Office, you should be given, and they should also care to obey the other ministers of the Holy Office, in testimony of all of this we order that you be given, and we give you the present commission signed by Our name, and sealed with the seal of the Holy Office, and undersigned by the Secretary

Sample Title and Commission of Notary of the Holy Office

We, the Inquisitors & Etc., because in the town of ———— and the places of its district it is necessary to name a notary before whom should pass all acts and documents in the presence of the Commissary of the said Holy Office who exists, or should exist in the said town, and out of our confidence in your legality and sufficiency, confiding in You, ————, resident of the said town, that with all secret, care, and diligence, you will do what is being committed to you and entrusted to you because we have had information that in your person exists the purity of blood and other qualities that are required, by means of the present we create and name you as Notary of this Holy Office before whom should pass all of the acts, documents, and other business and cases touching upon the Holy Office, and we give you full power to use and exercise the said office. Without you being present, the said Commissary cannot take testimony with any other notary before which passes the said business, and we exhort the existing Commissary or whoever may exercise that office in the said town and its district, that they have you for their said notary. And in the things of the Holy Office that may be reviewed (without there being present the Secretary of the Holy Office) before you should pass all of the said denunciations, information, acts, and diligences, and all of these things that should occur before you, you should remit the original copy of them, so that no copy should exist in your register. We exhort and require and, if it is necessary, order under Holy Obedience and under the penalty of major excommunication and a fine of fifty thousand maravedis for the extraordinary expenses of the Holy Office, we order that all judges and whatever judicial officials exist in the said town and all of its cities, villages, and districts, should hold you and have you as said notary and ensure you all of the immunities, benefits, and liberties enjoyed by all of the ministers of the Holy Office, and all that should be and is accustomed to be given as privileges, and that they should not take from you your weapons, nor should they attempt to have cognizance of criminal cases concerning your person, but instead they should remit them to us, as the competent judges that we are in these cases, and in testimony of all of this we order that you be given, and we give you the present commission signed by Our name, and sealed with the seal of the Holy Office, and undersigned by the Secretary

Sample Title of Familiar of the Holy Office

We, the Inquisitors & Etc., because in the town of ———— and the places of its district there occurs several things touching upon and belonging to the jurisdiction of this Holy Office, it is convenient that we have persons to whom we can entrust things concerning the Faith, and confiding in You, ————, resident of the said town, in your diligence and care, we have had information that in your person exists the purity of blood and other qualities that are required, and we believe that you will do all that is entrusted to you with all secret and legality concerning things that touch upon the Holy Office, and by means of the present we create, name, and deputize you as a Familiar of this Holy Office and it is our will that you, the said ———— should be one of the familiars among the number of those that should exist in the said town of ———— and so that you may enjoy and do enjoy all of the exemptions, privileges, and liberties that exist according to the laws and legislation of these Kingdoms, and the style and instructions of the Holy Office, and the Apostolic concessions, you should have and hold all of the said privileges that other familiars are accustomed and should enjoy, and we give you license and the faculty that you may go about carrying your weapons, both offensive and defensive, both by day and by night, both publicly and secretly, in whatever place or places in the said district you may be, without anyone else being able to place upon you an impediment, and we exhort, require, and admonish and, if it is necessary, order under Holy Obedience and under the penalty of major excommunication and a fine of fifty thousand maravedis for the extraordinary expenses of the Holy Office, we order that all judges and whatever judicial officials exist in the said town and all of its cities, villages, and districts, should hold you and have you as said familiar and ensure you all of the immunities, benefits, and liberties enjoyed by all of the ministers of the Holy Office, and that they should not take from you, nor remove your weapons, nor should they attempt to have cognizance of criminal cases concerning your person, but instead they should remit them to us, as the competent judges that we are in these cases, and that they should not bother you, and we order you, the said —————, that you should present this commission to the Town Council [cabildo] of the said town of ————— so that it should be made known that you are a familiar of this Holy Office, and that they should place you as such in their Cabildo book, and that the scribe of the town should make it known publicly within three days, and in testimony of all of this we order that you be given, and we give you the present commission signed by Our name, and sealed with the seal of the Holy Office, and undersigned by the Secretary.

DOCUMENT 5

General Rules and Orders Taken from the New Index of Prohibited and Purged Books for the Spanish Catholic Kingdoms of King Philip IV Written by Don Antonio Zapata, Inquisitor General

Seville, 1632

SOURCE: Partial text selected and translated from the original *Novus Index librorum prohibitorum et expurgatorum, editus auctoritate & iussu D. Antonii Zapata* (Sevilla: Francisco de Lyra, 1632), folios 24–33, available digitally online courtesy of the Biblioteca de la Universidad de Sevilla's Fondo Antiguo at http://fondosdigitales.us.es/fondos/libros/462/10 /nouus-index-librorum-prohibitorum-et-expurgatorum/.

NOTE: Don Antonio de Zapata y Cisneros (1550–1635) was the cardinal and archbishop of Burgos and inquisitor general of Spain from 1627 to 1632. He was commissioned on January 30, 1627, and resigned in 1632 shortly after publishing this updated Index of Prohibited Books cited here. The first section of this index was taken almost word from word from the Tridentine Index issued in 1564 after the conclusion of the Council of Trent.[36] The Tridentine Index would be the model for every subsequent Index of Prohibited Books released after 1564. One of the major differences in this new index was Cardinal Zapata's addition of specific orders and warnings to booksellers and book traders throughout the kingdoms of Spain and its colonies. The 1632 index was also the index that specifically prohibited the famous Spanish work known as *La Celestina*. Similarly, in the many specially issued Spanish indexes, the Inquisition both prohibited and expurgated books. This meant that, unlike the Roman indexes that completely prohibited most books, the Spanish index usually allowed some works that were prohibited to continue to circulate if the Inquisition could purge or erase the relevant passages that were cited as prohibited by the index.

Rules, Orders, and General Warnings

Rule I

All books that have been condemned either by the supreme pontiffs or by ecumenical councils before the year 1515 and are not contained in this list shall be considered condemned in the same manner as they were formerly condemned.

Rule II

The books of those heresiarchs,[37] who after the aforesaid year originated or revived heresies, as well as of those who are or have been the heads or leaders of heretics, such as Luther, Zwingli, Calvin, Balthazar Friedberg, Schwenkfeld, and others like these, whatever may be their name, title, or nature of their heresy, are absolutely forbidden. The books of other heretics, however, that deal professedly with religion are absolutely condemned. Those which do not deal with religion and have by order of the bishops and inquisitors been examined by Catholic theologians and approved by them are permitted. Likewise, Catholic books written by those who afterward fell into heresy, as well as by those who after their fall returned to the bosom of the Church, may be permitted if they have been approved by the theological faculty of a Catholic university or by the general inquisition.

Rule III

The translations of writers, also ecclesiastical, which have till now been edited by condemned authors, are permitted provided they contain nothing contrary to sound doctrine. Translations of the books of the Old Testament may in the judgment of the bishop be permitted to learned and pious men only, provided such translations are used only as elucidations of the Vulgate Edition[38] for the understanding of the Holy Scriptures and not as the sound text. Translations of the New Testament made by authors of the first class of this list shall be permitted to no one, since great danger and little usefulness usually results to readers from their perusal. But if with such translations as are permitted or with the Vulgate Edition some annotations are circulated, these may also, after the suspected passages have been expunged by the theological faculty of some Catholic university or by the general inquisition, be permitted to those to whom the translations are permitted. Under these circumstances the entire volume of the Sacred Books, which is commonly called the *biblia Vatabli,*[39] or parts of it, may be permitted to pious and learned men. From the Bibles of Isidore Clarius of Brescia, however, the preface and introduction are to be removed, and no one shall regard its text as the text of the Vulgate Edition.

Rule IV

Since it is clear from experience that if the Sacred Books are permitted everywhere and without discrimination in the vernacular, there will by reason of the boldness of men arise therefrom more harm than good, the matter is in this respect left to the judgment of the bishop or inquisitor, who may with the advice of the pastor or confessor permit the reading of the Sacred Books translated into the vernacular by Catholic authors to those who they know will derive from such reading no harm but rather an increase of faith and piety, which permission they must have in writing. Those, however, who presume to read or possess them without such permission, may not receive absolution from their sins till they have handed them over to the ordinary. Book dealers who sell or in any other way supply Bibles written in the vernacular to anyone who has not this permission, shall lose the price of the books, which is to be applied by the bishop to pious purposes, and in keeping with the nature of the crime they shall be subject to other penalties that are left to the judgment of the same bishop. Regulars who have not the permission of their superiors may not read or purchase them.

Rule V

Those books which sometimes reproduce the works of heretical authors, in which these add little or nothing of their own but rather collect therein the sayings of others, as lexicons, concordances, apothegms, parables, tables of contents, and such like, are permitted if whatever needs to be eliminated in the collections is removed and corrected in accordance with the suggestions of the bishop, the inquisitor and Catholic theologians.

Rule VI

Books which deal in the vernacular with the controversies between Catholics and heretics of our time may not be permitted indiscriminately, but the same is to be observed with regard to them what has been decreed concerning Bibles written in the vernacular. There is no reason, however, why those should be prohibited which have been written in the vernacular for the purpose of pointing out the right way to live, to contemplate, to confess, and similar purposes, if they contain sound doctrine, just as popular sermons in the vernacular are not prohibited. But if hitherto in some kingdom or province certain books have been prohibited because they contained matter the reading of which would be of no benefit to all indiscriminately, these may, if their authors are Catholic, be permitted by the bishop and inquisitor after they have been corrected.

Rule VII

Books that professedly deal with, narrate, or teach things lascivious or obscene are absolutely prohibited, since not only the matter of faith but also that of morals, which are usually easily corrupted through the reading of such books, must be taken into consideration, and those who possess them are to be severely punished by the bishops. Ancient books written by heathens may by reason of their elegance and quality of style be permitted but may by no means be read to children.

Rule VIII

Books whose chief contents are good but in which some things have incidentally been inserted that have reference to heresy, ungodliness, divination, or superstition may be permitted if by the authority of the general inquisition they have been purged by Catholic theologians. The same decision holds good with regard to prefaces, summaries, or annotations that are added by condemned authors to books not condemned. Hereafter, however, these shall not be printed till they have been corrected.

Rule IX

All books and writings dealing with geomancy,[40] hydromancy,[41] aeromancy,[42] pyromancy,[43] oneiromancy,[44] chiromancy,[45] necromancy,[46] or with sortilege, mixing of poisons, augury, auspices, sorcery, or magic arts are absolutely repudiated. The bishops shall diligently see to it that books, treatises, catalogs determining destiny by astrology, which, in the matter of future events, consequences, or fortuitous occurrences, or of actions that depend on the human will, attempt to affirm something as certain to take place, are not read or possessed. Permitted, on the other hand, are the opinions and natural observations that have been written in the interest of navigation, agriculture, or the medical art.

Rule X

In the printing of books or other writings is to be observed what was decreed in the tenth session of the Lateran Council under Leo X. Wherefore, if in the fair city of Rome any book is to be printed, it shall first be examined by the vicar of the supreme pontiff and by the Master of the Sacred Palace or by the persons appointed by our most holy Lord. In other localities this approbation and examination shall pertain to the bishop or to one having a knowledge of the book or writing to be printed appointed by the bishop and to the inquisitor of the city or diocese in which the printing is done, and it shall be approved by the signature of their own hand, free of charge, and without delay under the penalties and censures contained in the same decree, with the observance of this rule and condition that an authentic copy of the book to be printed, undersigned by the author's hand, remain with the examiner. Those who circulate books in manuscript form before they have been examined and approved shall in the judgment of the Fathers delegated by the council be subject to the same penalties as the printers, and those who possess and read them shall, unless they make known the authors, be themselves regarded as the authors. The approbation of such books shall be given in writing and must appear authentically in the front of the written or printed book, and the examination, approbation, and other things must be done free of charge. Moreover, in all cities and dioceses the houses or places where the art of printing is carried on and the libraries offering books for sale, shall be visited often by persons appointed for this purpose by the bishop or his vicar and also by the inquisitor, so that nothing that is prohibited be printed, sold, or possessed. All book dealers and venders of books shall have in their libraries a list of the books that they have for sale subscribed by the said persons, and without the permission of the same appointed persons they may not, under penalties of confiscation of the books and other penalties to be imposed in the judgment of the bishops and inquisitors, possess or sell or in any other manner whatsoever supply other books. Venders, readers, and printers shall be punished according to the judgment of the same. If anyone brings into any city any books whatsoever, he shall be bound to give notice thereof to the same delegated persons, or in case a public place is provided for wares of that kind, then the public officials of that place shall notify the aforesaid persons that books have been brought in. But let no one dare give to anyone a book to read that he himself or another has brought into the city or in any way dispose of or loan it, unless he has first exhibited the book and obtained the permission of the persons appointed, or unless it is well known that the reading of the book is permitted to all. The same shall be observed by heirs and executors of last wills, so, namely, that they exhibit the books left by those deceased, or a list of them, to the persons delegated and obtain from them permission before they use them or in any way transfer them to other persons. In each and all of such cases, let a penalty be prescribed, covering either the confiscation of books or, in the judgment of the bishops or inquisitors, another that is in keeping with the degree of the contumacy or the character of the offense.

Rule XI

With reference to those books which the delegated Inquisitors have examined and expurgated or have caused to be expurgated, or under certain conditions have permitted to be printed again, the book dealers as well as others shall observe whatever is known to have been prescribed by them. The bishops and general inquisitors, however, in view of the authority that they have, are free to prohibit even those books which appear to be permitted by these rules, if they should deem this advisable in their kingdoms, provinces, or dioceses. Moreover, the secretary of those delegated has by order of our most holy Lord [the pope] to hand over in writing to the notary of the holy universal Roman inquisition the names of the books which have been expurgated by the delegated Fathers as well as the names of those to whom they committed this task.

Finally, all the faithful are commanded not to presume to read or possess any books contrary to the prescriptions of these rules or the prohibition of this list. And if anyone should read or possess books by heretics or writings by any author condemned and prohibited by reason of heresy or suspicion of false teaching, he incurs immediately the sentence of excommunication. He, on the other hand, who reads or possesses books prohibited under another name shall, besides incurring the guilt of mortal sin, be severely punished according to the judgment of the bishops.

Rule XII

In general, it is declared and ordered that all printed books purged or prohibited in one language are also understood to be prohibited in all other languages, or printings.

Rule XIII

Concerning the Talmud and other books by Rabbis and Hebrews
The books of the Talmud are prohibited entirely, with all of their glosses, annotations, interpretations, expositions, and their other writings, along with all other nefarious books of the Hebrews, according to the constitutions of the Pontiffs, along with all other books of the Hebrews, Indians, or Moors, along with all things pertaining to the Mohammedans and their ceremonies and sect, whose principal arguments are all against our Holy Catholic Faith, and against good Christian customs, and the universal ceremonies of Our Holy Roman Church.

Rule XIV

Because it is the purpose of this Holy Office not only to tend to the conservation and purity of Our Catholic Faith, destroying all errors against it, but also to help and give all favor to those who defend it, declare it, and are illuminated by it and who write against the heretics and heresies, or who write about the Holy Scriptures, or who write other Scholastic things, and We advise all pious and learned men that when it is necessary to write in the service of the Church and Catholic Faith, and when it is necessary to consult by force one of the forbidden books in this Catalog, by asking us for a license, it will be permitted and allowed to have it, read it for whatever time may be necessary.

Orders to All Booksellers, Merchants, and Others Who Trade in Books

All those who have the office of booksellers, by table or shop, or the merchants or buyers and sellers of books, or those who trade in books by any other means, within seventy days of the publication of this index you are obligated to make an inventory or memorial of all of the books in your charge, by alphabetical order that begins with the names of the authors, declaring all of the books that you may have, swearing an oath and signing it with your names and handing it over to the Inquisitors, if there should be a Tribunal there, and if not handing it over to the Commissary who has been deputized, and it should be renewed each year during the first sixty days of the year, and this should begin with the year 1632, under the penalty of thirty ducats of gold for the expenses of the Holy Office for anything in the above orders that you should not comply with.

No one of you should from here onward have, buy, or sell any book or books that are prohibited by our Index, or by Edict of the Inquisitors, nor any other heretical books, under the penalty of suspension of office, or trade of books for two years for the first offense, and a penalty of exile for the same period of two years, and 200 ducats for the said expenses. And if this is violated for a second time, the penalty shall be doubled, as well as receiving other penalties either lesser or greater depending on the gravity of the guilt and at the discretion of the Inquisitors.

So that the above-mentioned should know which books are prohibited or permitted, we order that all of them should have a copy of this Index under the penalty of twenty ducats for the expenses of the Holy Office for each instance in which they are found not to possess this Index.

Orders to All Those Who Import and Bring in Books into These Kingdoms

All those who bring or cause books to be brought into these kingdoms, no matter what status or condition, should manifest them or by means of their agents, with a list or inventory signed in the same above-mentioned form, to be presented at the first seaport or landfall in these kingdoms to the Tribunal of the Holy Office if one exists and, if not, to a local Commissary of the Holy Office, under the penalty of losing the books, and the application of a 200-ducat fine for the said expenses of the Holy Office for each time that they do not show them. And if the books are taken to the customshouse or some other place, the public ministers of those places should not allow them to be released until a testimony of their contents should be made or signed by the Inquisitors or their Commissaries.

Also, because it is understood that many books have entered into these kingdoms clandestinely that have and preach bad doctrines by means of certain sheets of paper in the form of letters, by means of booksellers, ordering people to bring them, all in contravening against these orders and this Index, we order under the pain of Excommunication and a fine of fifty ducats for the expenses of the Holy Office, that similar sheets, packages, and boxes should not be allowed to arrive from outside of these kingdoms unless they should be first searched and examined by the ministers named for this purpose.

PART II

Documents concerning the Operations and
Procedures of the Inquisition in New Spain

Edicts of Faith of the Inquisition
in New Spain

[These edicts of faith] are the most efficacious defensive and offensive weapon that the Tribunals of Faith have, and they are the only precise means by which the faithful know their obligations and the best means of obligating them to comply with them.

Letter and Memorandum from the Suprema to the Inquisition in New Spain in 1657, Archivo Histórico Nacional, Sección de Inquisición, legajo 5048, caja 1.

Because most of the operations of the Inquisition in New Spain occurred in secret, the general public of the viceroyalty came to have knowledge of the Inquisition and its activities on only two occasions: the publication of the general edicts of faith (*edictos de fe*) and the final reading and proclamation of the sentences of convicted heretics at the public ceremonies known as the acts of faith (*autos de fe*).

The first of these two main contacts came during the public reading of one of the tribunal's edicts of faith. These edicts were documents that enumerated all of the crimes that fell under the jurisdiction of the Inquisition in New Spain and that the inquisitors had proclaimed publicly by town crier and by the clergy in the pulpit on specified Sundays after mass.[1] The Inquisition demanded by the public reading of these edicts that anyone who was guilty of the mentioned crimes should present himself to the tribunal. The edict also required that any who knew of someone "either living or dead or present or absent" who had committed one of these crimes should denounce what they knew.[2] The edict warned that anyone who refused could be considered suspect in the faith or guilty of covering up an act of heresy. According to Richard Boyer, the inquisition edicts served as "primers that listed errors, gave examples of suspicious behavior and urged the faithful to examine their consciences."[3]

When the Mexican Inquisition publicly proclaimed its first edict of faith on November 4, 1571, everyone in Mexico City over the age of twelve was legally required to attend its public reading or face possible excommunication.[4] From that date forward, the Inquisition in New Spain ordered that a general edict of faith be read out publicly on one of the Sundays during Lent each year in all of the cities and towns throughout the district of New Spain. In the outlying provinces, the duty of reading these public edicts fell to the local commissaries of the Inquisition.

In Mexico City, the capital of the viceroyalty and the seat of the tribunal, the public reading occurred during a great ceremony in which a sumptuous mass was said and a special guest, usually a famous orator or preacher, delivered a solemn sermon of the faith (*sermon de fe*).[5]

Besides these public edicts of faith, the Inquisition in New Spain also published and proclaimed special edicts of the faith dealing with crimes and practices that fell under the jurisdiction of the Inquisition. Frequently these periodic edicts included lists of prohibited books or focused on new types of crimes, heresies, or superstitious practices that the tribunal uncovered during its investigations. Most notable were those edicts of faith issued during the early seventeenth century concerning superstitions, such as divination and astrology, issued in 1616 (document 7), and the edict against the use of hallucinogens such as peyote, issued in 1620 (document 8).[6] These specialized edicts did not require all of the pomp and ceremony present in the public proclamation of the general edicts of faith. Instead, the inquisitors sent a printed version to their local commissaries with orders to have them publicly proclaimed in their towns and posted on the doors of the churches.

The documents collected in this section include some of the most important sources for the study of the Inquisition in New Spain. These edicts of faith and their public proclamation played an important role in the operations and process of the Inquisition. In fact, much of the entire process of the Inquisition's prosecution of heretics depended in a large part on the denunciations that came about after these public readings.

DOCUMENT 6
Edict of Faith Issued by Inquisitor Dr. Pedro Moya de Contreras
Mexico City, October 10, 1576

SOURCE: Archivo General de la Nación, Ramo de Inquisición, vol. 1511, exp. 13, folios 14r–19v.

NOTE: Modeled after a printed edict from Spain with addition of information for local needs, the following edict of faith is one of the first edicts issued by the tribunal in New Spain. In early 1576, the Suprema sent the inquisitors in New Spain a sample edict with instructions to describe in detail all of the rituals of the Jewish, Islamic, and Lutheran heresies, so that the people of New Spain could recognize these crimes against the faith. Nevertheless, the Suprema later criticized the Mexican tribunal for taking too many liberties and changing the wording in many of its edicts from the legal formulary that was supposed to be the general model for edicts of faith. The Suprema formally criticized this specific edict in a *carta acordada* of February 15, 1581. From that point onward, the Inquisition in New Spain issued edicts with detailed descriptions of all of the other crimes against the faith.

We, Dr. Pedro Moya de Conteras, by the grace of God and the Holy Apostolic See, Inquisitor General of New Spain against Heretical Depravity by appointment of His Majesty, and the other Inquisitors of this Holy Tribunal, etc.

We issue this edict and require that all people of any state, class, or condition, both ecclesiastics and seculars, within the present confines of this Kingdom of New Spain should come forth and denounce any and all crimes against the faith committed by them or another. Because it is our duty to ensure the spiritual health of the faithful entrusted to us, we exhort and order that all people who know anything about any of the crimes mentioned here in this edict should come forth and denounce them during the stated period of fifteen days.

1. If anyone knows that a priest or friar is guilty of misconduct, or if anyone publicly sins by committing fornication to the great scandal of the town and serving as a bad example for the rest of the faithful, or if someone has a female friend living with them or in their home, they should be denounced.

2. Also, if you should know about any person who uses spells, incantations, charms, or conjures up spirits, or commits any other type of superstitious enchantments, or uses any other type of witchcraft, even if they are medicinal curers, or if anyone should have a copy of any type of book of spells or other superstitions or any other type of prohibited book, they should be denounced. And we order that anyone who should possess these books or have read them should denounce themselves within the space of fifteen days before Us or Our other Inquisitors or their commissaries so that these writings can be examined and reviewed.

3. Also, if you should know about any other persons who have the custom of swearing oaths, or have blasphemed the name of God or of his Saints, or have issued statements saying that "I do not believe in God" or "I disbelieve in God" or "I renounce God," or who have committed blasphemy in any other type of word or deed, or have committed perjury before a court or have continued unrepentant in the face of excommunication without seeking absolution, or have not confessed at least one time a year—All of these must be denounced.

4. Also, you are required by this edict to depose against or denounce any married couples who do not conduct married life, living together in harmony; or any other persons who, having not received the sacrament of matrimony, live together in sin, as if they were married; or anyone who has married one of their close relatives. Also you are required to denounce all those who have married two or more times, if their spouse is still alive; or who are currently engaged in the crime of bigamy, having two spouses both living. Also you are required to denounce anyone who has committed the nefarious sin of sodomy[7] or other crimes against nature, such as incestuous relations with their relatives or bestiality.

5. Also, you are required to denounce and provide any information you may know of persons who have engaged in gambling or playing cards or dice or any other illicit games, especially those who profit from these illicit games.

6. Also, you are required to denounce any and all heretical propositions or statements that you may have heard, either in public or private or in the pulpit.

7. Also, you must denounce anyone whom you know to have ceased to pay the tithe according to what is owed to the Holy church by law.

8. Also, you are to denounce all persons who have committed some type of sacrilege, by fighting or engaging in a fight on Church grounds, in a cemetery, or other sacred place, or anyone who has placed his hands upon or attacked a member of the clergy, or anyone who has removed someone from the Church by force.

9. Also, you must denounce all persons who have usurped or stolen Church property or goods and then sold them for their own profit.

10. Also, You must denounce all those who charge exorbitant amounts of interest, more than 5 percent, on any moneys or goods that are loaned out.

Because all of these above-mentioned crimes result in infinite damages not only to the souls of our faithful sheep but also to the general state of government and public welfare we require you to denounce and give testimony against them.

Due to the seriousness of these crimes we admonish and exhort you under the sacred obedience to the Church that if you should know of or have heard of any of these public sins and crimes against the faith, you should manifest them and denounce them before Us and our Tribunal of the Holy Office of the Inquisition within the period of fifteen days from the publication of this edict so that this Tribunal may proceed and act upon what is in the service of Our Lord God and necessary for the salvation of the souls of the faithful. If you do not denounce what you know about these things within this time, you will be taken and considered as apostates, rebels, and heretics, and we will proceed against you and each and every one of you who may have secret knowledge of these public sins. The rigor of the laws under which you will then be placed will be upon your own consciences for not having come forth sooner and denounced what it is that you may have known about these public sins.

This Edict, we pronounce and issue on this day of the 10th of October 1576. The period of Grace will end on the 25th of October 1576, and upon that date this Tribunal will begin its Inquisition into matters of faith.

Dr. Pedro Moya de Contreras

Dr. Rivas

Dr. Palacios

DOCUMENT 7

Edict of Faith That Requires All to Denounce the Practitioners of Astrology, Necromancy, Geomancy, Hydromancy, Pyromancy, and Chiromancy, as Well as Anyone Who Possesses Books on These Themes

Mexico City, March 8, 1616

SOURCE: Archivo General de la Nación, Ramo Edictos de Inquisición, vol. 1, folios 2–5. Archival consultation and paleographic transcription of this edict, compliments of the Mexican historian Oscar Rodríguez Galicia (Universidad Nacional Autónoma de México).

NOTE: The edicts of the faith reveal not only perceptions on the part of the inquisitors and the general populace but also, in their denunciation of superstitious practices, the types of things that worried the residents of New Spain—for instance, how to ensure good health, wealth, and the safe journey of someone's loved one, or the protection of one's merchandise or the success of one's business venture. In the types of divination condemned here, we can see the preoccupations of the people who inhabited the cities, towns, and villages of New

Spain. In the same vein, the healthy skepticism and criticism of the inquisitors concerning the validity of these practices and the doubt of their efficacy show a somewhat enlightened approach to superstition and belief, ahead of its time (especially in comparison to the witch-craft craze that swept through colonial Massachusetts to the north several decades later).

✝

We, the Inquisitors against Heretical Depravity and Apostasy in the City of Mexico, states, and provinces of New Spain, New Galicia, Guatemala, Nicaragua, Yucatan, Verapaz, Honduras, and the Islands of the Philippines and their districts and jurisdictions by the Apostolic Authority & etc.

To all the residents, citizens, inhabitants, and other people in the cities, towns, villages, and other places of our district, of whatever quality, condition, and state, or preeminence or dignity, to each and every one of you to whose knowledge of this letter and Edict reaches, greetings and health in our Lord Jesus Christ, who is true health.

We make it known to you that before us the Prosecuting attorney of the Holy Office appeared and made us a relation stating that it has come to his attention that many people have come from many diverse parts of this our district with little fear of God and in great damage to their souls and consciences and that they have scandalized the Christian people, contriving against the precepts of the Holy Mother Church and against what we have ordered, including our General Edicts of the Faith, which we order published each year and:

Instead, they have given themselves over to the study of judicial Astrology, and they exercise this with mixtures of many other superstitions, making predictions by the stars and their aspects concerning future things, successes or other fortunes, or actions that depend on divine will or upon the free exercise of men; and others make predictions over the births of people through divinations concerning the day and the hour of birth, and they use other times and questionings concerning events and occurrences that they have had in the past or will have in the future, and they advise people about the path that their children should take or concerning dangers, disgraces, or other things concerning health, sicknesses, losses, or the gaining of great wealth, or advise them about the roads that they should take, or tell them about the manner in which they will die or other similar things they divine concerning future or past events.

And also others have come to exercise the arts of necromancy, geomancy, hydromancy, pyromancy, onomancy, chiromancy, using spells, enchantments, incantations, auguries, witchcraft and magic, characters, and other invocations of demons, having an expressed pact with them, or at least a tacit pact with them, by whose means they are able to divine the said future things to come, or the things in the past, or to discover hidden or stolen things, declaring which persons had stolen them, and the place in which they can be recovered, or revealing the places where treasures are hidden underneath the earth or the sea, and other hidden things.

And others who predict the successes of journeys and navigations, of the fleets or armadas at sea, and of persons or merchandise who go in them, and prognostications of things, deaths or events that occur in diverse distant provinces.

As well as others who declare to tell the future by means of the lines and wrinkles on peoples' hands, telling them their inclinations and characters, and what things will happen to them or should have happened.

As well as others who, by means of dreams that they have dreamt, give various interpretations.

As well as others who use various objects to cast fortunes, such as beans, wheat, corn, coins, other seeds, and similar things, mixing the sacred with the profane, such as combining these divinations with sayings from the Gospels, the *Agnus Dei, Ara Consagrada,* Holy water and other things, and sacred vestments that they bring with them to use and which they give to other people who bring with them certain *cédulas,* documents, and other printed things that had prayers or other superstitious words, with other circles, lines, and other types of similar spells, making known that with these things they can stop a violent death, or protect themselves from their enemies, or enable them to have success in battle or in business or trade or in marriage, or enable men to reach and gain many women and women to reach men whom they desire or to make sure that their husbands and friends treat them well and do not grow jealous with their wives or female friends or to "tie"[8] a man to a woman such as to make sure to impede the generative act of the man with anyone except for the woman who casts the spell, or to make and cause other damages and evils to persons, bodily members, or someone's health.

As well as those who use for these same results certain vain prayers, or superstitions, invoking in them God Our Lord and his Holy Virgin Mother and all of the saints, with a mixture of other invocations and other indecent words, continuing to pray them together for several days in front of certain images or at certain hours of the day or night, with a certain number of candles, glasses of water, and other instruments, and waiting afterward for the said prayers, auguries, and presages of what they pretend to know, by means of dreams while asleep, or by means of hearing voices in the street or what occurs to them on another day, or by means of the heavens or the birds that fly and many other types of vanities and madness.

Also, many people, and especially women, are easily given over to superstitions, which gravely offend God, Our Lord, and it is no doubt that through them they make a certain adoration of the devil, in order to know things that they wish, offering him a certain type of sacrifice, burning candles, and burning incense, and other odiferous things like perfumes and using certain unctions and ointments on their bodies, and invoking and adoring the Angel of Light[9] [Lucifer], and waiting for answers from him, or using images and representations of what they pretend, for all of these reasons the said women at other times go out into the fields during the day and at all hours of night, and they drink certain drinks of herbs and roots with which they grow drunk and dull their senses and have illusions and fantastic representations that they have there, and they ponder on them and speak of them publicly as if by revelation or a sure notice of what is to come.

Also, regardless of the prohibitions of the Index and Catalog of prohibited books published by the Holy See and by the Holy Office of the Inquisition, it is ordered now to collect all of the books that deal with Judicial Astrology, along with all other types of books or treatises, letters, printed pages, or all other printed papers that deal with or record any of these said pseudosciences, or arts, with rules on how to know future things, and it is ordered that no one should have them or read them, or show them, or sell them. Regardless of previous orders, many people have retained and continue to read such books and papers, and they read them and communicate their contents to other people, and these teachings have caused much damage.

Also, the absolution of all who commit these things shall be reserved to us, along with the absolution of all things or cases of things suspicious in the Faith, and other things dependent on heresies or any other crass ignorance or superstitions whatsoever. . . .

So that the above-stated may come to the attention of all and so that no one can claim ignorance, we order that this Edict be given and published in all of the churches of this District.

Given in the Audience Chamber of This Inquisition in Mexico, March 8, 1616

DOCUMENT 8
Edict of Faith concerning the Illicit Use of Peyote
Mexico City, 1620

SOURCE: Archivo General de la Nación, Ramo de Inquisición, vol. 289, exp. 12.

NOTE: This edict of the Mexican Inquisition specifically outlawing all uses of mind-altering substances such as peyote[10] shows the extent to which the Inquisition attempted to root out superstitions and superstitious practices that involved divination by the use of hallucinogens. Used by indigenous herbalists and shamanic healers, peyote, as this document attests, had already by 1620 become a mainstay of nonindigenous *curanderos* and healers. The Inquisition viewed the hallucinogenic state that such herbs and roots induced as being the work of the Christian devil, who attempts to deceive the user with false visions and illusions. From 1620 onward, the Inquisition in New Spain claimed for itself jurisdiction over cases of those who used peyote and other ritual intoxicants. However, as later documents in this volume show (see document 49), the Inquisition would be hampered in its effective eradication of the use of peyote because of its inability to prosecute indigenous practitioners, who were most often those who cultivated, traded, and taught the use of these substances to non-Indians.

†

We the Inquisitors against Heretical depravity and apostasy in the city of Mexico, states, and provinces of New Spain, New Galicia, Guatemala, Nicaragua, Yucatan, Verapaz, Honduras, and the Islands of the Philippines and their districts and jurisdictions by the Apostolic Authority & etc: Seeing that the use of the herb or root called *Peyote*[11] has been introduced in these provinces in order to divine and discover lost goods, and to divine or predict other things and future occurrences and other occult matters, we take it as a superstitious action that is to be reproved because it is against the purity and sincerity of Our Holy Catholic faith. Being as it is impossible that the said herb and any other herb can have the virtue or natural property that they ascribe to it for the stated effects nor can any herb cause imaginary illusions, phantasms, and other representations in which are based the foundations of such said predictions and divinations, and when using them the person sees them out of suggestion and with the assistance of the devil, the chief author of these vile illusions, who uses them in order to introduce and trick the simple minds of these Indians to their natural inclination toward idolatry and, by this way, deceive many other persons who are little fearful of God and the faith, and with these excesses this herb and its vice have taken root and occur with the frequency that has been seen. We are obligated by our office to attack this herb and see to the damages and the grave offenses that it offers against Our Lord God. Having treated of this matter and discussed it with other persons who are just and of a good conscience, we are in agreement to issue this present edict of faith and warn that under the penalty of Major Excommunication *Latae Sententiae trina canonica monitione praemissa*[12] and many other penalties both fiscal and corporal that from here onward no person of any status or condition whatsoever can use, grow, or make use of the said herb of Peyote. Nor can anyone use any other herb for the same effects or for any other similar effects under any other name, nor should anyone make or order that the Indians or any other person should take this herb or any like it. Anyone who does or says otherwise will be considered in rebellion and disobedience and will receive the said censures and punishments, and we will proceed against those who are rebellious and disobedient just as we would against any other persons suspect of committing a crime against our Holy Catholic Faith.

And because up until now this crime has been so frequent and used so commonly as is known, and our intention is to prohibit it and to remedy the use of this herb, we order anyone who has committed this sin to denounce it and repent so that we may absolve anyone who may have committed this sin using the benign mercy and the power given to us by the Lord Confessor, the Inquisitor General of Spain. . . . So that what is contained in this letter and edict should be made known to everyone, and so that no one can ignore it, we order that this edict of faith be published and placed on the doors of the churches of every one of the cities, towns, and villages of this our District.

Given in the Audience chamber of this Holy Office
on the nineteenth day of the month of July in the year 1620

DOCUMENT 9
Edict of Faith against Prohibited Books
Mexico City, June 12, 1621

SOURCE: Archivo General de la Nación, Ramo de Inquisición, vol. 289, exp. 13.

NOTE: In New Spain, booksellers and those who bought their books had apparently ignored the previous publication of the Index of Prohibited Books (published and proclaimed in 1613). As this edict argues, they had used loopholes in earlier versions of indexes of prohibited books in order to justify their continued sale and purchase of books the Inquisition had since purged. By having to submit detailed annual lists with the dates of purchase of the books they had in their inventory, booksellers in New Spain could no longer feign ignorance of any new index and justify their continued sale of prohibited books on the claim that those books had not been on the earlier index. The Inquisition issued and publicly posted many of these edicts concerning prohibited or purged books (more than fifty from 1571 to 1700, far outnumbering other types of edicts) to ensure that no one could claim ignorance of the index.[13]

✝

We the Inquisitors against Heretical Depravity and Apostasy in the City of Mexico, states, and provinces of New Spain, New Galicia, Guatemala, Nicaragua, Yucatan, Verapaz, Honduras, and the Islands of the Philippines and their districts and jurisdictions by the Apostolic Authority & etc.

Because, regardless of the many orders that have been given against incurring the grave damage that results from heretical and prohibited books, prohibited by the Catalogs of the Holy Office, and those which are not purged, but which have been marked to be purged by the newest edition of the *Expurgatorio*,[14] these prohibited books still do not cease from entering into these kingdoms, not even the booksellers or any other citizen appears to be purging those books which have been ordered to be purged as it has been dictated. For the remedy of this, we presently order that within six months time which begins with the publication of this Edict, all booksellers, and all other people of whatever rank, dignity, station, or preeminence, are obligated to purge the books that they have that have been ordered to be purged. Once this period has passed, any books that are found not to have been purged shall be confiscated and those who possess them shall be fined fifty ducats for each author. Those who are not booksellers and who are found to have the said books to be purged shall loose them, and they shall suffer the other penalties and censures described in the catalog and index of this Holy Office. And from here onward no one shall be permitted to bring into these kingdoms any books that have some type of purgation, and if someone brings in books that should be purged but are not purged, then they shall loose the said books and pay a fine of two hundred ducats each time. And under the said punishments we order the Commissaries, Qualifiers, and other people who conduct the said purges that they take all good care to erase what should be purged and make it so that it cannot be read by any means.

Also, having seen the Rule and orders that have been published in the said index and expurgatory which has as its title ORDER TO ALL BOOKSELLERS[15] and that then begins with the words ALL THOSE WHO HAVE AS THEIR TRADE BOOKSELLING, & etc., we order that, besides this memorial and inventory that the booksellers have the obligation of making each year, they should also have to add in their inventory all of the books that they receive and the year in which they were received in their power, and once this is written they cannot sell a book to anyone without first showing them to the people who are deputized by us, under the penalty contained in that rule and order concerning booksellers, merchants, and other book dealers, so that it can come to the notice of all other people, and so that no one can feign ignorance, we order that the present Edict be given.

Made in the City of Mexico, in the audience chamber on June 12, 1621

DOCUMENT 10
Edict of Faith concerning the Extirpation of the Abuses Committed by Priest Confessors against the Honesty and Purity of the Sacrament of Confession

Mexico City, March 31, 1783

SOURCE: Archivo General de la Nación, Ramo Edictos de Inquisición, vol. 2, folio 37.

NOTE: The problem of priests and confessors abusing the sacrament of the confession by soliciting sexual favors from their confessants was a widespread and prevalent charge, whether real or imagined, that occupies the pages of many inquisitorial denunciations and trial proceedings.[16] So great was the scandal and abuse of clergy in confessing especially female penitents that the Inquisition issued this present edict, although late, to curb many of the abuses by ordering the placement of screens and partitions in the confessionary used by the priest.[17] As the edict states, repeated warnings concerning the abuse of the sacrament were unheeded, thus necessitating these new orders. Although accusations of the solicitation of sex in the confessional continued after this edict, the entire nature of confession and the designs for confessionals had changed forever.

✝

We the Inquisitors against Heretical Depravity and Apostasy in the City of Mexico, states, and provinces of New Spain, New Galicia, Guatemala, Nicaragua, Yucatan, Verapaz, Honduras, and the Islands of the Philippines and their districts and jurisdictions by the Apostolic Authority & etc.

We order it known to all priests, prelates, and confessors of whatever grade or quality that reside and inhabit in this District: By our repeated orders, we have ordered and declared the means and form in which confessors should hear confessions from their penitents, and the places and circumstances in which this should be practiced, according to the distinction of the genders and states of people; and having understood with great experience of the damages and sufferings that occur due to the lack of observing these regulations concerning confessions, and knowing the many new abuses that have been invented in order to avoid them, we renew our Order that from here onward in especially cases dealing with women, that the priests should hear their confessions from behind the screens and gates of the closed confessionals, or of collateral seated confessionals separating the penitent from the confessor without any space in between them, and these being placed in the front of the church (whether it is a Cathedral, parish, or convent church), or in its chapels, which are public and clearly visible, without the use of any type of dividing screen, veils, fans, sheets, or any other type of invention which is not needed for such a sacred act. This should also be observed and practiced when the confession involves the use of a private family oratory, in which the Lady of the House and her servants may confess, ensuring that the door to these are open and with free access to the family, or any other person, during the confession. And even though the said confessors may listen to confessions in the chapels, clearings, and other places, they should always be seated inside of them, and the women should be seated on the outside of the chapel in the church, confessing through the gates whose doors should always be opened, as well as behind a screen or other type of enclosure. Even though the penitents may be hard of hearing, these things should be followed in the form referred to above. It is also equally forbidden to have in the convents of nuns confessionals or screens that are open to the living quarters or rooms of the clerics, religious, or their confessors, nor should there be any confessionals in any other place than inside of the church, and if there are any confessionals in any other place but these, they should within the space of three days of the publication of this our Edict, be closed, locked, and removed. Also, secular men can confess with a screen or without one, in the churches, sacristies, cloisters, or transepts of the Church, all of where people can pass through, particularly in cases or impediments such as indisposition due to the illness of a confessor, or a penitent, or the occupation of one or another. And in no case or any place should the confessors cover up with their capes the penitents, even if their faces and heads are uncovered. And they should not do this in their cells, except with their doors open, and only when there exists a good reason to make a confession there, nor should they do so in particular peoples' houses, except in the case of impediment etc., and we entrust and charge you that you should not have conversations with the penitent either before or after the administration of confession.

And we order that all of the priests, prelates, and confessors should comply with this concerning the part that touches upon them and should make this edict known to all confessors in all communities, either secular or regular, and this Edict, in order to avoid claims of ignorance, should be posted in the sacristies of the Churches as was ordered on November 14, 1781.

These orders and prohibitions are in conformity with all of the repeated orders that have been published by order of this Tribunal, principally with the Edict of March 24, 1713, which renewed one issued before on March 15, 1668, and one on November 23, 1679, and another one on April 15, 1692, and one on August 23, 1710, all of which have dealt with abuses of the Holy Sacrament of Confession.

But, having known of the inobservance and inaction in complying with these rules and because of the sad experience and damages that their violation has resulted in, it has been inexcusable not to remind you all of them by means of a new publication, so we shall explain the penalties so that no one can claim ignorance of them nor may gain absolution for their abuse.

For these powerful reasons, we order that all should comply with these following orders, and all priests, confessors, and penitents should follow the following form in confession:

1. Women should not confess anywhere except in closed confessionals with their own doors, by means of which the confessor remains without the ability to even casually touch or be touched by their feet. The screens that have to be there on both sides

should be composed in such a manner that you can hear the voices, without any fingers being able to enter into the holes, and much less the hands.

2. That by no means should any confessional under any pretext or motive be placed in a dark or obscure place, or set aside, but it should be placed so that any person without special intent can see the confessor.

3. That no confessor, either before or after the confession, should amuse himself or occupy himself in greeting, speaking with, or requesting so-called political conversation with his spiritual daughters, because all of this is very far from the point and out of place in such a holy spot, which deserves much reverence and reflection and penitence, and all doors or entranceways in which the devil can enter to cause illusions in the hearts of confessants should be closed.

4. That in all confessions of nuns, no priest, cleric, confessor, or prelate should enter into their cells, if not for the sole purpose of administering the Holy Sacrament of Penance, or some other spiritual direction, and they should not see them nor speak with them for any other reason. When they should confess them they should keep the two doors of the confessional opened so that they are visible to the church outside, as well as to the convent or cloister inside.

5. It should also be observed that no women should be confessed after sundown, or when night has arrived, and that all should cease to practice the confessions of women at night, except for when it is necessary for just causes that have an expressed license from Us, and all priests, prelates, chaplains, and others should not consent to this.

And so that all of the above contained and referred to has more weight, we order the publication of this present edict in all of the Churches, cathedrals, parishes, and whatever convent and chapel that exists within our district, and it should be placed upon their doors or in the accustomed places. In testimony of all of this, we sign it by our names, and seal it with the seal of the Holy Office, signed by our Secretaries of the Secret

Dr. Juan de Mier y Villar, Inquisitor
Dr. Antonio Bergosa y Jordán, Inquisidor
By order of the Holy Office, Lic. Don Matías López Torrecilla, Secretary

NO ONE SHOULD REMOVE THIS UNDER PENALTY OF EXCOMMUNICATION!

DOCUMENT 11
The Inquisition's Edict of Denunciation against the Priest Miguel Hidalgo y Costilla

Mexico City, October 13, 1810

SOURCE: Archivo General de la Nación, Ramo de Edictos de Inquisición, vol. 2, folio 69r–v.

NOTE: Often criticized for its involvement in political as well as religious censorship, the Inquisition in New Spain during the later eighteenth and early nineteenth centuries played an increasingly active role in censoring the publications and ideas of the Enlightenment, especially the revolutionary and anti-Catholic ideas of the French *philosophes*.[18] Facing outright rebellion and a war for independence that began in 1810, the Inquisition in New Spain took a very active part in suppressing the rebellion and its supporters through the use of its repressive apparatus of investigation and persecution. This edict against one of the leaders of the independence movement of Mexico is a prime example of the Mexican Inquisition's involvement in the suppression of not only religious heresy but also political dissent on the eve of independence and shortly before the tribunal's extinction.

†

We the Inquisitors against Heretical Depravity and Apostasy in the City of Mexico, states, and provinces of New Spain, New Galicia, Guatemala, Nicaragua, Yucatan, Verapaz, Honduras, and the Islands of the Philippines and their districts and jurisdictions by the Apostolic Authority & etc.

We order you, Br. Don Miguel Hidalgo y Costilla, Parish priest of the Congregation of Dolores in the Bishopric of Michoacán, self-titled Captain General of the Army of the Insurgents.

Be it know that before us appeared the Lord Prosecutor of this Holy Office, and he made presentation in the form of a formal trial against you, which began in the year 1800 and was continued until the year 1809, which was proved against you for the crimes of heresy and apostasy from Our Holy Catholic Faith, and that you are a seditious man, who has attempted to pervert and teach others, and heresies have been the rule in all of your conversations and conduct, and they are compiled into the following errors:

You deny that God punishes people in this world with temporal punishments and the sacredness of holy places.

You have spoken depreciatingly against the Popes, and against Church government as being driven by ignorant men, and one of which who was canonized is in Hell.

You are assured that no Jew who has his own judgment can convert, because there is no evidence of the arrival of a Messiah.

And you deny the perpetual virginity of the Virgin Mary.

You have adopted the doctrine of Luther concerning the Eucharist and auricular confession, negating the authenticity of the epistle of Saint Paul to the Corinthians[19] and assuring that the doctrine of the Holy Gospel on this sacrament is misunderstood concerning the existence of Jesus Christ.

You hold as innocent and licit the pollution of fornication as a necessary effect, and based on the mechanisms of nature, and through this error you have become libidinous and libertine.

And you have made pacts with your mistress so that she should look for women with whom you can fornicate, and you look for men with whom she can fornicate, assuring her that hell does not exist, nor does Jesus Christ.

And finally you are so bold as to say that you have not graduated as a Doctor in the Royal Pontifical University because its faculty is a squadron of ignorants.

And having feared or having learned that you have been denounced to the Holy Office, you have hidden yourself under the veil of hypocrisy in such a manner that one information has it as truth that you are so corrected and have arrived at a state of scrupulous conduct that you may convince us to suspend our zeal, suffocate the clamoring for justice, and offer you a truce based on the observation of your conduct.

But your repressed impiety has led to the corruption to the extent that your iniquity recently led you to place yourself at the head of a multitude of unhappy people, whom you have seduced, and declaring war against God, and his Holy Religion, and our Homeland, with a monstrous contradiction, now you preach, as the public papers proclaim, great errors against the faith, raising all of the villages to erupt in sedition with the cry of Holy Religion, with the name and devotion of the Holy Virgin Mary of Guadalupe,[20] and in the name of our beloved King Ferdinand VII, which I allege is proof of your apostasy from our Catholic Faith and your pertinacious errors.

Lastly, we cite you in our Edict, and underneath the penalty of Major Excommunication we order that you should appear before us in our Audience within the term of thirty days, which we fix by the date of this our Edict which we shall circulate throughout the entire kingdom, so that all faithful and good Catholic inhabitants of these realms should know that the promoters of this sedition and movement for independence has as its leader, an apostate from our religion, who is equally the one against whom the throne of King Ferdinand VII has declared war.

And in the case that you should not appear, we shall continue in the trial, which will be conducted *in absentia*,[21] until the relaxation of your person in effigy.

And since we believe that the prosecutor's petition is just and conforms to the law, and that the information that he has conducted against you for the crimes of heresy and apostasy is well proven, and seeing that you have eluded our zeal and have mocked the mercy of the Holy Office, and as it is impossible to cite you personally for being so well hidden and defended by the army of the insurgents that you have risen against religion and our homeland, we order that this our letter and edict should be read in the Cathedral of this city and in the parishes and convents of the bishopric of Valladolid and in neighboring dioceses until you should appear before us in our Audience, so that we should hear from you. Barring this we shall at the end of the said thirty days proceed with the case until the definitive sentence, and its execution.

And we order that this our letter and edict should be fixed upon all of the churches of our district, and that no person should remove it or deface it under the penalty of Major Excommunication, and a fine of five hundred pesos to be applied to the expenses of the Holy Office, and we order and declare as instigators and accomplices incurring said penalties all people without exception who approve of your sedition, receive your proclamations, or maintain correspondence with you or who aid you or give you favor in any way.

In testimony of this we order that this edict be given, and we give it and sign it with our names and seal it with the seal of the said Holy Office, certifying it with the signature of one of our Secretaries of the Secret.

Given in the audience chamber of the Palace of the Inquisition, in the City of Mexico, on October 13, 1810.

Dr. D. Bernardo de Prado y Ovejero
Lic. D. Isidro Sainz de Alfaro y Beaumont

NO ONE SHOULD REMOVE THIS UNDER PENALTY OF EXCOMMUNICATION.
By order of the Holy Office, Dr. D. Lucio Calvo de la Cantera, Secretario

Inquisition Prisons and Life in the Cells

The maintenance that should be given to prisoners of the Inquisition should be charged for according to the length of time of imprisonment and with consideration of the scarcity of foodstuffs. But if some person of quality who has goods in abundance should be imprisoned and if he wishes to eat and spend more than the ordinary ration, they should give him all that he desires and which appears honest for his person and his servants if he had any with him in jail.

"On the Rations That Should Be Given to the Prisoners," instruction 75 in the Compilation of the Instructions of the Holy Office, 1561

The documentary evidence appears to support the opinion that the Mexican tribunal's jails were more benign and offered better conditions than the civil prisons.[22] At least there were numerous cases of individuals who were imprisoned in the public jails who attempted to pretend to be heretics or blasphemers in order to be transferred to the Inquisition's prisons. While in the Inquisition's prisons, prisoners had access to a doctor as well as to a priest or confessor if they wished to have one. Inquisition prisoners received a standard diet of seasonal foods, and if they were wealthy enough and willing to pay, they could eat whatever they wished.[23]

By law, the inquisitors had to inspect their prisons several times a year in order to ensure that the conditions of the cells and their prisoners adhered to the regulations.[24] As the inquisitors often noted during their visitations, after the first few decades of the Inquisition's existence in New Spain, the prisons, located in the basements of the tribunal's palace, began to deteriorate. According to documents from the period, the prisons were excessively humid because the walls of the cells had been constructed of adobe; in addition, their dirt floors often became soaked with water and extremely muddy because of the seepage of groundwater into the lower levels.[25] On more than one occasion after flooding, the inquisitors commented that "it caused great compassion to see how the prisoners suffered."[26] Because of the frequent inundations, the adobe walls of the prison's cells could be easily chipped away, and many of the prisoners made small holes in the walls so that they could more easily communicate between cells with other prisoners.[27] Nevertheless, even with such porous walls, it is remarkable that few prisoners actually escaped from the prisons of the Inquisition.[28]

Not all of the Inquisition's cells exhibited such terrible conditions of darkness and humidity, because some received direct sunlight and air from the streets. The inquisitors often used the different cells for their own advantage: whereas the most obstinate and rebellious prisoners were forced to inhabit the worst cells in the dungeons where no light or fresh air entered, those prisoners who confessed or cooperated with the inquisitors often received the best cells.[29]

The cells themselves had no furnishings, and the Inquisition expected each prisoner to furnish his cell according to his or her social class, station, and economic resources.[30] As for clothing and other necessities, certain wealthy prisoners could request and pay for tablecloths and cloth napkins as well as other sundry personal effects. Most of the prisoners, however, were of more modest means and had only the clothing that they had been arrested with. These poorer prisoners occasionally asked for and received sewing needles and thread and an occasional change of shirt or pants, paid for out of the general funds.[31]

The daily routine of the Inquisition's prisons also saw the distribution of candles and bedpans and other pots for the prisoners' use for their bodily functions. Each of the prisoners could also request to have his hair cut by a barber, whom the Inquisition had on its staff, and men could ask for a shave from the same official.

Wealthy prisoners paid for their maintenance out of their own sequestered goods, so the jailers could purchase for them whatever they might desire. The poorer prisoners had to make do with the standard ration of foodstuffs valued at two silver reales a day;[32] occasionally, they received as extra rations some wine and a small portion of meat.[33]

Although Inquisition prisoners received these regular rations and medical treatment, in terms of their relative isolation and the prohibition of any contact between the prisoners, Inquisition jails might appear more rigid. Still, increased numbers of prisoners by the mid-seventeenth century required the Inquisition to force prisoners to share their cells with cellmates. Although sharing a cell would alleviate the isolation of the prisons, a cellmate could also be a curse, in that many of the Inquisition's prisoners often served as spies on behalf of the inquisitors and testified against their cellmates in order to receive better treatment or favorable circumstances for their own trials.[34]

The jails of the Inquisition, however, did not serve to punish but only to isolate and separate the prisoners during the processing of their cases. Nevertheless, accused heretics, especially accused Judaizers, could remain incarcerated in the secret prison (cárcel secreta) for years. Many even perished in jail before their trials were completed. Often, visiting judges sent from the Suprema in Spain found the tribunal guilty of abuses in procedures concerning both imprisonment and trials.[35]

DOCUMENT 12
Register and Account of the Pesos Spent by Order of Their Lordships in Order to Pay for Extraordinary Rations to the Following Prisoners

Mexico City, March 25, 1601

SOURCE: Archivo General de la Nación, Ramo de Inquisición, vol. 468.

NOTE: The Inquisition in New Spain often allowed its prisoners with sufficient financial means to purchase extraordinary rations beyond what they received in their daily allowances. A prisoner's extraordinary rations and other expenses were meticulously recorded by the jailer and other officials of the Inquisition's prisons. The document presented here lists the extraordinary rations given to several prisoners from the beginning of the year (January 15) until the end of March (March 25). The jailer carefully tallied the amount of moneys expended on these extraordinary rations and requested that the proper amounts be deducted from the prisoner's accounts, which contained the moneys and proceeds of the sale of their sequestered goods.

✝

Manuel Gómez Silbeyral, who has been given since the 15th of January 1600 until today March 25, 1601, thirty loaves of bread in extraordinary rations, at a half real[36] per loaf — 1 peso 7 ts

Antonio Gómez, who has been given since the 15th of January 1600 until today March 25, 1601, forty loaves of bread in extraordinary rations, at a half real per loaf — 2 pesos 4 ts

Jorge Rodríguez, who has been given since the 15th of January 1600 until today March 25, 1601, forty loaves of bread in extraordinary rations, at a half real per loaf — 2 pesos 4 ts

Enrique Montalvo, who has been given since the 15th of January 1600 until today March 25, 1601, twenty-six loaves of bread in extraordinary rations, at a half real per loaf — 1 pesos 5 ts

Lorenzo Machado, who has been given since the 15th of January 1600 until today March 25, 1601, forty-two loaves of bread in extraordinary rations, at a half real per loaf — 2 pesos 5 ts

Alberto Mayo, who has been given since the 15th of January 1600 until today March 25, 1601, thirty-two loaves of bread in extraordinary rations, at a half real per loaf — 2 pesos

Tomás de Fonseca, who was given while he was residing in the prison until today March 25, 1601, forty-four loaves of bread in extraordinary rations, at a half real per loaf — 2 pesos 6 ts

Manuel Tavárez, who has been given since the 15th of January 1600 until today March 25, 1601, forty loaves of bread in extraordinary rations, at a half real per loaf — 2 pesos 4 ts

Francisco Rodríguez de Ledesma, who has been given since the 15th
    of January 1600 until today March 25, 1601, thirty loaves of
    bread in extraordinary rations, at a half real per loaf   1 peso 7 ts

Juan Bautista, who has been given since the 15th of January 1600
    until today March 25, 1601, eight loaves of bread in extraordinary
    rations, at a half real per loaf   4 ts

Cristóbal Miguel,[37] who was given during the time of his imprison-
    ment fifty loaves of bread at a half real per loaf.   3 pesos 1 ts

Gregorio Miguel, who has been given since the 15th of January 1600
    until today March 25, 1601, sixty loaves of bread in extraordinary
    rations, at a half real per loaf   3 pesos 4 ts

Simón de Santiago, relaxed to the secular arm, who was given during
    his imprisonment until the 25th of March 1601 an extraordinary
    ration of fifty-five loaves of bread at a half real per loaf.   3 pesos 3 ts

The total and sum figure for the above-mentioned extraordinary
    rations for the said thirteen parties amounts to 31 pesos and
    6 grains of common gold as it appears in this account   31 pesos 0 ts 6 gs

Also, Pascual Sandre, who received six loaves of bread in addition to
    this usual ration, at a half real per loaf.   3 ts

Juan de León Plaza

Alcaide [Jailer] of the Prisons of the Inquisition

DOCUMENT 13

Register of Rations Given to Prisoners in the Prisons of This Inquisition, Order for Payment, and Receipt during Part of the Year

Mexico City, 1615

SOURCE: Archivo General de la Nación, Ramo de Inquisición, vol. 468.

NOTE: Unlike those prisoners with sufficient means and financial resources to pay for necessities during their imprisonment, poorer prisoners needed the Inquisition to cover their expenses and necessary funds from its own accounts. Not only did the Inquisition have to pay for the maintenance and upkeep of its poorer prisoners, but it also required that the expenses of the administration of torture and all other costs be paid by the general account. As illustrated by this document, the costs of these fees and other expenses could amount to a significant sum. The burden of having to pay for the expenses of poorer prisoners served to limit the inquisitors' desire to conduct interrogations under torture in such cases. No doubt this helps to explain why the use of torture is less frequent in cases that dealt with lesser crimes against the faith committed by common people.

Register of Rations Given to Prisoners in the Prisons of This Inquisition
during Part of the Year 1615

✝

Fray Pedro López[38] entered as a prisoner into the prisons of the Holy
   Office on Monday, January 7, 1615, and it was ordered that he receive
   an ordinary ration of 2½ reales per day.   9 pesos 5½ ts
Antón de los Reyes[39] entered as a prisoner into the said prisons, on
   Thursday, March 5, 1615, and it was ordered that he should receive
   an ordinary ration each day of 2½ reales, and he was in the prison
   for five days, totaling 12½ reales.   1 peso 4½ ts
Also, 12 more reales are owed for the payment for the town crier, trum-
   peters and the executioners, and for other miscellaneous things.[40]   1 peso 4 ts
Juan Vázquez[41] entered as a prisoner into the said jails of this Holy
   Office, on Thursday, March 5, 1615, and it was ordered that he be
   given a daily ration of 2½ reales, and he left the jail on the 9th of
   March, and for five days the ration amounts to 12½ reales.   1 pesos 4½ ts
He also owes 6 reales more for his service, plates, and bowls.   6 ts
He also owes more for his part of what was spent on axes and wax
   candles, 4 reales.   4 ts
He owes 2 more pesos for his share of the use of the town crier, trum-
   peters, and the executioner.   2 pesos

The total and sum figure of what is owed by these three above-named prisoners amounts
to 16 pesos and 4½ reales, and because these prisoners were poor and did not have anything to pay for their food that they ate during the time they were in the prison, they have
not paid me. I request that Your Lordship begs and requests that the Receptor of this Holy
Office, release the sums and pay me from the account of the Royal Fiscal Office of the
Inquisition, so that I may receive some mercy.

Juan de León Plaza
Alcaide [Jailer] of the Prisons of the Inquisition

Order for Payment Issued by the Inquisitors to Juan de León Plaza, the
Chief Jailor of the Secret Prisons of the Holy Office, August 23, 1615

✝

We the Apostolic Inquisitors order that you, Martín de Birviesca Roldán,[42] Receptor of
this Holy Office, should pay out of whatever moneys are in your charge within the armored
chest with the three keys that is placed in the Chamber of the Secret, to Juan de León
Plaza, Jailer of the Secret Prisons, 17 pesos and 4 reales (tomines) of common gold, which

are owed to him for the food rations and other things that he has spent on the following poor prisoners:

First of all, 9 pesos and 5½ tomines, which totaled the amount of the ordinary daily rations for Fray Pedro López of the order of Saint Francis, a poor prisoner from Monday the 7th of January 1615 until Monday March 9th, in which he was freed from the said prisons, at the daily rate of 2½ reales—9 pesos 5½ tomines.

Plus, another 3 pesos and 6 grains,[43] 1 peso and 4 reales and 6 grains, which comes to the amount of the ordinary ration of Antón de los Reyes, a free mulatto, prisoner here since Thursday the 5th of March until Monday the 9th of March, who was maintained in the secret prisons with a ration of 2½ reales each day, along with 12 reales for the town crier, trumpeter, and executioner amounts to a total of —3 pesos 6 grains.

Also, Juan Vázquez, a mestizo, he was also a prisoner in the secret jails of the Inquisition since Thursday the 5th of March until the 9th of March, whose daily ration was 2½ reales, which amounts to 1½ peso, and another half of one-third of a peso and 6 tomins for the plates and bowls he used, and four tomines for his part of what was spent on axes and wax candles and taken to the Cathedral, as well as 2 pesos for the expenses of the town crier, trumpets, and executioner, which amounts to 4 pesos, 6 tomins, 6 grains.

In this means, the sum total of all of the three accounts amounts to the said 17 pesos, 4 tomins, and 6 grains of common gold, and by means of this letter of payment, we order that you release the said 17 pesos, 4 tomins, 6 grains.

Signed in Mexico August 23, 1615
El Licenciado Gutierre Bernardo de Quiroz, Inquisidor
Juan Gutiérrez Flores, cleric and parish priest

Signed before me
Pedro de Mañozca, Secretary

Receipt and Bill of Payment from Juan de León Plaza, Alcaide of the Jails of the Holy Office, August 23, 1615

†

I, Juan de León Plaza, Jailer of the secret jails of the Holy Office, certify that I have received from you the Receptor Martín de Briviesca Roldán, out of the box of the three keys that is placed in the Chamber of the Secret, the said 17 pesos, 4 tomines, and 6 grains, and I sign it.

Executed in Mexico City, August 23, 1615
Juan de Léon Plaza.

DOCUMENT 14
Letter from Inquisitor Pedro Medina Rico, concerning the Plan and Layout of the Palace of the Tribunal of the Inquisition of Mexico

Mexico City, 1661

SOURCE: Translated and adapted from Francisco de la Maza, *El Palacio de la Inquisición* (México: Instituto de Investigaciones Estéticas, 1951), 26–27.

NOTE: The description of the interior of the first floor of the Inquisitorial Palace is very similar to one of the surviving schematic diagrams of the Holy Office made in 1650. Here we have one of the few written descriptions of what the early tribunal may have looked like on the inside of the structure (fig. 6).

✝

In conformity to what Your Lordship ordered, I am once again remitting to you a new plan of the Tribunal. I confide in God that it will arrive safely and appear well done, and that you may perceive well the care that has been placed in its construction, because in that plan you will see written information concerning its formation, and I will not say any more than is contained there.

What I can say and add more than this is that the room in which the Secret is sworn is on the right-hand side looking at the first floor after you come to the door labeled *ff*, and there they have placed a library, somewhat sparse, that will have about 1,000 volumes, because not all of the Inquisitors and Prosecutors have their own books, and it is convenient that here they may come to consult them, and especially, all of the Laws, compilations, and particular orders that deal and touch upon the Inquisition, and it appears that buying them all one by one will cost a considerable sum, it appeared better to us to buy the best volumes all together for 800 pesos; and if Your Lordship should not be pleased with this, it will be easy to resell them again.

On the left-hand side, looking at the said Chamber of the Secret, which is labeled *bb*, there is a room set aside, even though it is attached to the said Chamber, where the prohibited books have been collected and placed in stands and shelves; and here there are another 1,000 books. All of this works so that the Chamber of the Secret is divided into three separate parts:

1. One where the notaries dispatch current cases and there they placed the library of the Tribunal
2. Another part where the completed trials and protocols for finished cases and those to be proved are kept
3. And another one where the said prohibited books are placed and in this third part are also the two strong chests locked by three keys

And the Audience chamber of the Tribunal is also divided into three parts. One of them is the principal Audience chamber, and the other two chambers or parts are at either end of the main chamber, in such a way that neither one of these two chambers has communication between them, so that no prisoner may see any other, even though there may be three prisoners occupying the three chambers at any one time.

I hope to God that I have described it well for you, and I know that all have said that it appears to be very well done; but I have to add that if anyone saw the prisons, they would agree that they are all very bad, as I have complained before. If the prisons could be redone and renewed, then this Tribunal would be perfect, as I have stated before. The current prisons are almost uninhabitable because of the cold and moisture that exist on some days, and because of the humidity and the moisture, the beds on which the prisoners sleep and the clothing and linens that are on hand for the poor prisoners who have not brought their own beds are ruined, and all of it rots quickly.

Pedro de Medina Rico, Inquisitor

DOCUMENT 15
Letter and Description of the Interior of the Palace of the Extinct Tribunal of the Holy Office of the Inquisition of New Spain

Mexico City, July 10, 1820

SOURCE: Originally published in the *Semanario Politico y Literario* in 1820, this document was adapted and translated from Francisco de la Maza, *El Palacio de la Inquisición* (México: Instituto de Investigaciones Estéticas, 1951), 44–47.

NOTE: Once again, like another snapshot in time, we have a valuable description of the interior of the first and second floors of the Inquisitorial Palace as it looked in 1820 at the end of its history as the seat of the tribunal.

On July 10, 1820, the doors of the Palace of the Holy Inquisition were opened by force at ten o'clock in the morning by a group of seventy soldiers and two cannons under the command of Captain Pedro Llop and his lieutenant José María Caminos. The soldiers came out of their quarters and arrived at the door of the Inquisition Palace where they stopped. In a loud voice, the soldiers presented their arms and a notary read the text of the *bando*[44] that ordered the closing and extinction of the Holy Office of the Inquisition. After reading the edict, the notary fixed it on the corner of the building.

Captain Llop called out three times, banging on the door with his fist and sword. The doors did not open, so he exclaimed, "They will not open? Then blow them up!" Before they could do this the officials opened up the doors.

*   *   *

The public has shown a great interest in seeing for its own eyes what belonged to the extinguished Tribunal of the Inquisition, and we are persuaded that they will receive with benignity the following notes that we were able to write at the time that we examined the building that the Inquisition had occupied, without more aid than a paper and pencil.

In order to not make this article very long, we will not copy all of the many signs and writings that we found on the prison's walls and in the gardens; it is sufficient enough to say that the miserable prisoners used to distract themselves by writing on the walls and the doors, with pieces of metal, herbs, and pins, and they wrote texts from the scriptures that fit their own situations, implications against their judges, and even horrible exclamations filled with rage and desperation.

On the principal archway above the main stairway, and looking inward there is a stone plaque that has the following inscription:

DURING THE PONTIFICATE OF CLEMENT XII: WITH PHILIP IV REIGNING AS KING OF SPAIN; AND THE INQUISITORS GENERAL SUCCESSIVELY THEIR EXCELLENCIES LORDS DON JUAN DE CAMARGO, BISHOP OF PAMPLONA, AND DON ANDRÉS ORBE Y LARREATE-GUI, ARCHBISHOP OF VALENCIA: ACTUAL INQUISITORS OF NEW SPAIN THEIR LORDS LICENCIADO DON PEDRO DE NAVARRO DE ISLA, DON PEDRO ANSELMO SÁNCHEZ DE TAGLE, AND DON DIEGO MANGADO Y CLAVIJO, THIS WORK BEGAN ON DECEMBER 5, 1732, AND IT ENDED ON THE SAME MONTH IN 1736 TO THE HONOR AND GLORY OF GOD, AND THE TREASURER DON AUGUSTÍN ANTONIO CASTRILLO Y COLLANTES

To the right of the stairs, in the hallway that faces west, there is a door that gives entrance into the audience chambers and the other apartments of the officials and ministers.

In the first room are found oil paintings of the Inquisitors whose number reaches forty, with rounded shields on them that give the place of their birth, the years of their death, and even from what disease they died, as well as the diverse employments that they obtained in their respective careers, and the year and date of the collocation in this house, & etc.

By means of this hall or room one enters the Audience chambers, which are more than thirty *varas*[45] in length, and eight in width. The chamber is magnificently adorned. The columns and other architectural ornaments are all orderly composed, and the spaces between the columns are covered in fine damask silk. At the extreme end of the chamber that faces south, there is a very large altar very well decorated and on its centerpiece an image of Saint Ildefonso receiving the chasuble of the Holy Virgin Mary.

On the opposite side, placed upon a platform about one yard in height, is the table of the inquisitors, with their three high-backed chairs covered with velvet and crimson, and with edging and trimmings of gold, and each with their three cushions or corresponding pillows, encased in the same materials. There is also, nailed to the wall behind it, a velvet and crimson tapestry of the same color with edging and trimmings, and embroidery of gold. Emblazoned on this tapestry is the Royal Coat of Arms and standing upon the globe of the crown is a crucifix with a motto written around it that states: *Exurge Domine Judica Causam Tuam, Psalm 73.*[46] On either end of this are placed two angels: one of them has in its hand an olive branch and with the other one it holds a ribbon on which is read the motto: *Nolo mortem impii sed ut convertatur et vivat, Esequiel, Chapter 33.*[47] On the other side is another angel with a sword in its right hand, and in its left hand another ribbon with this motto: *Ad faciendam vindictam in nationibus: increpationes in populis, Psalm 148.*[48] All of these are covered in gold and silk, and they are much older than the building itself, because they were embroidered by Roque Zenón in Mexico in the year 1712.

On the wall of the said Audience Chamber which faces south, there is a little doorway that leads to the prisons, and another one that looks out to the west with a rounded motto above it that reads: *"The Lord Inquisitors order that no person may enter inside from this door even if they are officials of this Inquisition unless they are first sworn to the Secret, under the Penalty of Major Excommunication."* There is another door, next to the tapestry, filled with oblique circular sculptures and small windows so that the person who denounces an accused prisoner and the witnesses may look into the other chamber and see the prisoner, without being seen by him.

Going down the stairway that leads to the prisons there is a room with a winch and pulley from where they gave the food to the jailers so that they could distribute it to the cells. In the said room there are two doors, one of which opens to a spacious patio, in the center of which is a fountain and several orange trees, and around this there are nineteen prison cells. The other doorway leads to another larger prison, that the people in the Inquisition call the "coatroom" and which is composed of three or four rooms, of which the most interior one appears to have been the most used. On the walls of this last room or cell there are various pieces of poetry by A.C. y S. (Antonio Castro y Salgado),[49] who composed them during his imprisonment; and there are also some pictures and paintings of the same and among them one landscape that represents a campground, and in between the tents of the campground there are several trees, and in the distance the masts and sails of ships are distinguished.

Most of the prisons have cells that are about sixteen paces long and ten paces wide, even though there are several much smaller, and others much larger. Each of the cells has two very thick doors, each with a small opening or window with double iron bars where only a few scarce rays of light enter, and a raised platform of tiles where they can place their bed.

Behind these nineteen prison cells, there are other small gardens that are called "sunning places," where they brought the prisoners sometimes to take in the sun, but each of these little gardens were constructed in a manner so that it was impossible for one person to see another one.

It is also noted that these little gardens are much more overgrown than they had been in 1813.

*   *   *

On that 10th of July, 1820, Captain Llop ordered the opening of the prison cells of the Perpetual Prison:

They took out of one of them a man of gigantic stature who said he was the Jew Crisanto Gil Rodríguez nicknamed "The Guatemalan," a descendant of the Portuguese Jews who had been expelled from the peninsula in the eighteenth century. As he came out of his prison cell, he brought with him in his hat a treatise on Philosophy he had written there.

Out of another one of the cells came Padre Soría, who had been a prisoner for having defended, from the pulpit, the cause of Independence, as well as for having affirmed that logic is one of the faculties of reason.

Another one of the prisoners was an old man, now very worn, who had been imprisoned for thirty years.

Printed in the Office of Don Juan Bautista de Arizpe, Mexico 1820

Administration of Torture in
Inquisition Trials

The reader may judge, from the faint description, of the dreadful anguish I must have labored under, the nine different times they put me to the torture. Most of my limbs were put out of joint, and bruised in such a manner, that I was unable, during some weeks, to lift my hand to my mouth; my body being vastly swelled, by the inflammations caused by the frequent dislocations, I have but too much reason to fear, that I shall feel the sad effects of this cruelty so long as I live; I being seized from time to time with thrilling pains, with which I never was afflicted, till I had the misfortune to fall into the merciless and bloody hands of the Inquisitors.

John Coustos, English prisoner of the Inquisition, 1743[50]

At the fifth turn of the rack . . . he cried out like a wild beast.

Pedro de los Ríos, Notary of the Secret, Trial Proceedings against Michael Morgan, 1573[51]

Inquisitors were required to use every means possible to uncover the truth before they resorted to the use of questioning the defendant with the application of torture.[52] The Inquisition applied the use of torture far less frequently and less severely than popular myths suggest,[53] and its procedures limited the administration of torture itself by a series of official protocols and regulations. Any method of torture used could not cause death or permanent injury, and further limitations forbid the executioner to use any torture that might shed the blood of the prisoner. The Inquisition did not use torture systematically or indiscriminately throughout the investigative stage of its proceedings. Moreover, questioning under torture could occur only in cases in which the defendant had apparently conducted an act of formal heresy and was not allowed in cases where the alleged crime was only a minor infraction.

The Inquisition used torture only as its last means of obtaining full proof of an act of heresy (i.e., the defendant's full confession). Its severity and duration depended on the types or severity of the crimes alleged. In Mexico, apparently only those accused of being Protestants or apostate Christians who continued to use Jewish practices received interrogations under torture during this final phase of an inquisitorial trial.

The interrogation and questioning under torture occurred in the tribunal's torture chamber, a room specially set aside for this activity (see figure 2 for an example of a *sala de tormento* in the Mexican Inquisition). Because any torture session could end in either the death or permanent injuring of the accused, the inquisitors cleared their own consciences by stating that "if during the torture the accused should die, or be injured or that his blood should flow or his members be mutilated that it was under his own charge and guilt, not their own, for his not having said the truth and confessed earlier in the proceedings."[54]

Before the interrogation, a doctor or physician had to make a thorough medical examination to determine if the prisoner's health and physical situation could bear the ordeal. Both before and during the torture session, in order to ensure that the torture did not endanger the health or life of the prisoner, the Inquisition's medic assisted in the interrogation. Once the doctor certified that the prisoner could withstand the torture session, the Inquisition's constable escorted the accused into the torture chamber. In the company of the inquisitors, the tribunal's notary, a representative of the local bishop (or ordinary), and the hooded or veiled executioner of the torture, the ordeal began with the presentation before the prisoner of the instruments of torture (*in conspectu tormentorum*).

Upon showing the prisoner the torture devices, the inquisitors would officially admonish the prisoner one last time "for the love of God confess the truth." The inquisitors then gave the prisoner a few moments to confess in plain view of the implements of torture. If the defendant refused to confess at this point, the torture session began. The executioner stripped off all of the clothing of the prisoner, whether male or female, with the exception of the undergarment that covered the private parts. The vulnerability of the prisoner's nudity and the executioner's subsequent forcing of the prisoner back down upon a table where the torture would begin led many defendants to confess at this stage of the torture session.

The Inquisition most commonly used three major types of torture in these interrogations: the *potro*, the *garrucha*, and the *toca*. In the *potro*, or the rack, the prisoner was tied down on a rack with cords or ropes, which were gradually pulled tighter around the prisoner's limbs (especially his forearms and the calves of his legs) until he confessed (fig. 7). In this method, the executioner forced the prisoner to lay back on the rack or wooden board and then fastened his arms and legs into the iron shackles at each end. Then the executioner applied and tied a series of cords like tourniquets around various parts of the prisoner's body such as the wrists, forearms, waist, thighs, shins, or lower legs.

In the *garrucha*, a type of pulley system with ropes and weights, the prisoner had his hands tied (usually behind his back). With weights gradually attached to his feet, the executioner raised the prisoner abruptly upward toward the ceiling on the pulley before releasing him back to the ground (fig. 2). Use of the *garrucha* (also called the *strappado*) was considered by the jurists and inquisitors of the time the "queen of the torments."[55] Once hoisted up into the air, the prisoner remained suspended for some time and once let down, the inquisitors questioned him again, and if they did not appear convinced of the sincerity of his answers, the executioner was instructed to raise him again into the air.

The *toca* or the water torture (known today as waterboarding) involved gradual simulated asphyxiation (also see fig. 7). During this type of torture, the executioner immobilized the prisoner on top of a wooden table and then placed a linen cloth, called the *toca*, over the face of the prisoner making sure to cover both the nose and mouth of the defendant. At this point, the executioner began to simulate drowning and asphyxiation by means of the prisoner having jars of water poured over the linen cloth or sash pulled tightly across his face. As the executioner poured the water over the cloth and the prisoner gasped for air, the water soaked hood or cloth restricted his breathing by sealing off their nostrils and mouth, producing the sensation that the prisoner was drowning. After each jar of water, the inquisitors ordered the cloth removed from the prisoner to allow him to breathe and give him a chance to confess. The inquisitors measured the severity of this type of torture by the number of jars of water that each prisoner might be forced to endure. In some cases, the prisoner received more than six jars of water, which only the strongest prisoner could endure (see document 17).

After each phase of the administration of one of these methods of torture, the inquisitors continued to question the defendant under the threat of further torture. If the defendant did not answer or continued to deny the charges again, the inquisitors ordered the executioner to continue with the torture session until the prisoner made a full confession or until the attending physician declared that the prisoner had reached the limits of his physical ability to resist the torment. At either one of these points, the torture was suspended and postponed for another session if deemed necessary.

The Inquisition's notaries meticulously recorded everything that transpired within the torture chamber during these interrogations. As the Inquisition's documents gruesomely attest (see documents 16 and 17), the notaries diligently noted even the prisoner's painful exclamations and all of his implorations for mercy. Although the Inquisition in New Spain used torture frequently, not all of its prisoners were tortured. The Inquisition established strict guidelines for the administration and duration of torture sessions (document 1 and 3), but the process itself led to abuses (documents 17 and 18). According to the Inquisition's own instructions, torture sessions could not exceed more than an hour and

TABLE 11

Number and Types of Cases That Involved Interrogations or Confessions Conducted with the Use of Torture, 1571–1700

Type of Case/Crime	Total Number of Cases Tried	Cases Involving Use of Torture	Percentage
Lutherans/Protestants	91	27	29.6
Alumbrados	10	1	10.0
Judaizers	355	24	6.8
Superstitions	76	2	2.6
Crimes against the Holy Office	92	2	2.2
Heretical propositions	236	5	2.1
Various other crimes	68	1	1.5
Bigamy	219	1	0.5
Muslim practices	2	0	—
Solicitation	86	0	—
Total	1,235	63	5.1

Source: Herrera Sotillo, *Ortodoxia y control social*, 214–32.

fifteen minutes, and the law required that torture occur only once. In practice, however, inquisitors throughout Spain and the New World invented the legal fiction of suspending a torture session by means of which they could extend the application of a single session over a longer period. Many inquisitors and their aides "suspended" these torture sessions and resumed them over a period of several days.[56] Later, fearing further abuses, the Suprema in Spain again issued regulations that, even when suspended, a torture session could not extend for more than three individual sessions.[57] Although torture was always available, it was used as an interrogation technique in only a small percentage of cases in New Spain (table 11).

DOCUMENT 16
Instructions for Administering Questioning under Torture using the Rack
Madrid, Sixteenth Century

SOURCE: Archivo Histórico Nacional, Ramo de Inquisición, libro 1237, folios 130r–131r.

NOTE: This document and its transcription, given to the author courtesy of the church scholar Stafford Poole, is a rare source written by the Inquisition that delineates the specific instructions and methods on how the Inquisitions should go about administering the questioning of suspects with the use of torture on the rack (fig. 7). In an almost macabre mixture of questions and orders, this formal instruction requires the inquisitors to divide up the actual torture session into a series of orchestrated threats and interrogations, the goal of which was to make the prisoners confess fully to their guilt by gradually offering them several chances to recant and avoid the further application of more torture.

†

Once the prisoner has been taken to the torture chamber, the presiding judge should admonish the prisoner:
"Tell the truth for the Love of God if you do not want to see yourself facing such torment."
"Confess the truth."
"Confess the truth, or if you do not, orders will be given to bring in the executioner."
"Confess the truth."
If the prisoner makes a full declaration after he is initially notified of the sentence and order for the administration of torture, or if he should respond to these initial admonitions and warnings, [the torture session may be suspended]. Similarly, if he should have some apparent illness or other impediment so that torture cannot be administered, the inquisitors should order that the medic and surgeon enter into the torture chamber and examine the prisoner. On the basis of what these specialists declare to the judges, the torture session will either begin or be suspended. If there is no impediment, they should proceed with the torture, and even if there is one, they should proceed with more moderation according to what appears proper to them. At this point the medic and surgeon should be ordered to leave, and once they leave, the judge should pronounce formally, *"Bring in the Executioner of the Torture!"*

Once the executioner enters the inquisitor should make the sign of the cross with his fingers and then administer the oath of office to the executioner, stating:

"Do you swear before God and the symbol of this cross to execute fully and faithfully your office and to guard the secret?"

[The executioner] should respond, *"Yes, I swear."*

The inquisitor should then state, *"Then, we order you to do so under the penalty of major excommunication and two hundred lashes for failure to comply."*

Then the inquisitor should tell the prisoner, *"Confess the truth, or the order will be given to strip you naked. . . . Confess the truth!"*

If the prisoner does not confess, the inquisitor should give the order, *"Strip the prisoner naked."*

Once the prisoner is naked, the inquisitor should admonish him, *"Confess the truth, or the order will be given to have you examined. . . . Confess the truth."*

The inquisitor should order, *"Examine the prisoner!"*

The executioner [and his assistants] should then seat the prisoner on the rack, and the minister of justice should take a light or torch and examine the prisoner's mouth, behind his ears, and smell his breath,[58] and then the executioner should state, *"He is ready."*

[The inquisitor should warn the prisoner,] *"Tell the truth, or the order will be given to place you on the rack."*

"Confess the truth."

[The inquisitor should order,] *"Place him on the rack!"*

[The inquisitor should warn the prisoner,] *"Tell the truth or the order will be given to have your body bound."*

"Tell the truth."

[The inquisitor should order,] *"Bind him down on the rack!"*

[The inquisitor should warn the prisoner,] *"Tell the truth, or the order will be given to have the cords bind your right foot to the rack."*

"Tell the truth"

[The inquisitor should order,] *"Bind down his right foot!"*

[The inquisitor should warn the prisoner,] *"Tell the truth, or the order will be given to have the cords bind your left foot to the rack."*

"Tell the truth."

[The inquisitor should order,] *"Bind down his left foot!"*

[The inquisitor should warn the prisoner,] *"Tell the truth, or the order will be given to have the cords bind the lower side of your right arm to the rack."*

"Tell the truth."

[The inquisitor should order,] *"Bind down his lower right arm!"*

[The inquisitor should warn the prisoner,] *"Tell the truth or the order will be given to have the cords bind the lower side of your left arm to the rack."*

"Tell the truth."

[The inquisitor should order,] *"Bind down his lower left arm!"*

[The inquisitor should warn the prisoner,] *"Tell the truth, or the order will be given to have the cords bind the fleshy part of your upper right arm to the rack."*

"*Tell the truth.*"

[The inquisitor should order,] "*Bind down the fleshy part of his upper right arm!*"

[The inquisitor should warn the prisoner,] "*Tell the truth, or the order will be given to have the cords bind the fleshy part of your upper left arm to the rack.*"

"*Tell the truth.*"

[The inquisitor should then warn the prisoner,] "*Tell the truth, or the order will be given to apply the tightening cords for the torment.*"

[The inquisitor should order,] "*Tie him down for the application of the cords!*"

[The inquisitor should warn the prisoner,] "*Tell the truth, or the order will be given to administer the first turn of the cords on your right leg.*"

"*Tell the truth.*"

[The inquisitor should order,] "*Give him the first turn of the cords on his right leg!*"

[The inquisitor should warn the prisoner,] "*Tell the truth, or the order will be given to administer the first turn of the cords on your left leg.*"

"*Tell the truth.*"

[The inquisitor should order,] "*Give him the first turn of the cords on his left leg!*"

[The inquisitor should warn the prisoner,] "*Tell the truth, or the order will be given to administer the first turn of the rack.*"

"*Tell the truth.*"

[The inquisitor should order,] "*Give him the first turn of the rack!*"

[*On the left margin*: At each turn of the rack the executioner should tighten the cords and the inquisitors should tell him, "*Put force into it.*" And then the inquisitors should communicate to the prisoner that if he does not confess they will order the second turn of the cords to be given, and then they should repeat the same for all of the other turns of the cords.]

[The inquisitor should warn the prisoner,] "*Tell the truth, or the order will be given to administer the second turn of the rack.*"

"*Tell the truth.*"

[The inquisitor should order,] "*Give him the second turn of the rack!*"

[The inquisitor should warn the prisoner,] "*Tell the truth, or the order will be given to administer the third turn of the rack.*"

"*Tell the truth.*"

[The inquisitor should order,] "*Give him the third turn of the rack!*"

[The inquisitor should warn the prisoner,] "*Tell the truth, or the order will be given to administer the fourth turn of the rack.*"

"*Tell the truth.*"

[The inquisitor should order,] "*Give him the fourth turn of the rack!*"

[The inquisitor should warn the prisoner,] "*Tell the truth, or the order will be given to administer the fifth turn of the rack.*"

"Tell the truth."

[The inquisitor should order,] *"Give him the fifth turn of the rack!"*

"Tell the truth for the Love of God if you do not want to see yourself facing such torment."

[*Marginal note*: This should be said each time that the executioner ceases to administer the torture, and if the prisoner still does not confess, the session should continue.]

DOCUMENT 17
Inquisition Trial against Michael Morgan, Englishman and One of Those Who Came with the Armada of John Hawkins

Mexico City, 1572–1574

SOURCE: *Processo contra Miguel Morgan yngles de los que vinieron en la armada de Joan Aquines*, 1572–74, Inquisition Manuscript in the Marion L. Foster Collection, Tulane University, New Orleans, Louisiana, Latin American Library Manuscripts, Collection 113, 137 folios.

NOTE: The brief extract here from the case against the English sailor Michael Morgan is typical of the many cases in which torture was used to make a suspect confess his crimes. Michael Morgan had come to Mexico in 1568 with the John Hawkins expedition. Hawkins and his small fleet had been illegally trading in the Spanish Indies and, because of a storm, were forced to weather in the port of Veracruz. While docked in the harbor of Veracruz, an incoming Spanish fleet attacked Hawkins's ships, forcing Hawkins to abandon several dozen of his men on land while he escaped in his surviving ships back to England. The documents transcribed and translated here pertain to the initial arrest of the Englishman and the series of documents included in the official voting and decision for administering of torture. The remaining documents are the transcripts of the torture session and his eventual confession under torment. This torture session is quite similar to all of the others that were conducted by the Inquisition in Mexico. As such, this case is illustrative of the use of torture and its procedure in the inquisitorial courts of New Spain.

Arrest Warrant Issued against Michael Morgan and the Other Englishmen Who Came with Sir John Hawkins, December 3, 1572

†

We, Dr. Pedro Moya de Contreras, Apostolic Inquisitor against Heretical depravity and apostasy in this City of Mexico and its provinces of New Spain, Guatemala, Nicaragua, etc. We order that you, Antonio de Espejo, Familiar of this Holy Office, should go to the town of Texcoco and arrest the body of Michael Morgan [known as Miguel Morgan], an Englishman who resides in the said town. He is a short and heavy man with blond hair. You should arrest him no matter where he is, even if he is in a Church, monastery or other sacred place. After taking him prisoner you should bring him to these secret jails of the Holy Office and turn him over to the Jailer and sequester all of his said belongings, lands, properties, and goods and place them in the power of a bonded and secure person. You should also bring with you the sum of fifty pesos for the maintenance and food of the said prisoner along with all of the clothing and bedding necessary. We also order under the holy obligation of obedience to this Holy Office that all secular and ecclesiastical officials should aid you and help you in your duty and in the arrest of the accused. We also ordered him to arrest any other Englishmen that he should discover residing in the town.

Issued in Mexico City, December 3, 1572

Dr. Pedro Moya de Conteras
[Inquisitor General]

Act of Remission of the Prisoner to the Jailer, December 6, 1572

In the City of Mexico, December 6, 1573, Juan Ferrón, the Jailer of this Holy Office, said that he received the said prisoner in the middle of the night from the Familiar Antonio de Espejo. The said prisoner, Miguel Morgan, was searched, and they did not find anything prohibited on his person or in his belongings. The Familiar then officially handed him over and left him in his cell.

Pedro de los Ríos
[Notary of the Secret]

NOTE: After this there follows about fifty folios worth of testimony against Michael Morgan. Several witnesses then testified against him, stating that he was a Lutheran and that he practiced ceremonies and beliefs of the Lutheran sect. During the entire trial up to this point, Morgan refused to confess or declare anything.

Audience with the Defense Attorney, December 14, 1573

✝

In the city of Mexico, 14th of December 1573, the Lord Inquisitor Dr. Pedro Moya de Contreras ordered that the said Miguel Morgan should be brought before him for an audience in the presence of his defense attorney. Once he was present, he was asked if he had remembered anything concerning this business of the Lutheran sect, and he was urged to tell the truth under oath. He replied that he did not have anything else to say. He was told that the Licenciado Ávila would be his defense attorney, and he was present here to help him answer the specific charges that were leveled against him. The said Lawyer Ávila admonished him to tell the truth about the matter at hand. The said Miguel Morgan then replied that he had nothing to respond, and he referred the Inquisitors to the statements that he had already given. He requested mercy and justice and remained silent. The Inquisitors ordered him to be sent back to his prison cell.

All of this occurred in my presence.
Pedro de los Ríos
[Notary of the Secret]

Consultation and Vote on the Use of Torture, January 12, 1574

†

In the City of Mexico, January 12, 1574, during the afternoon the Lord Inquisitors and the consultants and qualifiers of the Holy Office met in consultation concerning this case. After reviewing the documents and the proceedings of the case, Dr. Pedro Moya de Contreras, Inquisitor General; and Dr. Esteban del Portillo, acting as Ordinary; Dr. Pedro Farfán, Doctor Lope de Miranda, and Dr. Francisco de Sande, judges of the Royal Audiencia of this city, and Dr. Francisco Cervantes de Salazar, consultant of this Holy Office, all decided to vote on the merits of the case concerning the Englishman Miguel Morgan. After having discussed the matter and argued the merits of the case, all were in favor and of one voice and vote. The decision was taken that the said Miguel Morgan would be put to questioning under torment so that the Inquisitors may know the truth concerning whether he had believed or followed the false sect of Martin Luther, a crime that has been testified to by many other witnesses. They decided to return and review the case again depending on what should be discovered under the administration of torture.

I testify to the consultation and the vote
Pedro de los Ríos
[Notary of the Secret]

Audience and Interrogation Held within the Torture Chamber, January 14, 1574

†

In the City of Mexico, January 14, 1574, having gathered together in the torture chamber, the Lord Inquisitor Dr. Pedro Moya de Contreras along and Dr. Esteban de Portillo, representative of the Ordinary, ordered that the prisoner, Miguel Morgan, should be brought before them. After being brought before them, he was questioned once again if he remembered anything concerning the matter of the case and he was admonished to tell the truth under oath.

He responded that he did not remember anything else.

Admonishment

He was told and admonished that he should know that on many occasions and at diverse times he was asked to tell the truth concerning everything that he had said and done, or had seen or heard in offense of Our Lord God and against his Holy Catholic faith and Evangelical law, especially concerning the things that he was accused of in these proceedings. . . . For all of these warnings, he has still not said a word or replied or wished to reply, but rather he has decided to remain silent and to cover up the truth. It appears from testimony that he is covering up many of the things that deal with the sect of Martin Luther, which he apparently has believed and practiced. Instead, regardless of the testimony against him, he persists in denying that he has ever believed or witnessed acts and other ceremonies of the said sect of Martin Luther. In order to investigate and discover the truth about what he knows, it has been ordered that he should be brought forth here and given one final chance to confess and tell the truth about his participation in these ceremonies and sects.

After having read him this admonishment, again he replied that he has never participated in or believed in the sect, or in the beliefs, of Martin Luther. After having seen and heard this final refusal to confess, their Lordships the Inquisitor and the Ordinary pronounced the following sentence:

CHRISTI NOMINE INVOCATO[59]

†

Believing that the evidence and testimony of this case against the said Miguel Morgan shows otherwise, and believing that he does now lie under oath, we condemn him and order him to be put to questioning under torment, asking him under the administration of torture concerning his intentions and participation in the sect of Martin Luther, which he has solidly denied ever having believed in. According to what has been voted on in these proceedings, we order that he be tortured and forced to confess the entire truth of these allegations. He is admonished under protest that if during the administration of torture he should die or remained crippled or maimed, this will be on his own conscience for not having confessed freely of his own free will. This we order as Holy Justice.

Dr. Pedro Moya de Contreras   Dr. Esteban de Portillo
[Inquisitor General]   [Ordinary]

After having pronounced and dictated the said sentence, they signed their names. The Defense Lawyer Ávila was also summoned and remained present serving as a witness to the torture with Gerónimo de Luguí and Juan Ferrón also serving as witnesses.

The sentence and order were then read out loud to the prisoner Miguel Morgan. Morgan then replied, *"For many other sins I deserve torture, but I deny ever having believed in my life in the said sect of Martin Luther even though I may have done many of the other things that I am accused of. . . ."*

With this final admonishment and his refusal to confess, the Inquisitor ordered that he be brought into the Torture Chamber. Once the prisoner was placed inside of the Torture Chamber, the Lord Inquisitor and the other witnesses entered with him. It was eight o'clock in the morning when the prisoner was shown the implements of torture as they lay before him upon the wooden table.

As the prisoner stood before the instruments of torture, he was admonished again out of obedience to Our Lord God that he should confess the truth. He did not say anything else.

The official who would administer the torture was called for and the prisoner was stripped naked. Standing naked before the Lord Inquisitor and the other witnesses, the official quickly fastened several ropes around his upper arms and his legs. Iron shackles were placed upon his ankles. He was asked once again to tell the truth concerning his beliefs in the sect of Martin Luther. He said, *"As God is my witness, I never did believe nor do I believe now in the said law of England and the sect of Luther and I commend myself to God and to his Mother and to Saint Bridget. . . ."*

It was ordered that the ropes be tightened around his arms and legs. He was forced to his knees, and there he prayed to an image of Christ. With the ropes tight around his arms and legs, he was admonished yet again to tell the truth. He said, *"I well understand that what you do is just and justice, but God who knows everything and all of the secrets of men knows that what I have said is the truth and I cannot say anything else even though I may die. . . ."*

FIRST TURN OF THE RACK

The prisoner was then forced to lay back upon the *potro* [the rack], and once fastened down upon the rack, he was admonished again to tell the truth. The Lord Inquisitor ordered that the official turn the rack and tighten it for the first time against his arms. He let out a loud yell and then lay quiet. Later he said, *"Lord God and Saint Mary knows that what I have said is the truth. . . . I beg God to come into my heart and see that it is the truth that I have told. . . ."* As the ropes tightened he cried out again and said, *"I am a great sinner, God Help me and have mercy on me. . . ."* Then he remained quiet and did not say anything else.

SECOND TURN OF THE RACK

Again he was admonished to tell the truth as the Official gave the rack another full turn, twisting the ropes around his arms and legs even tighter. He screamed out in pain and whimpered and cried out, *"My God, you have broken my arms. . . ."* Then he said, *"God knows that what I have already declared is the truth. . . ."*

THIRD TURN OF THE RACK

Once again he was admonished to tell the truth as the official gave another third turn of the rack. The ropes about his arms and legs were even tighter now. He gasped and began to cry. He screamed out several times *"Oh My God . . . My God, My God. . . . Holy Mother of God, help me!"* He then said that what he had told them before was the truth. He complained again much and cried for the pain. Whimpering he said that he had nothing else to confess.

FOURTH TURN OF THE RACK

Because he refused to confess anything else, the Lord Inquisitor signaled the Official to give a fourth turn of the rack. Admonished to tell the truth, the official put his force into it and turned the rack a fourth time. Immediately the prisoner cried out in pain and began to scream. He issued several cries of pain and exclaimed, *"For the Love of God, My God, My God. . . . Stop it!"* He then whimpered, *"I have told you the truth . . . what else do you want me to say. . . . I will say anything, just stop the torment. . . ."*

Asked the question again he responded, *"I will say what you want me to say even though it is not the truth. . . ."* He was told not to raise false testimony, but tell the truth. While screaming out he responded, *"The said Sanders, the master of the ship I was on said that we should incline our heads and hearts and keep the said Laws of the Lutheran sect . . . and the said Sanders read to them many of the laws and orders of the Lutheran sect and he warned them not to worship images nor to adore the things made by hand, nor any other thing in heaven above or on the earth below, but rather they should worship only God in Heaven. . . . He also alleged that this was based on the authority of the book of Exodus and that God had ordered it so . . . we were all on our knees and some of the men responded and agreed with him, but I did not respond to this. . . ."* He then said that he had nothing else to say.

Fifth Turn of the Rack

It was ordered that the Official give a fifth turn of the rack, tightening the ropes even more tightly about his arms and legs. When they were tight around his arms, he cried out like a wild beast and screamed out, *"For the Love of God. . . . Please loosen the ropes and I will tell you what you want to know . . . will tell you that I believe just as they believed and I beg for mercy."*

The ropes were loosened a bit and he then said, *"It is true that I believed in the said Law of England, which is the same as that which was stated in these proceedings and I saw in England the ceremonies of the Lutheran sect and I believed that I could and would save my soul by believing in these beliefs."* He then asked for mercy again.

He was then asked for how long did he believe in this sect that is taught and practiced in England. He responded that it is true that he believed in this sect and that he believed in it for about two and a half years while in England and while he traveled at sea. He said he believed in it until they arrived here at the port of San Juan de Ulua.

He was asked how long has it been since he stopped believing in the Lutheran sect. He said that, after he was briefly in Mexico, he went to the town of Texcoco, where he began to learn our language and to learn about Our Holy Catholic faith, and then it was that he separated himself from the Lutheran sect and felt shamed and sorry for having believed in it. He then returned to the belief in our Holy Catholic faith, and he wishes to continue to live and die with the Catholic faith.

He was then asked what things he had believed when he believed in the Lutheran sect. He said that he had believed that it was enough to confess ones sins in one's own heart to God and to propose to fix them.

He was then asked what did he think about confessing out loud to a priest. He said that he had no opinion concerning this except for what is in the books which he saw in England that say that God is merciful and that it was enough to confess one's sins directly to God, and this is what he believed, and even when there was a priest, he would not confess with him, instead only with God, believing that this was sufficient. He said that Francis Drake, a great English Lutheran who traveled with him, said that this was enough, and he converted him to Lutheranism and also spoke about other things based on the scriptures.

He was asked who were the authors of those books he mentioned, and he said that two of the English bishops who were Lutherans. One of them, he said, was burned by Queen Mary when she returned England to Catholicism.

He was then admonished a final time to tell the truth entirely. He said that all of this that he has said and confessed is the truth that he had believed in the Lutheran sect for the space of about two and a half years before he came to Mexico. He also believed that he could save himself by these beliefs, and if he had known anything else, he would have confessed it.

After hearing this, the Lord Inquisitor and the others believed that he had been suffi-ciently tortured and he had told the truth. They ordered that the torture should cease. At this point the torture ended, and he was released from the ropes. The official loosened the ropes and pulled him up off the rack. Once on his feet, the prisoner collapsed from ex-haustion and pain. He was then dressed, fed, and taken from the Torture Chamber to his prison cell. The entire procedure of the torment ceased at the hour of ten o'clock in the morning.

The entire torture occurred in my presence
Pedro de los Ríos
[Notary of the Secret]

Ratification of the Confession Taken under Torment, January 16, 1574

✝

In the City of Mexico, 16th of January 1574, at eight o'clock in the morning, the Lord Inquisitor Dr. Pedro Moya de Conteras ordered that the prisoner Miguel Morgan should be brought before him for an audience. He was brought before him and asked if he had remembered confessing something under torture. He was then told that now that he was outside of the Torture Chamber and free from torment that he should be read his confes-sion so that he could ratify it if it was well written and contained the truth. He was urged to amend it and correct it if there were errors. After taking the oath, he was read the con-fession. He responded after having listened to it that it was the truth and that he affirmed and ratifies it even though at the beginning of the torment he had denied it. He said that he had initially denied the truth because one of his companions in the jail said that he had seen in Spain at an auto-da-fé that those who confessed under torment were burned alive, and out of fear of this he had not confessed the truth. Now he ratifies that this is the truth and he asks for mercy.

Pedro de los Ríos
[Notary of the Secret]

DOCUMENT 18
Extract of the Sentence and Torture Session, Taken from the Proceedings of the Tribunal of the Holy Office against Rodrígo Franco Taváres, Native of Fondón, a Neighborhood of the Village of Cubillana, in Portugal, an Ambulant Merchant, for the Suspected Heresy of Being a Judaizer

Mexico City, February 7, 1601

SOURCE: Archivo General de la Nación, Ramo de Inquisición, vol. 254, exp. 4.

NOTE: In almost all cases of the use of torture, the suspects were accused of what the In-quisition believed were the worst heretical crimes, the practice of Judaism or the practice of a Protestant religion. The following document records an especially brutal session of torture enacted against a suspected Jew. As you will be able to see, in comparison with the case against the suspected English Protestant, prisoners accused of practicing the "Laws of Moses" were treated much more harshly. Cases like this dealing with accused Jews and crypto-Jews reveal that the Inquisition in New Spain, at least in dealing with suspected Jews, often lost control and went well beyond the letter of the law in its procedures and harsh torments.

The Sentence on the Use of Torture in the Case against Rodrígo Franco. Christi nomine Invocato

✝

In the City of Mexico, 7th of February 1601, having reviewed the merits of the case, along with the indications and suspicions which have resulted against the said Rodrígo Franco, we should condemn him, and we do condemn him to be put to questioning under torment, and it is justified by his stubbornness, and we order that the torment should be administered and should proceed as long as it is our will, so that he may tell and confess entirely the truth, according to how he has been admonished and warned, and if during the said torment he should be injured or should die or should suffer the loss of blood or mutilation of one of his members, the guilt of it shall be upon him for not wishing to tell and confess the truth, and this is the sentence that we pronounce.

Lic. Don Alonso de Peralta, Inquisitor
Lic. Gutierre Bernardo de Quiroz, Inquisitor
Dr. Don Juan de Cervantes, Inquisitor

PRONOUNCEMENT OF THE SENTENCE TO APPLY TORTURE

The said sentence was issued and pronounced by the said Lord Inquisitors and the Ordinary, and they signed their names, being in audience during the morning of the said day, month, and year above stated, with there being present Dr. Martos de Bohórques, the Prosecuting Attorney of the Holy Office, and the said Rodrígo Taváres, serving as witnesses, Pedro de Fonseca, the Notary of the Secrets, and Juan de León Plaza, Jailer of the Secret Jails of this Holy Office.

NOTIFICATION

The said Rodrígo Taváres having been read and notified of the sentence said that it had come in good time.

Audience Held within the Torture Chamber,

✝

After the notification, in the City of Mexico on February 7, 1601, having gathered together in the torture chamber, the Lord Inquisitors and the ordinary, at nine o'clock in the morning, they ordered that the prisoner be brought into the Torture Chamber.

After being brought before them he was questioned and admonished once again in reverence of God, to tell the truth under oath because no one wanted to see him suffer and that he would suffer greatly as he would soon see.

He responded that he already has told the truth for the account that he would give to God.

ENTRY OF THE EXECUTIONER OF THE TORMENT

With this, they ordered the entry of the minister who would execute the torture, and he entered, and they stripped the prisoner naked.

Being naked except for a linen loincloth, he stood before the instruments of torture, and he was admonished again out of obedience to Our Lord God that he should confess the truth. He said that he had already told the truth.

THE TORMENT OF THE CORDS UPON HIS ARMS

Standing naked before the Lord Inquisitors and the other witnesses, they ordered that they fasten several ropes around his upper arms, and he was asked to tell the truth.

He said, "*I have already said the truth, and it will aid me in this!*"

It was ordered that the ropes be tightened around his arms and that they give one turn of the cords around his arms.

FIRST TURN OF THE CORDS

He cried out in loud screams many times, "*Jesus, Holy Virgin, Help me!*" and then he did not say anything else.

SECOND TURN OF THE CORDS

With the ropes tight around his arms he was admonished yet again to tell the truth and they turned the cords again, and he said nothing more.

THIRD TURN OF THE CORDS

Admonished to tell the truth, he was given a third turn of the cords, he cried out, "*Jesus!*" and said, "*I have already told the truth,*" and then said nothing more.

FOURTH TURN OF THE CORDS

Admonished to tell the truth, he was given a fourth turn of the cords, he cried out, "*Jesus, Help me!*" and said, "*I have already told the truth, I told you.*"

Fifth Turn of the Cords

Admonished to tell the truth, he was given a fifth turn of the cords, and he cried out, *"I told you I have already told the truth."*

Sixth Turn of the Cords

Admonished to tell the truth, he was given a sixth turn of the cords, he cried out like a beast many times, *"Oh, sweet Jesus, take my soul, I have already said it!"*

Having been administered the said six turns of the cords, he was ordered to be taken and tied down to the rack and that the *garrotes*[60] be attached it his upper arms, his calves, and his shins.

The prisoner was then forced to lie back upon the rack, and once again he was admonished again to tell the truth because the torture would continue.

The prisoner said in a tearful voice crying out, *"Oh, My God, My God, My God"* sobbing while he said, *"I have already told the truth on my death, I swear it."*

The Turns of the Garrotes on the Rack

After the prisoner was admonished to tell the truth, the executioner drew tight the garrote on his right forearm. He murmured something in a low voice and said, *"I have already said it."*

After he was admonished to tell the truth, the executioner drew tight the garrote on his left forearm. He cried that he had already said it.

After he was admonished to tell the truth, the executioner drew tight the garrote on his left calf muscle and he murmured the same.

After he was admonished to tell the truth, the executioner drew tight the garrote on his left shin, and he said the same thing.

After he was admonished to tell the truth, the executioner drew tight the garrote on his right calf muscle, and he said the same thing.

After he was admonished to tell the truth, the executioner drew tight the garrote on his right shin and then he cried out something in a very low voice, exclaiming, *"Oh, Ah, my Lord, I believe in you, and in you I place my hope and my faith."* The he replied sobbing, *"I have already told the truth."*

They Ordered the Retraction of All of the Said Garrotes

After the prisoner was admonished to tell the truth, they ordered the executioner to retract and take off all of the said garrotes, and once they were released he said, *"Lord Inquisitor, I have already said the truth."*

The Water Jar Torment

After the prisoner was admonished to tell the truth, they ordered him to be strapped down on the rack and had him placed in restraints. Then they placed a linen hood over his head and began to pour a large jar of water forcing it through the hood into his mouth. Once they poured about a quarter of the jar, they took off the hood and asked him again. He said, *"I have already said it and that is the account that I will give to God."*

After he was admonished to tell the truth again, the executioner placed the hood back on his head and poured another jar of water into his mouth, and when the executioner removed the hood, the prisoner said the same thing.

After they removed the hood and his restraints, he was admonished to tell the truth, and he said with seriousness, *"I have already said the truth, and that is the account that I will render unto Jesus Christ."*

They ordered that all of the garrotes and restraints be removed and that he be lifted from the rack, and once he was lifted out, he was admonished again to tell the truth, and he said once again with a good semblance that that is what he had said.

He was ordered to be once again placed onto the rack, and he was restrained again and continued to say the same words.

After having seen this, and his resistance, the said Lord Inquisitors, and the Ordinary, ordered the cessation of the torment. Not believing him to be sufficiently tortured, they admonished him and promised that they would continue the torment whenever and however they believed most convenient. And he was notified of this, and he said, *"Let it continue and proceed in good time."*

With this he was taken off of the rack and brought back to a cell that stood near the Torture Chamber, where he was ministered to and looked over by the Surgeons of the Holy Office, who gave the opinion after they reviewed him that, even though he was very injured, nothing had been broken, and no cuts or lesions were apparent.

The session of torment ended at about half past ten o'clock in the morning.

All of this passed before me
Pedro de Mañozca

Consultation and Vote on the Sentence in the Case against Rodrígo Franco,

†

In the City of Mexico, Wednesday the 7th of February 1601, being gathered in the Audience chamber of the Holy Office, during the afternoon in consultation in view of the trials, the Lord Inquisitors Licenciados Don Alonso de Peralta and Gutierre Bernando de Quiróz, Dr. Juan de Cervantes, Archdeacon of the Holy Cathedral of this city who acts as Ordinary, and serving as consultants the Lords Dr. Santiago del Riego and Francisco Alonso de Villagrá, Judges of the Royal Audiencia of this city, and Dr. don Marcos Guerrero, Alcalde of the Court, and Licenciado Vasco López de Rivero, all of whom have seen the criminal proceedings of the faith against Rodrigo Taváres, native of the region of Fondón, a neighborhood of the village of Cubillana in Portugal, and having dealt with and conferred concerning the case, they voted in the following manner:

The Lord Inquisitors Lic. Gutierre de Quiroz, Dr. Juan de Cervantes, and Lic. Rivero were of the opinion that the said prisoner should be marched out in the next auto-da-fé, in the form of a penitent who will make an Abjuration *de vehementi*, and who should receive as justice 200 lashes.

The Inquisitor Lic. Don Alonso de Peralta, who was this day ill and in bed with poor health, was also of the same vote and opinion.

The Lord Alcalde, Dr. Don Marcos Guerrero, was of the same vote, and opinion, and added that he should serve in the Galleys of His Majesty, at the oars without a salary for the space of ten years.

Lord Dr. Francisco Alonso de Villagrá was also of the same opinion, without the sentence to the galleys, and only stated that the galleys should be his prison.

Lord Dr. Don Santiago del Riego was of the vote and opinion that the said suspect should be put to the torment once again, which should be done very well, and that once these diligences were made that they should come together and vote on this case again.

This is a copy of the original vote that is in the Second Book of Votes on Sentences, folio 34.

I testify to the consultation and the vote
Pedro de Mañozca
[Notary of the Secret]

Autos-da-fé in New Spain

At the end of seven months we were both carried to the high Church of Mexico to do open penance upon a high scaffold made before the high Altar upon Sunday in the presence of a very great number of people who were at the least five or six thousand. For there were some that came one hundred miles off to see the said Auto (as they call it) for that there were never none before that had done the like in the said Country nor could they tell what Lutherans were nor what it meant, for they had never heard of any such thing before.

Robert Tomson, Englishman who appeared at the auto-da-fé in Mexico City, 1560

The Inquisition and the secular authorities in New Spain publicly administered all definitive sentences at a formal function called an auto-da-fé, most often held on a particular Sunday. The Inquisition celebrated its "act of faith" with great pomp and ceremony, in the only public action in an otherwise secret tribunal. All of the tribunal's officials and assistants played their part in the solemn event, in what one modern scholar has termed "a dramatic mimesis of Christ's final judgment of sinners."[61] The Inquisition held these acts of faith in a large plaza and required all of the secular and ecclesiastical officials and the general populace to attend. The purpose of the gathering was to observe the procession of penanced, reconciled, and relaxed heretics and hear the announcement of the verdict of their individual sentences. Although the reading of the convicted heretics' sentences remained the main attraction, many other activities occurred at an auto-da-fé. Together, they served to manifest the power of the Catholic religion and to reinforce religious orthodoxy.

Preparations for the Ceremony

The preparations for an auto-da-fé began once the Inquisition had collected a significant number of reconciled and relaxed heretics. The ceremony most often occurred on a special feast day or coincided with another solemn religious holy day that served to bring together the largest viewing public possible. The formal preparations began with an official convocation and announcement of the event. Inquisitors ordered a formal procession through the major streets of Mexico City by the Inquisition's many familiars and notaries, who proclaimed the upcoming date of the ceremony and invited the public to attend the event with promises of gaining plenary indulgences and other spiritual benefits (fig. 8).

Carpenters and laborers then began constructing platforms, stages, and stadium-style seating, as well as the benches, tables, and other furniture the ceremony required. The project also included a specialized covered platform for the preferential seating of the inquisitors and other official guests. The Inquisition in New Spain often spent lavish sums of money to stage these celebrations, and the job often took the carpenters and laborers more than a month to complete. During the final weeks and days before the scheduled event, several other important activities occurred.

The night before the celebration of the auto-da-fé, the inquisitors organized the Procession of the Green Cross in which the familiars and other officials of the tribunal marched in procession with the Inquisition's central crucifix and its banner and emblem (fig. 9). The emblem held symbolic representations of the Inquisition's central duty to both offer mercy and punish wayward heretics. The biblical inscription in Latin from Psalm 73, verse 22 "Exurge, Domine, iudica causam tuam" (Rise up, Oh Lord, and Judge your Cause) surrounded the symbol and official shield of the Mexican Inquisition. The capital letters I and M on either side of Christ's crucifix symbolized "Inquisitio Mexici" or the Mexican Inquisition. The color of the cross on the shield and of the major crucifix that they marched in procession was green, symbolizing the hope of eternal salvation for those heretics reconciled by the Inquisition. The emblem was placed on a black flag or background symbolizing that the church mourned for the pertinacious heretics who refused to confess their crimes. The olive branch on the right-hand side of the emblem signified peace and mercy for those heretics who reconciled with the church, while the sword on the left-hand side symbolized justice and punishment for those unrepentant heretics.

The purpose of this procession was to escort the inquisition's standards to the place selected for the celebration of the auto-da-fé. The honor guard placed the standard and the crucifix on the highest spot on the platform and the staging and covered them with a black veil. Throughout the rest of the night, a select group of familiars and clergymen kept watch over these emblems to avoid their theft or damage.[62]

In the evening before the ceremony, special prayer vigils also occurred, while the inquisitors and other officials attempted to offer the impenitent heretics their final chance to confess and repent before the reading of their sentences and the execution of their punishments. Throughout the rest of the evening before the event, the familiars and other officials who served as the formal militia of the Inquisition kept watch and guard over the prisoners.

The Order of Events during the Ceremony

Before dawn on the day of the auto-da-fé, the Inquisition's prison officials and notaries prepared the prisoners and convicted heretics for their public procession. The officials ordered and dressed the penitents or reconciled heretics in their appropriate garments of shame, which they would wear throughout the ceremony. Afterward, the jailer and other officials arranged the prisoners in their positions for the solemn procession of the penitents, which would traverse the most prominent streets of the city to the main plaza.

The Public Procession of the Penitents

The procession began at the doorway of the Inquisition's palace, located on the plaza of Santo Domingo, and worked its way toward the central plaza (fig. 10). At the front of the procession, the inquisitors marched with their crucifix, whose black veil symbolized that Christ was in mourning for the heretics. The prisoners were escorted and guarded by the inquisitorial militia, and each was accompanied by two familiars of the Inquisition (fig. 8). The general procession and files of the penitents followed a specific order. In the first place, the inquisitors marched all of the penitent heretics who received sentences of penance. The penanced marched with their heads uncovered, wearing their *sanbenitos*, each according to the style of public abjuration they were expected to make. The penitent heretics also marched carrying a lighted green candle as a sign of their hope for forgiveness (fig. 11). Those who were sentenced to receive the punishment of public flogging also had a knotted noose or cord around their neck as a sign that they would receive lashes or go to the galleys.

In the second place came the reconciled heretics dressed in their own *sanbenitos* with the full Saint Andrew's crosses on the front and back. They also wore the conical dunce caps of shame with similar insignia. Next came the procession of those heretics sentenced with relaxation to the secular arm, that is, those condemned to receive the death penalty. They too wore the conical *coroza*, or fool's hat, and their *sanbenitos* not only contained the full Saint Andrew's cross but were also painted with flames and demons as a symbol of their ultimate fate: being burned alive. Finally, there came the statues or effigies of those heretics tried and convicted in absentia, along with the cadavers or bones of those deceased who had been tried for heresy posthumously. The solemn procession ended with a parade of the civil and ecclesiastical authorities, followed by the officials and functionaries of the Inquisition.

During the preceding weeks, the Inquisition had ordered two major platforms erected for the event in the central plaza: the prisoners and penitents sat on one of the platforms, and the guests of honor, including the viceroy and his retainers, and the inquisitors on the other.[63] The entire officialdom of Mexico City usually attended the auto-da-fé, with the secular town council and the bishop and his own cathedral chapter also seated in their own respective places on the platform and staging.

The prisoners were seated according to the order of the gravity of their crimes. At the highest level of the platform were those heretics sentenced to relaxation to the secular arm, below them in the middle of the staged seating sat those prisoners sentenced to reconciliation, and at the lowest level of seating sat those to be penanced (fig. 12).

The Oath of Loyalty

The official ceremony of the auto-da-fé began with the swearing of a mass public oath. All of the presiding officials together in unison with the gathered populace swore a public oath of fidelity to the Catholic faith and an oath of loyalty to the Holy Office of the Inquisition. By means of this oath, all of the attendees reaffirmed their fealty to the Catholic religion. In this manner, the public spectacle and didactic theater of judgment began.

The Opening Sermon

A sermon, usually by a prominent or prestigious religious cleric, began the ceremony of an auto-da-fé. The Inquisition in New Spain usually selected great orators and passionate speakers to deliver these sermons. For instance, on November 15, 1573, at the first auto-da-fé celebrated in New Spain, the newly consecrated bishop of Yucatan, Fray Diego de

Landa, presided.[64] One of the earliest monastic inquisitors in the Yucatan Peninsula, Bishop Landa delivered an hour-long sermon on the evils of heresy and the necessity of punishment for the wicked and impenitent. A solemn and formal celebration of the Catholic mass followed the sermon.

The Reading of the Heretics' Sentences

The culmination of the celebration focused on the formal reading of the official sentences against the heretics by the Inquisition's notary and his assistants. The senior inquisitor began the event with the ringing of a ceremonial bell, which was a signal to the notary and the chief constable to begin the reading of the sentences. The formal reading and proclamation of the crimes and sentences of the convicted heretics took most of the rest of the day. The notaries and inquisitors had the sentences proclaimed in the order of the gravity of their crimes.

The readings began with the sentences of those penanced for suspicions of minor crimes and heresy. One by one, the penanced heretics came up to a raised platform in the center of the stage and had their crimes and sentences read by the notary before the gaze of the entire town (fig. 12). After the sentences for those penanced, which often took much of the morning, the notary proclaimed the sentences of those reconciled for formal heresy. Again, one by one, the reconciled heretics stepped up to the central box to hear their sentences. Then came the reading of the crimes and sentences of those tried in absentia; those sentenced posthumously had their effigies or bones relaxed to the secular arm to be burned in effigy. The conclusion of the reading of the sentences occurred when those to be relaxed in person had their crimes and sentences read.

Public Absolutions, Abjurations, and the Procession
of the Condemned to the Stake

Once the reading of all of the sentences had occurred, the other convicted heretics sentenced to make public abjurations, either *de levi*, *de vehementi*, or *de formali*, made their public retractions and swore to remain faithful to the Catholic Church. Each of the prisoners stepped forward again and abjured publicly to never again fall into the errors of heresy.

At this point in the ceremony, a public act of vindication could occur in the rare cases in which the Inquisition absolved or acquitted an accused heretic. If an accused heretic was found innocent due to false-witness testimony, the Inquisition allowed the prisoner "to appear at the auto-da-fé carrying a palm branch as a symbol of his or her vindication before the Holy Office."[65]

After the public vindications and abjurations had occurred, the inquisitors proceeded to make a public absolution of the penitent heretics. The attendees then recited several prayers and chanted several hymns. At this point, the Inquisition's secretary and other officials handed over those condemned to death to the civil authorities. A final procession then began of the condemned along with the other effigies, statues, and bones of the deceased to be relaxed.

The ceremony concluded with the celebration of a Catholic mass. Then, a special procession and parade returned the green cross and the symbol of the Inquisition to its proper place in the Palace of the Inquisition. The entire spectacle had as its ultimate goal the inspiration of the public's reverential fear of the Inquisition and its abhorrence of heresy. Thus, the Inquisition, through the entire solemnity of the auto-da-fé, attempted to create what one scholar has called a mimicking of Christ's last judgment of the damned.[66]

DOCUMENT 19
Brief Relation of the Auto-da-fé

Mexico City, February 28, 1574

SOURCE: Archivo General de la Nación, Ramo de Inquisición, vol. 223, exp. 12.

NOTE: This document contains a brief relation of the penitents who were marched in one of the first autos-da-fé held in the New World. The crimes and types of accusations present illustrate the preoccupations of the first inquisitors in rooting out heretical practices and sacrilege in the kingdom of New Spain.

✝

List of the cases that were completed and dispatched in the auto-da-fé celebrated on the first Sunday of Lent, the 28th of February 1574:

Domingo de Torres, knife maker, native of the town of Azpeitia in the province of Guipúzcoa, resident in Mexico, tried for stating that if a man has carnal access with a woman one time, since they are not concubines, then it was not a mortal sin but rather a venial sin. He was sentenced to carry a candle and abjure *de levi* because he came to confess this spontaneously.

Hierónimo Pulo, French sailor, tried for having said that he renounced God and that he had a custom of saying this blasphemy. He was sentenced to carry a candle and make an abjuration *de levi*, he also received 100 lashes.

Juan de Valderrama, native of Guatemala, while a resident in Mexico made an abjuration *de levi* during a previous year for a sentence issued by the Provisor of this city, and afterward he made another abjuration *de vehementi* by order of the Provisor of Oaxaca for poorly understood things of little proof, and after that he was testified against before the Provisor in Mexico and remitted to this Holy Office for having said that the sacrament of confession and the Eucharist are just ceremonies, and not sacraments, and for saying that he could moralize about the gospels like any other theologian. He was sentenced to carry a candle and to make an abjuration *de levi*, and was sentenced to exile from this archbishopric for one year, according to the sentence of the Ordinary and the *Consultores*, and the Inquisitor Pedro Moya de Contreras freed him of this sentence because the evidence came from only one witness who was partial against him.[67]

Hernán Blanco, farmer, native of Parra in Extremadura, resident of Mexico, tried because while being married *in facie ecclesiae*[68] he went and became a Friar, and professed the order of Saint Francis, and afterward he became an apostate from the order and returned to live with his wife, and he requested this before the Ordinary Ecclesiastical Judge. He was sentenced to carry a candle with a noose around his neck, and also to wear a white conical *coroza* of shame, as well as to receive 200 lashes, and suffer exile from the archbishopric of Mexico for five years.

Isabel García, wife of Hernán Blanco, a *mestiza*[69] native of Mexico, tried because she tricked and persuaded him to join a monastery as a friar, pretending that she had been married before with another man, and this is what she confessed during her first hearing, and then she revoked this and said that her legitimate husband was Hernán Blanco, and if she had said anything differently, it was in order to end her marriage to him, and to stop from being punished by him for frivolous things that she did. She was sentenced to carry a candle, to wear a noose around her neck and a conical *coroza* of shame on her head, and to receive 200 lashes and exile from the archbishopric of Mexico for five years.

Marcos Prestes, also known as Francisco de Barbosa, resident of Xalapa in the bishopric of Tlaxcala, native of the town of Tambuxo, archbishopric of Lisbon, tried for being married two times. He was sentenced to carry a candle and wear a noose around his neck as well as a conical *coroza* of shame. He was also sentenced to receive 200 lashes and perpetual exile from the Indies, as well as a fine of 150 pesos for his first marriage in Lisbon, which was admitted to by his confession, whereas the second was not proved beyond the witnesses testifying to his living like husband and wife with the second woman.

Captain Juan Pablo de Carrión, a native of Valladolid in Castile, resident in the village of Purificación in the bishopric of Michoacan, tried for having been married two times, the first in Seville, and the other one in the village of Cuztalapa, province of Amula further away from Michoacan. He was sentenced to carry a candle, and to be exiled from the jurisdiction of New Spain for ten years. He was also fined 1,000 ducats due to the quality of his person and his high social standing.[70]

Pedro de Trejo, resident in Mexico, native of the city of Placencia in Spain, tried for having said and trying to amend two verses of the psalms of David, stating that with his amendment they made more sense, and he wrote it down and intended to consult with the Pope concerning it; he also tried to amend another prayer which is also commonly sung by the Church, saying that it did not work and that he would recompose it, communicating this with the Bishop of Michoacan, who could not satisfy him; and also for having written several works composed in rhyme and meter, as well as for reading several books which treated of profoundly deep spiritual things of the Faith and mysteries of the Holy Trinity, all of which, as an ignorant person, he should abstain from reading.[71] He was sentenced to carry a candle and then to be sent to the galleys as a soldier for a term of four years, based on the relation that he was a good Christian and an honest man, and he was warned not to write any similar works in the future.

DOCUMENT 20
Relation of the Order That Has Been Observed in the Holy Office of the Inquisition of New Spain since Its Founding on November 4, 1571, concerning the Celebrations of the Public Autos-da-fé

Mexico City, June 1594

Source: Archivo General de la Nación, Ramo de Inquisición, vol. 1510, exp. 1, folios 1–6, Lote Riva Palacios, vol. 35, no. 1.

NOTE: This document, written by the secretary of the Inquisition, Don Pedro de los Ríos, before his departure from office in 1595, reveals the standard operating procedures followed by the Holy Office of the Inquisition in New Spain concerning how to hold public autos-da-fé in which they would read the sentences and give penance to the convicted prisoners of the Inquisition. Not only does it recount in minute detail how the Inquisition celebrated autos-da-fé in Mexico, but it also shows the power of the Holy Office to humble even the figure of the viceroy. A mere complaint from the tribunal of Mexico could cause a series of reprimands for any incompliant viceroy or other government official.

✝

1. The consideration and good accord that commonly proceeds in the Inquisition concerning all things, not only the most essential but also the least important, led the Inquisitor Dr. Pedro Moya de Contreras to confer with the said Viceroy Don Martín de Enríquez[72] concerning things that might cause difficulties in the execution of the form of the autos-da-fé, especially the accompanying processions, precedents, places, courtesies, and respective seating arrangements, in order to formulate an accord and avoid all disturbances and disagreements that may occur, for all of which an order and procedure for the proper conduct was agreed upon. The Viceroy, out of his prudence wrote to Valladolid to the Inquisitor of that region, Licenciado Diego González, Abad of Arvas, a very close friend of his and a great person, requesting that he advise him concerning the customs used there between the Inquisition and the President and Audiencia, by means of which it would be easier to regulate the customs here. Accepting this accord, the Inquisition wrote and asked the same of Valladolid, as well as many other Tribunals concerning this same matter and others attached to it.[73] The Viceroy received a response, and taking out of the letter the substance which touched upon this question, he sent a record of it to this Holy Office on October 3, 1572, written in the hand of Juan Vázquez de Zearreta, his Secretary, and with the same whose original is in the Chamber of the Secret, signed and received in my name, with the responses of the said Inquisitions and that of Valladolid signed by the Inquisitors Licenciado Diego González, Doctor Quíjano de Mercado, Licenciado Sanctos y Realiego, which contains the substance of the said document.

During this time, the said Viceroy received a letter from the Lord Cardinal Don Diego de Espinosa, President of Castile and Inquisitor General in a mode of reprehension and complaint concerning the inhospitable and dismissive way in which he had received the arrival of this Inquisition on the day that it entered into Mexico City and the second day when the officials went to meet with him in the palace. Moreover, many other friends of his wrote this from court showing pity for what had been noted in this because of the complaint that the Holy Office had represented to the Cardinal and the General Council of the Inquisition in Spain. Feeling bad for this, the Viceroy sought to excuse his actions by stating that on that day he could not call for a good reception of the ministers, but rather instead he did it on the other day when he swore obedience in the church where he accompanied the Audiencia and the royal standard, and assisted in the administration of the oaths. He returned afterward to the Inquisition and, procuring to amend whatever had led to the misunderstanding before, and to avoid other new occasions for complaint, he retracted for his mistake and offered that, guarding his dignity as Viceroy and what should be given in preeminence, he would attend to the honor and the authority of the Holy Office. He said that even though he was the Viceroy and not only the president of the Audiencia like the leader of the state in Valladolid, that he would join in all of the processions of the Ministers of the Holy Office in all of the autos-da-fé just as the President does in Valladolid. From then onward, he always proceeded benignly and in accord with this agreement throughout my time as Secretary of the Holy Office.

The Celebration of the Public Autos-da-fé

2. Two or three days before the auto-da-fé, a town crier should announce that it was the intent of the last consultation of the Inquisitors with the consultants [who ordinarily were the Audiencia judges and magistrates], and conferring together and in accord with them, they have chosen a day that appeared convenient for this matter. Later, after this had been announced, in the afternoon they should send a message to the Viceroy to give him an account of how it had been decided to celebrate the auto-da-fé on that day and request that he should order the standard to be displayed and order the customary accompaniment, as well as beg him to be present personally so that, with his presence and greatness, the auto-da-fé will have the authority that is most convenient.

Who Should Take the Message to the Viceroy

3. In order to give the Viceroy this message, the Prosecuting Attorney and sometimes one of the Inquisitors, according to the devotion and contact that they may have with him, should go in order to assure and convince the Viceroy of his authority, and to pay him the respect that he is owed due to the fact that much is owed to his good will. They should decide there with him if there are any difficulties or other similar types of problems that most often concern the Audiencia. Then they should not deal more with the Audiencia, because they had already complied with its opinion in the consultation.

To the Town Council and the Cathedral Chapter

4. They should send the Chief Constable to the Cathedral Chapter,[74] and the Secretary to the *Cabildo*,[75] or Town Council, in order to notify them and request their presence, so that during the morning of the auto-da-fé they should accompany the Royal Standard in the solemn form as is accustomed to be done by both Councils [and the Town Council should be told not to display any other insignia or banner]. And this message should not be sent at the same time as that sent to the Viceroy, but instead it should be sent a day before they order the Town Crier to announce the auto-da-fé.

The Archbishop

5. If there is an Archbishop present in the consultation, whatever has been most recently practiced should be complied with, as in my own time it occurred that in several of the autos the Archbishop Don Pedro Moya de Contreras assisted. And if the archbishopric is in the period of a vacant seat,[76] or when the Archbishop is visiting his archdiocese or in Spain, I am not sure what else can be done in this respect.

The Proclamation

6. The day that the proclamation of the auto-da-fé should be made, one of the Secretaries with the other ministers, without anyone missing, should come out from the palace of the Inquisition at ten o'clock in the morning, all of them in their order. With many mounted gentlemen invited to join them from the city, they should march out with trumpets and drums sounding. Having made the first pronouncement by the town crier in front of the door of the Inquisitorial palace, or somewhere nearby so that the prisoners cannot hear it, they should then go on next to the Viceregal Palace and the House of the Town Council, and then on to the Public Square, and then to several other places, after which they should return from where they came. This should be done during the daytime during the week, and in some other Inquisitions it is done during the afternoon on feast days, and all of the Secretaries in these Tribunals go out if there is more than one. But it is understood that in none of the Tribunals does the Judge of Confiscations, or other officials, or even the Lawyers go out on these occasions.

The Stage and Scaffolding

7. Once the auto-da-fé has been proclaimed, it is up to the Receptor to arrange the construction of the stage and scaffolding, with the seating capacity, model, and design that is ordered (fig. 12). One section is for the penitents, and in it, if there are penitents to be relaxed or handed over to the secular arm, one or two semicircular benches or seats should be made. From these there should be built a narrow passageway about two varas in width and about ten or twelve varas long, with banisters and railings that lead to the elevated stage and scaffolding of the Tribunal, which should have below it a large-scale planned space from where they can erect six or seven stands of seats or terraces. Another smaller stand of seats and a terrace should be made for the Viceroy, the Inquisition, and the Royal Audiencia, which should be made of fine leather and walnut wood, without cushions nor any other thing except for a series of good carpets and coverings in the stands and terraces, except for the seat of the Viceroy, which should be covered with velvet and have two velvet pillows and cushions (without a footstool), one of the cushions for his feet and the other one for his seat. Even though the Archbishop should attend, or any other consecrated prelates, they should not receive this same singular honor.

8. The practice of placing seats in the Tribunal for everyone was introduced into this Inquisition of Mexico out of the necessity of the Viceroy's having one, and not wanting to restrict this singular benefit to him while everyone else sat on the hard benches covered only by carpets, as I have witnessed in Murcia, Llerena, and Seville, and as I understand is the procedure in all of the other Inquisitions of Spain.

The Adornment of the Stage and Scaffolding

9. The scaffolding and stage where the chairs and seating are to be arranged should be finely adorned with rich tapestries or with arches and other vaulted adornments along the wall where the seating is placed. In the middle of the entire structure, they should place the canopied arch and compartment of the Inquisition. At the feet of the staging, in the terraces, and on the ground of the staging, they should place good carpeting. It is a

good idea to place a small enclosed room at hand that is well concealed, for whatever occasion or necessity may be forcibly needed.

Concerning the Town Council and the Cathedral Chapter

10. Concerning the seating of the members of the Church, it is permitted that they be seated at the right hand of the Tribunal, at about half a vara below and attached to the Tribunal's raised dais. There a separate terrace of seats should be made where the Cathedral Chapter and the doctors of the University should be seated. And in the same form, on the left-hand side of the Tribunal's place, space should be reserved for the Town Council of the City, where there is accustomed to gather many gentlemen and other prominent people who do not fit into the said stands and lower staging.

Concerning the Prisoners

11. In the middle at the end of the said passageway, they should place a platform or pedestal with two small steps, where the prisoners will rise and stand when they are called forth to hear their sentence so that they may be viewed by all.

Concerning the Confessors

12. During the night of the auto-da-fé, at nine o'clock in the evening, the Inquisitors should enter into audience chambers, and there they should make the confessors who will take those to be relaxed to the secular arm to their seats make the oath that is accustomed and in conformity with the instructions. With the Prosecutor, Secretary, and the Chief Constable present, the eldest Inquisitor will then give them all a talk in reason of the obligation that they have in consideration of the sentence and justice of the Church, which the Holy Tribunal represents. He will also remind them that the Tribunal has declared the prisoners whom they will go to confess as heretics and that each one should go about his office according to his letters and with the confidence that he has in the integrity of their consciences as the selected persons. He must also advise them that the said crime of heresy had already been deduced from the evidence in their trials and that the prisoners were condemned and convicted and that they should not be absolved sacramentally until they have first confessed and made satisfaction judicially. They are to be advised that whatever they see and hear in the jails should be kept secret, that they should not give or take any news of what they had been given in confession, and that they should give notice of those who do confess to the said Tribunal. With this, the said Inquisitor should hand over to the confessors a small green cross that they have to give to the condemned (fig. 13). Then with the confessors, the Inquisitor should go down with them into the cells with the Jailer, the Secretary, and the Constable and the other Familiars, and they should place the prisoners hands in the hands of the confessor and tie them together, telling them to look to their conscience as a man who is about to die. Leaving them with the confessor, they should leave the cells and return to the Tribunal. This same thing should be done with each confessor, and the Jailer and the Familiars should watch over the jails with great care and security and give notice in the chamber of the secret if one of the prisoners requests an audience. If one is requested, one of the Inquisitors should go down with the Secretary to receive the testimony of the prisoner. Then the prisoner should be seen by the Inquisitors

and the Ordinary, who should be brought together before daybreak in the audience chamber in order to decide what to do in the case with the new testimony.

The Insignias for the Penitents and the Procedures for the Inquisitorial Procession

13. Two hours before dawn, the Jailer should order each jail lit with torches and wake the prisoners, instructing them to get dressed. And an hour later, in the company of an Inquisitor, the Secretary, the Constable, and the said Familiars, they should begin to call the prisoners forth and gather them in the patio of the secret jails, one by one. As the Jailer brings them, they should go placing on them each one their insignias according to the relation and sentences, which should have been brought and separated out according to the crime, so that there is no trick, equivocation, or error in the placing of the vestments and insignias of shame, because this would be a grave public error. Then they should seat the prisoners on a bench in the order that they should be brought out to hear their sentences. Once dawn and daylight has broken, they should go marching out in formation and procession with their Familiars each accompanying them as their guards through the chosen streets until they reach the scaffolding (fig. 8). By the quality of their crimes, they will begin in procession, with those guilty of the least serious crimes up front, followed by those associated with the serious crimes and those to be relaxed in person, and behind them the effigies or statues of those deceased or convicted in absentia. The Chief Constable with all of the most important Familiars with decency should go out mounted so that the procession shall not be interrupted. Then leaving them off, they should make the prisoners go up with the condemned to be relaxed in the highest terrace or seats, according to what has been ordered. Then the Familiars should return with the Inquisition in the company of the Tribunal, or quickly thereafter.

Accord with the Viceroy concerning the Hour for the Beginning of the Procession

14. The Viceroy should be advised on the evening before the auto concerning the hour of the next day in which the Holy Office will begin its procession. Once the Viceroy has arrived at the hour that is agreed upon with the two chambers of the Civil and Criminal courts at the doorway to the Inquisitorial Palace, without dismounting, the Inquisitors shall come forth and go up to the viceroy's procession, and the oldest Inquisitor with the due respect shall exclaim, "*Please Pass, Your Excellency,*" inviting him into the place at the head of the procession between the two Inquisitors. The viceroy should respond "*Please, After Your Mercy,*" and then passing a few words of courtesy between them, the Viceroy shall be given the best place. The rest of the accompanying officials and ministers shall go forth in the following order:

The Form and Order in Which the Procession Shall Proceed

15. The oldest Inquisitor and at his left-hand side the youngest Inquisitor, and at his right hand the Viceroy. In front of them the Judges of the Audiencia, two by two based on their antiquity, and then the Magistrates of the Civil and Criminal Courts, and the Civil Prosecutor; and then the Prosecutor of the Holy Office who holds the standard of the

Faith, either by himself, or with two gentlemen dressed in habits at either side of him, each one of them holding one of the tassels of the standard as is customary in Spain, and as I witnessed while I was the Secretary of the Inquisition in Llerena and as is practiced by the Inquisitors of Puebla and Medellin. After them the Judge of Confiscations and the Consultants who are not Audiencia Judges, and then the Qualifiers. Then after them the other officials, commissaries, and ministers of the Inquisition, two by two, because marching alongside the others is not very appropriate. Then, after them the Chief Constable of the Royal Chancellery by himself, with his Lieutenants ahead of him, and with him occasionally the Captain of the Guard went, if he was not placed behind the Viceroy. And after the Constable of the Court, commences the file of the members of the Cathedral Chapter and the University and other schools [all without their insignias] who at the said hour should all be assembled there in double files to the right of the procession, with the highest dignity of the Cathedral Chapter leading the file. And on the left-hand side of the procession all of the secular officials who had come with the Viceroy and the Corregidor, with all of the magistrates and other officials, in the manner that each one of them should march in line and lineup with a person in the right-hand column of the Cathedral Chapter matching the placement of a member in the line of the secular officials in imitation of the Inquisition of Seville where I saw this type of lineup practiced in an auto-da-fé conducted in October of 1570 in which I served as a member of the procession.[77] The remaining secular doctors, secretaries, and other ministers of the Royal Audiencia and others should be placed and accommodated in the column of the secular officials if they are not placed behind the Viceroy himself, because there is no other place assigned for them. And finally in the lead of the procession other gentlemen, personages, and other citizens and honored people who have come to accompany the procession.

The Place Reserved for a Consecrated Prelate

If there should attend some consecrated prelate, he should go in the procession and accompaniment right after the Viceroy and the Inquisitors, on the right-hand side of the oldest Audiencia Judge, because no other better place has been permitted them by order of the Viceroy Don Martín Enríquez, even though attempts were made to find one. And the Viceroy and the said Prelate should be seated on the stage and platform of the Tribunal with both of the Inquisitors in between them, as has been practiced in the two earliest and first autos-da-fé during the years 1574 and 1575, when the Bishop of Tlaxcala Don Antonio Morales de Molina attended the first one and preached a sermon and when the bishop of Yucatan [Fray Diego de Landa] attended and preached a sermon as well, and since then there has not occurred the attendance of another similar prelate.

How the Officials Are to Be Seated

16. Once they have arrived at the scaffolding and the seats, the Viceroy and the Inquisitors should be seated under the awning and enclosure for the Tribunal, each one sitting down in the order that they arrive. Then the oldest Audiencia Judge should be seated on the left-hand side of the awning to the left of the youngest Inquisitor, and the Viceroy [should be] seated on the right of the oldest Inquisitor so that the Viceroy and the oldest Audiencia Judge [if there is no prelate] will have between them the two inquisitors. All of

the rest of the Audiencia and the magistrates along with the Chief Constable of the Court shall be seated in French-styled chairs, without any velvet decorations, except for that of the Viceroy, which should have two cushions as has been stated, without any other person having them. Even though in the first auto-da-fé in the year 1574 the Inquisitor [Pedro] Moya de Contreras pretended to have a cushion at his feet because of his election as Archbishop of Mexico, and the Viceroy Don Martín [Enríquez] gave him tacit permission [by fortune a permission that he purged maliciously as many say] because of his own personal devotion, but he resisted it when attempted by his companion the Inquisitor Bonilla, and therefore since then no one else has been able to use one.

The Seat Reserved for the Prosecutor

17. The Prosecutor of the Holy Office, with his standard in hand, shall be seated in the middle of the last or bottom terrace right on the step or grade on which the Inquisitors place their feet. He shall be placed upon a platform several fingers' lengths high by himself, and by his side should stand the two gentlemen who came accompanying him.

Seating in the Other Levels and Terraces

18. In the next place, at their feet, in the middle grade or terrace toward the right-hand side should sit the Consultants who should be present [who are not members of the Audiencia], serving and seating near the head [of the terrace]. Behind them [should follow] the prelates of the religious orders by order of antiquity, and if they should not fit on that row of seats, they should continue in the next row. On the other left-hand side of the seating, the Qualifiers and Patrons shall be seated, also by order of antiquity. In one of these two parts, they should seat the Captain of the Guard because he is a functionary who is close to the Viceroy. And in the rest of the seats and terraces they should seat the other religious and secular gentlemen of the household of the Viceroy, and the other principal people of the City and kingdom who should attend, on the basis of the good election of their order and arrangement made by the person in charge of seeing to the seating and distribution of the scaffolding.

The Setup in the Plan and Enclosure

19. The plan and enclosure should have sufficient capacity and space to place on the right-hand side a raised bench with carpeting that runs from the seating where the lawyers of the Holy Office and the Accountant and other officials are seated according to the opinions of the Inquisitors. In the front of this, across the staging without carpeting, they should place the desk and space where those who will read the sentences should be placed. Here they should place a large table with a good covering, where the Secretary will be seated upon a small bench with all of the written sentences, which he will divide out and read in the order described in the relation of prisoners that he brings with him based on the orders of how he should go about reading the sentences.

The Rest of the Benches and Terraces

20. Behind the two benches and tables referred to, they should place two cleared areas with benches for the Secretaries of the Government and Audiencia and other ministers, and servants of the King, where they should be carefully seated if there is no more room

for them in the stands. And behind these benches they should place many others for the religious and clerics who could not fit in the stands, and for other persons who deserve to be accommodated at the discretion of the person in charge of the seating.

The Major Familiars

21. The major Familiars with their staffs of justice should be placed under the command of the Chief Constable. When they return with him to the stands and scaffolding they should accompany and escort the Tribunal and they should be seated near the place of the Councils.

The Seating of the Chief Constable and His Duties

22. At the beginning or entrance of the passageway that runs the length from the scaffolding of the penitents to that of the Tribunal, they should seat the Chief Constable of the Holy Office, placing him at the right-hand side, seated on a chair just like those of the Tribunal. It is his office not to return to his chair until he has left the Tribunal seated and has quieted the crowd. Once he is seated, it is a sign to the Preacher to begin his sermon. The Constable will also be able to attend from there to what other necessary things are needed in order to silence the crowd and to take away as prisoners anyone who disturbs the peace or interrupts the auto-da-fé, without it being necessary for him to be ordered to do so, so that all should be executed in a peaceful and solemn way. In front of the said Chief Constable, at the other end of the passageway, the Jailer should be seated upon a bench with a staff in his hand that belongs to his office. When the announcer calls out a prisoner, the Jailer will bring them forth in the company of the doorman of the Holy Office, who should be seated with him on his platform, so that the prisoner can hear his sentence read. They should be provided with cords, chains, and bridles and bits for those occasions when one of the most impertinent of the relaxed should take some liberty to disturb the peace, as usually occurs,[78] which makes it important that all commonly conduct their duties with attention and composure, because doing otherwise leads to a loss of respect for the necessary reverence in the auto-da-fé.

The Manner of a Declaration to Be Made by One of the Relaxed Penitents

23. If one of the relaxed penitents should wish to confess some other thing judicially, the Constable should make it known to the Tribunal. Then one of the Inquisitors should go down to the table in the staging area, where there will be a seat for this respect. Then the said Constable, with the Jailer, will bring the prisoner and force him to his knees so that he may declare what he has to state. After this declaration is seen by the Ordinary and the Consultants they may make an accord if it is convenient to suspend the pronouncement of the sentence and return the prisoner without the insignias of shame to the jail where he will be examined and where justice will be provided. They are then ordered to pronounce it and execute it as the Instructions demand.

Particular Autos-da-fé

24. Other smaller particular autos-da-fé have been made, and in none of them were there more than twelve or twenty persons marched in procession to the Cathedral Church.

In all of them there were no prisoners to be relaxed, and for the same reason they do not customarily take out the standard, nor is there usually an accompaniment. The order that should be kept in them, conferred and accorded between them and the same Viceroy Don Martín Enríquez, has been to make a small scaffold in the major chapel of the Cathedral, with its seats, stage, and awning. At the hour decided upon, the Inquisition leaves its palace, and with its officials and a small accompaniment of particular citizens it heads to the Cathedral. And at that point the Viceroy and his Audiencia leave from the palace and take their accustomed seats in the same form as they do in the other autos-da-fé. And the rest of the city takes its place in the pews, and the Town Council in its chorus. And at one of these autos in which the Archbishop [Pedro] Moya de Contreras[79] was present, he too came from his home and sat in the Tribunal as did the others at the side of the Inquisitors. When there is no prelate, his space is occupied by the Viceroy and the oldest Judge of the Audiencia. The other Judges and officials of the Audiencia are seated based on their antiquity. And the prisoners are placed on a smaller terraced scaffold set apart in the body of the Church, in front of the pulpit, where they do not pass further than a small platform at the entrance where each one is placed when they are to hear their sentence. When the reading of the sentences is over, each one returns just as he came. And in leaving the *auto,* the Viceroy leaves first with his Audiencia and after them the others, with the Inquisitors making the gesture of accompanying him without him permitting.

More Particular Rules concerning Smaller Autos-da-fé

25. This year there will be the need to dispatch several small batches of cases in the Cathedral of no more than six or eight prisoners, for which there is no need to form a formal procession, but rather only the Inquisitors shall go to the Holy Cathedral and take their seats at the section of the epistles, on top of a carpeting without cushions, with the officials of the Holy Office seated on small benches underneath them. Only the Viceroy will attend and not his entire Audiencia [who also do not attend for the reading of the edicts, only the viceroy]. When the prisoners are dispatched with the reading of their sentences, the officials go back to their houses, first the Viceroy, and then shortly after him the Inquisitors, who once again make gestures of wishing to accompany him, and this not being permitted. Several, however, have gone out with him, raising up the edge of his cape until they reached the chorus where they took their leave, exiting by different doors. It has also been the custom to dispatch smaller groups of prisoners in the Convent of Saint Dominic[80] without the Viceroy's assistance or any other procession, nor in any other form, except simply having the sentences solemnly read, as they do in Triana in Seville and in many other Inquisitions in Spain.

All of the practices referred to above in these pages have occurred in this Inquisition of Mexico during the time that I have served in it, from November 4, 1571, until the last part of June 1594, when I left the service of the Holy Office, and in certification of this I sign it.

Pedro de los Ríos,
Inquisition Secretary

DOCUMENT 21

Relation of the Auto-da-fé That Was Celebrated in the City of Mexico in the Major Plaza on the Second Sunday of Advent

Mexico City, December 8, 1596

SOURCE: Archivo General de la Nación, Ramo de Inquisición, vol. 1510, exp. 2, folios 7–12, Lote Riva Palacios, vol. 35, no. 2.

NOTE: This document contains an excellent description of the most common ordering, crimes, and sentences given by the Mexican Inquisition during its major autos-da-fé. The brief summaries of the penitent's crimes and their sentences and punishments reveal not only information concerning the Inquisition's procedures but also many aspects of daily life in the colony of New Spain.

Those Given Penitence for Diverse Crimes

✝

1. *Gonzalo de Salazar,* mestizo, resident of Mexico and native of the said city, tried for having removed several published edicts placed by order of the Holy Office and ordered to be fixed to the doors of the Cathedral, and then for having torn them to pieces. He was condemned to march in the auto-da-fé with a candle and a noose about his neck and to receive one hundred lashes and exile for precisely two years; he should leave the kingdom to comply with his exile within nine days, and if he does not do this, he will be condemned to double the sentence.

2. *Diego de Herédia,* a mestizo, native of the city of Oaxaca, a soldier in California, tried for having taking his hand to a sword in the attempt of freeing a woman from a Familiar of the Holy Office whom he was taking as a prisoner under the order of the local Commissary of the Holy Office, and who now resides in the city of Puebla de los Angeles; as well as for having taken and used a straw and made it a pen and having made ink with which to write letters inside of the jails.[81] He was condemned to be paraded in the auto-da-fé with a candle and noose about his neck; to receive two hundred lashes, one hundred in this city and one hundred in Cholula, where he committed the said crime; and to suffer the sentence of exile from this city and from that of Cholula for precisely three years. He will comply with the sentence of exile within the third day, and if he should break this, he is advised he will serve double the time.

3. *Domingo,* a creole[82] African slave of Gaspar de los Reyes Plata, Jailer of the secret prisons of the Inquisition, convicted of having taken notes and letters from some prisoners to others, and some even outside of the prisons to other people in the city. He was condemned to be paraded in an auto-da-fé with a candle and a noose and to receive two hundred lashes, and he is to be sold outside of this city, where he cannot return for precisely six years, under the penalty of a much harsher punishment.

Blasphemers Who Made an Abjuration *de Levi*

4. *Gaspar de Villafranca*, a young single man, native of the city of Orihuela in the Kingdom of Valencia, tried because, while he was playing cards and losing, with desperation he raised his eyes to heaven and exclaimed: *"It is possible that God exists in heaven, but for me I did not understand that God is in heaven, nor can I believe such a thing."* And having been reprimanded for this, he reaffirmed it, and he said very foul and dishonest words, and he was condemned to be marched in an auto-da-fé with a candle and a gag and bit in his mouth[83] and to make an abjuration *de levi*,[84] and he was also condemned to exile from this city of Mexico for precisely two years. And if he should disobey this he would have the punishment doubled, and that he should leave within three days.

5. *Juan Montes*, African slave of Cristóbal Rodríguez Callejas, hat maker, resident in this city of Mexico, for having renounced God and his Saints. He was condemned to appear in the auto-da-fé with a candle, a noose around his neck, and a gag and bit in his mouth and to give an abjuration *de levi*, with a punishment of one hundred lashes, and that his said master should imprison him for six months, indoctrinating and instructing him in the things of Our Holy Catholic Faith, under the penalty of two hundred pesos for the extraordinary expenses of the Inquisition if this is not complied with.

6. *Pablo Hernández*, creole African slave of Álvaro de Soria, resident of this city Mexico, convicted for renouncing God while he was being whipped by his master. After receiving three or four lashes, he renounced God and his Saints, and because they continued whipping him, he renounced God again and said that, if they continued whipping him, he would renounce him again. He was condemned to appear in the auto-da-fé with a candle, noose, and gag and bit and to give an abjuration *de levi*, as well as to receive one hundred lashes.

7. *Luis*, an African slave, native of Seville, slave of Don Juan de Sayavedra, resident in Mexico, convicted for having renounced God and his saints while he was being whipped, and when reprehended by the people standing present, he once again denied God and Our Lady, continuing in the said blasphemy, repeating it ten times; and he was condemned to appear in the auto-da-fé with a candle, a noose, and a gag and bit, to make an abjuration *de levi*, and to receive two hundred lashes.[85]

8. *Juan Carrasco*, African slave of Juan Vanegas, resident of the city of Puebla de los Angeles, a creole native of the said city, for having renounced God and his saints and having said that he does not know God. He was condemned to appear in the auto-da-fé with a candle, noose, and a gag and bit in his mouth, to make an abjuration *de levi*, and to receive two hundred lashes, one hundred lashes in this city and one hundred lashes in Puebla, where he committed the crime, and his master shall be ordered to have him imprisoned for six months and to not release him, under the penalty of two hundred pesos for the expenses of the Holy Office.

9. *Sebastián Juárez*, Ladino African slave, native of Lisbon, slave to Master Pedro Círujano, resident of Mexico, convicted because when he was being whipped by his master, having been stripped naked for this punishment, he had renounced God and his Saints two times. He was condemned to appear in the auto-da-fé with a candle, noose, and a gag and bit, to make an abjuration *de levi*, and to receive two hundred lashes,

and his master was ordered to imprison him for six months and not to release him, under the penalty of two hundred pesos for the expenses of the Holy Office.

10. *Francisco Jasso,* mulatto slave of Martín de Jasso, resident of Mexico, native of Villa de Jeva in Andalucia, convicted for having renounced many times God and his blessed mother the Virgin Mary, and his saints, saying that it was better to be a monkey than to be a Christian and that he hoped to be burned so that he would not have to live in this world and that he was already proscribed to go to hell. And reprehending him, he went on again to deny God and to state that he thought it was better to believe in the religion of Mohammad than in the evangelical law, and he then spit on a crucifix six times and has done many other sacrilegious things, pretending afterward to be a Jew and a Moor, thinking in this way to avoid by this means several of the serious crimes for which he was imprisoned in the Royal Jail and sentenced for by the Judges of the criminal court. He was condemned to appear in the auto-da-fé with a candle, noose, and a gag and bit, to make an abjuration *de levi,* and to receive two hundred lashes, and then be returned to the Royal criminal jail where he was a prisoner before he was brought to this Holy Office, so that the Criminal judges can execute his sentence.

Fornicators

11. *Master Domingo Nicolás,* Constable and artillery officer on the ship San Jorge, son of the Master Lorenzo Grifo, native of the city of Antújar in the province of Macedonia, for having said that it was not a sin to have carnal access with a single woman if she was not married and, besides this, for having committed the sin of sodomy which was an abominable sin. He was condemned to appear in the auto-da-fé with a candle, to make an abjuration *de levi,* and to suffer exile from all of the Indies for the time and space of ten years. He should embark on his exile on the first fleet that leaves for Spain.

12. *Sebastián Caracho,* a single young Portuguese man, apprentice tailor of tapestries, resident in Mexico, native of the village of Munchig in Algarve, for having said that it was not a mortal sin, but rather a venial sin, to have carnal access to a woman who gave her body freely if she was asked for it. He was condemned to appear in the auto-da-fé with a candle and to make an abjuration *de levi,* and he was ordered to be raised by a good religious person who can teach him the Christian doctrine and to instruct him in the things of our Holy Catholic faith.

Those Guilty of Sorcery and Witchcraft

13. *Magdalena Hernández,* widow, resident of Veracruz, native of the city of Malaga, in the kingdoms of Castile, for having used sorcery and witchcraft and other superstitions invoking the name of God and his saints, having used prayers to commit vile and dishonest acts, having made a consecrated altar so that men would come to love certain women, having used several consecrated words with one of her lovers so that he would love her better,[86] having said the prayer of the star[87] and that of Santa Marta[88] and that of the souls, and having made conjures with Barabbas and with Satan. She was condemned to appear in an auto-da-fé with a candle, a *coroza,* and a *sanbenito* with a noose around her neck, to make an abjuration *de levi,* to receive two hundred lashes, and to be exiled from this city and that of Veracruz for the period of

precisely six years, and that she should abstain from using such superstitions, under the penalty that, if she did not, she would be more severely punished.

14. *Inés de Villalobos,* resident of Veracruz, wife of Bartolomé García, carpenter, native of this city of Mexico, for having used sorcery and superstitions and conjures for vile, unchaste, and dishonest things; for mixing holy and saintly things and the names of God and his saints; for saying the prayer of Santa Marta; for blessing the water in a cup for the said effects; and for invoking the name of the Father, Son, and Holy Ghost. She was condemned to appear in the auto-da-fé with a candle, *coroza,* and a *sanbenito,* to make an abjuration *de levi,* to pay a fine of one hundred pesos for the expenses of the Holy Office, and to be exiled from the city of Veracruz for precisely the time of one year. The said exile she will began within nine days, and she shall not disobey this or the punishment will be doubled (fig. 11).

15. *Lucía de Alcalá,* widow, and wife of the deceased Coachman Juan García, resident of Veracruz, for having used sorcery and cast fortunes; having blessed the water in a cup in the name of the Father, Son, and Holy Ghost; looking into it and seeing a pregnant woman; and doing this for vile, unchaste, and dishonest means in order to know more about a man with whom she dealt. She was condemned to appear in an auto-da-fé with a candle, *coroza,* and *sanbenito,* to make an abjuration [*de levi*], to pay a fine of four hundred pesos for the extraordinary expenses of the Holy Office, and to suffer exile from this city and that of Veracruz for precisely two years (fig. 14).

16. *Catalina Ortiz,* wife of Juan Alemán, a resident of the city of Veracruz and native of Gerona in the region of Seville, for having used sorcery and witchcraft, having believed in her own power to know future things that depend on the free will of men, for unchaste and dishonest things, for mixing the names of God and his saints, for saying prayers and casting lots and fortunes with dried beans and others by means of the cup, and for naming the three persons of the Holy Trinity. She was condemned to appear in an auto-da-fé with a candle, *coroza,* and *sanbenito,* to make an abjuration *de levi,* to pay a fine of three hundred pesos for the extraordinary expenses of the Holy Office, and to suffer exile from this city and that of Veracruz for precisely one year.

17. *Catalina Bermúdez,* wife of Baltasar de Espinosa, barber, and a resident in the city of Veracruz, native of Seville, for having used sorcery and superstitions and having cast lots and fortunes for evil ends and unchaste acts; for naming the Father, Son, and Holy Ghost and blessing a cup of water to see in it what she pretended to know; for praying the prayers of San Julián[89] and Saint Erasmus and saying other conjures, naming Saint Peter and Saint Paul, and Saint James, and God and the Holy Mary; and for casting fortunes in the sea with an image of Saint Julián, according to which there were good omens if the sea took them away and an even better omen if the sea sent them back. She did this in order to know if her Husband had other women. She was condemned to appear in an auto-da-fé with a candle, *coroza,* and *sanbenito,* to make an abjuration *de levi,* to pay a fine of two hundred pesos for the extraordinary expenses of the Holy Office, and to suffer exile from this city and that of Veracruz for precisely six years.

18. *Juana Pérez,* wife of Sebastián de Luenda, tailor, resident of the city of Mexico, native of Seville, for having used sorcery and superstitions and having baptized water in the

name of the Father, Son, and Holy Ghost in order to use it to tell fortunes; for pretending to know things yet to come; and for asking if a certain person she dealt with would marry her. She was condemned to appear in an auto-da-fé with a candle, *coroza,* and *sanbenito,* to make an abjuration *de levi,* to pay a fine of four hundred pesos for the extraordinary expenses of the Holy Office, and to suffer exile from this city and ten leagues around for precisely two years.

19. *Ana de Herrera,* widow and wife of the late Cristóbal Núñez de la Jurada, Scribe in the city of Veracruz, and resident there, native of Mexico, for having used sorcery and superstitions and having cast lots and made conjures for unchaste and dishonest things, for mixing divine and holy things, for saying the name of God and his saints and the persons of the Holy Trinity, and for blessing a cup of water where she predicted fortunes so that a man she knew would love her well and in order to know if he was to marry her or not. She was condemned to appear in the auto-da-fé with a candle, a noose, and a *coroza,* and *sanbenito,* to make an abjuration *de levi,* to pay a fine of four hundred pesos for the extraordinary expenses of the Holy Office, and to be exiled from Mexico and Veracruz for two years.

Those Guilty of Having Been Married Two Times

20. *Bernabé Galán,* native of Almodóvar del Campo, in the kingdoms of Castile, resident of the village of Izúcar in the Bishopric of Tlaxcala, for having been married a second time while his first wife was alive. He was condemned to appear in the auto-da-fé with a candle, noose, a *coroza,* and *sanbenito,* to make an abjuration *de levi,* and to receive one hundred lashes and four years in the galleys without a salary.

21. *Francisca López,* mulatta, native of Mexico, convicted because she married a second time while her first husband was still alive. She was condemned to appear in the auto-da-fé with a candle, noose, a *coroza,* and *sanbenito,* to make an abjuration *de Levi,* and to receive two hundred lashes and exile from Mexico and six leagues around it for three years.

22. *Juana Agustina,* mulatta, native of the village of Guaxacatlan and its mines in the bishopric of Guadalajara, because she married for a second time while her first husband was alive. She was condemned to appear in the auto-da-fé with a candle, noose, a *coroza,* and *sanbenito,* to make an abjuration *de levi,* and to receive one hundred lashes and exile for precisely one year from the mines where she married for the second time, and she is to be secluded in the prison for women called Santa Mónica[90] in Mexico.

Those Guilty of Being Accomplices [*Fautores*]

23. *Francisco Rodríguez,* a single young Portuguese boy, native of San Vicente de Abreu in the Kingdom of Portugal, for suspicion of covering up and hiding those who are in observance of the Law of Moses and for being an accomplice of heretics. He was condemned to appear in the auto-da-fé with a candle and a noose, to make an abjuration *de levi,* and to receive one hundred lashes and two years' exile from Mexico.

24. *Gerónimo Rodríguez,* Portuguese, a resident of the city of Puebla de los Angeles, and a native of San Vicente de Abreu in Portugal, convicted of being an accomplice to Judaizing heretics and for having received and covered up persons who maintained the Law of Moses, whom the Holy Office had ordered to be arrested. He was condemned to appear

in the auto-da-fé with a candle, to make an abjuration *de levi,* and to pay a fine of four hundred pesos of common gold for the extraordinary expenses of the Holy Office.

Those to Make an Abjuration *de Vehementi*

25. *Ana Báez,* native of the city of Seville, wife of Jorge Álvarez, also Portuguese, and a resident of Mexico, descendant of Jews who were testified against for having guarded and observed the Law of Moses. She was condemned to appear in the auto-da-fé with a candle, to make an abjuration *de vehementi,* and then to be given back all of her goods that had been sequestered during the time of her apprehension (fig. 14).

Those to Be Reconciled for Guarding and Observing the Dead Law of Moses

26. *Víolante Rodríguez,* Portuguese, native of the Village of Salceda in Portugal, widow of Símon González, of the generation of Jews, for having continued to guard the Law of Moses, its rites, and ceremonies, for waiting for the return of the Messiah, and for having covered up heretics whom she hid from justice. She was sentenced to appear in the auto-da-fé with a candle and a habit or the *sanbenito* and to perpetual imprisonment with the confiscation of her goods.

27. *Léonor Díaz,* wife of Francisco Rodríguez Deza, Portuguese, native of Seville and resident of Mexico, daughter of Diego López Regalón, convicted for having continued to guard the Laws of Moses, its rites, and ceremonies, for waiting for the return of the Messiah, for fasting on the Great day that they Jews call the day of Penitence,[91] and for not eating pig fat or any other pork. She was sentenced to appear in the auto-da-fé with a candle and a habit or the *sanbenito* and to be placed in the perpetual prison for six years with the confiscation of her goods.

28. *Isabel Rodríguez,* daughter of the said Víolante Rodríguez, wife of Manuel Díaz who was relaxed in person in this auto-da-fé, native of Salceda in Portugal, of the generation of new Christians, descendants of Jews, for having continued to guard the Law of Moses, its rites, and ceremonies and for waiting for the return of the Messiah. She was sentenced to appear in the auto-da-fé with a candle and a habit or the *sanbenito* and to perpetual imprisonment with the confiscation of her goods.

29. *Ana López,* the wife of Diego López Regalón, native of Fondón in Portugal, for having continued to guard the Law of Moses, its rites, and ceremonies, for waiting for the return of the Messiah, and for having fasted on the great day the Jews call the Day of Penitence. She was sentenced to appear in the auto-da-fé with a candle and a habit or the *sanbenito* and to perpetual imprisonment with the confiscation of her goods.

30. *Constanza Rodríguez,* wife of Sebastián Rodríguez, Portuguese native of Seville, resident in Mexico, for having continued to guard the Law of Moses, its rites, and ceremonies, for waiting for the return of the Messiah and not believing Our Redeemer Jesus Christ was the same, and for her bad confession. She was sentenced to appear in the auto-da-fé with a candle and a habit or the *sanbenito* and to perpetual imprisonment with the confiscation of her goods.

31. *Clara Enríquez,* Portuguese, wife of Francisco Méndez, Portuguese Merchant, resident in Mexico, native of Fondón in Portugal, of the caste and generation of the New

Christians, descendants of Jews, for having continued to guard the Law of Moses, its rites, and ceremonies, for waiting for the return of the Messiah and not believing him to be Our Redeemer Jesus Christ, and for having fasted the fasts of the said law and celebrating the Sabbaths and Passover. She was sentenced to appear in the auto-da-fé with a candle and a habit or the *sanbenito* and to perpetual imprisonment with the confiscation of her goods.

32. *Justa Méndez,* young virgin daughter of the said Clara Enríquez and the said Francisco Méndez her husband, native of Seville, resident in Mexico, for having continued to guard the Law of Moses, its rites, and ceremonies, for waiting for the return of the Messiah, and for having covered up heretics whom she hid from justice. She was sentenced to appear in the auto-da-fé with a candle and a habit or the *sanbenito* and to perpetual imprisonment with the confiscation of her goods.

33. *Catalina Enríquez,* native of Seville, daughter of Simón Pavía, deceased, and of Beatríz Enríquez Lapavía who was relaxed in this auto-da-fé in person for guarding the Law of Moses, Portuguese, of the caste and generation of the New Christians descendants of Jews, wife of Manuel de Lucena, resident of the mines of Pachuca also relaxed in person in this auto-da-fé for the guarding of the Law of Moses, convicted for having continued to guard the laws of Moses, its rites, and ceremonies, and for using its prayers; for not eating bacon, pig fat, or any other pork; for guarding the Sabbaths and Passover and other feasts of the said Law; and for waiting for the return of the Messiah and not believing Our Redeemer Jesus Christ was the same. She was sentenced to appear in the auto-da-fé with a candle and a habit or the *sanbenito* and to perpetual imprisonment with the confiscation of her goods.

34. *Sebastián de la Peña,* a single young boy, also known by the name of Sabastián Cardoso, native of San Juan de Pesquera in the Bishopric of Portugal, of the caste and generation of the New Christians whose descendants were Jews, for having continued to guard the Law of Moses and to believe in its rites and ceremonies, along with those above. He was sentenced to appear in the auto-da-fé with a candle and a habit or the *sanbenito* and to perpetual imprisonment with the confiscation of his goods. The first two years of his imprisonment he should be placed in whatever monastery that may be selected, and in it he should be entrusted to a religious person who can instruct him in the things of Our Holy Catholic faith.

35. *Sebastián Rodríguez,* Portuguese, married to Constanza Rodríguez, native of the village of San Vicente in Portugal, for having continued to guard the Law of Moses, its rites, and ceremonies, for having made the fast of Queen Esther,[92] and for waiting for the return of the Messiah. He was condemned to appear in the auto-da-fé with a candle and a habit or the *sanbenito* and to perpetual imprisonment with the confiscation of his goods.

36. *Diego Díaz Nieto,* single young Portuguese boy, native of the city of Oporto, for having continued to guard the Law of Moses and for having awaited the Messiah like the others. He was sentenced to appear in the auto-da-fé with a candle and a habit or the *sanbenito* and to imprisonment for one year and the confiscation of his goods.

37. *Pedro Rodríguez,* Portuguese, native of Fondón in the bishopric of La Guardia, of the caste and generation of the New Christians whose descendants were Jews, for having

continued to guard the Law of Moses and to believe in its rites and ceremonies, along with those above. He was condemned for his bad confessions to wear a habit or the *sanbenito* and to perpetual imprisonment, along with a sentence of four years in the galleys as a rower without a salary. The *sanbenito* should be taken off of him when he reaches the sea, and once his term is up he should once again wear the *sanbenito* and comply with the rest of his imprisonment in the perpetual jails in the city of Seville and also the confiscation of his goods.

38. *Marco Antonio,* a single young master at arms, native of Castelo Blanco in Portugal, of the caste and generation of the New Christians whose descendants were Jews, resident in the town of Trinidad in the province of Guatemala, for being a Judaizing heretic like all the others and for his slight confessions. He was condemned to appear in the auto-da-fé with a candle and a habit or the *sanbenito* and to perpetual imprisonment with the confiscation of his goods.

39. *Domingo Cuello,* native of the village of Almofala in Portugal, in the Bishopic of Amego, an itinerant cattle trader, of the caste and generation of the New Christians whose descendants were Jews, for being a Judaizing heretic along with the others. He was condemned to appear in the auto-da-fé with a candle and a habit or the *sanbenito* and to perpetual imprisonment with the confiscation of his goods.

40. *Jorge Laís,* native of the village of San Vicente in Portugal, resident in the city of Puebla de los Angeles, a merchant and trader, of the caste and generation of the New Christians whose descendants were Jews, for having continued to guard the Law of Moses and to believe in its rites and ceremonies. He was condemned to appear in the auto-da-fé with a candle and a habit or the *sanbenito* and to imprisonment for four years wherever he should be sent, along with the confiscation of his goods.

41. *Manuel Rodríguez,* single young man, native of Fondón, jurisdiction of the village of Cubillana in the Bishopric of La Guardia in Portugal, a Merchant and trader, for having guarded the Law of Moses and its rites and ceremonies. He was condemned to appear in the auto-da-fé with a candle and a habit or the *sanbenito* and to imprisonment for six years and the confiscation of his goods.

42. *Pedro Enríquez,* young single Portuguese man, son of Simón Pavía and of Beatriz la Pavía both relaxed in person in this auto-da-fé, a native of the city of Seville, of the caste and generation of the New Christians whose descendants were Jews, for having continued to guard the Law of Moses and to believe in its rites and ceremonies and having kept the Sabbath; having placed clean linens on the bed on Fridays in the evening; for having fasted the fasts of the said Law, including that of Passover; and especially for doing some of these said things in the jails of the Holy Office after having stated and sworn that he was a convert, for making holes in the walls of the said prisons, and for having communicated with other prisoners and attempting to hide all of this. He was condemned to appear in the auto-da-fé with a candle, a noose about his neck, and a habit or the *sanbenito;* to perpetual imprisonment and to one hundred lashes and the confiscation of his goods; and to five years in the galleys as a rower without a salary. And it is ordered that his *sanbenito* should be removed when he reaches the water, and after the said five years of imprisonment, he should put it on again and finish the rest of his sentence in the perpetual jails of the Inquisition of Seville.

43. *Manuel Francisco del Belmonte,* native of the village of Cubillana in the Kingdom of Portugal, merchant in the mines at Cultepeque and resident there, for having continued to guard the Law of Moses and to believe in its rites and ceremonies, for having said the prayers and stories that reproved Christ Our Lord, for having covered up heretics who observed the said laws of Moses, and for his bad confessions. He was condemned to appear in the auto-da-fé with a candle, a noose about his neck, and a habit or the *sanbenito* and to imprisonment for three years and the confiscation of his goods, as well as one hundred lashes in the form of justice.

44. *Diego López,* native of the village of San Vicente de Abreu in Portugal, a single young man, of the caste and generation of the New Christians whose descendants were Jews, for having continued to guard the Law of Moses and to believe in its rites, for saying the prayers of the said law facing to the east, for having communicated with other prisoners while in the jails of the Holy Office, and for varying his confessions. He was condemned to appear in the auto-da-fé with a candle, a noose about his neck, and a habit or the *sanbenito* and to imprisonment for three years and the confiscation of his goods as well as one hundred lashes in the form of justice.

45. *Manuel Gómez Navarro,* native of San Martín de Trebejos, in the Kingdom of Portugal, a young single trader in the mines of Xichu, for having for having continued to guard the Law of Moses and to believe in its rites, for using clean clothing on Fridays in the night and changing his bed linens then, for praying the prayers while facing east, for having fasted and awaited the promised Messiah, for denying that it was Our Lord and Redeemer Jesus Christ and saying that he was no more than a false Prophet and that for this he had been crucified, for denying the Holy Trinity and saying that it was a bunch of lies and that the Holy Sacrament was a piece of dough, and for other blasphemies, and he had procured to teach the said Law of Moses to other persons, tricking the Holy Office, stating that he was a convert, maintaining the same Law of Moses even while he was in the jails of the Holy Office, and communicating with other prisoners for this. He was condemned to appear in the auto-da-fé with a candle, a noose about his neck, and a habit or the *sanbenito* and to perpetual imprisonment and the confiscation of his goods, as well as two hundred lashes in the form of justice and six years' service in the galleys as a rower. His *sanbenito* should be removed from him when he leaves land, and replaced when he returns, and then he should be placed in the perpetual prison of the Holy Office in Seville.[93]

46. *Jorge Álvarez,* son of Manuel Álvarez, native of Fondón in the bishopric of La Guardia in Portugal, a merchant and trader, resident of Mexico, for having continued to guard the Law of Moses and to believe in its rites and ceremonies. He was condemned to appear in the auto-da-fé with a candle, a noose about his neck, and a habit or the *sanbenito* and to perpetual imprisonment and the confiscation of his goods as well as one hundred lashes for his bad confessions.

47. *Duarte Rodríguez,* a young man, native of Villana in the Bishopric of La Guardia, in the Kingdom of Portugal, trader and resident in Mexico, of the caste and generation of the New Christians whose descendants were Jews, for having continued to guard the Law of Moses and to believe in its rites and ceremonies. He was condemned to appear in the auto-da-fé with a candle, a noose about his neck, and a habit or the *sanbenito*

and to perpetual imprisonment and the confiscation of his goods, and for having communicated with other prisoners in the jails, he will receive as well one hundred lashes in the form of justice.

48. *Andrés Rodríguez,* young single man, native of the said village of Fondón in Portugal, merchant and trader, resident in the city of Texcoco, for having continued to guard the Law of Moses and to believe in its rites, for changing the linens on his bed on Friday at night and wearing his best clothes on Saturday, also for continuing to practice the said Law of Moses even after he confessed and begged for mercy from the Holy Office, for having given poor confessions, for lifting false testimony against people who he claimed were Jews and who were not, and for having communicated with other prisoners in the said prisons. He was condemned to appear in the auto-da-fé with a candle, a noose about his neck, and a habit or the *sanbenito* and to face perpetual imprisonment and the confiscation of his goods. He is also to receive two hundred lashes and five years' hard labor as a rower in the galleys, removing his *sanbenito* when he reached the sea, and replacing it when he returned. He should then serve out the rest of his sentence in the secret prisons of the Holy Office in Seville.

49. *Daniel Benítez,* tailor, native of the city of Ambure [Hamburg] in the States of Lower Germany, resident as a soldier in the fort of San Juan de Ulua, for suspicions of heresy and belief in the sect of Martin Luther and afterward based on his belief in the teachings of one of his companions, for having believed and observed the Law of Moses and their rites and ceremonies, and for awaiting the promised Messiah. He was condemned to appear in the auto-da-fé with a candle, a noose about his neck, and a habit or the *sanbenito* and to perpetual imprisonment and the confiscation of his goods. The first two years of his imprisonment he should be secluded in a monastery, where he may be instructed in the things of Our Holy Catholic faith. And for having communicated in the prisons and written notes and messages, he shall receive two hundred lashes in form of justice.

All of these above-mentioned reconciled penitents made an abjuration de vehementi of the errors that they were convicted of making.

Those to Be Relaxed in Person

50. *Manuel Díaz,* Merchant, resident of Mexico, native of the said village of Fondón in Portugal, of the caste and generation of the New Christians whose descendants were Jews, for having continued to guard the Law of Moses and to believe in its rites and ceremonies and for being convinced in them, with a large number of witnesses against him, and for having been impenitent and having denied the accusations. He was condemned to appear in the auto-da-fé with a candle, a *coroza,* and *sanbenito* with the insignias of fire,[94] to be relaxed in person to the justices and secular arm of government, and to suffer the confiscation of his goods (fig. 3).

51. *Beatríz Enríquez La Pavía,* wife of the deceased Simón Pavía, a resident of Mexico, native of the said village of Fondón in Portugal, of the caste and generation of the New Christians whose descendants were Jews, for having continued to guard the Law of Moses and

to believe in its rites and ceremonies and for being convinced in them, with a large number of witnesses against her, and for having been impenitent and having denied the accusations. She was condemned to appear in the auto-da-fé with a candle, a *coroza*, and *sanbenito* with the insignias of fire, to be relaxed in person to the justices and secular arm of government, and to suffer the confiscation of her goods, and be burned alive (fig. 14).

52. *Diego Enríquez*, a single young man, son of the said Beatríz Enríquez, convicted of being a relapsed heretic in the Law of Moses, and its rites, and ceremonies and for being an impenitent and consummate heretic, he was condemned to be relaxed in person and handed over to the justices and secular arm of government and to suffer the confiscation of his goods.

53. *Manuel de Lucena*, native of the village of San Vicente de Abreu in the bishopric of La Guardia in Portugal, resident and Merchant in the mines of Pachuca, of the caste and generation of the New Christians whose descendants were Jews, son-in-law of the said Beatríz Enríquez and brother-in-law of the said Diego Enríquez, for having continued to guard the Law of Moses and to believe in its rites and ceremonies, for awaiting the promised Messiah, for keeping the Sabbath and Passover of the said Law of Moses, for fasting the fasts, for teaching and dogmatizing the said Law of Moses to many persons and having done great harm with his teachings, for having said many blasphemies against our Savior Jesus Christ, for having fulfilled his doubts, and then for having returned to the said belief in the Law of Moses, in which he said he wished to die, even though he faked being converted in order to deceive the Holy Office. He was condemned to appear in the auto-da-fé with a candle, a *coroza*, and *sanbenito* with the insignias of fire, to be relaxed in person to the justices and secular arm of government, and to suffer the confiscation of his goods as a heretical Judaizer and teacher of the said Law of Moses. As an impenitent heretic who denied confession, he was burned alive.

54. *Doña Francisca de Carvajal*, a widow, wife of the deceased Francisco Rodríguez de Matos, native of Benavente in the kingdoms of Castile, who was burned in statute and whose bones were burned, of the caste and generation of the New Christians whose descendants were Jews, for having continued to guard the Law of Moses, and believed in its rites, and ceremonies and for relapsing into them. She remained an impenitent and was condemned to appear in the auto-da-fé with a candle, a *coroza*, and *sanbenito* with the insignias of fire, and to be relaxed in person to the justices and secular arm of government, and to suffer the confiscation of her goods.

55. *Doña Isabel Rodríguez de Andrade*, daughter of the said Francisco Rodríguez de Matos, and of the said Doña Francisca Carvajal, widow and wife of the deceased Gabriel de Herrera, native of Benavente, who was reconciled by this Holy Office in the year 1590 for guarding and observing the Law of Moses, and now having relapsing into them, she remains impenitent and was condemned to appear in the auto-da-fé and to be relaxed in person to the justices and secular arm of government and to suffer the confiscation of her goods.

56. *Doña Catalina de León y de la Cueva*, daughter of the said Francisco Rodríguez de Matos, and the said Doña Francisca de Carvajal, sister of the said Doña Isabel Rodríguez de Andrade, wife of Antonio Díaz de Cáceres, Portuguese, resident in Mexico,

reconciled by this Holy Office in the year of 1590 for guarding and observing the said Law of Moses and its rites and ceremonies, convicted now for relapsing into the said beliefs in the said Law of Moses. She had been impenitent when she had been reconciled the first time, and now, imprisoned for this again, she is condemned to appear in the auto-da-fé and to be relaxed in person and handed over to the justices and secular arm of government and to suffer the confiscation of her goods.

57. *Doña Leonor de Carvajal,* wife of Jorge de Almeyda, Portuguese, resident of Mexico, and daughter and sister of the above mentioned, who was also reconciled by this Holy Office in the year 1590 for having guarded and observed the said Law of Moses and its rites and ceremonies. Now she is convicted for relapsing in it, and as an impenitent, she was condemned to appear in the auto-da-fé and to be relaxed in person and handed over to the justices and secular arm of government and to suffer the confiscation of her goods.

58. *Luis de Carvajal,*[95] a single young man, son and brother of the above mentioned, was reconciled by this Holy Office in the year 1590 for guarding and observing the said Law of Moses and its rites and ceremonies. Now he is convicted for relapsing in the said law, for dogmatizing and teaching them, and for having written books and prayers in the said Law. An impenitent, pertinacious, and consummate heretic, he was condemned to appear in the auto-da-fé with a *coroza* and *sanbenito* with the insignia of the flames and to be gagged with a bit due to his many blasphemies against Jesus Christ Our Lord. He was relaxed in person and handed over to the justices and secular arm of government, and he was ordered to be burned alive, with the confiscation of his goods. Once they led him to be burned alive, he gave signs of willingness to convert, and he died instead, strangled.

Those Who Are Deceased and Who Are to Be Relaxed in Effigy

59. *Domingo Rodríguez,* a reconciled Portuguese man who was tried in this Holy Office for guarding and observing the Law of Moses, its rites and ceremonies, keeping the Passover and fasts. He was a young man who was a deceased resident of Mexico, against whose memory and fame a trial was conducted after his reconciliation for having been lax in his confessions that he made at the time of his first imprisonment. For notable deeds that cannot be forgotten and for having died in the belief of the said Law of Moses, he was relaxed in effigy and his bones were taken out of the sacred place where they had been buried and handed over with the statue and effigy to the justices and secular arm. They were burned, and his goods were confiscated.

60. *Antonio Rodríguez,* Portuguese, native of the Village of San Vicente de Abreu in Portugal in the Bishopric of La Guardia, now deceased, against whose memory and fame a trial was conducted for having guarded and observed the Law of Moses, its rites and ceremonies. He was condemned to be relaxed in effigy to the justices and secular arm. His remains were burned, and his goods were confiscated.

Those Who Are to Be Relaxed and Are Absent and Who Are to Be Burned in Effigy

61. *Francisco Jorge,* Portuguese, resident and married in the village of Benavente in the Kingdoms of Castile, resident in the mines of Taxco, an absent fugitive, for a convic-

tion as a Judaizing heretic and observer of the Law of Moses, relaxed in effigy and handed over to the justices and secular arm to be burned. His goods were confiscated in legal form.

62. *Fabián Granados,* Portuguese, native of Lamego in the Kingdom of Portugal, resident in Mexico, absent and fugitive, for guarding and observing the Law of Moses, relaxed in effigy to the justices and secular arm, and his goods confiscated.

63. *Antonio López,* Portuguese, native of Orico in the Kingdom of Portugal, resident in Mexico, absent and fugitive, for the guarding and observance of the Law of Moses, relaxed in effigy with the confiscation of his goods.

64. *Doña Isabel Pérez,* wife of Licenciado Manuel de Morales, absent and fugitive, for the guarding and observance of the Law of Moses, relaxed in effigy to the justices and secular arm, and her goods confiscated.

65. *Antonio López de Morales,* absent and fugitive, for the guarding and observance of the Law of Moses, relaxed in effigy with the confiscation of his goods.

66. *Manuel Rodríguez de Matos,* a Portuguese young man, native of Medina de Campos, in the kingdom of Castile, son of the said Francisco Rodríguez de Matos, relaxed in effigy by this Holy Office, and of Doña Francisca Carvajal, relaxed in person in this present auto-da-fé, and brother of the said Luis de Carvajal, doña Isabel Rodríguez de Andrade, doña Catalina de León y de la Cueva, y doña Leonor, all relaxed in person, who is absent and fugitive, for the guarding and observance of the Law of Moses, relaxed in effigy with the confiscation of his goods.

67. *Francisco Báez,* a Portuguese young man, resident of the mines of Pachuca, absent and fugitive, for the guarding and observance of the Law of Moses, relaxed in effigy with the confiscation of his goods.

DOCUMENT 22
Relation of the Preliminary Preparations for the Small Public Particular Auto-da-fé Celebrated with Thirteen Prisoners in the Church and Convent of Santo Domingo on June 1, 1783

Mexico City, May–June 1783

SOURCE: Archivo General de la Nación, Ramo de Inquisición, vol. 1510, exp. 22, folios 215–41, Lote Riva Palacios, vol. 35, no. 22.

NOTE: The Inquisition sponsored many smaller, routine celebrations called *autos particulares,* or *autillos* (small autos-da-fé), which would occur frequently throughout the years whenever the inquisitors collected and convicted a critical mass of anywhere between ten and twenty suspected heretics. In this way, the Inquisition was able to publicly punish lesser criminals more often throughout the years at a much lower cost. In comparison with these smaller *autillos,* the larger public autos-da-fé were much more lavishly decorated, better attended, and much more costly.

Inquisitorial Order, May 26, 1783

✝

In the Holy Office of the Inquisition in Mexico, on the 26th of May 1783, while in audience during the morning, the Lord Inquisitors Dr. Juan de Mier y Villar, and Don Antonio Bergosa y Jordán, stated: That in addition to having concluded and sentenced thirteen cases against several prisoners in the secret prisons of this Holy Office, including Josef Joaquín or Josef de Jesús María Martínez, for having given confession without being ordained; Josef María de Esparza y Escobar, for heretical blasphemy; Josef Antonio Trinidad, condemned for having extracted from his mouth a sacred prayer and then having wrapped it up in a paper that contained love poems; Francisco Téllez Girón, for heretical propositions; Juan Gutiérrez, for having made his second escape from the distant mission presidio where he had been condemned for the previous crime of polygamy; Manuel Payés y Mora, for celebrating mass without Holy Orders; and the cases against Josef Lázaro del Castillo, Juan Eusebio de Luna, or Laureano González, Josef Anastasio Zarasúa, Santiago Pantaleón Contreras Estrada y Silva, María Josefa Sayavedra, María de la Encarnación Taváres, and María Gertrudis, by the evil name of Mocha, Martínez, all for the crimes of polygamy.

And having conferred concerning the date on which to pronounce their said sentences, they decided to order and then ordered that a special particular auto-da-fé should be held in the Church and Imperial Convent of Saint Dominic on the coming 1st of June in the accustomed form, and in order to comply with this they give the necessary orders to the Messenger and the Provider/Overseer of this Holy Office with the list of the numbers of prisoners so that they can respectively provide for the insignias and vestments necessary. And so that everything should be executed in the style and manner necessary, the Secretary Don Juan Nicolás Abad will go this coming Wednesday and give notice from this Tribunal to his Excellency the Viceroy, letting him know the date selected for the auto and that the hour of its commencement will be seven o'clock in the morning, so that if His Excellency wishes to attend, he may sit behind the curtain that is to be provided for in the construction of the stands for the auto according to the proper manner. And also they order that the Reverend Father Prior of Saint Dominic should be given the same notice, so that he may select a religious friar to say the mass, and the sacristan of the Church of Saint Dominic should be ordered to have the church unoccupied. The Treasurer should also be notified of the date of the auto so that he can make the preparations in proper style. The Master Laborer should be notified to place the wooden stands and bleachers and to construct the pulpit and the benches for the ministers of the Holy Office. And the Messenger of the Holy Office should notify on this coming Wednesday that all of the qualified ministers should come gathered on Sunday at the entranceway to the Tribunal at six o'clock in the morning, and at the following Monday at eight o'clock. Those who are not ecclesiastics (i.e., the Familiars) should come dressed in their finest clothing and mounted on horseback, in order to assist and accompany the execution of the sentences, all of which they will execute and comply with under the penalty of fifty pesos for the extraordinary expenses of this Holy Office, as it is that they are irremissibly obliged to attend.

Dr. Mier

Dr. Bergosa

D. Santiago Martínez Rincón, Secretary

And later, while in Audience during the morning, the said Inquisitors ordered that the Reverend Father Prior of the convent of Santo Domingo be called forth,[96] and having entered, they presented him with their orders concerning what he had to do and have disposed of for the coming Sunday, 1st of June, concerning what had been ordered in the previous document. And the Reverend Father Prior responded that he now was informed and that the Tribunal would be served well in what he could provide.

So that it is made known I sign it.

Martínez

On the same day the orders and news were given to the said Provider, Messenger, and Treasurer, concerning what pertained to them. And on May 27, 1783, the messenger was given the second order to bring all of the ministers and familiars etc.

So that it is made known I sign it.

Martínez

Order Given to Don Vicente de las Heras, Treasurer of this Holy Office, May 26, 1783

✝

The Tribunal by means of its order today, directed that on the following Sunday, the 1st of June, there should be celebrated a public auto-da-fé in the Church of Saint Dominic in this court, and we order that you should provide for a lunch in the same form that has been accustomed on other similar occasions, to be held on the morning of that said day. Your Mercy should also provide for the Soldiers and ministers of the executions of the sentences what is necessary for their offices, and also bear the cost of constructing the benches and bleachers which are accustomed to be built in similar functions. All of this has been provided for by the order of the said Tribunal so that it should be complied with.

Given in the Chamber of the secret, May 26, 1783

D. Santiago Martínez Rincón, Secretary

Order Given to the Messenger of the Holy Office, Don Andrés López Barba, to Prepare the Vestments and Other Insignia for the Prisoners to Be Paraded in the Public Auto-da-fé, May 26, 1783

✝

It is ordered that the Messenger of this Holy Office in compliance with this order should have prepared for the coming Sunday, the 1st of June, all of the corresponding *corozas*, nooses, and candles for prisoners numbered 6, 7, 10, 11, 17, 18, and 20, who are being made to make penitence for being married two times, and for prisoner number 4 for having confessed people without Holy Orders; and the same items, as well as the vestments and a metal bit or gag, for prisoner number 5 for blasphemy; also a similar bit for prisoner number 9 for having uttered a sacred prayer in vain, as well as for prisoner number 11 for heretical propositions, for prisoner number 15 for having made his second escape from his *presidio,* and for prisoner number 19 for celebrating mass without Holy Orders. All of this was communicated by order of this Holy Tribunal.

Given in the Chamber of the secret, May 26, 1783
D. Santiago Martínez Rincón, Secretary

Order Given to the Provider/Overseer of the Holy Office to Order the Making of the *Sanbenitos* and Other Vestments Needed for the Public Auto-da-fé, May 26, 1783

✝

It is ordered that the Provider/Overseer of this Holy Office should order the making of the *sanbenitos* and other vestments needed for the procession of the auto-da-fé for the coming Sunday, the 1st of June, especially the garments for the prisoners numbered 4, 5, 6, 7, 9, 10, 11, 12, 15, 17, 18, 19, and 20, all of them to be labeled with the insignia with respect to the qualities of their sentences given in the attached relation. At the appropriate time, he is ordered to present them and to present the account of moneys spent, so that an order for payment may be given in his favor for the quantity of money he has advanced. All of this was communicated by order of this Holy Tribunal.

Given in the Chamber of the secret, May 26, 1783
D. Santiago Martínez Rincón, Secretary

Order Given to All of the Ministers and Familiars of This Holy Office by the Messenger Don Andrés López Barba, Ordering Them to Appear to Attend and Assist in the Public Auto-da-fé, May 26, 1783

✝

It is ordered that the Messenger of this Holy Office in compliance with this order should go and alert all of the qualified ministers and familiars, so that they should come gathered at six o'clock in the morning on next Sunday, the 1st of June, at the entranceway to the Tribunal with their various accoutrements, and at the following Monday at eight o'clock, and those who were not ecclesiastics (i.e., the familiars) should come dressed in their finest clothing and mounted on horseback, in order to assist and accompany the execution of the sentences, all of which they will execute and comply with under the penalty of fifty pesos for the extraordinary expenses of this Holy Office, as it is that they are irremissibly obliged to attend.

All of this was communicated by order of this Holy Tribunal.

Given in the Chamber of the secret, May 26, 1783

D. Santiago Martínez Rincón, Secretary

Text to Be Publicly Read by the Town Crier, May 27, 1783

✝

This is the justice that has been ordered to be made by the Holy Tribunal of the Inquisition with these men and women. The first seven, prisoners numbered 6, 7, 10, 11, 17, 18, and 20 have been convicted for having been married twice; the eighth prisoner number 11 has been found guilty of heretical propositions, and the ninth (prisoner number 5) has been convicted of blasphemy; the tenth (prisoner number 15) was convicted of having escaped from his presidio twice; and the eleventh (prisoner number 4) has been found guilty of confessing people without Holy Orders, and the twelfth (prisoner number 19) is convicted of having celebrated mass without being ordained, and the thirteenth (prisoner number 9) has been convicted of uttering a sacred verse and then having wrapped it up in several papers with love poems written on them. All of them are to receive two hundred lashes, and their respective years of imprisonment. He who commits the sin shall pay the price!

Order in Which the Prisoners Should Be Placed in the Procession of the Auto-da-fé in the Church of Saint Dominic

Place	Number of the Prisoner
First	Number 10
Second	Number 7
Third	Number 20
Fourth	Number 14
Fifth	Number 15

Sixth	Number 11
Seventh	Number 19
Eighth	Number 6
Ninth	Number 5
Tenth	Number 17
Eleventh	Number 9
Twelfth	Number 4
Thirteenth	Number 18

Order in Which the Sentences of the Thirteen Prisoners Who Will Be Marched in Procession in the Auto-da-fé on Sunday, the 1st of June Should Be Read by the Secretaries and the Officials of the Secret

Places	*Number of the Prisoner*	*Minister to Read the Sentence*
First	Number 10	Abad
Second	Number 7	Martínez
Third	Number 20	Torrecilla
Fourth	Number 14	Beica
Fifth	Number 15	Ruiz
Sixth	Number 11	Nájera
Seventh	Number 19	Torrecilla
Eighth	Number 6	Beica
Ninth	Number 5	Martínez
Tenth	Number 17	Ruiz
Eleventh	Number 9	Martínez
Twelfth	Number 4	Torrecilla
Thirteenth	Number 18	Beica

Invitation to Attend Given to the Viceroy, May 28, 1783

†

I certify that I, the above-cited Secretary of the Secret, having gone out in compliance with the order given me on the 26th of this month to the Royal Palace requested that the page of the palace guards advise his Excellency the Viceroy, Don Matías de Gálvez,[97] that a Secretary of the Holy Office came to give His Excellency a message from the Tribunal. Shortly thereafter they bade me enter, and finding myself in the presence of the Viceroy, he asked me: "*Does this deal with a matter that must be communicated in secret?*" to which I responded that, even though it was not a matter that fell underneath the rigor of the secret of the Holy Office, it still was from the Tribunal. And immediately he asked his accompanying gentleman who was there to leave the chamber. He ordered me to take a seat on a bench in front of his chair, and once seated, I gave to His Excellency the message in this form: "*Excellent Lord, the Tribunal of the Holy Office of New Spain has ordered the celebration of a public auto-da-fé next Sunday at the Church and Convent of Santo Domingo, and if Your Excellency should wish to attend, the Tribunal will have that which it desires, but because this attendance demands the preparation of a curtain behind which you may attend conforming to the manner of the attendance of the Lord Viceroys in all particular autos-da-fé along with other particular preparations, I have come to let them know your desires.*" And he responded to me that he felt esteemed and honored by the attention given to him by the Holy Office, but that he was impeded to walk even one step due to his suffering from gout, which will make it unable for him to attend. With that I began to take my leave, requesting his license to pass and kiss the feet of His Excellency's wife, the *Virreina*[98] and give her the same message from the Tribunal. He immediately called a page and ordered him to tell his mistress that she was to be presented to a Gentleman Secretary of the Holy Office, and as I arose from the seat His Excellency attempted to do the same thing, but the gout did not permit him to do so, and he instead waved at me a parting greeting of "*Adios Lord Secretary, Your mercy should go and see the Lady Virreina.*" Having found her without any previous etiquette and forewarning, I came to her chambers where she stood to listen to me (allowing me to see her gentle character and the simplicity of her treatment), and I proceeded to give her the same message in the equivalent terms as those expressed before, to which she answered showing great willingness and thanks, and no light indications that she may attend, if not the auto, then for sure on the next day in the palace of the Inquisition. And with this motive I procured to make the insinuations that appeared necessary to me to make known her resolution; but she responded without giving a positive response, and she remained somewhat indecisive, and I took my leave of Her Excellency, and entrusted her with the best wishes of the Tribunal. And so that it will be certified in virtue of the above-cited order, I give this certification, today Wednesday when I conducted the said request, which is the 28th of May 1783.

Juan Nicolás Abad, Secretary

Order and Writ of the Inquisitors concerning the Auto-da-fé, May 28, 1783

†

In the Holy Office of the Inquisition in Mexico, on the 28th of May 1783, while in audience during the morning, the Lord Inquisitors Dr. Juan de Mier y Villar, and Don Antonio Bergosa y Jordán, stated: In order to ensure that the auto-da-fé that has been ordered to be celebrated on the coming Sunday, the 1st of June, should be conducted without the chaos and turbulence that often gives occasion to the gathering of large numbers of people usually in attendance at such functions,[99] they order that the said Secretary Don Juan Nicolás Abad should take another message to His Excellency on the part of the Tribunal, requesting that he should see it fit to order a military escort of forty men with their respective corporals to assist in complying with the orders of the Tribunal from half past six o'clock in the morning until the conclusion of the auto, and also request that the following Monday, the 2nd of the said month of June, that another squad of twenty-five soldiers and dragoons with their corporal should attend from seven o'clock in the morning in order to escort the prisoners to the execution of their sentences and to accompany the parade under the orders of the person whom the Tribunal should select, which is according to custom. And they give another order to the Messenger that he should take another message to the Lord President of the Royal Court of Criminal Law, so that according to the style and manner of custom, they should give the necessary orders to the executioner and the town crier, so that they should attend at the required hour with the necessary instruments and beasts of burden, whose number will be expressed in good time. And they gave the corresponding order to the Provider so that he may prepare the lunch that is accustomed to be given to the prisoners who are marched in the auto, and also orders went out to the doctors and surgeons so that they may equally attend for the exercise of their offices.

All of this was ordered, and signed

Dr. Mier

Dr. Bergosa

D. Santiago Martínez Rincón, Secretary

Relation of the Message Given to the Viceroy, May 30, 1783

✝

I certify that I, the above-cited Secretary of the Secret, having gone out in compliance with the order on the same day, to the Royal Palace, and requested that the page of the palace guards advise His Excellency that a Secretary of the Holy Office came to kiss his hands and give His Excellency another message from the Tribunal. Shortly thereafter I was told to enter, and I went into the office of His Excellency, where he was on foot and apparently about to leave [and without engaging in other formalities because I knew that he had urgent business to care for] I requested on the part of the Tribunal the aid of forty men of the infantry with their corresponding corporals for their service on the next Sunday, the day of the auto-da-fé, and also twenty-five cavalrymen for the next Monday, to which he responded that he would quickly give the order to the Major of the Plaza, and he entrusted me with the message that he would give any other necessary aid requested by the Holy Office as quickly as possible in order to show his affection and particular esteem to the Tribunal. With this I made leave after giving His Excellency the thanks he was owed. And so that it will be certified in virtue of the above-cited order, I give this certification, today Wednesday when I conducted the said request, which is the 30th of May 1783.

Juan Nicolás Abad, Secretary

List of Expenses of the Public Auto-da-fé Celebrated on June 1, 1783, Recorded June 6, 1783

✝

The Treasurer and Receptor of this Holy Office, in compliance with the previously ordered lineup of prisoners, has covered the costs of the lunch held for the Ministers of the Tribunal, the familiars, and soldiers of the Regiment, along with the other expenses charged to the said account, which I give now as dutifully presented in the following form:

For the cost of the lunch   62 pesos 5 reales 6 grains
For the alms for the use of the church   2 pesos 0 reales 0 grains
For the placement of the stage and other seating and the
    enclosure   5 pesos 0 reales 0 grains
For the two corporals of the twenty-four Soldiers and
    Dragoons   28 pesos 0 reales 0 grains
To the executioner   12 pesos 0 reales 0 grains
For ropes and nooses   0 pesos 4 reales 0 grains
The total expense   110 pesos 1 real 6 grains

All of this appears to be the costs and expenses, except for any error, which totals 110 pesos, one real, and six grains of gold, all of which I request Your Lordships to make an order of payment to me for the said expenses.

I swear in the proper form in this Inquisition of Mexico, on June 4, 1783
Vicente de las Heras Serrano,
Treasurer and Receptor of the Holy Office

The Order for Payment Made by Their Lordships the Inquisitors, June 6, 1783

✝

Their Lordships the Inquisitors Mier and Bergosa recognize this account, which has been presented by the Secretary and in which there has resulted no error, and they issue the said order for payment in favor of the said Treasurer.

Dr. Mier
Dr. Bergosa

Finances and Assets of the Inquisition
in New Spain

> This inquisition tribunal's finances are such a disgrace in terms of confiscations that only now with the confiscation of these Jews are there enough funds to pay for the food of the prisoners, which appears to be an incredible thing here in the Indies . . . for all of this the ministers [of the tribunal] are so despondent that they have to instead pay for their salaries out of the fines and minor fees charged as penance.
>
> Report of the Inquisitors of New Spain to the Suprema, 1595

The Inquisition of New Spain counted on a variety of sources of income in order to pay for its operational expenses. Although problems existed in its funding during the later sixteenth century, from the middle of the seventeenth century onward, the Inquisition in New Spain accumulated enough capital to allow it to come to serve as one of the major sources of credit in colonial Mexico.[100]

One of the major sources of income for the fiscal office of the Inquisition in New Spain remained the funds and goods confiscated from the Inquisition's prisoners and suspected heretics. One of the first things that the officials of the Inquisition did when they arrested a suspected heretic included taking an inventory of the suspects' moneys and other goods and possessions. After taking the inventory, the Inquisition embargoed these goods and confiscated them. If the Inquisition later found the suspect innocent of the charges, it would return his goods, except for a certain amount for the maintenance of the prisoner during the extent of the trial. On the other hand, if the Inquisition found a suspect guilty, it sold the suspect's goods and possessions, either completely or partially confiscating the proceeds, depending on the final sentence in the case.[101]

A second type of income for the Inquisition in New Spain came from the funds granted to the institution from a portion of the annual tithe revenues from the bishoprics of the Kingdom of New Spain, including the bishoprics of Mexico, Puebla, Oaxaca, Yucatan, Chiapas, Guatemala, Michoacan, and Manila. These funds had been set aside for the payment of a number of canons for the Cathedral Chapter in each of these regions. The funds gained from the requisite proportion of these suppressed "cannonries" were meant to help support the activities of the Inquisition in New Spain.[102] The income from these funds remained significant, so much so that as late as 1813 an Inquisition official in New Spain recorded that the total amount of 32,000 pesos in that period covered close to half of the expenses of the Inquisition.[103]

Another important source of income came from private personal donations or alms, with some larger sums coming from bequests in the wills of wealthier citizens. The Mexican Inquisition received smaller quantities of private donations or alms from the faithful throughout its existence, but these funds remained irregular and sporadic.[104] The Inquisition also came to own a significant number of urban houses and other property bequeathed to it by prominent citizens in their wills. On some occasions, the funds and properties gained from these bequests amounted to a small fortune. Most notable among this type of bequest was the estate of the wealthy lawyer of the Royal Audiencia, Dr. Agustín de Vergara, who died without heirs and bequeathed his entire estate to the Mexican Inquisition in 1749.[105] From the rents and sale of this type of property, the Inquisition in New Spain came to hold a significant amount of capital. Once all of the expenses of the Inquisition were considered, any capital remaining in the accounts of the fiscal office were then invested, most often in interest-bearing loans to prominent citizens of the viceroyalty.[106]

Nevertheless, the costs of maintaining the Inquisition and its palace and properties remained a significant financial burden. All of the activities of the Inquisition, including its annual celebrations for its patron saints, as well as the formal processions and the elaborate staging and ceremonies of the many autos-da-fé, represented enormous expenses and costs. Other continuing expenses included not only the sustenance of its prisoners in the secret prisons (see documents 23–24) but also repairs and maintenance on the palace of the Inquisition and its many other urban properties, which it used for its offices and the living quarters of its ministers and its prisons (see documents 25–26). Testimonies of the great expenses for upkeep and repair exist in numerous account books that have survived in the archives of the Fiscal Office of the Inquisition.[107]

DOCUMENT 23

Register and Account of the Pesos that I, Juan de León Plaza, Alcaide of the Secret Prisons of this Holy Office, Have Paid for Necessary Things for the Operation of the Prisons by Order of Your Lordships from the 17th of July 1599 When I Was Received as the Said Jailer until the End of July 1600

Mexico City, July 17, 1599– July 31, 1600

SOURCE: Archivo General de la Nación, Ramo de Inquisición, vol. 468, folios 86r–92v.

NOTE: This account offers a view into the day-to-day operations in the secret jails of the Holy Office, giving us many details of the prison, including a glimpse into the lives of the prisoners, the jailors and other people who had contact with the prisoners, and the types of expenses that would have been incurred.

First, on July 21, 1599, 2 pesos and 2 tomines were paid to the three Indians who served during the week in the said prisons.

2 ps 2 ts

On July 29, 2 pesos and 2 tomines were paid to the three Indians who served during the week in the said prisons.

2 ps 2 ts

On the 29th, 2 pesos and 2 tomines were paid for four dozen plates and bowls.

2 ps 2 ts

On this same day, six tomines were paid for several small notebooks for the said jails.

6 ts

On the same day, large pots and kettles for the cooking of the prison's food were purchased for one peso.

1 ps

On the 29th of the said month, seven tomines were paid for a number of reed mats purchased for the prisons.

7 ts

On the same day, another 1 peso and 1 tomines were paid for two dozen more plates and bowls for the said prisons.

1 ps 1 ts

On August 6, 2 pesos and 2 tomines were paid to the three Indians who served during the week in the said prisons.

2 ps 2 ts

On August 14, 2 pesos and 2 tomines were paid to the three Indians who served during the week in the said prisons.

2 ps 2 ts

On August 22, 2 pesos and 2 tomines were paid to the three Indians who served during the week in the said prisons.

2 ps 2 ts

On August 25, 2 pesos and 2 tomines were paid for the purchase of twelve large containers that were bought to bring water in the service of the said prisons.

2 ps 2 ts

On the same day, one peso and seven tomines paid for seven metal strainers that were purchased for the service of the said jails.

1 ps 7 ts

On the same day, one peso and four tomines paid for the ropes and cords used to bring the said water containers to the prison.

1 ps 4 ts

On August 30, 2 pesos and 2 tomines were paid to the three Indians who served during the week in the said prisons.

2 ps 2 ts

On the 8th of September, 2 pesos and 2 tomines were paid to the three Indians who served during the week in the said prisons.

2 ps 2 ts

On September 16th, 2 pesos and 2 tomines were paid to the three Indians who served during the week in the said prisons.

2 ps 2 ts

On September 24th, 2 pesos and 2 tomines were paid to the three Indians who served during the week in the said prisons.

2 ps 2 ts

On the same day, two tomines were paid for ceramic jars for the said jails.

4 ts

On the 1st of October, 2 pesos and 2 tomines were paid to the three Indians who served during the week in the said prisons.

2 ps 2 ts

On October 7th, 7 tomines were paid for the use of seven servants in the said prisons.

7 ts

On October 9th, 2 pesos and 2 tomines were paid to the three Indians
who served during the week in the said prisons.   2 ps 2 ts

On October 17th, 2 pesos and 2 tomines were paid to the three Indians
who served during the week in the said prisons.   2 ps 2 ts

On October 25th, 2 pesos and 2 tomines were paid to the three Indians
who served during the week in the said prisons.   2 ps 2 ts

On the 3rd of November, 2 pesos and 2 tomines were paid to the three
Indians who served during the week in the said prisons.   2 ps 2 ts

On 11th of November, 2 pesos and 2 tomines were paid to the three
Indians who served during the week in the said prisons.   2 ps 2 ts

On November 19th, 2 pesos and 2 tomines were paid to the three
Indians who served during the week in the said prisons.   2 ps 2 ts

On November 27th, 2 pesos and 2 tomines were paid to the three
Indians who served during the week in the said prisons.   2 ps 2 ts

On the 4th of December, 2 pesos and 2 tomines were paid to the three
Indians who served during the week in the said prisons.   2 ps 2 ts

On the same day, 1 peso and 2 tomines were paid for two dozen plates
for the service of the said prisons.   1 ps 2 ts

On the same day, 5 tomines were paid for straw mats to be used in the
said prisons.   5 ts

On the same day, 1 peso and 2 tomines were paid for cushions for the
said prisons.   1 ps 2 ts

On the same day, 1 peso and 1 tomines were paid for the purchase of six
large containers that were bought to bring water in the service of
the said prisons.   1 ps 1 ts

On the same day, four tomines paid for the ropes and cords used to
bring the said water containers to the prison.   4 ts

On December 20th, 2 pesos and 2 tomines were paid to the three
Indians who served during the week in the said prisons.   2 ps 2 ts

On the same day, another 1 peso and 1 tomines were paid for two dozen
more plates and bowls for the said prisons.   1 ps 1 ts

On the 24th of the said month, 10 tomines were paid for straw mats to
be used in the said prisons.   10 ts

On December 28th, 2 pesos and 2 tomines were paid to the three
Indians who served during the week in the said prisons.   2 ps 2 ts

On December 29, 1599, were paid 1 peso and 4 tomines to Jurado de
Herrera, the blacksmith, for the making of the two heavy locks
for the prisons, and for a iron knocker for the inside of the door
placed on the stairways leading to the portal and entrance of the
prisons.   1 ps 4ts

On the same day, one tomine was paid for ceramic jars for the said
jails   1 ts

On the 5th of January, 1600, 2 pesos and 2 tomines were paid to the
three Indians who served during the week in the said prisons.   2 ps 2 ts

On the 13th of January, 1600, 2 pesos and 2 tomines were paid to the
    three Indians who served during the week in the said prisons.   2 ps 2 ts

On the same day, 7½ tomines were paid for cushions for the said
    prisons.   7½ ts

On the 21st of January 1600, 2 pesos and 2 tomines were paid to the
    three Indians who served during the week in the said prisons.   2 ps 2 ts

On the same day, 3 pesos and 1 tomine were paid for five dozen sets of
    plates and bowls for the service of the said prisons.   3 ps 1 ts

On the 29th of January 1600, 2 pesos and 2 tomines were paid to the
    three Indians who served during the week in the said prisons.   2 ps 2 ts

On the 6th of February 1600, 2 pesos and 2 tomines were paid to
    the three Indians who served during the week in the said
    prisons.   2 ps 2 ts

On the same day, one tomines was paid for ceramic jars for the said
    jails   1 ts

On the same day, three tomines were paid for ceramic jars and candle-
    holders for the said jails   3 ts

On this same day, Cristóbal Verdugo was paid four tomines for a secret
    execution conducted in the prisons   4 ts

On the 14th of February, 2 pesos and 2 tomines were paid to the three
    Indians who served during the week in the said prisons.   2 ps 2 ts

On the same day, 1 peso and 2 tomines were paid for straw mats pur-
    chased for the prisons.   1 ps 2 ts

On the 22nd of February, 2 pesos and 2 tomines were paid to the three
    Indians who served during the week in the said prisons.   2 ps 2 ts

On the 1st of March, 2 pesos and 2 tomines were paid to the three
    Indians who served during the week in the said prisons.   2 ps 2 ts

On the 9th of March, 2 pesos and 2 tomines were paid to the three
    Indians who served during the week in the said prisons.   2 ps 2 ts

On this same day was paid the royal tax of 4 pesos and 5 tomines for the
    rights to Indian porter services for 27 weeks for the use of three
    Indians each week from the 14th of July 1599 until the end of
    December of the same year   4 ps 5 ts

On the 17th of March, 2 pesos and 2 tomines were paid to the three
    Indians who served during the week in the said prisons.   2 ps 2 ts

On the 25th of March, 2 pesos and 2 tomines were paid to the three
    Indians who served during the week in the said prisons.   2 ps 2 ts

On the 2nd of April, 2 pesos and 2 tomines were paid to the three
    Indians who served during the week in the said prisons.   2 ps 2 ts

On the 10th of April, 2 pesos and 2 tomines were paid to the three
    Indians who served during the week in the said prisons.   2 ps 2 ts

On the 18th of April, 2 pesos and 2 tomines were paid to the three
    Indians who served during the week in the said prisons.   2 ps 2 ts

On the 26th of April, 2 pesos and 2 tomines were paid to the three
    Indians who served during the week in the said prisons.   2 ps 2 ts

On the 4th of May, 2 pesos and 2 tomines were paid to the three
    Indians who served during the week in the said prisons.   2 ps 2 ts

On the 12th of May, 2 pesos and 2 tomines were paid to the three
    Indians who served during the week in the said prisons.   2 ps 2 ts

On the 14th of May, were paid 2 pesos of common gold for 16 large water
    containers that were purchased for the service of the said prisons.   2 ps

On the 20th of May, 2 pesos and 2 tomines were paid to the three
    Indians who served during the week in the said prisons.   2 ps 2 ts

On the same day, 2 tomines were paid for straw mats for the use of the
    prison.   2 ts

On the same day, 1 peso was paid to Jurado Herrero, the blacksmith for
    the repair of the lock mechanism of the large door to the prisons   1 ps

On the 28th of May, four tomines paid for the ropes and cords used to
    bring the said water containers to the prison.   4 ts

On the same day, 2 pesos and 2 tomines were paid to the three Indians
    who served during the week in the said prisons.   2 ps 2 ts

On the 29th of May, 2½ pesos were paid for four dozen sets of plates
    and bowls for the service of the said prisons.[108]   2 ps 4 ts

On the 3rd of June, 2 pesos and 2 tomines were paid to the three
    Indians who served during the week in the said prisons.   2 ps 2 ts

On the 13th of June, 2 pesos and 2 tomines were paid to the three
    Indians who served during the week in the said prisons.   2 ps 2 ts

On the 15th of June, 2½ pesos were paid for four dozen sets of plates
    and bowls for the service of the said prisons.   2 ps 4 ts

On the 21st of June, 2 pesos and 2 tomines were paid to the three
    Indians who served during the week in the said prisons.   2 ps 2 ts

On the 29th of June, 1 peso was paid for twelve small registry books for
    the service of the said prisons.   1 ps 3 ts

On the 29th of June, 2 pesos and 2 tomines were paid to the three
    Indians who served during the week in the said prisons.   2 ps 2 ts

On the 7th of July, two pesos were paid by order of their Lordships to
    be given to Cristóbal Verdugo, who came to make certain
    executions.[109]   2 ps

On the 8th of July, 4 tomines were paid by order of their Lordships to
    be given to Cristóbal Verdugo, who came to make another
    execution.[110]   4 ts

On this same day, 6 tomines were paid to repair the feet of two inmates   6 ts

On this same day, 1 peso was paid for one large blank registry book to
    record the visitations of the prisoners.   1 ps

On July 8th were paid 1 peso and 1 tomin for several registry books for
    the service of the said prisons.   1 ps 1 ts

On the same day, one tomin was paid for ceramic jars for the said jails.   1 ts
On the 8th of July, 2 pesos and 2 tomines were paid to the three
    Indians who served during the week in the said prisons.   2 ps 2 ts
On the 15th of July, 2 pesos and 2 tomines were paid to the three
    Indians who served during the week in the said prisons.   2 ps 2 ts
On the last day of July, 2 pesos and 2 tomines were paid to the three
    Indians who served during the week in the said prisons.   2 ps 2 ts

All of this passed before me,
Juan de León Plaza,
Jailor of the Prisons of the Holy Office

DOCUMENT 24

Relation of What Has Been Spent since the 8th of January 1616 in the Purchase of Pens, Ink, String, Wafers, Canvas, and Other Miscellaneous Items for Use in the Chamber of the Secret of This Holy Office

Mexico City, 1616–1617

SOURCE: Archivo General de la Nación, Ramo de Inquisición, vol. 468, folios 196r–205v.

NOTE: This account enables us to understand the average costs of running the court and maintaining its archive throughout the year and helps illustrate the day-to-day operations of the tribunal in minute detail.

†

On the 19th of January 1616, two pesos worth of ink   2 pesos
On the 23rd of January 1616, four reales worth of ink   4 reales
On the same day, four reales worth of string to bind letters   4 reales

On March 23, 1616, two reales worth of ink   2 reales

On April 11, 1616, four reales worth of ink   4 reales
On this same day, four reales worth of wafers[111]   4 reales

On May 11th, five reales worth of string to bind letters   5 reales
On the same day, four reales of ink   4 reales
On May 18th, 1616 pesos worth of ink   2 pesos

On July 1, 1616, two reales worth of ink   2 reales
On July 6, 1616, two reales worth of wafers   2 reales

On August 12, 1616, I paid to Diego de la Rivera, bookseller, nine
    pesos for a Dominical (Sunday) missal[112]   9 pesos

On August 30, 1616, two reales of ink		2 reales
On September 10, 1616, two reales of ink		2 reales
On September 26, 1616, I paid 10 reales for twelve registers		
of silk with their buttons for the Sunday missals	1 peso	2 reales
On the 5th day of October, 1616, two reales worth of ink		2 reales
On the 8th day of October, four reales of wafers		4 reales
On this same day, two reales worth of ink		2 reales
On the 29th of October, four varas' length of coarse linen		
cloth, priced at 4 reales and ¼ per vara, which amounts		
to 13 reales	1 peso	5 reales
On this same day, five reales worth of packaging string		
for the large cover sheets of document bundles		5 reales
On the 14th of November, 1616, I paid Diego de Castro, the Jailer		
of the Perpetual Jail of this Inquisition, twelve reales for		
opening and storing two crates of twenty bundles of paper		
for the Chamber of the Secret	1 peso	4 reales
On this same day, two reales worth of ink		2 reales
On the 7th of January,[113] four reales worth of ink		4 reales
On the 13th of February, four reales worth of ink		4 reales
On this same day, two reales worth of wafers		2 reales
On the 3rd of April of the said year two pesos of ink	2 pesos	
On the 24th of April, two reales worth of ink		2 reales
On the 2nd of May 1617, two reales worth of ink		2 reales
On the 9th of May, four reales for ink and wafers		4 reales
On the 24th of May, for six varas of vellum[114] at four reales per		
vara for the coversheets and letters to Spain	3 pesos	
On this same day, for the same reason, 1½ pesos for the		
thin waxed string and balls of string to close letters	1 peso	4 reales
On this same day, two reales worth of wafers		2 reales
On June 20th, 1617, two pesos worth of ink	2 pesos	
On the 1st of July, Juan de Cervantes, resident of Tepexoxuma		
was paid six pesos for bringing the Indian servant		
women Magdalena María and Juana María to serve in		
this Tribunal	6 pesos	
On the 8th of July, two reales worth of ink-		2 reales

On the 8th of August of the said year, a new key for the door and lock of the Chamber of the Secret, which cost 14 reales	1 peso	6 reales
On the 19th of August, two pesos worth of ink	2 pesos	
On the 7th of September 1617, four reales of wafers		4 reales
On the 27th of September, four reales of ink		4 reales
On the 19th of October 1617, two reales worth of ink		2 reales
On the 24th of October, two reales worth of ink		2 reales
On the 3rd of November of the said year, two reales of ink		2 reales

In all a sum and total of 38 pesos and 1 real were spent on miscellaneous expenses for the Chamber of the Secret from January 1616, until the end of November 1617.

Signed and executed by me on November 30, 1617
Pedro de Vega

DOCUMENT 25
Documents Relating to the Making of an Inventory of the Assets, Goods, and Estate of the Palace of the Extinguished Tribunal of the Holy Office of the Inquisition of New Spain

Mexico City, April 1814

SOURCE: Archivo General de la Nación, Ramo de Intendentes, vol. 42.

NOTE: This document contains just a few pages extracted from a three-hundred-page inventory of the goods, decorations, furniture, and other assets held by the Tribunal of the Inquisition and confiscated from the Palace of the Tribunal during the first extinction of the Inquisition in 1813–14. The wealth and sumptuous decorations described in these pages made the Inquisition tribunal one of the most lavishly decorated palaces in New Spain. Second only to those of the palace of the viceroy, the Inquisition's wealth and its treasures had never been seen by the public before. Only those unfortunate enough to have been involved in inquisitorial proceedings would have had any idea of the wealth and majestic decorations held by the tribunal.

Relation of the Inventory and Examination of the Palace, Contents, Assets, and Other Goods Belonging to the Extinguished Tribunal of the Inquisition, April 19, 1814

✝

In the City of Mexico, on the 19th of April 1814, I the Scribe in virtue of what has been ordered by the Superior Government, went to the building and Palace that served as the

Extinguished Tribunal of the Inquisition, in the company of the Evaluator, Don Manuel Carvajal, for the effect of making an evaluation of all of the goods that remain in the said Tribunal and with an initial manifest of the goods handed over by the pensioner Don Manuel Martínez de Cosío, who had served as a minister of the said Tribunal, we began to evaluate the value of the goods in the following form.

The Principal Great Hall

In the principal great hall in the entrance of the ground level of the Palace we found nine major wall hangings made out of Damask silk, with forty-five large tapestries each measuring five varas in width, which totaled together measured 225 varas, along with 14 curtains of damask silk, which made a sum total of 239 varas of silk at 14 reales a vara.	418 pesos 2 reales 0 grains
Another wall hanging made out of fine red velvet, five varas in width and thirty-nine varas in length	160 pesos 0 reales 0 grains
A large table, three varas long, with a cloth table covering	8 pesos 0 reales 0 grains
A smaller hanging cloth of damask silk, with another 14 varas of edging and border made of gold at 14 reales a vara.	42 pesos 4 reales 0 grains

Since it was now 12 o'clock midday, the evaluation was suspended at this point so that lunch can be eaten. All of which I certify.

Joseph Manuel Carvajal   Manuel Martínez de Cosío
José Ignacio Cano y Moctezuma

Continuation of the Inventory and Evaluation of the Assets of the Extinguished Tribunal of the Inquisition

In the afternoon of the said day, the evaluation and inventory continued in the following form:

First, a comforter of fine red velvet with a golden border, stuffed with cotton	28 pesos 0 reales 0 grains
Five well made chairs, covered with red velvet, and edged in gold	50 pesos 9 reales 0 grains
A wooden floor made of closely fitted hard wooded planks	35 pesos 0 reales 0 grains
A large modern styled carpet measuring 73½ varas at 4 pesos a var	294 pesos 0 reales 0 grains

Because it was now half past five o'clock in the afternoon, the inventory and evaluation was suspended.

Carvajal   Cosío
José Ignacio Cano y Moctezuma

Continuation of the Inventory and Evaluation of the Assets of the Extinguished Tribunal of the Inquisition, April 20, 1814

In the City of Mexico, on the 20th of April 1814, I the Scribe in virtue of what has been ordered by the Superior Government continued in the making of an evaluation of all of the goods that remain in the said Tribunal, in the following form:

3 large curtain rods with 18 glass insets at 24 pesos for each window set	72 pesos o reales o grains
3 large curtains with their cords and iron rods, at 4 pesos each	13 pesos 4 reales o grains
4 large benches upholstered with tapestries and covered by covers of fine velvet and silk	12 pesos o reales o grains
2 oval glass mirrors each with three Roman glass mirrors	6 pesos o reales o grains
A cloth frieze 84 varas in length and a door covering of rough cloth at 2 reales a vara	21 pesos o reales o grains

Since it was now 12 o'clock midday, the evaluation was suspended at this point so that lunch can be eaten. All of which I certify.

Joseph Manuel Carvajal   Manuel Martínez de Cosío
José Ignacio Cano y Moctezuma

Continuation of the Inventory and Evaluation of the Assets of the Extinguished Tribunal of the Inquisition

In the afternoon of the said day, the evaluation and inventory continued in the following form:

THE SECOND MAIN HALL

A wall covering made of damask silk and another twenty-one oil paintings each 31 by 2 varas, which make 77 covered varas at 14 reales each one, and 17½ varas of fine damask silk at 4 reales each vara	135 pesos 4 reales o grains
2 large curtain assemblies with 16 inset pieces of Roman glass each ½ a vara, at 27 pesos each one	54 pesos o reales o grains
2 large curtains of heavy cotton cloth and their fittings	2 pesos o reales o grains
1 large covered wooden paneled screen	3 pesos o reales o grains

Because it was now half past five o'clock in the afternoon, the inventory and evaluation was suspended.

Carvajal   Cosío
José Ignacio Cano y Moctezuma

Continuation of the Inventory and Evaluation of the Assets of the Extinguished Tribunal of the Inquisition, April 21, 1814

In the City of Mexico, on the 21st of April 1814, I the Scribe in virtue of what has been ordered by the Superior Government, continued in the making of an evaluation of all of the goods that remain in the said Tribunal, in the following form:

CONTINUING ON TO THE REAR OF THE CHAPEL

2 large covered wooden paneled screens with linen coverings	5 pesos 0 reales 0 grains
A large circled window with twelve good glasses	6 pesos 0 reales 0 grains

THE ENTRANCEWAY AND ANTECHAMBER

A large circled window 5 varas in width worth 6 pesos, with 6 windows of ¾ vara valued 46 pesos	52 pesos 0 reales 0 grains
A large orbital window with four large sheets of Roman glass, each measuring ½ a vara	8 pesos 0 reales 0 grains
Three more oval windows with ordinary glass panes, and several of them broken	30 pesos 0 reales 0 grains
Eleven small benches each 2½ varas in length, covered with fine yellowed sheepskin, valued at 18 reales each	24 pesos 6 reales 0 grains

Since it was now twelve o'clock midday, the evaluation was suspended at this point so that lunch can be eaten. All of which I certify.

Joseph Manuel Carvajal   Manuel Martínez de Cosío
José Ignacio Cano y Moctezuma

Continuation of the Inventory and evaluation of the assets of the Extinguished Tribunal of the Inquisition

In the afternoon of the said day the inventory and evaluation continued in the following form:

THE CHAMBER OF THE LORD PRADO

The room to the right, where there is a large glass lantern.

There is a window set with seven glass panes, and eight smaller pieces	3 pesos 0 reales 0 grains
A large lantern with its board and table	3 pesos 0 reales 0 grains
A small paneled screen	2 pesos 0 reales 0 grains
Another window set with two sheets of twelve window panes of ¼ vara each	5 pesos 2 reales 0 grains

The Dining Room

Another window with 27 small glass panes, at 2½ reales
    each, and 19 smaller pieces of glass at 12 reales   9 pesos 7 reales 6 grains
Another window with 10 Roman styled glass panes   10 pesos 0 reales 0 grains

The Chamber before the Dining Room

Another window with 28 glass panes at 10 pesos, 4 reales,
    and 18 pieces of glass at one peso   11 pesos 4 reales 0 grains

NOTE: As you can see from this brief extract of an inventory that continues on for pages, in just wall coverings, glass windows, and furniture alone, the Inquisition's assets were valued at more than 68,000 pesos of gold. Once the final amount included all of the tribunal's other assets and properties, the total was far greater than 2 million pesos, a staggering sum for those days.

DOCUMENT 26
Documents of the Minister of Finance of the Intendancy of Mexico concerning the List of the Employees of the Extinguished Tribunal of the Inquisition

Mexico City, 1823

SOURCE: Archivo General de la Nación, Ramo de Intendentes, vol. 42.

NOTE: As in all changing bureaucracies, the extinction of the Holy Tribunal of the Inquisition led to the unemployment of many ministers and other officials. The new government of an independent Mexico attempted to reincorporate many members of the tribunal in its various offices of government. This document, one of the final documents concerning the Inquisition in Mexico, deals with an exchange between the new ministries of State and the Treasury, which had to find out how to settle with the ex-employees of the Holy Office and how to recuperate any pensions that were paid.

Letter to the Excellent Lord Minister of Finance Requesting the List of the Employees of the Extinguished Tribunal of the Inquisition, February 28, 1823

✝

Lord Super-Intendant of this Court:

I requested that Your Lordship send me a list of all of the Pensioners of the Extinguished Inquisition with an expression of where they are presently occupied in the Treasury and Accounting offices of this branch of Government. Also list those who are now in other offices, and those who are unemployed, either by their choice or being dedicated to other labors, or because they are not needed.

May God guard Your Lordship for many years
Mexico 28th of February 1823
The Lord Minister of State

List of the Ex-employees of the Extinguished Tribunal of the Inquisition, March 10, 1823

†

1. Lord Licenciado Don José María Rosas, Honorary Judge of the Audiencia, who was the Prosecuting Attorney of the Holy Office	750 pesos salary
2. Presbiter Don Félix Loperena, official who served in the Holy Office, who is now working in the Archbishopric	700 pesos salary
3. Presbiter Don Antonio Cano, who was Lieutenant Jailer in the Holy Office, who now is in the Archbishopric's employment	351 pesos salary
4. Juan Antonio Carvajal, a physician in the Holy Office, and now an aide in the Archbishopric	280 pesos salary
5. José Antonio López, who was the doorman of the said Tribunal, and who remains the doorman still in the same building	180 pesos salary
6. Don José Antonio Zúñiga, Master Architect in charge of the construction labors of the said Tribunal	296 pesos salary
7. Presbiter Don Ignacio Calapiz, an official of the Holy Office who is now the Chaplain of alms in the Jail of the Civil Court	100 pesos salary
8. Doña Josefa Velandia and Doña María de las Heras, both enjoy a pension as widows based on their husbands service in the Holy Office	300 pesos pension

Other Pensioners Who Are Now Living in Spain

1. Lord Dr. Don Antonio Pereda, minister of the said Tribunal	3,580 pesos pension
2. Don Venancio Pereda, Secretary of the Tribunal	1,600 pesos pension
3. Don Pedro Pereda, an official of the Tribunal	600 pesos pension
4. Don Tomás Perojo	100 pesos pension

Nominal List of the Individuals Who Receive Pensions from the Extinguished Tribunal of the Holy Office of the Inquisition, March 11, 1823

1. Don Matías de Nájera, Secretary of the Secret of the said Tribunal, who because of his advanced age was not given any other post, who enjoys a salary of	1,600 pesos

2. Don José María Ruiz, Secretary of the Secret, who is also not
   currently employed due to his bad vision and constant illness,
   who enjoys a salary of   1,600 pesos
3. Don Manuel Orvé, who was also a Secretary of the Tribunal,
   and who is now a secretary in the Accounting Office, who
   enjoys a salary of   1,600 pesos
4. Don Casiano Chavarría, also a Secretary of the Tribunal, and
   who now serves as an auxiliary of the Treasury, who enjoys a
   salary of   1,600 pesos
5. Don Francisco Regueron, Account of the said Tribunal   1,200 pesos
6. Don Manuel Martínez de Cosío, who was Secretary of the
   Sequestered Goods of the cited Tribunal, and who now
   serves in the Treasury since the extinction of the Tribunal,
   has occupied a position there since the illness and death
   of the officeholder there, a man named Zuazola, and he
   only enjoys a fixed salary of 1,000 pesos with the proviso
   that for his pension for holding the place of secretary, he
   had enjoyed another 1,000 pesos, as has been manifested
   to the Ministry of the Treasury in a set of documents
   formed in this ministry, and he is now assigned above his
   salary as Treasurer, in recompense of his services
   another 1,000 pesos.
7. Presbiter Don José Miguel Vega, who was an official of the
   Secret of the said Tribunal, and today he is in charge of the
   arrangement and care of the papers of the Archives of the
   Archbishopric, who enjoys a salary of   544 pesos 4 reales

Given by the Lord Minister of the Treasury
March 11, 1823

Letter to His Excellency, the Lord Minister of State, March 11, 1823

†

Excellent Lord,

In compliance with what Your Lordship requested in your letter dated the last 28th
of February, I send Your Excellency the list that I have composed of the Pensioners of
the Extinguished Tribunal of the Inquisition as requested. And I remind Your Excellency of the request by Don Manuel Martínez de Cosío, who on April 30, 1822, was elevated as Treasurer of this ministry, whose tenure in the said office he wished to be
conferred in perpetuity, and whose office he has occupied provisionally since the death
of Don José Zuazola, and until this is decided, I cannot request him to renounce his
pension.

I request that Your Lordship should let me know about your determination in this matter so that I can arrange the procedures here.

May God guard Your Excellency
March 11, 1823
The Lord Minister of the Treasury

FIGURE 1 The Initial Hearing and First Interrogation. From Antonio Puigblanch, *The Inquisition Unmasked: Being an Historical and Philosophical Account of That Tremendous Tribunal* (London: Baldwin, Cradock, and Joy, 1816). Photo from author's private collection.

FIGURE 2 Questioning the Accused Suspect under Torture. From Antonio Puigblanch, *The Inquisition Unmasked: Being an Historical and Philosophical Account of That Tremendous Tribunal* (London: Baldwin, Cradock, and Joy, 1816). Photo from author's private collection.

FIGURE 3 Images (*left to right*) of a Relaxed Heretic, a Penanced Heretic, and a Reconciled Heretic in *Sanbenitos*. Detail of a 1722 engraving by Bernard Picart. Photo from author's private collection.

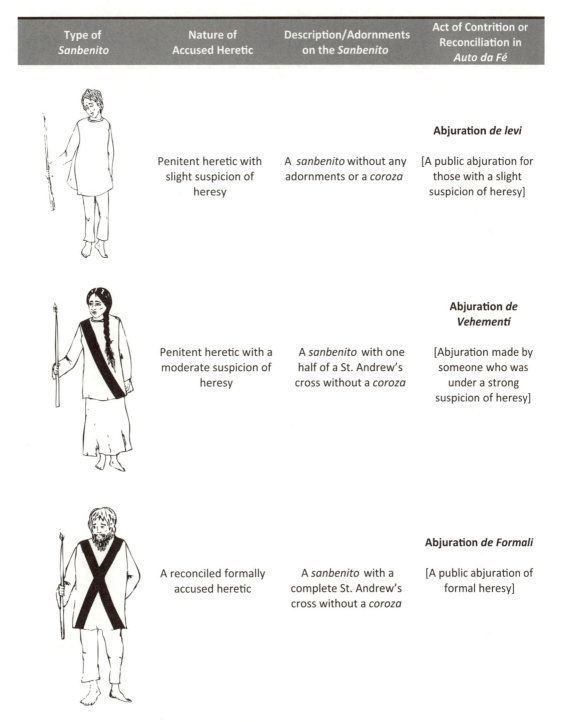

Type of *Sanbenito*	Nature of Accused Heretic	Description/Adornments on the *Sanbenito*	Act of Contrition or Reconciliation in *Auto da Fé*
			Abjuration *de levi*
	Penitent heretic with slight suspicion of heresy	A *sanbenito* without any adornments or a *coroza*	[A public abjuration for those with a slight suspicion of heresy]
			Abjuration *de Vehementi*
	Penitent heretic with a moderate suspicion of heresy	A *sanbenito* with one half of a St. Andrew's cross without a *coroza*	[Abjuration made by someone who was under a strong suspicion of heresy]
			Abjuration *de Formali*
	A reconciled formally accused heretic	A *sanbenito* with a complete St. Andrew's cross without a *coroza*	[A public abjuration of formal heresy]

FIGURE 4 Major Types of *Sanbenitos* Used for Accused Heretics in Typical Auto-da-fé in Colonial New Spain, 1571-1821. Drawings by Argelia Segovia Liga.

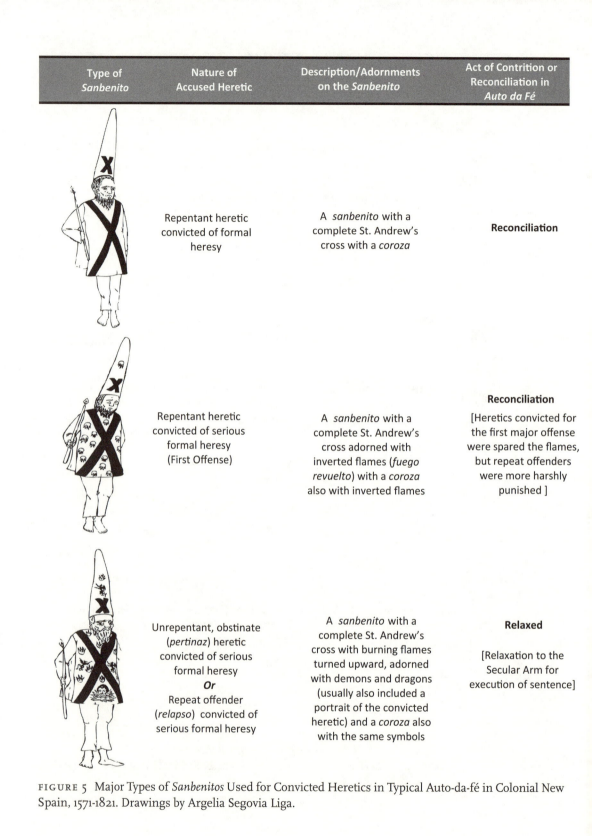

Type of *Sanbenito*	Nature of Accused Heretic	Description/Adornments on the *Sanbenito*	Act of Contrition or Reconciliation in *Auto da Fé*
	Repentant heretic convicted of formal heresy	A *sanbenito* with a complete St. Andrew's cross with a *coroza*	**Reconciliation**
	Repentant heretic convicted of serious formal heresy (First Offense)	A *sanbenito* with a complete St. Andrew's cross adorned with inverted flames (*fuego revuelto*) with a *coroza* also with inverted flames	**Reconciliation** [Heretics convicted for the first major offense were spared the flames, but repeat offenders were more harshly punished]
	Unrepentant, obstinate (*pertinaz*) heretic convicted of serious formal heresy *Or* Repeat offender (*relapso*) convicted of serious formal heresy	A *sanbenito* with a complete St. Andrew's cross with burning flames turned upward, adorned with demons and dragons (usually also included a portrait of the convicted heretic) and a *coroza* also with the same symbols	**Relaxed** [Relaxation to the Secular Arm for execution of sentence]

FIGURE 5 Major Types of *Sanbenitos* Used for Convicted Heretics in Typical Auto-da-fé in Colonial New Spain, 1571-1821. Drawings by Argelia Segovia Liga.

Palace of the Inquisition

Convento de Santo Domingo

FIGURE 6 Location of the Palace of the Inquisition in the Plaza of Santo Domingo in Mexico City, ca. 1749. Drawing adapted by the author from a 1749 plan of the City of Mexico by Carlos López.

FIGURE 7 The Water Torture Combined with the Torment of the Cords. From Antonio Puigblanch, *The Inquisition Unmasked: Being an Historical and Philosophical Account of That Tremendous Tribunal* (London: Baldwin, Cradock, and Joy, 1816). Photo from author's private collection.

FIGURE 8 Procession of an Auto-da-fé. Detail of a Print from John Joseph Stockdale, *The History of the Inquisitions: Including the Secret Transactions of Those Horrific Tribunals* (London, 1810). Photo from author's private collection.

FIGURE 9 Emblem of the Mexican Inquisition. Photo from author's private collection.

FIGURE 10 Solemn Procession of Prisoners. From Antonio Puigblanch, *The Inquisition Unmasked: Being an Historical and Philosophical Account of That Tremendous Tribunal* (London: Baldwin, Cradock, and Joy, 1816). Photo from author's private collection.

FIGURE 11 Images of Penitents Wearing *Sanbenitos*. From Antonio Puigblanch, *The Inquisition Unmasked: Being an Historical and Philosophical Account of That Tremendous Tribunal* (London: Baldwin, Cradock, and Joy, 1816). Photo from author's private collection.

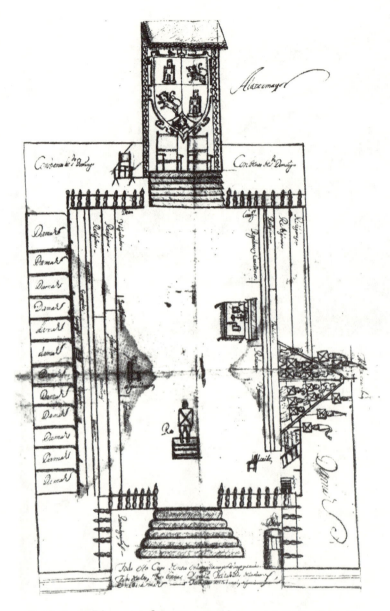

FIGURE 12 Diagram of Staging Used in an Auto-da-fé in New Spain, ca. 1699. From Archivo General de la Nación (México), vol. 707, folio 544.

FIGURE 13 The Execution of Sentences. Detail of an image of an Auto-da-fé in M. Victor Férél, *Mystères de l'inquisition et autres sociétés secretes d'Espagne* (Paris: P Boizard Editeur, 1846). Photo from author's private collection.

FIGURE 14 Images (*left to right*) of a Relaxed Woman Wearing a *Sanbenito* with the Insignias of Fire, a Penanced Woman Wearing a *Sanbenito* Who Made an Abjuration *de Levi*, and a Reconciled Woman Wearing a *Sanbenito* Who Made an Abjuration *de Vehementi*. From Antonio Puigblanch, *The Inquisition Unmasked: Being an Historical and Philosophical Account of That Tremendous Tribunal* (London: Baldwin, Cradock, and Joy, 1816). Photo from author's private collection.

PART III

Selections of Trials and *Procesos de Fe* of the Inquisition in New Spain, 1536–1820

Blasphemy Trials

By God's body, he who doesn't blaspheme is not a man!

Blasphemous phrase reportedly uttered by a Spanish conquistador of Mexico, Rodrigo
Rengel, 1527.[1]

Although one of the most common crimes prosecuted by the Inquisition in New
Spain was the crime of blasphemy, inquisitors in both Spain and the New World often de-
bated exactly what the crime of blasphemy actually entailed. According to ancient church
doctrine, blasphemy was any type of ill- or vile-sounding word or other derogatory comment that insulted or offended God or the saints. Medieval Spanish theologians and inquisitors came up with two strict definitions of blasphemy, which divided the crime into
two categories: simple blasphemy and heretical blasphemy.

The difference between the two was a fine one but a difference that became very
important to the Inquisition. According to the manual of Spanish inquisitor Nicolas
Eimeric, the *Directorium Inquisitorium,* an act of blasphemy was considered simple blasphemy and nonheretical when the insult or swearing reviled God or the Virgin or expressed ingratitude to them. The more serious heretical blasphemy entailed denial of
the articles of the faith or of God, the Virgin, or the saints. To deny God's existence in an
utterance of blasphemy was considered heretical blasphemy, whereas to curse God for
not helping you in a game of dice was considered only simple blasphemy. Thus, as far
as the Inquisition was concerned, the utterance of words in anger while a person
was emotionally distraught was generally considered to be simple blasphemy and not
heresy. Apparently, only the worst public cases of blasphemy were tried. In Spain and New
Spain, furthermore, most Spaniards commonly used expletives considered indecent and
irreverent, but not necessarily heretical. It was common to hear in Spanish gambling
houses and taverns such expletives as *Mal grada haya Dios* (In spite of God), *Pese a
Dios* (May God regret it), *Reniego a Dios* (I renounce God), and *Descreo de Dios* (I disbelieve in God).

The sin of blasphemy in Mexico was punished by the Inquisition in different ways,
depending on the quality or status of the accused. Race played a very important role
in the Inquisition's developing focus on blasphemy cases. Figures collected by Richard

Greenleaf and Solange Alberro indicate that in the first years of the Mexican Inquisition during the sixteenth century, Spaniards were the main focus of inquisitorial zeal.[2] Their habitual swearing and usage of foul and sacrilegious language was seen as a bad example for the rest of the population. From the middle of the seventeenth century, however, Africans and mulattoes became the target of inquisitorial activity. Blasphemy among people of African descent took the form of *reniegos* (denials), which in the case of enslaved men and women served the very practical purpose of calling the attention of the Holy Office to their victimization at the hands of their masters.[3]

Regardless of the race or quality of the accused, as the colonial period advanced, the Inquisition in New Spain prosecuted fewer people for charges involving blasphemy. The resulting lack of vigilance concerning the use of profane language by Spaniards, mulattoes, and mestizos gradually led to the common usage of cultural expletives even of a sacrilegious nature.

DOCUMENT 27
Inquisition Trial and Proceedings against Juan de Pórras, for Gambling and Blasphemy
Mexico City, 1536

SOURCE: Archivo General de la Nación, Ramo de Inquisición, vol. 14, exp. 3.

NOTE: This early trial conducted by the episcopal inquisition led by the first bishop of Mexico, Fray Juan de Zumárraga, explicitly shows the relationship between gaming and gambling and the crime of blasphemy. Blasphemous expletives such as those uttered by Juan de Pórras during a losing hand at cards or dice often brought about accusations and investigations for the crime of simple blasphemy.

Denunciation and Testimony of Cristóbal de Benavente against Juan de Pórras for the Crime of Blasphemy, July 1, 1536

†

In the great city of México-Tenochtitlan, in this New Spain in the chambers of the Holy Office of the Inquisition[4] on this first Saturday, July 1, 1536, before his Reverence Don Fray Juan de Zumárraga, first bishop of this said city and Apostolic Inquisitor of New Spain . . . Cristóbal de Benavente appeared before this Holy Office and in the presence of Martín de Campos, Secretary of this Holy Office, in order to denounce Juan de Pórras for the crimes of gambling and blasphemy. This witness declares that on many occasions he has seen the said Juan de Pórras gambling and playing cards and that on those occasions he has heard him utter several blasphemous things such as *"May God regret this"* and *"I'll make God and that woman who gave birth to him regret this,"* and he also uttered many other vile things against the saints stating that he did not believe in God and that *"I can do God more harm than this!"* and he often said that he could do whatever he wanted to. He also declared that the said Juan de Pórras said these things every time he played cards and gambled. When he lost at cards or dice, he proclaimed these blasphemies. He said all of these things every time he played cards and lost. The witness swore the oath to tell the truth and he swore to the secret of the Holy Office.

Cristóbal de Benavente
Martín de Campos [Secretary]
Fr. Juan de Zumárraga [Inquisitor]

Denunciation and Testimony made by Diego de la Palma against Juan de Pórras for the Crime of Blasphemy, Friday, July 7, 1536

†

On Friday, July 7, 1536, Diego de la Palma appeared before his Lordship the Inquisitor in order to denounce and declare against Juan de Pórras. He stated that, while they gambled and played cards, he had seen and heard him say that he did not believe in God. Especially when he last played cards with him, he heard him say this and exclaim when he lost, "*By the life of God and the Saints.*" He states that he has heard him say this many times.

He was then asked if he knew that it was public knowledge that the said Juan de Pórras used blasphemy publicly and said these things in the presence and in front of many people. He said that he saw and heard Juan de Pórras use these and other blasphemous words publicly in front of many people. He stated that he had blasphemed the name of Our Lord God and many of his saints on many occasions. He then swore the oath and declared this all to be the truth.

Diego de la Palma
Martín de Campos [Secretary]
Fr. Juan de Zumárraga [Inquisitor]

Denunciation and Testimony Made by Hernán Pérez against Juan de Pórras for the Crime of Blasphemy, Friday, July 7, 1536

†

On Friday, July 7, 1536, Hernán Pérez de Carrión, scribe of His Majesty, appeared before his Lordship the Inquisitor and the secretary in order to denounce and declare against Juan de Pórras. He stated that he denounced and denounces Juan de Pórras for blaspheming on several occasions while he was playing cards and gambling. He said that while he played cards he heard him say, "*I renounce God*" and "*May God regret this!*" and "*I don't want God to do me any and I won't thank him even if he does!*" He declares that these words are often exclaimed by Pórras when he plays cards. He has the custom of saying them when he plays and loses. Publicly he exclaims these things and others much worse before all of the men he plays with. He swears the oath and declares that all of this is the truth and not declared out of malice or ill will, but for the good of his own soul.

Hernán Pérez de Carrión
Martín de Campos [Secretary]
Fr. Juan de Zumárraga [Inquisitor]

Arrest and Confession of Juan de Pórras, Tuesday, October 10, 1536

✝

On Tuesday, October 10, 1536, His Lordship ordered that Juan de Pórras be brought before him in the audience chamber of the Holy Office.[5] Pórras, who has been a prisoner here in this Holy Office was then brought before him and received the oath and promised to tell the truth according to the following questions he was asked.

He was asked what he was called. He replied that he was called Juan de Pórras.

He was asked where he was from and he said that he was a native of Cuellar and that he was raised in the town of Medina del Campo in the Kingdom of Castile.

He was asked who were his parents and grandparents and where were they from. He said that he was clean of heretical blood in the generation of his father who was called Gonzalo de Pórras, native of Valdeporras, who was a nobleman, and that his mother was called Francisca de Toledo, native of Cuellar, and this confessant believes that she came from a family of converted Jews because this is what he had heard said by many people.

He was asked if any of his relatives were punished or tried by the Inquisition or cited by the Holy Office for any crimes against the faith. He said that he did not know, and he did not believe that any of his parents had been prisoners or penitents of the Holy Inquisition, and moreover he had always believed them to be good Christians and they were held as such in their towns.

He was asked if he had been punished or sentenced by the Inquisition for blasphemy or for any other things or crimes against the faith by any judge. He said that no, he had not.

He was asked what type of blasphemies or renunciations had he said or made against God in front of other people or in the presence of others and how many times had he made such blasphemies. He said that he has said several blasphemous things and that he had come to denounce himself to the Holy Office. He also stated that he had reported himself to the Inquisition and his blasphemies were recorded here, and he thus asks for mercy and penitence.

He was asked again if at any other time he remembered having said shameful things such as, "*I renounce God*" or "*I detest God and his saints*" or many other vile blasphemies against God, the Virgin, or the saints.

He said that he had already denounced himself of all of these sins and blasphemies contained in this said question. Again he asks for penance and mercy and declares that he cannot remember any other specifics about the instances of his blasphemy, and he remits himself to his earlier confessions concerning his frequent anger and ill temper and his tendency to blaspheme and say vile words every time he could.

He was asked if he knew that blaspheming and renouncing God and his saints was a very grave sin against Our Lord. He said that he knew that blaspheming and renouncing God was a very abominable sin and because of this terrible sin he had come to denounce himself and again he asks for mercy and penance, and he promises to be a faithful Christian and not to commit the said crime and sin of blasphemy again. He added that he was truly sorry in his deepest heart for having committed the sin of blasphemy and he asks for God's pardon and the penance that Your Lordship should impose upon him. He did not sign because he did not know how to sign.

Final and Definitive Sentence in the Blasphemy Trial against Juan de Pórras, October 14, 1536

✝

We find that we must order and condemn and we do condemn the said Juan de Pórras of the crime of blasphemy. We order that on the following Sunday that the said prisoner Juan de Pórras should appear before the cathedral of this city and hear a Mass. He shall be placed standing before the congregation, naked from the waist up. With his head and feet uncovered, he shall hold a long candle in his hands. He shall also have a metal gag placed in his mouth, and he shall have his tongue slit as a punishment.[6] After the Mass he shall publicly say the Ave María and the Pater Noster, and he will beg the Lord God to forgive him publicly. He shall also be condemned to pay a fine of ten gold pesos.

Fr. Juan de Zumárraga [Inquisitor]
Martín de Campos [Secretary]

DOCUMENT 28
Inquisition Trial and Proceedings against the Tailor Juan de Villate for Blasphemy and Heretical Propositions

Mexico City, May 1539

Source: Archivo General de la Nación, Ramo de Inquisición, vol. 2, exp. 9.

Note: This brief trial for blasphemy depicts aspects of daily life in early colonial New Spain. Like Juan de Villate's wife, Juana Gómez, many women in New Spain may have accused their husbands of crimes against the faith for real or perceived personal abuses. Although there was another declaration against the tailor Villate, Inquisitor Zumárraga's lenient sentence in this case reveals that he viewed with some skepticism the veracity of the wife's denunciation and her apparent confession against her husband to a third person, which she did no doubt because of her jealously over her husband's philandering ways.

Denunciation made by Lope Gallego against the Tailor Juan de Villate for Blasphemy and Heretical Propositions, May 12, 1539

✝

In the great city of México-Tenochtitlan, in this New Spain in the presence of his Reverence Don Fray Juan de Zumárraga, first bishop of this said city and Apostolic Inquisitor of New Spain and before the secretary of the Holy Office, Lope Gallego appeared in order to denounce to the Holy Office what he knew about the Tailor Juan de Villate. He said that about a month ago, more or less, when this witness was a worker in the house of the said Villate, he had heard Juana Gómez, the wife of the said Tailor, say several things about her husband. She had said that her husband had rebuked her for praying before an image of Our Lady the Virgin Mary. She had told him that he had taken from her the rosary beads that she used to pray to the Virgin, ripped them from her hand, and told her "*You should not pray so much to God; it is better to pray to the Devil!*" She also told him that they had fought because she had prayed to the Virgin. Again, he declared that last Sunday he had heard from a mestizo laborer named Marco who worked for Juan de Villate that the night before Juan de Villate had found his wife praying again and he had fought with her and taken from her the beads that she was praying with and he slapped her in the face several times and told her, "*I swear to God if I find you praying again with those beads I will throw them into a well and I will burn your hands.*" And this said Marco had told him this and also that an Indian woman named Catalina who was a slave to the household was also present when this occurred. He swore that this is the truth and that he does not declare it out of malice or hatred toward the said Juan de Villate. He does not sign it because he said that he does not know how to sign.

Miguel López [Secretary]
Fr. Juan de Zumárraga [Inquisitor]

Testimony of Juana Gómez, Wife of the Tailor Juan de Villate, May 16, 1539

✝

His Lordship the Inquisitor ordered that Juana Gómez, wife of the said Tailor, appear before the Holy Office to testify concerning the case. She swore to the oath and promised to tell the truth.

She said that her name was Juana Gómez and that she was the wife of Juan de Villate.

She was asked if her husband had fought with her because she was praying. She replied that yes, on many occasions her had fought with her and he had taken from her the prayer beads she used, ripping them out of her hands and saying, "*You should not pray to God, but rather you should pray to the Devil!*" She also said that it was true that her husband, Juan de Villate, on many occasions found her praying and that he similarly ripped the beads away from her and told her, "*Why do you pray so much. . . . You are going to the Devil. . . . he will take care of you.*" She also said that on two other occasions he fought with her when he found her praying, slapping her and placing his hands violently on her.

She was asked if she had seen him conduct any Jewish or other pagan ceremonies. She said that she had not.

She was then asked to what caste or group does her husband belong. She said that she does not know anything else than what he tells her and that is that he is of a better caste and genealogy than this witness.

She was asked if her husband confessed or if he was living in concubinage with any other women. She replied that he did not confess and that he had been denounced before in the church for not having confessed. She also said that he was and is presently living in sin in concubinage with an Indian woman, and he also has relations with one of their slaves. All of this he uses to give her a bad life, and she admits that she prays when he wishes to come and lay with her.

She was asked if she had heard or seen her husband renounce God or say any other blasphemies. She said that several times she had heard him say that he *"spites God"* and that she has not heard any other blasphemies, nor has she heard him renounce God and that all of this is the truth under oath.

She also stated that this morning her husband had threatened her and told her not to tell the Holy Office that he gave her such a bad life. He warned her that if the Holy Office asked her if he gave her a bad life that she should deny it and said that he gave her a good life. This too is the truth. She does not sign because she said she does not know how to sign.

Miguel López [Secretary]
Fr. Juan de Zumárraga [Inquisitor]

Confession and Testimony of the Prisoner Juan de Villate, Tailor, May 17, 1539

†

His Lordship ordered that the prisoner, Juan de Villate be brought before the Holy Office and questioned according to the accusations placed against him. He was sworn in and promised to tell the truth.

He said that his name was Juan de Villate and that he was a native of the Kingdom of Castile, and that he came from the town of Villa de Llerena in the province of Leon.

He said that concerning his caste and race that he was born in the town of Villa de Llerena and that he was born in the house of the Inquisitor Villate[7] and that the said Inquisitor had him and kept him as his son and that his mother was a woman from the Canary Islands.[8]

He was asked if he was baptized. He said that he had always heard that he was baptized.

He said that he was married to Juana Gómez.

He was asked if he had fought with his wife on several occasions when she was praying and if he had said that she *"should not pray so much to God but rather to the Devil."* He said that he denies this, and instead he has said on many occasions that she should pray and remember God so that God will remember her. He declared that many times when he came home to eat he found that his food had not been cooked and that instead of preparing the food, he found his wife praying with the said prayer beads in her hands. He also stated that on another occasion he came again and saw this and out of anger that she had not made the food he angrily exclaimed, "*You never take out those beads until you see me coming home to eat. . . . To the Hell with your damn beads because these beads don't commend you to God, but rather to the Devil!*"

He was asked if he had been denounced in his church for not having gone to confession. He declared that it was the truth that he had not confessed and for this he had been excommunicated and that this very morning he went to ask for penance and absolution, but he was taken here to this prison instead before he could gain absolution.

He was asked if he had a lover and lived in sin with an Indian woman and if he had other lovers, and he was asked to declare all of his lovers. He declared that he had no concubines at all but that he has slept with and had relations with a few Indian women from time to time.

He was asked what blasphemies he had spoken. He said that on a few occasions he had said "*I swear to God*" and "*By God I swear*" and that he has said no other blasphemies and all of this is the truth under oath.

Juan de Villate
Miguel López [Secretary]
Fr. Juan de Zumárraga [Inquisitor]

Definitive Sentence against Juan de Villate, May 20, 1539

✝

After having seen the confession and denunciations against Juan de Villate, His Lordship said that he condemns and does condemn him to pray five times a day the Rosary of Our Lady and that he pay a fine of one peso of gold to be given as an alms to the Syphilitic hospital here in this City. Besides this he condemns him to pay a fine of ten pesos of gold to be applied and paid to the Fiscal of the Holy Office and to be paid before he may leave the said jails and secret prisons of the Holy Office. He also condemns him to pay for the costs of this trial and all other costs associated with his case. This condemnation was given as his definitive sentence and it was pronounced and ordered by His Lordship the Inquisitor

Fr. Juan de Zumárraga [Inquisitor]
Lic. Loaisa [Inquisitor]
Juan Rebollo [Secretary]

DOCUMENT 29

Self-Denunciation and Sentence against Alonso Bueno
for the Crime of Blasphemy

Mexico City, January 7, 1541

SOURCE: Archivo General de la Nación, Ramo de Inquisición, vol. 14, exp. 40.

NOTE: Fear of being denounced by others might prompt self-denunciation in order to protect oneself from later prosecution or to gain leniency if brought before the Inquisition. Apparently, Alonso Bueno acted out of fear that someone might have denounced him for a supposed act of blasphemy.

Self-Denunciation Made by Alonso Bueno for the Crime of Blasphemy

✝

In the great city of México-Tenochtitlan, in this New Spain in the presence of his Reverence Don Fray Juan de Zumárraga, first bishop of this said city and Apostolic Inquisitor of New Spain and before the secretary of the Holy Office, Alonso Bueno appeared in order to denounce himself for the crime of blasphemy. He appeared in order to denounce himself because several days ago when two other people were fighting he was able to stop their fight and regain the peace. He declared that one of them had proclaimed, "*By the Love of all of the Saints I do not have to be your friend!*" Then, not watching his own words, he replied, "*The Saints be Damned. . . . By the Love of God, who is more powerful than the saints, I will be your friend.*" He declared that he said this without paying attention to what he was saying. Seeing that he had sinned, he went before the Provisor[9] so that he could absolve him, but the Provisor ordered him to go and denounce himself to the Inquisition. He declared that this is the truth under oath.

He concluded that he does not have anything else to add to a confession and that as a good Christian and fearful of God he asks for mercy and penitence from Your Lordship.

Alonso Bueno

Miguel López [Secretary]

Fr. Juan de Zumárraga [Inquisitor]

Definitive Sentence against Alonso Bueno

✝

After having seen the confession and self-denunciation given by Alonso Bueno, His Lordship said that he condemns and does condemn him to a fine of three pesos of gold to be given to the Fiscal of the Holy Office and to be paid before he leaves this said building and seat of the Holy Office. This condemnation was given as his definitive sentence, and it was pronounced and ordered by His Lordship the Inquisitor.

Fr. Juan de Zumárraga [Inquisitor]
Miguel López [Secretary]

DOCUMENT 30
Inquisition Testimony against Pascuala, a Mulatta Slave on the Sugar Plantation of Tlacomulco in the Region of Cuernavaca, for the Crime of Blasphemy
Tlacomulco, Cuernavaca, April 1710

Source: Archivo General de la Nación, Ramo de Inquisición, vol. 470, exp. 45.

Note: It was quite common for slaves in New Spain to use blasphemy as a means of relief or resistance to harsh labor and other desperate situations.[10] Sometimes slaves could even avoid harsher punishments from their owners or other civil authorities by committing blasphemy and having themselves removed to an Inquisition jail. In this case against Pascuala, a mulatta slave on a sugar plantation, one slave who testified against her was able to use his knowledge to gain his own release from a civil prison (at least temporarily) in order to denounce her blasphemy.

Letter and Remission of a Denunciation of Blasphemy against a Mulatta Slave, April 23, 1710

†

I am remitting this denunciation of blasphemy against a mulatta slave from the Sugar mills at Tlacomulco, so that once you have reviewed the case Your Lordship can order me to do what is most convenient.

May God guard Your Lordship for many years for the defense of our Faith.
Signed in Cuernavaca, April 23, 1710
Bachiller Juan de Roa
Commissary of the Inquisition in Cuernavaca

Received in this Holy Office in Mexico City on April 28, 1710
Advise the commissary and the secretary who serves
as the prosecutor of the receipt of this denunciation.

Signed The Lord Inquisitors Deza and Garzarón

Denunciation of Juan Antonio de Gama, Mestizo, against the Suspected Blasphemy of a Mulatta Slave, April 20, 1710

✝

In the town of Cuernavaca, of the valley district, on the 20th of April 1710, before Bachiller don Juan Simón de Roa, cleric of this archbishopric and commissary of the Holy Office in this jurisdiction, during the afternoon, a man called Juan Antonio de Gama appeared without having been summoned, stating that he was a single mestizo native of Mexico and resident of this jurisdiction, a muleteer by trade, and he appeared to be of the age of twenty-five years old. The said mestizo stated and declared that for the discharge of his conscience, that when he had been at the Sugar mill at Tlacomulco during the past month of March aiding the carpenter Juan García, he heard it said that Francisco, a mulatto slave owned by Bachiller Don Felipe Salazar, had to denounce someone to the Inquisition, but being a prisoner at the time he could not do it.

Asked if he had been told about whom or about what he had to denounce, he said that he did not want to say who it was, and the only other thing that he told him was that there at that Mill was someone who constantly blasphemed and renounced God, and that he could, upon being summoned, say who it was, and that only if someone would call for him would he say who it was.

He stated that this was the truth and that it had been well written, and thus he swore the oath to God and the Holy Cross and stated that he did not denounce this out of hatred.

He promised to keep the secret and he signed it with the Commissary.

Bachiller Juan de Roa   Juan Antonio de Gama

This passed before me,
Francisco Ximénez Cubero, Notary

Testimony of Francisco de la Cruz, Mulatto Slave of Bachiller Don Felipe de Salazar, April 20, 1710

✝

In the said town, on the same day, month, and year, before the Commissary there appeared, having been summoned, Francisco de la Cruz, a mulatto slave of Bachiller Don Felipe de Salazar, who swore to God Our Lord and before the sign of the cross to tell the truth in all that he would be questioned.

Questioned what was his name, he said that it was Francisco de la Cruz and that he was a single mulatto slave of the age of sixteen years, native of this town of Cuernavaca.

Asked if he knew why he had been called, he said no.

Asked if he had heard of or seen something against Our Holy Catholic Faith, he said that during the second week of Lent,[11] one day on Saturday in the morning he heard Pascuala, a mulatta slave of the said Mill, blaspheme. After her other female companions

went into the fields to work, without having been whipped there in the fields after her labors and work, she exclaimed that she renounced the Holy Virgin and her precious son.
And after that instance, several other weeks later he also heard the said Pascuala talking to
her brother who urged her to go to confession. He stated, *"Why should she go, what could she
say"* and that *"she had renounced God and the Saints many times that year."* On another occasion when her husband asked her why she did not pray to the Saints or light candles to
them, she said that she did not want to do it because she had not obtained her children. All
of this was also heard by Juan de Dios, another mulatto slave of the said Mill.

And asked if he knew any other thing or had heard any other thing said by other persons, he said that he did not, and that all he had stated was the truth under the oath that he
had taken. Being read what had been written, he stated that he did not denounce this out
of hatred. He promised to keep the secret and did not sign it because he did not know how
to write.

Bachiller Juan de Roa
This passed before me,
Francisco Ximénez Cubero, Notary

Testimony of Juan de Dios, Slave of the Tlacomulco Mill, April 25, 1710

✝

On the 25th of April 1710, before the said commissary in the morning, there appeared,
having been summoned, Juan de Dios, slave of the Tlacomulco Mill, married with Andrea
de la Concepción, a slave native of Peru, of the age of thirty years old, a miller and wood-
cutter by trade.

Asked if he knew why he had been called, he said no.

Asked if he had heard of or seen something against Our Holy Catholic Faith, he said
that about a month and a half ago while being in the Mill house, at about around eight
o'clock at night, he heard that when the Overseer threatened her, Pascuala, a slave of the
said Mill, said that *"Even if the Devil will take me, I will renounce the Holy Virgin, and all her
Saints, even if they whip me,"* and she has the custom of whenever she receives a whipping
or a punishment to call out to the devils to take her away, and speak other blasphemies.
And he stated that, even though on that occasion it was the Overseer involved, he did not
reproach her, nor did he make an account of it, because no one pays her any attention.

He stated that this was the truth under the oath that he had taken before God and the
cross, and being read what had been written, he stated that he did not denounce this out
of hatred. He promised to keep the secret and did not sign it because he did not know
how to write.

Bachiller Juan de Roa
This passed before me,
Francisco Ximénez Cubero, Notary

Testimony of Miguel Ramírez, a Mulatto Muleteer, April 25, 1710

✝

In the said town, on the same day, month, and year, before the Commissary, there appeared, having been summoned a man called Miguel Ramírez, a single mulatto muleteer, native of Valladolid, twenty years old.

Asked if he knew why he had been called, and he said no.

Asked if he had heard of or seen something against Our Holy Catholic Faith, he said that about a month before, while this witness and Francisco de la Cruz were seated near a windmill, he heard it said that a mulatta slave named Pascuala had renounced the Holy Virgin and her precious son, and that someone should denounce it to Father Roa, and that this witness knows that the said Pascuala on many occasions while they have been in the fields has uttered curses and other vile and profane words out of desperation.

Asked if he knew anything else, he said that he did not, and he stated that this was the truth under the oath that he had taken before God and the cross, and being read what had been written, he stated that he did not denounce this out of hatred. He promised to keep the secret and did not sign it because he did not know how to write.

Bachiller Juan de Roa
This passed before me,
Francisco Ximénez Cubero, Notary

NOTE: The preceding documents contain only a series of commissary investigations and denunciations. There was no formal accusation of the fiscal or any arrest warrant or further proceedings in this case. Apparently the inquisitors took into consideration the quality and status of those who testified to crimes against the faith and put little value in the veracity of testimony provided by the slaves and mestizo overseers.

Bigamy, Polygamy, and Crimes against
the Sacrament of Matrimony

[He was] dragged down in human weakness because he wanted her so much and, since
she was a virgin, there was no other way to gain access to her because Juana said he could
have her only if they married. Thus, carried away and defeated by passion, he committed
the error.

Confession of Marcos de la Cruz, a Spaniard accused of having committed bigamy by marrying Juana Montaño while he himself was already married, 1671[12]

Soon after its establishment in Spain, the Inquisition came to include among its
jurisdictions control over a series of crimes of the faith concerning the sacrament of
matrimony. For centuries the royal and ecclesiastical courts in Spain had punished the
crime of bigamy, but once the Inquisition arrived, it claimed the exclusive right to punish
bigamists and other transgressors against sexual morality.[13] The initial justification for
the Inquisition's claim of jurisdiction lay in the fact that many bigamists held erroneous ideas about the church's belief in the undissolvable bonds of holy matrimony. Consequently, some of the first questions asked of any suspected bigamist focused on his understanding of matrimony.[14] As early as 1575, however, the inquisitors in New Spain wrote
to the Suprema that the bigamists they encountered revealed no erroneous beliefs concerning matrimony.[15] More often than not, these bigamists claimed that their second marriage came only after they had to abandon their first spouses for a variety of reasons, such
as abuse, neglect, and adultery. As most bigamists argued, they had believed that they were
acting properly as good Christians in contracting a second marriage in order not to live in
open sin with their second spouse.[16] The inquisitors of New Spain deduced, as they wrote
in another letter in 1576, that the real cause behind most of the cases of bigamy was the
"little care that the bishops and their clergy take in giving marriage licenses to men they
do not know without any more information than their own personal declarations that they
are single and unmarried, without any proof of another witness."[17] As a result, the Inquisition in New Spain issued stern warnings to the region's bishops not to issue marriage licenses without taking precautions in order to avoid these crimes.

The immigration of a preponderance of males during the first decades of the colony
explained most cases of bigamy as a simple result of the distance and difficulty of communication. Many argued that they had heard, through third parties, that their first spouses

had died in the interim and, without the possibility of verifying the death, accepted these communications and contracted a second marriage out of necessity. In New Spain, both women and men committed the crime of bigamy. Women often claimed the same reasons for leaving their spouses or marrying a second time (document 31).[18] The prevalence of bigamy in the Indies led the crown to pass laws, ordering "all those who were married in Spain who resided in the Indies and who were absent from their women and wives" to return to Spain to live with their wives.[19]

Nevertheless, as María Asunción Herrera Sotillo discovered in her own research, the crime of bigamy appears to have been more actively prosecuted in New Spain than in the Peninsular tribunals.[20] According to the figures compiled by Gustav Henningsen for the tribunals in Spain, cases against bigamy amounted to just over 5 percent of all crimes punished by the Spanish Inquisition.[21] In New Spain, on the other hand, bigamy cases amounted to more than 18 percent of all of the cases from 1571 to 1700.[22]

Of 219 bigamy cases prosecuted in New Spain during this time period, only 24 cases pertain to women, and only 7 of those cases included white Spanish women.[23] Most involved mestizas and mulattas born in New Spain who had received little religious or educational instruction and whose sexual customs and relationships apparently were more liberal than their white Spanish counterparts. Of the 155 white Spanish men tried for the crime of bigamy, most had been born in Spain. The Inquisition in New Spain tried only 40 men of other ethnicities for the same crime.[24]

The most common punishments for the crime of bigamy included having the guilty verdict read publicly to a suspect wearing a *sanbenito* and holding a burning candle, with a noose tied around his or her neck as a symbol of their ultimate public flogging.[25] According to the documents, 171 of those convicted for bigamy made a public abjuration *de levi* in combination with receiving a certain number of lashes and other public humiliations. Other more serious cases received harsher sentences of exile or forced service, sometimes as a rower in the royal galleys.[26]

Some prisoners received lighter sentences, such as Gonzalo de Ávila, who was punished by having to make publicly an abjuration *de levi* and pay a fine of seven hundred pesos. The lenience of this sentence, as the inquisitors stated in a copy of the relation of the auto-da-fé of 1574, was "based on his quality and his appearing to have had a good intention without much bad faith in contracting his second marriage."[27] Similarly, as Herrera Sotillo discovered, the Inquisition in New Spain diminished the rigor of its punishment from 1670 onward, when almost no one was sentenced to galley service for the crime of bigamy.[28]

DOCUMENT 31

Inquisition Trial against María de Sotomayor, for the Crime of Polygamy

Mexico City, 1538–1540

SOURCE: Archivo General de la Nación, Ramo de Inquisición, vol. 36, exp. 6.

NOTE: The following trial for polygamy shows the lengths to which women in New Spain would go in order to avoid an unwanted or abusive husband. In this case, the accused woman, María de Sotomayor, wished to avoid her original first husband so much that, even after the trial and sentencing, she refused to return to her husband in Spain.

Denunciation and Testimony of Cristóbal de Cañego against María de Sotomayor for Suspected Polygamy, July 2, 1538

✝

Very Reverend Inquisitor,

I, Cristóbal de Cañego, official constable of the Inquisition, discharge my conscience and denounce and make it known to Your Mercy, in order to avoid public scandal and in order to ensure that those who commit crimes are punished, that María de Sotomayor, a woman who says that she is married to Gaspar Hurtado, now a prisoner in the public jail of this city of Mexico, is already a married woman who has procured the holy bonds of matrimony to another man back in Spain by a ritual of the Holy Mother Church. She has contracted matrimony before in the town of Toledo with a man known as Juan de Castro, a resident in the said kingdom of Castile, who is presently still alive. With her husband still living, the said María de Sotomayor through vile duplicity and against the laws of our Holy Mother Church, contracted holy matrimony a second time with Gaspar de Hurtado here in this city of Mexico as is publicly known. Because this second matrimony is public and common knowledge, I will present information proving that she has thus engaged in a second marriage while she knew that her first husband is still alive.

I denounce her so that the Holy Office can begin to proceed against the said María de Sotomayor with all the rigor and justice necessary, punishing her for her sins with all of the punishments possible under civil and ecclesiastical law.

Cristóbal de Cañego

After having heard and read this denunciation, it was ordered by his Lordship the Apostolic Inquisitor that María de Sotomayor should be arrested and her goods seques-tered while public information and testimony is taken in the case.[29]

Testimony of Alonso de Alarcón, July 13, 1538

✝

After the said denunciation, the Inquisitor summoned and received the oath from Alonso de Alarcón, a resident of this city who promised to tell the truth.

He was asked if he knew the said María de Sotomayor, now a prisoner in this prison, while he had lived in the town of Toledo in the kingdom of Castile. He replied that yes, he did know her when he lived in the city of Toledo. He also said that he knew her husband, Juan de Castro, and he knew that he was apparently married to the said María de Sotomayor and that they had been married in the church of San Lázaro. He knew this because he lived with Juan de Ávila, who had been one of the godparents of the said wedding ceremony.

He was asked if he had seen that the said María de Sotomayor and the said Juan de Castro had lived together as one and if the said María de Sotomayor had left her husband and fled from him or abandoned him. He said that he saw them married and living together in one house, concerning the rest of the things questioned, he does not know.

He was asked if, at the time he had left Toledo to come to this kingdom of Mexico, he had known or seen that the said Juan de Castro was still alive. He said that he had left from Toledo only recently, more or less, about two years ago, and when he left he knew that Juan de Castro was alive because he had spoken with him in Seville.

He was asked if he had since found out that the said Juan de Castro, husband of María de Sotomayor, had died or had been killed and, if so, how long ago. He replied that he did not know and that he believed he was still alive.

He was asked if he knew that the said María de Sotomayor had married once again here and that she was now married to Gaspar de Hurtado. He said that he had heard it said that she had married him and that he had seen her imprisoned here in this jail at the request of Gaspar de Hurtado.

He did not sign it because he did not know how to write.

Juan Rebollo [Notary]

Testimony of García de Medina, Resident of the City of Mexico, August 2, 1538

†

The Inquisitor summoned and received the oath from García de Medina, a resident of this city who promised to tell the truth.

He was asked if he knew the said María de Sotomayor, now a prisoner in this prison, while he had lived in Spain. He said that he had known her for six years more or less and that he had met her in Seville in the house of a silversmith named Castro who lived in the Barrio of Santa Cruz, and he counted her as one of his friends.

He was asked if he knew that the said María de Sotomayor had been married to a Juan Castro. He said that what he knows is that during that time a man came to Seville from Toledo, and this witness remembers him calling himself Castro, and that he came to Seville to find the said María de Sotomayor. The said Castro then found and hid María de Sotomayor for two or three months in a house there because he said publicly in the barrio of Santa Cruz that she was his wife and that they had been married. This is the truth under oath, and he did not sign because he did not know how to sign.

Juan Rebollo [Notary]

Testimony of Hernando Díaz, August 7, 1538

✝

After the said denunciation, the Inquisitor summoned and received the oath from Hernando Díaz, a resident of this city who promised to tell the truth.

He was asked if he knew María de Sotomayor and if he knew a Juan Castro, her husband. He said that he did know María de Sotomayor for about fourteen years more or less and that he knew the said Juan de Castro her husband for about twenty years more or less.

He was asked if he knew that María de Sotomayor was married in Toledo with the said Juan de Castro and if they had lived together as man and wife and if he knew whether Juan de Castro was dead. He said that in Toledo about twelve or thirteen years ago [1526] the two of them fell in love while the said María de Sotomayor lived in her mother's house. They eloped and went to Toledo and were married, and that the priest Francisco de Reynosa, priest of the church of San Lázaro of Toledo married them. He said that he knew this because the said Juan de Castro was a very good friend of his, and he remembered that one Juan de Ávila and his wife were the godparents of the couple. He said that he did not know if the said Juan de Castro was alive or dead, but he added that when he left Toledo he was still alive, and this is the truth under oath.

Hernando Díaz
Juan Rebollo [Notary]

Testimony of María Maldonado, August 8, 1538

✝

After the said denunciation, the Inquisitor summoned and received the oath from María de Maldonado, a resident of this city who promised to tell the truth.

She was asked if she knew María de Sotomayor and if she knew Juan de Castro, her husband. She said that she knew María de Sotomayor for about thirteen or fourteen years more or less and that she also knew the said Juan de Castro, her husband.

She was asked if she knew that María de Sotomayor had married Juan de Castro in Toledo and if they had lived as husband and wife and if she knew if the said Juan de Castro was dead. She said that it must have been about twelve or fourteen years ago when she was in the city of Toledo in the company of the Licentiate Castellón when she witnessed the marriage of María de Sotomayor and Juan de Castro. She saw them married in the church of San Lázaro by the parish priest Francisco Reynosa, and she knows this because she was present at the marriage ceremony. She also knew that Juan de Ávila and Elena de Aguilar, his wife, served as the godparents of their wedding. She said that she does not know if the said Juan de Castro is now dead or if he lives, because when she left Toledo he was still alive, and this is the truth under oath.

Cristóbal de Torres [Notary]

Testimony and Confession of María de Sotomayor, August 26, 1538

✝

After the said denunciation, the Inquisitor summoned and received the oath from the said prisoner María de Sotomayor, who promised under oath to tell the truth and confess the truth of all that she was asked.

She was asked what her name was, and she replied that she was called María de Sotomayor and that she was a native of the city of Toledo in the kingdom of Castile.

She was asked how long had she been living in the Kingdom of New Spain. She replied that she had been in these lands for three years.

She was asked if she was married. She said that yes she was married and that she had been married in a public ceremony with Gaspar de Hurtado, who is now living in this city of Mexico.

She was asked how long ago it was since she was married with the said Gaspar de Hurtado. She said about fifteen months ago, more or less, she married him in this city in the Cathedral and a priest whose name she could not remember married them.

She was asked if she had ever been married before she had married with the said Gaspar de Hurtado. She said yes, she had been married to Juan de Castro, a native and resident of the town of Toledo and the son of Juan Castellón and that she married him in a church there that was called San Lázaro, and a priest called Francisco Herrera de Reynosa had married them.

She was asked how long she had been married with the said Juan de Castro. She replied that she had been married with him for fourteen years more or less.

She was asked if he was dead or alive. She said that, when she left Toledo for these kingdoms, she left behind the said Juan de Castro, her first husband, alive. After she had arrived in Mexico, she was told that he had died and for this reason she had married again with the said Hurtado. Then she said about eight months ago, more or less, her sister had written her a letter from Toledo telling her that the said Juan de Castro, her first husband, was still alive and that he wanted her to return to him to make a married life with him again. She stated that this was the truth under oath.

Cristóbal de Torres [Notary]

On September 4, 1538, the Inquisitor ordered that all of the belongings of the said María de Sotomayor should be confiscated and sequestered.

Audience and Testimony of Gaspar de Hurtado, August 30, 1538

✝

After the said confession, the Inquisitor summoned and received the oath from Gaspar de Hurtado, present and second husband of the accused María de Sotomayor, who was summoned by the Inquisitor and made aware of the denunciation placed against his wife by Cristóbal de Cañego and the confession of the said María de Sotomayor. He was also told that her said first husband, Juan de Castro, was still alive and thus her legitimate husband and that he should renounce all rights and obligations being as he was in illegitimate matrimony with the said María de Sotomayor, now accused of the crime of polygamy. Gaspar de Hurtado then said that he renounced and accepted the confession and accusation against his wife, and he requested that the Inquisitor absolve him of ill guilt, for he said that he did not know that her first husband was still alive. He then requested that the Inquisitor close the case and quickly sentence her.

Gaspar de Hurtado
Cristóbal de Torres [Notary]

Review of the Case and Definitive Sentence in the Trial, September 4, 1538

†

After reviewing the said documents, accusations, and denunciations in this case and after the said accused María de Sotomayor rejected the request to present evidence in her favor, his Lordship the Inquisitor said that he decided, sentences, and condemns the said María de Sotomayor that on the first feast day possible she should be placed and stripped naked before the congregation and forced to kneel and hear a penitential mass in the Cathedral. She should have a candle in her hand and remain naked from the waist up and barefoot. She should be paraded before the congregation and after the mass she should be forced to kneel before the images of the saints and listen to a sermon concerning the holy bonds of matrimony. We also condemn her to the confiscation and loss of half of all of her belongings as a fine that is to be applied to the fiscal office of this Holy Inquisition, and under the threat of excommunication we order that she be placed on the next available ship bound for Spain and that she return to the kingdom of Spain where she is to again go and live a married life with her first and only legitimate husband, Juan de Castro. After she has done her penance, we order any priest to absolve her of her sins, and we sentence her now with these punishments and with the admonition that, if she should not obey these sentences, then she will suffer harsher sentences.

Fr. Juan de Zumárraga [Apostolic Inquisitor]
Licentiate Loaisa [Inquisitor]

On September 10, 1538, María de Sotomayor was notified of her sentence and all of her belongings were confiscated and applied as a fine to the fiscal office of the Inquisition. She was also ordered to remain ready to be sent back to Spain on the next available ship.

Letter and Petition from María de Sotomayor, September 10, 1538

✝

Reverend Sir,

I kiss the hands of your Excellency and Lordship and I wish to tell you that I have been ordered by this Holy Office that I should be sent back to Spain to make once again married life with my husband, Juan de Castro. I wish by means of this letter to say I cannot return as of yet. I cannot comply now with this order due to the distance between this city and the city of Toledo where my said husband resides. By means of this letter and my petition, I beg your Mercy before God and in his service that you extend the time limit for my return to the period of a year and a half so that I can send for my husband to come here to live in New Spain since this is a land of opportunity.[30] Surely, Your Lordship should prefer that he come here to live with me as my husband instead of sending me back to Spain, alone and poor. I am afraid that if I was to return to Spain now I will lose my wealth and my health and any other number of dangers or inconveniences could occur. Your Lordship, as a Holy and just Judge should see the evil in forcing me to return to Spain. I beg Your Lordship on your Holy Office and out of the love to God to grant me this petition and allow me to stay here in this kingdom of Mexico.

María de Sotomayor

Interview and Documents concerning the Case of María de Sotomayor, May 21, 1540

✝

On May 21, 1540, his Lordship the Apostolic Inquisitor while holding an audience in these chambers of the Holy Office, received word that María de Sotomayor had once again been arrested. He ordered her to be brought before him from her prison cell. She was given the oath and promised to tell the truth.

She was asked her name. She said that she was called María de Sotomayor. She was asked if it was true that she had been brought here before, sentenced and punished by this Holy Office of the Inquisition for the crime of having been married two times and having lived in polygamy and that the said sentence had ordered her to return to Castile to live in marriage with her first husband, Juan de Castro. She said that it was true that she had been punished and had received penance from this Holy Office and that she remits to the trial proceedings that were completed about two years ago.

She was asked if it was true as it was reported to his Lordship that instead of going to Spain she decided to go to the Kingdoms of Peru and that she was ordered not to leave this city without the explicit license of his Lordship. She said that it was true that she had been notified of the sentence.

She was asked if it was true that she ignored the sentence and left the said city and went to Peru and that she did leave on a ship and stayed there in Peru for many days. She said that yes it was true.

She was asked if it was true that she had returned later again to this city of Mexico and had been here for many days living in this city. She said that yes this was also the truth under oath.

His Lordship, having before treated María de Sotomayor benevolently now orders that she should be taken in chains and irons to the port of Veracruz and that there she should be forcibly placed upon one of the ships that waits there and taken by force back to Spain where she has been ordered to return and live with her first husband. It was furthermore ordered that she was to forfeit all of her remaining belongings to the Holy Office and that at her own expense she should be taken to the Port of Veracruz. Under the threat of excommunication, she is to return to Spain and never again return here to these kingdoms of New Spain without the express license of His Majesty or of the Lord Inquisitor General in Spain, under the penalty of three hundred lashes and then being considered a relapsed heretic. She will then be released to the secular arm and executed if she should disobey these orders.

Fray Juan de Zumárraga [Apostolic Inquisitor]
Licentiate Loaisa [Inquisitor]

Inventory of the Sequestered Goods Taken from the Possession of María de Sotomayor

✝

This is a list of the goods and valuables taken from the prisoner María de Sotomayor and sold to pay for her passage back to Spain.

First, five large pieces of cloth from Holland	6 pesos
Two blue pillows	3 pesos
Eight other pillows, five black ones and three red ones	5 pesos
A black bed covering	6 pesos
Several cotton long-sleeved shirts	4 ½ pesos
A white cotton bed	8 pesos
Nine other bed coverings	5 pesos
Two small wooden boxes embossed with gold	8 pesos
One cape and dress for a young child	3 pesos
Several large metal buttons	2 pesos
Three large tablecloths	3 pesos
Four light bed sheets	4 pesos
Two bedspreads, partially embroidered	2 pesos
A native blanket	1 peso
A ream of paper with silk and linen attachments	3 pesos
Several cotton mantles and scarves	½ peso
A pound of thread and a comb	½ peso
Several small silver buttons and a rosary along with a red carpet and several other pieces of cloth	1 peso

A large wooden box and several iron nails	6 pesos
A box of spices and several pieces of cotton underwear	1½ peso
A red silk bag and mirror and porcelain dish	2 pesos
Several old shirts and rags	1 peso
Several small pieces of gold jewelry and a rosary made out of amber	3 pesos
A straw and woolen hat	½ peso
Several other cushions and rags	2 pesos

DOCUMENT 32
Proceedings before the Holy Office of the Inquisition against Nuño Méndez for the Crime of Incestuous Liaisons
Mexico City, 1537–1538

SOURCE: Archivo General de la Nación, Ramo de Inquisición, vol. 42, exp. 12.

NOTE: This document depicts how far the Inquisition in New Spain would go in its attempts to control the sexual morality and sexual practices of the colonists. Even someone's youthful sexual indiscretions could lead to a later denunciation for sexually amoral practices or other sexual crimes punished by the Inquisition. The danger of bragging about one's sexual exploits or telling someone else of one's earlier indiscretions is also evident in the testimony published here.

Denunciation and Testimony of Gonzalo Hernández against Nuño Méndez, January 16, 1537

†

In the City of Mexico, January 16, 1537, Gonzalo Hernández, a resident of this city was called before his Lordship the apostolic Inquisitor and received the oath and promised to tell the truth. When he was asked what it was that he knew about Nuño Méndez, the Constable of the City, he said that what he knows is that about a year and a half ago more or less, when this Méndez was in the house of this witness, he heard him say that he had had carnal relations with a mother and a daughter in Portugal. He also said that Méndez had said that the mother was a miller's wife, and she had told Nuño Méndez to go and get some wine, and she gave him some medicines for her daughter, and she told him *"for the love of God go to my daughter who is ill and give her a few drinks of the wine and give her this medicine."* Then apparently, Méndez went to the daughter, and he had carnal relations with her after he had already had relations with her mother. When the mother arrived to get the wine, her daughter told her that Nuño Méndez had had carnal relations with her. The mother grew angry and picked up a knife and attacked the said Méndez, yelling, *"Traitor, how could you have taken the virginity of my daughter!"* The mother sent him away and, while chasing after him, tripped over a dog and later died. All of this Nuño Méndez said in his house in the presence of witnesses, including Leonora Morisca, whom the said Méndez now has as his mistress. He stated that this is all true under oath. He was then administered the oath of the secret and promised not to reveal anything that he had seen or heard under the penalty of excommunication. He signed it by his name and the entire denunciation passed before the secretary.

Gonzalo Hernández
Martín de Campos [Secretary]
January 16, 1537

Testimony and Confession of the prisoner Nuño Méndez, March 1, 1538

✝

In the City of Mexico, in the chambers of the Holy Office of the Inquisition on the first day of March 1538, Nuño Méndez appeared before his Lordship the Apostolic Inquisitor,[31] and he received the oath in the form required by law and was examined according to the following questions.

He was asked what his name was. He replied that it was Nuño Méndez.

He was asked where he was from, and he replied that he was a native of the region of Olivencia in the kingdom of Portugal and that he was Portuguese because both his mother and father were Portuguese, or at least he believes this because his father is Portuguese, even though his mother speaks Castilian.

He was asked the name of a certain female miller who resided not far from where his father lived in the village. He said that she was called Leonora Álvarez.

He was asked if the said Leonora Álvarez had any daughters. He said that she had two daughters, one who was married and one who was unmarried and still a virgin.

He was asked how long he had been a friend of Leonora Álvarez. He said that he had never had her as a friend but that he had had carnal relations with her once.

He was asked if, after he had had carnal access and relations with her, he had had carnal relations with either one of her two daughters. He replied that he did not have carnal relations with anyone else but with the said mother.

He was asked if the said Leonora Álvarez had given him some medicines to take to her daughter, who was sick in bed. He replied that he did not take any medicines to the girl. He added that the mother had gone outside of the door after she took a straw hat from him and she told him that she was going out and that her daughter would stay behind and that he should give the girl what she needed. Then he said when he passed by her house the said daughter, named Catalina, told him that her mother was out and that she told her that if she needed anything that he would give it to her. The said Catalina then told him that she did not need anything and that he should leave there.

He was asked if it was because he had had carnal relations with the daughter Catalina that the mother Leonora Álvarez attacked him with a knife. He was also asked if it was true that she had attacked him and yelled at him that he had dishonored her daughter. He replied that it is true that the said Leonora Álvarez attacked him with a knife, but it was not because of this reason but rather for another reason. He said that she was angry at him and for this reason she attacked him. He also stated that all of this was the truth under oath, and he signed it with his name.

Nuño Méndez

And after the said testimony and confession, on the fifth of March 1538, Nuño Méndez was summoned again before the Holy Office of the Inquisition and his Lordship and the said Nuño Méndez stated that, on the day that his confession was taken, he had been upset and did not respond honestly according to the truth in answer to the questions. Even though he believed that he was not guilty of this crime, he now wishes to clarify his confession and statements and to tell the truth. He stated that the truth is that he did have carnal relations with the said Leonora Álvarez, the mother of the said girl Catalina Alfonso, but he did so when he was only fourteen years old more or less, and he did it out of ignorance and the impetuous nature of youth, and he thought that he did not commit sin in the act. He also stated that he did not know what he was doing when he lay with her, because she was much older than he was. He then stated that, after he had had carnal relations and lain with the mother, he did have carnal relations with the said daughter. He admits that he did have carnal access to her body, and he did fornicate with her. Now he asks for the definitive sentence and the conclusion of this case based on this his true confession because he has nothing else to add to or allege concerning this case.

In light of the documents of the case and the merits of the confession and the fact that when he had carnal relations with mother and daughter he was of a young age and that he now appears to be poor, the sentencing will be passed quickly.

Diego de Mayorga [Notary]

Final Sentence and Condemnation in this Case, March 6, 1538

†

We order and condemn the said Nuño Méndez to appear before the Cathedral of this city and that he should be forced to hear a mass with his head uncovered and with a candle in his hand while he kneels in front of the public throughout the entire mass. He is also to chant out loud several penitential psalms that deal with the reason of his penitence. Also, so that God, Our Lord, may pardon him, we condemn him and order him to pay a fine of twenty gold pesos, which he will pay before he is released from jail and the fine shall be applied to the Fiscal office of the Inquisition, and the Receptor will receive them. Once his fine has been paid and he has heard the penitential mass, we authorize any Priest or clergyman to absolve the said Nuño Méndez of his excommunication. Thus, we pronounce and proclaim our definitive sentence in this case.

Fr. Juan de Zumárraga [Apostolic Inquisitor]
Lic. Loaisa [Inquisitor]
Diego de Mayorga [Notary]

Execution of the Punishments, Thursday, March 7, 1538

✝

On the morning of Thursday, March 7, 1538, I the said Secretary and Notary of the Holy Office testify to and notarize the fact that the said Nuño Méndez complied with and made penance according to his sentence. He heard a mass while being uncovered and kneeling before the public without his cape, hat, or other coverings, and he knelt on his knees throughout the entire mass in the Cathedral of this City of Mexico. The Provisor Miguel de Barreda said the mass and His Reverend Lordship the Archbishop absolved him after the mass from the excommunication that he had incurred in his crime.

Diego de Mayorga [Notary]

DOCUMENT 33
Documents and Accusations Presented to the Commissariat of the Inquisition in the Province of Yucatan by the Maya Villagers of the Town of Hocaba against Their Parish Priest, Padre Cristóbal de Valencia, for the Crime of Solicitation, Fornication, and Other Nefarious Acts against Nature

Merida, Yucatan, 1609

SOURCE: Archivo General de la Nación, Ramo de Inquisición, vol. 472, exp. 5.

NOTE: The following accusations and trial transcripts come from a very long Inquisition trial (more than 2,000 pages long) against the sexual crimes of the priest Cristóbal de Valencia, who served as the parish priest of the Maya town of Hocaba in the province of Yucatan. Although many of these testimonies may have been falsified by the Maya in order to get rid of their parish priest, who had punished them for continued idolatry, the evidence was enough to have the priest removed from their parish and punished with severe penalties.[32]

Translation of a Petition and Denunciation Written in the Maya Language by Clemente Ek and His Father Francisco Ek, Natives of the Town of Hocaba, July 6, 1609

✝

We come before your Excellency, the Lord Commissary of the Holy Office here in this province of Yucatan, in order to tell you and let you know how it is that Father Cristóbal de Valencia perverts the good Christian doctrine of the town of Hocaba. First of all, Clemente Ek, a native of the town of Hocaba, said that father Cristóbal de Valencia called him into his house and, while he stood naked before him, told Ek: *"Come and take my private parts in your hands and play with them because this is the service of God and it is the office of the saints who are in heaven . . . and if you do not comply with this and play with my private parts go and bring me your wife because she has a large vagina and has slept with the entire village."*

Clemente Ek then responded in shock to the priest, *"Why do you say this Father, this is a very shameful thing . . . look here is the sacred chalice and you say this in front of it."* The said priest Cristóbal de Valencia responded, *"Don't you come here and preach to me . . . I will have my way with you without anyone ever knowing it and if not I will kill you tonight!"* and when he said this, the said priest said many other vile words and insults to Clemente Ek, and he attacked him and cut his genitals saying, *"Go and complain about this to the Bishop or the Inquisitor . . . I have the power to burn you alive and I am not afraid even if four hundred bishops come here I will not dirty my pants out of fear . . . I am the bishop here."*

Francisco Ek, the father of the said Clemente Ek, denounces and requests that your Reverence, the Commissary of the Inquisition here, should look into the matter and procure justice in the service of God due to the bad treatment that the priest had given to his son, cutting and causing his genitals to bleed. The cacique, and other native leaders of the town are witnesses, and they have seen his injured member and they know about the other sins that the padre commits.

Fr. Rodrigo Tinoco translated this document from Maya in the town of Hocaba on July 6, 1609.

Fr. Rodrigo Tinoco

NOTE: After several months of testimony and the interviews of hundreds of Maya witnesses from several towns, the commissary of the Inquisition arrested and accused the parish priest of the sexual crimes alleged by the Maya. In the following document the priest answers the major accusations placed against him and gives his response to the charges.

Confession of the Prisoner Padre Cristóbal de Valencia in the Trial That the Holy Office Is Conducting against Him for Abuses and Other Crimes, October 11, 1609

†

In the city of Merida, bishopric of Yucatan, His Mercy Br. Francisco de Ávila, Commissary of the Inquisition in these provinces, ordered Padre Cristóbal de Valencia, a prisoner here in this secret jail, to appear before him and answer to the specific charges alleged against him. He was questioned and answered according to the following questions.

Asked what was his name and if he was a priest and for how long he had been a priest.

He said that his name was Cristóbal de Valencia, and that he was forty-five years old more or less and that Bishop Gregorio de Montalvo had ordained him a priest more than twenty years ago and during those twenty years he had been occupied as a priest in Indian parishes in this province where he administered the holy sacraments to the Maya natives and where he preached to them in their own language. Currently he is the parish priest of the town of Hocaba.

He was asked if he had taken any theology courses or if he knew anything about theology and the teachings of the Holy Catholic Church.

He said that he had heard many sermons on theology and that he had studied theology and grammar in the college of the Jesuits in Mexico City, and there his teachers had been good Catholics and they taught healthy doctrine.

He was asked if he was a parish priest, what were his obligations, and what were the duties of his office as a parish priest.

He said that he ignored this question and that he well knows the obligations that he has as a priest and that he has always attended to his obligations in the administering of the sacraments to the Maya with total devotion and with a dedication to God.

He was asked if he knew that all parish priests and clergymen had the obligation of guarding all decency and clean habits and composure and that they should show a better example than any other layperson in their habits and lifestyles and avoid all public scandals and indignities which might affect their service in office.

He said that he had always lived with the proper composure and decency according to the office and duties of a priest and that until now he has not committed any scandalous or indecent things, but instead he has lived in decency and purity as a chaste and holy priest.

He was asked if he knew the witness Clemente Ek, a resident in the town of Hocaba, and if it was true that, when he was in the said town of Hocaba, he called the said witness and Juan May and Alonso Huchim and that he told them that all three of them should lay down with him in his room where he was lying on a bed and that they should lay with their feet on a mat. And once they lay on the mats at the foot of the bed, he ordered them to blow-out the candle and come to him. Then he called to the said Clemente Ek and, with little reverence for the holy orders that he had received, he gave them a bad example and told them to play with his virile member, and combining that crime with other crimes, he told them that this would be in the service of God and other vile-sounding and scandalous words, and he told them *"This is the pathway to heaven which he would teach them because even the saints did this."* And that the said Clemente Ek responded, *"Father, why do you tell me this, you lift up the host and the chalice, you can't say these things . . . they are wrong."* Then, out of vile desire, he told him that if he did not play with his member, then he should bring his wife. Then he rose up from the bed and went to the door and with little fear of God and in sacrilege he told Ek, *"Now I am going to kill you tonight so that no one will see it."* And then he placed his hands on Ek's private parts and squeezed them with such force that he caused his virile member to explode and begin to bleed and much blood came out, and even though Clemente Ek complained, saying that it hurt him very much, he continued to squeeze and not release him until he was very much injured from the ordeal leaving his member damaged and bruised.

He said that he denies the principal statements of this question, and he does not believe that any Christian person could have done such an awful thing, less a priest. The reason, he said, that the native raised this testimony against him was that he often had an itch on his back and ordinarily he would lift his shirt and scratch his back. One night when he was lying on the bed, he had the said itch and, not being able to reach the spot on his back, called to one of the boys who lived in the church there, the said Clemente Ek, to help him and scratch his back. The said boy woke up and began to scratch his back, and while he was scratching his back, the boy fell asleep, and due to the terrible itch he screamed at him, "*By the Devil! You are sleeping. . . . Wake up and Scratch!*" and what he re-members is that he hit the boy to wake him. Without any intention of hurting the boy, he hit him in his private parts, and they began to bleed and this is what happened and noth-ing else. Then he said that the boy ran away and he never saw him again. He said that since the boy was frightened, he raised false testimony like all of the other Indians, falsely accusing their priests of any type of crime that enters their vile and devilish minds.

He was asked if he knew Pablo Chan, a resident of the town of Hoctun, and if it was true that this confessant with a diabolical soul and indignant in the ministry and office of a priest, called the said Indian one day and ordered him to put his virile member into his mouth and that the said Indian placed his virile member into the mouth of this confes-sant, and he took his own member into his hands and he played with it until he spilled his own natural seed. And also if on the day of Saint John[33] while in the said village this con-fessant again called the said Indian and ordered that he once again place his member into his mouth and that then this confessant once again began to agitate his member and make the said Pablo Chan spill his own natural seed into his mouth. Also that the said confes-sant made the said Indian also play with his member on other occasions, and each time he made him spill his seed, which fell onto the hands of the said Indian.

He said that he did not remember any such Indian and that he denies that this had ever occurred and that the native is giving false testimony against him based on the in-ducement of his enemies. Again he said that he is a good priest of good and strong Chris-tian morals and that he has never engaged in any type of perverted or depraved action such as that described in this question. Also he states that the natives give this false testi-mony against him because he had punished them for their own crimes against the faith and their idolatries and drunkenness, which they engage in frequently, and for this reason they declare these falsehoods against him.

Asked if he knew Pedro Couoh, a native of the town of Sahcaba, and if it is true that on the feast of the Holy Sacrament[34] he had engaged in similar deviant acts with this native as he had with the native in the previous question. Also, he was asked if it was true that he had asked the said Indian to play with his virile member and, when the Indian refused, yelled vile and evil sounding insults at him and said, "*You have to touch my member because this is in the service of the Church and by doing this you will go to heaven and be an angel,*" and because the Indian still refused to do it, he attacked him and beat him several times until, out of fear, the native got up on the bed and sat on his chest, placing his member in the mouth of this confessant, and he forced him to rock back and forth and commit a nefarious act with him. Also that he then took the virile member of this Indian into his hands and that he fiercely began to play with it with great violence until he forced him to spill his seed. After he had done this, he told him, "*Now I love you and you are now my own blood and my son and I will do everything I can to help you,*" and not content with this, he forced him to engage in other nefari-ous acts on several occasions, and when he did not want to go to him, he ordered him whipped.

He said that the truth is that he did know the said Pedro Couoh and he knew that he was the Sacristan of the church of the town of Sahcaban, and that on one occasion he had punished the said Pedro Couoh for various errors that he had committed in his duties as Sacristan and that he had him whipped for failing to comply with his orders. He denied ever having committed the vile acts that are alleged in this question. As a good Christian, fearful of God, he denies ever having committed any act like those described in this question. He also said that he and the other natives testify falsely against him out of the hatred that they have for his having punished them for their crimes against God and their other vices and sins, which he preached against publicly. He refers the Inquisitor to the testimony and opinions of the other parish priests who have served in the province of Hocaba who know and can tell him how it is public knowledge that the Maya from the town of Hocaba have a common practice of raising false testimony against their priests in order to get rid of them.

And because it was late in the afternoon on this day, the confession of the priest was postponed until the following day when it will be taken up again and he may answer to the charges and allegations placed against him. His Mercy the Commissary of the Inquisition signed it together with the said Padre Cristóbal de Valencia before me, Gonzalo Pérez Camelo, Apostolic Notary and Secretary.

Br. Francisco de Ávila, Commissary of the Inquisition
Cristóbal de Valencia
Gonzalo Pérez Camelo, Apostolic Notary and Secretary

Trials and Testimonies against Jewish
and Crypto-Jewish Practices

Spanish debtors of Jews knew very well that the fastest way to free themselves from a persistent creditor was to report them to the Inquisitors.

Seymour Liebman, *The Jews in New Spain: Faith, Flame, and the Inquisition,* 1970, 50.

The Inquisition's active persecution of Jews is one of the most studied aspects in the academic literature on the Spanish Inquisition.[35] Although in Spain cases brought against suspected Judaizers amounted to more than 29 percent of the total, in New Spain such cases were less than 6.8 percent of the total number of crimes prosecuted from 1571 to 1700.[36]

In order to understand the presence of Judaizers in the New World, it is necessary to understand the impact of the Spanish expulsion of the Jews by the Catholic monarchs Ferdinand and Isabella in 1492. Many of the expelled Jews who fled Spain in 1492 took up residence in the neighboring kingdom of Portugal. Unfortunately for those Jews who fled to Portugal, another expulsion edict followed five years later, but unlike the Catholic monarchs of Spain, the king of Portugal, not wanting to lose so many of his productive citizens, ordered the forced conversion, even using violence if necessary, of the remaining Jews in Portugal.[37] The situation for Jews in Portugal worsened when the Portuguese crown founded the Portuguese Inquisition in 1574.[38] Nevertheless, a new avenue of escape came in 1580 when the crowns of Portugal and Spain united under the Spanish monarch Philip II. With the annexation of Portugal, the *conversos* of Portugal could more easily reside in Spain or its New World colonies. Some of these Portuguese *conversos* and crypto-Jews who had only partially been converted, or had converted out of fear but continued to practice their previous religion in private, immigrated to the New World. The first group arrived in Brazil because the region offered greater freedom to continue to practice Judaism. This freedom quickly ended when in 1591 the Portuguese Inquisition conducted its first visitation of Brazil.[39] With the arrival of the Inquisition in Brazil, these Portuguese *conversos*, who now had become quite wealthy through their mercantile trade with the Old World, fled to the more distant Spanish colonies of the New World.[40]

These Portuguese Jews migrated to the Spanish colonies of Peru and Cartagena de Indias, where they continued to develop a thriving mercantile trade, especially in slaves and other imported goods.[41] By means of their commercial connections, many of these Portuguese *conversos* made their way to New Spain by the end of the sixteenth century and beginning of the seventeenth. Other Portuguese *conversos* made their way to New Spain directly from the Iberian Peninsula after 1580, regardless of the prohibitions that the crown had passed forbidding Jews and their *converso* descendants to migrate to the New World.[42] Many of these *conversos* falsified documents concerning their *limpieza de sangre,* purchased licenses, or offered outright bribes to the officials of the House of Trade (Casa de Contratación), who controlled the granting of licenses to immigrate to the Indies. Many of these Portuguese *conversos* made their way to New Spain. Although it is impossible to know how many of these *conversos* emigrated to New Spain, Herrera Sotillo notes in her own study of the Mexican Inquisition that most of the 324 cases against suspected Judaizers prosecuted in New Spain from 1571 to 1700 involved Portuguese New Christians.[43]

According to the surviving trial documents, the Inquisition in New Spain irregularly prosecuted cases against suspected Jews. A majority of the existing cases occurred during two periods, from 1590 to the first part of the seventeenth century and during the decade of the 1640s.[44]

In terms of the punishments and sentences of convicted Judaizers, the Inquisition in New Spain handed out some of its harshest verdicts and penalties. Nevertheless, it has to be noted that those convicted of Judaizing were in fact guilty of true formal heresy.[45] The majority of the convicted Jews sentenced by the Inquisition in New Spain received sentences of reconciliation and relaxation to the secular arm. The death penalty of burning at the stake occurred in almost all of the cases where the convicted Judaizer had been previously sentenced for the same crime on an earlier occasion. Still, of the total number of 130 Judaizers sentenced to be relaxed to the secular arm, only 29 received this exemplar punishment of being burned alive.[46] Even among this number, all but four of them, received the mercy (if it can be considered one) of having been garroted before being burned. In more than 101 cases of those Jews sentenced to be relaxed to the secular arm, the Mexican Inquisition sentenced the convicted Jews in absentia or *post mortem,* after the suspect had been deceased.[47] Others had fled the region, and only their statues or effigies were burned after the auto-da-fé at the execution of the sentences. The fines and pecuniary penalties paid by convicted Judaizers amounted to about 30,000 pesos, while confiscation of the goods and estates of convicted Judaizers arguably brought the Inquisition's fiscal office millions of pesos in net worth.[48]

The documents in this section corroborate and emphasize the Portuguese origin of most of those suspects accused of either openly or secretly practicing the Jewish religion. The large number of wealthy merchants of Portuguese origin found themselves swept up in a transatlantic wave of persecution that increased with malignant fury during the decade of the 1640s in New Spain. In the cases that dealt with accused Jews, the Inquisition in New Spain most frequently disobeyed its own orders and violated many of its established procedures.

DOCUMENT 34

**Proceedings before the Holy Office of the Inquisition against the Barber
Juan de Salamanca for the Crime of Judaism, or Jewish Practices**

Mexico City, August 1539

SOURCE: Archivo General de la Nación, Ramo de Inquisición, vol. 125, exp. 1.

NOTE: The brief extract here from a case against an apparent crypto-Jew, a resident in
Mexico City, is fairly representative of Inquisition cases dealing with accusations and confessions of crypto-Jews. Note the types of practices that the Inquisition labeled as "Jewish."

Denunciation against Juan de Salamanca, Barber, Resident in this City
of Mexico for Jewish Practices, August 17, 1539

†

In the City of Mexico, August 17, 1539, there appeared before their Lordships the Inquisitors and before the Secretary of the Holy Office, Miguel López, Francisca Hernández,
the wife of Francisco de Tapia who stated that she came to discharge her conscience and to
reveal what she knows about Juan de Salamanca, a barber and resident in this city.

She stated that about twenty days ago more or less, while she was on the roof of her
house, she saw in the corral and yard of the house of Juan de Salamanca, which is only a
few houses away from her own house, that an Indian slave named Catalina was washing
and lathering with soap a bundle of clothes.

She also stated that this occurred on a Saturday during the morning, and while the
said Indian was washing the clothes, Juan de Salamanca came and yelled at her with angry words and stopped her from washing the clothes. He fought with her and asked her,
"*Why are you washing these clothes on a Saturday?*" and then he began to fight with his wife
Ana Martín, asking her "*Why have you ordered the Indian servants to wash our clothes on
Saturday?*" All of this occurred in the presence of this witness, because she watched the
whole thing from her rooftop.

Later she asked Salamanca's wife Ana Martín why she had fought with her husband
concerning the washing of the clothes on Saturday. Ana Martín told her that her husband did not allow anyone to do anything in their household on Saturdays, and he ordered
them all to guard and keep Saturdays sacred just like Sundays saying, "*In my homeland this
is the way we treated Saturdays.*"

And this is all that she knows concerning this case, and she came to denounce it to the
Holy Office for the discharge of her conscious, and she swears that it is the truth before
God and the sign of the Cross and that she does not declare it out of hatred or animosity
nor ill will that she may have for the said Salamanca, nor out of any inducement from any
other person, but rather out of her own will.

She was then asked who else was present when she had witnessed the said fight with the
Indian servant and Salamanca's wife when they washed clothes on a Saturday. She said that

she did not see anyone else at the time except for Ana Martín and the Indian servant, and this is the truth under oath. She did not sign it because she said she did not know how to sign.

Miguel López
[Secretary of the Holy Office]
The Inquisitors

Testimony and Confession of Juan de Salamanca, August 20, 1539

†

On August 20, 1539, the Lord Inquisitors ordered that Juan de Salamanca should be brought before them to give testimony. While in audience on this day, the Inquisitors ordered Juan de Salamanca, the Barber, to appear and he was administered the oath according to law and he swore before God and the cross to tell the truth.

He was made several questions, and he responded the following.

When he was asked what was his name he responded that his name was Juan de Salamanca.

When he was asked where he was from, he responded that he was a native of the kingdoms of Castile and a native of a place called Almenara, which is in the lands of the Duke of Albuquerque close to Salamanca.

He was questioned about how long he had been in New Spain. He said that he had been there for about fifteen years more or less.

He was asked who his parents and grandparents were, and if they had been natives of the place called Almenara and what they were called. He said that his mother was a native of Almenara, and she was called María Hernández, daughter of Pedro de Parada, and his father was named Juan García and he does not know where he was from. He also stated that he did not know his grandparents.

He was asked if he was married. He said that he was married in this city with the daughter of Alonso Guisado and that before he had been married in Castile with a servant of the house of Villafaña whom he brought to New Spain, but who had died.

He was asked what age he had presently. He said that when he came to New Spain he was about twenty-five years old and that he had lived there for about fifteen years so that he believes he is about forty-five years old.

He was asked what was his race and category. He responded that on his father's side he was related to Old Christian Spaniards on both sides of his family.

He was asked if he could read and write. He responded no.

He was asked if he had lived with some Jew or with someone who knew of the Jewish ways. He said that he had had many patrons and sponsors and he does not know if they were Jews or Moors, but that he took them all for Christians because many of them were clergymen, others were the Count of Lemos[49] and the Great Captain, Hernán Cortes, all his employers and all Christians.

He was asked if he had been baptized. He said that he believed that he was baptized because he heard it said that he had been baptized.

He was asked if he was circumcised. He said no.

He was asked if in his homelands they guarded and kept Saturdays sacred just like Christians hold Sundays. He said that he does not hold Saturdays as sacred unless they are feast days.

He was questioned if he did hold Saturdays sacred and had ever fought with his wife or servants concerning this. He said that he had never done any such thing unless it was a Holy Feast day and that he had fought with his wife so that the Indian servants learn the Pater Noster and the Ave María and other prayers.

He was then asked if he held or had any error that he committed against Our Holy Catholic Faith, or if he believed in any Jewish superstition. He said no.

He was asked how long had it been since he confessed. He said that he had confessed during the previous Cuaresma.[50]

All of this he said and declared under oath.

Juan de Salamanca
The Inquisitors
Miguel López [Secretary]

Testimony of Ana Martín, Wife of the Said Juan de Salamanca, August 20, 1539

†

On the same day, the Inquisitors ordered that Ana Martín be brought before them in audience in order to examine her and take her testimony. She received the oath and promised to tell the truth.

She was asked if her husband Juan de Salamanca knew how to read and if he had any books from which he read. She said that no, he did not know how to read nor did he have any books.

She was asked if her husband, Juan de Salamanca, ordered her and her household to hold Saturdays as sacred days even when they were not Holy feast days and if she had fought with him over the said issue of keeping Saturdays as sacred as Sundays. She said that what her husband told her was that in his homeland on Fridays they prepared and cleaned the house, not on Saturdays, but that he had never told her to keep or guard Saturdays as sacred days nor did they believe them to be such.

She was asked if she had ever told anyone that her husband had ordered her to guard and keep Saturdays as sacred. She said that she had never said any such thing nor has she seen him conduct any Jewish ceremony.

She swore that this was all the truth under oath, and she did not sign because she said she did not know how to sign.

Juan Ricalde [Secretary]
Inquisitors

NOTE: In the end, Juan de Salamanca was eventually convicted on the basis of these and other testimonies. The only evidence against him was that he told his wife and others that he had always refrained from cleaning on Saturdays.

DOCUMENT 35

Selected Autos and Proceedings of the Second Trial against Luis de Carvajal the Younger, Reconciled by This Holy Office as a Judaizer, a Relapsed Practitioner of Judaism, and a Formal Heretic

Mexico City, 1594–1596

SOURCE: Archivo General de la Nación, Ramo de Inquisición, vol. 1489, exp. 1.

NOTE: The final proceedings and definitive sentencing of the famous Mexican crypto-Jew Luis de Carvajal serve as an example of the harshness with which the Inquisition in New Spain dealt with recidivists or repeat offenders, especially those suspected or convicted of Jewish practices.[51]

Auto and Proceedings of the Second Trial against Luis de Carvajal the Younger, 1596

✝

Luis de Carvajal the younger, reconciled by this Holy Office, son of Francisco Rodriguez Matos, deceased and condemned, and of Doña Francisca Núñez de Carvajal, reconciled, of the generation of New Christians, alias *Joseph Lumbroso*.[52]

As seen by us, the inquisitors against heretical depravity and apostasy in the City and Archbishopric of Mexico and the provinces of New Spain and its district, by the apostolic and ordinary authority, a lawsuit and criminal case that was pending before us and was pending between Dr. Martos de Bohórquez, the Prosecutor of this Holy Office and accusing member, and the other, the accused defendant, the said Luis de Carvajal the younger, reconciled and changed in name in the Law of Moses, Joseph Lumbroso, who presently is accused of the crimes of heresy, apostasy, pertinacious belief in Judaism, and a formal relapse as a dogmatizing Judíazante, master and teacher of Judaism, for which reason the said Prosecuting Attorney denounced and criminally accused him before us, saying that the above-mentioned in previous years was imprisoned in this Holy Office, testifying and accused, despite being a baptized and confirmed Christian, he had guarded and believed in the Old Law and the death of Moses, his rites and ceremonies, and seemingly by exterior trial to be satisfied with the proof and testimony received against him, and that of true heart and faith not feigned he converted to our Holy Catholic Faith, repenting and separating from his errors and heresies, and from his feigned tears and signs that he used in the Public Act of faith that was celebrated in this city this past year of 1590, using with him the leniency and clemency that he did not merit, having been admitted and reconciled to the fold of the Holy Catholic Church, under the promise and solemn judgment that was publicly done then that he not return again to those heresies or to other persons, who abjured and detested, and submitted himself to the just and severe punishment of fire constituted by relapse, and he had signed his name; and he was like a dog who returns to his own vomit after his abjuration and reconciliation, with the natural ingratitude of Jews and their hardness and perverseness, forgetting the undeserved mercy and benefit that he had received, he returned to his previous beliefs and keeps the Law of Moses, and its rites and ceremonies, that in the milk and hopes of his parents, he was suckled, thinking and believing to be saved in it as in the Good Law given by God to Israel, that promised to those who kept its glory, riches, and worldly goods, and not in our Lord Jesus Christ, whom they do not have as God.

That the said Luis de Carvajal the younger does not believe, nor has he ever believed in Christ our Lord, [and he has] made jests of the Holy Sacraments that were left instituted in his church, and excluding all of that he rejected oral confession and confessed only to God, making laughs and jokes about the Consecrated Host and how His precious and true body was moldy, calling Him inappropriate and strange names concerning His Divinity and Holy Humanity, and others about Our Lady, insulting her dignity; affirming that he was a truly baptized person. He was circumcised, which was ordered by God to Abraham, by means of which men were saved and by no other manner, and it was done in this New Spain, under a palm tree, and he was circumcised with some scissors, with which he arrived at the point of losing his life.

Vote for the Administration of Questioning under Torment in the Case against Luis de Carvajal the Younger, February 6, 1596

†

In the City of Mexico, Tuesday, 6th of February of the year 1596, being present in the audience chamber of the Holy Office, during the afternoon, in consultation and after having seen the proceedings in the case, the Lord Inquisitors Dr. Lobo Guerrero and Licenciado Don Alonso de Peralta, Dr. Juan de Cervantes the Archdeacon of the Holy Cathedral of this city and the governor of the Archbishopric who serves as the ordinary, and in the presence of the consultants the Lords Dr. Saavedra Valderrama, Dr. Santiago del Riego, and Licenciado Francisco Alonso de Villagra, Judges of the Audiencia and Royal Chancery of this city, and Licenciado Vasco López de Vivero, Corregidor in this city by order of His Majesty, the criminal case against Luis de Carvajal the younger was reviewed, and all where in conformity and voted that it was their opinion that the above-said should be put to questioning under torment *in capit alienum* so that he should state and declare the truth concerning his accomplices and other people who know and continue to guard the Law of Moses, and depending on what should result, the case should be seen again.

Dr. Lobo Guerrero

Lic. Don Alonso de Peralta

Mtro. Don Juan de Cervantes

Lic. Saavedra Valderrama

Dr. Santiago del Riego

Lic. Francisco Alonso de Villagra

Lic. Vivero

Before me, Pedro de Mañozca, Secretary

Second Vote concerning the Continued Administration of Questioning under Torment in the Case against Luis de Carvajal the Younger, February 14, 1596

✝

In the City of Mexico, during the afternoon of Wednesday the 14th of February of the year 1596, being present in the audience chamber of the Holy Office in consultation and after having seen the proceedings in the case, the Lord Inquisitors Dr. Lobo Guerrero and Licenciado Don Alonso de Peralta, and Dr. Juan de Cervantes, the Archdeacon of the Holy Cathedral of this city and the governor of the Archbishopric who serves as the ordinary, and in the presence of the consultants, Lords Dr. Saavedra Valderrama, Dr. Santiago del Riego, and Licenciado Francisco Alonso de Villagra, Judges of the Audiencia and Royal Chancery of this city, and Licenciado Vasco López de Vivero, Corregidor in this city by order of His Majesty, the criminal case against Luis de Carvajal the younger was reviewed again, concerning the article of whether to continue the questioning under torment which was begun on the 8th of this present month and year, and concerning the diligences made with the accused in the torture chamber, and they voted in the following form:

The Lord Inquisitors Dr. Lobo Guerrero, Dr. D. Juan de Cervantes, the ordinary, and Licenciado Francisco Alonso de Villagra were all in agreement and voted that the torture should not continue, because it is their belief that it is sufficient.

The Lord Inquisitor Licenciado Don Alonso de Peralta, was of the vote and opinion that they should give him three or four more turns of the cords of the rack on his arms.

Their Lords Licenciado Saavedra Valderrama and Dr. Riego were of the vote and opinion that the torture should be continued.

The Lord Corregidor voted that the accused by placed under an order of *Conminatio*[53] and admonished under pains of punishment to tell the truth.

Dr. Lobo Guerrero

Lic. Don Alonso de Peralta

Mtro. Don Juan de Cervantes

Lic. Saavedra Valderrama

Dr. Santiago del Riego

Lic. Francisco Alonso de Villagra

Lic. Vivero

Before me, Pedro de Mañozca, Secretary

Vote and Definitive Sentence against Luis de Carvajal, the Younger, February 16, 1596

✝

Attending to the acts and merits of the case, the Promotor Fiscal has fully proven his accusation according and how it should be done, and we find and pronounce that he has submitted sufficient proof, in consequence of which we must and do declare that the said Luis de Carvajal, having been and being a practicing Jewish heretic and apostate to our Holy Catholic Faith, an accomplice and one who hides heretical practicing Jews, a false converted Jew, an impenitent, relapsed and pertinacious dogmatist and by this having fallen and incurring the sentence of High Excommunication, and to be combined with this the confiscation and loss of all his goods from the time that he began to commit his crimes of heresy, the proceeds of which we order applied to the Royal Treasury of your Majesty and your Receptor should receive them in your name. We also declare that we must relax and we do relax the person of the said Luis de Carvajal to the Justices and Secular Arm, especially to Licenciado Vasco López de Vivero, Corregidor of this City, so that the punishments should be executed.

Dr. Lobo Guerrero

Lic. Don Alonso de Peralta

Mtro. Don Juan de Cervantes

Lic. Saavedra Valderrama

Dr. Santiago del Riego

Lic. Francisco Alonso de Villagra

Lic. Vivero

Before me, Pedro de Mañozca, Secretary

Revision of the Case by the Corregidor on Behalf of the Secular Authorities, December 8, 1596

✝

In the city of Mexico, Sunday, the eighth day of the month of December of 1596, being in the central Plaza in the Building of the Cabildo, conducting and celebrating the public act of Faith [*auto-de-fé*] by the Lord Apostolic Inquisitors of this New Spain, the case and sentence against the reconciled Luis de Carvajal the younger was read as it was done in this Holy Office, which is here present, and it is ordered that the said Carvajal be relaxed to the Justice and Secular Arm as a relapsed, pertinacious nonpenitent. The said case having been seen by the Licenciado Vasco López de Vivero, Corregidor of this said city for Your Majesty, he confirmed both the sentence and date of remission and concurred with the guilt which resulted against the said Luis de Carvajal, pronounced against him as settled in the tribunal, where for this effect he was handed over and the sentence is of the following tenor.

Judgment and Definitive Sentence of the Corregidor Licenciado Vasco López de Vivero, in the Case against Luis de Carvajal, for the Crime of Relapsing into Judaism after Having Been Reconciled in the Auto-da-fé of 1590,[54] December 8, 1596

✝

Attending to the guilt of the said Luis de Carvajal, I must condemn and order that he be led through the public streets of this city, mounted on a saddled mule. With the voice of a town crier his crimes shall be proclaimed, and he shall be carried to the marketplace of San Hipólito, and in the part and place which has been designated, he shall be burned alive and thrown into the living flames of fire until he is turned to ashes, and of him there will remain no memory. By this means I give my definitive sentence, and thus I pronounce it and order it.

Licenciado Vivero

Execution of the Sentence against Luis de Carvajal, the Younger, December 8, 1596

✝

In the city of Mexico, on the same day, month, and year, in completion of the said sentence, being the said Luis de Carvajal on a saddled horse, was carried through the customary street with the voice of a public crier proclaiming his crime. During the procession, there was a demonstration that the prisoner had been converted and took in his hand a crucifix, and he said some words by which it was understood that he had converted and repented. And due to this, having arrived at the bonfire which was in the marketplace of San

Hipólito, he was garroted until he died naturally, and having appeared [dead] he was put on the fire and his body remained burning within the flames until it became a cinder.[55]

Present as witnesses were Baltazar Mexía Salmerón, Chief Constable, and Pedro Rodríguez, and Juan de Budía and Francisco de Benavides, and their lieutenants and many other persons.

Before me, Alonso Bernal, Public Notary

DOCUMENT 36
Relation of the Prisoners of This Holy Office of the Inquisition in Mexico Who Have Been Penanced and Have Been Punished in Two Autos-da-fé That Have Been Celebrated Along with Others for Their Observance of the Laws of Moses and Subsequently Exiled Permanently from These Kingdoms and Provinces of New Spain and Peru

Mexico City, 1647

SOURCE: Archivo General de la Nación, Ramo de Inquisición, vol. 1510, exp. 18, folios 126–31, Lote Riva Palacios, vol. 35, no. 18.

NOTE: This relation of convicted prisoners, and several more like it, describes the crimes, sentences, and punishments for Inquisition prisoners who were accused or convicted for Jewish practices. In the details and punishments, those who were apprehended for committing Jewish practices (called Judaizantes) and those who were New Christians who still practiced Judaism, some even unknowingly (called crypto-Jews), were the most repressed and most rigorously punished group who came under investigation by the Holy Office. It will be no surprise that the inquisitorial tribunal, in its zeal to prosecute Jews and crypto-Jews, often violated many of the Inquisition's own laws concerning due process and proper procedure.

†

Testimony of the prisoners' sentences, ages, and physical features [is provided] in order to present them to the Tribunal of the Holy Office in the city of Seville. Within one month's time they should arrive there and be shown in which place they shall reside. They were sent back by ship in the fleet under the command of Lorenzo Rodríguez de Córdova, during this present year of 1647.

Antonio Méndez Bilón, merchant, and resident of the city of New Veracruz, a native of Lisbon in Portugal, fifty-three years old, rich, with a robust stature, with big eyes, well placed, and a thick beard and moustache that is black with some graying, fluent in the Spanish language, and who bears the symbol of circumcision.[56] While being observed naked by four surgeons of this Holy Office, he had the markings of a longitudinal incision that runs from the front of the foreskin until the base of the genital member, with an apparent scar which was made by a cutting instrument; and the said surgeons took it as a sign of circumcision or retraction, which is consistent with the various rites and ceremonies of the Jews; and he said that he did not know what had caused that mark.

Doña Beatriz Enríquez, native of the city of New Veracruz, wife of Tomás Méndez, Portuguese, reconciled, resident and merchant of the said city, thirty-three years old, of a dusky complexion, very thin, with a mole on her chin, black eyes, and a birthmark on her nose. She is the daughter of Fernando Rodríguez and Doña Blanca Enríquez, both observers of the Law of Moses.

Clara Antunes, native and resident of this city of Mexico, married with Manuel Ríos Núñez reconciled by this Holy Office, twenty years old, with a fine figure, large black eyes, and bushy eyebrows, with very dark black hair, she is very presentable, and has a birthmark above her mouth on the left side, and others on her face.

Diego Méndez de Silva, who made an abjuration *de vehementi,* a Merchant, resident of the city of Seville where he is married, and his wife Luisa de Mercado, and Blanca, his daughter, all of whom were accused by witnesses of being observers of the Law of Moses in this Inquisition. He is a native of Albuquerque in Portugal, and forty-seven years old, with a light complexion, very bald, of a good height, with a thick gray beard and moustache.

Esperanza Ríos, mulatta, with a dark complexion, native of the city of Puebla and resident in Mexico City, widow of Juan Batista del Bosque a deceased native of Germany, fifty years old more or less, and of a tall stature, with graying hair.

Francisco de Acosta, single, native of the city of Lisbon in Portugal, resident in Guatemala, thirty-four years old, tall, with ample eyebrows, a black beard and hair, of a very white complexion, with large black eyes, and a narrow forehead, speaks only Portuguese.

Francisco Núñez Navarro,[57] a single native of the village of Chazin in Portugal, resident in New Galicia in this kingdom of New Spain, a merchant, forty years old, grayish hair, of a medium build, with fat legs, a rounded face and closely set eyes, speaks only Portuguese.

Hernando Rodríguez, native of the village of Aveiro in Portugal, resident in the city of New Veracruz where he was the local agent for the sale of African slaves for the Portuguese crown, a widower of Doña Blanca Enríquez, an observer of the laws of Moses who died in the secret jails of this Holy Office. He is more than sixty years old, of a good build, white with freckles on the right side of his face, blue eyes, with white hair and beard, and he speaks mostly Portuguese, and he has the sign of circumcision. Having been seen and examined by the surgeons of this Holy Office, he was found to have a longitudinal scar which begins at the end of the genital member and appears to show that it was made by a cutting instrument, a very old scar, and the said surgeons took it as a sign of circumcision or retraction. He denied it and said that he did not have such a sign.

Francisco López Correa, his son and that of the said Doña Blanca Enríquez, native and resident of the city of Veracruz, a young man, single without a profession; twenty-eight years old, of a good stature, white complexion, with large crop of black hair, black eyes, and a sparse beard and moustache.

Francisco Díaz de Montoya, native of Castelo Blanco in Portugal, merchant and resident of the city of Manila in the islands of the Philippines, where he is married to Doña Nicolasa de Bañuelo, forty-seven years old, more or less, and who is of a good stature, dark complexioned, with a black beard and hair, who has two marks on his face, one on the right cheek, and another one between his eyes, both appear to be wounds. He too has the sign of circumcision. After he was examined and reviewed, the surgeons of the Holy Office found that he had a mark on the prepuce of his genital member with a circular scar, and he was missing his foreskin which appeared to be cut with a cutting instrument, and on his genital member he had a birthmark, as well as another birth mark on his chin along with other pox marks that indicate that they came from some illness, as well as two small scars or cuts on either side of his forehead which appear to have been made by a cutting instrument, and the said surgeons judged that he had been circumcised and retracted, and he said that he had been circumcised as a child due to several open sores that he had due to an illness that he had in those private parts.

Gerónimo Núñez de Rojas, single, native of the city of Guardia in Portugal and resident in this city of Mexico, without a profession, thirty-four years old, of a tall stature, thin, with thin legs and large feet, both his hair and his beard are black, and he is cross-eyed, and in between his eyes he has a scar that appears to come from an injury. He said it came from a stabbing that someone had given him. He also has the sign of circumcision. He was examined and reviewed by the said Surgeons of the Holy Office, who found a similar longitudinal scar on the left hand side of his member from his foreskin which ran down to almost the middle of his genital member, which appeared to be old, and made by a cutting instrument, and they judged it as a sign that he had been circumcised and retracted, and he said that he did not know where it came from.

Gabriel de Granada, native and resident of the city of Mexico, a young man, single, without a profession, son of Manuel de Granados deceased in the Philippine islands, and of Doña María de Ribera deceased in the secret jails of this Holy Office,[58] observant of the Law of Moses, nineteen years old, of a thin body, with black eyes, well formed face, black hair with a budding beard. He was examined and reviewed by Surgeons of the Holy Office, who found a similar longitudinal scar which ran down to the beginning of his genital member with an apparent scar that appeared to be recently made with a cutting instrument, and the Surgeons judged it as a sign that he had been circumcised and retracted. He said that he did not know who could have done that to him.

Isabel Rodríguez del Bosque, a mulatta with a light complexion, single, native, and resident of this city of Mexico, daughter of the said Esperanza Rodríguez, mulatta, and of the said Juan Bautista del Bosque, twenty-five years old, thin with a good figure, and black eyes.

Juan Rodríguez Suárez, single, native of the city of Lisbon, Merchant and resident in this city of Mexico, thirty-five years old, of a good build, stocky, and well proportioned, with a large nose, chin and with a black moustache and hair, who speaks the Portuguese language. He was examined and viewed by the Surgeons of the Holy Office, who found a similar longitudinal scar on the left hand side of his member, which denoted that it had been made with a cutting instrument, and which appeared to be old, because the scar was faded. The said Surgeons judged it as a sign that he had been circumcised and retracted. He said that he did not know about the sign, and that he had suffered a sickness in that private part.

Juan Cardoso, single, native of the Village of Simide in Portugal, resident and Merchant in the village of Orizaba in this New Spain, fifty-five years old, with very gray hair, dark complexion, and well proportioned with large eyes, who had a scar from an injury on the joint of his middle finger, and who speaks only the Portuguese language. He was examined and reviewed by the Surgeons of the Holy Office, who found a circular scar around the prepuce of his genital member, which indicated that it had been cut by a sharp instrument long before, and they took it for a sign that he had been circumcised and retracted, and he confessed and said that it was true.

Juana Rodríguez del Bosque, a mulatta with a light complexion, who was married to Blas López, a Portuguese man observant of the Law of Moses who has been a fugitive for many years who was a native of the city of Cartagena de Indias, and resident in this city of Mexico, daughter of the said Esperanza Rodríguez and Juan Bautista del Bosque, twenty-nine years old, of a good figure, and pretty with a large rounded face.

Juan Méndez de Villa Viciosa, single, native of the Village of Villa Viciosa in Portugal, resident and Merchant in the city of Mexico, forty years old, more or less, tall in stature, with somewhat rounded shoulders, well proportioned, white with a black beard and hair. This man was condemned to five years in His Majesty's galleys.[59]

Luis de Amézquita Sarmiento, single, native of the city of Segovia, and resident and Merchant in this city of Mexico, forty years old, of a medium stature, dark complexion, with a chubby face, a little bald, and with much gray hair, narrowly placed eyes, and a poorly fashioned nose.

Manuel Rodríguez Núñez (alias Caraballo), married with the said Clara Antunes, a native of Castelo Blanco in Portugal and resident in Mexico, without a profession, thirty-six years old, of a medium build, with a sparse beard and a think black moustache, thin, with a sunken mouth and a forehead that had a scar from an injury.

Manuel Díaz de Castilla, a single, native of the City of Rodrigo, resident and Merchant in this city of Mexico, forty-four years of age, of a good build, thin, with a pale color, a black beard and hair, and some gray hair. He was examined and reviewed by the Surgeons of the Holy Office, who found a similar longitudinal scar on his member only a little longer than a grain of hops placed at about a finger's length from the top of his member, apparently made with a cutting instrument, which appeared to be an old scar. They judged it as a sign that he had been circumcised and retracted, and he denied it, instead stating that he had suffered an illness in that part.

Manuel Carrasco, a single native of Villa Flor in Portugal, resident in the Valley of Amilpas, without a profession, thirty-five years old, of a good build, presentable, with narrowly placed eyes, and a brown beard and hair, narrow forehead, with a scar from an injury on his upper left lip.

María Rodríguez del Bosque, mulatta, white complexion, single, daughter of the said Esperanza Rodríguez and Juan Bautista del Bosque, native of the city of Guadalajara in New Spain, twenty years old, of a tall stature, black eyes, and a pretty face.

Nuño de Figerora (alias Don Nuño Perea), a single native of the city of Lisbon, resident and Merchant in Guadalajara in this New Spain, forty-five years old, of a good build, thin, with a black beard and hair which is turning gray, and missing a few teeth in his lower jaw.

Cristóbal de Castro, native of the city of Valladolid in Castile, resident in the Villa de los Valles in this New Spain, without a profession, married with Leonor Báez, observer of the Law of Moses, resident in the city of Valladolid, thirty-four years of age, of a medium build, dark complexion, with a thin gaunt face, with a black beard, large eyes; who was condemned to five years in the Galleys. He was examined by the Surgeons of the Holy Office, who found three scars from incisions in the prepuce of his member, with recent scarring that appeared to have been made by a cutting instrument which they judged to be a sign that he had been circumcised and retracted. He confessed that it was true.

Bachiller Rodrigo Fernández Correa, practitioner of medicine, single, son of the said Fernando Rodríguez and Doña Blanca Enríquez, native of the city of New Veracruz, twenty-four years old, of a thin build, with black hair, a sparse beard and moustache, thin, with a dark complexion, with a scar on his forehead from a fall.

Rafael de Granada, a young man, single and without a profession, a student of Rhetoric, and son of the said Doña María de Rivera and Manuel de Granada, native of this city of Mexico, twenty years old, of a tall stature, white and poorly proportioned, pox-marked by smallpox, with several freckles on his face, with black hair and the beginnings of a moustache of the same color. He was examined by the Surgeons of the Holy Office, who found a somewhat transversal scar that began underneath the head of his member and went down to the middle of his genital member. The scar appeared recent and having been made by a cutting instrument. They judged it as a sign that he had been circumcised and retracted. He said that he did not know who had made the said mark.

Simón Fernández de Torres, single native of the village of Dobla in Portugal, resident and Merchant in the city of Guadalajara in this New Spain, thirty-five years old, of a tall stature, white, with a scarred face, and thin with brownish hair, and a thin beard and moustache with some graying. He was examined by the Surgeons of the Holy Office, who found a similar transversal scar about the length of a grain of hops down underneath the head of his member which appeared to be old, so much so that the Surgeons could not be sure that it had been made with a cutting instrument. The said Simon told them that he did not know where it came from.

Tomás López Monforte, single native of Monforte in Portugal, without a profession nor residence, thirty-five years old, tall, thin, and with blond hair and beard, and narrow eyes, who only speaks Portuguese.

Tomés Méndez, resident and Merchant in the city of New Veracruz, husband of the said Doña Beatriz Enríquez, reconciled; forty-four years old, of a medium stature, not very heavy, and of a dark complexion, with a black beard and hair that is graying, and he has a mark above the right eye and his left hand is somewhat injured.

(End of the list of Prisoners who were exiled for their Observance of the Laws of Moses from this New Spain, 1647)

DOCUMENT 37

Summary Report on the Visitation and Examination of the Proceedings of the Holy Office of the Inquisition in New Spain, by Don Pedro de Medina Rico, Citing the Inconsistencies, Negligence, and Violations of Inquisitorial Procedures in the Trials of Faith Pursued by the Said Inquisition against Various Persons and Prisoners in the Secret Jails of the Holy Office

Mexico City, September 28, 1656

SOURCE: Archivo Histórico Nacional, Sección de Inquisición, legajo 1738, exp. 1.

NOTE: As this document attests, when visited and examined for the legality of its procedures, the tribunal of Mexico was on occasion found to be negligent and operating in violation of the Inquisition's laws and regulations. In this brief report, the notary of the special

visitation of the Mexican tribunal sent from the Supreme Council of the Inquisition in
Spain uncovered many inconsistencies and errors, omissions, and violations, especially, as
he notes here, in cases concerning accused Jews and others convicted of practicing Jewish
rites and ceremonies.[60]

✝

Don Marcos Alonso de Huidobro, notary of the Holy Office of the Inquisition of
Cordoba and notary named in the investigation of the Inquisition of Mexico of which the
Inquisitor Doctor Don Pedro de Medina Rico[61] was presiding.

I certify and give my word that I saw and examined the lawsuits and trials of the faith
pursued by the Inquisition of the said city of Mexico against various persons, criminals,
and prisoners held in the secret prisons and in others, and those accused of being fornica-
tors, the deluded, witches, bigamists, heretics, members of heretical sects, and more, and
almost all the trials that have serious errors and lack of proper procedures were for followers of the Law of Moses, and in these there were few acquittals, or suspended sentences,
and few other convicts reconciled or released and there are many other lawsuits yet to be
concluded. In all of these trials I observed some defects in each lawsuit, which I put forth
in the form of a warning written into the records of the criminals so that the defects may
be declared and the said faults should be evident so that they, the said Inquisitors, should
reform their procedures and end many other abuses. Because of tediousness I will not
point out all of the errors here, except for a few that will be added here at the end as a warning. I began witnessing the said Trials in the Chamber of the Secret of the said Inquisition
on September 28, 1656, in the following manner.

I warn that I will not relate everything, simply all that seemed to me to have been
delinquent either by omission, or by neglect, or out of malice or outright negligence and
ignorance, reviewing first the trials since the year 1640 and following the trials up until
the arrival of the two inquisitors who have presently entered into the exercise of these
offices.

In reviewing the case against *Manuel de la Serda,* a resident of Maracaibo [tried as a
Jew], the proceedings contained only the attorney general's petition, which concerned the
imprisonment of the criminal, without a presentation of testimonies or any other efforts,
or edicts, and with this the lawsuit ended. Also, since Maracaibo is within the district of
the Cartagena inquisition, this body should have been notified, but there is no record of
this or of remitting the testimonies to the Cartagena inquisition as should have been done.

Melchor Rodríguez López [tried as a Jew]. The denunciation or presentation was written without a presentation or an edict. No information was given on the prison judgment.
He entered into the prisons on the 2nd of February 1645, and the first hearing was held on
the 4th of February. The accusation was on the 20th of July 1646. The testimony of fifteen
witnesses was given in publication. Negative. The definitive decision was made on the 26th
of March 1648, and he was condemned to abjuration (*de vehementi*) and a fine of 3,000
ducats. The sentence was not pronounced, and at the end of the abjuration there is a signature that seems to be that of Melchor Rodríguez, but between the end of the text and the
beginning of the signature there is at least five fingers' space left blank. There is no signature

of the prison notaries authenticating the said abjuration.[62] There is no record of whether the attorney general was notified of the verdict or sentence.

Melchor Rodríguez de Huerta, deceased [with a trial against his memory and fame as a Jew]. No denunciation or initial petition. No information pertaining to his death or to his supposed crimes. The edict of the 9th of May 1645 was written with the petition of denunciation and the information used to dispatch the edicts, citing the interested parties who spoke against his memory. The accusation was signed by the lawyer Tomás López de Erenchun, who served as the Prosecutor. The testimony of five witnesses was given in publication. No definitive decision is given.

Manuel Antunez [tried as a Jew]. Only one witness appeared at the trial and his testimony was simply without authorization or demonstration of faith. The prisoner entered the prisons on the 13th of July 1642. A hearing at his own request was given on the 14th of July 1642. He showed himself repentant. The first official hearing was on the 3rd of August, but the accusation was not made until the 5th of October 1644. The publication was on the 11th of November 1644. The testimony of twenty-seven witnesses was given in publication. No definitive sentence given and the pronouncement of the sentence remained simple without any signature and with two blank pages. On a separate sheet, the abjuration was given without a signature.

Marina de la Mota [Beata]. The denunciation or petition said that she pretended to have many revelations, using superstitions and witchcraft, and that she predicted certain events, convincing many people of this. The inventory of her goods is included with the proceedings of faith, and the original information was also placed in with the formal proceedings. She entered the prisons on the 9th of May 1652. The first hearing was on the 23rd of May 1652. The testimony of fourteen witnesses was given in publication. It was decided to reprimand her in the Audience Chamber. They did not qualify the evidence of the deeds or discern if the revelations or events were certain.[63]

María Rodríguez del Bosque, mulatta [tried as a Jew]. There was no petition, information, or prison judgments. She entered the prisons on the 13th of July 1642, and the first hearing was not held until 11th of October 1644.[64] On the 4th of November the testimony of twenty-six witnesses was given in publication. No definitive decision exists. She was repentant. The pronouncement of the sentence was simple without a signature and on a separate sheet, and the abjuration had no date.

Manuel Coronel, deceased [with a trial against his memory as a Jew]. Without any information the testimony of six witnesses was given in publication. No definitive decision. The Archbishop was placed at the head of the sentence followed by the inquisitors. The case was terminated in 1648.

Manuel Álvarez de Arellano [tried as a Jew]. The denunciation or petition was without a presentation or an edict. Two witnesses appeared simply without authorization or any oath. No prison judgments or any other orders. He entered the prisons on the 23rd of March 1643. The first hearing was on the 14th of April, and another hearing was held on the 9th of June. He confessed and the accusation was on the 13th of May 1644. There is a letter from the Council which contains a petition from Francisco Núñez, the brother of the criminal, which faulted the relatives of Doña Raphaela, a married woman, because they tried to kill the criminal for having an illicit relationship with this lady. This was put before the accusation. On June 3, 1644, the testimony of twenty-five witnesses was given in publication. No definitive decision was made. He was reconciled. The pronouncement of the sentence was simple, leaving the rest of the page blank, and on a separate sheet, the abjuration appears without a date.

Manuel de Acosta [tried as a Jew]. The denunciation was made without a presentation. Eleven witness testimonies appeared in the trial, sixteen simply without authorization or signature and without demonstrating their oath. No prison judgments. He entered the prisons on the 15th of March 1643. The testimony of sixteen witnesses was given in publication on the 26th of August 1643. There is no vote or verdict on the use of torture, but it states that he confessed after the publications and in the torture chamber.[65] He was reconciled. The pronouncement of the sentence was simple without signature, leaving the rest of the page blank. The abjuration was on a separate sheet without a date, and it should have been continued by the pronouncement of the sentence.

Manuel Rodríguez (alias) Manuel Caraballo [tried as a Jew]. No information appears. He entered the prisons on the 1st of December 1642. The first hearing was on the 9th of December. He confessed on the 8th of January 1643. The accusation was on the 9th of July 1643. The publication of testimony was on the 18th of May 1644. The testimony of fourteen witnesses was given in the publication. No definitive decision or sentence was given. The pronouncement of the sentence was simple, leaving the rest of the page blank and the abjuration was on a separate sheet without a date.

Mathías Rodríguez de Olvera [with a trial as a Jew], twenty-nine witnesses appeared at the trial, nine simply without any authorization or oath. He entered the prisons on the 9th of April 1643. The first hearing was on the 11th of May. The accusation was on the 8th of May 1646. The testimony of thirty-one witnesses was given in the publication. They administered torture. The result was negative, no confession. He was condemned to a fine of 6,000 Castilian ducats. The pronouncement of the sentence was simple, without any signature, leaving the rest of the page blank. The abjuration was on a separate sheet without a date; it should be followed by the pronouncement of the sentence. The Archbishop was at the head of the sentence, which is a violation, and after him the inquisitor appeared.

Doña María de Rivera [tried as a Jew]. No information given. She entered the prisons on the 19th of May 1642. A hearing at her own request was given on the 20th of May. She was repentant. The first hearing in which they asked her about her genealogy was given on the 27th of May. On the 16th of November 1643, she died before dawn in her cell. Doña Margarita Moreira, her cellmate, declared that the day before the criminal was sick. The jailor was aware of her condition but just left her there in the cell. That night, she died. The fault of the jailor Marañon was in not notifying anyone of her condition. She died repentant, without reconciliation, abjuration, absolution, or the sacraments. She feared that false testimony that she had whipped the figure of a Christ would be used against her. This was a lie. In another declaration, Margarita Moreira revealed that the prisoner developed a great hatred for the inquisitors. They ordered surgeons to examine the body, and they opened it and declared that she died of starvation. The surgeons attributed her behavior to her desperation. A second case was made against her memory as impenitent and for having despaired of the mercy of God and letting herself die of hunger. The Prosecutor presented the denunciation and asked that her mother and sisters be notified so that they could defend her, if they so desired.

The testimony of fifty-two witnesses was given in publication; none appeared at the trial. They decided to release her. There was no order to exhume her bones or any effort made on her behalf since she died in prison, at least there is no record of it.

María Gómez, wife of Tomás Treviño relaxed [tried as impenitent relapsed Jew]. The denunciation or petition was without formal presentation. No prison judgments exist in the documentation. She entered the prisons on the 11th of October 1644. The first hearing was on the 29th of November. In the hearings of the 14th and 18th of January, they gave her the second and third warnings, with a blank page and without a reprimand or any signatures. The accusation was on the 6th of May. The testimony of twenty-five witnesses was given in publication on the 1st of September 1648. They decided to release her on the 31st of January 1649. In the case of the sentence, the bishop's name came first then the inquisitors.

Doña Margarita de Rivera [tried as a Jew], as testified by fifty-six witnesses. Twenty of these appeared simply without any authorization, or any recorded oaths and without a definitive sentence. The writing does not seem to be that of the notaries or assistants of the Secret prisons. It must be the handwriting of one of the assistants at the time of the plot, and therefore the testimony cannot be used and must be taken over again. The twenty-seven witnesses who appeared at the trial were all given in publication. She entered the prisons on the 17th of May 1642. A hearing was held at her request on the 19th of May, and in it she began to confess. The first hearing was held on the 31st of May. There was no definitive decision. The pronouncement of the sentence was simple without the signature of the notary, leaving the rest of the page blank and the abjuration on a separate sheet without a date.

Miguel Núñez de Huerta [tried as a Jew], with only one witness in his first case. He entered the prisons on the 16th of December 1642. A hearing at his own request was given on the 17th of January 1643. He began to confess in the first hearing. He was very sick in the prison on the 22nd of April 1643. On the 24th of April, they accused him. The same day he was reconciled. On the 27th, they administered the sacraments to him since his life was at risk due to his illness. On the 13th of July 1643, they took him to the hospital. He returned on the 5th of December. They accused him a second time to which he responded on the 28th of February 1644. The surgeons reported that he would not live much longer, so the tribunal ordered a monk to confer with him according to Theology. On the 4th of March, they visited him, and he declared that he had nothing more to say other than that he was dying, and they left him in this state. On the morning of the 7th of March, the jailor found him dead as he was inspecting the prisons. He died alone, without the tribunal ordering anyone to take his confession. The monk did not say whether he had confessed before dying. The second case was against his memory and against him for being a diminished repentant. The denunciation was notified to Doña Blanca de Rivera and his children. No information exists. The testimony of seventeen witnesses was given in publication. He [his memory] was released.

Manuel de Mella [tried as a Jew]. No information exists. He entered the prisons on the 2nd of September 1642. A hearing at his own request was held on the 5th of September 1642. He confessed in the first hearing on the 8th of January 1643. The accusation was on the 4th of May 1645. The publication was on the 11th of September 1647. The testimony of thirty-nine witnesses was given in publication. The pronouncement of the sentences was like the others, simple, leaving the rest of the page blank, and the abjuration on a separate page.

Doña Micaela Henríquez, wife of Sebastián Cardoso [tried as a Jew]. Three witnesses appeared at her trial testifying simply, without authorization or oath. She entered the prisons on the 4th of July 1642. A hearing at her own request was held on the 15th of July 1642. The first hearing was held on the 25th of February 1643. She confessed. The accusation was on the 24th of January 1648, and the publication of testimonies was on the 18th of February; forty-nine testimonies were given in publication. The pronouncement of the sentence was simple, leaving the rest of the page blank and the abjuration was on a separate sheet.

Manuel Coronel [tried as a Jew and as an absent fugitive]. No information of the crime, his escape, or his absence is given. The edict which brought his case to attention was dated the 9th of February 1649 and was made with this information. The declaration had no warning of the notary, publication, or record of the testimony of three witnesses given in publication. No definitive decision. At the head of the sentence the Archbishop signed and then, after, the inquisitors. The prisoner was relaxed [in effigy] to the secular arm.

Doña Mariquita Moreira [tried as a Jew]. Seven witnesses appeared at her trial, one testified simply. She entered the prisons on the 31st of January 1643. The first hearing was held on the 11th of February 1643. The accusation was on the 6th of May. The testimony of eight witnesses was given in publication. No definitive decision. She confessed while under torture. They also violated the regulations when they decided to torture her and then executed it without the ordinary being present.[66] The pronouncement of the sentence was simple, with four pages left blank, and on a separate page the abjuration, which should have been continued by the pronouncement of the sentence, which is absent.

Manuel Díaz de Castilla [tried as a Jew]. Four witnesses appeared at the trial and testified simply. He entered the prisons on the 13th of July 1642. A hearing at his own request was given on the 30th of July, and he confessed at this time. The first formal hearing was on the 7th of August and the accusation on the 4th of May 1643. The publication of the witnesses occurred on the 7th of June 1643. No definitive sentence. The pronouncement of the sentence was simple without any signature. The abjuration was on a separate sheet.

Manuel Ramírez de Montilla, deceased [with a trial against his memory as a Jew]. No information. The testimony of seven witnesses was given in the publication. No definitive decision. At the head of the sentence the Archbishop and, after, the inquisitors appear.

Manuel López Núñez, deceased [with a trial against his memory as a Jew in the year 1648]. There was no information or testimony of his death or his crimes. The testimony of nine witnesses was given in publication with their full names listed in violation of the regulations.[67] No definitive decision. At the head of the sentence the name of the Archbishop appears and then, after him, the inquisitors.

Manuel Méndez [tried as a Jew]. He entered the prisons on the 2nd of October 1655. The first hearing was on the 13th of November 1655. The accusation was on the 23rd of May 1646. The testimony of eight witnesses was given in publication. No judgments exist on the application of torture, but he was submitted to questioning under torment. The result was negative; he did not confess. No definitive decision. The sentence was ordered in the proceedings after the abjuration on its own. At the head of the sentence, the Archbishop's name appears and then, after him, the inquisitors. They ordered that the relations of the sentence with the signs and description of the criminal be sent to the Councils of the Inquisition in Seville, Cartagena, and Lima, but there is no record of this being done.

Mayor López, deceased [with a trial against his memory as a Jew, 1645]. The case is without testimony or information concerning his death. The testimony of three witnesses was given in publication with their names, against regulations. No definitive decision. At the head of the sentence the Archbishop's name and then, after, the inquisitors.

Miguel Tinoco [tried as a Jew]. Seventeen witnesses appeared at his trial, and fifteen of them testified simply without authorization or the oath. No prison judgments or orders exist, yet he entered the prisons on the 9th of September 1642. On the 6th of October he asked for a hearing, and it was accorded to him, and he confessed to his crime. On the 13th of October the first formal hearing was held. The accusation occurred on the 28th of January 1643. On the 22nd of February 1646, he communicated concerning the accusation with his lawyer. The testimony of nineteen witnesses was given in publication. He was declared repentant, without any definitive decision. The pronouncement of the sentence was simple, without a signature, leaving the rest of the page blank, and the abjuration was without a date, and it should have been continued by the pronouncement of the sentence.

María de la Encarnación [and her trial as an impostor and an enlightened woman who pretended to have revelations]. No petition. No prison orders. No information. Apparently she did not enter the prisons. No rations were allocated to her. The first hearing was held on the 11th of September 1649, and she confessed to lying about all the revelations and rapture and other things, and she made many confessions in this manner. She died in prison on the 11th of September 1650. There was no qualification of the evidence or even an accusation in this case.

Nicolasa de Santo Domingo [denounced for following the sect of the enlightened and for using revelations with heretical propositions to deceive many people]. She said that she had revelations of heaven and that she had ordinary conversations with our Lord Jesus Christ and his blessed Mother, and with other saints. In the proceedings, there are nineteen testimonies and no prison judgments or any imprisonment recorded. On the 17th of September 1649, she was given a hearing at her own request since she was in the secret prisons. In this hearing she confessed to have devotions and meditations on the passion of Our Lord and other works of virtue. She gave the names of her confessors and her genealogy. Then she stated that she had become a prisoner on the 9th of September. The qualification of her propositions and other things that were testified to was not done until the 10th of October 1654, five years after her initial imprisonment. The accusation was not made until the 2nd of March 1655, and they were provided with an edict to qualify the case on the 10th of October. By an edict of the inspecting inquisitor, it was ordered, on the 7th of May 1655, that the testimony in the case of this criminal be found. The publication of testimonies was on the 13th of May 1656, and the testimony of nineteen witnesses was given in publication. The sentence condemned her to abjuration (*de levi*) and other penances. The pronouncement of the sentence was simple without the signature of the notary, with a page and a half left blank and on a separate page. The abjuration, without a date, should have been continued by the pronouncement of the sentence.

Nuño Suárez de Figueroa [tried as a Jew]. No testimony. No prison judgments exist. He entered the prisons on the 13th of July 1642. The first hearing was on the 24th of July. In the hearing of the 22nd of December 1642, he confessed, but it was not until the 9th of July 1646 that he was accused. On the 17th of October the testimony of twenty-seven witnesses was given in publication. He was repentant, and the pronouncement of the sentence was simple, without the signature of the notary, leaving the rest of the page blank and on a separate page the abjuration without a date.

Marcos Rodríguez Tristán, deceased [with a trial against his memory as a Jew, in the year 1645]. The petition had no presentation, testimony, or information concerning his death. The testimony of seven witnesses was given in publication, with their full names listed. No definitive decision exists. No sentence or any other efforts in the case are recorded.

All of this was conducted during the visitation of the Holy Office in the Secret Chambers of the Tribunal by me, July 18, 1656.

Marcos Alonso Huidobro, Secretary of the Visitation

Trials and Testimonies against Lutherans, Calvinists, and Other Protestants

> The Lutherans are not as bad as they say, actually there are some things good about them.
>
> Reportedly said by Gerónimo Monti, a Milanese resident of Guatemala, denounced to the Inquisition in 1582

The Inquisition in New Spain confused many of the actual beliefs and practices of the new Protestant religions and used the term *Lutheran* to describe all Protestants, even those who did not follow the teachings of Martin Luther.[68] Among the wide variety of Protestant beliefs held by those tried for Lutheranism in New Spain were Calvinism, Anglicanism, Anabaptism, Quakerism, and Puritanism. The accused were usually foreigners or had lived in a foreign country where the Protestant religion was practiced,[69] with a majority coming from England, Holland, Germany, and the Protestant regions of France.[70] Most cases against foreign Protestants occurred during the first four decades of the Mexican tribunal's existence, from 1571 to 1610.[71] Other than "foreigners and outsiders,"[72] heretics in New Spain were relatively rare. Many of those tried in the early period had been sailors or even pirates captured on the coasts of New Spain.[73] Because of the immense territory controlled by the tribunal of New Spain, prosecution and apprehension proved difficult. Its northern and southern districts remained outside of the effective control of the tribunal and together witnessed the prosecution of less than 10 percent of the total number of cases tried by the Mexican Inquisition (map 2).[74]

After the decade of 1610, prosecution of cases against Lutherans and Protestants declined significantly. Between 1610 and 1700, only seven cases occurred in New Spain.[75] Political rather than religious reasons motivated this change. After Philip II's death in 1598, his successor Philip III signed the Treaty of London of 1603, in which it was agreed not to permit the prosecution of English sailors and merchants in Spanish ports.

Before this agreement, the Inquisition had issued harsh sentences against convicted Protestants. Although, according to Herrera Sotillo, punishments given to convicted Lutherans ranged from total absolution to relaxations to the secular arm,[76] in some cases the harshness of their trials was outdone only by those against suspected Jews. Most notably, in the administration of interrogations under torture, the Mexican inquisition exceeded its usual cruelty in dealing with suspected Protestants, especially foreigners. It is not surprising that the largest share of all cases involving the use of torture, almost 30 percent, occurred

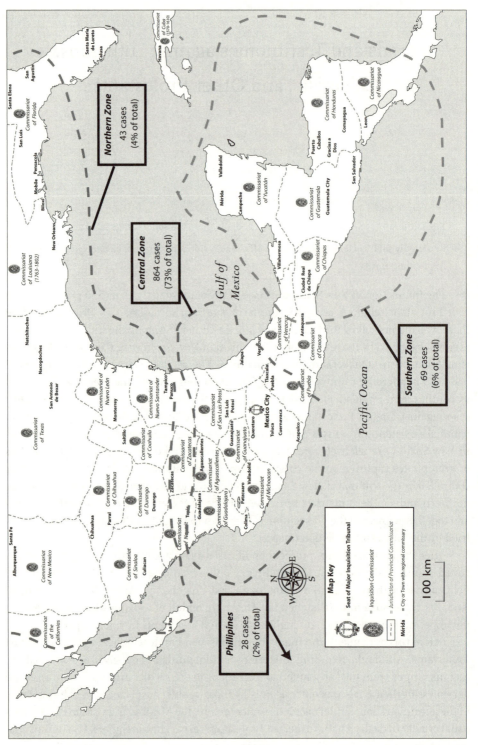

Northern Zone
43 cases
(4% of total)

Central Zone
864 cases
(73% of total)

Southern Zone
69 cases
(6% of total)

Phillipines
28 cases
(2% of total)

*Gulf of
Mexico*

Pacific Ocean

Santa Maria
de Loreto
Caluza
San
Agustín

Santa Elena

San Luis

*Commissariat
of Florida*

Mobile
Pensacola
Biloxi

New Orleans

Natchitoches

*Commissariat
of Louisiana*
(1763–1802)

Nacogdoches

San Antonio
de Bexar

*Commissariat
of Texas*

Alburquerque
Santa Fe

*Commissariat
of New Mexico*

La Paz

*Commissariat
of the
Californias*

*Commissariat
of Sinaloa*
Culiacan

Chihuahua
Parral

*Commissariat
of Chihuahua*

*Commissariat
of Durango*
Durango

*Commissariat
of Nayarit*
Tepic

*Commissariat
of Nuevo León*
Monterrey

Saltillo

*Commissariat
of Coahuila*

*Commissariat
of Nuevo Santander*

Tampico
Pánuco

*Commissariat
of San Luis Potosi*
San Luis
Potosí

*Commissariat
of Zacatecas*
Zacatecas
Aguascalientes

*Commissariat
of Aguascalientes*

Guanajuato
*Commissariat
of Guanajuato*

Querétaro

*Commissariat
of Guadalajara*
Guadalajara

Colima

Pátzcuaro
Valladolid

*Commissariat
of Michoacan*

Mexico City
Toluca
Cuernavaca

Acapulco

*Commissariat
of Puebla*
Tlaxcala
Puebla

Jalapa

Veracruz
*Commissariat
of Veracruz*

Antequera
*Commissariat
of Oaxaca*

Ciudad Real
de Chiapa
*Commissariat
of Chiapas*
Villahermosa

Mérida
Campeche

*Commissariat
of Yucatán*

Valladolid

*Commissariat
of Guatemala*
Guatemala City

San Salvador

Puerto
Caballos
Gracias a
Dios

*Commissariat
of Honduras*
Comayagua

León

*Commissariat
of Nicaragua*

*Commissariat
of Cuba*
(1570–1610)
Havana

Map Key

= Seat of Major Inquisition Tribunal

= Inquisition Commissariat

= Jurisdiction of Provincial Commissariat

Mérida = City or Town with regional commissary

100 Km

N
W—E
S

MAP 2. Regional Distribution of Place of Origin of Completed Inquisition Trials in New Spain, 1571–1700

when the Inquisition in New Spain dealt with cases against suspected Protestants. This use of torture likewise reveals that the Inquisition's repressive dealings with foreign Protestants during the reign of Philip II had more to do with politics than religion.[77]

DOCUMENT 38
Inquisition Trial against Cristóbal Miguel, the Official Who Separates Out the Gold from the Silver, Reconciled by This Holy Office for Believing in the Sect of Calvin and Who Continues to Ride on Horseback and Wear Silk and Carry Arms, Things Forbidden to Those Who Have Received Penance from the Holy Office

Mexico City, 1604

SOURCE: Archivo General de la Nación, Ramo de Inquisición, vol. 274, exp. 8.

NOTE: Of note in this series of denunciations of a previously convicted Calvinist is the impact of an inquisitorial conviction on one's lifestyle, dress, and privileges. Restrictive sumptuary regulations prohibited convicted heretics and reconciled penitents from wearing fine fabrics, carrying arms, and enjoying other privileges of their class or position.

Denunciation by the Prosecuting Attorney of the Holy Office, Dr. Martos de Bohórques, against Cristóbal Miguel, for Guarding and Observing the Calvinist Sect, June 21, 1604

✝

Dr. Martos de Bohórques, Prosecuting Attorney for the Holy Office of the Inquisition in this City of Mexico, its regions and provinces of New Spain, in all solemnity and in the proper form according to law, I denounce and formally charge Cristóbal Miguel, the official who separates gold and silver bullion, and a member of those reconciled by this Holy Office for guarding and observing the Calvinist sect and its followers.

I state that by information that is contained in the numbered registers of this Holy Office, which I now make presentation of so that it can certify to the above stated, it has been prohibited him by law as it is of all said people who have been reconciled, that he should bear arms and wear clothing of silk and go about mounted on horses. In violation of this precept he goes about publicly using them, and without respect and in detriment to the orders of this Holy Office, he continues to use them, and for this he should be punished.

I beg your Lordship to request an order that he should be arrested and taken to one of the prisons of this Holy Office where he should be made prisoner, and I declare that I will make the accusation in the proper form and continue a case against him as is my right by justice, all of this I request and implore all that is necessary for the completion of this Holy Office.

Dr. Martos de Bohórques, Prosecutor

Presentation of the Petition Made by the Prosecutor Dr. Martos de Bohórques against Cristóbal Miguel, June 21, 1604

✝

In the City of Mexico, 21st of June 1604, being present the Inquisitors Licenciado Don Alonso de Peralta and Gutierre Bernardo de Quiroz in their audience during the morning, there appeared the Prosecutor of the Holy Office, Dr. Martos de Bohórques, who presented this petition and requested what he asked and implored justice.

And once the said petition was seen by the said Lord Inquisitors, they agreed and took it as presented, and they provided for justice.

This all passed before me,
Pedro de Mañozca
(Secretary of the Holy Office)

The Testimony of Pedro Álvarez, Smelter of Gold, against Cristóbal Miguel, March 22, 1604

✝

In the City of Mexico, 22nd of March 1604, being present the Inquisitor Licenciado Don Alonso de Peralta in his audience during the morning, there appeared out of his own free will and swore the oath to tell the truth a man who said he was called Pedro Álvarez, a smelter of gold who worked on San Francisco street in the house of Hernán López Xardon, who said he was about twenty-six years old.

He said that he had heard about the Edict of this Holy Office and about what it ordered,[78] and he came to state and manifest for the discharge of his conscience that about one and a half or two months ago he and the said Pedro de Rivera had seen Cristóbal Miguel, the separator of gold and silver bullion who had been reconciled by the Holy Office, riding on horseback on a high saddle, breaking his horses stride and going about dressed in fine woolens with silk stockings. The said Pedro de Rivera stated that he had run into the said Cristóbal Miguel again last night and that he went about armed with a sword, and that this was all that he had to state.

He stated that it was the truth under his oath, and he stated it not out of hatred. After having been read his statement, he approved and agreed to the secret and signed.

Pedro Álvarez
This all passed before me,
Pedro de Mañozca
(Secretary of the Holy Office)

The Testimony of Pedro Carrillo de Rivera against Cristóbal Miguel, March 22, 1604

✝

In the City of Mexico, 22nd of March, 1604, being present the Inquisitor Licenciado Don Alonso de Peralta in his audience during the morning, there appeared out of his own free will and swore the oath to tell the truth a man who said he was called Pedro Carrillo de Rivera, a smelter of gold, resident of this city who lives on Tacuba street and who smelts gold in the house of Hernán López Xardon,[79] who stated to be about thirty-three years old.

He said that because he had heard the General Edict of Faith, he came to make a statement to discharge his conscience for having seen last night between seven and eight o'clock, Cristóbal Miguel, the Official separator of gold and silver bullion reconciled by this Holy Office, wearing a sword, and that Luisa Hernández, wife of this witness, and Pedro Becerra, painter and goldsmith who lives on Tacuba street, and his wife Juana de Torres, all saw the same thing.

Also, he said that this witness and Pedro Álvarez had seen two or three times during the day the said Cristóbal Miguel passing by mounted on a horse riding through San Francisco street, using a saddle and spurs. Similarly he had seen him dressed in fine woolens and with stockings of silk, and he was not sure if they were the thick kind, because he wore a long black cape, but that there were many witnesses because he went about publicly dressed like this.

He stated that it was the truth under his oath, and he stated it not out of hatred. After having been read his statement, he approved and agreed to the secret and signed.

Pedro Carrillo de Rivera
This all passed before me,
Pedro de Mañozca
(Secretary of the Holy Office)

The Testimony of Fructuoso Díaz against Cristóbal Miguel, March 22, 1604

✝

In the City of Mexico, Monday, the 22nd of March 1604, being present the Inquisitor Licenciado Don Alonso de Peralta in his audience during the afternoon, there appeared out of his own free will and swore the oath to tell the truth a man who said he was called Fructuoso Díaz, a silversmith, resident of this city who works on San Francisco street, and who stated to be about twenty-eight years old.

He said that, because he had heard yesterday the Edict of Faith of this Holy Office read in the convent of Santo Domingo, he came to make a statement that about eight days before as this witness arrived at the shop of a silversmith in the said street, he heard it said *"Look there goes Cristóbal Miguel mounted on horseback!"* and when this witness turned to look, he had already entered into the small alleyway of Doctor Alemán. Then this witness told Martín de Uribe and Gaspar Páez that they should not be shocked by that, because on the morning of the day of Saint John the year before others had seen the said Cristóbal Miguel going through the orchards mounted on a horse with saddle and spurs and a golden sword, and with a woman behind him. All of these things this witness heard said by someone whom he does not remember. And this witness has also seen the said accused going about dressed in fine woolens, and he heard it said that all of this was prohibited him for having been reconciled by this Holy Office.

He stated that it was the truth under his oath, and he stated it not out of hatred. After having been read his statement, he approved and agreed to the secret and signed.

Fructuoso Díaz
This all passed before me,
Pedro de Mañozca
(Secretary of the Holy Office)

The Testimony of Gaspar Páez against Cristóbal Miguel, March 22, 1604

†

In the City of Mexico, Monday, the 22nd of March 1604, being present the Inquisitor Licenciado Don Alonso de Peralta in his audience during the afternoon, there appeared out of his own free will and swore the oath to tell the truth a man who said he was called Gaspar Páez, a silversmith, resident of this city who works on San Francisco street at the shop of Martín de Uribe, and who stated he was about thirty-two years old.

He said that because he had heard the Edict of Faith of this Holy Office read about eight days before in the Cathedral, he came to make a statement to discharge his conscience that he saw Cristóbal Miguel, reconciled by this Holy Office, riding two times on horseback with a saddle and spurs close to La Concepción, wearing a sheathed sword. On one of those occasions, he saw that he had a woman behind him, all of which he did publicly, which all of the people of this city should know about, and that Fructuoso Díaz, the silversmith, said to this witness that he had been seen on the day of Saint John during the previous year riding on horseback through the orchards with a golden sword, and he understood this to be very bizarre. And when he encountered him near La Concepción, he was alone, and he does not know anyone else who can testify to this.

He stated that it was the truth under his oath, and he stated it not out of hatred. After having been read his statement, he approved and agreed to the secret and signed.

Gaspar Páez
This all passed before me,
Pedro de Mañozca
(Secretary of the Holy Office)

The Testimony of Alonso de Sotelo against Cristóbal Miguel, March 22, 1604

✝

In the City of Mexico, Monday, the 22nd of March 1604, being present the Inquisitor Licenciado Don Alonso de Peralta in his audience during the afternoon, there appeared out of his own free will and swore the oath to tell the truth a man who said he was called Alonso de Sotelo, major Official of the Royal Factory of His Majesty, resident of this city, who stated to be about thirty years old more or less.

He said that because he had heard the reading of the Edict of Faith of this Holy Office read in the convent of Santo Domingo yesterday, he came to make a statement to discharge his conscience, that just after leaving the church and hearing the reading of the Edict, he saw Cristóbal Miguel, reconciled by this Holy Office, riding on horseback between the Royal houses and the schools. Juan de Escobar went in the company of this witness at that time, and he lives in the middle of the street from this witness, which is at the rear of the said schools and that he had nothing else to declare.

He stated that it was the truth under his oath, and he stated it not out of hatred. After having been read his statement, he approved and agreed to the secret and signed.

Alonso de Sotelo
This all passed before me,
Pedro de Mañozca
(Secretary of the Holy Office)

The Testimony of Pedro Becerra against Cristóbal Miguel, March 26, 1604

✝

In the City of Mexico, Friday, the 26th of March 1604, being present the Inquisitor Licenciado Gutierre Bernardo de Quiroz, in his audience during the morning, there appeared out of his own free will and swore the oath to tell the truth a man who said he was called Pedro Becerra, a painter, who lives on Tacuba street, who stated he was about twenty-seven years old.

He said that because he had heard the reading of the Edict of Faith of this Holy Office as it was read in the convent of Santo Domingo last Sunday, he now came to make a statement and discharge his conscience, stating that on that said Sunday evening when the palace had *luminarias*,[80] this witness went to view them with his wife and with Pedro de Rivera and his wife, and in the small plaza of the Marqués they saw Cristóbal Miguel, who had been reconciled by this Holy Office, with a woman holding her by the hand as they approached Santo Domingo street, and he wore a sword underneath his arm. And he also said that he had seen the said Cristóbal Miguel later after having been recognized riding on horseback on a bridled and saddled horse, well fitted with a black cloth, dressed in woolens, and this is what he has to declare.

He stated that it was the truth under his oath, and he stated it not out of hatred. After having been read his statement, he approved and agreed to the secret and signed.

Pedro de Becerra
This all passed before me,
Pedro de Mañozca
(Secretary of the Holy Office)

DOCUMENT 39
Documents Pertaining to the Reconciliation to Our Holy Catholic Faith of Joshua Morton, Native of England and Protestant Heretic Who Has Followed the Rites of the Anglican Church

Mexico City, October 8, 1720

SOURCE: Archivo General de la Nación, Ramo de Inquisición, vol. 787, exp. 2.

NOTE: In this eighteenth-century case of self-denunciation and reconciliation, a captured English Protestant sailor attempted to convert to Catholicism to relieve himself of his imprisonment and gain permission to live freely in Mexico. These types of spontaneous confessions and conversions were encouraged by the Inquisition in New Spain, though the supposed convert placed himself in greater danger if he was found later to persist in his Protestant beliefs. As an unconverted Protestant, an English sailor would have remained a prisoner during wartime, but once a new convert he would find himself under the surveillance and jurisdiction of the Inquisition.

Self-Denunciation, Audience, and Reconciliation of Joshua Morton, an Englishmen, before the Holy Office, October 8, 1720

✝

In this Holy Office of the Inquisition of Mexico on the 8th of October 1720, sitting in Audience, the Lord Inquisitor Licenciado Don Francisco de Garzarón, Visitor General of New Spain, ordered the entry of a man who came of his own free will, who being present received the oath before Our Lord God and the sign of the cross in true legal form under which he promised to state and respond to the truth in everything that he should be questioned, and he promised to maintain the secret of all that transpired here.

He said that his name was Joshua Morton, and Englishman, native of London, single and a sailor by trade, twenty years old, and he stated that he requested this audience because he has come to recognize by the mercy and grace of God, the errors in which he has until now lived by belonging to the English Anglican Church due to his birth and raising in it, and he realizes that salvation can be obtained only through the belief in the Holy Catholic Church of Rome, which he now recognizes as the only true Church, and he requests to be brought back into the fold and company of its faithful which is made clear in the writing that he presented to his Illustrious Lordship the Archbishop of Mexico, which he shows here, and in order to achieve his goal he was sent here to this Holy Office.

He was asked to state and declare the errors that he says that he had professed in the belief of the English Anglican church in which he was raised.

He said that he could not declare all of the errors of the Anglican Church individually because he has not had or received the Catechism used in this church, and as a sailor by trade he has taken little care in instructing himself in this religion.

He was asked to give an account of his life.

He said that he was raised and lived much of it in London until more or less five and a half years ago when he began to navigate and he has made many different voyages to Lisbon, Cartagena, Santiago de Cuba, Jamaica, and lastly he came to Veracruz in the ship named the *San Jorge,* which arrived last year in 1719, and there due to the war they brought him to Mexico City.[81] He has been living in Chapultepec Castle for about a year, where he has been instructed in the doctrine of the Roman Catholic faith by Father Castro, who is the parish priest in that mountain, and afterward he was instructed by Father Julián Gutíerrez Dávila, the cleric of the oratory of San Felipe de Nerí, where he has been for the past four months.

He was asked if during the time that he was in the ports of Spain, if he had done anything in the observation of the laws of the Anglican Church, which he then professed, and if his soul is now in firm resolution to detest his errors in which he was raised and lived until the present day, and to live and to die in the faith of the Holy Roman Church?

He said that only in Lisbon did he assist at one of the preaching sessions of the English Anglican Church, but that in the rest of the Ports of Spain there are no Anglicans, nor are Anglicans permitted, so in this way he has not done any of these things either then or now, and since he has been in New Spain he has not exercised any of the ceremonies which are proper in the Anglican Church. Having recognized out of the mercy and grace of God the trickery and errors in which he was raised and has lived until now, he seeks to be restituted to the fold of the True Church of Our Lord Jesus Christ, which is the Roman Catholic church, in whose faith and by whose Articles of belief he has been well instructed, and he wishes to live in it and die in it, and thus he now abjures and detests all of the other errors that he had professed and believed, including all of those of the Anglican Church, and all of those of the other sects that are opposed to the doctrine of the Holy Catholic Church of Rome in which he now believes firmly.

He was asked if he knows someone, or anyone in this Kingdom, or in those of Spain, and if he has had contact with them.

He said that he only knows those of his companions who were brought with him to Chapultepec, and all of the other people whom he has treated with have been and are Catholics.

All of this he said was the truth under the oath that he had taken and he affirmed it, ratified it, and signed it.

Joshua Morton

This passed before me,

Don Eugenio de las Peñas (Secretary of the Holy Office)

Order of Restitution Made by His Lordship the Inquisitor Don Francisco de Garzarón Bringing the Said Joshua Morton Back into the Fold of the Holy Catholic Church, October 8, 1720

†

And later on the same day, month, and year, the said Lord Inquisitor Don Francisco de Garzarón, having seen the declaration above made by Joshua Morton, a native of England, by which it appears that the said Morton has been raised, instructed, and educated in the dogmas and errors of the Anglican Church, and that he had not been instructed in the mysteries and beliefs of Our Holy Catholic Faith, until he had been brought to this City of Mexico and taken to the Royal Palace of Chapultepec, where they were proposed by Father Castro who assists to the ministry at the said mountain of the Royal Palace, and he quickly embraced them with promptness and docility, and he now requests to be reinstituted in the fold of the Holy Catholic Faith of Rome, His Lordship orders and ordered that the said Joshua Morton should be absolved *ad cautelam*[82] of the censures in which he could have incurred for the errors which he has previously held and believed, and now has detested in his said declaration, and which touch upon the Holy Office, and he orders him restituted and reinstated into the unity of the Sacrament of the Holy Mother Church of Rome, and concerning this he should be given testimony and certification in the proper form held by law.

Licenciado Don Francisco de Garzarón
This passed before me,
Don Eugenio de las Peñas (Secretary of the Holy Office)

Act of Absolution and Reinstitution into the Fold of the Holy Catholic Church of Rome for Joshua Morton, October 8, 1720

†

And later on the same day, month, and year, the said Lord Inquisitor Don Francisco de Garzarón, ordered that the said Joshua Morton return to the audience chamber, and in conformity to the previous order and having had the said Morton make all the acts of Faith of the Catholic Church, he absolved him *ad cautelam* of the ecclesiastical censures in which he could have incurred for his errors, and he proclaimed to the said Joshua Morton that for all things touching upon this Office, he was once again reinstituted into the fold of the Our Holy Mother Church of Rome, and as a testament of this he issued this certification and placed it at the end of the list of papers that he brought to this Audience, and he returned them to him so that he could go and show his priest who had sent him here to this Tribunal, so that it will serve as proof of his reconciliation.

All of this passed before me,
Don Eugenio de las Peñas
(Secretary of the Holy Office)

DOCUMENT 40
Documents Pertaining to the Reconciliation to Our Holy Catholic Faith of Jacob Fors, Native of Sweden and a Lutheran Heretic

Mexico City, October 8, 1720

SOURCE: Archivo General de la Nación, Ramo de Inquisición, vol. 787, exp. 3.

NOTE: As in the previous document, a sailor, a native of Stockholm, seeks to gain release from imprisonment and permission to reside permanently in Mexico by means of a certified conversion to Catholicism before the Inquisition in Mexico. Once again, whether a sincere conversion or not, the very act of reconciliation conducted here would place the sailor under the future jurisdiction of the Inquisition and make him a relapsed heretic if he should continue in his previous Lutheran beliefs.

Self-Denunciation, Audience, and Reconciliation of Jacob Fors, a Native of Stockholm, in the Kingdom of Sweden, before the Holy Office, October 8, 1720

✝

In this Holy Office of the Inquisition of Mexico on the 8th of October 1720, sitting in Audience, the Lord Inquisitor Licenciado Don Francisco de Garzarón, Visitor General of New Spain, ordered the entry of a man who came of his own free will; who being present received the oath before Our Lord God and the sign of the cross in true legal form under which he promised to state and respond to the truth in everything that he should be questioned, and he promised to maintain the secret of all that transpired here. He said that his name was Jacob Fors, a native of the town of Stockholm in the royal court of Sweden, single and a sailor by trade, thirty-one years old.

He was asked what he wanted and why he had requested this audience.

He said that he requested this audience because he has the desire to reconcile himself to the Holy Catholic Church of Rome and seek to be admitted to the fold of its faithful, which he had lived apart from until now due to his birth and raising in the dominions and Kingdom of Sweden, as he has said, where he was instructed until now and has held and believed in the dogmas of the Lutheran sect, which is the only religion professed publicly there.

He was asked to state and declare what are the dogmas that he was taught in the name of Christian Doctrine.

He said that the particular differences between Lutheranism and the other sects and religions are the following: the principal difference is that Lutherans deny that in the Holy Sacrament of the Eucharist the consecration of the host by the priest leads to transubstantiation, or the miraculous conversion of the substance of the bread and the wine into the body and blood of Our Lord Jesus Christ, all of which they do not believe. . . . Besides this dogma, which is the principal belief, they also deny and call Idolatry all of the invocations of the saints, and the cult and veneration of their images and relics, and they also deny the existence of purgatory. And concerning the sacraments, they only believe in two, that of the Eucharist and that of Baptism, whose form is the same as that of the Catholic Church, such that the minister who baptizes the infant immerses him into the water without any other mixture or oils on their forehead, pronouncing the words *"Ego te baptizo in nomino Patris et Fili, et Spiritu Santi"*[83] and this is the form of baptism practiced in all places and parts of the Kingdom of Sweden.

He was then asked to give an account of his life.

He said that he was raised and lived in Sweden until he was sixteen years old when he took to sea with the English. He has done the same throughout the rest of his life, navigating with them to Guinea, New England, Virginia, and no other Catholic countries, except for one trip that he took to Lisbon in the year 1716, staying in that port for about two months until about the time of October 1718 when he arrived at the Port of Veracruz in the small ship called the *Albertus,* which belongs to the London Company. He is in doubt as to whether it was in the month of September or October of the said year, and on the occasion of the breaking of peace with England he was detained with the others who came with him on the said ship, and they were brought to the Royal Palace of Chapultepec, where he lived for about a year, and the rest of the time he has been in Mexico. During the time that he was in Chapultepec, he was instructed in the faith and belief of the Holy Catholic Church by Father Castro, who assisted to the ministry in the region of Chapultepec, and having recognized that his Lutheran sect was not the true way toward salvation, and that he could only achieve salvation by professing the Roman Catholic religion, he sent to the Lord Archbishop in order to be admitted to the fold, as appears in the documents that he presents to Your Illustrious Lordship, which he showed and had returned to him. From there he has come to this Holy Office for the same effect.

He was asked if during the time that he was in Lisbon, or during the two years or more that he has resided here in New Spain, if he practiced any of the ceremonies in observance of the laws of the Lutheran sect, and if he is now firm and faithfully instructed in what Our Catholic Church of Rome teaches, and if his soul is firm to live and to die in the faith of the Holy Roman Church, detesting from now on and forever Lutheranism and all of the other sects and errors against the Faith.

He said that during the time he was in Lisbon he prayed prayers that he had been taught as a boy, without having gone to or attended any other ceremony which may have been against the Catholic Religion, and that he practiced the same thing in New Spain before he was instructed in the truth of the faith of the Roman Catholic religion. He did this until he went to Chapultepec where the said Father Castro instructed him. Recognizing the grace of God, and the errors in which he had been raised and lived until now, he now solicits his restitution into the fold of the True Church of Our Lord Jesus Christ, which is the Catholic Roman church in whose faith, articles, and beliefs he is now well instructed, and he wishes to live and die in it, and from now on he abjures and detests all of the other errors that he had professed and believed, including all of those of all other sects opposed to the doctrine of the Holy Catholic Church of Rome in which he now believes firmly.

Asked if he knows someone, or any other heretics in this kingdom, or in those of Spain, and if he has had contact with them.

He said that he only knows those of his English companions who were brought with him to Chapultepec, but besides them he does not deal with any others who are not Catholics.

All of this he said was the truth under the oath that he had taken and he affirmed it, ratified it, and signed it.

Jacob Fors

This passed before me,

Don Eugenio de las Peñas

(Secretary of the Holy Office)

Order of Restitution Made by His Lordship the Inquisitor Don Francisco de Garzarón Bringing the Said Jacob Fors Back into the Fold of the Holy Catholic Church, October 8, 1720

✝

And later on the same day, month, and year, the said Lord Inquisitor Don Francisco de Garzarón, having seen the declaration above made by Jacob Fors, a native of Sweden, by which it appears that the aforesaid has been raised, instructed and educated in the dogmas and errors of the Lutheran sect, and that he had not been instructed in the mysteries and beliefs of Our Holy Catholic Faith until he had been brought to this City of Mexico and taken to the Royal Palace of Chapultepec, where they were proposed by Father Castro who assists to the ministry at the said mountain of the Royal Palace, and he quickly embraced them with promptness and docility. Seeing that he now requests to be reinstituted in the fold of the Holy Catholic Faith of Rome, His Lordship orders and ordered that the said Jacob Fors should be absolved *ad cautelam* of the censures in which he could have incurred for the errors which he has previously held and believed, and now has detested in his said declaration, and which touch upon the Holy Office, and he orders him restituted and reinstated into the unity of the Sacrament of the Holy Mother Church of Rome, and concerning this he should be given testimony and certification in the proper form held by law.

Licenciado Don Francisco de Garzarón

This passed before me,

Don Eugenio de las Peñas (Secretary of the Holy Office)

Act of Absolution and Reinstitution into the Fold of the Holy Catholic Church of Rome for Jacob Fors, October 8, 1720

✝

And later on the same day, month, and year, the said Lord Inquisitor Don Francisco de Garzarón, ordered that the said Jacob Fors return to the audience chamber, and in conformity to the previous order, and having had the said Jacob Fors make all the acts of faith of the Catholic Church, he absolved him *ad cautelam* of the ecclesiastical censures in which he could have incurred for his errors, and he proclaimed to the said Jacob Fors that for all things touching upon this Office, he was once again reinstituted into the fold of the Our Holy Mother Church of Rome, and as a testament of this, he issued this certification and placed it at the end of the list of papers that he brought to this Audience, and he returned them to him so that he could go and show his priest who had sent him here to this Tribunal, so that it will serve as proof of his reconciliation.

All of this passed before me,
Don Eugenio de las Peñas
(Secretary of the Holy Office)

DOCUMENT 41
Spontaneous Denunciation Made against Himself by Edward Rivet, Native of England, for Having Been Raised and Lived in the Sect of the Quakers, or Tremblers, Seeking to Be Reincorporated to the Fold of Our Holy Catholic Faith

Mexico City, November 1719

SOURCE: Archivo General de la Nación, Ramo de Inquisición, vol. 777, exp. 2.

NOTE: Albert Edward Rivet reveals through his lack of Spanish and other hints that his desire to convert to Catholicism may not have been motivated by true belief or desire for conversion. As opposed to both Joshua Morton and the Swede Jacob Fors in the preceding documents, Edward Rivet would not be absolved and, instead, would later find himself on trial for heretical beliefs. His later trial would be concerned with many of the same beliefs that he hinted at in this document. This document shows the dangerous and double-edged nature of self-denunciations.

Denunciation Made against Himself by Edward Rivet, November 3, 1719

✝

In this Holy Office of the Inquisition of Mexico on the 3rd of November 1719, sitting in Audience, the Lord Inquisitor Licenciado Don Joseph Cienfuegos, ordered the entry of a man who came of his own free will; who being present received the oath before Our Lord God and the sign of the cross in true legal form under which he promised to state and respond to the truth in everything that he should be questioned, and he promised to maintain the secret of all that transpired here.

He said that his name was Albert Edward Rivet, native of the city of London, twenty-two years old, and that about nine months before he had been taken prisoner in the town of Puerto Caballos in the province of Honduras, and that he had been taken to the prison of San Juan de Ulua, and from there they brought him to this city where he was been for five months.

He was asked what he wanted and why he had requested this audience.

He said that he requested this audience because he wants to be an Apostolic Roman Christian because he was born in the said city of London as he has said, and that he was raised in the religion of the Quakers which his father proclaimed, and whose sect was permitted in England, and where there are temples were it is preached, to which he attended, and his father brought him where they made the prayers and other things that the others do until his father died more than seven or eight years before.

Because the aforesaid could not express himself well enough in Spanish, the said Lord Inquisitor suspended the audience until tomorrow, and he ordered him to return to this Holy Office so that he could be understood by interpreter. With this he ordered him to leave the Audience chamber, and before this he signed

Edward Rivet
This passed before me,
Don Eugenio de las Peñas
(Secretary of the Holy Office)

Act of the Acceptance and Oath of the Interpreter, November 4, 1719

✝

In the palace of the Holy Office of the Inquisition in the city of Mexico, 4th of November 1719, being in Audience in the morning, the Lord Inquisitor Licenciado Don Joseph Cienfuegos, ordered the entrance of a man called Don Gerardo Moro who came when called, and being present he was told that the Tribunal called upon him so that he could serve as an Interpreter in a certain diligence that had to be done with an Englishman, and having accepted the said charge he received the oath by God Our Lord and the sign of the cross in true and legal form, and under it he promised to use his charge faithfully and truthfully, and he promised to keep the secret concerning all that transpired there. He then signed it, and I certify it.

Gerardo Moro
This passed before me,
Don Eugenio de las Peñas
(Secretary of the Holy Office)

Second Audience with the Englishman Edward Rivet, concerning His Desire to Be Reconciled with the Holy Catholic Church, November 4, 1719

✝

And later on the same day, month, and year, the said Lord Inquisitor Don Joseph Cienfuegos, being in Audience in the morning, ordered the appearance of the same man who had come earlier on his own will, then in the presence of the Interpreter contained in the oath and act before, he was asked to receive the oath before God Our Lord and the sign of the cross, under which he promised to tell the truth and respond truthfully to all he was questioned about and to keep the secret of all that transpired there.

He said that his name was Edward Rivet, native of a place close to London called White Island, and that he was twenty-two years old, and that he has been in this kingdom for about seven months, and that he was taken prisoner in the Bay of Honduras by an Irish Captain with a patent and orders from the Governor of Havana, and that a few days after having been taken prisoner, they fell upon bad weather, and this man, along with four other companions came to arrive at Veracruz where they were imprisoned in this city where he has been a prisoner of the Vice-regal bodyguards, where they sent him to work with an artilleryman, which is his own trade.

He was asked what he wanted and why he had requested this audience.

He said that he requested this audience because he wants to be reincorporated to the Holy Catholic Church of Rome and baptized because having been born close to the city of London in England and raised in the sect of the Quakers or Tremblers[84] until he left his home and came to these kingdoms, he has desired to acquire this benefit, and he wants to place this in execution now that he is in a place where this can be done.

He was asked what motive he had to desire baptism, and for how long he had desired it.

He said that he has desired it since he has come of the age of reason, and now he desires it much more because of what he has read of the Divine Word.

Asked why he has desired baptism since he had reached the age of reason. He responded that he wanted to do it in order to imitate Our Lord Jesus Christ because he believes and believed that he should be baptized, and this has been the reason why he desired it, but that he had not been able to achieve this desire because it was not permitted him.

He said that ever since he had left London for the first time, being away from the power of his Parents, he had always followed the religion of High Anglicanism, and he went with them to the temples and prayers that they accustomed to give, unless he found several Quakers and then he would pray with them.

He was asked if he believed that in that religion and in no other he could be saved.

He said that as a boy he never paid much attention or consideration to this, and that he always desired baptism in his heart and he did not care about the rest.

He was asked what it was that he believed in at present, and what did he think about Our Holy Catholic Apostolic Roman Faith.[85]

He said that what he believes now and will believe in until he dies is that only through the Catholic and Apostolic religion of Rome is there true salvation, and not in any other, and that he wished he had known this before and believed in it many years before.

He was asked if in the time that he has been in the cities and ports referred to, if he has dealt with or had communication with other Catholics concerning matters of religion.

He said that he had only met in Falmut an Irishman by the name of Buli, who had asked him why his father had not baptized him, and realizing that the guilt belonged to his father he made signs as if out of compassion, but being a Catholic Christian there [in England] he did not dare tell him more so that he would not be accused of catechizing and suffering a trial for this. He also stated that even though he had several Catholic books on his table, he did not dare give them to him for the same reason. And this witness declared that in things of religion he was always a little embarrassed, and this is why he did not care much about things of religion or in which religion he should live in order to gain salvation.

He was asked if he had been well instructed in the mysteries of Our Holy Faith. He said that he knew the prayers of Our Father, the Ave María, the Creed, Salve Regina, the Ten Commandments of the Laws of God, and of the Church, and several other things he learned in catechism.

Asked if after having come to these kingdoms, he has dealt with someone of his same religion, or if he knows that they exist here either publicly or secretly, or anyone of another sect. He said that the only communication he has had since he came to this kingdom is with two Irishmen belonging to his companions, who were also Catholic Christians, and that he does not know if there are any other sectarians in this kingdom except for the prisoners of war.

All of this that he has said is the truth under the oath that he has taken, and he affirms it and ratifies it and signed it with the Interpreter, which I certify.

Gerardo Mora, Interpreter
Edward Rivet
This passed before me,
Don Eugenio de las Peñas (Secretary of the Holy Office)

Trials and Testimonies against *Alumbrados* (Illuminati) and Others for Heretical Acts and False Revelations

[Sentencing the said Juan Gómez to be relaxed to the secular arm] for having sown and practiced many doctrines against the purity of Our Holy Catholic Faith, by following the sects of the sacramental Iluminist heretics.

Relation of the Case and Sentence against Juan Gómez as an *Alumbrado* in New Spain, 1659

The term *alumbrado* (illuminist in English) refers to men and women who, according to the Inquisition, were false mystics who pretended or faked having direct contact with God. The Inquisition did not fear only that their pretended contact with God was heretical but also that it served to attack the very organized structure of the Catholic Church and its hierarchy. According to the inquisitors, a false mystic, by claiming revelations and communications with God or his saints, attacked the very basic precepts of Christian morality and the church's teachings concerning the necessary role of priests as mediators between God and the Christian faithful.

The Inquisition's persecution of false mystics had deep roots in Spain, and with increasing contacts between Spain and its New World colonies, the phenomenon of *alumbradismo* (illuminism) arrived in the New World in the later sixteenth century. The designation of a false mystic being "illuminated" came from the general belief that these mystics held that the Holy Spirit had inspired them and "enlightened" them as it had illuminated the early Christian apostle Saint Paul.[86] In Spain, the illuminists lacked any formal doctrine or dogma and remained only loosely affiliated, sometimes holding meetings clandestinely. The Inquisition in Spain had nearly extinguished the followers of illuminism by the end of the 1530s.

The most common forms of punishment in the Spanish Inquisition for *alumbrados* and false mystics remained a sentence of public abjuration *de levi* in combination with a few other lesser spiritual penances. Only in rare cases in Spain did the Inquisition use harsher punishments, such as galley service or long terms of imprisonment.

Because most of the *alumbrados* in Spain had been eradicated by active prosecution on the part of the Inquisition, those cases conducted by the Inquisition in New Spain focused on a confused understanding of the formal nature of the crime of illuminism and its conflation and misidentification with other simpler crimes of false revelations and charlatanism.[87] Nevertheless, the Inquisition often handed out harsh sentences against these suspected false mystics and falsifiers of revelations. In a few cases, such as the trial against Don Joseph Bruñón Ortiz, it even sentenced a convicted *alumbrado* to be relaxed to the secular arm.[88]

The documents in this section offer examples of false revelations and the supposed mystical experiences that made up the typical cases against *alumbrados* in New Spain,[89] in investigations involving both men and women.

DOCUMENT 42

Inquisition Proceedings against Padre Fray Juan de Santa Ana, a Religious Carmelite Friar, for Dreams, Revelations, and Other Disparate Prophesies

Mexico City, 1690–1691

SOURCE: Archivo General de la Nación, Ramo de Inquisición, vol. 680, exp. 33.

NOTE: There are many hundreds of denunciations for the crime of having false revelations and other prophetic visions. As the documents from this case against a Carmelite friar show, however, the inquisitors often remained skeptical and found it difficult to either believe in these denunciations or have the heretical nature of the alleged revelations qualified. The lack of any arrest warrant, formal accusation, or other documentation in this case, perhaps due to the inability to gather enough proof, most likely meant that the allegations were dropped without further investigation.

Denunciation of the Franciscan Fray Pedro de Ortiz against Fray Juan de Santa Ana, a Carmelite, for Various Supposed Revelations and Prophesies, November 10, 1690

✝

In the Holy Office of the Inquisition in the city of Mexico, 10th of November 1690, while the Lord Inquisitor Licenciado Don Juan de Armesto y Ron sat in Audience during the morning, the doorman gave notice that at the doorway appeared a religious friar of the order of Saint Francis who requested an audience. He was ushered into the audience chamber and once present swore the oath to tell the truth in legal form and promised to keep the secret. He said that his name was Fray Pedro de Ortiz, Lector of the Order of Saint Francis, and actual Vicario of the convent of religious nuns of the order of Saint John the Penitent here in this city, and that he was forty-three years old.

He said that he came to denounce a Discalced Carmelite friar,[90] named Fray Juan de Santa Ana, who at present is a member of the monastery of his order in this city.

The said Fray Pedro Ortiz then showed three sealed papers that he brought with him for this Holy Tribunal, in which he said contained what he came here to denounce against the said Carmelite friar Juan de Santa Ana.

Having opened one of them, it was read and seen that it was signed by this witness and the nun Nicolasa de San Antonio, and apparently it was written in the said convent on December 20, 1689, and what it denounces is the following proposition:

"I dreamed the other night that the Holy Pontiff was dead and that he appeared in a comet as a sign of the event."

And this and everything else in the said paper was signed by his name, and that of the nun, and the said paper was also signed by Teresa de la Encarnación, another religious nun of the same convent, and what it denounces is the following proposition:

"Tomorrow, Holy Saturday of the Incarnation, once the holy mass is said, while I am saying mass and you are standing in the choir, you will die all of a sudden."

And this proposition was written by Fray Juan de Santa Ana, and this witness requested the said nun to give him the letter in which he had written this proposition, and the said nun, Teresa de la Encarnación, by the advice of Father Fray Lorenzo de Montealegre, a friar of her same order and the confessor of the said nun, had burned the letters and that he had also counseled her not to pay attention to other similarly disparate things, but that she declared what those papers had said to this witness who was her confessor and for that which touches upon confession she gave him license to denounce these things to the Holy Office. This paper was also signed by Petronilla de San Joseph, a professed nun of the same convent, and the principal that she denounces is that the said Fray Juan de Santa Ana had written to the said nun Petronilla and ordered her to confess two sins that she had committed before, the first one when she was a novice, and the other one a few days before the feast of Saint Joseph.[91] She had written it down, but she had since lost it since she did not pay it much attention. The Mother Superior of the said convent believing that all three of these propositions were evil and pernicious, authorized this witness to come to denounce these things to the Holy Office and to declare extrajudicially that the friar was the said Fray Juan de Santa Ana, and that he has since been made a prisoner by his order for crimes he has committed. But about a month before they told him, he had escaped his prison and had appeared in the neighborhood of Saint John, and the said religious nun Teresa de la Encarnación had since asked this witness for his mantle and hat for whom she said was a Carmelite who was coming to see her. This witness sent her his mantle and hat, though he thought it a strange request, and he later saw that she had given the said Carmelite (Fray Juan de Santa Ana) advice to use the said mantle and hat to enter into one of the lecture halls of the said convent. He stated that he later found out that it was the said Fray Juan de Santa Ana who had done this and that his fellow Carmelites had taken him back again in their convent, and based on this, the witness had requested an audience here.

And he stated that the beginning of all of this occurred when Bachiller Francisco Xavier, cleric and priest of the Oratory of San Felipe Nerí, went to the said Convent or nunnery of Saint John the Penitent and required the Abbess and this witness as the Vicar of the Convent on the part of God Our Lord to collect all of the letters and papers that speak about things of the spirit written by the said Fray Juan de Santa Ana. He requested it with such urgency that this witness thought that the said Bachiller Francisco Xavier was a minister of this Holy Office and that his orders were directly from the Inquisition, to all of which the said Bachiller responded that he was not a minister of the Holy Office, nor did he come under its orders, and that he had ordered him to collect the papers out of his own order for the service of God Our Lord. With this, the present witness conducted the diligences in the convent and ordered that all of the nuns who knew of or had papers from the said Carmelite friar had to turn them over to him. On the basis of this request, several of them handed them over, although he did not remember how many, but that among them were three biographies or Lives of three Carmelites, which had been written and begun by the said friar, concerning three religious nuns of the said convent. Along with the other papers these were handed over to the said Bachiller Franisco Xavier, more or less a month before. This witness stated that he did not insist nor did he make any other diligence in order to know or question any more about the end to which the said Bachiller requested the said papers, except that which he has declared here.

And having been read his statement, he said that it was well written and truthful, and that he had nothing more to add to it, nor to alter or amend it, and he was entrusted with the secret and he promised it and signed.

Fray Pedro Ortiz
This passed before me,
Don Diego de Vergara, Secretary

Letter Written by Fray Juan de Santa Ana to Sister Nicolasa de San Antonio, Nun of the Order of Saint John the Penitent, December 20, 1689

My Dear Angel and Lady,

It is not yet time to write getting ahead of myself in giving Your reverend Ladyship season's greetings, because this may arrive after it is over because the porters go about busy at work. I do not have to tell nor desire Your Ladyship how much I have you in my soul. I only ask your Ladyship that she ask the Holy Christ child to give me his love so that I do not go about omitting to supplicate him for Your Ladyship. I dreamed the other night that the Holy Pontiff was dead and that he appeared in a comet as a sign of it, and it was about fifteen days ago that I dreamt this, and because of the esteem that his Lord the Archbishop has for His Holiness, and for the honor of Rome, he merits particular prayers from Your Ladyship, and if it is as I dreamed or in case of doubt, I commend him to God, and even there the most powerful need the prayers of the poorest in this life. And also I must say that in dreams not imagined, they seek them and to seek out a hidden poor person like myself there must be a great need. This is all between Your Ladyship and myself. It may be that it was a true dream, and we should not believe in dreams, but we should also not dispose of them when they ordain us to do something good.

May God guard you as I most desire.
From the Convent, December 20, 1689
To the Beloved Angel of my Soul

Chaplain of Your Ladyship, Fray Juan

P.S. Also give my best to your mother Isabel, and to my beloved Mariquita. I do not intend to be without my Mariquita from Antigua, and after the Holidays I will return for her.

Letter Denouncing Fray Juan de Santa Ana Written by Fray Pedro Ortiz and Signed by Nicolasa de San Antonio, November 8, 1690

✝

To Your Very Reverend Lordships and the Sacred Tribunal of the Holy Office,

Fray Pedro de Ortiz of the order of Saint Francis, Lector and Vicar of the convent of nuns of the order of Saint John the penitent in this city of Mexico: I state that having found out clearly that Father Fray Juan de Santa Ana, a religious professed discalced Carmelite friar, wrote to Mother Nicolasa de San Antonio, a professed nun of the said convent of Saint John, several papers and letters, several of them (which are included together with this one) contain this proposition: *I dreamed the other night that the Holy Pontiff was dead, and that he appeared in a comet as a sign of it.* This with the rest of the comments sounds evil to me, and out of the discharge of my conscience and in order to observe Our Holy Faith, I admonished the said nun to take as suspicious this letter and to include it in this original letter to be presented before the Holy Office in order to see if this statement was dignified of being corrected. Together we jointly defer and denounce this letter to your attention, denouncing its author and we sign it in this city of Mexico

Fray Pedro Ortiz
Nicolasa de San Antonio

Letter Denouncing Fray Juan de Santa Ana Written by Fray Pedro Ortiz and Signed by the Nun Teresa de la Encarnación, November 9, 1690

✝

To Your Very Reverend Lordships and the Sacred Tribunal of the Holy Office,

Fray Pedro de Ortiz of the order of Saint Francis, Lector and Vicar of the convent of nuns of the order of Saint John the penitent in this city of Mexico: I state that having found out clearly that Father Fray Juan de Santa Ana, a religious professed discalced Carmelite friar, wrote a letter to Mother Teresa de la Encarnación, a professed nun of the said convent of Saint John, with several papers and letters, one of which contained this proposition: "*Tomorrow, Holy Saturday of the Incarnation, once the holy mass is said, while I am saying mass and you are standing in the choir, you will die all of a sudden.*" This with the rest of the comments sound evil to me, and out of the discharge of my conscience and in order to observe Our Holy Faith, I admonished the said nun to take as suspicious this letter and to include it in this original letter to be presented before the Holy Office in order to see if this statement was dignified of being corrected. Together we jointly defer and denounce this letter to your attention, denouncing its author, and we sign it in this city of Mexico

Fray Pedro Ortiz
Teresa de la Encarnación

Letter Denouncing Fray Juan de Santa Ana Written by Fray Pedro Ortiz and Signed by the Nun Petra de San Joseph, November 9, 1690

✝

To Your Very Reverend Lordships and the Sacred Tribunal of the Holy Office,

Fray Pedro de Ortiz of the order of Saint Francis, Lector and Vicario of the convent of nuns of the order of Saint John the penitent in this city of Mexico: I state that having found out clearly that Father Fray Juan de Santa Ana, a religious professed discalced Carmelite friar, wrote a letter to Mother Petra de San Joseph, a professed nun of the said convent of Saint John, in which he told her that she had to confess two sins that she had committed, one when she was a novice, and the other a few days before the feast of Saint Joseph. This with the rest of the comments sound evil to me, and out of the discharge of my conscience and in order to observe Our Holy Faith, I admonished the said nun to take as suspicious this letter and to include it in this original letter to be presented before the Holy Office in order to see if this statement was dignified of being corrected. Together we jointly defer and denounce this letter to your attention, denouncing its author and we sign it in this city of Mexico

Fray Pedro Ortiz

Petronilla de San Joseph

Review of the Testimony by the Prosecutor of the Holy Office and His Decision to Continue the Proceedings, January 11, 1691

✝

Illustrious Lord,

The Prosecuting attorney, having seen this denunciation made by Fray Pedro Ortiz, religious friar of the Order of Saint Francis, and vicar of the nuns of Saint John the Penitent in this city, against a religious Carmelite friar named Fray Juan de Santa Ana, and also having read the papers presented by the said Padre Ortiz, and the letter sent by the said Carmelite friar to a nun in the said convent of Saint John the Penitent, he states that the person who seems to have more information concerning the writings of the friar is the said Bachiller Fray Xavier, priest who assists in the oratory of Saint Felipe de Nerí of this city. It would be well done if Your Lordships would order that Bachiller Francisco Xavier be examined according to all that can be answered in order to plainly investigate the case further to understand all that was done by the said Fray Juan de Santa Ana, and that he should remit all of the papers from the said Padre Santa Ana and exhibit all the papers that he collected both from him and the other nuns in the said convent.

Dr. Don Francisco de Deza y Ulloa, Fiscal

Testimony and Questioning of Bachiller Francisco Xavier de Velasco y
Oviedo in the Proceedings against Fray Juan de Santa Ana,
January 29, 1691

✝

In the Holy Office of the Inquisition in the city of Mexico, on the 29th of January 1691, while in Audience in the morning, Lord Inquisitor Licenciado Don Juan de Armesto y Ron ordered the entrance in the chambers of a cleric who came having been called. Once present, he took the oath in due form and said that he was called Bachiller Don Francisco Xavier de Velasco y Oviedo, a cleric domiciled in this Archbishopric, twenty-seven years old.

He was asked if he knew or presumed why he had been called for before this Holy Office.

He said that he presumed that it had to do with things concerning the discalced Carmelite friar named Fray Juan de Santa Ana, who as he remembers was a preacher and confessor, and concerning what occurred he stated that during the past year of 1689, the said friar one Saturday came between eight and nine o'clock at night and came to present himself to this witness at the oratory of Saint Felipe de Nerí. Others at the oratory told him that this witness was conducting his duties with the other priests, and that they would advise him when he finished that the friar wished to speak with him, but the others did not tell him that it was a friar who wished to speak to him, because the man came disguised with a red handkerchief on his head and wearing a Franciscan mantle wrapped around himself as if it were a cape. In this means he recognized him and gave him lodging for the night with the license of the Rector of the said Oratory.

The witness did not attribute it to malice that the friar came disguised that night without his own habits, but rather out of caution because of the constitutions of his order that require any of their brothers who are in habit not to lodge themselves in any other house except for their monastery if it existed in the place, not even permitting him to stay in the house of his own parents.

And in the discourse of their conversations that they had that night concerning things of the spirit and other exercises, he asked this witness if he could say mass there, and he said that yes he could, even though he did not know him, since there was a chapel in the house. But the said friar told him, trying to instigate him to say the mass himself, that *"I have not been able to say mass for four months since the Devil or my sins have made it impossible for me to make the offering of the mass . . . and I am unable to say mass because my throat closes up tight leaving me unable to pronounce a word. . . ."* And then the friar asked him for a cape and other things to go out in disguise to check on his horses that he stated he had stabled there close to the house. This witness then loaned him these things, and then he went down to say mass. Once he had finished, he returned to the room and the said friar took his leave of him, saying that he would return after he saw to his horses. Then this witness went down to his confessional and went about his other priestly duties in the oratory. Even though he waited the whole day and night for the said friar to return to eat and have dinner with him, he did not return, which caused this witness to doubt his scruples. He then commented all that he had said and done with the said friar to his Spiritual Father in confession, who advised him and told him to inquire and learn where the said Friar was and to give an account to the friars of his order so that they could bring him back to their monastery. And this witness then did this, making the diligences and learning that the said friar was in the house of Maestro Joseph Gallegos de Velasco, father of this witness, who had a pharmacy in the center of town. There he encountered this friar disguised and wearing his habit and a symbol of Diego,[92] and he spoke with him about returning to the monastery. Shortly after, for this effect the Prior of the monastery and another religious friar of the order came and took him away, placing on him his proper habit as a Carmelite. And while they dressed him, the prior and the other friar spoke with the father of this witness and his other family members, and in the best means possible the said Fray Santa Ana came and gave this witness several letters and papers and said that if he did not return for them in fifteen days or send for them, then he should burn them. He also mentioned that he had left other papers like these in the care of a potter who sells dishes in the plaza, but this witness does not remember the name of this potter. Then, shortly after night fell, the said Prior and the friar left and took the said Fray Juan de Santa Ana with them.

The next day, this witness went to look for the potter so that he could hand over the papers, which he did, and collecting them all, he read them, and they appeared to be very bad, because in their text they abused the Holy Scriptures and other spiritual things such as hymns, and there were other things, many disparate things written in those papers, all of which this witness cannot remember, and he remits to the said papers for their content.

He noted that several of them were correspondence with several nuns from the convent of Saint John the Penitent, and fearing some damage to the friar or the nuns, this witness went to the convent to speak at the door of the gates where he spoke with a nun whose name he did not remember, requesting that they all hand over all of the papers that they may have had written by the said friar. All of which the nun gave account to her prelate, who in the company of the Vicar Fray Ortiz, passed forward to the gate with this witness, and the three stood talking concerning all of this, and this witness insisted that they turn over all of the papers written by the friar. Although he was motivated by the truth, he also wanted to collect them so that he could give an account of them to his order, so that they would punish him for the errors that the writings contained. Although they did not hand over any papers at that time, later the Vicar collected several papers that appeared to be the written lives of some saints, exactly whom he did not remember, even though he had seen them. He also stated that he did not know if these papers remained in the hands of the said Vicar Ortiz.

After talking with several people, they all convinced him that he should come to denounce these things to the Holy Office, for which effect he came before the presence of the Lord Inquisitor Don Juan Gómez de Mier and communicated to him what he has stated here. The Inquisitor told him to take the papers to Padre Diego Marín, a Jesuit Qualifier of the Holy Office, so that he can examine them, and this is what he did, and he left the said papers with him there, and several days later returned to see if he had recognized them. The said Padre Marín told him that he still had not had time to read them because it was a matter that would take a great deal of time, and he asked this witness where he lived so that later he could send for him, and that he has not been called for yet, except for the summons by this Holy Office, and this is all the truth under his oath that he has sworn.

The said Lord Inquisitor ordered that the ministers go and search for the said papers in the house of the said Padre Marín and that they should bring them and present them here in this Holy Office. And he swore to keep the secret.

Bachiller Francisco Xavier de Velasco y Oviedo
This passed before me,
Don Diego de Vergara, Secretary

Presentation of the Requested Documents and Papers, January 30, 1691

†

In this Holy Office of the Inquisition of Mexico, on the 30th of January 1691, while in Audience in the morning, their Lordships the Inquisitors Licenciado Don Juan Gómez de Mier and Don Juan de Armesto y Ron were interrupted by the doorman Bernardo de Navia, who gave notice that the said Bachiller Francisco Xavier de Velasco was at the door. They ordered him to enter into the said Audience Chamber. Once present, the said Bachiller presented and exhibited the said papers that were handed over to him by Padre Fray Juan de Santa Ana, discalced Carmelite, which were in the power of Padre Diego Marín, according to what he had declared in his testimony yesterday before this Holy Office and complying with all that he had been ordered to do, and the said Inquisitors accepted the papers as submitted and exhibited.

He was asked if he thought that the said friar Santa Ana was lucid and how long he had known him.

He said that he had known him for about three years and that he had spoken to him at length two times and had taken him for a good and virtuous religious man, even though based on his last action, he presumes that he had been a fugitive from his religious order, but that he does not take him to be insane, nor demented, because he always appeared to speak with good judgment and was easily understood by him. And he signed it.

Don Francisco Xavier de Velasco y Oviedo
This passed before me,
Don Diego de Vergara, Secretary

Declaration of Bachiller Don Francisco Xavier Exhibiting Several Papers, February 12, 1691

†

In this Holy Office of the Inquisition of Mexico, on the 30th of January 1691, while in Audience in the morning, their Lordships the Inquisitors Licenciado Don Juan Gómez de Mier and Don Juan de Armesto y Ron ordered the appearance of the said Bachiller Don Francisco Xavier de Oviedo, who came of his own free will, and who received the oath in legal form under which he promised to tell the truth of all he would be questioned.

He stated that he came to request this audience so that he could hand over and make presentation of several signed and sealed papers from his Lord Maestro Joseph Gallegos de Velasco, which appear to be from the said Fray Juan de Santa Ana, discalced Carmelite, and one of them written by the friar to the said Maestro is in his handwriting and signed by his name, which comes opened, and having been read, it appears that its content is reduced to requesting that he guard and collect several papers and documents, which are those this witness presented before this tribunal before this day, and its date is January 10, 1691. This witness said that the said Maestro turned the papers over because he was asked to do so without opening them up. The other papers that came sealed include the following:

A letter written on the envelope, addressed to Captain Juan de Sobresilla, and in his absence his daughters, and this witness declares that he does not know this said Captain or his daughters.

Another sealed letter whose envelope reads in the middle

Don Diego, Whom May God Guard for Many Years
Tacuba Street, Santiago House

Another one that says in the middle:

My brother, Thomas de Herrera

Another one that says:

My dear Mother, Madre Angela de Cristo
Who May God Preserve for many years
To be placed in your hands and no one else's
At the first gate of the Convent of Saint John

Another one that says in the middle:

To my beloved Father and Nephew
Reverend Francisco Xavier

(This witness did not wish to read or open it until he brought it to this Holy Office)
Another one addressed to:

Doña Josepha de Velasco, my dear Niece

(Who is the sister of this witness)

He stated that he requested this audience to hand over these papers and for no other reason.

The Inquisitors accepted and exhibited these letters and ordered that the said Bachiller Don Francisco Xavier should wait in the colonnaded patio, and he left the Audience chamber after promising to keep the secret.

Don Francisco Xavier de Velasco y Oviedo
This passed before me,
Don Diego de Vergara, Secretary

Final Decision and Orders of Their Lordships the Inquisitors
February 12, 1691

✝

And shortly after, the said Inquisitors, being in Audience, ordered that the said letter addressed to Madre Angela de Cristo be opened and read, and having been read and found not to contain anything of substance, ordered that it be placed with the rest of the unopened letters and given back to Bachiller Don Francisco Xavier so that he may hand them over to their owners.[93] They placed the opened letter into the proceedings, placing it with its envelope, which was opened and addressed to the Bachiller and Maestro Joseph Gallegos de Velasco, and then they ordered that Don Francisco Xavier be ordered back into the room and handed over to him the sack of papers so that he could return them to the people addressed, unopened. And he said that he would do this and was then ordered to leave the audience chamber.

This passed before me,
Don Diego de Vergara, Secretary

Document 43
Inquisition Trial Proceedings against Thomasa González, Who Wears the Habit of a *Beata*, for Suspicions of Being an *Alumbrada*
Aguascalientes, 1692–1695

Source: Archivo General de la Nación, Ramo de Inquisición, vol. 685, exp. 11.

Note: This document is an excellent example of the length of time that it often took to investigate and follow the cases of suspected heretics. Beginning in 1692 and lasting until 1695, these documents were compiled with several testimonies against a woman named Thomasa González, who many believed to have had false revelations. It is interesting to note that, regardless of this information, the prosecuting attorney remitted the papers to the local commissary to collect more evidence, doubting the strength of the case on the basis of the hearsay that appears here. The burden of proof often dictated that trials, testimonies, and cases could drag on for years before an accusation, arrest, or imprisonment could occur. Apparently, Thomasa González may have never become aware of the case that was being built against her—another testament to the power of the "Secret" maintained in inquisitorial proceedings.

Testimony of the Cleric Sebastián González de Espinosa against Thomasa González for Suspicions of Being an *Alumbrada*, June 5, 1692

✝

In the city of Guadalajara, 5th of June 1692, during the afternoon, before the Lord Licenciado Don Joseph Meléndez Carreño, Archdeacon of the Cathedral of this city and Commissary of the Holy Office, there appeared without being called and swore the oath to tell the truth, a man who said that he was called Sebastián González de Espinosa, cleric of minor orders, resident in the town of Aguascalientes, who was thirty-six years old. For the discharge of his conscience he declared the following.

He stated that he heard Juan de Soto, resident of the said town of Aguascalientes, state that about a year before when he found himself in the village of Cuquio, in the jurisdiction of Tacotan, he had heard from the Indians who lived there in that village about a woman named Thomasa González who wore the garments of a *beata*, with a dark habit, whom they said was a saint. They had said that she had told them that she had been sent by God from faraway lands to admonish a certain woman, the wife of a merchant called Ordóñez of the said village and to tell her that she should be disposed to die, because a disastrous death awaited her and only by intercession with the Virgin had she not died before. Hearing this, the woman and wife of the merchant fell into deep despair.

On the same day that the said *beata* came to the village, she went from door to door at night telling everyone that they should be alert because death was near. This entire event he heard from the said Juan de Soto who had procured to find the said *beata*. He said that he met her and that she was a woman born in Zelaya who had been married in the town of Aguascalientes. He also added that he takes her to be an imposter.

And feeling for the despair that the natives told him that the wife of the said merchant Ordóñez suffered, this witness stated that Juan de Soto went to visit her. He discovered that it was true what the Indians had told him and he heard it directly from the wife of the said Ordóñez. She confirmed all of what he had heard and even more that the said *beata* had told her. She had said that she came on behalf of God with an angel to admonish her to dispose herself and prepare for a terrible death that awaited her and that only by the intercession of the Virgin it had not occurred before. She also stated that the *beata* told her not to be afflicted and that she could, with her prayers, oblige God to save her.

Hearing all of this, Juan de Soto told her to relax and not to pay any attention to what the *beata* had said to her, because he told her that she was not a foreigner, or even a saint, but that he knew very well that he had seen her in the town of Aguascalientes going about begging in the streets and that she was an imposter. With all of this the woman relaxed and settled down.

And this witness, having heard all of this from the said Juan de Soto in front of his wife and two daughters said that the *beata* appeared more to be an *alumbrada* than a saint, to which Juan de Soto's wife, who is called Sebastiana de Esguera, responded that she had heard of the said *beata* many times and that she received favors from the Virgin. She added that whenever this *beata* had a necessity for something, she placed herself in prayer and whatever she desired appeared on her bed, things such as chocolate, shoes, and other things. She stated that the *beata* had told her that while she was in prayer a snake would come down from the wall in order to disturb her, and in this way it circled around her, but that even this did not cause her to cease her prayers. She also stated that many times when she went to lie down in bed, she found serpents and other animals underneath the bed and in her clothing, but that they did not do anything to her, and that she would then lie down without care, because she had it for certain that they would not harm her.

And this is the truth under the oath he had taken. Being read what he stated, he said that it was well written and that he did not state this out of hatred, and he signed it and promised to keep the secret.

Sebastián González de Espinosa
This passed before me,
Tomás Romero Villalón
Notary of the Holy Office

NOTE: This denunciation was remitted by the commissary of Guadalajara, Don Joseph Meléndez Carreño, along with a letter dated July 4, 1692, on the occasion of the publication of the Edict of Faith.

Decision of the Prosecutor of the Holy Office concerning the Denunciation Made before the Commissary of the Inquisition in Guadalajara against Thomasa González for Suspicions of Being an *Alumbrada*, January 27, 1694

†

Illustrious Lord,

The Prosecutor of this Holy Office has seen the denunciation made before the Commissary of Guadalajara against a woman who appears to go about in the garb of a *beata* who is called Thomasa González, and who appears to reside in the village of Cuquio in the jurisdiction of Tacotan and claims to have revelations from God. And he states that the said denunciation was made by a clergyman on the basis of hearsay from another man named Juan de Soto, resident of Aguascalientes. Because this man may give a better testimony against the said *beata* concerning her residence, her appearance, and age, Your Lordship is best served by making a copy of the said denunciation and remitting it to the Commissary in the said village of Aguascalientes so that, after reviewing its contents, he may examine the said Juan de Soto and other people implicated in the denunciation, asking them questions concerning the particulars of the case, and so that all of the witnesses who should be called should be ratified *ad perpetuam*[94] in seeking justice.

Signed in the Secret Chamber of the Holy Office of Mexico, January 27, 1694
Dr. Don Francisco de Deza y Ulloa
Prosecutor of the Holy Office

Title and Commission Given by the Inquisitors to the Commissary of the Holy Office in Aguascalientes, or the Parish Priest in His Absence, concerning the Information against the Alleged *Beata* Thomasa González, May 16, 1694

†

Along with this order, we remit to Our Commissary in the town of Aguascalientes, or in his absence to the Parish Priest or Minister of the Doctrine of the said town, an authentic copy of the said denunciation made by Sebastián González de Espinosa against a *beata* named Thomasa González, who is said to go about begging, and who was a resident of the said town where she was married. Once our Commissary should receive this, he should order that Juan de Soto appear before him and Sebastiana de Espinosa, his wife, and their two daughters, all of them residents of the said town. And in secret and before the Notary of the Holy Office in conformity with the style and instructions of the Holy Office, he should examine each of them concerning the things mentioned in the denunciation, making them express with clarity and distinction all that they may have heard and seen executed by the said *beata* Thomasa González, in the order in which the said denunciation reports it. He should also ask them about whatever else they may know or may have heard said and at what time and on what occasions, and what persons were present.

And our Commissary should also examine the wife of a Merchant named Ordóñez, residents of the village of Cuquio in the jurisdiction of Tacotlan, so that they can declare what has occurred with the said *beata* on the occasion when she admonished her to dispose herself to die because a terrible death awaited her, and to report with what motive she had said this, and when, and who were present, and all of the other things that they may know or have heard said by the said *beata*.

And also our Commissary should examine other witnesses cited in their testimonies, asking them where does this said *beata* reside now, her appearance, age, and other things about her life and customs. Once three days have passed from the depositions, they should be ratified at the continuation of each one *ad perpetuam rei memoriam* against the said *beata* Thomasa González.

He should make all of the arrangements and documents and testimonies in the style and form printed in the instructions given to our Commissaries,[95] which we remit to you, and if in the village and its environs there does not exist a notary of this Holy Office, we give the power to our Commissary so that he can act and proceed before whatever ecclesiastical notary may exist to his satisfaction, and so that they serve as notary, after first receiving the oath of secrecy in all things and promising to fulfill the duties of the office faithfully. Once you have completed all of the diligences in all brevity, remit the originals back to us with this commission and the said printed instructions for Commissaries.

Signed in the Audience Chamber of the Holy Office, May 17, 1694
Don Juan Domingo Mier, Inquisitor
Don Juan de Armesto y Ron, Inquisitor

By order of their Lordships the Inquisitors,
Don Benito Núñez de Rumbos

Letter from Don Sebastián Munillo Ordóñez, Parish Priest of the Town of Aguascalientes, to Don Carlos de Andrada Sotomayor, Commissary of the Holy Office and Parish Priest in the Town of La Cienaga, April 14, 1695

✝

Health and Grace in Our Lord Jesus Christ,

I am writing in order to inform you that during the night on Sunday, April 3, 1695, the first day of Easter and the Resurrection of Our Lord, I had a terrible attack which has left me ill, and I fear another similar one due to a lack of medicine. Seeing that Your Mercy had presented me on that same day with a Commission from the Holy Tribunal of the Inquisition of Mexico, which I obeyed and received in my said parish church, and because the Synod and Constitutions of this Bishopric have ordered under the pain of excommunication and the loss of office that we parish priests cannot absent ourselves from our benefices without express license from the Bishops, Provisors, or Governors of the Bishopric. By means of this letter, as the said Parish priest, vicar and ecclesiastical judge in this town, I must inform you that during the month of May last year 1694 a great flood and continual rainfall occurred that lasted sixty days, more or less, causing the streams and trickles to rise and overflow the waters of the rivers, in such a manner that it was impossible to pass through them or wade across them from one bank to another without evident danger to one's life and risk of the loss of whatever papers may be exposed to such inclement weather. For all of these reasons, when I received the letter and dispatch concerning the commissary of the Holy Office or in his absence the local parish priest of the town, I was unable to execute the order due to the difficulties and distance by means of roads and rivers to the said village, and since I lacked a license given to me by the venerable Dean of the Cathedral in the City of Guadalajara, which was not dispatched until March 11, 1694 (which I had requested before Easter last year), and now seeing that my health has been affected, I remit to Your Mercy the sealed dispatch from the Holy Office, so that as the said Commissary you can execute what the order contains and make an account of it all to the Holy Tribunal as I am sure of your care and diligence in this matter.

May God guard you many happy years.
Signed in Aguascalientes, April 11, 1695
Sebastián Murillo Ordóñez

Declaration and Testimony of Juan de Soto in the Case against Thomasa González, April 22, 1695

✝

In the Hacienda of Huiquinaqui, jurisdiction of the town of Aguascalientes, on the 22nd of April 1695, at five o'clock in the afternoon, before the Lord Commissary of the Holy Office of the said town of Aguascalientes and its jurisdiction, there appeared, having been called, a man who said he was Juan de Soto, a mestizo muleteer, married, forty-seven years old, and he swore to tell the truth in the proper form of all that he was questioned.

He was asked if he knew why he was called.

He said that he did not know, nor did he presume why he was called.

He was asked if he knew Thomasa González, and he said that he knew her and that she wore a dark habit of a *beata* and that she is the widow of Nicolas Macías, a deceased Spaniard, and that he believed she was a Spaniard, because he had heard it said of her and she is taken as such.

Asked about her life and customs, he said that he had heard it said in the village of Cuquio, jurisdiction of Tacotlan from several Indians of the said village, that the *beata* Thomasa González went about the village stating that the world was about to end, and this is what she said to the wife of Don Juan Ordóñez, merchant of the said village of Cuquio. He also heard it said from the Indians of the said village, that she went about from door to door, shouting "*Be careful, be alert, death is close by.*" This witness also stated that he heard from the wife of Don Juan Ordóñez that the said *beata* had told the woman that she should dispose of her things, because she was to have a terrible death. Then this witness told Don Juan de Ordóñez not to believe that *beata* because she was an imposter, and that a while back he had known her and that she went about begging from door to door in Aguascalientes, and that she was no saint in order to know this, and this all occurred about two years ago.

And all of this was the truth under the oath that he had taken and stated in discharge of his conscience, not out of hatred, and he promised to keep the secret. Being read his statement, he said that it was well written and he did not sign because he did not know how to write; instead the Commissary signed it.

Don Carlos de Andrade Sotomayor, Commissary
Before me, Juan López de Lizardi, Notary

Declaration and Testimony of Don Juan de Ordóñez in the Case against Thomasa González, May 5, 1695

✝

In the village of Cuquio, jurisdiction of Tacotlan, in the district of the town of Aguascalientes, on the 5th of May 1695, at nine o'clock in the evening, before the Lord Commissary of the Holy Office of the said town of Aguascalientes and its jurisdiction, there appeared having been called a man who said he was Don Juan de Ordóñez, a married merchant, resident of this town of the age of forty years old. He swore to tell the truth in the proper form of all that he was questioned.

He was asked if he knew why he was called.

He said that he did not know.

He was asked if he knew Thomasa González, and he said that he knew her and that about two years before he saw her wear a dark habit of a *beata* in this town. He said that she was a widow and that she appeared to be a Spaniard, probably about fifty years old, and he does not know where she was from originally, but that she is a tall woman, with a complexion of a wheat color, and that the said woman came into his house six or seven times. He said that he never liked anything that the woman did because, on the basis of her actions, what she did was not virtuous. Once he heard her ask for alms with some kind of impatience, and he heard his wife say that on five or six times she had asked to see the hands of one of their daughters, or some other person in his house at the time, so that she could see them and predict what kind of luck they would have.[96]

He stated that this is the truth under the oath that he had taken and he stated in discharge of his conscience, not out of hatred. He promised to keep the secret, and being read his statement, he said that it was well written, and he did not sign because he did not know how to write; instead the Commissary signed it.

Don Juan de Ordóñez

Don Carlos de Andrade Sotomayor, Commissary

Before me, Juan López de Lizardi, Notary

Declaration and Testimony of Juana de Ordóñez Marañon in the Case against Thomasa González, May 7, 1695

✝

In the village of Cuquio, jurisdiction of Tacotlan, in the district of the town of Aguascalientes, on the 7th of May 1695, at nine o'clock in the evening, before the Lord Commissary of the Holy Office of the said town of Aguascalientes and its jurisdiction, there appeared, having been called, a woman who said she was Juana de Ordóñez Marañon, married to Don Juan de Ordóñez, resident of this said village and a native of Irapuato, twenty-six years old, who swore to tell the truth in the proper form of all that she was questioned.

She was asked if he knew why she was called.

She said that she did not know.

She was asked if she knew Thomasa González, and she said that she did know her and that she had seen her in this village in the habit of a *beata* more than about four years ago now, and that she believed that she was probably about fifty years old. She stated that she is of a good stature with a mole on her face and a wart on her forehead, and she knows that she is a widow because she told her so. She also knows that she told her she was a native of Zelaya and that, one night when she was having dinner with her, she asked a girl to show her hand so that she could see it, because she was going to be very disgraced in the next life. She also told another girl, who was only two years old, that this century would be a terrible one, but she will be blessed in the afterlife. She said that the *beata* also told her that only by looking at someone's face she could know the future luck that each one would have, and this witness heard it from many other people that the said Thomasa González went about saying this to many people, telling each one what luck they would have.

She also said that the *beata* told her that she went to see a little girl who was in bad shape, more than a league away from the town of Aguascalientes, to whom she told that she should separate herself from sin, because if she did not do it, she would die soon and then be condemned to hell. When this same witness asked the said *beata* what happened, she told her that the girl separated herself from sin, and a few days later she died.

And she stated that the said *beata* told her that at several instances there appeared before her a demon and that the demon whipped her and that he covered her body in serpents, frogs, and other things while she was ill and that she could not move, because, when she did, snakes, frogs, and other creatures came out of her.

Then this witness was told that in the Holy Office there is a certain information against the said Thomasa González that stated that the said *beata* told this witness that she should dispose herself because she was about to have a terrible death and that she would be condemned.

This witness responded that the said Thomasa González never told her any such thing.[97]

And that this is the truth under the oath that she had taken and stated in discharge of her conscience and not out of hatred. She promised to keep the secret. Being read her statement, she said that it was well written, and she did not sign because she did not know how to write; instead the Commissary signed it.

Don Carlos de Andrade Sotomayor, Commissary
Before me, Juan López de Lizardi, Notary

Trials and Testimonies against Superstitions, Sorcery, and Magical Practices

These territories are very contaminated with similar superstitions, the people even desire to believe thus and do not wish to believe that the illnesses they suffer are the will of God our father, but rather they vacillate and then believe that they are bewitched.

Report of the Inquisition Commissary of Guanajuato, to the Inquisitors of New Spain, 1772[98]

Under the general category of superstitions, the Mexican Inquisition included witchcraft (*brujería*), sorcery (*hechicería*), divination, and other types of prophecies or predictions, and heretical practices involving an explicit or implicit pact with the devil (*pacto con el demonio*).[99]

Although the Inquisition received thousands of denunciations and accusations against suspected witches and other superstitious practitioners, the Mexican Inquisition proceeded beyond these initial investigations to engage in only seventy-six actual trials for superstition during the period from 1571 to 1700.[100] During the first few decades of the Inquisition in New Spain, a diverse series of superstitions punishable by the Inquisition found their way into several edicts of faith. Among the punishable offenses mentioned in these special edicts of faith (see document 7), divination or prognostication using water (hydromancy), fire (pyromancy), air (aeromancy), and other substances or devices such as reading cards, dice, and bones served as the most common.[101]

In terms of superstitions punished by the Inquisition in New Spain, most cases dealt with charms, spells, and incantations used by women of all *castas* and classes in order to attract and retain the love of a man. Although this type of superstitious practice remained common in Spain, in New Spain new adaptations included the admixtures of practices of African and indigenous origins, including the addition of herbs and potions to "tame" a difficult spouse or "tie" a wayward lover to the suspected witch.[102]

Moreover, unlike the crime of bigamy, which involved mainly men, those classified as general superstitions involved mostly women. Fifty-seven women were convicted of superstitious practices but only nineteen men. Men tried for superstitious practices represented a very diverse group, including such unlikely candidates as a Franciscan friar and a royal gold assayer, as well as soldiers, cowboys, and slaves.[103] Similarly, even the women were a diverse group, including six African women manifesting magical practices of African origin, eleven mestizas, and forty Spanish women, many of whom exhibited and used a mixture of indigenous and Spanish witchcraft and magic, though most of them implicated indigenous women as the guilty parties in their cases. In one interesting case, the inquisitors showed compassion for a wealthy Spanish woman, Doña Leonor Maldonado, who, thanks to her station, was fined four hundred pesos but was spared having to endure the humiliation of marching in a public auto-da-fé. The inquisitors reasoned in this case that "she should not go out in an auto because she was a noble woman married to a very honorable man, and even though she lacked honesty in her person, she had a young daughter of marriageable age who might have lost her chance to be married had she been given such a public punishment."[104] Such consideration of class and station occasionally served as a mitigating factor in the decisions of the inquisitors of New Spain.

On occasions, the suspected practitioners of these superstitions admitted to the inquisitors that they engaged in the practice only to earn money. Many further admitted during their trials that they did not believe in the efficacy of these actions and had only pretended to do them or used trickery to deceive their clients who sought their magical powers.[105] Relatively rare are the cases of malignant witchcraft in New Spain, which so frequently filled the archives in Spain, and overwhelmed the judges of witchcraft in other European nations. Herrera Sotillo argues that the Mexican inquisitors did not make a distinct difference between the charges of sorcery (*hechicería*) and malignant witchcraft (*brujería*), something that the Peninsular tribunals took great care to separate. In New Spain, it appears that most cases of witchcraft did not contain the typical characteristics of malevolent magic prevalent in Spain, that is, the desire of the witch to harm individuals, provoke illness, or destroy crops.[106] Absent also in New Spain is evidence of witches' covens, the witches' Sabbath, and other witches' tricks, such as flying. Instead, the witches and sorceresses appeared to be interested in more mundane things, such as attracting a lover, finding lost objects, and punishing a wayward husband with impotence.[107] Instead of casting curses and spreading diseases, sorceresses preferred to cast lots and predict the future. In many of the practices in New Spain, the superstitions did have a sacrilegious mixture of Christian and pagan elements, but most of them did not constitute outright heresy as many of the practices in Spain did.[108] Thus, the inquisitors for the most part left these women alone, which explains why so many denunciations resulted in so few cases. Rather than a religious role, the use of superstition and magic may reflect more on its social aspect. The fact that women from all *castas* and social classes resorted to the use of superstition, often the only outlet at their disposal to better their lives, may also be a consequence of women's limited access to power in colonial Mexico.[109]

DOCUMENT 44
Trial Proceedings against María de Armenta, for the Crimes of Sorcery and Witchcraft Involving a Demonic Pact

Mexico City, 1536–1537

SOURCE: Archivo General de la Nación, Ramo de Inquisición, vol. 38, exp. 3.

NOTE: The alleged crimes committed and the types of sorcery and superstitious acts conducted by María de Armenta were commonplace in colonial New Spain. Although most sorceresses received fairly light punishments, unlike the harsh punishments given to witches throughout Europe, those who relapsed or refused to make the light penances required by the Mexican Inquisition could be dealt with more harshly, as this case suggests.

Denunciation of Ana Pérez against María de Armenta for Superstitious Acts and Sorcery, October 9, 1536

✝

In the great City of Mexico in this kingdom of New Spain, before the Holy Office of the Inquisition on this day of October 9, 1536, Ana Peréz, the widow of Juan López, deceased, appeared before the Apostolic Inquisitor Fray Juan de Zumárraga, to denounce things she believed were against our Holy Catholic Faith. She swore the oath and then denounced what she knew about María de Armenta:

She said that about twenty days ago more or less, this witness went into the door of her house, and there she saw María de Armenta with an old Indian woman whom she called "Mother" who sat on a cushion in front of her. This witness then quickly asked her, *"What are you doing there? . . . Are you casting spells and enchantments?"* The said María de Armenta responded nervously, *"If you have seen anything that I have been doing here, you must not tell anyone."* Then she told this witness, *"If you wish, I can make any man come to you and be with you just as if he had had his hands tied behind him. . . . I can make them come to you, because I can make whoever I wish go wherever I want them to. . . . I can give you anything or anyone. . . ."* This witness then told her that she did not need anything or anyone and that she was going to denounce her and what she saw to the Holy Inquisition.

Also, this witness said that she had seen the said María de Armenta have carnal relations with two brothers and one cousin. She said that María de Armenta was proud of this and that she bragged about it. This witness then asked her, *"Aren't you afraid of God and that he may harm you for this?"* The said María de Armenta responded to this witness, *"God does not have the power to do me any harm, and you should mind your own business."* She stated that she believed this was a terrible heresy. She also said that she knew it was true, because she had seen on several occasions each of the brothers lying naked beside her on her bed. When she saw them both naked together, she was surprised, but María de Armenta told her to look at their nakedness and that she was proud of it. This witness said that Beatriz Nieta also knows about this.

She swears that all of this is the truth under oath and that she does not denounce her out of malice or hatred, but rather as a means of discharging her own conscience. She does not know how to sign, so the Bishop of Oaxaca will sign it for her.

Fr. Juan de Zumárraga, Apostolic Inquisitor
Juan López de Zárate [Bishop of Oaxaca]
Juan Javier Zárate, Notary of the Holy Office

Confession of María de Armenta, October 11, 1536

✝

On this 11th day of the month of October in the year 1536, the Apostolic Inquisitor ordered that María de Armenta should appear before the Inquisition, confess, and give testimony. She was questioned under the penalty of the punishments that those who commit perjury receive and admonished that she should answer the following questions honestly.

She was asked what was her name, and she replied that she was called María de Armenta.

She was asked where she had been baptized. She replied that she had been baptized in the islands of the Grand Canaries and that she was born there and she did not know who had baptized her because she had been a young girl then.

She was asked who had taught her about our Holy Catholic faith and what she knew about the Faith. She said that a lady who raised her named Francisca de Robayna taught her things about the Catholic faith and that she knows the Ave María and the Pater Noster and that she does not know the Creed or the Salve Regina.

She was asked why she did not learn the Creed and the Salve, and she replied that when they had shown her the Ave María and the Pater Noster, she had been a young girl, and that now as a grown woman she cannot learn the Creed and the Salve.

She was asked if she knew that God granted her a great mercy in making her a Christian and if she believed and held the beliefs of the Holy Catholic Church. She said yes.

She was asked if she knew what a sin was and what things were prohibited and sinful against our Holy Catholic faith, and that it was sinful for women to live in public sin outside of the Church. She said yes she knew.

She was asked if she knew that casting spells or making enchantments or believing in auguries or invoking demons in order to know or discern the truth about future things to come or to divine the future or to ensure her own will and make things she desired come to pass, or if by any other means one invoked the Devil, if she knew all of these were sins. She said that she knew this.

She was asked if it was true that she knew that all of these things were sins against Our Holy Catholic faith, then why did she do and commit these sins. She was also asked to declare and confess all of the different types of spells and auguries that she consulted and made or were made with her consent and who made them or taught them to her. She declared that she had not made any spells or enchantments on her own nor did she know how to make them, but that what she knew was that when she had wanted to get married with a man and when she sought some way of doing this, a black woman named Marta told her that she could ensure that the said man would marry her. Then the said Marta brought a handful of dirt, and she placed it on the doorsteps of her house. Then she took off her clothes and while she was naked, she began to blow away the dirt. Also, she knew that several Indian women had asked her to divine the whereabouts of several lost goods.

She was asked if she knew who these Indians were and if she knew one of them, and if at the present she has contact with them. She replied no, she did not.

She was asked if she had ever told anyone that she knew how to cast spells and make enchantments, or if she had done them any time before any other person. She said no.

She was asked if now she had any Indian women who knew how to cast spells or divine and predict the future. She said no.

She was then asked if she had had carnal relations with any close relatives. She said that what is the truth was that she had intended to come before the Inquisition and denounce that she had had carnal relations with two brothers without knowing that they were brothers. She said that after she had asked them, they denied that they were brothers and told her that they were very distant relatives. Only after this did this witness discover that they were truly brothers. After she discovered this, she did not continue to have relations with them.

She was asked who the two brothers were. She said they were called Pedro de los Ríos and Diego de Proano.

She was asked if anyone had asked her why she had had carnal relations and committed such a grave sin with them. She said that it was true that several people had told her and asked her why she had had carnal relations with the two brothers. She said that she had told them that it was the truth and that she was going to denounce herself.

She was asked if she had ever told anyone that she believed that Our Lord had no power to do her any harm. She said that she had never said anything like that.

All of this she swore under oath.

Fr. Juan de Zumárraga, Apostolic Inquisitor

Juan Javier Zárate, Notary of the Holy Office

Admonishment of María de Armenta to Tell the Truth, October 13, 1536

†

On October 13, 1536, the Apostolic Inquisitor ordered María de Armenta to be brought before him again. This time he admonished her that she had to tell the truth concerning everything that she was questioned about and she should do so truthfully and openly. Then he told her that certain denunciations and testimonies existed against her for the crimes of sorcery and witchcraft, and if she told the truth, his Lordship would deal with her benignly and kindly according to justice. By any other means she was admonished that he would proceed against her with the full severity of the law. The said María de Armenta stated that what she knew was that she did not do anything else but have carnal relations with two close relatives and that she had come to denounce this before the Inquisition. She also said that what she knows is that when the Lord Bishop of Tlaxcala[110] lost a gold ring, an Indian woman had told her that she could bring an old Indian woman who could divine the future and discover its whereabouts. This confessant told her to bring the Indian woman and the said old woman came and with several grains of corn, she divined the whereabouts of the ring, but the ring was never found. She had paid the Indian woman a cotton mantle for this, and this is all that she knows under oath.

Inquisitor

Juan Javier Zárate, Notary of the Holy Office

After this, the Inquisitor ordered the Prosecutor to present the formal accusation against María de Armenta in due form.

Formal Accusation of the Prosecutor of the Holy Office against María de Armenta for Suspected Witchcraft and Sorcery, October 13, 1536

✝

The Chief Prosecutor of the Holy Office appeared before the Apostolic Inquisitor and presented the case and made a formal accusation against María de Armenta based on her confession and the testimony against her. He accuses her of all of the alleged sins and any sins that will result from the inquisition and investigation into the matter. He requests and asks that His Lordship order her to be punished for her said crimes and sins that she had committed with the most severe and rigorous of punishments prescribed by law.

Dr. Rafael de Cervantes, Fiscal

María de Armenta was notified of the formal accusation, and she replied that she had no formal defense or any other thing to say or add to her confession. Both she and the Fiscal asked for the definitive conclusion of the case, and they both requested the sentence.

Definitive Sentence in the Case against María de Armenta

✝

We order that we should condemn and we do condemn the said María de Armenta, prisoner here in these jails of the Holy Office, that she is to be taken from the jail with a pointed *coroza* on her head and that tomorrow, October 15, 1536, a Sunday, she should be taken to the Cathedral of this City and that she should be forced to stand with the cap of shame on her head throughout the whole mass. Then she is to be stripped naked to the waist and her crimes and sins are to be announced before the whole City while she stands upon several steps so all can see her.[111] After this sentence is executed, she should be brought back to the jail so that she can begin to serve the imprisonment for the time and period that we should see fit. This is our definitive sentence and we pronounce it as just and necessary.

Fr. Juan, Episcopus Mexicanus, Apostolic Inquisitor
El Licenciado Loaisa, Inquisitor

Audience and Inquisition of María de Armenta, Penitenciada and Reconciliada, October 15, 1536

✝

After having complied with her sentence, the Inquisitors ordered that María de Armenta be brought before them. She was ordered to learn the Pater Noster, the Ave María, and the Creed and that she should appear every Friday before this Holy Office to show the Inquisitors how she had learned them, and if she did not comply with this, she was to be punished more harshly. She was then ordered to be released from her imprisonment.

Consultation and Audience concerning María de Armenta's Rebellion and Scorn for the Holy Office, June 26, 1537

✝

In the chambers of the Holy Office on June 26, 1537, his Lordship the Apostolic Inquisitor against Heretical Depravity noted that the said María de Armenta had not come before the Holy Office and given an account of how she had or had not learned the Pater Noster, the Ave María, and the Creed as it was ordered. Out of rebellion and scorn for the Holy Office, she has not come before the Tribunal. Seeing that her evil way of living and her bad lifestyle is notorious and public, his Lordship ordered the said María de Armenta arrested and again brought to the jails of the Holy Office.

Audience of the Inquisition with the Prisoner María de Armenta, July 3, 1537

✝

His Lordship the Inquisitor ordered the prisoner María de Armenta to appear before the Tribunal in chains and irons. She was sworn in and asked the following questions.

She was asked if she had received penitence ordered by this Holy Office and if she had been in the Cathedral dressed in a *coroza* last year. She said yes she had.

She was asked if it was true that when she was absolved after her sentence was executed that it was ordered that she come before the Holy Office every Friday in order to learn the prayers and the creed because she did not know them. She said yes it was true.

She was asked if it was also true that she was ordered to appear every fifteen days in order to give testimony and show the Inquisitors how she had learned the prayers. She said that it was true but that she had been a prisoner in the Public and Civil jails of this city and so she had been unable to come to the Holy Office.

She was asked if now she had learned the Pater Noster, the Ave María, and the Creed as she had been ordered to do. She said that it was true that she knew the Pater Noster and the Ave, and she said almost all of the Creed before his Lordship.

She was asked what was the name of the Indian woman whom she had had in her home and whom she ordered to make spells and enchantments and which enchantments had she made since she had received her penitence from this Holy Office. She said that the Indian that she had in her house did not know how to make spells or enchantments nor does she know how to cast spells.

Signed,

María de Armenta

Inquisitors

Order and Sentence of Exile and Banishment Issued against María de Armenta, September 19, 1537

✝

In this City of Mexico on the 19th of September 1537, Pedro de Medinilla, the Chief Constable of the Holy Office Proclaimed:

Hear Ye, Hear Ye, to all of the citizens and residents of the said City of Mexico, since several days ago María de Armenta, a single woman residing in this city, has lived a vile and bad life of poor example, and she was sentenced by the Holy Office of the Inquisition by His Reverence to perpetual exile and banishment from these Kingdoms of New Spain, and this has been ordered by the Holy Office many days ago, and still she remains in New Spain in great affront and scorn for the Holy Office and the Holy Mother Church. His Lordship issues this proclamation of exile again, so that anyone who is seen or known to harbor or give her aid shall be accused formally and be tried by this Holy Office for disobedience and scorn for the sanctity of this Holy Office. Under the penalty of excommunication, no one is to help, aid, shelter, or feed the said María de Armenta, now or in the future. Anyone who knows about her whereabouts or knows of those who have so sheltered, fed, or protected her are under the Holy obligation to denounce them to the Holy Office.

DOCUMENT 45
Trial Proceedings against Br. Pedro Ruiz Calderón, Clergyman, for Superstitions, Witchcraft, and Practicing the Black Arts of Necromancy

Mexico City, 1540

SOURCE: Archivo General de la Nación, Ramo de Inquisición, vol. 40, exp. 12.

NOTE: This case involved an alleged male warlock who practiced the black arts. The clergyman Pedro Ruiz Calderón apparently practiced the male magic related to the manipulation of arcane and secret knowledge, to be distinguished from female magic, whose practitioners were believed to use simpler types of superstitious magic for more emotional or physical reasons.

Denunciation and Testimony of Miguel López de Legaspi, Secretary
of the Holy Office, against Pedro Ruiz Calderón, Clergyman,
for Practicing the Black Arts, January 30, 1540

✝

In the City of Mexico, Miguel López de Legaspi, the Secretary of the Holy Office, appeared before his Lordship the Apostolic Inquisitor against Heretical Depravity and Apostasy in order to denounce Br. Pedro Ruiz Calderón, a clergyman residing in this city for
having made a certain conjuring in order to discover treasures by means of these ceremonies and other invocations of demons. Also he stated that many persons have made it
known before him that the said Calderón knows of the Black Arts and that he learned
them from others and that he can make himself invisible when he wishes and that in one
hour he can go from these kingdoms to Castile and return again. Many people also say
other vile sounding things against this clergyman Calderón, saying that he practices and
believes in superstitious things and that he can wish illness upon anyone. It has also come
to his attention that the said Pedro Ruiz Calderón has in his possession many forbidden
books of superstitions with many conjures and other spells and other suspicious things
touching upon heresy. For this reason, he denounces him so that the Holy Office can make
a thorough inquisition into the matter and discover the truth of the accusations.

Miguel López de Legaspi, Secretary of the Holy Office

Testimony of Juan Báeza de Herrera, Secretary of the Royal Audiencia in
the Information Compiled against Pedro Ruiz Calderón, January 30, 1540

✝

Having taken the oath, Juan Báeza de Herrera testified the following according to the
questions he was asked.

He said that what he knew about the situation was that one day during this month
Luis Gómez came to his house and said that a clergyman was living in the house of Juan de
Ávila who practiced the Black Arts and who could divine or discover the whereabouts of any
hidden treasure. The said Luis Gómez told this witness that on purpose he had gone to the
town of Antelco in the lands of the Marquis of the Valley of Oaxaca[112] and to the town of
Suchilapan, and in his presence the said priest went to a little hill of rocks close to this city
called Tepancingo, and there he told them to look for the said treasures. He went with him
and there they had several Indians dig and excavate the area and a few hours later they discovered some gold that the Aztecs had left behind after the conquest. Luis Gómez had said
that he did not remember how much gold was found, but it was at least fourteen or fifteen
baskets full of golden ornaments. When he asked the clergyman how he had known that
they would find the gold there, the said Calderón told him, "*In the Levant and in Italy I
learned the Black Arts of divination and prognostication and there I learned the arts with several
others.*" He told him that he had lived there for six years and that he had seen demons who

told them about the whereabouts of lost treasures. Then this witness asked him in what language did the demons tell him about the treasures. The priest replied, *"They spoke in Aramaic, Hebrew, and Greek and in another language that I do not know."*

He also said that he was told that this said Calderón had a spirit familiar whom he held in great esteem and who helped him in finding lost articles and in predicting the future. On one occasion, the said spirit or demon told him not to go forward on his horse because he would fall and impale himself upon his sword. The said Calderón listened to his spirit familiar and watched as another horseman advanced and fell off his horse, falling upon his own sword and killing himself.

He also stated that the said Calderón had told him that he had used the Black Arts to just look into a woman's eyes and cause her to fall under his spell, enchanting her with a mere glance. He said that he had told him that any woman would fall helplessly in love with him and desire him beyond all reason.

He said that he had heard it said that, in Italy and Sicily, the said Calderón had discovered many treasures by his use of the Black Arts and by using conjures and other spells invoking demons.

Juan Báeza de Herrera

Testimony of Gil González de Benavides against Pedro Ruiz Calderón for Practicing the Black Arts and Necromancy, February 3, 1540

✝

Gil González de Benavides, after having sworn the oath, testified the following:

This witness stated that he had heard it said that the clergyman Calderón would often go into a room with a young boy and that by means of the Black Arts and Necromancy he could turn stones and other metals into gold and silver and by saying several words he could also make things invisible and then visible again. He could turn coal into gold and gold into coal.[113]

He also said that he had witnessed that the said Calderón had discovered the whereabouts of several baskets filled with golden ornaments and items that the natives had hidden from the Spaniards.

He also knew that he engaged in carnal relations with many women and that he had bewitched them with certain spells and enchantments that he reads from certain books written in strange characters that only those knowledgeable of the Black Arts can read.

All of this he states is the truth under oath.

Gil González de Benavides

NOTE: After these two testimonies, several other witnesses testified to the same things. Pedro Ruiz Calderón denied the charges, but the inquisitors discovered several books of "strange characters" in his possession. This in combination with the testimony of the witnesses was enough to sentence him.

DOCUMENT 46
Denunciation against María de Bárcena, the Wife of Medina the Tailor, for Suspected Sorcery and Sexual Magic

Mexico City, 1570–1572

SOURCE: Archivo General de la Nación, Ramo de Inquisición, vol. 380, exp. 5.

NOTE: The most common type of magic practiced by women from all walks of life in New Spain involved spells, charms, and incantations either to tame an abusive husband or to seduce and maintain the affections of a lover or wayward husband. Sometimes, as in this case, women were alleged to have used potions and other herbs to cause the death or illness of an abusive husband or lover.

Denunciation and Testimony of Juana Pérez, Wife of the Merchant Gerónimo León, June 30, 1570

✝

In the City of Mexico before their Lordships the Inquisitors, a woman named Juana Pérez appeared in order to offer a denunciation and testimony against María de Bárcena, the wife of Medina the Tailor, both residents of this City. She swore the oath and said the following.

She stated that about three years ago, more or less, when María de Bárcena was in her house this witness discussed certain problems she was having with her husband. She told Bárcena that her husband abused her and he cheated on her with several other local women. The said María de Bárcena told her, *"Look, don't be sad, be happy . . . you should kill your husband and I know how to do it!"* Then the said Bárcena told her, *"Look, I have certain powders and roots and with one of them if you place it under your husband's pillow where he sleeps it will cause him to quickly die!"* She then told her that even then she was waiting for an Indian to bring several of these herbs to her. This witness then told her that she should not say those types of things and that she should not believe in them because they were tricks and lies of the demons.

She declares this all under oath as the truth and she does not denounce it out of malice or hatred for the said María de Bárcena.

Inquisitors, Moya de Contreras
Br. Miguel de la Barreda, Notary

Denunciation and Testimony of Teresa Gutiérrez, wife of Rodrigo Donís, July 10 1572

†

In the City of Mexico before their Lordships the Inquisitors, a woman named Teresa Gutiérrez appeared in order to offer a denunciation and testimony against María de Bárcena, the wife of Medina the Tailor. She swore the oath and declared the following.

She and her husband came to these kingdoms from Guatemala, and they stayed in the house of Medina the Tailor and his wife. When this witness once spoke to the said wife, María de Bárcena, about her own husband, she told her, "This husband of mine is a lost man, and I don't know what I am going to do with him." She said that María de Bárcena responded, "Give me one thousand cacao beans and one of the pins from your husband's pants, and I will give the chocolate to a Moorish black slave of Diego de Ocampo's house, and she will cast a spell with the pin so that your husband will never again in his life love or desire another woman, only you." She also told this witness that she had several powders which could be placed in the bed of her husband and others that she could place in his drinks. Then she told this witness that if she did not want to do this that she should find the blanket from a young horse that had just given birth and that she should place it around her husband to ensure his affection forever.

She swore that this was the truth and that she did not denounce her out of malice or hatred.

Inquisitors
Br. Miguel de la Barreda, Notary

NOTE: After a few other similar testimonies, and the accused witch's vehement denials of any guilt, the inquisitors sentenced María de Bárcena to appear naked from the waist up in the cathedral. In addition to this, she was sentenced to three years in prison and had to pay a fine of twenty gold pesos (a large sum).

DOCUMENT 47
Denunciation against Several Acts of Supposed Sorcery and Witchcraft Presented by Doña Juana Rosado

Merida, Yucatan, September 4, 1672

SOURCE: Archivo General de la Nación, Ramo de Inquisición, vol. 150.

NOTE: Because the local commissaries of the Inquisition were not permitted to do more than collect evidence and depositions for crimes of witchcraft and sexual sorcery, often there would be no further investigation into the allegations beyond the initial denunciation and these types of secret depositions.

✝

In the city of Merida in the provinces of Yucatan, in the evening after the final prayers on September 4, 1672 a woman named Doña Juana de Rosado appeared after having been summoned before his Lordship Don Antonio de Horta y Barroso, the Commissary of the Holy Office of the Inquisition in these provinces. Before his Lordship and a notary, the said woman declared that she was the widow of Pedro Cervera and a native of this city. She said that she was twenty-six years old, and she swore the oath and then declared that she came to denounce certain things that she had heard and witnessed that are against our Holy Catholic faith.

She was asked if she knew of the reason why she had been summoned before the Inquisition. She said that she presumed that it was in order to know what a woman named Ignacia López had told her. She stated that the said woman was married with Joseph de Lugo and that she was a witch who knew how to enchant and cast spells over bones and roses.

Also, she stated that she had heard that several mulatto women, one of whose names she remembered as Leonora de Toribio, and the others whose names she forgets, were all witches. She does not remember who told her this.

She also denounces that a mestizo woman, the widow of Juan de Tolosa the Tailor, a woman named Agustina, whose last name she forgot, told her that a mulatto woman who lived in the neighborhood of San Juan knew how to enchant and cast spells over roses and by using the roses she could gain the amorous attentions of any man. She was also told that the said mulatto woman had driven a man crazy with her enchantments and spells and that the man had died from these malicious spells.

She also presumes that she was called here in order to tell what she knows about what she had heard about five or six months ago from the mouth of Gertrúdis de Lara, a resident here in the neighborhood of San Cristóbal. She had told her that a free mulatto woman of the said neighborhood named Micaela Montejo was another enchanter of roses and other things and that she had a small doll and with the doll she said a few words, words that this witness did not know, and it transformed into a man or a woman of full size. Also, she testifies that she also cast fortunes over a bowl of water in which she placed several herbs and she chanted over them several words.

She also stated that she knew that a mulatto woman who had been the slave of Captain Tomás Gutiérrez de Páramo, and who is now free, was also a malicious witch who knew how to cast spells and enchantments over both men and women.

She was then asked if she knew that any woman had enchanted or kept some man enchanted with spells or potions that she gave them in their food or drink. She said that she did know that a certain woman had given her husband a spell or enchantment by putting a potion or poison in his food and that shortly thereafter he had died. She also knew that a certain woman had killed another woman by placing a spell or enchantment over her plate of food. She also said that she knew that Doña Brigida Pacheco killed her first husband with a spell that she had given him. Her first husband Sancho del Puerto suffered greatly from her spells and enchantments, and he eventually died from them. This she said that she knew because she had heard it said publicly and often.

She also stated that what else she knew was that in the town of Campeche one of Doña María Rejón's sisters had died from a spell or enchantment and this she had heard from the Sacristan of the Church there, Pedro Vázquez, who had visited this city about a year and a half ago.

She says that she states all of this under oath in answer to the questions, and she does not state it out of malice or hatred for those who she denounces, but rather as a means of discharging her conscience, and she does not sign because she did not know how to sign.

Dr. Antonio de Horta y Barroso, Inquisition Commissary
Bernarbé de Fuentes, Notary of the Holy Office

DOCUMENT 48
Denunciation against Several Acts of Supposed Sorcery and Sexual Magic Presented by Lorenza Márquez

Merida, Yucatan, April 1672

SOURCE: Archivo General de la Nación, Ramo de Inquisición, vol. 150.

NOTE: Hearsay evidence was often denounced to the local Inquisition commissaries in the outlying regions of New Spain. Most of these spontaneous denunciations and depositions were often motivated out of spite, malice, or a desire for revenge. The fact that few of these denunciations led to further trial proceedings meant that the inquisitors in New Spain were often cautious in issuing arrest warrants and formulating trials on the basis of such hearsay evidence for alleged minor infractions such as witchcraft and sorcery.

Denunciation and Testimony of Lorenza Márquez, April 22, 1672

✝

In the city of Merida in the provinces of Yucatan, in the evening after the final prayers on April 22, 1672, a woman named Lorenza Márquez appeared spontaneously without having been called before his Lordship Don Antonio de Horta y Barroso, the Commissary of the Holy Office of the Inquisition in these provinces. Before his Lordship and a notary, the said woman declared that she was the wife of Francisco Osorio and a resident here in this city. She swore the oath and then declared that she came to denounce certain things that she had heard and witnessed that are against our Holy Catholic faith. She declared that she wished to discharge her conscience and denounce the following.

She said that about one month before, more or less, when she was talking in the plaza with Bernarbé de Herrera, known as *Barracillo,* he had told this witness how several women had cast spells and enchantments so that his virile member was "tied" [*ligado*] and that when he had told a certain Indian man about this, he responded to him that he would be unable to undo the damage unless he had him cast another spell that would place a curse on these women. She declares that he told her that he did have the Indian cast a spell, which left the women "stupid," and only then did he return to normal, and only then did his virile member continue to function as it should. He also told her that if he wished to force them to come to him to beg him to have carnal relations with him, he could do it. She asked him how he could do this, and he replied that he could do it by killing a horse and placing its private parts in the fire. He also told her that he knew how to know if certain women were witches when they came into the Cathedral. She asked him how he could know this, and he replied that by taking a little piece of bacon that had been placed in a pot on Fat Tuesday before Lent and then on Holy Thursday at night placing the bacon on the Church doors. Thus, if there were witches or warlocks in the church at that time they would not be able to open the doors without having someone remove the bacon, and by this means, you can discover who is a witch.

She also denounces that several years before she had sent one of her Indian servants named Diego Chab on an errand. She declared that he came upon a mestizo tailor named Agustín Sosa who was a resident of this city and he took him by the hand and forced him to go into an abandoned plot of land where he persuaded him to let him commit the nefarious crime of sodomy with him. The said Indian responded, *"I am not a woman to do this thing with you,"* but Sosa insisted, and Diego Chab quickly escaped from him and ran to this witness to tell her what had happened.

Also, she denounces that about two years before one of her nephews, Iñigo Sugastí, told her that an Englishman named Ricardo Luis conducted curing ceremonies and surgery, but that he did not do this with goodness, but rather he cured people by a diabolical art. When she asked him how he knew this, her nephew responded that he had seen it when he saw him curing Br. Francisco Sugastí, his uncle in the town of Sotuta where he was the parish priest. There, the Englishman opened a little book where he saw a figure drawn in it that appeared very evil to him, and he read a few things that caused him great horror and he became afraid and he threw the book aside.

This is all that she has to declare, and she states that it is the truth under oath. She did not sign it because she does not know how to write, the Lord Commissary signed it on her behalf.

Br. Antonio de Horta y Barroso
It passed before me, Br. Gerónimo de Sepúlveda, Notary of the Holy Office

Testimony of Iñigo de Sugastí, April 23, 1672

✝

In the city of Merida in the province of Yucatan, His Lordship the Commissary General of the Holy Office of the Inquisition ordered that Iñigo de Sugastí should give testimony before this Tribunal. Iñigo de Sugastí, a native of this City and now residing in the town of Yaxcaba appeared and said that he was about twenty-six years old, married, and he swore the oath.

Asked if he knew why he had been summoned before the Inquisition. He said that he did not know why.

He was asked if he had heard or, seen, or done anything that was against Our Holy Catholic Faith or contrary to the free and liberal exercise of the Holy Office. He said that what he knows is that while he was in the town of Sotuta, caring for his uncle Br. Francisco de Sugastí, the parish priest of the town, he witnessed that an Englishman named Ricardo Luis was curing him. The said Englishman was talking to his uncle, and he heard his uncle say that an Indian woman had been bewitched by a spell or enchantment that had been placed upon her, and his uncle asked him if he wished to see her and cure her. The said Ricardo said that he would see her, and later the same day they brought the said bewitched Indian woman and the supposed spell or object of enchantment that had been used against her. The object was a little bundle of meat fashioned into the form of a bull's heart, and this witness saw it and he saw the said Englishman Ricardo Luis study the said amulet or bewitched object, and this all occurred about three years ago. He also said that he has a great suspicion that the said Ricardo Luis understands spells and incantations and knows a great deal about witchcraft and sorcery. He also knows how to remove spells and bewitchments, and this he has heard from many people in the town who say that he has also removed on another occasion a cursed object of bewitchment made out of a bundle of bones and herbs that had been used by a witch against a woman named Doña Catalina de Vargas, who this witness knows now lives in Campeche. He also said that all of this appears to touch upon the Holy Office and its duties and he declares it under oath.

He was told that in this Holy Office there was a formal statement and testimony that the said Ricardo Luis, besides what he has declared, is accused of having a book which he uses to cure people and that it was stated that this witness saw in this book a figure that appeared evil to him and which caused him great horror and that this witness supposedly knows that he does not cure people out of a good art but rather from a diabolical practice of witchcraft. He responded that, even though it is the truth that he believes that the said Englishman cures people by using a diabolical art, using the Devil to divine and discover the causes of diseases, he knows this only because he has heard it said. He also said that he saw a strange book that he had, but he does not remember having seen in it a strange and horrible figure.

All of this he declares under oath
Iñigo de Sugastí
Dr. Don Antonio de Horta y Barroso

The testimony was presented before me, Bernarbé de Fuentes, Notary of the Holy Office.

Trials and Testimonies against the Use
of Peyote and Other Herbs and Plants
for Divination

We have it for certain that [this herb] should not be taken, even for use in medicinal remedies, due to the danger and suspicion that it gives of the Devil having a pact with the said herb or of his having taken advantage of the custom of its use for his evil ends.

Qualification of the Supreme Council of the Inquisition against the use of the indigenous herb Peyote, 1620

Ingestion of native herbs such as pipiltzintzintli and the cactus peyote was another target for eradication in the minds of the inquisitors. For centuries the indigenous peoples of Mexico had used similar herbs, mushrooms, and cacti in their curing and medical rituals.[114] During the colonial period in New Spain, apparently the use of peyote and other hallucinogens as a means of divination and communication with the spirit world spread far beyond their traditional pre-Hispanic geographic limits and came to cross ethnic, social, and gender boundaries.[115] The Mexican Inquisition discovered the use of these hallucinogens as far away as Guatemala and other parts of Central America. The rapidly expanding use of these substances for magical and healing practices even among nonindigenous people in the early seventeenth century was for the inquisitors of New Spain evidence of a diabolic conspiracy between the indigenous shamanic users of these substances and a growing number of Spanish and other *castas* who consulted them and spread the use of peyote among non-Indians.[116] The Inquisition in New Spain became so alarmed at the spread of peyote that it consulted with the Suprema concerning the situation.[117] A series of testimonies and reports flowed back and forth across the Atlantic until the Suprema finally decided to permit the Inquisition in New Spain to add cognizance of the illicit use of peyote and other hallucinogens to its jurisdiction.[118] It issued a special edict of faith against the use of peyote in 1620 (document 8).[119]

Nevertheless, as the documents in this section illustrate, the Inquisition's attempt to eradicate the use of peyote and other indigenous herbs such as pipiltzintzintli as divinatory and medicinal aids ultimately failed because the very people who cultivated and collected these herbs and spread their use among the nonindigenous people of New Spain remained outside of the jurisdiction of the Inquisition.[120]

DOCUMENT 49
Denunciation and Inquisition Investigations and Documents concerning the Prohibited Herb and Hallucinogen Pipiltzintzintli,[121] Which Was Discovered in the Village of Tepepan and Xochimilco, Valley of Mexico

Tepepan, Xochimilco, October 1698

SOURCE: Archivo General de la Nación, Ramo de Inquisición, vol. 706, exp. 27.

NOTE: Following the 1620 inquisitorial edict prohibiting the use of peyote and other native herbs and mushrooms for the purposes of divination, healing, and witchcraft, the Inquisition continued to investigate and examine the continued use of other native herbs, flowers, and plants that had similar hallucinogenic effects. Several interesting aspects of inquisitorial procedures and the use of native herbs can be gained from this brief document. Apparently even the Franciscan friars in this case had mixed messages concerning the nature of herbs and other native plants prohibited by the Inquisition. Only one of the several friars questioned remembered the Holy Office officially issuing an edict against several native herbs and other plants. In terms of local native knowledge of herbs and plants, most natives were familiar with the use of the plant called pipiltzintzintli, because they could identify the dried hallucinogenic version of the plant and distinguish it from similar fresh plants that did not have the hallucinogenic effects. There was some confusion, as late as the seventeenth century, of who actually had jurisdiction over investigating, punishing, and rooting out the use of similar native hallucinogens. Apparently, the Inquisition prohibited the use of the herbs but had no direct control or jurisdiction over the extirpation of their use in the indigenous communities. The Franciscan friar guardians of the monastic regions were also unsure of how to proceed. Such jurisdictional confusions, as Richard Greenleaf points out, became quite common in the seventeenth and eighteenth centuries.[122]

Denunciation and Testimony of Fr. Pedro de Echevarría, Guardian of the Convent of Tepepan, October 15, 1698

✝

Very Illustrious Lords,

I, Fr. Pedro de Echevarría, the procurator and Guardian of the Franciscan convent of this town of Tepepan, appear before Your Lordships and declare that under the clerical oath of obedience and in accord with the published edicts of the faith of this Holy Tribunal, I am moved to declare and give notice of how the magistrate of the town of Xochimilco, Juan de Saavedra sent two constables named Juan de Morales and Cristóbal Amparador to arrest several Indians from the town of Tepepan concerning their growing and using certain herbs and roots called *Pipiltzintzintli*, the said herb being one that they planted and use in their idolatrous and superstitious rituals. Having heard this and having learned that this said herb is one of many prohibited by the Holy Office and because I know that the jurisdiction over the confiscation of the said herb and the forming of a legal proceedings against such sins best belongs to this tribunal, I denounce this before you so that you may do what is most convenient in the service of God our Lord.

Given this day in the city of Tepepan, October 15, 1698
Fr. Pedro de Echeverría

Order of the Holy Office of the Inquisition, October 17, 1698

✝

Having learned by way of a denunciation that the magistrate of the town of Xochimilco sent several constables to arrest and apprehend several Indians from the town of Tepepan for growing and using the prohibited herb and hallucinogen called *Pipiltzintzintli,* we order that you, Fray Nicolás Matías, Qualifier of the Holy Office and Guardian of the convent of Xochimilco, should go and investigate into the matter and inform us of what you may discover concerning the circumstances involved.

Dr. Don Juan de Armesto y Ron [Inquisitor]
Dr. Don Francisco de Deza y Ulloa [Inquisitor]
Don Vicente Adel y Piñarosa [Secretary]

Information Remitted by Fr. Nicolás Matías concerning the Issue of the Pipiltzintzintli, October 21, 1698

✝

In response and under the orders of the Holy Office, I investigated into the nature of the issue and devised the following series of questions for all witnesses.

First, if they knew the said Magistrate of Xochimilco.

Second, if they knew that the said Magistrate Don Juan de Saavedra sent several constables to the town of Tepepan in order to arrest and proceed in a case against several Indians who had planted the said prohibited herb called Pipiltzintzintli. If they knew this then they should state who they were and what their names were.

Third, if they know that the said constables punished the natives and then took from them a fine of a certain number of pesos.

Fourth, if they know that the said Magistrate Juan de Saavedra had stated by what means and jurisdiction he arrested and proceeded against the said natives.

Fifth, if they are related to anyone named in the case.

Sixth, if they know that this is all public and common knowledge.

Testimony of Fr. Miguel Bravo, October 21, 1698

✝

On the same day, the commissary judge for the investigation of the case called before him Fr. Miguel Bravo, friar here in this convent. He swore the oath in proper and due form and then replied.

First, that he knows the said Magistrate of Xochimilco, Don Juan de Saavedra.

Second, that he knows that, in the town of Tepepan, the Magistrate ordered two constables to go and arrest several Indians who had the said prohibited herb Pipiltzintzintli. He also said that he had seen two of the constables go to the fields and pull out the said herbs called Pipiltzintzintli that they found there. They ripped out the herbs that the Indians had planted. Then they said that they had ripped out the said herbs since they were prohibited by the Holy Office, and the said Constable Juan de Morales had said this. Then he stated that the said constable came to this convent, and he sent a message to the guardian and asked for his advice. The Guardian urged him to use caution in punishing the natives and asked him not to fine them in cash. Then another friar, Fr. Donado, told him that there was an order and edict of prohibition from the Holy Office against the said Herb. After this the friars discovered that the Constables had extorted moneys from the Indians and they went to complain against them to the magistrate, who did nothing. The only thing that the Magistrate did was to show the friars a piece of the plant or herb that the constables had ripped out of the ground.

Fr. Nicolás Matías [Commissary]   Fr. Pedro de Echevarría [Secretary]

Fr. Miguel Bravo

Testimony of Fr. Manuel Cabello, October 21, 1698

✝

On the same day, month and year, Fr. Manuel Cabello from the convent at Tepepan testified and swore the oath as required by law. He stated that one of the said constables, who he believes is called Cristóbal and whose last name he does not recall, came to him and showed him an herb which he said was called Pipiltzintzintli. He had in his hand a bit of dried herb and in the other hand some fresh herbs that he took from off of the wall. The said Cristóbal then said, *"This dry herb here is the one that has the effect, and this fresh green herb does not."* Then the said Cristóbal took out of the Indians' houses, in the presence of Don Juan de Sosa and the Licenciado Quixada, a handful of the said dried herb, and he showed it again to this witness and the others. Then he said, *"There is a declaration and order of excommunication issued against anyone who uses these said herbs!"* Then this witness and all of the others left the Indian's house and took their own roads.

Fr. Nicolás Matías [commissary]   Fr. Pedro de Echevarría [secretary]

Fr. Manuel Cabello

Testimony of Fr. Pedro Sánchez, October 21, 1698

✝

On the same day, month, and year, Fr. Pedro Sánchez from the convent at Tepepan testified and swore the oath as required by law. He stated that one day he walked through the town of Tepepan and passed by a house where he saw a great number of Indians who appeared to be drunk or inebriated. He returned to the convent and told his superior. He then said that they both witnessed that two Spanish constables came and took from the said group of Indians a large amount of the prohibited herb, Pipiltzintzintli. This is all that he knows.

Fr. Nicolás Matías [commissary]   Fr. Pedro de Echevarría [secretary]
Fr. Pedro Sánchez

Testimony of Fr. Joseph de la Concepción Donado, October 21, 1698

✝

On the same day, month, and year, Fr. Joseph de la Concepción Donado, from the convent at Tepepan, testified and swore the oath as required by law. He stated that about a month ago two Spanish constables came to this town from Xochimilco in order to confiscate and take away from the Indians a prohibited herb that they call Pangui, and by another name Pipiltzintzintli, and that one of the constables was called Morales and the other one he forgets. He discovered this when several Indians came to the convent to warn him that the constables had arrested and punished several Indians. He then went to the town and saw the constables and asked them what they were doing there. The constable who was called Cristóbal then told him, "*We came to take this herb from these natives.*" With this he showed him some of this herb and then said, "*It is not permitted nor is it good that they drink this herb because with it they see many vile and evil things and visions and when they take it they speak with demons and other vile monsters.*" He then said that, "*This herb is prohibited and forbidden by the Inquisition.*"
This is the truth under oath.

Fr. Nicolás Matías [Commissary]   Fr. Pedro de Echevarría [Secretary]
Fr. Joseph de la Concepción Donado

Sentence and Final Decision of the Commissary Judge, October 22, 1698

✝

In this village of San Bernardino de Xochimilco, on October 22, 1698, after having examined the said testimony and information, the Lord Commissary Fr. Nicolás Matías decided not to continue with the examination of the Indians of the town of Our Lady of Tepepan because the Indians are not to be trusted to maintain and keep the secret necessary for the oath of the Holy Office. In order not to risk detection and the revelation of the secret proceedings, the Commissary decided to conclude this information and enclose it and send it along with another letter to their Lordships the Inquisitors at the seat of the Holy Tribunal in the City of Mexico.

Fr. Nicolás Matías [Commissary]   Fr. Pedro de Echevarría [Secretary]

DOCUMENT 50
Inquisition Trial against a Mulatta Named María, for the Use of the Herb Pipiltzintzintli and Other Diverse Charges

Texcoco, 1704

Source: Archivo General de la Nación, Ramo de Inquisición, vol. 727, exp. 24.

Note: Following the Edict of Faith of 1620 (document 8) that outlawed the use of herbs such as peyote and pipiltzintzintli, the Inquisition and its commissaries became vigilant in their denunciation of the continued use of these plants in curing, divination, and other magical practices and witchcraft. In this case, the mulatta woman named María apparently served as a type of midwife or herbal healer, and her confiscated medicine bag reveals the type of materials used by rural medicinal healers in colonial Mexico.

Letter and Remission of a Denunciation against a Mulatta named María for the Use of the Prohibited Herb Pipiltzintzintli, January 25, 1704

✝

Along with this letter I forward a denunciation against a mulatta from whom we took a small leather bag that had inside of it several dried plants of Pipiltzintzintli, as well as the umbilical cord of a child, and other types of herbs, all of which I send along with this letter so that they can be identified. I have not gone as far as taking the declaration of the said mulatta until I was able to give notice to Your Lordship, so that you may order what should be done in this case, as well as all others that occur in that Holy Tribunal.

May the God guard Your Lordship for many years for the defense of our Faith

Signed in the house and Hacienda of Santa Catarina Martyr, Texcoco
January 25, 1704
I kiss the hands of Your Lordship,
Your Very secure servant and Chaplain

Licenciado Bartolomé Camacho
Commissary of the Inquisition in Texcoco

Received in this Holy Office in Mexico City on January 25, 1704

Place the leather bag in the chamber of the secret, and place it in an assigned spot with a note concerning its owner.

Signed the Lord Inquisitor

Denunciation of Don Antonio Joseph Cantero, Cleric and Notary of the Holy Office in the City of Texcoco against a Mulatta Named María, January 3, 1704

†

In the town of Texcoco, on 3rd of January 1704, in the morning before Licenciado Bartolomé Camacho, commissary of the Holy Office in this jurisdiction, during the afternoon, there appeared, without having been summoned, and swore an oath *in verbo sacerdotis*[123] with his hand placed on his chest, Bachiller Don Antonio Joseph Cantero, cleric and notary of the Holy Office in this city and resident therein, who said that he was twenty-nine years old. He stated and declared that for the discharge of his conscious, he denounces that on the 29th of December 1703, while at home in his house, he was called for on the part of Father Fray Joseph Muñetones, a Franciscan and a minister of the doctrine of that city, who told him to go to the house of Andrés de Vicuña, resident and merchant in this said city, in order to observe and study a leather bag with several suspicious herbs inside, which was found on a young woman, apparently a mulatta. Having gone to the said house, he asked the said mulatta if it was true that she had brought that said leather bag, and she replied that yes, that she rightly brought it and held it without malice, and that she only knew that one herb that she brought in that bag was good for curing ant bites and the said bag was shown to the Commissary.

He was asked if he knew what was the name of the said mulatta, and if she was single or married, or what personal signs or features she might have had. He responded that her name was María, and that he did not know if she was married or single, and that her personal characteristics are that she is small in stature, dark skinned, apparently belonging to the Lobo caste,[124] with short hair that is not obviously curly or straight.

He stated that this was the truth and that it had been well written, and thus he swore the oath to God and the Holy Cross, and stated that he did not denounce this out of hatred.

He promised to keep the secret and he signed it with the Commissary.

Antonio Joseph Cantero

This passed before me,
Bachiller Joseph Camacho, Notary

Ratification of the Testimony and Denunciation Made by Don Antonio Joseph Cantero, Cleric and Notary of the Holy Office in the City of Texcoco against a Mulatta Named María, January 5, 1704

✝

In the town of Texcoco, on 5th of January, 1704, in the morning before Licenciado Bartolomé Camacho, commissary of the Holy Office in this jurisdiction, Bachiller Don Antonio Joseph Cantero, a cleric and resident of this town appeared and stated that he was about twenty-nine years old, and in the presence of honest and religious persons, including Bachiller Don Felipe Arias Río Frío, and Bachiller Francisco Javier García de la Mora, Presbiters who had sworn the secret, he received the oath and promised to tell the truth. Being questioned if he remembered having been deposed before a Judge testifying against some person concerning things touching upon the Faith, he said that he remembered having testified before the Lord Judge Don Bartolomé Camacho, commissary, against a mulatta women named María, and he refers in substance to the contents of that testimony, and he asked that it be read to him. He was told that the Lord Prosecutor of the Holy Office will present him as a witness *ad perpetuam rei memoriam*[125] in a case against the said María, and he should be attentive to this, and he was read his testimony, and he requested that if he had to alter, add to, or amend it, he should do so in such a manner that everything tells the truth. He affirmed and ratified it, because anything he said now would be prejudiced against the said mulatta María, and then he was read his testimony *verbo ad verbum*,[126] and the said Bachiller Don Antonio Joseph Cantero said that he had heard it and understood it and that it was his said testimony, and that he had stated it just as he had heard it and that he did not have anything to alter, add, or amend because as it was written it was the truth. He affirmed this and ratified it, and if it was necessary, he would state it all again against the said mulatta María, not out of hatred, but rather for the discharge of his conscience.

He promised to keep the secret and he signed it with the Commissary.

Antonio Joseph Cantero   Bachiller Felipe Arías Río Frío
Bachiller Javier García de la Mora

This passed before me
Bachiller Joseph Camacho, Notary

Testimony Taken from Doña Petrona de Herrera, Spanish Wife of Don Andrés de Vicuña, Resident and Merchant of This Town of Texcoco, January 3, 1704

✝

In the town of Texcoco, on 3rd of January 1704, during the afternoon, the Licenciado Bartolomé Camacho, commissary of the Holy Office in this jurisdiction, went to the house and dwelling place of Andrés de Vicuña, resident and Merchant in the said city, and there appeared Doña Petrona de Herrera, his wife, a Spaniard, more or less twenty-nine years old, and she swore the oath in the proper form and promised to tell the truth concerning all that she was questioned.

She was asked concerning the small leather bag of herbs and questioned about who she had taken it from, and how it came into her possession, and she replied that the past Saturday which was the 29th of December 1703, while in her shop, a mulatta woman came in to buy several things, whose name she does not remember or know. Once she left with her packages this witness discovered a small leather bag on the floor, which she judged belonged to one of the Indians who came into her shop to purchase goods. Out of curiosity, she cut the small bag open with a pair of scissors in order to see what was inside, and at that time the said mulatta woman returned frantically looking for the small bag, saying that it contained relics. This witness reprehended her, stating that if she brought that bag with her she should know that it only contained herbs, which symbolized something evil. To this the mulatta freely responded that she carried them as something good without any evil, and then she left. Then she shamelessly returned a second time telling this witness *"You understand better than I things concerning witchcraft because you recognize the herbs that are in that bag"* and still this witness did not want to give it back to her.

She was asked if she knew what she was called, or knew or had heard from some other person that she had conducted some curse or witchcraft. She responded that she had never seen her another time and that she did not know her, except for that occasion and that this is the truth based on her oath that she has made, and she said that it all appeared well written.

She promised to keep the secret and did not sign it because she did not know how to write. The Commissary signed it for her.

Licenciado Bartolomé Camacho

This passed before me
Bachiller Joseph Camacho, Notary

Ratification of the Testimony of Doña Petrona de Herrea, against an Unnamed Mulatta Woman, January 5, 1704

✝

In the town of Texcoco, on 5th of January 1704, in the morning before Licenciado Bartolomé Camacho, commissary of the Holy Office in this jurisdiction, appeared Doña Petrona de Herrera, legitimate wife of Don Andrés de Vicuña, resident and Merchant of this city, aged twenty-nine years more or less, and in the presence of honest and religious persons, including Bachiller Don Felipe Arías Río Frío, and Bachiller Francisco Javier García de la Mora, Presbiters who had sworn the secret, she received the oath and promised to tell the truth

Questioned if she remembered having been deposed before a Judge testifying against some person concerning things touching upon the Faith, she said that she remembered having testified before the Lord Judge Don Bartolomé Camacho, commissary, against a mulatta women named "The María," and she refers in substance to the contents of that testimony.

He asked that it be read to her, and she was told that the Lord Prosecutor of the Holy Office will present her as a witness *ad perpetuam rei memoriam* in a case against the said María and she should be attentive to this, and she was read her testimony, and requested that if she had to alter, add to, or amend it, she should do so in such a manner that everything tells the truth. She affirmed and ratified it, because anything she said now would be prejudiced against the said mulatta María, and then she was read her testimony *verbo ad verbum,* and she said that she had heard it and understood it and that it was her said testimony, and that she did not have anything to alter, add, or amend because as it was written it was the truth. She affirmed this and ratified it, and if it was necessary, she would state it all again against the said mulatta María, not out of hatred, but rather for the discharge of his conscience.

She promised to keep the secret, and she did not sign because she did not know how to write, so the Commissary signed it for her in the presence of the said witnesses

Licenciado Bartolomé Camacho

Bachiller Felipe Arías Río Frío   Bachiller Javier García de la Mora

This passed before me,
Bachiller Joseph Camacho, Notary

Auto and Review of the Material in This Case by the Tribunal of the Holy Office, January 5, 1704

✝

Reviewed on the same day, month, and year by the said Lord Inquisitor, who stated that due to the short distance between this city and the town of Texcoco, these original diligences and documents should be returned to the Commissary so that he may once again examine the witness who first denounced this case, requesting him to state before what witnesses did this confession occur in the said shop in which the denounced declared that the bag was hers, and that they should all declare this under examination. Also he should examine the friar who it says called him to come and denounce it, so that he can declare what he knows and the motive by which he called for the man to denounce the mulatta. And also, he should return and examine Doña Petrona de Herrera, so that she should state which other persons where there as witnesses to what she refers occurred between her and the denounced mulatta when she returned for the bag. Then the commissary should examine those people whom she remembers as witnesses, and they should all ratify their testimonies according to the style and instructions of the Holy Office. He should be cautious concerning the denounced mulatta, and in the case that she attempts to flee, he should ensure that she should be arrested under some other pretext in the royal jail, and all that should be declared and testified to should be sent back to this Tribunal in all brevity, and this I order and attest to.

The Inquisitor

This passed before me,
Don Eugenio de las Peñas, Secretary

Trials and Testimonies Related
to Prohibited Books

In some parts of that diocese there was no notice of the Index and because in some towns of Spaniards it would be possible for some prohibited books to circulate, we therefore send with this the list of those books which are most likely to continue to circulate.

Letter from the inquisitors of New Spain to the regional commissary of Guadalajara, 1587

The Holy Office controlled dissenters and those who went against established laws and policies by limiting the spread of information. Its censorship of prohibited books and ideas averted serious religious movements that might challenge Spanish Catholicism and helped stifle the advent of Protestantism in New Spain.[127] Through its review of all printed material and its control over the licensing of permissions to read prohibited books (see documents 51 to 56), the Inquisition directly controlled education, literature, and other intellectual pursuits, including ideas spread by word of mouth—evident in many cases involving heretical propositions or evil-sounding words.[128] Through its contact with the Supreme Council of the Inquisition in Spain, the Holy Office was able to monitor all vessels traveling between Mexico and Spain and thus limit the number of foreigners who might introduce the contaminating influences of Protestantism and other undesirable people with histories of heretical crimes and other social undesirables such as those convicted of theft and prostitution.[129] The final period of the Mexican Inquisition (1700–1820) included its growing political use for the punishment of non-Catholic foreigners and political dissenters. Hundreds of residents of New Spain faced Inquisition trials during this period for their political views, including two of the most famous leaders of the Mexican Independence movement, Father Miguel Hidalgo and José María Morelos (documents 11 and 57).

Soon after the installation of the tribunal in New Spain, the inquisitors began to preoccupy themselves with discovering what types of books and printed materials had made their way to the new colony.[130] In terms of the Index of Prohibited Books, even in Europe the enforcement of the index varied from place to place. Nevertheless, in New Spain the enforcement of the index remained most effective in the many cities and urban areas.[131] It was in the ports and more distant provinces where the Inquisition's control over prohibited books and other publications broke down, as the endless numbers of reports with complaints from local regional commissaries attested. Most notably lacking was the surveillance in the major port of Veracruz, the exclusive entrepôt of all European merchandise throughout the colonial period. Apparently, as the inquisitors soon discovered, there had been almost no regulation of the book trade through the port of Veracruz before 1572. The inquisitors quickly attempted to remedy this because they believed, as did Francisco Peña, the sixteenth-century scholar and commentator on the famous *Directorium Inquisitorum*, that the port cities remained the main sites of "the viral spread of heresy."[132]

A new inquisitor, Dr. Pedro Moya de Contreras, began a widespread purge of prohibited books between1571 and 1572. His activities "demonstrated that both lay and clerical Spaniards in Mexico read and possessed a wide range of prohibited works between 1559 and 1572."[133] According to the records of the inquisitor's visitations, people in New Spain read and possessed copies of the scriptures, prayer books, the works of Erasmus, and other spiritual works specifically prohibited by the index. Although apparently few copies of any of the works of Martin Luther and John Calvin existed at that time, things would change with the influx of foreigners in the later sixteenth and early seventeenth centuries.[134]

Censorship of printed materials remained an area of divided jurisdiction, with both the crown and the Inquisition attempting to control aspects of pre- and post-production publishing. Through its Council of Castile, the Spanish crown approved book projects and thus could "prevent the publication of any book simply by refusing a license for its publication," although, in practice, this rarely happened. After a book's publication, the Inquisition laid claim to censorship. If a book contained anything that it believed to be worthy of censure, the Inquisition, even its distant regional tribunals such as the one in New Spain, held the right to prohibit its distribution, order material expurgated, or remove it from circulation.[135]

The Inquisition in New Spain, as its many particular edicts of faith illustrate, took this power of censorship seriously. However, the Inquisition had the power not only to prohibit books but also to investigate, prosecute, and punish everyone who read, possessed, or distributed books on the index or had knowledge of them.[136] These powers granted the Mexican inquisitors a wide field of jurisdiction over intellectual pursuits, and throughout the later colonial period, the Mexican tribunal even attempted to go beyond its established limits by granting permissions and licenses to read prohibited books, a prerogative that belonged only to the Suprema or to direct papal review.[137]

In its edicts (e.g., document 9) and periodic communications with local regional commissaries (e.g., documents 50 and 51), the Inquisition often demanded that regional officials force their local citizens to catalog and submit lists of the books they owned, with the names of the authors, book titles, and date and place of publication. The Mexican Inquisition periodically issued edicts with lists of additional prohibited books to augment the general index.

The tribunal also required regional commissaries to conduct the important visitations of ships (*visitas de naos*) whenever a ship arrived at their port in order to ensure that no prohibited materials made their way into the colony.[138] One of the most onerous of duties of the nonsalaried commissaries, such visitations often involved days and sometimes even weeks of work. The local commissary and his appointed notary had to examine every piece of cargo on board. No other official, not even the royal judges, were permitted to open the crates or other merchandise until the Inquisition's commissaries had conducted their official visitation and taken their inventory.

Although a highly regulated and structured activity, the visitation of ships varied from region to region and often depended on the zeal of the local commissary.[139] On some occasions, even in the important port city of Veracruz, the local commissaries disobeyed the regulations and either conducted their visitations in a haphazard manner or remained lax in enforcing the index, "despite the clarity of the law and the theory of the Inquisition."[140] As the documents reproduced here illustrate, the Inquisition in New Spain had a difficult time enforcing the Index of Prohibited Books under the best of circumstances, even in the urban areas and regions under better surveillance.

DOCUMENT 51

Correspondence of the Commissary of the Holy Office of the Inquisition in the Province of Yucatan with the Inquisitors in the City of Mexico concerning Prohibited Books

Merida, Yucatan, 1574–1587

SOURCE: Archivo General de la Nación, Ramo de Inquisición, vol. 142, exp. 2.

NOTE: This series of exchanges between the inquisitors of New Spain and one of their local commissaries in the distant region of Yucatan is an example of the extent to which the Inquisition in Mexico kept in close contact with its regional commissaries concerning the catalogs and lists of prohibited books. The local commissaries often served as the most important agents in the Inquisition's attempt to create vigilance and control over the trade. They were required to actively seek out and order the confiscation of prohibited books in their own regions, a daunting task when most of these commissaries had no real coercive means to enforce their orders and edicts.

Letter from the Inquisitors of the Tribunal of the Holy Office in Mexico City to the Commissary of Yucatan, May 4, 1574

✝

Along with the old catalog of Prohibited Books that we have ordered published, it is necessary to publish the following listing that is included along with this letter. It is again necessary to prohibit and collect several small paintings and writings concerning the saints that were published in Holland. We order that, on a set Sunday, Your Lordship should publish this listing and require all Christians to denounce and hand over all copies of these books, especially the barbarous works of the Heretic Erasmus, along with other works such as *The Triumph of Petrarch* and any other of his works if they were not published in the printing house in Valladolid in the year 1541.

Also, concerning the amendments and changes to the Vocabulary of the Nahuatl language published by Fr. Alonso de Molina in Mexico City, your Lordship should only collect the books and amend one single word.[141] Once the word is fixed, you may return the books to their owners with the correction because the author, Fr. Alonso de Molina, was a good Catholic and lived an exemplary life and his book is a good book filled with healthy doctrine and very helpful and necessary for the Christian doctrine of the natives.

May Our Lord God guard your Lordship for many years!
Lic. Bonilla [Inquisitor]
Dr. Pedro Moya de Contreras [Inquisitor General]
Pedro de los Ríos [Secretary of the Holy Office]

Letter from the Commissary General of the Holy Office in the Province of Yucatan to the Inquisitors in Mexico City concerning Prohibited Books, April 27, 1587

On December 20, 1586, I received in the town of Mani a broadside from your Lordships the Inquisitors along with a commission concerning what I should do in the issue of the prohibited books. Afterward, on January 12, 1587, I received a second order from your Lordships in the city of Merida containing a listing and an index of prohibited books that your Lordships have recently purged. After receiving these orders I set about publishing the index here in the city of Merida as your Lordships ordered. I also set about collecting the prohibited books and burning them as your Lordships ordered secretly in the presence of a friar within the monastery of the order of Saint Francis in this city. I also ordered that the book *Pontifical History* be handed over and burned since it appeared to me that it was published before the year 1569 and that in that year it was on the Papal Index of Prohibited Books.

Knowing your Lordships' desire and zeal in purging these prohibited books, both Padre Bustemante and I occupied ourselves in seeking out and purging several other books, especially those that were contained in three important libraries in this province. I have issued an order that everyone, both secular and ecclesiastic, should make an inventory and list of the books that they have in their libraries, and the catalogs they make will be checked against the Index of Prohibited Books.

Also according to your Lordships orders, we are diligently going throughout the countryside and taking from the Indians all copies that they may have of the Holy Gospel and the Scriptures. As your Lordships ordered we are taking from the Indians all copies that they may have of the Holy Bible and reserving and restricting them to be held only by their parish ministers who administer the doctrine to them, and only they are allowed to own copies of the Holy Bible and only under your explicit license or that granted by any other Inquisitor in these Kingdoms.

Later, seeing that your Lordships also prohibited all of the Prayer books and other spiritual devotionaries that have been published in the Spanish language, we have gone among the Spaniards and mixed castes of this city and inquired about the existence of these volumes. I have collected a great number of them, and they too were burned secretly with the other prohibited books as ordered.

Only ten days ago, I received a letter from a parish priest in the distant province of Tabasco, Padre Gabriel de Rueda, along with all of the inventories and lists of the books held and owned in that province. After this arrived, Padre Bustamante and I examined them diligently to discover if any of the books were on the lists or the Index.

After I had received the most recent updated list of prohibited books, I issued orders and advised all of the preachers and parish priests in the towns and villages that they should announce and make the list and index known to all people so that they will denounce any prohibited books so they can be burned as well.

I swear that any of these prohibited books that we find will be gathered up, purged, and burned secretly as ordered.

May God be served to guard and keep your Lordships healthy and safe and may he grant you long lives.

I kiss the hands and feet of Your Lordships
Fray Hernando de Sopuerta
Commissary of the Holy Office
In the Province of Yucatan
April 27, 1587

DOCUMENT 52
Order and Information Given to the Commissaries of the Inquisition concerning Prohibited Books in the Kingdom of New Spain

Mexico City, September 22, 1587

SOURCE: Archivo General de la Nación, Ramo de Inquisición, vol. 140

NOTE: Once lists and catalogs of prohibited books arrived in New Spain, the Inquisition would issue new instructions such as in this document to ensure that the local Inquisition commissaries in the outlying provinces would remain vigilant and continue to censor prohibited books and pamphlets and encourage their collection and destruction.

†

Orders and Instructions concerning prohibited books that are to be purged by the Holy Office and which are believed to be owned by several Spaniards in these kingdoms. All of the Commissaries of our district and kingdoms should order this list published, and they should collect these books from any and all persons both ecclesiastic and secular. The following books should be included among those prohibited by the General Catalog and Index.

All types of books of prayers published in the Spanish language.

All types of prayer books, gospels, and spiritual devotionaries that are published by a named author or anonymously.

A treatise on the "Peace of the Soul" published by the author Fr. Juan de Bonilla of the Order of Saint Francis.[142]

The Devotionary or the book *Treasury of Devotions* compiled by Marco Antonio Ramírez and corrected by the reverend Father Fray Diego Hernández, the Reader of Sacred Theology of the Order of St. Bernard, which was printed in the printing house of Hernán Ramírez during the years 1584–85 and any and all other editions of this work.

The *Manual of Prayers*, translated into Spanish from the original Latin by Master Fr. Gerónimo de Campos and printed in Seville in the year 1580 and in the town of Alcala de Henares in the year 1584 and any other impression or printing of the book in any other common language. This same book is prohibited by the Catalog in Latin with the Title of *Enchiridion Piarum Precationum*, whose author is Simon Verrepeo.[143]

Another manual of *Prayers and Spiritual Exercises of the Christian Soul* taken from the Holy Scriptures and the early Church Fathers in Greek and Latin, composed by the same Fr. Gerónimo de Campos and printed in Madrid in the year 1585 and any and all copies in any language are prohibited.

Also prohibited is the book entitled, *A Bouquet of Spiritual Flowers*, whose author is Fray Pedro de Padilla, a Carmelite and this was published in Alcala in the year 1585 and also any other printing is forbidden.

Also especially prohibited are any of the letters or epistles of the Apostles in the Spanish language, either published by themselves or taken and published together as sermons or declarations of Catholic authors.

Also any and all copies of the Holy Gospel or Scriptures written and published in the vernacular Spanish language are prohibited, along with any and all books published in the Hebrew languages of the Jews, even though they are published without any of these sermons or epistles. Only parish priests may have these works under special licenses from the Holy Office.

Also prohibited is the work called *Pontifical History* composed by Dr. Gerónimo de Yllescas and printed before the year 1569, because any of the printings or published works of that year and after it are not forbidden.

This directory and Index of Prohibited Books was issued in this city of Mexico on September 22, 1587

By the Order of the Holy Office

Pedro de los Ríos [Secretary of the Holy Office]

DOCUMENT 53

Documents Pertaining to Licenciado Don Manuel Abad Queipo's Petition to Request a License to Read Prohibited Books

Valladolid (now Morelia), Michoacan, 1796

SOURCE: Archivo General de la Nación, Ramo de Inquisición, vol. 1094.

NOTE: In this document, a clergyman requests permission from his local tribunal to have a license to read prohibited books. The petitioner, born in Spain about 1760, came to Mexico the year before this petition (about 1795), and as governor of the bishopric of Michoacan during the beginning of the strife for independence, he became noted for his violent measures and publications against the patriots. He was later to write several historical publications concerning the Miguel Hidalgo revolt. He wrote "Edicto instructivo sobre la revolución del Cura de los Dolores y sus Secuaces" (México, 1810); "Carta Pastoral sobre la Insurrección de los Pueblos del Obispado de Michoacán" (1811); and "Carta Pastoral sobre el riesgo que amenaza la Insurrección de Michoacán a la Libertad y a la Religión" (1813). Apparently he was never given the license to read prohibited books. In Spain in 1815 he ran into trouble with the Inquisition for reading prohibited books and opposing the Inquisition's procedures concerning the purging of books.

Letter from Don Manuel Abad Queipo, Visiting Judge and Provisor of the Bishopric of Michoacan Requesting a License to Read Prohibited Books, February 11, 1796

†

Illustrious Lord,

Licenciado Don Manual Abad Queipo, cleric, forty-four years old, Visiting Judge Ordinary of wills, chaplaincies, and pious works in this bishopric of Michoacan, and Interim Provisor in the same bishopric, before Your Illustrious Lordship in all due course, I state that for reasons of my priestly ministry, and my referred to employments, there are offered and will be offered occasions when I must impugn at least in word against false, erroneous, and dangerous doctrines that are contained in the books that are prohibited from the community of the faithful by the Holy Tribunal of Faith. In order to better execute my duty by necessary instructions either by word or in writing, as may be demanded by occurring circumstances, it is convenient and even necessary that I be able to read with reflection these said books. In this knowledge, I humbly request Your Illustrious Lordship to concede to me the necessary license to read and retain prohibited books with all the ample powers of the highest degree, based on the knowledge that you have concerning my person, age, and conduct.

For this reason, I request and petition that you grant this request based on my merits, and I swear that I do not request this with malice, but rather out of what is necessary, & etc.

Licenciado Manual Abad Queipo

Letter to Don Antonio Bergosa concerning Prohibited Books, February 6, 1796[144]

†

My Dear Antonio:

Someone recently gave me as a gift the *Ecclesiastical History* of Racine,[145] and having begun to read it, someone told me that he believed that it was prohibited, and I told him that it did not seem out of the ordinary, and it appeared to me that it was very pure in its doctrine concerning dogma. After this someone else told me (a very passionate supporter of the Jesuits) that Racine was a Jansenist, and with this I went to look him up in the biographical pieces in the *Dictionary of Illustrious Men,* and he appeared to be good, but apparently he was very prejudiced against the Jesuits. Due to this circumstance and the justification of the work that I discovered at the end of it, it seemed to me that there was no such prohibition, and I continued to read it until I reached the end of the fifth century where I left off reading it because the Jesuit supporter assured me that it was effectively a prohibited book. With this motive, and on the basis of others that may arise, I determined to put forward a petition to read prohibited books, which is added to this letter, requesting that the Inquisition favor me with sending forward my petition if there is nothing inconvenient in it.

Also, last Tuesday evening at night I had an accident and had a bad case of stomachache and flatulence, but God was served to shorten it later by means of an enema. I was remedied by it, thank God.

I celebrate in the fact that Your Mercy is in good health and your most appreciated friend sends you his best wishes

Manuel Abad

Opinion of the Holy Office concerning This Issue of Prohibited Books, February 11, 1796

†

The Lord Inquisitors Mier, Bergosa, and Prado answer this individual and order him to hand over this *History* by Racine to the local Commissary of the Holy Office in that city, and we order that His Excellency Lord Inquisitor General be informed and requested to respond to what is most convenient concerning this ecclesiastic, sending him the accompanying testimony and the petition where he requests the privilege.

Inquisitor Mier
Inquisitor Bergosa
Inquisitor Prado

DOCUMENT 54
Documents and Papers concerning Several Printed Cloths or Handkerchiefs Remitted to This Holy Office by the Chief Constable of the City of Veracruz Which Contain Inscriptions in the English Language

Veracruz, 1775

SOURCE: Archivo General de la Nación, Ramo de Inquisición, vol. 1170, exp. 25.

NOTE: The index and the Holy Office prohibited not only books and pamphlets but also all other types of drawings, paintings, and other printed material that may have contained heretical beliefs, statements, or other errors against the faith. In this interesting 1775 case involving several large cloths or handkerchiefs, we see the extent to which the Holy Office attempted to control what was read and distributed to the people of New Spain. One surviving copy of this printed handkerchief is held by the collections of Colonial Williamsburg in Virginia.[146]

Letter from Manual Arroyo, the Chief Constable of the City of Veracruz, August 11, 1775

✝

Very Illustrious Lord,

In complying with my obligation and out of the zeal that I have exercised, I have discovered the enclosed printed cloth or handkerchief along with four others that remain in my power which have come to be shown to this Commissariat here by me. Because they contain what appears to be sacred history and because their examination touches upon Your Illustrious Lordships whose opinion is needed, I remit this to you in the disposition of the said Commissary. And if in any part of this I have erred, I await the just correction of Your Lordships, which I may deserve, as well as any advice on what I should do with the other ones that are still in my power.

May God Our Lord guard Your Lordships many years.
Signed in Veracruz, August 11, 1775

Manuel Arroyo
Alguacil Mayor

(Received September 5, 1775)

Response and Order of the Inquisitors of the Holy Office, September 5, 1775

✝

Respond to this minister that what he has done was done well, and order him to retain the other handkerchiefs until he receives further orders. And with respect to the writing and printing, seeing that Dr. García Bravo is competent in the English language, place the handkerchief in his care so that he can translate what is written on them and what he may find there.

The Inquisitors

At the same time, what their Lordships ordered was executed.

Order from the Tribunal of the Holy Office to Dr. Don Joseph García
Bravo, Ordering Him to Translate the Text of the Enclosed Handkerchief
and Its Drawings, September 5, 1775

✝

By Order of the Tribunal of the Holy Office, we send Your Mercy the enclosed handkerchief so that at the bottom and continuation of this you should write and explain your
opinion concerning the meaning of all of the figures and text, and translate all of the
stamped inscriptions into Spanish, dividing them into sections based on their respective
medallions. All of this, the Tribunal wishes you to conduct with exactitude and brevity.

May God Guard Your Mercy for many Years.
Signed in the Chamber of the Secret of this Inquisition of Mexico on September 9, 1775

Don Juan Nicolás Abad, Secretary

Certified Translation and Opinion of Dr. Joseph García Bravo concerning
the Text and Images of the Remitted Handkerchief, September 18, 1775

✝

Illustrious Lord,

We have examined, in compliance with the superior order of Your Illustrious Lordship, the handkerchief that you have remitted and I find the following.

That the principal idea in general is reduced to what is indicated in the rounded border that it has placed above in big characters, or INDUSTRY AND IDLENESS REWARDED or
what appear to be various types of recompense that waits for one or the other. This handkerchief intends to show this through various figures and symbols distributed all around
the handkerchief. In all of this I advise you there is a strange mixture of the sacred and the
ridiculous, presupposing the uniformity of all peoples who understand them.

At first in the middle there is someone who appears to be sleeping with a pen in his
hand, and several papers or fallen books all around, among them the Holy Bible. The figure
that is placed behind him, without a doubt, must symbolize sleep, or tiredness. In front of
him stands an angel, leading a child to a building that is uncovered, perhaps it is a temple.

In the part above this there is a beehive and several bees, and these words: *Frugality
and Industry are the hands of Fortune* and below these *Run from Idleness, which is a cancer, or
corruption of all things good, such as health, wealth, honor, and the arts.*

Based on the order of the medallions that occupy the entire surface of the handkerchief, as Your Lordships ordered, I will distinguish them by numbers, commencing with
the one that is in the top left hand side of handkerchief of the viewer.

1. A loom with a man working, and on the other opposing side someone sitting down in
   idleness, both of whom are referred to in the inscription which below reads: *The Good*

and Bad Worker at work and below this a small caption on the wall that reads *Good and Bad,* and in the smaller box *Industry is the servant of fortune; while the idle one is covered in rags.*

2. A man who is about to attack another man who is lying down with a sword. The surrounding rounded border reads *Johnny the lazy boy wastes away the Sabbath.* And in the text box *No Good comes from idleness, and by wasting away a Sabbath other evil things can come.*

3. A man kneeling down, who is reading prayers in a book and behind him other smaller figures that represent the same thing. The rounded border reads *William, the good child in church.* And in the text box below *Teach me Lord your wisdom and knowledge so that I can obey your commandments.*

4. Three men in a boat, and the man in the middle is apparently threatening the man at the end of the boat with a noose, which reveals behind it in the distance the inscription *The evil servant who goes to sea.* And below it *The wise one will inherit substance, but shame and infamy are all that the stubborn will receive.*

5. Two men who appear to be making accounts, as the books appear to signify, along with the boxes and crates of merchandise. The inscription reads *The faithful servant rewarded by his Master.* And below *You have been faithful above all things, and I give you the government and direction of much more.*

6. Two people in a bed, jumping out of bed because of a shield that they perceived has fallen, knocked over by a jumping cat. The rounded border reads: *Johnny the idle one wakens frightfully from sleep.* And in the box *The sound of a leaf falling can frighten him.*

7. This image represents a marriage ceremony, and in the border it reads: *William the good, or the good boy, marries the daughter of his Master.* And below *Your Wife will be like the fertile vine on the walls of your house, and your children like olive branches around your table.*

8. Various persons, some with hatchets in their hands, and others with other things such as coins that they display denoting what the inscription says: *Johnny the idle one, imprisoned for a robbery.* And in the box *Because his feet take him to evil, and they pressure him to spill blood.*

9. A man with a staff of justice, and a paper in his hand, and another one there appearing as a supplicant with the inscription: *William the good child, elected Mayor of London.*[147] And below *Lucky is the one who gains a recompense for a good deed, so as to put in their place and silence the ignorance of stubborn men.*

10. An act of justice appears in which a man appears as a prisoner with his accusers who present him with the instruments of his crime. The inscription reads: *Johnny the idle one, turned over as a prisoner by his companion.* And below *You do not respect nor look upon persons in judgment, but rather you will punish those who have left behind the road of justice.*

11. A man dressed in a mantle, who carries another one, heading for a government house. The inscription reads: *Yours are the riches and honor, and in your hand you hold the power of justice and good judgment* and above this *William the good boy enters into his government.*

12. An image of a prisoner being led away in a cart and one of the ministers of justice is exhorting against him. The inscription reads: *Johnny the condemned goes to his final end.* And in the box *You fell out of your own iniquities.*

In all of these, as I perceive them, the object or idea is to make known the parable in the Gospels of the two servants, and this is done by using the images, the texts, and the Holy Scriptures all placed in English, and taken out of the Bible, and out of the book of Psalms, and from other learned books. And this is what I have to state as my opinion as to the meaning of them all as ordered by superior order of Your Lordships.

September 18, 1775

Josef García Bravo

Order of the Inquisitors of the Holy Office to the Lord Qualifiers of this Holy Office, Fr. Francisco Larrea, and Fray Nicolás Troncoso, to Review and Decide upon the Contents and Merits of the Case, Qualifying It in Order to Proceed, October 11, 1775

✝

By Order of the Tribunal of the Holy Office, we send Your Reverend Fathers the enclosed handkerchief along with its description that accompanies the figures and characters, so that once you have studied it, you can give your opinions concerning its context with respect to the rules of the Index, the *Expurgatorio,* and the Edicts.

May God Guard Your Reverend Fathers for many Years.

Signed in the Chamber of the Secret of this Inquisition of Mexico on October 11, 1775

Don Juan Nicolás Abad, Secretary

Certified Opinion of the Qualifiers of the Holy Office concerning the Text and Images of the Remitted Handkerchief, October 15, 1775

✝

Having understood and received the superior order that appears before this document, we have examined and read with reflection on the description of the figures and medallions that are stamped and printed on the handkerchief. The object of the present examination, following the rules and regulations concerning prohibited things in the *Expurgatorio,* is the qualification of what appears to be represented by the symbols, as well as their meaning that has been translated. Taken all into account, we must together uniformly state that the printing and stamped symbols in these medallions are of their entirety prohibited based on the eleventh Rule of the mentioned *Expurgatorio,* as being parodies of sacred figures, regardless of the texts in the writing, and by this reason great inconveniences could occur that could cause irreverence. We are of the opinion that the said handkerchiefs should be collected and erased of their printing. Also the sixteenth rule is even more explicit in this individual case, because it says that all words in foreign languages should be purged.

This is our opinion and qualification in this case as ordered.

Dr. Francisco Larrea   Fr. Nicolás Troncoso

Decree and Order of the Holy Office of the Inquisition concerning the Printed English Handkerchiefs, October 19, 1775

✝

We inform our Commissary in Veracruz that in a letter dated August 11, 1775, the Chief Constable of Veracruz, Don Manuel de Arroyo, remitted to us a printed handkerchief that he stated appeared to have images and inscriptions on it that were sacred stories, informing us that four other similar handkerchiefs remained in his power. And having seen it and examined it, we have found that its representations are not of sacred things, but regardless of this, we have decided to prohibit it because in many parts of its inscriptions there are sections taken from the Holy Scriptures applied to profane things, and they are printed and stamped in an indecent manner considering its use. In consequence of this, we order that Our Commissary once he has received this order should go and collect the other four handkerchiefs, and all others he may find like them, which may have similar inscriptions. And he should order them to be prohibited and consider them prohibited, and he should try to discover who is their owner, in order to receive his testimony concerning the original number of them, and how many he may have sold or given away, and to whom, so that we can better commence with their collection. He should give notice of this.

Regardless of their provenience, which is important to be known, if the owner of the said handkerchiefs did not proceed in malice (as it is presumed), we offer the chance that if the inscriptions and the Angel in the center can be erased by the means of washing them so that they do not reappear, then you may concede to them that they may keep them, making them understand the benign nature of the Holy Office, under the qualification that they will have to show them again to the commissary, who should order that the test of washing them should be made. If what had been erased by washing it should not reappear, they can have them returned to them. And in the contrary case, that they cannot be erased by washing them, then they should be collected and burned and a certification of all of this should be returned to us.

May God Guard Our Commissary.
Signed in the Audience of the Inquisition of Mexico, October 19, 1775

Dr. Don Manuel Ruiz de Vallejo
Licenciado Don Nicolás Galante y Saavedra
Inquisitors

By order of this Holy Office
Don Juan Nicolás Abad, Secretary

Testimony of Ángel de Cires, Merchant in Veracruz before the Commissary of the Inquisition, October 30, 1775

✝

In the city of Veracruz, on the 30th of October 1775, in the morning before the Lord Commissary Don Miguel Francisco de Herrera, there appeared having been called and sworn in due form, a man who said he was called Ángel de Cires, native of the province of Leon, twenty-nine years old, a single resident of this city and for the past seven years by profession a Merchant.

Asked if he knew or presumed the reason why he was called.

He said that he presumed that it was in order to answer for several handkerchiefs made of linen that the Chief Constable of the Holy Office took from him that contained sacred things.

He was asked from whom he bought the said handkerchiefs, and how many of them were there.

He said that he bought them from a man named Cueto Viafante, who came from Havana, and whom he believes today lives in Cadiz, who brought piecemeal twenty-three of the said handkerchiefs, which were purchased between himself and Don Ventura Urisar, a resident and merchant of this city. Out of the thirteen that he bought, he sold two of them to someone who took them to Mexico City, and another one to Don Miguel de Tocano, Chief Magistrate of Cosamaluapan, and the seven left over handkerchiefs he sold to another man named Foro, a resident of *Barlovento*,[148] but he does not know where.

He was told that out of the mercy and benign nature of the Holy Office, he may consider still using them if he is able to discover some way of erasing the text and the Angel that is in the middle, either by washing them, or by some other means.

He responded that he knew of no other way than to throw them into the fire because the colors and ink were very permanent, and that he was glad to do so and he wished he had all of the others in his power so that he could turn them over to the Holy Office.

And this is the truth under the oath that he has taken. Having read him his statement he said that it was well written, and he swore to keep the secret, and signed it with his name.

Ángel de Cires
Don Miguel Francisco de Herrera, Commissary

This passed before me,
Fr. Agustin de Burgos
Notary of the Holy Office

Testimony of Don Ventura Urisar, Merchant in Veracruz before the Commissary of the Inquisition, October 30, 1775

✝

In the city of Veracruz, on the 30th of October 1755, in the afternoon before the Lord Commissary Don Miguel Francisco de Herrera, there appeared having been called and sworn in due form, a man who said he was called Don Ventura Urisar, a single native of Venes in the kingdom of Biscay, merchant in this city for more than nineteen years, who said he was thirty-five years old.

Asked if he knew or presumed the reason why he was called.

He said that did not know.

He was asked if he knew or remembered dealing with someone called Cueto during the previous months who had brought some goods from the city of Havana,[149] and to state what goods he may have bought from him.

He said that it is the truth that from this man named Cueto, whom he knew only from his last name, he bought in the company of Don Ángel de Cires, another merchant from this city, twenty-six handkerchiefs and they divided them, each receiving thirteen of them.

He was asked how many of these handkerchiefs were still in his power.

He said that none of them were left to him because a woman from *Barlovento*, who came into his shop, bought them all so that she could take them to her land, and he does not know from where she came, nor does he know her name.

And this is the truth under the oath that he has taken. Having read him his statement he said that it was well written, and he swore to keep the secret, and signed it with his name.

Ventura de Urisar
Don Miguel Francisco de Herrera, Commissary

This passed before me,
Fr. Agustín de Burgos
Notary of the Holy Office

Certification of the Notary of the Holy Office of the Intent to Wash the Handkerchiefs to Erase Them, October 30, 1775

†

I certify that having made the experiment of washing the handkerchiefs in water we were still not able to erase the text, nor the images of the Guardian Angel that they have painted on them. Instead we burned them all in obedience of the order of the Holy Office, and I give this in testimony and so that it should be confirmed, I sign it this day 30th of October 1775

Fr. Agustín de Burgos
Notary of the Holy Office

Letter from the Local Commissary of the Inquisition in Veracruz, Br. Miguel Francisco Herrera, concerning the Orders Dealing with the Said Handkerchiefs, October 30, 1775

✝

In obedience of the decree dated the 19th of October 1775, which included the diligences and documents conducted in this case, I have recognized that the subjects in this case proceeded without malice in the purchase and sale of these said handkerchiefs, and because we have not been able to erase the writing with the benefit of washing them in water, we have burned them all in the flames, by means of which we have complied with the tenor of the said decree.

> May God Our Lord guard Your Lordship for many years.
> Signed in Veracruz, October 30, 1775
> Miguel Francisco de Herrera, Commissary of Veracruz

(Received in the Tribunal, November 5, 1775)

DOCUMENT 55
Documents Relating to the Petition of the Surgeon and Doctor Don Anacleto Rodríguez Requesting Permission to Read Prohibited Books

Veracruz, March–April 1799

SOURCE: Archivo General de la Nación, Ramo de Inquisición, vol. 1094, exp. 6.

NOTE: Many clergy and other scholars in the New World often petitioned the local tribunal of New Spain for permission or license to read prohibited books, but all of their petitions were merely forwarded to the Suprema with a brief opinion from the local tribunal concerning the request. In this document, one of the young professors of medicine at the naval hospital at Veracruz in Mexico requests permission to read prohibited books from the tribunal. The response is not what the professor had hoped to receive, and eventually he abandons his attempt.

Letter and Petition by Don Anacleto Rodríguez Requesting a License to Read Prohibited Books, March 9, 1799

✝

Don Anacleto Rodríguez, native of the village of Estepa in the kingdom of Seville, *bachiller* and second Professor of surgery and medicine of the Royal Navy and its hospital here at this city, before Your Lordship with respect I state that I am desirous to contribute to the defense of the Faith and the propagation of the Catholic Religion, and therefore I request Your Lordship to deign to concede to me the title as a Familiar, a privilege that I hope to merit from your Lordship, and in that capacity I will apply myself until I have exhausted all of my forces.

Also, desirous of making progress in my profession, I request Your Lordship concede to me the privilege to read and have in my power the prohibited books in all languages, especially in French, which deal with my profession as well as all of the auxiliary sciences attached to it, and I protest and swear to subject myself to the will of Your Lordship, and credit that my soul is righteous and Christian and that I will die as such.

I request and petition Your Lordship to concede to me the privileges that I request.

May your Lordship live perpetually
Anacleto Rodríguez

Letter from the Commissary of the Inquisition in Veracruz, Don Ignacio José Ximénez, to the Inquisitors in the Tribunal of Mexico, March 29, 1799

✝

Your Lordship,

Along with this letter, I send an accompanying memorial from Br. Don Anacleto Rodríguez, a medical surgeon of the Navy, who is presently stationed in this city, who based on information solicited from the secular town council appears to be of good conduct and known virtue. He has requested from this commissariat of the Holy Office that Your Lordships should see to it to grant his petition and concede him a license to read prohibited books, especially those that deal with his profession and duties. I can attest to the fact that having dealt with him somewhat face to face I believe I recognize in him a solid and virtuous person, who wishes to excel in his profession, not out of vanity but to improve his talents to help humbly and with charity all those who have need of his services. I also believe that he shows the moderation that makes all of his merits relevant and sets him apart from his colleagues and fellow associates in general. And this is all that I can state for your Lordships.

May the God Our Lord guard you for many years.
Signed in Veracruz, March 9, 1799

I kiss the hands of Your Illustrious Lordships
Ignacio José Ximénez, Commissary of the Holy Office

Response and Order to the Commissary from the Lord Inquisitors of the Tribunal of Mexico, April 3, 1799

✝

Illustrious Lord,

Give this answer and order to the Commissary, stating that concerning the license to read prohibited books that is solicited by the petitioner, that it is not in the powers of this

Tribunal to concede any such license, and that only the Lord Inquisitor General has the private power to concede any such license. Let the petitioner know that he can request the said license by means of a formal request. As for that which concerns the petitioner's request to be named a familiar, in respect to his office in the Navy it is possible that he may be exposed to being transferred, we request that the Commissary investigate the matter of his stationing in Veracruz, and if he will be permanently stationed there, and if he has the competent abilities and decency and corresponding character of the ministry and office of Familiar, then in that case he may begin to inquire into the proofs of his merits within two years.

Inquisitor Mier

Inquisitor Bergosa

Juan Antonio Ibarra, Secretary

Letter and Response from the Commissary of the Inquisition in Veracruz, Don Ignacio José Ximénez, concerning the Petitions of Don Anacleto Rodríguez, April 10, 1799

✝

Your Lordship,

As a consequence of what has been issued by superior order of their Lordships, I made it known to Don Anacleto Rodríguez the orders concerning his petition for a license to read prohibited books. Concerning his tenure and presence in this city, I have to state that even though it has been my experience that others who have been stationed in this city in similar circumstances and in similar positions have not left the city except under their own wishes and at their own will, but they were always exposed, as is this petitioner, to the possibility that they may be ordered to move to another Port, or enter into the service of some Ship that may have need of them. I must also add that Don Anacleto Rodríguez has become frustrated as he remembers the French *Encyclopedia* and the *Natural History* written by the Count Buffon that he studied in his college, and he has insinuated that he will suspend any further petition.

May God Our Lord guard Your Lordships many years.

Signed in Veracruz, April 10, 1799.

Ygnacio José Ximénez

Commissary of the Holy Office in Veracruz

DOCUMENT 56

License to Read Prohibited Books Issued to Don Josef García Armenteros, Consul of the Royal Merchant Guild of the Philippines and Royal Historian, so That He May Acquire, Have, and Read All Books concerning Political and Natural History Forbidden by the Holy Office

Madrid, October 5, 1799

SOURCE: Archivo General de la Nación, Ramo de Inquisición, vol. 1314, exp. 21.

NOTE: Although it was done rarely, the inquisitor general of Spain did have permission and the ability to grant, on a limited basis, licenses permitting clerics, scholars, and other Christians with good reasons to read prohibited books. As seen in this document, usually the license was granted to permit the reading of only certain classes or types of books, such as in this case natural and political histories. No blanket waivers or licenses to read all prohibited books were ever given. Similarly, no license could be issued by the local tribunals of the Inquisition; instead, only by direct appeal and response from the inquisitor general in Spain could a petition be granted. Many clergy and other scholars in the New World often petitioned the local tribunal of New Spain for this permission or license, but all of their petitions were merely forwarded with a brief opinion from the local tribunal concerning the request.

✝

We, Don Ramón Josef de Arce, by the Grace of God and the Holy Apostolic See, Archbishop of Burgos and Inquisitor General in all of the Kingdoms and Districts of His Most Catholic Majesty, Knight of the Great Cross of the Royal Spanish Order of Charles III, member of the Council of his Majesty & etc.

By means of the present document and the apostolic authority conceded to us, which we use on our behalf, we give our license and abilities to You, Don Josef García Armenteros, Consul of the Royal Merchant Guild of the Philippines, so that you can acquire, have, and read all of the books of political and natural History that are prohibited by the Holy Office, which ever ones that you deem necessary in your conscience, so that you may continue and conclude the work that you are conducting in writing the manuscript that you are writing for the benefit of the natives of the Islands of the Philippines, and their state. And we entrust that you will present this license before you use it to the Tribunal of the Inquisition in Mexico, to whose prudence and judgment we will leave it either to hand it back to you or to withhold it, if they do not believe that you are filled with the required capacity to promise to make a good Christian use of these prohibited books. All of the books that you will have in your good custody you should reserve so that they do not arrive in the hands of any other person. All of these prohibited books should be handed over to the said Tribunal or to any local minister of the Holy Office upon your death, which will prevent any damage upon the consciences of your heirs or those who deal with your last will and testament.

Given in Madrid, on October 5, 1799

Ramón Joseph Archbishop of Burgos, Inquisitor General

By order of His Excellency
Licenciado Josef Ortiz de Solórzano. Secretary

DOCUMENT 57
Self-Denunciation of Don José Ignacio Sánchez concerning His Support for the Miguel Hidalgo Revolt
Mexico City, April 19, 1811

SOURCE: Archivo General de la Nación, Ramo de Inquisición, vol. 416.

NOTE: This self-denunciation provides details concerning daily life and common late colonial opinions concerning the Inquisition and its edicts, especially those aimed against the insurgents led by Father Miguel Hidalgo. This document also shows that news and speculation were widespread during the period of the Hidalgo insurrection and that Padre Hidalgo apparently received support from members of all walks of life.

†

In the oratory of Saint Felipe Nerí of Mexico, at seven o'clock at night before the Presbítero Don José Antonio Tirado y Priego, Presbítero of the said oratory and Commissary of the Holy Office of the Inquisition in this Court, and before me, Doctor Don Juan Bautista Díaz Calvillo, Presbítero of the cited congregation, named Notary for this diligence: There appeared without having been called a person who swore before Our Lord God and the Holy Cross to say the truth and guard the secret in that which he would be asked concerning his name, age, quality, state and employment.-

He said that his name was Don José Ignacio Sánchez, forty years old, a single Spaniard without occupation; residing at the street of Los Bajos de San Augustín, number 4.

He was asked why he wanted this audience.

He said that he wanted to denounce himself before the Holy Office, for having been a partisan of the present insurrection according to the following terms:

1. At the beginning he aided the insurrection thinking it to be just and necessary.
2. He begged God for its happy success in his private prayers, and he even asked others with whom he shared news to do the same.
3. He even criticized the proclamations of the Archbishop and Viceroy.

He said that his father, Don Matías Sánchez, having heard what was contained in the Edict of the Holy Office of October 13 (see document 11), responded something uncomfortable, saying that what it said about the Padre Hidalgo was slanderous and a supposition. He also talked with several other individuals, arguing that the Lord Bishop of Valladolid[150] had no power, for he was not consecrated.

Later, this witness had heard two other edicts that were promulgated one day, exactly which one he does not know, but he does remember that they were from the Lord Archbishop, and they made him change his concept of the situation entirely, for which he had a discussion one Sunday with Don Ignacio Fernández, now deceased, one of the subjects with whom he had spoken about the affairs of that period.

He stated that he had said to Fernández that Padre Hidalgo was supposedly a heretic, and he declared himself his enemy and opponent, and he protested saying that he would speak no more about such matters. The said [Ignacio] Fernández responded, "*Does Your Mercy, my namesake, believe that everyone has told me the same,*" and then "*No, it is stupid to get involved?*" However, at that time, Don Félix de la Campa Coz, a tobacco employee entered the room and this witness silenced himself fearing that another person would hear this discussion, for this said Campa Coz had a loose tongue and he would reveal it to everyone. The said Campa Coz asked about any new occurrences or news, and since the witness cannot remember if Fernández was present, because he was Master of the pharmacy on the corner of *Los Medinas* street and the merchants distracted him many times from his conversations, he told him about the news concerning the Insurgents. Passing on to (talking about) the edicts, Campa Coz dissuaded this witness in his modes of thinking that he had formed on that day, telling him that the contents of the edicts were lies or suppositions, and even in its literal sense he declared it slanderous, adding "*How Hidalgo had said that one of the Popes whom they venerate in the altars is in hell, contradicting himself and as a consequence negating that there even is a hell. We should not believe anything, for Hidalgo is a very devoted Catholic, and everyone knows this.*" Furthermore, with these expressions, this witness remained hesitant, and he believed that at least that which was denounced before the Holy Office was slander, consequently blaming the Holy Office for not having punished Hidalgo, supposing that he was heretic during the period of ten years in which he had been denounced.

Furthermore, on the Monday after this conversation, this witness being with Don Vicente Rodríguez, a merchant of the *Parián*[151]—to whose dry goods store he went every day to give him the latest news—talked about the edict, which it appeared that Rodríguez had not read. This witness then presented the same objections to Rodríguez that he had said before Campa Coz with which Rodríguez persuaded himself to the same opinion.

Then this witness continued in his daily visits to the said dry goods store until the beginning of December, and they both reservedly discussed these matters even in front of Rodríguez's youngest son-named Don Manuel, focusing on the news of the insurrection that several people used to bring them.

He stated that several people used to bring them news such as one crippled man named Romero and a deaf womanizer from Oaxaca whose name this witness ignored. They all criticized the edict (of the Holy Office), declaring themselves to be partisans of the insurrection. Also on these occasions Don José Gil de Rosas used to be present, but he is a kindhearted man, and he did not go to denounce the conversations believing that there was nothing that merited excommunication.

The witness said that from this dry goods store he went on to the store of Don Agustín Alcalá, in the same Parián market in which one Don Salvador Marengo, Alférez of the Militia frequented, and the three of them were talking together in the company of a merchant named Don Manuel Miranda. He stated that they were speaking about the state of things, and they desired a happy outcome, and they all scorned the Edict, criticizing it and then later forgetting about it. They openly talked about and desired the conclusion of the rebellion against the Europeans.

He also stated that during the night, this witness went to Indio Triste street to the house of Licenciado Don Ignacio Espinosa, even though the Licenciado was never at home at that hour, but on occasions others were there, including the Licenciado's father don Ramón, another relative, his sister Doña Maríana Espinosa, a young lawyer who recently passed his comprehensive exam, and one of this witnesses' aunts named Doña Pascuala Sánchez, as well as one of his cousins named Doña Magdalena Sánchez. During these visits this witness tried to persuade the women who were fearful that they should not be afraid, for the insurgents were not going to harm anyone and that they came to favor the creoles. These said women sometimes were consoled by his words, and other times they were saddened by them. The men supported the sedition as a good thing.

The witness also declares that at other hours of the day and night he went to the cited Bótica, in which there used to also go a man named "el Güero" whose first and last name the witness ignored. On one or two other occasions Don Ignacio Cisneros (owner of a *hojalateria* in front of the gates of this oratory) met with them. On another three or four occasions a Pharmacist named Laguna met with them. All of them made mention of other individuals who had acquired other news and information. They were happy with the exploits of the insurgents.

Also, on another three occasions a colleague of the witness from the College of San lldefonso named Llano, met with them, and he loaned the witness an extract of the *Rendición de Zamora,* which contained an image of one Huidoro, Field Marshall of the American (Insurgent) army of the Ayuntamiento of the said town of Zamora. The witness took a copy of this and gave it to Don Agustín Alcalá.

Also he states that in the doorway of the Mercaderes at night there gathered a man who had declared himself with the name of Licenciado Don Vicente whose last name the witness ignored (but he was the man who helped with the dispatch to the Lord Prosecutor Robledo, and he lives in his lower apartments). This man gathered with a scribe of the lawyer named Dávalos, who lived near San Pablo, and these two met with this witness and on two or three other occasions with one of their acquaintances (the witness did not remember his name, though he knew him by sight). They spoke openly in the same doorway about the news, rejoicing over those who favored the insurrection, and feeling the contrary for those American partisans (creoles) of the Europeans whom they spoke against.

Also he declares that on several nights he went to the house of one of his uncles named Don Francisco Sánchez, at #12 Calle de los Donceles, and in the presence of his aunt Doña Josefa Villagran and their daughters Doña Gregoria and Doña María Loreto and their sons Don Pablo and Don Fernando Sánchez, the witness tried to reassure them not to have fear of the insurgents, because they would not do anything to them. On four occasions the witness discussed with the said Don Francisco, his uncle, the matter of the insurrection with indifference, one time telling him that he had read several broadsides of the battle of Calderón made in Guadalajara, the same broadsides that this witness declared having read.

He stated that on several other nights he went to the house of his sister, named Doña Gregoria Sánchez (who is married to Don José Jiménez Casarín), located in front of the doorway or gate number 3. On these occasions the witness told the news of the insurrection to his sister and her mother-in-law, Doña Ana Cruz, whose conversations were reduced to speaking badly of the Europeans and feeling pains at the deaths of the insurgents, for by this means they made themselves partisans of the insurgents.

Also, in the street he had discussions on two or three occasions with a certain Quijano, who is married to Doña María Cerendieta and is employed in the Secretariat of the Viceroyalty, and their conversations were reduced to satirizing the government because of their hatred of it, and supporting the insurrection.

Similarly, on two or three other occasions the witness conversed with Don Ignacio Cubas, another employee of the same Secretariat, who lives on the corner of the calle Las Cocheras, with whom the witness poured out his heart since the said Cubas shared his same means of thinking and his opinions.

The witness also states that on another night he met with Don Manuel de la Torre, a merchant from the Parián, and he told him about the actions of the insurgents extolling them as good and just in punishment of the Europeans for their sins.

In a shop near the front of the Gate of Santa Clara, the witness was present daily, conversing with several people, including the owner of the shop, Don Cristóbal Orozco, now deceased, one Romero (a confectioner near the Mail office), a salesman whose name and address he ignored, a corporal or sergeant of the Mexico City Militia (who he also did not know), one Mansilla (a member of the Franciscan Third Order), a medicinal curer (he ignored his name), and an Indian painter, owner of a office on the calle de Vergara. They all met, giving the most recent news, speaking against the Europeans, and rejoicing at the advantages of the insurgents. This witness, afraid of them because he did not know them well, refused to speak, only adding an occasional flourish.

He declares that on one or two occasions, a religious of the Mercedarian order named Fr. José Huerta met with them at the watchmaker's shop, though his conversations were a little indifferent.

The witness also denounces that in his own house, in front of his father and his sister Doña Josefa Sánchez and sometimes in the company of her husband Don Francisco de la Colina, he had spoken about the insurrection, and he saw them filled with passion by it.

On another afternoon, in the company of Don Salvador Marengo, cited above, the witness went to see a cleric from Valladolid, who according to Marengo was being tried by the government (though he ignored his name). The cleric was staying in front of the Casa de Moneda in the house of a Mayorazgo (which appeared to him to be that of Moctezuma), the said ecclesiastic came down the stairway to converse with Marengo, who brought him the news that the insurgents had entered Valladolid, to which the said cleric showed great joy saying that "*That is how it should happen in all of the places in the Kingdom and in Mexico City too!*" To this Marengo answered "*Amen!*"

On another afternoon the same Marengo brought this witness to speak to, several "good patriots" (the name that they both gave to the partisans of the insurrection) on the comer of the las calles segunda de San Ramón, Calle de Ortega, and the callejón de Santa Clara. However, none of these subjects were present in their own homes, and they did not know the witness.

He also denounces that in the end of January or the beginning of February, with the motive of having a small house appraised, the witness went to see Don José del Mazo, Master of public works of this noble city, who lived on the bridge of the old customshouse in front of the Pharmacy of San Gerónimo. As the said Mazo made the appraisal, they spoke about new occurrences, and Mazo asked him if he had examined the Edict of the Holy Office (which was published on January 28), and this witness responded no. Mazo then took out a proclamation of Hidalgo, published in Guadalajara, which had been publicly burned by the superior government and prohibited under the punishment of excommunication by the said Edict. Mazo read it to this witness, and after this the said Mazo gave him several broadsides about the battle of Calderón to read (the same ones mentioned above), which mentioned the heroic deeds done by various insurgents among them, according to his memory, extolling the murder of the Lord Coronel Flon, which was attributed in one of the broadside's notes to one of their heroes, a man named Aldama or Abasolo. Concerning this meeting with Mazo, the witness spoke about it with no one, he had spoke about having read the broadsides only with his uncle Don Francisco Sánchez, as he has declared above.

Also on one occasion, according to his memory, in the month of October while being in the Alameda with Don Manuel Sarmiento, who lives in the house of the deceased regidor Rodríguez Velasco, he had another conversation about hatred of the Europeans.

Similarly, he had another one of these conversations in the Alameda with one Velázquez, nephew of the Secretary of this Viceroyalty, who is employed in the Tribunal de Minería.

With Miguel Benítez, the cashier of a store that is on the bajos de Mireles calle primero, he had various conversations of the same type, though he adds that the already-mentioned Sarmiento and Velázquez did not show themselves to be such great partisans of the Insurrection as Benítez, for he denied the victory gained by the King's troops on the Bridge at Calderón and other favorable news of the just cause of the government.

He was asked about the addresses of the men he named.

He said that the booth of Don Vicente Rodríguez in the Parián is the one called "The Sun" and it is behind the ones which are in front of the Diputation.

He said that Don Agustín Alcalá lives with his uncle el Senor Magistral.

He does not know where Don Salvador Marengo lives, but he knows that he is married with the stepdaughter of Don Felipe Ferris, who lives on the street of San Lorenzo.

He states that the relative of Licenciado Espinosa already went to Guanajuato. Also the *boticario* Laguna is a resident of Puebla, and he does not know if he would have returned.

He says that this is what he has to say about himself and his accomplices and that he does not make this denunciation out of hatred or ill will, but rather in order to relieve his conscience. He adds that since the beginning of the revolution in Spain, he has always fed his hatred of the Europeans with many frequent conversations, and he did not want to believe or he grew saddened at the good news and he rejoiced over the bad news, not because he was a partisan of the French, but rather out of hatred for the Europeans.

He was asked why he waited until now to denounce himself and his accomplices and why he had not done it previously.

He said that in confessing himself in these past days in a general confession with the present notary, he felt repentant of such unjust conduct and the confessor exhorted him to voluntarily denounce himself to the Holy Tribunal, asking it for pardon and absolution for the repeated excommunications which he incurred through these crimes, subjecting himself to the punishment or punishments that the Holy Office would impose on him.

He also states that he knows of no other person than those against whom he has declared that has said or done anything that is against our Holy Faith, or the righteous conduct of the Holy Office.

Being read what he had declared, the witness said that it was correctly written and he affirmed and ratified under the oath taken. He was once again charged with the secret, promising to guard it and he signed it with the said commissary of the Inquisition, which I certify:

Dr. José Antonio Tirado y Priego,
José Ignacio Sánchez
Before me, Dr. Juan Bautista Díaz Calvillo

GLOSSARY

abjuración. A denial, disavowal, or renunciation under oath. In common ecclesiastical language this term is restricted to the renunciation of heresy made by the penitent heretic on the occasion of his reconciliation with the church. In Inquisition trials there are three sorts of abjuration that could occur.

abjuración de formali. An abjuration made by someone who was found to be a notorious heretic or an apostate. This was the strongest form of penitential abjuration and was reserved for those usually condemned of formal heresy (those who had sufficient proof against them to convict them to a sentence of death).

abjuración de levi. An abjuration made by someone who was found to have a slight suspicion of heresy. It was a lesser abjuration than abjuration *de vehementi,* which connoted serious wrongdoing.

abjuración de vehementi. An abjuration made by someone who was found to have a strong suspicion of heresy. It was a stronger form of penitence than an abjuration *de levi,* which connoted a less serious wrongdoing.

abogado de presos. Advocate appointed to defend the inquisition's accused prisoners.

absolución ad cautelam. Absolution with caution was a type of verdict and sentence where the suspected heretic is absolved with some minor censure, which declared that some slight suspicion of guilt existed but that the suspect still deserved absolution.

absolución total. Total absolution was a type of verdict in an inquisition case that amounted to a total declaration of innocence where no suspicion of heresy remained concerning the accused.

adulterio. Adultery.

adúltero/a. Adulterer/adulteress.

aeromancy. The practice of divination by means of measuring the atmosphere or changes in the weather.

alcaide. Jailer or warden; keeper of the local jail.

alcaide de las cárceles secretas. Jailer or warden of the secret prisons of the Inquisition in New Spain.

alcalde de corte. Judge of the civil division of the Audiencia.

alcalde del crimen. Judge of the criminal division of the Audiencia.

alcalde ordinario. A judge, usually located in a city, who had original jurisdiction in both civil and criminal cases.

alguacil mayor. Chief constable, the official who served as the major arresting officer of the Inquisition.

alumbrados. Illuminists, a mystical sect of Christians who believed union with God was possible without a priestly intercessor.

aráncel. Ecclesiastical fee list.

arcédiano. The archdeacon was the official of the Cathedral Chapter who examined all who presented themselves for ordination and sometimes acted as administrator of a diocese in the absence of a bishop.

arroba. Unit of weight, about twenty-five pounds.

Audiencia. The highest royal court of appeals within a jurisdiction, serving at the same time as a council of state to the viceroy or governor. It was also a court of first instance in certain cases (*casos de corte*), usually involving higher officials. It was divided into two chambers, one for criminal cases (*sala del crimen*) and one for civil suits (*sala de corte, sala de provincia*). The judges of the Audiencia (called *oidores*) varied in number. In 1583 the Audiencia of Mexico had six of these judges. The term was also applied to the area of district under the Audiencia's jurisdiction.

autillo de fé. A small auto-da-fé usually held in audience chambers or courtroom of the tribunal of the inquisition. These smaller *autillos de fe* could either be *a puertas abiertas* (open doors) in which as many people as could fit inside the chambers could attend; or *a puertas cerradas* (closed doors) where only the persons authorized by the tribunal could attend.

auto. Decree or edict referring to various legal documents, including judicial sentences in secondary matters that ordinarily did not demand a sentence.

auto de fé. Auto-da-fé, or act of faith. Public ceremony at which the sentences of the Inquisition were pronounced along with the reading of the resulting punishments. It often occurs in its Portuguese form *auto da fe*. No punishments or executions occurred at the auto-da-fé, only the reading of the sentences.

auto general de fé. General act of faith. These were large public auto-da-fé celebrated with a large number of prisoners of all types and classes, including those condemned to be relaxed to the secular arm for execution of a death sentence (see *relajado; relajación al brazo secular*).

auto particular de fé. Particular auto-da-fé. Similar to the *autillo de fe*, the *auto particular* was a smaller auto-da-fé in which only a few prisoners had their sentences read in public, also usually held in a church. Most often only the officials of the inquisition were in attendance, without the pomp and ceremony involved in larger general auto-da-fé.

auto singular de fe. Singular auto-da-fé. These ceremonies were autos-da-fé that were celebrated with a single prisoner. These occurred most often in a church or in a public plaza, depending on the circumstances.

ayuda de costa. Stipend derived from Indian tribute.

Bachiller. Holder of the equivalent to a bachelor's degree in the colonial period. Less common and more prestigious in the sixteenth century than at present.

bando. Proclamation.

barbero. Barber.

barrio. Neighborhood. Settlement subordinate to a village, usually within or next to the main town or village.

beata. A single woman, usually a widow, who led a form of religious life without belonging to any order, often wearing distinctive garb and occasionally engaging in charitable works. Most often, however, these *beatas* were poor women who occupied themselves in prayers and spiritual exercises.

beneficio. Benefice. An ecclesiastical office with an income attached.

bienes. Assets.

blasfemia. Blasphemy. An ecclesiastical crime related to an irreverent or impious act, attitude, or utterance against God or the Catholic saints or other precepts, the sacraments, or other things considered inviolable or sacrosanct by the Catholic Church.

boticario. Pharmacist.

bozal. Muzzle (literal meaning). A slave newly arrived from Africa, presumably without knowledge of the Spanish language, religion, or customs.

Br. Abbreviated form of *Bachiller,* for holder of a bachelor's degree; also the honorific title of a secular priest.

breve, bula. Brief, bull. A bull (from the medieval Latin *bulla,* referring to a lead seal) was a papal pronouncement or letter, whereas a brief was a shorter form of a bull.

bulas de santa cruzada. Bulls of the Holy Crusade. Papal indulgences sold to support war against infidels, collected for the crown.

bulto. Religious image usually carved in a type of cedar, pine, or cottonwood.

cabeza de proceso. An initial *auto* whereby a judge provides for the investigation of a crime and the delinquents.

caja. The Royal treasury, as well as a strongbox. Also the district administered by the royal treasury officials (*oficiales reales*).

Caja de tres llaves. Royal strongbox for holding money and revenues. The Fiscal Office of the Inquisition was required to keep the moneys it acquired from confiscations, rents, and other income in these strongboxes.

calabozo. Dungeon.

calidad. The condition or quality of one's character, nature; nobility, rank; personal qualifications. In colonial New Spain, the term indicated aspects of color, occupation, wealth, purity of blood, honor, integrity, and place of origin.

calificación. Qualification. The inquisition used this term to describe the formal review and censure of the deeds or statements of a suspected heretic by the theological advisers called the qualifiers (see *calificadores*). Once a case received a qualification, the inquisitors could proceed with the case and issue an arrest warrant and proceed with a formal trial.

calificado/a. Qualified. Authorized, competent. This term was used to describe the document or certification that an act of heresy had occurred during a Inquisition Qualifier's review of the initial investigation in an inquisition case.

calificador. Qualifier. An unsalaried inquisition official or consultant, usually a priest or clergyman trained in theology, who reviewed the initial investigations, denunciations and testimonies collected against a suspected heretic in order to assess whether or not heresy was involved in the case. These qualifiers also served as censors who reviewed, purged, and helped the Inquisition censor books and other publications.

capellan. A priest who has a chaplaincy, or says mass in a private Chapel and who is paid by a trust fund or private individual.

cárceles comunes. The common prisons where the prisoner was allowed to have communication with people from outside of the Tribunal. Most often the inquisition would place people accused of lesser crimes in this type of prison.

cárceles de penitencia. The penitential prisons were usually housed outside of the palace of the inquisition, or close by them, and they served as the place where those penitents sentenced to serve short term imprisonment could serve out their sentence. These prisons were also often called *cárceles de misericordia* (prisons of mercy) or *cárceles de piedad* (prisons of clemency).

cárceles perpetuas. The perpetual prisons of the inquisition were where the inquisition kept those convicted heretics condemned to spend long periods of incarceration for their heresy. The Inquisition sentenced few people to perpetual imprisonment. Many times the inquisitors commuted the sentence of perpetual imprisonment for reclusion in a monastery.

cárceles secretas. The secret prisons were used by the Inquisition for holding accused heretics incommunicado during the duration of their trial. A prisoner in these secret cells was not allowed to have communication with anyone.

carga. Charge, burden. Maximum load that could legally be carried by Indian bearers, equal to two arrobas (fifty pounds).

cartas acordadas. Circulars or letters of instruction sent to the Inquisition in New Spain from the Supreme Council of the Inquisition (the Suprema).

casado/a. Married.

casado dos veces. The Inquisition crime of having been married twice while the first spouse still lived.

casamiento. Marriage, wedding.

casar. To marry.

castas. Generic term for racial mixtures.

cédula real. Royal decree or order.

censo. A mortgage or lien on land or real estate, one of the ways in which the Inquisition financed its operations. There were many varieties and forms. It was a contract in virtue of which an immovable good (real property) was subjected to the payment of an annual pension as interest on a sum of money received. Failure to repay brought loss of property to the benefit of the holder of the *censo.* It was a form of an interest-bearing lien or mortgage loan or *préstamo hipotecario a interés.*

censura. Censure was a category of ecclesiastical penalties whose purpose was to bring about the reformation or reconciliation of the person penalized. The principal censures were excommunication, suspension, and interdict.

chantre. Official of the Cathedral Chapter who was in charge of the cathedral choir.

clérigo. A diocesan priest.

cofradía. Confraternity was a religious fraternity or brotherhood.

comisario. A local commissary judge or commissioner of the Inquisition, most often a priest or clergyman responsible for taking witness testimony, investigating acts of heresy, and collecting other testimony in distant regions or provinces far away from the seat of the tribunal. These commissaries also had to post and proclaim the tribunal's edicts of faith and conduct any other business that the inquisitors entrusted to them.

comisión. A special commission or appointment, one that carried unusual or additional duties. Much of the Inquisition of New Spain's work was conducted by commissioning distant priests or other ecclesiastical officials with the power to serve as a commissary judge.

compadrázgo. God-parentage was a very important social institution that established ties between parents of a baptized child and the child's godparents. The mother and godmother are *comadres;* the father and godfather are *compadres.* Especially important in Indian communities.

competencia. Conflict of jurisdiction.

Concilio de Trento. Council of Trent, the nineteenth ecumenical council, which opened in Trent, Italy on December 13, 1545, and closed there on December 4, 1563. There were a total of twenty-five sessions that created Catholic dogma that would be enforced by the Inquisition.

concordias. Agreements between the Inquisition and cities, defining the limits of the tribunal's jurisdiction, especially in relation to local fueros.

consanguinidad. Consanguinity is the degree of blood relation, related by blood.

Consejo de Indias. The Council of the Indies was the chief administrative body of Spain regarding the New World.

consulta de fé. The consultation of faith was an official meeting or jury made up of inquisitors, consultants, theologians, and a representative of the local bishop (the *ordinario*) who passed judgment on an suspected heretic at the end of a inquisition trial.

consultor. A consultant was a legal and theological adviser to the inquisitors who helped them pass judgment and sentence a convicted heretic in inquisition trials. In New Spain these consultants usually came from the local royal judges of the Audiencia and other lesser courts, along with the prelates and other learned clergymen from the religious orders.

contador. An accountant or salaried official of the Inquisition who was in charge of all of the accounts and investments of the Tribunal.

converso. A convert from Judaism to Catholicism.

cópula ilícita. Unlawful sexual relationship.

cópula lícita. Lawful sexual relationship.

coroza. A certain type of miter or pointed cap made out of pasted papier-mâché that was placed on the head of a penitent heretic as a type of punishment, or shame. The pointed cap was about one yard tall and painted with different figures according to the crime or act of heresy that the penitent had committed. The wearing of the *coroza* was one of the sentences of public shame and humiliation that a penitent or reconciled heretic had to undergo (see *penitenciado*; *reconciliado*).

corregidor. Spanish official in charge of a province or district. Local magistrate and administrator with jurisdiction over an Indian polity.

criollo. A creole is a person of European blood born in the New World.

Cristiano Nuevo. New Christian usually refers to Jews who accepted baptism into the Catholic faith.

crypto-Jew. An individual who practiced Judaism (illegal in New Spain).

cuestión de tormento. The formal interrogation of a prisoner under torture by the Inquisition.

culpa. Sentence of proven guilt issued in a formal verdict in an inquisition trial.

cura. A parish priest, curate, or rector; member of secular clergy.

cura benificiado. Secular parish priest was a priest subordinate to a bishop who held a benefice.

curador. A curator, tutor, or guardian was appointed by the Inquisition for any prisoner under the age of twenty-five years old to represent him in response to the formal accusation and during the duration of the trial. The curator could not be a member of the tribunal, but should be a good Christian of sufficient quality to be above reproach.

curandero/a. Medical practitioner without official degree, an herbal healer, herbalist.

deán. Dean or president of a cathedral chapter who presided over its meetings in the absence of the bishop. He also acted as the pastor of the cathedral church.

denuncia/delación. A denunciation was a judicial accusation or statement given to the Inquisition concerning deeds or statements that a witness or deponent had seen, heard, or witnessed which appeared to him to be against the Catholic faith, or something that he felt either criticized or hampered the free exercise of the Inquisition.

depositada. Woman who is removed from her home by authorities and placed in another house when her parents object to her pending marriage.

depositario general. A bonded official in charge of sequestered goods and other moneys under litigation. In terms of the inquisition, this official served as the public treasurer of the sequestered goods.

derecho. Right, justice, law.

desposar. To be betrothed or married.

diezmo. Tithe (literally "one tenth"), one-tenth share of agricultural products and animals paid to the church.

dignidades. The top five ranks in a Cathedral Chapter: the *deán, arcediano, maestrescuelas, chantre,* and *tesorero.*

diligencias. Obligations, duties, and other judicial formalities, procedures.

diócesis. Diocese is the unit of the Catholic Church presided over by a bishop.

dispensa. Dispensation is a waving of a certain rule or regulation, such as when one is given a dispensation in order to marry someone who is a close relative such as a first cousin (which is normally prohibited by law).

doctrina. Religious jurisdiction. Also, a parish or missionary jurisdiction consisting of recently converted Indians administered by regular clergy.

doctrina cristiana. Christian doctrine.

doctrinero. Priest or friar entrusted with providing Christian training to an indigenous community.

don, doña. A title of honor for men and women, denoting someone from an important, respected family.

doncella. Maiden; unmarried woman.

ducado. A ducat is a coin equivalent to 375 maravedís.

edicto de fé. An edict of Faith is a published list of the existing heresies and other crimes against the faith printed so that it could be read out in all of the churches in New Spain on Sundays after mass. It was the duty of local Inquisition commissaries to read these edicts of faith publically to solicit denunciations and testimonies against people who may have committed one of the mentioned heresies or crimes against the faith. The Inquisition in New Spain also periodically issued specific smaller edicts of faith that condemned any new types of heresies or issued others to censor one or more books.

edicto de gracia. The edict of grace mentioned specific new types of heresy and then offered a grace period, or time limit, for voluntary confessions of self-denunciations without sanction or punishment.

encomendero. A trustee or holder of an Indian *encomienda.*

encomienda. A tribute institution used in Spanish America in which a Spaniard received Indians in trust (*encomienda*) to protect and to Christianize them, but in return this person could demand tribute including labor.

entredicho. Interdict was an ecclesiastical penalty whereby church services were forbidden in a certain church or district.

escribano. A notary was a secretary or scribe primarily expert in executing documents in correct legal format.

escribano apostólico. Ecclesiastical notary.

excomunión. Excommunication was an ecclesiastical penalty whereby a person was barred from receiving the sacraments and participating in public worship. An *excomunión mayor* barred him from all church actions, including Christian burial, and made him a *vitandus. Excomunión menor* was not so drastic. The penalty was used frequently in the sixteenth century.

expediente. File of documents bearing on an Inquisition case.

expurgatorio. Expurgatory was the term used to describe the book or catalog of all of the prohibited publications, books, and other printed works that the Inquisition ordered purged.

familiares. Familiars were deputies or police agents of the Inquisition. These officials were unsalaried secular, civilian representatives of the Inquisition that served as a type of militia and acted as deputized constables and local officials. These familiars also had the duty and obligation to serve as "spies" and informers, make denunciations, and aid in other duties as required. These officials, as a privilege of their office, received immunity from prosecution in civil and criminal cases in any court outside of the Inquisition.

fanéga. Measurement of grain and seed; usually equal to about two and one-half bushels.

fiscal. The chief prosecutor of an inquisition court, this salaried official served as the second most important position in an Inquisition tribunal. Often in New Spain one of the inquisitors had to serve as the prosecutor due to the lack of a separate official. When this occurred, he was called *inquisidor fiscal,* to signify that he held both prestigious positions.

Fisco. Royal treasury; also called *camara del rey.*

fraile. Friar, a member of a mendicant order.

fray. Title used before the first name of a friar, from the Latin for "brother."

fuero. A local right or privilege recognized by the crown.

garrúcha. A block and pulley system used to inflict torture during an Inquisition interrogation session to gain a confession.

gente de razón. "People of reason," civilized people, or Spanish settlers; educated or rational persons in contrast to unconquered Indians.

geomancy. The practice of divination by means of the use of geographic features.

grano. The smallest denomination of Spanish currency. They were ninety-six to a gold peso and there were twelve granos in one silver real.

hidalgo. A member of the lower nobility. An untitled noble, literally meant a "son of somebody."

hijo/a de la iglesia. Child born of unknown or undeclared parentage.

hijo/a natural. A child born out of wedlock from unwed parents who could have been legally married.

hydromancy. The practice of divination by the observation of water.

idolatry. The worship of idols, images, or other objects of perceived supernatural power.

ilegítimo/a. Illegitimate child born of an adulterous relationship.

ilícita. Unlawful.

incontinencia. Incontinency, unchastity, sexual promiscuity, lewdness.

información. Term used by the inquisition to refer to the compilation of a number of declarations or witness testimonies taken under oath by witnesses who were interrogated judicially.

información sumaria. This term describes the information of interrogated witnesses at the beginning of an inquest, or *proceso,* before the qualification of the case and before an arrest occurred and a confession was made by a suspect. This part of the trial, once concluded and qualified, led directly to the opening of the second formal trial phase when a formal trial began, and the case was opened *a prueba* or "opened for proof."

Inquisición. The Inquisition (from the Latin *inquirere* "to look into") was a special ecclesiastical institution established in the thirteenth century to suppress heresy. The Spanish Inquisition was a more recent and distinctive tribunal on the eve of the Reformation, established specifically to deal with the problems of pseudo-conversions of Jews (*Marranos*) and Moors (*Moriscos*) to Christianity.

instrucciones. The term given to the formal ordinances, rules, and instructions given by the inquisitor general and the Suprema and approved by the king, which all of the Inquisition tribunals had to observe as force of law in their internal proceedings, governance, and form of processing and determination of Inquisition cases.

interrogatorio. List of questions to be asked of a sworn witness in a formal judicial proceeding.

inventario. A list made of sequestered goods, or other inventoried goods, including moneys and accounts.

Judaizante. A Judaizer was Jewish convert to Catholicism who continued or was suspected of continuing the covert practice of Judaism.

juez. Judge.

juez eclesiástico. Ecclesiastical judge.

juramento. A formal oath taken on a Bible or before a cross swearing that the oath taker will tell the truth in the subsequent deposition.

jurisdicción. Jurisdiction.

juro. Long-term, interest-paying bonds issued by the crown. The interest formed a kind of annuity and was guaranteed by a lien on specific crown revenue, such as a sales tax.

juro al quitar. A *juro* that was redeemable at a particular date rather than being perpetual.

juro de heredad. A *juro de por vida* that could be inherited.

juro de por vida. A *juro* redeemable at the end of a lifetime.

juro de resguardo. A *juro* that carried additional collateral as a guarantee against default, together with the right to sell part or all of the collateral before repayment by the crown.

juro situado. A *juro* based on a specific source of revenue. *Situado* meant that the income was burdened or mortgaged in advanced of being collected.

Juzgado de indios. General court with jurisdiction over Indians.

legajo. Bundle of loose papers that are usually tied together because they deal with a common subject; most common unit of filed papers in Spanish inquisition archives.

legua. A league is the distance that can be traveled on horseback in an hour. The Spanish league was roughly measured at 5,000 varas or meters and was the equivalent of about 3 miles.

le tocan las generales. The legal formula "the general questions pertain to him" indicated that the witness was related to one or both persons contracting marriage, or to the accused in a Inquisition trial.

letrado. Holder of a law degree, who was a professional lawyer or offered legal counsel.

libro de votos. Book of votes was the formal book in which each Inquisition tribunal recorded the signed original collection of the votes of the inquisitors and their theological and legal consultants in their juried decisions (*consultas de fe*) concerning Inquisition cases. These books contained the votes on the administration of torture, as well as the definitive sentences decided in Inquisition cases.

licencia. Permission, leave, license, liberty.

licenciado. Someone who had a master's degree. In terms of Inquisition officials, a licentiate usually had a master's degree in law or theology. In general this title was given to lawyers and university students who held the degrees between the baccalaureate and the doctorate.

lícita. Lawful.

ligado/a. In New Spain, the term came to signify an illicit magic spell cast by a witch that "tied" or made a male impotent, causing his penis to be "bound" and thus not function properly.

limpieza de sangre. Purity of blood was a certification that a person and his ancestry were not contaminated with heretical religion or the blood of Moors (Moriscos), Jews, or Africans; also a type of document or record showing the purity of ancestry of the person applying for a position. The Inquisition required that all of the candidates to its positions, as well as all its employees, have one of these certifications conducted before they could hold office.

maestre. Master artisan, non-degreed medical practitioner.

maestrecuelas. Member of the Cathedral Chapter in charge of the cathedral school.

maestro de idolatría. A native indigenous ritual specialist or shaman.

mandamiento de apremio. Judicial order that one must appear in court within a specified time.

maravedí. An invented unit of Spanish currency that was used as the standard of value for the coinage. Ancient Spanish coin, 450 to the gold peso. A maravedi was worth one thirty-fourth of a silver real coin.

marrano. A slang word for pig or swine used in a derogatory sense for a converted Jew.

mestizaje. Miscegenation, crossbreeding.

mestizo/a. Person of mixed European and Indian blood.

mordaza. A term that described an instrument, usually made of iron, that served as a bit placed into the mouth of a prisoner so as to inhibit his speech. These iron bits were most often used in cases of blasphemy and were worn when the penitent was marched out in an auto-da-fé to hear the reading of their sentences in public.

moreno. A free African.

morisco/a. Those baptized Moors who lived in Spain and the colonies; in Mexico it refers more to a type of blood mixture: Spanish and mulatto.

mujeres perdidas. Lost women were sexually promiscuous women or prostitutes.

mulato. A mulatto, a person of mixed Spanish and African parentage.

no le tocan las generales. If the witness was not related to the accused, then this legal formula, "the general questions do not pertain to him," was used in Inquisition cases to signify for the record that the witness was not related to the accused.

notario y alguacil mayor. The notary and chief constable were two local nonsalaried deputized officials of the Holy Office of the Inquisition who would be expected to seek out or report cases of heresy and aid the local commissary of the inquisition in his local region. The notary served as the recorder of all regional inquisition documents, and the chief constable aided in any arrests and sequestration of goods that might be ordered in the region.

Nueva España. New Spain or colonial Mexico.

Nueva Extremadura. The territory of Coahuila, Mexico.

Nueva Galicia. Colonial Aguascalientes, Jalisco, and parts of Durango, Zacatecas, Nayarit, San Luis Potosi, and Coahuila, Mexico (its capital was the city of Guadalajara).

Nueva Vizcaya. New Biscay was separated from Nueva Galicia in 1573–76; included Sinaloa, Sonora, Durango, Chihuahua, and parts of Coahuila, Mexico (its capital was Durango).

Nuevo León. Mexico and its surrounding areas including part of modern state of Tamaulipas.

obispado. A bishopric was an episcopate or diocesan territory administered by a bishop.

oidor. A "listener" or high court judge of the Audiencia.

Old Christians. Cristianos Viejos. Those without Jewish or Muslim ancestry (see *limpieza de Sangre*).

ordinario. An ordinary is an ecclesiastical official who exercised jurisdiction on his own name, not that of another. The opposite of *vicario* (vicar).

parda/o. A dark-skinned casta, or person of mixed African blood.

pariente. Kinsman/kinswoman.

pena. A punishment or penalty given in a formal Inquisition sentence.

pena pecuniaria. A pecuniary fine was an Inquisition penalty to be paid in money.

penitencia. A type of punishment, or penitence, usually a spiritual one, to atone for a sin or a crime against the faith.

penitenciado. Penanced was a term used to describe someone who was formally punished by the Inquisition. Usually a convicted heretic condemned for lesser crimes who was formally accepted back into the church, but who had to renounce and publicly "abjure" his sins and receive a fine or other punishments, including the wearing of the *sanbenito*, or garment of shame.

peso. This Spanish silver coin (also called a piece of eight) was the most widely used denomination of Spanish American coinage; smaller denominations of eight silver reales or "bits" added up to one peso (a piece of eight).

portero. A lesser salaried official of the Inquisition who served as a doorman, bailiff, and minor messenger of the tribunal. One of the main functions of this official was to help escort new prisoners to their cells. This official also had access to the inquisition's prison keys.

potro. The rack (or wooden horse) was one of the most common instruments of torture employed by the Inquisition and civil courts during the early modern period.

prebendado. Cleric whose income came from the income of the cathedral.

pregonero. Public announcer of the edicts and laws that had to be publicly proclaimed.

las [preguntas] generales de la ley. General exemptions from testifying, such as minority of age, friendship, or kinship with the defendant or accused.

preso/a. Prisoner.

principal. A native indigenous noble or notable, member of the Indian elite.

proceso. A formal inquisitorial trial proceeding that included all of the legal proceedings, or the collection of all the papers and autos that went to make up a specific legal case.

proposición errónea. An erroneous proposition is one that is contrary to good Christian doctrine but
for which the church has not issued a definitive dogma.

proposición herética. A heretical proposition is a statement that is completely contrary to the Catholic
faith and expresses a complete denial or rejection of a religious truth as revealed by God.

proposición malsonante. A vile-sounding proposition was one that held a double meaning that perverted the proper meaning of the phrase or words and smacked of heresy or hinted at an implicit anti-Catholic or antireligious meaning.

proposición sediciosa (cismática). A seditious or schismatic proposition was a statement that attacked
the unity or proper form of the Catholic Church or its members, especially the clergy.

protomédico. Official authorized to inspect and license medical practitioners.

provisor. Chief ecclesiastical judge of a diocese, sometimes also the vicar general. This judge served
as an inquisitor for the indigenous people of the dioceses in New Spain. He presided over an
Indian court or inquisition called a *Provisorato de Indios.*

Provisorato de Indios. The Provisional Court of the Indians created to supervise and inquire into the
religious crimes of the Indians. Also known as the Indian Inquisition. After the creation of the
Tribunal of the Holy Office of the Inquisition in New Spain in 1571, the local diocesan *provisora-
tos* gained exclusive jurisdiction over the crimes committed by indigenous peoples.

pureza de sangre. Purity of blood or the absence of Moorish, African, Indian, or Jewish blood was required of nobles and officials of the colonial church and state.

quemadero. The site or place set aside for the execution of the sentence of burning at the stake of those
whom the Inquisition sentenced to "relaxation." Usually this stake or place of execution was at the
outskirts of the city. In New Spain, the *quemadero* was placed in the public plaza of the Alameda.

querella. Criminal accusation or complaint.

ramo. A section of an archive.

real. A silver coin, worth one-eighth of a peso, also called a tomin in colonial New Spain.

real cédula. A royal order.

real patronazgo. Royal patronage (also *real patronato*) was a right of Spanish monarchs to make nominations for ecclesiastical appointments and to control ecclesiastical and church revenues.

recogimiento. A "house of penitence," a place where women were collected and enclosed to "remedy"
their defects.

reconciliado. Reconciled is an Inquisition term used to describe a relapsed penitent heretic (one who
had been punished lightly before for a crime of the faith). On a second offense, a penitent heretic was considered "reconciled" to the church by the Inquisition but was forced to undergo a
harsher punishment, including either partial or total confiscation of their property, flogging,
galley service, and the wearing of the garment of shame, the *sanbenito,* either perpetually or for
a specific period of time.

reconciliados por diminutos. Persons punished by the Inquisition on the basis of partial confessions.

recusación. Recusation was one of the possible means of defense of a suspected heretic. The formal
process of removing an inquisitor or judge by means of alleging partiality and animosity toward the accused.

regidor. A town official whose most important duties in the sixteenth century dealt with supervising foodstuffs and the distribution of public lands.

relaciones de causas. Regular summaries of completed cases sent to the Supreme Council of the Inquisition in Madrid by the provincial tribunals.

relajado. Relaxed is an Inquisition term used to describe those convicted heretics guilty of serious formal heresy and sentenced to death by burning at the stake. These convicted heretics were to be "relaxed" or handed over to the secular authorities in order to have their death sentences executed. Those given this sentence were either burned alive or in effigy.

relajado al brazo seglar. Relaxed to the secular arm is a euphemism used by the Inquisition in order to designate those condemned to die by burning at the stake, either in person or in effigy. The prisoner was literally turned over to the civil officials of the city and then executed by ordinary civil justices.

relapso. A relapsed heretic was one who had been previously declared a formal heretic, or who had been under a strong suspicion of heresy (*vehementi*) or one previously absolved *ad cautelam* (under censures) who had become a recidivist and relapsed in the same heretical acts as before.

reo/a. A defendant or criminal imprisoned in an inquisition case.

sanbenito/sambenito / saco bendito. Distinctive garment, a "sacred cloth," worn by those reconciled or condemned by the Inquisition. The term refers to the penitential garments worn in public by the condemned at the various autos-de-fé. The garment usually consisted of a long, one-piece robe made out of either white or yellow cloth that was adorned with a version of the Saint Andrew's cross with addenda such as demons or flames (either upright or inverted) depending on the severity of the convicted heresy or crime. Those sentenced to wear the garment of shame, or *sanbenito*, also wore a conspicuous conical hat (or dunce cap). After the period of shame had passed for the reconciled heretic, or after the death sentence in the case of a relaxed heretic, the *sanbenito* was publicly displayed in the local parish church of the offender in perpetuity as a reminder of their shame, and the continued shame of the victim's family.

Santo Oficio. A term used to describe the Holy Office, or the Inquisition.

secreto. The inquisition used this term, "the secret," to describe two things. 1. The secret archive of the tribunal where all of the *procesos* and trials of each inquisition were archived. The door of this chamber usually had three keys, two of which were in the possession of the secretaries, and the third one held by the prosecutor. The chamber of the secret was divided into four separate sections. In one of these sections they placed the pending trials. In a second section they archived those trials that had been suspended for lack of evidence, and in a third section they housed the completed trials, subdividing them into those of the relaxed heretics and those of the reconciled or penanced heretics. The fourth section contained all of the documentation pertaining to the local commissaries and familiars who served in the distant provinces. 2. The term also described the formal oath of secrecy that everyone who appeared before the tribunal had to swear.

sede vacante. Vacant bishopric.

señor. Sir/lord.

sermón de la fé. A sermon of the faith was a special public sermon preached by a prominent cleric or ecclesiastic before the gathered public attending the formal act of faith, or auto-de-fé, where the sentences of the convicted heretics were read publicly.

sumaria. Summary is the formal series of Inquisition documents that includes all of the declarations of witnesses and depositions taken under oath in secret from subsequent witnesses implicated under interrogation concerning supposed acts of heresy or crimes against the faith contained in an initial denunciation or accusation. This collection of documents made up the initial pretrial inquest or investigation into an act of heresy. No arrest order or trial could occur until the inquisitors submitted the *sumaria* to a formal review called a "qualification" from one or more theological advisors called qualifiers (see *calificadores*).

sumaria suspensa. A suspended summary is a case, or *proceso*, that contained the sworn interrogations and depositions of witnesses and an initial denunciation or accusation that was suspended and not carried forward due to a lack of evidence or proof of a crime sufficient enough to "qualify" the crimes and justify the issuing of an arrest order.

Suprema. The Supreme Council of the Inquisition, or the superior governing council of the Spanish Inquisition founded in 1483 and seated in Madrid. Under the leadership of the inquisitor general, the Suprema was the supreme governing body of the Inquisition and as such controlled all of the other regional tribunals underneath it. The Suprema communicated with its subordinate courts and inquisitors by means of *cartas acordadas,* circulars or letters, which held instructions that had the binding force of law on all of the subject tribunals.

tacha. Disqualification or disabling of a witness in an Inquisition case for enmity by the use of one or more allegations or the presentation of evidence that casts doubt upon the veracity or truth of a hostile witnesses' testimony.

testigo. Witness.

testigos de abono. The presentation of character witnesses, who could swear and testify to the good Christian character of an accused suspect, combined with the use of *tachas* (or the disqualification of prosecution witnesses by means of proving enmity) and *recusación* (or the recusation or disqualification of an inquisitor or judge for apparent animosity toward the suspect), served as the most important means of a suspected heretic's defense against the charges of heresy.

testimonio. Written testimony of a witness; a deposition.

toca. A porous linen cloth placed over the face and mouth of an Inquisition prisoner who was about to receive the water jar torture (called water-boarding today). The cloth would constrict the breathing passages of the victim who was placed laying back on the rack. As the water poured over the *toca,* the victim would strain to breath, but the water-drenched linen cloth would restrict his ability to breath giving the victim the sensation of impending suffocation.

tomín. A small silver coin worth one-eighth of a peso, also called a silver real.

tormento in caput alienum. This type of torture (literally, in Latin, torture on the head of another) is given in cases where the inquisitors want to force the prisoner to serve as a witness in the trial of another suspect where this prisoner had been cited as a material witness of an act of heresy. This means of torment and of forced interrogation under torture was permitted only after the inquisitors had questioned the prisoner and the suspect denied any knowledge of the event or act of heresy. If the inquisitors had a strong suspicion that the prisoner lied maliciously to conceal a truth or hide an accomplice, they could order this type of questioning under torture.

tormento in caput proprium. This type of torture (literally, in Latin, torture on one's own head) was ordered to be given in cases when a prisoner was to be interrogated under the effects of torture in reference to his own case or suspected act of heresy.

trapiche. Animal-driven sugar mill. An arrangement of a press, a cauldron, and a fireplace that allowed sugar cane juice to be extracted and boiled down to produce crude sugar.

vecino. A resident or citizen of a city, town, or a mine, usually restricted to whites in colonial times.

vicaría. Vicarage is the territory over which a vicar presides: an area similar to a parish in size but not yet advanced in its development sufficiently to be elevated to the position of a parish; a vice-parish.

vicario. A vicar exercising power in the name of another rather than in his own right. His authority is called vicarious.

violar. To ravish, force, or violate; to profane a church.

visita de distrito. Visitation of the district was a provincial or regional inspection that included the holding of sporadic investigations, denunciations, and hearings conducted by a visiting local inquisitor. The Inquisition required that the local inquisitors conduct these regional visitations of their district periodically in order to actively seek out and punish crimes against the faith.

visitas de naos. Visitation of ships was the formal process by which an inquisitor or an Inquisition commissary in outlying districts boarded and inspected all incoming ships in port for the existence of prohibited books or other religious contraband. A record of all visitations of ships would be created and sent to the tribunal for its review.

votos. Votes were the formal opinions of the inquisitors and their consultants concerning what should be decided as a final sentence in a case against a convicted heretic.

NOTES

Preface

1. See Henry Charles Lea, *A History of the Inquisition of Spain*, 4 vols. (New York: Macmillan, 1906), 1: Preface.

2. Juan Antonio Llorente, *Historia Crítica de la Inquisición en España*, vols. 1–4 (Madrid: Hiperión, 1980).

3. Juan Antonio Llorente (1756–1823) was born in Rincon de Soto, Spain. He studied at the University of Saragossa and, having been ordained priest, became vicar-general to the bishop of Calahorra in 1782. This position gave him ample experience in the methods and procedures of ecclesiastical court cases. Three years later, in 1785, Llorente became a commissary of the Holy Office in the region of Logroño. On the basis of his proceedings and competence, in 1789 he was appointed as general secretary of the Suprema of the Holy Office in Madrid.

4. See Jaqueline Vassallo, "La Inquisición en los archivos: Una historia de organización, destrucción y dispersión," paper presented at VII Congreso de Archivologia del Mercosur, Santiago, Chile, 2007.

5. See Lorenzo H. Feldman, "La inquisición y otros archivos hispánicos tempranos," *Biblios Revista Electrónica de Bibliotecología, Archivología y Museología* 4, no. 13 (2002): 3.

6. Vassallo, "La inquisición en los archivos."

7. Virgilio Pinto Crespo "La documentación Inquisitorial," in *La Inquisición* (Madrid: Ministerio de Cultura, 1982), 98.

The Holy Office of the Inquisition in New Spain (Mexico)

1. See Lu Ann Homza, *The Spanish Inquisition, 1478–1614: An Anthology of Sources* (Indianapolis: Hackett, 2006), x–xi.

2. Edward Peters, *Inquisition* (Berkeley: University of California Press, 1989), 12–17.

3. Ibid., 14.

4. Richard L. Kagan and Abigail Dyer, eds. and trans., *Inquisitorial Inquiries: Brief Lives of Secret Jews and Other Heretics* (Baltimore: Johns Hopkins University Press, 2004), 11.

5. Ibid., 15.

6. Edward Peters, *Torture* (Philadelphia: University of Pennsylvania Press, 1996), 53.

7. Richard E. Greenleaf, *The Mexican Inquisition of the Sixteenth Century* (Albuquerque: University of New Mexico Press, 1969), 4.

8. See Homza's *The Spanish Inquisition*, xv–xxxvii, for her excellent discussion of the origins and development of the Spanish Inquisition.

9. The grant of royal patronage not only gave the Spanish monarchs control over the naming and appointment of inquisitorial officials but also ensured royal control over all aspects of the Catholic Church in the Spanish realms, especially in terms of naming personnel, collecting and levying church taxes and fees, and missionizing the recently conquered indigenous people of the New World. For more information concerning royal patronage and the church, see John Frederick Schwaller, *The Church and Clergy in Sixteenth-Century Mexico* (Albuquerque: University of New Mexico Press, 1987), as well as Nancy Farriss, *Crown and Clergy in Colonial Mexico, 1759–1821: The Crisis of Ecclesiastical Privilege* (London: Athlone Press, 1968).

10. Lester R. Kurtz, "The Politics of Heresy," *American Journal of Sociology* 88, no. 6 (1983): 1085–1115, especially 1086.

11. Saint Jerome is credited with giving one of the first discussions of the etymological origins of the term *heresy*; for a more in-depth examination of the origin and development of the concept of heresy and its use by the Inquisition, see Peters, *Inquisition*, 61–65.

12. For a detailed examination of the relationship between the early Christian Church, its ecumenical councils, and the development and definition of Christian heresies, see Jean Guitton, *Great Heresies and Church Councils* (New York: Harper & Row, 1965).

13. Henry Charles Lea, *A History of the Inquisition of Spain* (New York: Macmillan, 1906), 2:3.

14. For a discussion of the complexities of Catholic Church dogma and its conceptual relationship to a Catholic understanding of God's will, or the truth, as revealed to man (*veritas revelata*), see Karl Barth, *Church Dogmatics: The Doctrine of the Word of God,* ed. and trans. Geoffrey William Bromiley and Thomas Forsyth Torrance (London: T & T Clark International, 2004), 1:12, 111–20, 270–94.

15. For a more complete examination of the Catholic belief in the role of Christ in the creation of the "One, Holy Catholic and Apostolic Church," see Jaroslav Pelikan, *The Christian Tradition: A History of the Development of Doctrine,* vol. 4: *The Reformation of Church and Dogma (1300–1700)* (Chicago: University of Chicago Press, 1985), 69–126. For the Catholic Church (and the inquisitors), "True catholic doctrine could never go wrong, for Christ, who was the way and the truth, had promised to abide with his catholic church forever through the successors of the apostles" (ibid., 100).

16. Kurtz, "The Politics of Heresy," 1087.

17. Ibid., 1088.

18. Homza, *The Spanish Inquisition*, xi.

19. Margaret Mott, "The Rule of Faith over Reason: The Role of the Inquisition in Iberia and New Spain," *Journal of Church and State* 40, no. 1 (1998): 57–81.

20. Ibid., 61.

21. Lea, *History of the Inquisition of Spain*, 2:4.

22. For a detailed description of the Inquisition's stance on ignorance and heresy, see Martin Nesvig, *Ideology and Inquisition: The World of the Censors in Early Mexico* (New Haven: Yale University Press, 2009), 51–54.

23. Ibid., 52.

24. Lea, *History of the Inquisition of Spain*, 2:4.

25. See María Asunción Herrera Sotillo, *Ortodoxia y control social en México en el siglo XVII: El Tribunal del Santo Oficio* (Madrid: Universidad Complutense de Madrid, Departamento de Historia de América, 1982), 74.

26. Henry Kamen, *The Spanish Inquisition: A Historical Revision* (New Haven: Yale University Press, 1998), 213.

27. Lea, *History of the Inquisition of Spain*, 2:20.

28. This list is based on the tenets of canon law and the laws of the Indies. For fuller discussion, see Ángel Martínez González, *Gobernación espiritual de las Indias, código Ovandino; Libro 10* (Guatemala: Instituto Teológico Salesiano, 1978), 184–87; also see *Recopilación de leyes de los reynos de las Indias: Mandadas imprimir y publicar por la Majestad Católica del rey Don Carlos II, nuestro señor* (Madrid: Imprenta de Julian de Paredes, 1681); Ignacio López de Ayala, *El Sacrosanto y Ecuménico Concilio de Trento Traducida al idioma Castellano* (México: Librería de Garnier Hermanos, 1855); Mariano Galván Rivera, *Concilio III Provincial Mexicano celebrado en México el año de 1585* (México: Eugenio Mallefert y Compañia, Editores, 1859); and T. Lincoln Bouscaren, S.J., and Adam C. Ellis, *Canon Law: A Text and Commentary* (Milwaukee: Bruce Publishing, 1951). For an older book on canon law as practiced in the Spanish provinces, see *Diccionario de Derecho Canónico arreglado a la jurisprudencia eclesiástica Española antigua y moderna* (Paris: Librería de Rosa y Bouret, 1853).

29. Kamen, *Spanish Inquisition,* 137.

30. See Henry Charles Lea, *The Inquisition in the Spanish Dependencies* (New York: Macmillan, 1908), 203.

31. For the specifics concerning the inquisitor general's removal of the necessity of consultation with the Suprema in cases concerning the permission to use torture during the Mexican Inquisition's questioning of accused heretics, see document 3, instruction 24.

32. For the specific royal laws and regulations against interfering with the Inquisition's ministers and its trials, see *Recopilación de las Leyes de los Reynos de las Indias,* tomo I, libro I, titulo XIX, legajo IV, 160–61.

33. For a detailed discussion of the nature of the crimes of heresy punished in New Spain, see Yolanda Mariel de Ibáñez, *El Tribunal de la Inquisición en México (siglo XVI)* (México, D.F.: Universidad Nacional Autónoma de México, Instituto de Investigaciones Jurídicas, 1979), 16:61–85.

34. See Richard E. Greenleaf, "Historiography of the Mexican Inquisition: Evolution of Interpretations and Methodologies," in *Cultural Encounters: The Impact of the Inquisition in Spain and the New World,* ed. Mary Elizabeth Perry and Anne J. Cruz (Berkeley: University of California Press, 1991), 255.

35. See Greenleaf, *Mexican Inquisition,* 6–12; for information on the inquisitorial activities of Fray Diego de Landa, see John F. Chuchiak, "*In Servitio Dei*: Fray Diego de Landa, the Franciscan Order, and the Return of the Extirpation of Idolatry in the Colonial Diocese of Yucatán, 1573–1579," *The Americas* 61, no. 4 (2005): 611–46.

36. See John F. Chuchiak, "The Holy Office of the Inquisition," in *Oxford Encyclopedia of Mesoamerican Cultures,* ed. David Carrasco (Oxford: Oxford University Press, 2001), 2:46–48.

37. For a general discussion of the continued existence of the episcopal courts as a type of "Indian Inquisition" as well as the many conflicts of jurisdiction between these bishop's courts and the Holy Office, see Richard E. Greenleaf, "The Inquisition and the Indians of New Spain: A Study in Jurisdictional Confusion," *The Americas* 22 (1965): 138–66; for the activities of these episcopal courts in the diocese of Yucatan, see John F. Chuchiak, "La inquisición Indiana y la extirpación de idolatrías: El castigo y la Represión en el Provisorato de Indios en Yucatán, 1570–1690," in *Nuevas Perspectivas Sobre el Castigo de la Heterodoxia Indígena en la Nueva España,* ed. Ana de Zaballa Beascoechea (Bilbao: Universidad del Pais Vasco, Spain, 2005), 79–94.

38. See Joaquín Pérez Villanueva and Bartolomé Escandell Bonet, eds., *Historia de la Inquisición en España y América,* vol. 1 : *El conocimiento científico y el proceso histórico de la Institución (1478–1834)* (Madrid: Biblioteca de Autores Cristianos / Centro de Estudios Inquisitoriales, 1984), 662.

39. See Greenleaf, *Mexican Inquisition,* 6–12.

40. The only surviving documents concerning these early trials by the Franciscan inquisitor include fragments of several cases. See, for example, *Proceso contra Marcos, Indio de Acolhuacan por*

amancebamiento, 1524, Archivo General de la Nación (hereafter AGN), Ramo de Inquisición, vol. 1, exp. 1; as well as fragments found in vol. 1, exp. 7, 13.

41. Greenleaf, *Mexican Inquisition,* 11–12.

42. Ibid. Also see the extant trial proceedings conducted by the Dominican inquisitors in AGN, Ramo de Inquisición, vols. 1, 1A, 2, and 14.

43. See Richard E. Greenleaf, "The Persistence of Native Values: The Inquisition and the Indians of Colonial Mexico," *The Americas* 50, no. 3 (1994): 351–76, especially 368–70.

44. See France V. Scholes and Ralph Roys, *Fray Diego de Landa and the Problem of Idolatry in Yucatán* (Washington, D.C.: Carnegie Institution, 1938).

45. For the documents concerning the Landa affair, see France V. Scholes and Eleanor B Adams, eds., *Don Diego Quijada, Alcalde Mayor de Yucatán, 1561–1565,* 2 vols. (México: Editorial Porrua, 1938). For Diego de Landa's return to Yucatan as its second bishop and his renewed inquisitorial activities, see John F. Chuchiak, "El regreso de los autos de fe: Fray Diego de Landa y la extirpación de idolatrías en Yucatán," *Península: Revista semestral de la Coordinación de Humanidades* 1, no. 0 (2006): 29–47.

46. See *Proceso del Santo Oficio de la Inquisición contra Tacatetl y Tanixtetl, indios de Tanacopan, por idolatras y sacrificadores,* 1536, AGN, Ramo de Inquisición, vol. 37, exp. 1.

47. See *Proceso del Santo Oficio de la Inquisición contra Don Carlos, Cacique de Texcoco, por idolatra y dogmatizador,* 1539, AGN, Ramo de Inquisición, vol. 2, exp. 10. A transcript of the entire proceedings of this trial is found in Archivo General de la Nación, *Proceso Inquisitorial del Cacique de Texcoco,* vol. 1 of the *Publicaciones del Archivo General de la Nación* (México, 1910).

48. See Greenleaf, *Mexican Inquisition,* 130–32.

49. On the episcopal inquisition, see Jorge Traslosheros, *Iglesia, justicia y sociedad en la Nueva España: La Audiencia del Arzobispado de México, 1528–1668* (México: Editorial Porrúa y Universidad Iberoamericana, 1994). Similarly, for more specifics on the development of proper inquisitorial theory and methods of processing indigenous cases, see Consuelo Maqueda, "Mundo indígena e Inquisición: Conflicto de fe en Nueva España," in *Intolerancia e Inquisición,* ed. José Antonio Escudero (Madrid: Sociedad Estatal de Conmemoriaciones Culturas, 2006), 47–96.

50. On the confusing nature of the jurisdiction of the Inquisition and the punishment of the indigenous peoples of Mexico, see Greenleaf, "Inquisition and the Indians of New Spain."

51. See John F. Chuchiak, "The Inquisition in New Spain," in *Encyclopedia of the History of México,* ed. Michael Werner (New York: Fitzroy Dearborn Publishers, 1997), 704–8.

52. Greenleaf, *Mexican Inquisition,* 170–74.

53. During this final phase of the Inquisition, its direct impact on Mesoamerican culture was minimal; see Chuchiak, "The Holy Office of the Inquisition," 48.

54. For the role of the Inquisition and the episcopal courts in the punishment of indigenous practices, see John F. Chuchiak, "The Indian Inquisition and the Extirpation of Idolatry: The Process of Punishment in the *Provisorato de Indios* of the Diocese of Yucatan, 1563–1812" (Ph.D. dissertation, Tulane University, 2000).

55. See especially Antonio Pompa y Pompa, *Procesos inquisitorial y militar seguidos a D. Miguel Hidalgo y Costilla* (México, D.F.: Instituto Nacional de Antropología e Historia, 1960).

56. One of the five major councils of state created by the Spanish crown, the Suprema often conflicted in its jurisdiction with other councils and tribunals. For the documentation concerning the major power struggles between the Suprema and other branches of Spanish royal government, see *Índice general de Decretos Reales y consultas originales sobre diversos negocios que se contienen en los 20 libros formados de ellos y pertenecen a la Secretaría de Castilla, del Real y Supremo Consejo de la Santa y General Inquisición, sobre competencias de jurisdicción entre el Consejo de la Inquisición y otras Justicias Reales (1535–1738)* (Madrid: Archivo Histórico Nacional), Inquisición, libros 3 y 4.

57. Greenleaf, *Mexican Inquisition*, especially 5.

58. Solange Alberro, *Inquisición y sociedad en México, 1571–1700* (México, D.F.: Fondo de Cultura Económica, 1988), 31.

59. Herrera Sotillo, *Ortodoxia y control social*, 116.

60. Lea, *Inquisition in the Spanish Dependencies*, 215.

61. For sources that have examined the intimate workings of the three major tribunals of the Holy Office of the New World, the most important would include Pérez Villanueva and Escandell Bonet, *Historia de la Inquisición en España y América*, vol. 1, as well as the classic studies of Juan Antonio Llorente, *Historia Crítica de la Inquisición en España*, vols. 1–4 (Madrid: Hiperión, 1980), and Lea, *History of the Inquisition of Spain*. For any study of the Holy Office in New Spain, essential works include Greenleaf, *Mexican Inquisition*; Julio Jimenez Rueda, *Herejías y supersticiones en la Nueva España* (México, D.F.: Imprenta Universitaria, 1944); Jimenez Rueda, *Don Pedro Moya de Contreras, primer Inquisidor de México* (México, D.F.: Imprenta Universitaria, 1944); and the classic work by José Toribio Medina, *El Tribunal del Santo Oficio de la Inquisición en México* (Santiago: Imprenta Elzeviriana, 1903). For the tribunal in Perú, see José Toribio Medina, *El Tribunal del Santo Oficio de la Inquisición en Lima* (Santiago: Imprenta Gutenberg, 1887), and the studies of the Lima tribunal published by Paulino Castañeda Delgado, Pilar Hernández Aparicio, René Millar, and others in Peru (see *La Inquisición de Lima*, vols. 1–3 [Lima: Editorial Deimos, 1989–95]). For perhaps the best synthesis of the history of all of the New World tribunals, see Lea's *Inquisition in the Spanish Dependencies*.

62. Just as in the Inquisition tribunals in Spain, the inquisitors and prosecutors in New Spain were always named by the inquisitor general in Madrid. See Herrera Sotillo, *Ortodoxia y control social*, 111.

63. Lea, *History of the Inquisition of Spain*, 2:236.

64. For the role of theological consultants and censors in the Mexican tribunal, see Nesvig, *Ideology and Inquisition*, 70–74.

65. See Peña comment, 51, 3a pars (as cited in ibid., 67, n. 11).

66. Ibid., 67.

67. Lea, *History of the Inquisition of Spain*, 2:235.

68. For an excellent summary of this phenomena throughout the Spanish world, see Ricardo Juan Cavallero, *Justicia inquisitorial: El sistema de justicia criminal de la Inquisición española* (Buenos Aires: Ariel Historia, 2003), 56–58.

69. Cathedral canons were clerics who served as members of a Cathedral Chapter and formed the senate or council of the bishop. A canon was an integral member of the Cathedral Chapter, and the clergymen who held this position were usually trained in canon law. For more information, see Schwaller, *Church and Clergy in Sixteenth-Century Mexico*, 14–18.

70. The Cathedral Chapter was the ecclesiastical council made up of clerics who held various offices and served to advise the local bishop and aid the bishop in the administration of his diocese. For the best study of the Cathedral Chapter in New Spain, see John Frederick Schwaller, "The Cathedral Chapter of Mexico in the Sixteenth Century," *Hispanic American Historical Review* 61 (1981): 651–74.

71. For the career paths of Spanish inquisitors, see Kimberly Lynn Hossain, "Arbiters of Faith, Agents of Empire: Spanish Inquisitors and Their Careers, 1550–1650" (Ph.D. dissertation, Johns Hopkins University, 2006).

72. See Herrera Sotillo, *Ortodoxia y control social*, 118.

73. In 1695 King Charles II added to this restriction that not only the inquisitors but also the secretaries and prosecutors should not serve in a tribunal if they were natives of the region. For more information on this and other requirements, see Lea, *History of the Inquisition of Spain*, 2:236.

74. The instructions explicitly forbade the naming of an inquisitor or any official who was a relative or close associate of any member of the tribunal. See *Compilación de las instrucciones del oficio de la Santa Inquisición hechas por fray Tomás de Torquemada e por los otros Inquisidores Generales cerca de la orden que se ha de tener en el exercicio del Santo Oficio* (Madrid: impreso de nuevo por el señor Joan Everardo Nidardo, Inquisidor General, 1667), folio 13r.

75. See *Carta del inquisidor de México, Juan Gómez de Mier, al Consejo de Inquisición*, 21 de Agosto, 1684, Archivo Histórico Nacional (Madrid) (hereafter AHN), Sección de Inquisición, legajo 2274.

76. See Herrera Sotillo, *Ortodoxia y control social*, 115. According to Herrera Sotillo, there were many examples of this type of "inheritance" of positions in the Mexican tribunal. For instance, Eugenio de Saravia, a notary of the secret, was succeeded by his son Diego de Saravia in the same office. Other examples include the Rey y Alarcón family where the grandfather Bartolomé Rey y Alarcón served as the Mexican tribunal's accountant and was succeeded sequentially by his son Florian and then his grandsons Bartolomé and Florian.

77. Lea, *History of the Inquisition of Spain*, 2:233.

78. Herrera Sotillo, *Ortodoxia y control social*, 119. Many of the early inquisitors of Mexico went on to the post of bishop. Several of the more prominent examples include Inquisitor Alonso Granero de Ávalos (inquisitor from 1574 to 1579), who became the bishop of Charcas; Inquisitor Francisco Santos García (inquisitor from 1580 to 1591), who served as bishop of Guadalajara; and Inquisitor Dr. Bartolomé Lobo Guerrero (inquisitor from 1593 to 1598) who became archbishop of the New Kingdom of Granada and later archbishop of Lima, Peru.

79. For specific examples of the instructions concerning the *fiscal*, or prosecutor, see document 1, instructions 18–37. Also see the section on rules concerning the prosecutors of the Inquisition in *Compilación de las instrucciones del oficio de la Santa Inquisición*, 1667, especially folios 8r, 20v–23r.

80. See instruction 19 in document 1.

81. See *Carta acordada del Consejo de Inquisición*, 1632, AHN, Sección de Inquisición, libro 939, folio 68.

82. See Herrera Sotillo, *Ortodoxia y control social*, 117.

83. Ibid., 118.

84. Ibid.

85. Ibid. These included Dr. Bartolomé Lobo Guerrero (who served as prosecutor from 1581 to 1593), Dr. Gonzalo de Martos Bohórques (prosecutor from 1593 to 1609), and Dr. Francisco de Deza y Ulloa (prosecutor from 1685 to 1695).

86. For more details on the duties and responsibilities of the notary of the secret, see "Las instrucciones que tocan al Notario del Secreto," in *Compilación de las instrucciones del oficio de la Santa Inquisición*, 1667, folios 15v–16v.

87. Lea, *History of The Inquisition of Spain*, 2:244.

88. Ibid.

89. Ibid.

90. On the duties and responsibilities of the *alguacil*, see "Las instrucciones que tocan al Alguacil," in *Compilación de las instrucciones del oficio de la Santa Inquisición*, 1667, folios 16v–17r.

91. Ibid., 245.

92. Herrera Sotillo, *Ortodoxia y control social*, 120.

93. See *Carta de los inquisidores de México al Consejo de Inquisición*, 28 de diciembre, 1607, AHN, Sección Inquisición, legajo 2270.

94. See document 3, instruction 13.

95. See "Intrucciones que tocan al Cárcelero," in *Compilación de las instrucciones del oficio de la Santa Inquisición*, 1667, folio 17r.

96. Herrera Sotillo, *Ortodoxia y control social*, 124.

97. On the duties and responsibilities of the receiver, see "Las instrucciones que tocan al Receptor," in *Compilación de las instrucciones del oficio de la Santa Inquisición*, 1667, folios 17v–20r.

98. Lea, *History of the Inquisition of Spain*, 2:446.

99. Herrera Sotillo, *Ortodoxia y control social*, 122.

100. Ibid.

101. *Carta y autos sobre las cuentas dadas por el receptor Francisco López Sanz, quien ha fallecido*, 1672, AHN, Sección de Inquisición, libro 1062, folios 5r–6v, 10–15, 25–28.

102. See Pilar Huertas, Jesús de Miguel, and Antonio Sánchez, *La Inquisición: Tribunal contra los delitos de fe* (Madrid: Editorial Libsa, 2003), 225.

103. On the duties and responsibilities of the accountant, see "Las instrucciones que tocan al Contador," in *Compilación de las instrucciones del oficio de la Santa Inquisición*, 1667, folio 25r–v.

104. On the structure of the finances of the Inquisition, see José Martínez Millán, "Estructura de la hacienda de la Inquisición," in *Historia de la Inquisición en España y América*, vol. 2: *Las estructuras del Santo Oficio*, ed. Joaquín Pérez Villanueva and Bartolomé Escandell Bonet (Madrid: Biblioteca de Autores Cristianos, Centro de Estudios Inquisitoriales, 1993), 885–1076.

105. See Lea, *History of the Inquisition of Spain*, 2:251.

106. Ibid.

107. *Carta acordada del Consejo de Inquisición*, 18 de Junio, 1608, AHN, Sección de Inquisición, libro 942, folio 64.

108. Kamen, *Spanish Inquisition*, 193.

109. Lea, *History of the Inquisition of Spain*, 2:246.

110. Herrera Sotillo, *Ortodoxia y control social*, 124–25.

111. Ibid., 124.

112. Ibid., 125.

113. Lea, *History of the Inquisition of Spain*, 2:263.

114. Ibid.

115. On the development of inquisitorial law concerning these qualifiers and consultants, see Nesvig, *Ideology and Inquisition*, 71–74.

116. Ibid., 263.

117. This duty of the *calificadores* in New Spain made them important players in the censorship of religious and political publications. For a discussion of the role of these *calificadores* relative to book censorship, see ibid., 141–63.

118. Ibid., 136–42.

119. Ibid., 142.

120. On the role of the ordinary in inquisition cases in Mexico, see Lea, *Inquisition in the Spanish Dependencies*, 203–4.

121. For the specific orders sent to the Inquisition of New Spain concerning the necessity of conducting a formal *limpieza de sangre* of all candidates for the office of familiar, see *Carta acordada del Consejo de Inquisición ordenando a los inquisidores de México de tomarles las informaciones sobre sus geneaologías y limpieza de sangre a los familiares*, 6 de Julio, 1575, AGN, Ramo de Inquisición, 1511, folio 9r–v.

122. See *Lista de los Familiares del Santo Oficio con Noticia de la fecha del nombramiento y de los Inquisidores que la firmaron, de marzo 3, 1660 hasta 19 de enero, 1701*, AGN, Ramo de Inquisición, vol. 87, exp. 2, 17 folios.

123. The territory granted to the Tribunal of the Holy Office in New Spain encompassed much more than the lands directly controlled by the Audiencia and viceroyalty of Mexico. In several instances, especially concerning Cuba and lower Central America, difficulties and jurisdictional disputes over regional districts eventually led to the removal of several territories from the geographic control of the tribunal of Mexico. For instance, in 1610 the island of Cuba was removed from the control of the Mexican tribunal and handed over to the newly created tribunal of Cartagena de Indias, supposedly because of the closer administrative distance of Cartagena. The southern portion of Central America also passed over to the control of the tribunal of Peru based in Lima, with especially Panama and the region of Costa Rica residing in the tribunal of Lima's territorial district by 1650. For more information on the territorial extensions of the New World tribunals of the Inquisition, see Mariel de Ibáñez, *El Tribunal de la Inquisición en México*, 60–61.

124. Alberro, *Inquisición y sociedad*, 23–24.

125. The instructions given to the inquisitions sent to the Spanish American colonies stated that the inquisitors should create commissaries of the Holy Office in every city that served as the head of a bishopric as well as in all of the major port cities. See Herrera Sotillo, *Ortodoxia y control social*, 128.

126. On the Inquisition commissaries and their duties in New Spain, see *Instrucción que deben observar los comisarios y notarios del Tribunal de la Santa Inquisición de México en el despacho de los negocios de fe y demas tocantes a su conocimiento* (México, 1667) (consulted in AGN, Ramo de Inquisición, vol. 1519, exp. 5, folios 276r–293v).

127. See *Carta del tribunal de México al Consejo de Inquisición sobre nombramientos de calificadores, comisarios y familiares en el distrito de México*, 8 de Mayo, 1572, AHN, Sección de Inquisición, libro 1047, folio 98.

128. See *Instrucción que deben observar los comisarios y notarios del Tribunal de la Santa Inquisición de México*, AGN, Ramo de Inquisición, vol. 1519, exp. 5, folio 280r–v.

129. For a list of the major inquisition commissaries in New Spain from 1572 to 1655 and their backgrounds, see Alberro, *Inquisición y sociedad*, 85–96.

130. Nesvig, *Ideology and Inquisition*, 142.

131. See Alberro, *Inquisición y sociedad*, 50. Alberro cites his excessive zeal in collecting information against large numbers of people in the region of Celaya. See AGN, Ramo de Inquisición, vol. 278.

132. lberro, *Inquisición y sociedad*, 51.

133. See *Denuncias contra Diego de Herrera Arteaga, comisario de Zacatecas* (1613), AGN, Ramo de Inquisición, vol. 303, folio 392.

134. Alberro, *Inquisición y sociedad*, 51.

135. For the naming of local notaries and their specific duties, see *Instrucción que deben observar los comisarios y notarios del Tribunal de la Santa Inquisición de México*, AGN, Ramo de Inquisición, vol. 1519, exp. 5, folio 278v.

136. Lea, *Inquisition in the Spanish Dependencies*, 212.

137. Ibid., 213.

138. For a detailed description of the finances and activities of the Real Fisco de la Inquisición in New Spain, see Gisela von Wobeser, "La Inquisición como institución crediticia en el siglo XVIII," *Historia Mexicana* 39, no. 4 (1990): 849–79.

139. Lea, *Inquisition in the Spanish Dependencies*, 212.

140. See ibid. Few sources have been compiled for the formal study of the salaries and finances of the Inquisition of New Spain. Comparative material does exist for the tribunal in Peru. For excellent information of the salaries and finances of the Tribunal of the Holy Office in Lima, see Casta-

ñeda Delgado et al., *La Inquisición de Lima*, vol. 1: *1635–1696*, 201–52; vol. 2: *1635–1696*, 209–59; and vol. 3: *1697–1820*, 165–250.

141. For the primary early interpretations of the inquisition as a corrupt institution bent on the confiscation of as much wealth as possible, see Medina, *El Tribunal del Santo Oficio de la Inquisición en México*; Lea, *A History of the Inquisition of Spain* and *Inquisition in the Spanish Dependencies*; and Helen Phipps, "Notes on Medina Rico's 'Visita de Hacienda' to the Inquisition of Mexico," in *Todd Memorial Volumes: Philological Studies*, ed. John D. Fitzgerald and Pauline Taylor, 2 vols. (New York: University of Columbia Press, 1932; reprint of 1930 edition), 2:78–89.

142. See Stanley Hordes, "The Inquisition as Economic and Political Agent: The Campaign of the Mexican Holy Office against the Crypto-Jews in the Mid-Seventeenth Century," *The Americas* 39, no. 1 (1982): 23–38, especially 28.

143. Ibid., 28.

144. Ibid.

145. Lea, *Inquisition in the Spanish Dependencies*, 212.

146. See ibid., 212–17.

147. Ibid., 219.

148. Although Herrera Sotillo argues that most of the early inquisitors' complaints about lack of funds appeared to have been feigned (Herrera Sotillo, *Ortodoxia y control social*, 155–99; Alberro (*Inquisición y sociedad*, 41, n. 47) and others claim that the Mexican tribunal did appear to have severe financial difficulties in the earlier period before 1630. Most scholars agree, however, that after the massive confiscation of the wealth of accused Portuguese merchants as Judaizers, the Inquisition's financial situation improved.

149. For information on the goods and assets of the early tribunal, see *Petición del Tribunal de la Inquisición de México pidiendo a la de España un receptor para un capital de 4,283 pesos*, 1579, AGN, Ramo de Inquisición, vol. 85, exp. 27, 2 folios.

150. In 1814 the notaries who sequestered the goods of the tribunal of Mexico at its first extinction claimed that the earnings during that preceding year amounted to 117,000 pesos, whereas their expenses did not surpass 60,000 pesos. See Lea, *Inquisition in the Spanish Dependencies*, 289.

151. See *Inventario de los bienes del extinguido Tribunal del Santo Oficio de la Inquisición de México*, AGN, Ramo de Intendentes, vol. 42. Part of this documentation is described in document 25.

152. On the rights of the accused in an inquisition trial, see José María García Marín, "Proceso inquisitorial-proceso regio: Las garantias del procesado," *Revista de la Inquisición*, no. 7 (1998): 137–49.

153. See Peters, *Torture*, 62–66.

154. See Kagan and Dyer, *Inquisitorial Inquiries*, 17.

155. Kamen, *Spanish Inquisition*, 193.

156. It is not surprising to see the impact of post-Enlightenment thought on the development of the legal system in the United States as a direct and conscious attempt to avoid the creation of a judicial system that resembled the Inquisition. The major guarantees of the U.S. legal system (e.g., habeas corpus, the concept of a presumption of innocence until proven guilty, the right to know ones accuser, right to remain silent so as not to incriminate oneself) are in a very direct way the Founding Fathers' purposeful attempt to avoid inquisitorial style proceedings in the creation of the U.S. judicial system.

157. The necessity of keeping the prisoner in the prison secretly and in isolation appears prominent in the many printed manuals and instructions of the Inquisition. For an early compilation of the instructions and orders on this, see Pablo García, *Orden que comúnmente se guarda en el Santo*

Oficio de la Inquisición acerca del procesar en las causas que en él se tratan conforme a lo que está proveído por las instrucciones antiguas y nuevas (Madrid, 1622).

158. Lea, *History of the Inquisition of Spain*, 2:475.

159. Kamen, *Spanish Inquisition*, 182.

160. *Instrucciones del Rey al Inquisidor Don Alonso Manrique de Lara*, 1595, AHN, Sección de Inquisición, libro 939, folio 273r–v.

161. *Carta acordada del Consejo de Inquisición a los inquisidores de México sobre el secreto*, 17 de Junio, 1595, AGNRamo de Inquisición, vol. 1511, folio 44r–v.

162. Lea, *History of the Inquisition of Spain*, 2:476.

163. See *Carta acordada del Consejo de la Inquisición a los inquisidores de México sobre el secreto*, 26 de Febrero, 1607, AGN, Ramo de Inquisición, vol. 1511, folio 55r–56v. This order demanded the same punishment for the violation of the oath of secrecy as formal perjury. The Suprema required that it be read each year during the first meeting of the tribunal along with the official instructions, which also had to be publicly read in the tribunal before all of the ministers.

164. Lea, *History of the Inquisition of Spain*, 2:477.

165. *Carta acordada del Consejo de Inquisición a los inquisidores de México sobre la impresión en letra de molde de unos abjuraciones*, 10 de Septiembre, 1590, AGN, Ramo de Inquisición, vol. 1511, folio 41r–v.

166. Lea, *History of the Inquisition of Spain*, 2:473.

167. For the text of the oath and its administration during the first audience, see García, *Orden que comúnmente se guarda en el Santo Oficio de la Inquisición acerca del procesar en las causas*, folios 8r–9r.

168. Lea, *History of the Inquisition of Spain*, 2:473.

169. For a discussion of the development of inquisitorial legislation and procedural manuals, see Cavallero, *Justicia inquisitorial*, 59–60; also see Kamen, *Spanish Inquisition*, 139.

170. The Mexican Inquisition's archive retains copies of many of the manuals and instructions published by the inquisitors general of Spain. These manuals used in New Spain included the most important compilations of these instructions, most notably that of 1561 (printed by order of Inquisitor General Fernando de Valdés in Toledo) and those of 1667 (ordered compiled and printed by Inquisitor General Juan Everardo Nidardo). See *Instrucción que deben observar los comisarios y notarios del Tribunal de la Santa Inquisición de México*, AGN, Ramo de Inquisición, vol. 1519, exp. 1–6, for the copies of these manuals used in New Spain.

171. *Carta acordada del Consejo de la Inquisición a los inquisidores de México sobre las Instrucciones*, 17 de Febrero, 1592, AGN, Ramo de Inquisición, vol. 1511, folios 42r–43v.

172. On the significance of Eimeric's manual and Peña's important commentaries on the text, see Edward Peters, "Editing Inquisitors' Manuals in the Sixteenth Century: Francisco Peña and the Directorium Inquisitorum of Nicholas Eymeric," in *Bibliographical Studies in Honor of Rudolf Hirsch*, ed. William E. Miller and Thomas G. Waldman, with Natalie D. Terrell, *Library Chronicle* 60 (1974): 95–107.

173. For an excellent discussion on the use of these inquisition manuals in New Spain, especially Eimeric's manual with Peña's commentaries, see Nesvig, *Ideology and Inquisition*, 35–44.

174. According to Nesvig, the *Directorium Inquisitorium* was published by itself in Rome in 1587 and 1595 and with commentaries by Peña in 1578, 1583, 1585, 1587 1595, and 1607 (Nesvig, *Ideology and Inquisition*, 287, n. 41).

175. Ibid., 43.

176. Even the Jesuit College library in the remote town of Durango in the far northern region of New Spain possessed a copy of Eimeric's manual commented on by Peña as early as 1610 (ibid., 44).

177. Kamen, *Spanish Inquisition*, 193.

178. Peters, *Torture*, 46–47.

179. Peters, *Inquisition*, 65.

180. Peters, *Torture*, 50–51.

181. See the order concerning confessions taken during a torture session and the requirement that they be ratified at least twenty-four hours later in García, *Orden que comúnmente se guarda en el Santo Oficio de la Inquisición acerca del procesar en las causas*, folio 30r–v.

182. For a complete discussion of the methods and procedures of the use of torture throughout Europe, see Peters, *Torture*, 60–89; also for more detailed information on the juridical use of torture in western Europe, see Julius Ralph Ruff, *Violence in Early Modern Europe, 1500–1800* (Cambridge: Cambridge University Press, 2001), especially the section on "Judicial Torture," 92–96.

183. On the nature of proof and a suspect's confession during inquisition trials, see Kamen, *Spanish Inquisition*, 183–92.

184. See Peters, *Torture*, 46–47.

185. Lea, *History of the Inquisition of Spain*, 2:491.

186. See *Compilación de las instrucciones del oficio de la Santa Inquisición*, 1667.

187. See Instructions from the Inquisitor General Cardinal Don Diego de Espinosa given to the Inquisitors of New Spain, 1570 (document 3, especially instructions 24 and 25).

188. For an in-depth discussion of the defense of the accused in inquisition trials, see María García Marín, "Proceso inquisitorial-proceso regio: Las garantias del procesado"; also for an interesting view on the Inquisition and the issue of human rights, see Regina María Pérez Marcos, "Derechos humanos e Inquisición, ¿Conceptos contrapuestos?" *Revista de la Inquisición*, no. 9 (2000): 181–90.

189. The following pages and narrative description of the various stages and subsequent phases of a typical Inquisition trial come from the author's exhaustive review of thousands of folios of trials from the Inquisition in New Spain and a comparison and analysis of their procedures with the official manuals and orders established by the Spanish Inquisition. The narrative also owes much of its structure and content to the major secondary sources on the Inquisition's procedures in Spain and New Spain, including the works of Henry Charles Lea (*History of the Inquisition of Spain* and *Inquisition in the Spanish Dependencies*); José Toribio Medina (*Historia del tribunal del Santo Oficio de la inquisición en México* [México: Ediciones Fuente Cultural, 1952]); Richard E. Greenleaf (*Zumárraga and the Mexican Inquisition, 1536–1543* [Washington, D.C.: Academy of American Franciscan History, 1966] and *Mexican Inquisition*); Herrera Sotillo (*Ortodoxia y control social*); Solange Alberro (*Inquisición y sociedad*); Henry Kamen (*Spanish Inquisition*); Edward Peters (*Inquisition* and *Torture*); Helen Rawlings (*The Spanish Inquisition*); and Joseph Pérez (*The Spanish Inquisition: A History* [New Haven: Yale University Press, 2006]); Lu Ann Homza (*The Spanish Inquisition*).

190. Kamen, *Spanish Inquisition*, 193–94.

191. Ibid., 174–75.

192. Lea, *History of the Inquisition of Spain*, 2:554; also see the discussion of false witness in Kamen, *Spanish Inquisition*, 181–83.

193. See Rawlings, *The Spanish Inquisition*, 31.

194. For the source of Voltaire's quotation, see William Jones, *The History of the Christian Church from the Birth of Christ to the XVIII Century* (Philadelphia: R. W. Pomeroy, 1832), 367.

195. See Peters, *Torture*, 66.

196. See García, *Orden que comúnmente se guarda en el Santo Oficio de la Inquisición acerca del procesar*, folios 1v–2r.

197. See *Compilación de las instrucciones del oficio de la Santa Inquisición*, 1667, folios 3v–4r.

198. Even in the district commissariats, the commissaries were cautioned to scrupulously follow these procedures. See *Instrucción que deben observar los comisarios y notarios del Tribunal de la Santa Inquisición de México*, AGN, Ramo de Inquisición, vol. 1519, exp. 5, folios 277r–279r.

199. For more detailed information on the weight of witness testimony in heresy cases, see Lea, *History of the Inquisition of Spain*, 2:561–68.

200. See Castañeda Delgado et al., *La Inquisición de Lima*, vol. 3: *1697–1820*.

201. For instructions on the responsibilities and duties of the commissaries, see *Instrucción que deben observar los comisarios y notarios del Tribunal de la Santa Inquisición de México*, AGN, Ramo de Inquisición, vol. 1519, exp. 5, folios 276r–293r.

202. For a discussion of this process and the creation of the initial *sumaria*, see Lea, *History of the Inquisition of Spain*, 2:486–89. In the case of an Inquisition commissary's initial investigations, the official instructions of commissaries in New Spain required them not only to compile their own opinions and include them along with the denunciations and witness testimonies but also to compile "a separate information concerning the style of life, customs and public fame and opinion of both the persons denounced and the witnesses." The commissaries were also warned to conduct these investigations "cautiously and impartially." See *Instrucción que deben observar los comisarios y notarios del Tribunal de la Santa Inquisición de México*, folio 5r.

203. Kamen, *Spanish Inquisition*, 183.

204. García, *Orden que comúnmente se guarda en el Santo Oficio de la Inquisición acerca del procesar*, folio 5r–v.

205. See section 10, "On Prisoners," in *Copilación de las Instrucciones del Santo Officio de la Santa Inquisición* (Madrid: Alonso Gomez, 1576).

206. See instruction 6 in Valdés's *Compilation of the Instructions of the Holy Office*, 1561 (document 1), as well as the similar order and reference to these instructions in García, *Orden que comúnmente se guarda en el Santo Oficio de la Inquisición acerca del procesar*, folio 6r.

207. See *Compilación de las instrucciones del oficio de la Santa Inquisición*, 1667.

208. García, *Orden que comúnmente se guarda en el Santo Oficio de la Inquisición acerca del procesar*, folio 8r–v.

209. Ibid., folio 6r–v.

210. See Greenleaf, *Zumárraga*, 22; also see *Compilation of the Instructions of the Holy Office*, 1561 (document 1, especially instructions 13–14).

211. The instructions formally demanded that the suspect recount his genealogy in detail. See García, *Orden que comúnmente se guarda en el Santo Oficio de la Inquisición acerca del procesar*, folios 9r–10r. Many scholars have used the so-called incidental autobiographies compiled during these trials to study various classes of people; see, for example, Kagan and Dyer, *Inquisitorial Inquiries*.

212. García's *Orden que comúnmente se guarda en el Santo Oficio de la Inquisición acerca del procesar* specifically states that the suspect should be asked to cross himself and then state the "Pater Noster, Ave María, Credo, and Salve Regina in Latin or in Spanish" (folio 10r). For a detailed discussion of these requirements of religious instruction in inquisition trial proceedings, see Rawlings, *The Spanish Inquisition*, 115–16.

213. See document 31 for an early 1539 example of the Mexican Inquisition's requiring a defendant to recite these prayers.

214. The official instructions ordered the inquisitors during this first audience to issue the first warning to the suspect to confess because they had evidence against him for a crime against the faith. The orders specifically told the inquisitors to formally warn the prisoner, "This Holy Office does not have the custom to arrest any person without sufficient information or proof of their having

said, done, or committed . . . something against the faith." See Pablo García's *Orden que comúnmente se guarda en el Santo Oficio de la Inquisición acerca del procesar*, folio 10v.

215. Ibid., folio 11r.

216. Ibid.

217. See instruction 19 in Valdés's *Compilation of the Instructions of the Holy Office*, 1561 (document 1). Moreover, the secretary of the Suprema, Pablo García, in 1622 noted that the prosecutor was still required to formally charge the prisoner even if he gave a full confession. See García, *Orden que comúnmente se guarda en el Santo Oficio de la Inquisición acerca del procesar*, folio 14v.

218. García, *Orden que comúnmente se guarda en el Santo Oficio de la Inquisición acerca del procesar*, folios 13r–14r.

219. Peters, *Inquisition*, 93.

220. Ibid., folios 14v–15r.

221. See Kamen, *Spanish Inquisition*, 194.

222. See García, *Orden que comúnmente se guarda en el Santo Oficio de la Inquisición acerca del procesar*, folio 15v.

223. Kamen, *The Spanish Inquisition*, 194.

224. Henry Kamen noted that the Spanish Inquisition, unlike the medieval inquisition, allowed the accused to have the services of an advocate or defense attorney (ibid., 194).

225. Kamen noted that "by the middle of the sixteenth century the prisoners' lawyers, or *abogados de los presos*, were recognized as officials of the Inquisition, dependent upon and working with the inquisitors" (ibid., 194).

226. See Herrera Sotillo, *Ordoxia y control social*, 124.

227. See instruction 23 in Valdés's Compilation of the Instructions of the Holy Office, 1561 (document 1). Also see García, *Orden que comúnmente se guarda en el Santo Oficio de la Inquisición acerca del procesar*, folio 16r–v.

228. The attorney-client privilege, a hallmark of the U.S. legal system, was another right of defendants denied in inquisitorial proceedings.

229. Rawlings, *The Spanish Inquisition*, 32.

230. Ibid.

231. See García, *Orden que comúnmente se guarda en el Santo Oficio de la Inquisición acerca del procesar*, folio 17r–v.

232. *Compilación de las instrucciones del oficio de la Santa Inquisición*, 1667, folio 6r.

233. See instruction 30 in Valdés's *Compilation of the Instructions of the Holy Office*, 1561 (document 1).

234. See García, *Orden que comúnmente se guarda en el Santo Oficio de la Inquisición acerca del procesar*, folio 20v.

235. See instruction 36 in Valdés's *Compilation of the Instructions of the Holy Office*, 1561 (document 1).

236. Kamen, *The Spanish Inquisition*, 195.

237. Lea, *The Inquisition in Spain*, 3:63.

238. Ibid., 63–64.

239. See García, *Orden que comúnmente se guarda en el Santo Oficio de la Inquisición acerca del procesar*, folio 25r.

240. Lea, *The Inquisition in Spain*, 3:64.

241. Pérez, *The Spanish Inquisition*, 146.

242. Lea, *The Inquisition in Spain*, 3:64.

243. On the process of *tachas* in inquisition trials, see Andrew W. Keitt, *Inventing the Sacred: Imposture, Inquisition, and the Boundaries of the Supernatural in Golden Age Spain* (Leiden: Brill, 2005), 21.

244. Ibid., 57.

245. See instruction 52 in Valdés's *Compilation of the Instructions of the Holy Office*, 1561 (document 1).

246. On the relationship between a full confession as evidence or proof of a crime and the relationship between a confession and torture, see Peters, *Torture*, 40–73.

247. See the detailed instructions on when and how to administer an interrogation or confession using torture in García, *Orden que comúnmente se guarda en el Santo Oficio de la Inquisición acerca del procesar*, folios 26r–28r.

248. Peters, *Torture*, 57.

249. See Kamen, *Spanish Inquisition*, 188–92; Peters, *Inquisition*, 92–93; and Rawlings, *The Spanish Inquisition*, 33.

250. Rawlings, *The Spanish Inquisition*, 33.

251. See the figures on number of cases involving torture in the Inquisition in New Spain in Herrera Sotillo, *Ortodoxia y control social*, 214–32.

252. On the administration of torture in inquisition proceedings, see Lea, *History of the Inquisition of Spain*, 3:1–35; as well as Lea, "An Essay on Torture," in *Superstition and Force: Essays on the Wager of Law, the Wager of Battle, the Ordeal, Torture* (Philadelphia: Collins Printers, 1866), 281–391; also see Peters, *Torture*, 62–67.

253. Kamen, *Spanish Inquisition*, 189.

254. García, *Orden que comúnmente se guarda en el Santo Oficio de la Inquisición acerca del procesar*, folios 26r–27r.

255. There are cases in New Spain in which defendants over the age of eighty were submitted to questioning under torture, but these cases were rare. According to Kamen, "There seems to have been no age limit for victims, nor was there any limit on the torture" (Kamen, *Spanish Inquisition*, 190).

256. García, *Orden que comúnmente se guarda en el Santo Oficio de la Inquisición acerca del procesar*, folio 30r.

257. Ibid.

258. Ibid., folio 30v.

259. See instruction 40 in Valdés's *Compilation of the Instructions of the Holy Office*, 1561 (document 1).

260. A review of the mandatorily recorded first book of votes from the many *consulta de fe* in New Spain shows that in the voting on the administration of torture or in the final sentences the Mexican Inquisition involved from six to ten consultants. See *Libro primero de votos de la Inquisición de México, 1573–1600* (México: Imprenta Universitaria, Archivo General de la Nación, 1949).

261. Rawlings, *The Spanish Inquisition*, 34.

262. See instruction 66 in Valdés's *Compilation of the Instructions of the Holy Office*, 1561 (document 1 in this volume). Also see *Compilación de las instrucciones del oficio de la Santa Inquisición*, 1667, folio 13r.

263. Again, see instruction 66 in Valdés's *Compilation of the Instructions of the Holy Office*, 1561 (document 1).

264. See Cavallero, *Justicia inquisitorial*, 157–67. Also see *Manual de Inquisidores: Directorium Inquisitorum de Fray Nicolas Eymeric*, with translation, notes, and introduction by José Antoinio Fortea (Madrid: La Esfera de los Libros, 2006).

265. On the nature of inquisition sentences and punishments in New Spain, see Antonio M. García-Molina Riquelme, *El régimen de penas y penitencias en el Tribunal de la Inquisición de México* (México: Universidad Nacional Autónoma de México, 1999).

266. Richard Dugdale, *Narrative of Unheard of Popish Cruelties towards Protestants beyond Seas; or, A New Account of the Bloody Spanish Inquisition. Published as a Caveat to Protestants* (London: Printed for John Hancock at the Three Bibles in Popes-Head-Alley over against the Royal Exchange in Cornbil, 1680), 13.

267. For a discussion of the process of acquittal or suspension, see Lea, *History of the Inquisition of Spain*, 3:105–10.

268. For a complete description of the nature of the sentence of absolution (or the *sentencia absolutoria ab instantia*), see García, *Orden que comúnmente se guarda en el Santo Oficio de la Inquisición acerca del procesar*, folios 41v–42r. However, Valdés's *Compilation of the Instructions of the Holy Office*, 1561 (document 1) states that this type of a sentence of vindication should be used sparingly by the inquisitors (see instruction 47).

269. Valdés, *Compilation of the Instructions of the Holy Office*, 1561 (document 1), instructions 46 and 47.

270. Herrera Sotillo notes that during this period from 1571 to 1700, the Inquisition in New Spain absolved or acquitted only forty-five persons for lack of proof or because their trials revealed that they had been testified against falsely. See Herrera Sotillo, *Ortodoxia y control social*, 231.

271. Instructions on the cautious use of a sentence of compurgation are detailed in García, *Orden que comúnmente se guarda en el Santo Oficio de la Inquisición acerca del procesar*, folios 69r–73r. Special care, according to this manual, had to be taken to examine and cross-examine the witnesses whom the accused presented as his *compurgadores* (or oath takers). Similarly, they could not be witnesses presented during his defense or a close relative or servant or employee of the accused.

272. In New Spain, the Inquisition likewise suspended only a small minority of the cases (less than 5 percent of the 1,235 cases tried from 1571 to 1700) for lack of evidence. Most of these cases, according to the scholar María Herrera Sotillo, concerned the crime of bigamy, which became difficult to prove when the first marriage occurred across the Atlantic or in another distant district far from New Spain. See Herrera Sotillo, *Ortodoxia y control social*, 231–32.

273. Alberro, *Inquisición y sociedad*, 208.

274. See García-Molina Riquelme, *El régimen de penas y penitencias en el Tribunal de la Inquisición de México*, 11–32.

275. Lea, *History of the Inquisition of Spain*, 3:93–104.

276. For the significance of this public retraction or abjuration, see ibid., 123–26.

277. Pérez, *The Spanish Inquisition*, 150.

278. See García-Molina Riquelme, *El régimen de penas y penitencias en el Tribunal de la Inquisición de México*, 563–69, 583–86, 588–92.

279. For the specific formula and process of a convicted heretic's abjuration for slight suspicion of heresy, see the instructions on *"Abjuracion de levi,"* in García, *Orden que comúnmente se guarda en el Santo Oficio de la Inquisición acerca del procesar*, folios 39r–40r.

280. The specific formula and instructions on the issuing of a sentence of *abjuración de vehementi* is detailed in ibid., folios 38r–39r.

281. Ibid., folio 34r.

282. García-Molina Riquelme, *El régimen de penas y penitencias en el Tribunal de la Inquisición de México*, 559–63, 582, 587–88.

283. See García, *Orden que comúnmente se guarda en el Santo Oficio de la Inquisición acerca del procesar*, folios 37r–39r.

284. Alberro, *Inquisición y sociedad*, 208.

285. García, *Orden que comúnmente se guarda en el Santo Oficio de la Inquisición acerca del procesar*, folios 34v–36r.

286. Pérez, *The Spanish Inquisition*, 150.

287. García, *Orden que comúnmente se guarda en el Santo Oficio de la Inquisición acerca del procesar*, folios 32r–34r.

288. Rawlings, *The Spanish Inquisition*, 35. Also see Kamen, *Spanish Inquisition*, 200–201.

289. Alberro, *Inquisición y sociedad*, 208.

290. For a complete description of the *sanbenito* and *coroza*, see Lea, *History of the Inquisition of Spain*, 3:162–72.

291. For more information on the punishments and penances of those reconciled by the Inquisition in New Spain, see García-Molina Riquelme, *El régimen de penas y penitencias en el Tribunal de la Inquisición de México*, 343–45, 599–602, 628–30.

292. On the sentence of relaxation of prisoners, see ibid., 79–212.

293. Ibid., 88–115.

294. Ibid., 132–44.

295. See Kamen, *Spanish Inquisition*, 202–3; also see Rawlings, *The Spanish Inquisition*, 35; as well as Pérez, *The Spanish Inquisition*, 169–75.

296. Alberro, *Inquisición y sociedad*, 208. Herrera Sotillo also notes that during this period, only forty people were sentenced to be relaxed in person for execution by the Inquisition in New Spain (*Ortodoxia y control social*, 230–31). The total number of all relaxations in person in the Inquisition in New Spain amounted to only forty-five people from 1571 to 1820.

297. Dugdale, Narrative of Unheard of Popish Cruelties towards Protestants beyond Seas, 13.

298. Lea, *History of the Inquisition of Spain*, 3:100.

299. Pérez, *The Spanish Inquisition*, 152.

300. For more on fees and other fines collected by the Inquisition in New Spain, see Lea, *Inquisition in the Spanish Dependencies*, 218; as well as García-Molina Riquelme, *El régimen de penas y penitencias en el Tribunal de la Inquisición de México*, 395–99.

301. See "Inquisitorial Proceedings in Mexico City against Robert Tomson, 1559–1560," in G. R. G. Conway, *An Englishmen and the Mexican Inquisition* (México: privately published, 1927), 23–77; quotation, 11–12.

302. On the history and development of the *sanbenito* and its use by the Inquisition, see Shelomo Alfassa, "The Origin and Stigma of the Iberian Garment of Shame, the San Benito," *International Sephardic Journal* 1 (September 2004): 1–13.

303. See García-Molina Riquelme, *El régimen de penas y penitencias en el Tribunal de la Inquisición de México*, 539–34.

304. See Antonio M. García-Molina Riquelme, "Una propuesta del Tribunal de México: El Sambenito de Media Aspa," *Revista de la Inquisición* (Spain) 9 (2000): 241–49.

305. For information on the *quemadero*, or place of execution for those sentenced to be burned at the stake in Mexico, see Lea, *Inquisition in the Spanish Dependencies*, 206.

306. Pérez, *The Spanish Inquisition*, 166.

307. See García-Molina Riquelme, *El régimen de penas y penitencias en el Tribunal de la Inquisición de México*, 197–200.

308. See especially Greenleaf, "Historiography of the Mexican Inquisition." For other discussions of historiography, see Rawlings, *The Spanish Inquisition*, 1–20; and Kimberly Lynn Hossain, "Unraveling the Spanish Inquisition: Inquisitorial Studies in the Twenty-first Century," *History Compass* 5-4 (2007): 1280–93.

309. For just one example of the use of Inquisition sources in the study of the religion, morality, and sexuality of New Spain, see Asunción Lavrin, "Aproximación al tema de la sexualidad en el México colonial," *Encuentro* 2, no. 1 (1984): 23–40. For a synthesis on the colonial church's stance on sexuality in New Spain, see Asunción Lavrin, "Sexuality in Colonial Mexico: A Church Dilemma," in *Sexuality and Marriage in Colonial Latin America*, ed. Asunción Lavrin (Lincoln: University of Nebraska Press, 1989), 47–95. For other examples of Lavrin's analysis of inquisition materials for the investigation of the history of women and nuns in New Spain, see Asunción Lavrin, "Women and Religion in Spanish America," in *Women and Religion in America*, vol. 2: *The Colonial and Revolutionary Periods*, ed. Rosemary Radford Ruether and Rosemary Skinner Keller (San Francisco: Harper & Row, 1983), 42–78; Lavrin, "Espiritualidad en el claustro novohispano del siglo XVII," *Colonial Latin American Review* 4, no. 2 (1995): 155–79; and Lavrin, "La escritura desde un mundo oculto: Espiritualidad y anonimidad en el Convento de San Juan de la Penitencia," *Estudios de Historia Novohispana* 22 (2000): 49–76.

310. Kamen, *Spanish Inquisition*, 317–18.

311. On the use of inquisition sources by historians, see Thomas Kuehn, "Reading Microhistory: The Example of Giovanni and Lusanna," *Journal of Modern History* 61, no. 3 (1989): 512–34.

312. Ibid., 318.

313. See Keitt, *Inventing the Sacred*, 22.

314. See Lu Ann Homza, review of Stuart Schwartz, *All Can Be Saved: Tolerance and Salvation in the Iberian Atlantic World*, *William and Mary Quarterly*, 3rd ser., 66, no. 2 (2009): 409–11 (quote from p. 411).

315. See Jean Pierre Dedieu, "The Archives of the Holy Office of Toledo as a Source for Historical Anthropology," in *The Inquisition in Early Modern Europe: Studies on Sources and Methods*, ed. Gustav Henningsen and John Tedeschi, in association with Charles Amiel (DeKalb: Northern Illinois University Press, 1986), 158–89.

316. Ibid.

317. Ibid., 177.

318. See John Edwards, "Review: Was the Spanish Inquisition Truthful?" *Jewish Quarterly Review* 87 (1997): 351–66.

Part I. Laws, Regulations, and Instructions concerning the Holy Office

1. For a discussion of the development of inquisitorial legislation and procedural manuals, see Ricardo Juan Cavallero, *Justicia inquisitorial: El sistema de justicia criminal de la Inquisición española* (Madrid: Ariel Historia, 2003), 59–60.

2. For a review of the literature on the juridical procedures, laws, and instruction manuals of the Holy Office, see Joaquín Pérez Villanueva and Bartolomé Escandel Bonet, *Historia de la Inquisición en España y América*, vol. 1. *El conocimiento científico y el proceso histórico de la Institucion (1478–1834)* (Madrid: Biblioteca de Autores Cristianas / Centro de Estudios Inquisitoriales, 1984), especially 41–167.

3. The collection of royal cédulas concerning the Holy Office can be found in book XIX of *Recopilación de leyes de los reynos de las Indias: Mandadas imprimir y publicar por la Majestad Católica del rey Don Carlos II, nuestro señor*, titulo XIX, "De los Tribunales del Santo Oficio de la Inquisición y Sus Ministros" (Madrid: Imprenta de Julian de Paredes, 1681), folios 91–105.

4. Cavallero, *Justicia inquisitorial*, 60.

5. Solange Alberro, *Inquisición y sociedad en México, 1571–1700* (México: Fondo de Cultura Económica, 1988), 69.

6. See José Toribio Medina, *Historia del Tribunal Santo Oficio de la Inquisición de México*. edited and expanded by Julio Jiménez Rueda (México: Ediciones Fuente Cultural. 1952), 182–83.

7. The Supreme Council of the General Inquisition (known as the Suprema) was the chief governing body of the Spanish Inquisition. Presided over by an inquisitor general, the Suprema became modeled on the system of governing councils in use by the Spanish Hapsburg kings. It joined the other governing councils of the Spanish crown such as the Consejo de las Indias (which administered Spain's colonial possessions in the New World) and the Consejo de Castilla (which administered the Kingdom of Castile).

8. The person chosen to sequester the goods and hold them for the Inquisition had to be bonded and prove that he was a good Christian and of a high moral character.

9. The historian Henry Charles Lea noted that the job of serving as a trustee of the sequestered goods "involved labor, anxiety and responsibility without payment but, when selected and approved, the appointee was obliged to serve, under penalty of excommunication and a fine of ten or twenty thousand maravedís" (Henry Charles Lea, *A History of the Inquisition of Spain* [New York: Macmillan, 1906], 502). The law also required that the trustee should not be a relative of the prisoner and that he should be of good repute and standing in the community.

10. A Spanish *ducat* (*ducado*) was a gold coin equivalent to a value of 375 maravedies. The *maravedí* was a fictitious Spanish money of account that came to serve as the smallest fraction of Spanish currency. The ducat was replaced by the Spanish gold coin known as an *escudo* after the monetary reforms of the Spanish king Charles V in 1537. The escudo was a debased form of the earlier ducat and worth only 350 maravedies.

11. The most common prayers of the Christian doctrine that the inquisitors requested the prisoners to recite were the Our Father (Pater Noster), the Ave María, and the Salve Regina. They also often requested the accused heretics to recite the Creed and the Articles of Faith.

12. The *curador* (a guardian or trustee) was usually named in Spanish law to protect and represent minors in legal cases and judicial proceedings. Following the traditions of Roman law, Spanish legal proceedings "provided that in suits and actions involving those who had not attained the full age of twenty-five years, the assent of a *curador,* either permanent or temporary ad hoc, was necessary to validate the legal acts of a minor" (Lea, *History of the Inquisition of Spain,* 50).

13. In the Spanish colonial period, a *procurador* (procurator) was someone who had the legal right (by delegation through the use of a power of attorney) to act and conduct legal business in the name of another person. A procurator was not necessarily a trained lawyer but could help a defendant litigate his or her case. In Inquisition cases, permitting prisoners to have access to an external procurator would have given them access to the outside world, something that in effect defeated the necessary secret isolation of inquisitorial prisoners.

14. The Inquisition conducted two specific types of questioning under torture: *tormento in caput proprium* (on one's own head), used to force a suspect to make a confession in his own case or trial; and *tormento in caput alienum* (on someone else's head), which was torture used to force a suspected or convicted heretic to identify and testify against his accomplices. This second type of torture was used only when a suspect refused to give information about or name his accomplices and the inquisitors had strong suspicions that the suspect was withholding the names of the accomplices.

15. The use of torture during the questioning of a suspected heretic did not occur until the final proof stage of an Inquisition trial right before the prosecutor made his formal accusation against the suspect. The Inquisition used torture as a means of proof *ad eruendam veritatem* (in order to discover the truth). Questioning under torment was reserved for only those suspects accused of formal heresy and not those suspected of lesser ecclesiastical crimes and minor infractions such as blasphemy, witchcraft, and bigamy. For the use of judicial torture, see Edward Peters, *Torture* (Philadelphia: University of Pennsylvania Press, 1996), especially 11–73.

16. This instruction to confessors of Inquisition prisoners actually violated the canonically mandated orders to confessing priests not to reveal that which was confessed to them in the sacrament of the confession.

17. An Audiencia, the highest royal court of appeals within a jurisdiction, was also a court of first instance in certain cases. In the kingdom of New Spain (Colonial Mexico and Central America) there were three separate *audiencias* or appellate court districts: The Audiencia of Mexico (founded 1529), the Audiencia of Guatemala (founded 1544), and the Audiencia of Nueva Galicia (founded in Guadalajara in 1549).

18. *Oidores* (literally listeners) were the judges of these local *audiencias* or appellate courts. By the later colonial period the Audiencia of Mexico had six of these *oidores* or judges.

19. The *sanbenito* was the official garment of shame that the Inquisition used to stigmatize the convicted heretics who were reconciled or relaxed to the secular authorities for execution. Other penitents, even those who may have abjured suspicions of heresy, would often be sentenced to wear this garment for specified lengths of time as a punishment and a reminder to the faithful of the danger of heresy.

20. *Tierra Firme* was the Spanish term derived from the Latin *terra firma* meaning "dry land" (i.e., the mainland).

21. *Alcaldes* were local administrative officials with administrative and judicial functions.

22. *Corregidores* were Spanish officials or magistrates in charge of a province or district.

23. *Alcaldes mayores* were the chief political and military officials who served as the administrator of a province, or a governor.

24. For more specific information on Espinosa's career as inquisitor general, see José Antonio Escudero, "Notas sobre la carrera del inquisidor general Diego de Espinosa," *Revista de la Inquisición* 10 (2001): 7–16.

25. The term Temistitán-México was used during the early colonial period in New Spain to identify the capital city of the viceroyalty rebuilt on the ruins of the Aztec capital of Tenochtitlan. The term fell out of use by the end of the sixteenth century when the capital was simply referred to as Mexico, or Mexico City (*la ciudad de México*).

26. A *legajo* was a bundle of papers dealing with a common subject or theme that were held or fastened together.

27. The value of a maravedís was fixed at 375 maravedis for a gold ducat and 34 maravedis for one silver real. Eight silver reales made up 1 silver peso (commonly known as a "piece of eight").

28. The "poor person's ration" was the set and established minimum standard or ration of food to be paid for poor prisoners whom the Inquisition had to support from its own funds. In 1641, for example, the standard ration given to the poor prisoners in Toledo was apparently valued at 1½ reales per day (see Lea, *History of the Inquisition of Spain*, 531–32). In comparison, the daily ration of the poor prisoners apparently was much higher in New Spain because of the higher cost of living in the colonies. As early as 1615, the daily ration for poor prisoners was set by the Mexican Inquisition at 2½ reales a day (see documents 12 and 13).

29. Blood purity, or *limpieza de sangre*, was a formal legal certification that a person and his ancestors were not "contaminated" with the blood of heretics, or the blood of Moors (Muslims), Jews, or Africans. Records and documentation proving the purity of one's blood ancestors were necessary in order to apply for a government or ecclesiastical position. Detailed records on this certification of blood purity of those who applied for a position in the Inquisition were meticulously collected and archived by each tribunal.

30. The "Festival of the Three Kings" refers to the *Day of the Three Wise Men*, and it was celebrated in colonial Mexico on January 6 (also known as the Feast of the Epiphany).

31. The *Domingo de cuasimodo,* called Quasimodo Sunday, was the Sunday after Easter Sunday. The word *cuasimodo* apparently comes from the Latin word that means "Al modo de," and it refers directly to the words spoken at the beginning of the mass on the Sunday after Easter Sunday, "Quasi modo géniti infants . . ." (Just like newborn children . . .).

32. This is a reference to the *Compilation of the Instructions of the Inquisition* (see document 1).

33. The "ordinary" was either the local bishop or his selected representative.

34. The initial order that established the Inquisition in the New World also removed from its cognizance all cases dealing with the indigenous peoples of the New World. Instead, a separate court was formally established under the powers of the local bishops. This separate "inquisition of the Indians" was called the *Provisorato de Indios.* For more information concerning the removal of the indigenous people from the jurisdiction of the Inquisition, see Richard E. Greenleaf, "The Persistence of Native Values: The Inquisition and the Indians of Colonial Mexico," *The Americas* 50, no. 3 (1994): 351-j75; as well as his earlier article "The Inquisition and the Indians of New Spain: A Study in Jurisdictional Confusion," *The Americas* 22 (1965): 138–66.

35. *Ad verbum* (word for word).

36. The Council of Trent (1545–63) was one of the most important Catholic Church councils and played a major role in developing and reforming Catholic doctrine and dogma in reaction to the Protestant reformation. During the twenty-five sessions that made up this council, the Catholic bishops issued condemnations against what they defined as Protestant heresies and solidified, codified, and defended the Catholic Church's teachings in the areas of scripture, the sacraments, and the Eucharist, as well as the veneration and cult of saints. The Council of Trent was significant in terms of the development of the Inquisition in that it further defined the concept of heresy and issued important decrees concerning prohibited books and heretical beliefs.

37. A *heresiarch* is defined as someone who originates or is the chief proponent of a heresy or heretical movement.

38. The Vulgate was the Latin edition or translation of the Bible made by Saint Jerome at the end of the fourth century A.D., and for the Roman Catholic Church, it was the only authorized version of the Bible for use by the clergy. No Bibles translated into the vernacular languages were permitted.

39. The *Bible of Vatable* first published by Robert Estienne (1503–59) in Paris in 1545 and reportedly annotated with notes by the French Hebrew scholar François Vatable (d. 1547) or his students, contained two Latin editions of the Bible. The Inquisition eventually banned and prohibited this version of the bible because of the discovery that the second version of the Latin text in this Bible was translated by a Protestant. For more information on the significance of this edition of the Bible, see Alice Philena Hubbard, "The Bible of Vatable," *Journal of Biblical Literature* 66, no. 2 (June 1947): 197–209.

40. *Geomancy* is the practice of divination by means of the use of geographic features.

41. *Hydromancy* is the practice of divination by the observation of water.

42. *Aeromancy* is the practice of divination by means of measuring the atmosphere or changes in the weather.

43. *Pyromancy* is the practice of division using fire or flames.

44. *Oneiromancy* is the practice of divination using dreams.

45. *Chiromancy* is the practice of divination by means of reading palms.

46. *Necromancy* is the practice of communicating with the spirits of the dead to predict the future.

Part II. Documents concerning the Operation and Procedures of the Inquistion in New Spain

1. For a discussion of these two public activities of the otherwise secret tribunal in New Spain, see María Asunción Herrera Sotillo, *Ortodoxia y control social en México en el siglo XVII: El Tribunal del Santo Oficio* (Madrid: Universidad Complutense de Madrid, Departamento de Historia de América, 1982), 207–13.

2. See Pablo García, *Orden que comúnmente se guarda en el Santo Oficio de la Inquisición acerca del procesar en las causas que en él se tratan conforme a lo que está proveido por las instrucciones antiguas y nuevas* (Madrid, 1622), folios 49r–50r.

3. See Richard Boyer, *Lives of the Bigamists: Marriage, Family and Community in Colonial Mexico* (Albuquerque: University of New Mexico Press, 1995), 19.

4. Herrera Sotillo, *Ortodoxia y control social,* 207.

5. Ibid., 208.

6. For information on this correspondence with the Suprema concerning peyote and other new crimes identified by the Mexican Inquisition, see *Testificación por uso del peyote,* AHN, Sección de Inquisición, libro 1051, folios 199r–200v.

7. The Inquisition in Spain did not actively pursue or prosecute those who committed sodomy, but the Inquisition in New Spain did include sodomy prosecution in its edicts of faith. For Spain, see Christian Berco, *Sexual Hierarchies, Public Status: Men, Sodomy, and Society in Spain's Golden Age* (Toronto: University of Toronto Press, 2006). This is just one more example of how the Inquisition in the New World became more interested in controlling the morality and behavior of its colonists than attacking purely heretical beliefs.

8. To "tie" or *ligar* a man meant to use a series of spells, incantations, and often some ritual object to make the man impotent or incapable of having sexual intercourse with another woman by "tying" his virile member and making it impossible for him to have an erection with another woman. For more information on this type of sexual magic in New Spain, see Noemí Quezada, "Sexualidad y magia en la mujer novohispana, siglo XVIII," *Anuario de Antropología* 26 (1989): 261–95.

9. "Angel of Light" is in reference to the Christian devil (Satan or Lucifer), and it comes from the scriptural passage found in 2 Corinthians 11:14, which reads, *"And no marvel; for Satan himself is transformed into an angel of light."*

10. A great deal of correspondence occurred between the Suprema and the Inquisition in New Spain concerning the edict of faith against peyote. The Inquisition in Peru issued similar edicts of faith against the practice of divination using the coca leaf. For information on this correspondence with the Suprema concerning peyote and other new crimes identified by the Mexican Inquisition, see *Testificación por uso del peyote,* AHN, Sección de Inquisición, libro 1051, folios 199r–200v; the final decisions in the Suprema concerning this crime in *Calificación en la Suprema sobre el uso del peyote,* 26 de Octubre 1619, AHN, Sección de Inquisición, libro 1051, folios 205–6v; and *Calificación hecha en la Suprema sobre uso del peyote y diferentes clases de pacto con el demonio,* AHN, Sección de Inquisición, libro 1051, folios 201r–202v. The Suprema finally ordered the Mexican tribunal to issue a special edict of faith concerning the use of peyote on January 1, 1620; see *Carta de la Suprema al tribunal de México con orden para que publiquen edicto contra el uso del peyote,* AHN, Sección de Inquisición, libro 353, folio 128r–v.

11. Peyote (from the Nahuatl or Aztec word *peyoltl*) is a small, spineless cactus that is known for its hallucinogenic and psychoactive properties. The Mesoamerican indigenous people have a long tradition of the use of peyote for religious and medicinal purposes.

12. *Latae sententiae* is a Latin term used by Catholic canon law that literally meant an "already passed sentence." Officially a *latae sententiae* penalty in canon law comes automatically, by force of the law itself, as soon as the law or regulation is violated.

13. These many edicts are found in AGN, Ramo Edictos de Inquisición, vols. 1–4. For a complete list of the dates and reasons for these many edicts against prohibited books, see Solange Alberro, *Inquisición y sociedad en México, 1571–1700* (México, D.F.: Fondo de Cultura Económica, 1988), appendix 6, 127–36.

14. The *expurgatorio* was the Inquisition's list of purged or prohibited books. For a discussion of these lists, see Antonio Sierra Corella, *La censura de libros y papeles en España y los indices y catálogos españoles de los prohibidos y expurgados* (Madrid: Cuerpo facultativo de archiveros, bibliotecarios y arqueólogos, 1947).

15. For the updated Index of Prohibited Books, see document 5.

16. See Stephen Haliczer, *Sexuality in the Confessional: A Sacrament Profaned* (New York: Oxford University Press, 1996), on the crime of solicitation. For a detailed study of the use of Inquisition denunciations of solicitation against priests and friars by indigenous people in New Spain, see John F. Chuchiak "The Secrets behind the Screen: *Solicitantes* in the Colonial Diocese of Yucatán, 1570–1770," in *Religion in New Spain*, ed. Susan Schroeder and Stafford Poole (Albuquerque: New Mexico University Press, 2007), 83–109.

17. This edict against solicitation was preceded by several other edicts issued by the Inquisition in New Spain throughout the seventeenth century. The more important edicts include *Edicto de fe de los Inquisidores de México contra el crimen de la solicitación*, 30 de Abril, 1620, AGN, Ramo Edictos de Inquisición, vol. 1; *Edicto de fe de los Inquisidores de México contra los solicitantes*, 13 de Mayo, 1624, AGN, Ramo Edictos de Inquisición, vol. 3, folios 45–46; *Edicto de fe de los Inquisidores de México contra los solicitantes*, 13 de Mayo, 1651, AGN, Ramo Edictos de Inquisición, vol. 3, folios 69–73. For a study of these edicts and the crime of solicitation, see Jorge René González Marmolejo, "El delito de solicitación en los edictos del tribunal del Santo Oficio, 1576–1819," in Solange Alberro et al., *Seis ensayos sobre el discurso colonial relativo a la comunidad doméstica: Matrimonio, familia y sexualidad a través de los cronistas del siglo XVI, el Nuevo Testamento y el Santo Oficio de la Inquisición* (México: Departamento de Investigaciones Históricas, INAH, 1980), 169–201. Also see Jorge René González Marmolejo, *Sexo y confesión: La Iglesia y la penitencia en los siglos XVIII y XIX en la Nueva España* (México: Conaculta-INAH/Plaza y Valdés Editores, 2002), especially 47–66.

18. For information on the Mexican Inquisition's persecution of the ideas and writings of the French *philosophes*, see Jacques Houdaille, "Frenchmen and Francophiles in New Spain from 1760 to 1810," *The Americas* 13, no. 1 (July 1956): 1–29; as well as Lewis A. Tambs, "The Inquisition in Eighteenth-Century Mexico," *The Americas* 22, no. 2 (Oct. 1965): 167–81.

19. Saint Paul's first letter (epistle) to the Corinthians establishes and justifies the Catholic Church's belief in the mass and the importance of the Eucharist (or the act of taking communion) as the major act of unity of the church.

20. The parish priest Miguel Hidalgo y Costilla (1753–1811) used the symbol of the mestizo Virgin of Guadalupe as his banner when he led a disaffected group of Indians and mestizos in a revolt against the peninsular Spanish viceroyalty in 1810.

21. *in absentia* is Latin for "in the absence of," meaning that a trial against him would be conducted even without his physical presence.

22. For one of the best descriptions of life in the prisons of the inquisition of New Spain, see Alberro, *Inquisición y sociedad*, 223–76.

23. Ibid., 225.

24. See instruction 80 in *Copilación de las Instrucciones del Santo Officio de la Santa Inquisición* (Madrid: Alonso Gomez, 1576).

25. See Alberro, *Inquisición y sociedad*, 223.

26. Ibid., 223, n. 1.

27. Ibid., 223.

28. Although the walls of the cells were easily excavated, few prisoners actually managed to escape from the prisons. Two notable cases are the escape of Gullén de Lampart and another young prisoner, Diego de Maqueda. See José Toribio Medina, *Historia del Tribunal del Santo Oficio de la Inquisición en México* (Santiago: Imprenta Elzeveriana, 1903), 121.

29. Alberro, *Inquisición y sociedad*, 224.

30. Ibid., 225.

31. Ibid.

32. As late as 1650, the Mexican Inquisition still only paid two reales per day for the rations of its poorer prisoners. For specific information on what this ration contained, see *Cuaderno en que constan las raciones que se dan a los presos de las cárceles secretas del Santo Oficio en los meses de marzo 1594 hasta diciembre de 1596*, AGN, Ramo de Inquisición, vol. 216, exp. 22.

33. Alberro, *Inquisición y sociedad*, 225.

34. Entire volumes of the Inquisition archive contain collections of these secret conversations of the prisoners or the testimonies taken from spies sent into the cells of other prisoners. For several of these confidential informants' testimonies (or *confidencias*), see the case of the Inquisition spy Gaspar de Alfar, who informed on the conversations and communications of two accused crypto-Jews held in the secret prisons (Juan de León and Francisco Botello). Part of the informant's reports are contained in Boleslao Lewin, "'Las Confidencias' of Two Crypto-Jews in the Holy Office Prison of Mexico: 1654–1655," *Jewish Social Studies* 30, no. 1 (1968): 3–22.

35. For specific information on the Medina Rico visitation, see Richard E. Greenleaf, "The Great Visitas of the Mexican Holy Office, 1654–1669," *The Americas* 44, no. 4 (1988): 399–420.

36. A *real* was a Spanish silver coin that served as the basic unit of currency. One real was one-eighth of a silver peso. In colonial Mexico, silver real coins were also called tomins (abbreviated as ts).

37. See document 38 in this volume for more information concerning the crimes of this wealthy prisoner who was imprisoned for suspicion of Calvinism.

38. Fray Pedro López de San Francisco was imprisoned in the jails of the Inquisition in 1615 for accusations of having committed solicitation of sex in the confessional. See *Abecedario general de los relajados, reconciliados y penitenciados por el Santo Oficio de esta Inquisición de la Nueva España desde su fundacion en 1571 hasta 1726*, AGN, Ramo de Inquisición, vol. 1265, exp. 09.

39. Antón de los Reyes was a mulatto laborer from Guadalajara who was imprisoned in 1614 in the civil prisons in Guadalajara for a crime. The harsh conditions of the prison apparently forced Antón to utter blasphemous words in front of his jailers. Nevertheless, Antón was not imprisoned in the Inquisition's jails for blasphemy until March 1615. The delay from his initial denunciation in 1614 until his arrest in mid-1615 illustrates how long it often took for the Inquisition to compile enough evidence in order to issue an arrest warrant. Nevertheless, simple cases such as this case of blasphemy were usually dispatched quickly. Anton remained in the Inquisition's prison for only five days. See *Proceso contra Antón de los Reyes, mulato libre, porque estando preso muerto de hambre y puesto en el cepo con toba y cadena renege "de la madre que lo pario, de Dios y de los Santos . . .*," AGN, Ramo de Inquisición, vol. 300, exp. 11, 90 folios.

40. This seemingly innocuous entry of fees paid to the "Executioner" under the expenses of Antón de los Reyes suggests that during his brief imprisonment he was questioned under torture at

the end of his trial. The use of torture for the minor crime of blasphemy would have been excessive and in violation of Inquisition procedures. The entry may, however, refer to the executioner who administered the lashes that were no doubt given to him in his definitive sentence.

41. Juan Vázquez was a mestizo native from the town of Taximaroa in Michoacan imprisoned by the Holy Office for bigamy in 1615. Although he was not arrested until March 5, 1615, the inquest into his alleged crime of bigamy began by secret inquisition in 1614. See *Testificación contra Juan Domínguez o Juan Vázquez, mestizo nativo de Taximaroa, obispado de Michoacan por casado dos veces*, AGN, Ramo de Inquisición, vol. 302, exp. 5.

42. Martín de Birviesca Roldán served as the receptor of the Mexican Inquisition from 1592 until 1620.

43. The term *grains* refers to the smallest unit of Spanish currency, granos. There were ninety-six grains for every peso and each silver real coin was made up of twelve grains.

44. A *bando* was an official printed proclamation.

45. The term *vara* was a Spanish measurement of length roughly equivalent to the English yard, or three feet.

46. The motto of the Inquisition, *Exurge Domine Judica Causam Tuam* (Rise up, O Lord and judge thy cause), came from Psalm 73.

47. The scriptural passage in the Latin Vulgate actually reads *Nolo mortem impii, sed ut convertatur impius a via sua, et vivat* (I do not want the heretic's death, but rather that he changes his path [road] and lives) (Ezekiel 33.11).

48. There is an apparent error here in the document. The inscription comes from Psalm 149 in the Latin Vulgate, not Pslam 148. The scriptural passage reads *Ad faciendam vindictam in nationibus: increpationes in populis* (To do revenge in the nations, chastisements amongst his peoples).

49. The priest Antonio de Castro y Salgado had been imprisoned and tried early in 1803 for the crime of soliciting sex in the confessional.

50. See *An Account of the Sufferings of John Coustos in the Inquisition at Lisbon* (Norwich: J. Trumbull, 1798).

51. See the section on the prisoner's exclamations after the first turn of the rack in *Confesión debajo del tormento del reo Miguel Morgan, Ingles*, 14 de enero, 1574, in *Processo contra Miguel Morgan yngles de los que vinieron en la armada de Joan Aquines*, 1572–1574, Inquisition Manuscript in the Marion L. Foster Collection, Tulane University, New Orleans, Louisiana, Latin American Library Manuscripts, Collection 113, 137 folios.

52. Edward Peters, *Torture* (Philadelphia: University of Pennsylvania, 1996), 57.

53. Helen Rawlings, *The Spanish Inquisition* (London: Blackwell, 2006), 33.

54. García, *Orden que comúnmente se guarda en el Santo Oficio de la Inquisición acerca del procesar en las causas*, folios 26r–27r.

55. Peters, *Torture*, 68.

56. Richard E. Greenleaf, *The Mexican Inquisition of the Sixteenth Century* (Albuquerque: University of New Mexico Press, 1969), 22–23.

57. See *Carta acordada del Surpema al Tribunal de México*, 1625, AHN, Sección de Inquisición, libro 353.

58. This examination was conducted to make sure that the prisoner had not taken either drugs or alcohol to be able to resist the torture session.

59. Literally, "The name of Christ being invoked."

60. The Spanish term *garrotes* referred to cords or tourniquets that were applied to the arms, legs, thighs, and calves of prisoners and tightened and loosened during the process of interrogations under torment.

61. See Maureen Flynn, "Mimesis of the Last Judgement: The Spanish Auto de Fe," *Sixteenth Century Journal* 22, no. 2 (1991): 281–97.

62. Joseph Pérez, *The Spanish Inquisition* (New Haven: Yale University Press, 2006), 161.

63. For a complete description of the staging and seating autos-da-fé in New Spain, see document 20.

64. See John F. Chuchiak, "El regreso de los autos de fe: Fray Diego de Landa y la extirpación de idolatrías en Yucatán," *Península: Revista semestral de la Coordinación de Humanidades* 1, no. 0 (2006): 29–47.

65. Rawlings, *The Spanish Inquisition*, 36.

66. See Francisco Bethencourt, "The Auto da Fé: Ritual and Imagery," *Journal of the Warburg and Courtauld Institutes* 55 (1992): 15–168.

67. Unique and partial witnesses, though admitted by the Inquisition, were often given little credence in the final sentencing, as this case suggests.

68. The term *in facie ecclesiae* (in the presence of the congregation) meant that someone had a public marriage in a church before witnesses.

69. *Mestiza* meant someone of mixed indigenous and Spanish blood.

70. Those convicted of heretical acts or sins against the faith were often punished with pecuniary fines depending on the "quality of their persons" or their level or rank in the social hierarchy of New Spain. This example of a steep fine of 1,000 pesos was meant to serve as an example to those members of the upper stratus of colonial society, since they were to serve as the best examples of good Christian citizens.

71. The sentence against Pedro Trejo is a good example of the Inquisition's fear that colonists who were without the benefit of a theological education would pervert the faith of others by their meddling with the psalms, prayers, and Holy Scriptures and rendering them in the vernacular.

72. Don Martín Enríquez de Almansa served as the fourth viceroy of New Spain from 1568 to 1580. During his tenure as viceroy, the first Tribunal of the Inquisition was formally established in Mexico.

73. In matters of procedure, the Inquisition in New Spain frequently corresponded with other tribunals back in Spain. The inquisitors in Mexico also routinely reported back to the Suprema on matters of concern or on contentious issues.

74. The *cabildo eclesiástico*, or Cathedral Chapter, was the governing and consultative body of a bishopric that was attached to the major cathedral or seat of the bishop. The Cathedral Chapter administered the bishopric or archbishopric in the absence of a bishop or in between bishops during a vacant episcopal seat (*sede vacante*). Like the secular town council, there were various officials who made up this Cathedral Chapter. The executive officers of the Cathedral Chapter included the dean, the archdeacon, schoolmaster, choirmaster, and the treasurer. Underneath them there were at least ten canons and other lesser officials.

75. The *cabildo* was the municipal government of Mexico City, which served as the town council and was composed of several officials including two *alcaldes* (or chief magistrates) and a number of *regidores* (councilmen or aldermen) along with several other minor officials.

76. A vacant episcopal seat meant that the resident archbishop or bishop had either died or been transferred and that no official occupied the position. In cases where this occurred, the members of the Cathedral Chapter governed the archbishopric or bishopric until a new official arrived to occupy the position.

77. As in all things concerning the procedures and orders of the trials, processions, and the autos-da-fé, the Inquisition in Mexico looked to the standard practices and procedures used by inquisitorial tribunals back in Spain. Many of the inquisitors and other officials who arrived in New

Spain, like the secretary Pedro de los Ríos, had experience working in various Inquisition tribunals back in Spain. For more information on the transatlantic nature of inquisitorial careers, see Kimberly Lynn Hossain, "Arbiters of Faith, Agents of Empire: Spanish Inquisitors and Their Careers, 1550–1650" (Ph.D. dissertation, Johns Hopkins University, 2006).

78. As the secretary Pedro de los Ríos noted here, in many instances the condemned heretics in New Spain took any chance possible to resist and protest against their condemnation. Those that did disrupt the proceedings were often gagged and thrown into chains, as this document attests.

79. Dr. Pedro Moya de Contreras (1528–91) served as the third archbishop of Mexico from 1573 to 1591. After receiving a doctorate in canon law, he became a member of the Cathedral Chapter in the Canary Islands and later served as the inquisitor of the tribunal of Murcia. In 1571 he was named as the first inquisitor general of New Spain and arrived late in 1571 to formally establish the Inquisition in Mexico. He presided over the first auto-da-fé celebrated in New Spain in 1571. In early June 1573 he was chosen as archbishop of Mexico. For more information on Pedro Moya de Contreras and his significance as an inquisitor general, see Stafford Poole, *Pedro Moya de Contreras: Catholic Reform and Royal Power in New Spain, 1571–1591* (Berkeley: University of California Press, 1987).

80. The Convent of Santo Domingo, or Saint Dominic, was placed adjacent to the palace that housed the Tribunal of the Inquisition in New Spain. Its close proximity to the Inquisitorial Palace made it the most convenient place to conduct these smaller individual autos-da-fé (fig. 6).

81. Diego de Herédia's conviction on having made a pen and ink drawing and illegally writing messages while in the Inquisition's prisons testifies to extent to which the Inquisition went in maintaining the secrecy of its trials and imprisonments.

82. A creole African slave was one who was born in the New World.

83. The placing of a gag or bit in a penitent's mouth was one of the most common punishments given for those convicted of the minor crime of blasphemy by the Inquisition.

84. An abjuration was a denial, disavowal, or renunciation under oath. In common ecclesiastical language, this term is restricted to the renunciation of heresy made by the penitent heretic on the occasion of his reconciliation with the church, usually done in an auto-da-fé. An abjuration *de levi* was made by someone who was found to have a slight suspicion of heresy. It was a lesser abjuration than abjuration *de vehementi*, which connoted serious wrongdoing.

85. African slaves were often given much harsher physical punishments by the Inquisition than non-African citizens of New Spain. The race or *calidad* (quality) of the person was often a major consideration in the deliberations on which punishments to impose. Harsher physical punishments often went to the members of what were considered lesser races or castes and to those of lesser "quality." Members of the higher castes or those considered to have more *calidad* often received harsher pecuniary fines and other fiscal punishments such as confiscations and exile.

86. For more information concerning these types of sexual magic and love sorcery, see María Helena Sánchez Ortega, "Sorcery and Eroticism in Love Magic," in *Cultural Encounters: The Impact of the Inquisition in Spain and the New World*, ed. Mary Elizabeth Perry and Anne J. Cruz (Berkeley: University of California Press, 1991), 58–92.

87. The Prayer of the Star (*Oración de la Estrella*) was a common conjure or spell used by women in Spain and the Spanish New World in order to ensure the affections of a lover. It was recited by the woman casting the spell like this: "*Conjuróte estrella la más alta y la más bella-Conjuróte con la una, con las dos, y con las tres y desta suerte hasta nueve, por el monte Olivete entra, por el monte olibete entréis—tres—baras de enebro negro me cortéis en las muelas de barrabas, las amoléis y traigáis a fulano atado y amarrado a mi querer y a mi mandar y a toda mi voluntad sin que nadie se la puede estorbar*" (AGN, Ramo de Inquisición, vol. 366, exp. 3, fol. 224r). For more information on these types of prayers and enchantments used in sexual magic in New Spain, see Araceli Campos Moreno, *Oracio-*

nes, ensalmos, y conjuros mágicos del Archivo Inquisitorial de la Nueva España (México: El Colegio de México, 2001).

88. The prayer of Saint Marta or *Conjuro de Santa Marta* was also used similarly by women in New Spain to attract the affections of a specific lover. The spell and prayer went like this: "*Señora sancta Marta, digna sois y sancta. De mi señor Jesucristo querida y amada; de la virgin Maria huéspeda y convidada. Señora sancta Marta, por el Monte Olivete entrastes, con la serpiente brava encontrastes, con una cinta la atastes, y al pueblo la entregastes. Asi como esto es verdad, roguéis a mi señor Jesucristo me dé remedio y gracia para que le sirva.*" For other variant spells and conjures, see Campos Moreno, *Oraciones, ensalmos, y conjuros mágicos*, 95–132.

89. The *Conjuro* or Conjure of San Julián was also used by women in New Spain again to gain power over their lovers. This prayer was usually used in junction with acts of hydromancy using a cup or other receptacle of water, which the sorceress looked into to divine the future and cast fortunes. As the sorceress peered into the container of water, she chanted: "*Señor San Julián. suertes echastes en la mar. Si buenas suertes echastes, mejores suertes sacastes. Ansí lo saque yo, sancto, con lo que os pido, que lo vea esta criatura.*"

90. The women's house of seclusion, or *casa de recogimiento*, of Santa Mónica was established in 1582. Founded by an endowment from the conquistador Pedro de Trujillo and his wife, Isabel López, it served throughout the late sixteenth century as a place of reclusion of women sentenced by the ecclesiastical and secular courts. Although ostensibly a house of reclusion like a nunnery, the punitive nature of most of the women's seclusion made it more of a prison than a house of seclusion. For more information on the Prison of Santa Mónica and other places of imprisonment for women in Mexico, see Jacqueline Holler, *Escogidas Plantas: Nuns and Beatas in Mexico City, 1531–1601* (New York: Columbia University Press, 2005).

91. This "Jewish Day of Penitence" refers to Yom Kippur, which was one of the most important Jewish holy days held sometime from September to October. Jews consider Yom Kippur a day of fasting and penitence. This date marked the end of the ten days of penitence that followed Rosh Hashanah, or the Jewish New Year.

92. The Fast of Esther (called the Ta'anit Ester in Hebrew) is a Jewish fast from dawn until dusk on the eve of the Jewish celebration of Purim which celebrates the deliverance of the People of Israel from a Persian plot to annihilate them.

93. Because throughout the sixteenth century the Inquisition in New Spain lacked any permanent perpetual prisons, the most serious heretics sentenced to perpetual imprisonment were most often ordered sent to serve out their sentences in the perpetual prisons of the Inquisition in Seville, Spain.

94. The *sanbenito* "with the insignias of fire" was worn by those penitents who were to be relaxed to the secular authorities and burned at the stake. See the introduction for more information on the types and significance of the *sanbenito* garment of shame.

95. His sentence and partial trial documents are contained in document 35.

96. The Convent of Saint Dominic (Santo Domingo) was conveniently located across the street in front of the Palace of the Inquisition in Mexico City (fig. 6).

97. Don Matías de Gálvez y Gallardo, the captain general of Guatemala was the forty-eighth viceroy of New Spain, who was appointed on April 28, 1783, and died shortly after on November 3, 1784, perhaps from complications from his gout (mentioned in this document) or perhaps kidney failure, due to an advanced stage of this disease.

98. The *virreina,* or the wife of the viceroy, María Josefa de Madrid, was the mother of Bernardo de Gálvez de Madrid, their son who would later replace his father as the forty-ninth viceroy of New Spain. Before taking his place as viceroy, Don Bernardo served as the governor of Spanish

Louisiana from 1776 to 1785. In this post he aided the American Revolutionaries in their battle against the British, seizing the ports of Mobile (Alabama) and Pensacola (Florida) for Spain.

99. The public and theatrical nature of the Inquisition's autos-da-fé made then popular events in colonial New Spain. Large crowds often gathered to witness the events and later attend the executions on the Monday morning after the sentences were read at the auto-da-fé the preceding Sunday.

100. For more specific information on this phenomenon, see Stanley M. Hordes, "The Inquisition as Economic and Political Agent: The Campaign of the Mexican Holy Office against the Crypto-Jews in the Mid-Seventeenth Century," *The Americas* 39, no. 1 (July 1982): 23–38.

101. For more details of this type of Inquisition income, see Gisela von Wobeser, "La inquisición como institución creditícia en el siglo XVIII," *Historia Mexicana* 39, no. 4 (1990): 849–79.

102. For the most complete coverage of the finances of the Mexican Inquisition, see Medina, *Historia del Tribunal del Santo Oficio de la Inquisición en México*.

103. Ibid., 344.

104. For an excellent description of these types of donations and their significance for the Mexican tribunal, see Alfredo Ruiz Islas, "Ingresos y Egresos del Tribunal del Santo Oficio de la Nueva España en el siglo XVIII," *Revista de Indias* 65, no. 234 (2005): 511–34.

105. Ibid., 529, n. 34.

106. See von Wobeser, "La inquisición como institución creditícia en el siglo XVIII," 853–55.

107. For specific information on the costs of repairs and upkeep on the Inquisition's palace and its other urban properties, see AGN, Ramo de Real Fisco, vol. 103, exp. 1; vol. 115, exps. 1 and 2; vol. 23, exps. 1–17; vol. 27, exp. 2; vol. 29, exps. 1–2.

108. The numbers of sets of plates and bowls may possibly give us a hint at the numbers of prisoners who resided in the various Inquisition prisons in the summer of 1600. Apparently from twelve to forty-eight people resided in the Inquisition's prisons during that time.

109. As this record shows on July 7–8, 1600, several of the Inquisition's inmates were questioned under torment by Cristóbal Verdugo, who was the paid torturer of the Holy Office at that time. The subsequent entry referring to the need to "cure and repair" the feet of two inmates gives an apparently mundane yet terrible look at the impact of torture on those imprisoned by the Inquisition.

110. Apparently in 1600 the executioner of torture received a fee of four reales (or tomines) per torture session as evidenced by this registry's entry. The fee of two pesos paid to the same executioner the day before (July 7, 1600) most probably meant that he had conducted four other torture sessions on the previous day.

111. The holy wafers referred to here were used for the customary daily masses, which were held in the audience chambers of the Inquisition in New Spain.

112. A Dominical, or Sunday, Missal was a Catholic prayer book that contained all the prayers and responses necessary for celebrating the mass throughout the year.

113. The officials of the Holy Office of the Inquisition routinely had an extended Christmas vacation from the middle of December until the feast of the Epiphany (January 6). Their first audiences and new activities did not occur until January 7 of the following year.

114. Vellum was a type of thick parchment made from calfskin or lambskin used for the binding of books and documents.

Part III. Selections of Trials and *Procesos de Fe* of the Inquisition in New Spain, 1536–1820

1. For the nature of the crime of blasphemy in New Spain, see Javier Villa-Flores's *Dangerous Speech: A Social History of Blasphemy in Colonial Mexico* (Tucson: University of Arizona Press, 2006). For the source of this quotation and more specific information on the case of Rodrigo Rengel, see ibid., 37–38.

2. See Richard E. Greenleaf, *The Mexican Inquisition of the Sixteenth Century* (Albuquerque: University of New Mexico Press, 1969); and Solange Alberro, *Inquisición y sociedad en México, 1571–1700* (México, D.F.: Fondo de Cultura Económica, 1988).

3. See Alberro, *Inquisición y sociedad en México,* 75.

4. This document was created by the early episcopal inquisition in New Spain. Fray Juan de Zumárraga, along with the title as first bishop of Mexico, brought with him a commission as an apostolic inquisitor for the entire region of New Spain. On the basis of this early commission, Bishop Zumárraga conducted the first episcopal inquisition trials during the years 1536–43. For more information on the initial phases of the Inquisition in New Spain, see Richard E. Greenleaf, *Zumárraga and the Mexican Inquisition, 1536–1543* (Washington, D.C.: Academy of American Franciscan History, 1962); as well as the Introduction to this volume.

5. After the testimony and declarations of three witnesses, Zumárraga ordered the arrest of the suspected blasphemer. The procedures of the Inquisition appear to have been violated in this case because no document concerning a consultation appears to have been made in order to qualify Juan de Pórras's statements as blasphemous. There is also no document concerning his arrest or the constable's handing of the prisoner over to a jailer. Nevertheless, Zumárraga's dual position as apostolic inquisitor and bishop granted him absolute authority over crimes against the faith. As the chief arbiter of ecclesiastical justice, Zumárraga as inquisitor-bishop could justify proceeding summarily in the dispatch of inquisitorial trials.

6. Slitting of the tongue was a harsh punishment for the crime of simple blasphemy. The only recorded instances of this punishment for minor infractions occurred during the earlier monastic and episcopal inquisitions. The formal tribunal of the Inquisition in New Spain would not issue such harsh punishments.

7. Bachiller Juan de Villate was one of the two inquisitors of the tribunal of Llerena in Spain around 1510–12. The suspect Juan de Villate was most probably born the illegitimate son of Bachiller Villate and a woman from the Canary Islands during this period. His father, the Bachiller Villate, had been the archdeacon of the Cathedral of Ronda in Malaga and had served since 1499 as an inquisitor in the city of Cartagena (1499–1507) and then in the city of Leon (1507–10), and eventually in the tribunal of Llerena.

8. It is possible that Juan de Villate was the illegitimate son of one of two inquisitors from the tribunal of Llerena. This might have explained the lenient sentence that he was given by Inquisitor Zumárraga.

9. The provisor was the chief ecclesiastical judge of a Bishopric.

10. For the role of the crime of blasphemy and African slaves in New Spain, see Javier Villa-Flores, "To Lose One's Soul": Blasphemy and Slavery in New Spain, 1596–1669," *Hispanic American Historical Review* 82, no. 3 (2002): 435–68.

11. The second week of lent in 1710 would have been March 17–23. That means that the Saturday referred to must have been March 22, 1710.

12. The bigamy case against Marcos de la Cruz is found in AGN, Ramo de Inquisición, vol. 608, exp. 3, folios 216–99. For more information, see Richard Boyer, *Lives of the Bigamists: Marriage, Family, and Community in Colonial Mexico* (Albuquerque: University of New Mexico Press, 1995), 85.

13. See María Asunción Herrera Sotillo, *Ortodoxia y control social en México en el siglo XVII: El Tribunal del Santo Oficio* (Madrid: Universidad Complutense de Madrid, Departamento de Historia de América, 1982), 288.

14. Ibid., 288. For a more nuanced discussion of the crime of bigamy in New Spain, see Boyer, *Lives of the Bigamists,* 13–32.

15. See *Carta de los inquisidores al Consejo de Inquisición sobre el delito de bigamía,* 23 de Septiembre, 1575, AHN, Sección de Inquisición, libro 1047, folio 383r–v.

16. Ibid., 288.

17. *Carta de los inquisidores al Consejo de Inquisición sobre el delito de bigamía y su causa,* 22 de Mayo, 1575, AHN, Sección de Inquisición, libro 1066, folios 297r–298v.

18. Again, see Boyer, *Lives of the Bigamists,* 43–44.

19. See *Recopilación de las Leyes de Indias,* tomo II, libro VII, titulo III.

20. See Herrera Sotillo, *Ortodoxia y control social,* 289–90.

21. See Henningsen, "El 'banco de datos' del Santo Oficio: Las relaciones de causas de la Inquisición española, 1550–1700," *Boletín de la Real Academia de la Historia* 174 (1977): 547–70, especially 564.

22. Herrera Sotillo, *Ortodoxia y control social,* 290.

23. Ibid., 292.

24. Ibid., 292–93.

25. Ibid., 293. For several instances of these punishments for bigamy, see documents 19 and 21 in the section on the autos-da-fé.

26. Ibid., 293.

27. See *Relación del auto de fé de 28 de Febrero,* 1574, AHN, Sección de Inquisición, libro 1064, folios 48r–62v.

28. Ibid., 294.

29. The issuing of an arrest warrant on the simple accusation of just one minister of the Inquisition (the chief constable) was a violation of proper inquisitorial proceedings. Again, these types of violations of standard Inquisition procedure were commonplace in the early episcopal inquisition in New Spain.

30. The New World remained a land of opportunity for Spaniards, especially those of the lower classes. Apparently more chances of social mobility existed in New Spain than in Spain.

31. Again, proper inquisitorial procedures were not followed in this case. The arrest warrant was apparently issued on the basis of only one denunciation.

32. For further cases of similar Maya denunciations of the alleged sexual abuses of their parish priests, see John F. Chuchiak, "The Secrets behind the Screen: *Solicitantes* in the Colonial Diocese of Yucatán, 1570–1770," in *Religion in New Spain,* ed. Susan Schroeder and Stafford Poole (Albuquerque: University of New Mexico Press, 2007), 83–109.

33. The feast day of Saint John the Baptist was held on June 24.

34. The feast of the Holy Sacrament (also known as the feast of Corpus Christi) is a movable feast day of the Catholic Church that occurred sixty days after Easter Sunday and could be held anywhere from May 21 to June 24. In 1609 the feast of the Holy Sacrament (or Corpus Christi) would have been held on June 18.

35. For an excellent compilation of Inquisition documents from New Spain concerning the prosecution of Jews and crypto-Jews, see Alfonso Toro, *Los judios en la Nueva España* (México: Fondo de Cultura Económica, 1993). For other studies, see, for example, the works of Seymour Liebman, *The Inquisitors and the Jews in the New World: Summaries of Procesos, 1500–1810, and Bibliographical Guide* (Coral Gables, Fla.: University of Miami Press, 1974); Stanley Hordes, "The Inquisition and the Crypto-Jewish Community in Colonial New Spain and New Mexico," *Western States Jewish History* 29, no. 1 (1996): 689–701; and Eva Uchmany de de la Peña, *La vida entre el Judaísmo y el Cristianismo en la Nueva España, 1580–1606* (México, D.F.: Archivo General de la Nación, 1992).

36. See Herrera Sotillo, *Ortodoxia y control social,* 235.

37. See Antonio Domínguez Ortiz, *Los judeo conversos en España y América* (Madrid: Ediciones Istmo, 1971), 60–62.

38. Ibid., 236.

39. Ibid.

40. Some Portuguese crypto-Jews migrated to the northern region of New Mexico. See Stanley M. Hordes, *To the End of the Earth: A History of the Crypto-Jews of New Mexico* (New York: Columbia University Press, 2005).

41. For the Jewish and Portuguese background of this mercantile elite, see Robert Ferry, *The Colonial Elite of Early Caracas: Formation and Crisis, 1567–1767* (Berkeley: University of California Press, 1989).

42. Ibid., 237.

43. Ibid.

44. Ibid., 238.

45. Ibid., 248.

46. Ibid.

47. Ibid.

48. For the economic activity of the Mexican Inquisition in terms of confiscations and fines, see Solange Alberro, "Indices economicos e inqusisición en la Nueva España, siglos XVI y XVII," *Cahiers des Amériques Latines*, nos. 9–10 (Paris, 1974), 247–64.

49. Juan de Salamanca most probably referred here to one of his previous patrons, Rodrigo Henríquez de Castro-Osorio, the 5th Count de Lemos, Grandee of Spain, who was born in 1459 and died in Spain in 1522, buried at the Convent of San Anthony of Padua in Monforte de Lemos, Lugo, Galicia, Spain. It may have been the death of his patron that caused Juan de Salamanca to come to New Spain in 1524 and join in the service of Hernán Cortes.

50. *Cuaresma* was the period of Lent, or the forty-day period before Easter Sunday. Lent traditionally begins on Ash Wednesday and ends on Palm Sunday. In 1539 Lent began on Wednesday, February 19, 1539 (Ash Wednesday) and ended on Sunday, March 30, 1539 (Palm Sunday).

51. For more information on the trial and proceedings against the famous Mexican crypto-Jew, Don Luis de Carvajal the younger, see Martin Cohen, *The Martyr: The Story of a Secret Jew and the Mexican Inquisition* (Philadelphia: Jewish Publication Society, 1973); also for the surviving writings and last will and testament of Luis de Carvajal the younger, see Seymour B. Liebman, *The Enlightened: The Writings of Luis de Carvajal, El Mozo* (Coral Gables, Fla.: University of Miami Press, 1967).

52. While in prison, Luis de Carvajal took the Hebrew name of Joseph Lumbroso (or "the enlightened"); for more information, see Liebman, *The Enlightened*, 31.

53. An order of *cominatio* (Latin meaning "a threat or the act of threatening") was one in which the prisoner or suspect was threatened with further violence and the addition of harsher punishments during the subsequent questioning under torment.

54. It was the secular justices who actually issued the final sentence of death against relapsed and relaxed impenitent heretics. The Inquisition only passed judgment and declared the prisoner a heretic. It was the civil judges who would then give the order for the death sentence to be executed. Nevertheless the process of "relaxing" or handing the impenitent heretic over to the civil authorities was in effect a death sentence.

55. Luis de Carvajal's last-minute confession and repentance spared him the torture of having been burned alive. Instead he was given the so-called mercy of being strangled to death before his lifeless body was burned on the pyre.

56. Any signs of male circumcision served as definitive proof for the inquisitors that the suspect was a practicing Jew. Most of the cases and accusations dealing with suspected male Jews involved a

medical examination by the doctors and medics of the Inquisition. No such similar medical proof was available in terms of identifying Jewish women. Unjustly, the mere fact that a woman's husband was circumcised and possibly a Jew meant that the woman would most likely be convicted as a Jew as well.

57. Information on this penitent and suspected Judaizer is also found in document 21 concerning the auto-da-fé of 1596.

58. A large number of penitents and suspected heretics often died in the Inquisition's prisons during the lengthy imprisonment while their trials proceeded.

59. The sentence of imprisonment in the galleys was one of the worst sentences that a man could be given. The galleys were large wooden ships propelled solely by human oarsmen. This sentence of imprisonment was actually a sentence of harsh labor at the oars below the deck of one of these wooden ships. Poorly fed and overworked with few chances to even glimpse the sun, galley prisoners faced a fate worse than death.

60. For similar visitations of the Mexican tribunal by visiting judges, especially the visitation of Inquisitor Pedro de Medina Rico's investigation of the mishandling of ecclesiastical justice, see Richard E. Greenleaf "The Great Visitas of the Mexican Holy Office," *The Americas* 44, no. 4 (April 1988): 399–420. The revised instructions of 1561 issued by Inquisitor Fernando Valdés (document 1) were Medina Rico's and Huidobro's primary guide for measuring the Mexican Tribunal's performance between 1640 and 1657.

61. According to Richard Greenleaf, "The Great Visitas of the Mexican Holy Office," the Suprema chose Dr. Pedro Medina Rico to serve as the visiting judge. A distinguished attorney and university professor in Cordoba and Seville, Dr. Medina Rico served as visitor general of the archbishop of Sevilla before he became the prosecuting attorney of the Inquisition tribunal of Zaragosa in 1645 and later an inquisitor of Seville in 1646. Greenleaf also notes that he was sent to Cartagena de Indias to conduct an investigation of the tribunal there in 1647. It was not until May 9, 1651, that he was ordered to Mexico with full power to bring order to the Mexican tribunal, a process that took fifteen years.

62. This was in violation of article 42 of the 1561 instructions, which served as the official procedures for the Inquisition in New Spain (document 1).

63. In this case, the Mexican Inquisition again violated procedures by not qualifying if the supposed revelations were heretical. This was in violation of article 1 as ordered by the 1561 instructions.

64. According to proper procedures, the first hearing should have been held within ten days after the official arrest unless the prisoner requested an earlier audience. This was in violation of article 18 of the Instructions of Toledo of 1561. The investigating judges discovered that in more than 110 cases the ten-day limit was violated. Often the first hearing was delayed anywhere from six months to seven years after an initial arrest, violating the rights of the accused and all due process (see Greenleaf, "Visitas of the Holy Office," 414).

65. This is only one instance of the irregularities in the use and administration of torture in the Mexican Inquisition's proceedings against Jewish prisoners. The visiting judges found several dozen more instances of apparent violations from 1640 to 1650.

66. This was in violation of article 48 of the 1561 Instructions of Toledo.

67. The listing of the names of witnesses in the formal publications of testimonies (in violation of articles 31 and 32 of the 1561 instructions) was a serious violation of inquisitorial procedures that in effect negated the entire secret nature of the proceedings.

68. For a discussion of this confusion in terminology and a lack of understanding of the subtle differences between Lutheranism and Calvinism, see Richard E. Greenleaf, *The Mexican Inquisition of the Sixteenth Century* (Albuquerque: University of New Mexico Press, 1969), 76–85.

69. Herrera Sotillo, *Ortodoxia y control social,* 254–55.

70. Ibid., 254.

71. Ibid., 253; also see Alberro, *Inquisición y Sociedad,* 172–77.

72. Alberro, *Inquisición y sociedad,* 174.

73. Herrera Sotillo, *Ortodoxia y control social,* 256–59.

74. Ibid., 175.

75. Ibid., 253.

76. Ibid., 258–59.

77. For the political nature of the punishment of foreign sailors by the Mexican Inquisition, see Michael S. Hale, "Behold These English Dogs! Englishmen in the Atlantic World before the Holy Office of the Inquisition, 1560–1630" (M.A. thesis, Missouri State University, 2005).

78. In early 1604 the Mexican Inquisition issued a special edict of faith requiring the denunciation of all those reconciled or convicted of heresy who continued to violate the sumptuary prohibitions against their wearing silks and other fine fabrics and carrying arms or riding on horseback. See AGN, Ramo de Inquisición, 1495, for several other trials for other violations of sumptuary prohibitions.

79. These fellow gold smelters and other artisans may have denounced Cristóbal Miguel not out of their good Christian conscience but rather because of their business rivalry; Cristóbal Miguel's success in business is suggested by his continued use of fine woolens and silks.

80. In the sixteenth and seventeenth centuries small bonfires called *luminarias* were burned alongside the roads and churchyards to commemorate Christ's birth at Christmas and also to commemorate the Easter resurrection. They served to guide people to midnight mass held at the end of both celebrations.

81. The war referred to here was the War of the Quadruple Alliance (1718–20), in which the new Spanish Bourbon king Philip V attempted to retake territories in Italy and to claim the French throne. A four-way alliance of England, France, Austria, and the Dutch Republic eventually defeated Spain. The war was officially declared in December 1718, and many English sailors who were unaware of the declaration of war were arrested in Spanish New World ports such as Veracruz.

82. *Ad cautelam* (Latin for "by precaution"). An ecclesiastical judge absolves an accused suspect *ad cautelam* when there is doubt whether the accused has committed the crime or merited the punishment.

83. Latin for "I baptize thee in the name of the Father, the Son, and the Holy Ghost."

84. The Quakers (or Society of Friends, also known as the "Tremblers in the presence of the Holy Spirit") were a Protestant sect founded in 1652 by George Fox. Quakers were pacifists and refused to take oaths or practice traditional Anglican Church services, such as participating in sermons or choirs.

85. As the flow of the questioning suggests, the inquisitors were not convinced by Edward Rivet's line of reasoning favoring his conversion to Catholicism. His testimony and answers to the questions reveal that he held little belief or loyalty to any faith since he quickly changed his beliefs and practiced Anglicanism and then confessed in the same breath that he went back to praying with Quakers if he came across them.

86. For the phenomena of illuminism (*alumbradismo*) in Spain and its New World colonies and the Inquisition's reaction to these false mystics, see Álvaro Huerga, *Historia de los alumbrados,* vol. 3: *Los alumbrados de Hispanoamérica 1570–1605* (Madrid: Fundación Universitaria Española, 1986).

87. For a discussion of the cases against *alumbrados* in New Spain, see Herrera Sotillo, *Ortodoxia y control social,* 262–67. Also see Daniel Patrick Dwyer, "Mystics in Mexico: A Study of Alumbrados in Colonial New Spain" (Ph.D. dissertation, Tulane University, 1995).

88. For more information on the nature of female false mystics in New Spain, see Antonio Rubial García, "Las santitas del barrio. 'Beatas' laicas y religiosidad cotidiana en la ciudad de México en el siglo XVII," *Anuario de Estudios Americanos* 59, no. 1 (2002): 13–37.

89. On the nature of these false mystics and the state of popular religion in terms of divine revelations, see Antonio Rubial García, *Profetisas y solitarios: Espacios y mensajes de una religión dirigida por ermitaños y beatas laicos en las ciudades de Nueva España* (México: Universidad Nacional Autónoma de México, 2006), especially 67–122, 189–242.

90. The Catholic mendicant order of the Discalced Carmelites (Barefoot Carmelites) was a hermetic religious order founded in 1593 and later reformed by the Spanish saints Teresa de Ávila and John of the Cross.

91. The feast of Saint Joseph was celebrated on March 19.

92. The symbol of the Spanish Franciscan San Diego de Alcalá (or Saint Didacus of Alcalá, d. 1463) was a particular type of cross symbolic of the saint's devotion.

93. Apparently the inquisitors were not interested in censoring or reading private correspondence.

94. *ad perpetuam* (Latin for "everlasting" or "permanently") meant that the Inquisition could call them back as a witness indefinitely.

95. These printed instructions for commissaries of the Holy Office in New Spain are reproduced in document 4.

96. The practice of chiromancy (reading of the hands or palms) was one of the types of fortune-telling prohibited by the Inquisition (document 7).

97. Doña Juana de Ordóñez Marañon's denial of the initial allegations apparently caused the Inquisition commissary to drop any further investigation of the case. There are no other allegations or testimonies extant against the said *beata*, and it must be assumed that the Inquisition ceased investigating the case.

98. Quoted from Noemí Quezada, "The Inquisition's Repression of *curanderos*," in *Cultural Encounters: The Impact of the Inquisition in Spain and the New World*, ed. Mary Elizabeth Perry and Anne J. Cruz (Berkeley: University of California Press, 1991), p. 54, n. 18.

99. Herrera Sotillo, *Ortodoxia y control social*, 316.

100. Ibid.

101. Ibid., 318.

102. On sexual magic and witchcraft, see Noemí Quezada, "Sexualidad y magia en la mujer novohispana, siglo XVIII," *Anuario de Antropología* 26 (1989): 261–95.

103. Herrera Sotillo, *Ortodoxia y control social*, 317.

104. See ibid., 317–18. For the interesting 1596 case of Doña Leonor Maldonado, see *Relación de las causas de 1596*, AHN, Sección de Inquisición, libro 1064, folio 211.

105. Herrera Sotillo, *Ortodoxia y control social*, 323.

106. Ibid., 324.

107. For interesting examples of love magic, see María Helena Sánchez Ortega, "Sorcery and Eroticism in Love Magic," in *Cultural Encounters: The Impact of the Inquisition in Spain and the New World*, ed. Mary Elizabeth Perry and Anne J. Cruz (Berkeley: University of California Press, 1991), 58–93.

108. On this contemporary mixture of superstitious magic with pagan and Christian elements in Spain, see Pedro Ciruelo, *A Treatise Reproving All Superstitions and Forms of Witchcraft*, ed. and trans. Eugene Maio and D'Orsay W. Pearson (London: Associated University Presses, 1977).

109. For the connection between women's proper roles and their use of witchcraft to manipulate those around them, see Martha Few, *Women Who Live Evil Lives: Gender, Religion, and the Politics of Power in Colonial Guatemala* (Austin: University of Texas Press, 2002).

110. The bishop of Tlaxcala at this time (1536) was the Dominican Fray Julián Garcés (1457–1547), who had been the court preacher and chaplain of the Spanish king and Holy Roman emperor Charles V.

111. This early sentence gives an example of the Inquisition's use of public shame in its punitive sentences against heretics and sorceresses.

112. The Marquis of the Valley of Oaxaca in 1540 was Hernán Cortes, the conquistador of Mexico.

113. Apparently the clergyman Calderón had a reputation as an alchemist.

114. See Herrera Sotillo, *Ortodoxia y control social*, 322.

115. For the case of peyote, see Irving A. Leonard, "Peyote and the Mexican Inquisition, 1620," *American Anthropologist* 4, no. 2 (Apr. 1942): 324–26.

116. For one case in point of the expanding use of this hallucinogen in regions far beyond its natural habitat, see John F. Chuchiak, "The Medicinal Practices of the Yucatec Maya and Their Influence on Colonial Medicine in Yucatán, 1580–1780," in *Change and Continuity in Mesoamerican Medicinal Practice*, ed. John F. Chuchiak and Bodil Liljefors Persson, special edition of the Swedish Americanist Society's *Acta Americana* 10, nos. 1–2, (2006): 5–19.

117. For information on this correspondence with the Suprema concerning the use of peyote and other new crimes identified by the Mexican Inquisition, see *Testificación por uso del peyote*, AHN, Sección de Inquisición, libro 1051, folios 199r–200v.

118. A great deal of correspondence occurred between the Suprema and the Inquisition in New Spain concerning the edict of faith against peyote and other hallucinogens. See *Testificación por uso del peyote*, AHN, Sección de Inquisición, libro 1051, folios 199r–200v; as well as the final decisions in the Suprema concerning this crime in *Calificación en la Suprema sobre el uso del peyote*, 26 de Octubre 1619, AHN, Sección de Inquisición, libro 1051, folios 205–206v; as well as *Calificación hecha en la Suprema sobre uso del peyote y diferentes clases de pacto con el demonio*, AHN, Sección de Inquisición, libro 1051, folios 201r–202v.

119. The Suprema finally ordered the Mexican tribunal to issue a special edict of faith concerning the use of peyote on January 1, 1620; see *Carta de la Suprema al tribunal de México con orden para que publiquen edicto contra el uso del peyote*, AHN, Sección de Inquisición, libro 353, folio 128r–v.

120. Nevertheless, the episcopal courts of the *provisorato de indios* did focus efforts on the eradication of the use of peyote and other ritualized intoxicants but with little overall success. For an early source on the episcopal campaigns to root out the indigenous use of peyote, see Hernando Ruiz de Alarcón, *A Treatise against the Heathen Superstitions in New Spain*, ed. J. R. Andrews and R. Hassig (Norman: University of Oklahoma Press, 1984). For a similar attempt elsewhere in New Spain, see John F. Chuchiak, "'It is Their Drinking That Hinders Them': Balché and the Use of Ritual Intoxicants among the Colonial Yucatec Maya, 1550–1780," *Estudios de Cultura Maya* 24 (2003): 137–71.

121. Pipltzintzintli (a Nahuatl or Aztec word) is believed to be the leaves of the plant known as *Salvia divinorum*, which was a psychoactive and hallucinogenic herb used in traditional Mexican indigenous ritual divination and healing.

122. For a complete discussion of the most important cases of the conflict of jurisdiction concerning the prosecution of indigenous cases involving the use of native superstitions, herbs, and witchcraft, see Richard E. Greenleaf, "The Inquisition and the Indians of New Spain: A Study in Jurisdictional Confusion," *The Americas* 22, no. 2 (1965): 138–66.

123. *in verbo sacerdotis* (Latin for "upon the word of a priest").

124. Someone of the *lobo* caste was the mixed offspring of an Indian and an African.

125. *ad perpetuam rei memoriam* (Latin for "for a continual remembrance thereof").

126. *Verbo ad verbum* (Latin for "word for word").

127. See Irving A. Leonard, "Spanish Shipboard Reading in the Sixteenth Century," *Hispania* 32, no. 1 (Feb. 1949): 53–58; as well as Irving Leonard, *Romances of Chivalry in the Spanish Indies with Some Registros of Shipments of Books to the Spanish Colonies* (Berkeley: University of California, 1933).

128. On the censorship of prohibited literature, see Martin Nesvig, "Pearls before Swine: Theory and Practice of Censorship in New Spain, 1527–1640" (Ph.D. dissertation, Yale University, 2004); as well as his recent book, *Ideology and Inquisition: The World of the Censors in Early Mexico* (New Haven: Yale University Press, 2009).

129. For more information on the licensing and revision of passengers to the Indies and the restrictions placed upon certain categories of people, see Juan Friede, "The Catálogo de Pasajeros and Spanish Emigration to America to 1550," *Hispanic American Historical Review* 31, no. 2 (May 1951): 333–48. For other information on passengers who booked passage to the Indies and their applications for licenses, see Luis Romera Iruela and María del Carmen Galbis Diez, *Catálogo de Pasajeros a Indias, Siglos XVI, XVII y XVIII*, vol. V, tomos I and II (1567–77), Archivo General de las Indias, Ministerio de Cultura, 1980; as well as María del Carmen Galbis Diez, *Catálogo de Pasajeros a Indias, Siglos XVI, XVII y XVIII*, vol. VI (1578–85), Archivo General de las Indias, Ministerio de Cultura, 1986; and María del Carmen Galbis Diez, *Catálogo de Pasajeros a Indias, Siglos XVI, XVII y XVIII*, vol. VII (1586–99), Archivo General de las Indias, Ministerio de Cultura, 1986.

130. For a general description of the Inquisition's censorship of books during this early period, see Yolanda Mariel de Ibáñez, *El tribunal de la Inquisición en México (siglo XVI)* (México: Universidad Nacional Autónoma de México, Instituto de Investigaciones Jurídicas, 1979), 81–83.

131. Nesvig, *Ideology and Inquisition*, 242.

132. Ibid., 235.

133. Ibid.

134. Ibid., 228.

135. Ibid., 229–30.

136. Ibid.

137. For several specific instances where the Mexican tribunal received letters of reprimand in terms of its activities in relation to prohibited books, see various *Cartas Acordadas* contained in AHN, Sección de Inquisición, libros 353, 1053, 1064–65.

138. See Juan Carlos Galende Díaz and Bárbara Santiago Medina, "Las visitas de Navíos durante los siglos XVI y XVII: Historia y documentación de una práctica inquisitorial," *Documenta y Instrumenta* 5 (2007): 51–76.

139. Nesvig, *Ideology and Inquisition*, 230–42.

140. Ibid., 236.

141. As this document aptly illustrates, the Inquisition not only prohibited books but also took an active role in purging or editing out supposed heretical passages in many other unlikely books and sources, such as this famous 1571 Spanish-Nahuatl dictionary by the Franciscan missionary linguist Fray Alonso de Molina. For more information on the Inquisitions purging of heretical passages and its prohibition of books and other media, see Nesvig, *Ideology and Inquisition*.

142. The Franciscan Fray Juan de Bonilla published his *Breve tratado donde se declara cuán necesaria sea la páz del alma* in 1580 in Alcalá de Henares. Although he had received permission to publish his treatise on the peace of the soul in 1568, by the later decade of the 1580s his treatise was placed on the Index of Prohibited Books due to the Inquisition's suspicions that it revealed similarities with several doctrines of the *alumbrados* (illuminists).

143. The correct title of the book is *Precationum piarum Enchiridion*. Compiled around 1570 by Simon Verepaeus and published first in 1572, this work remained a popular prayer book with fifteen editions published in three languages from 1564 to 1591.

144. Don Antonio Bergosa y Jordán (1748–1819) served for twenty years as an inquisitor and prosecuting attorney for the Inquisition in New Spain (1781–1801). He later served as bishop of Oaxaca from 1801 to 1817. He eventually received a promotion to the post of archbishop of Mexico, where he served for two years before his death in 1819. Apparently Manuel Abad knew the inquisitor personally, as indicated by the informal nature of this letter. He no doubt believed that his familiarity with the inquisitor would lead to his eventual receipt of a license from the tribunal to read prohibited books.

145. Bonaventure Racine (1708–55) was a Jansenist (or a believer in the Catholic heresy of Jansenism, which like Calvinism held a belief in predestination). His encyclopedic ecclesiastical history *Abrégé de l'histoire ecclesiastique* in 13 volumes published in Paris from 1762 to 1767 was added to the list of prohibited books shortly after the expulsion of the Jesuits from the New World in 1767.

146. An interactive digital image of the handkerchief described here can be consulted online at www.history.org/history/teaching/enewsletter/volume4/november05/primsource.cfm.

147. The Inquisition's informant and translator are in error here. The real inscription notes that he was elected as the "Sherriff" of London, not the mayor.

148. *Barlovento* (Spanish for "windward") was a term used to describe the windward islands of the Lesser Antilles.

149. In 1762, at the end of the Seven Years' War, Britain declared war on Spain and invaded Cuba, occupying Havana and the rest of the island for almost a year. During the British occupation, the Spaniards of Havana were allowed to trade with all countries. It was no doubt during or shortly after the British invasion of Havana that English goods such as these handkerchiefs entered into the markets of Cuba.

150. The bishop of Valladolid (or Michoacan) during this time was the same Manuel Abad y Queipo referred to in document 53.

151. The Parián was a famous marketplace in Mexico City.

SELECTED BIBLIOGRAPHY

Archival Sources
Archivo General de la Nación, México City

Abecedario general de los relajados, reconciliados y penitenciados por el Santo Oficio de esta Inquisición de la Nueva España desde su fundación en 1571 hasta 1726, Ramo de Inquisición, vol. 1265, exp. 09.

Carta acordada del Consejo de Inqusición a los inquisidores de México sobre el secreto, 17 de Junio, 1595, Ramo de Inquisición, vol. 1511, folio 44r–v.

Carta acordada del Consejo de Inquisición a los inquisidores de México sobre la impresión en letra de molde de unos abjuraciones, 10 de Septiembre, 1590, Ramo de Inquisición, vol. 1511, 3 folios.

Carta acordada del Consejo de Inquisición ordenando a los inquisidores de México de tomarles las informaciones sobre sus genealogías y limpieza de sangre a los familiares, 6 de Julio, 1575, Ramo de Inquisición, 1511, folio 9r–v.

Carta acordada del Consejo de la Inquisición a los inquisidores de México sobre las Instrucciones, 17 de Febrero, 1592, Ramo de Inquisición, vol. 1511, folios 42r–43v.

Cartilla de Comisarios del Santo Oficio de la Inquisición de México, Impreso en la Ciudad de México, 1667, Ramo de Inquisición, vol. 1519, exp. 5, folios 276r–293v.

Compilación de las instrucciones del oficio de la Santa Inquisición, hechas en Toledo en 1561 y impreso en Madrid, 1574, Ramo de Inquisición, vol. 1480, exp. 1, folios 1r–12v.

Confesión debajo del tormento del reo Miguel Morgan, Ingles, 14 de enero, 1574, Ramo de Inquisición, vol. 10, 12 folios.

Denuncias contra Diego de Herrera Arteaga, comisario de Zacatecas (1613), Ramo de Inquisición, vol. 303, folio 392.

Indice general de las causas de fe, que se han seguido en este Tribunal del Santo Oficio de la Inquisición de México, desde su fundación en el año de 1571 hasta el de 1719, Ramo de Inquisición, vol. 1524, folios 1–223.

Instrucçiones del Ilustrísimo Señor Cardenal Don Diego de Espinosa, Inquisidor General para la implantación desta Inquisición, 1570, Ramo de Inquisición, vol. 1519, exp. 2, folios 41r–47r, Lote Riva Palacio, vol. 44, no. 2.

Instrucción que deben observar los comisarios y notarios del Tribunal de la Santa Inquisición de México en el despacho de los negocios de fe y demás tocantes a su conocimiento, printed in Mexico, 1667, Ramo de Inquisición, vol. 1519, exp. 5, folios 276r–293v, Lote Riva Palacio, vol. 44, no. 2.

Instrucción que han de guardar los comisarios del Santo Oficio de la Inquisición en las causas y negocios de fe, 1667, Ramo de Inquisición, vol. 1479, exp. 2, folios 51r–57v, Lote Riva Palacio, vol. 3, no. 2.

Inventario de los bienes del extinguido Tribunal del Santo Oficio de la Inquisición de México, 1813, Ramo de Intendentes, vol. 42.

Lista de los Familiares del Santo Oficio con Noticia de la fecha del nombramiento y de los Inquisidores que la firmaron, de marzo 3, 1660 hasta 19 de enero, 1701, Ramo de Inquisición, vol. 87, exp. 2, 17 folios.

Petición del Tribunal de la Inquisición de México pidiendo a la de España un receptor para un capital de 4,283 pesos, 1579, Ramo de Inquisición, vol. 85, exp. 27, 2 folios.

Proceso contra Antón de los Reyes, mulato libre, porque estando preso muerto de hambre y puesto en el cepo con toba y cadena reniegue "de la madre que lo pario, de Dios y de los Santos . . .," Ramo de Inquisición, vol. 300, exp. 11, 90 folios.

Testificación contra Juan Domínguez o Juan Vázquez, mestizo nativo de Taximaroa, obispado de Michoacán por casado dos veces, Ramo de Inquisición, vol. 302, exp. 5.

Archivo Histórico Nacional, Madrid (Sección de Inquisición)

Carta acordada del Consejo de Inquisición, 18 de Junio 1608, libro 942, folio 64.

Carta acordada del Consejo de Inquisición, 1632, libro 939, folio 68.

Carta del inquisidor de México, Juan Gómez de Mier, al Consejo de Inquisición, 21 de Agosto, 1684, legajo 2274.

Carta de los inquisidores de México al Consejo de Inquisición, 28 de diciembre, 1607, legajo 2270.

Carta del tribunal de México al Consejo de Inquisición sobre nombramientos de calificadores, comisarios y familiares en el distrito de México, 8 de Mayo, 1572, libro 1047, folio 98.

Cartas y autos sobre las cuentas dadas por el receptor Francisco López Sanz, quien ha fallecido, 1672, libro 1062, folios 5r–6v, 10–15, 25–28.

Instrucciones del Rey al Inquisidor Don Alonso Manrique de Lara, 1595, libro 939, folio 273r–v.

Printed Primary Sources

An Account of the Sufferings of John Coustos in the Inquisition at Lisbon. Norwich: J. Trumbull, 1798.

Arguëllo, G. *Instrucciones del Santo Oficio de la Inquisición sumariamente, antiguas y modernas.* Madrid: Imprenta Real, 1630.

Carena, Caesare. *Tractatus de Officio Santissimae Inquisitionis.* Cremona: Baptistam Belpierum, 1655.

Compilación de las instrucciones del oficio de la Santa Inquisición hechas por fray Tomás de Torquemada e por los otros Inquisidores Generales cerca de la orden que se ha de tener en el ejercicio del Santo Oficio. Madrid: impreso de nuevo por el señor Joan Everardo Nidardo, Inquisidor General, 1667.

Copilación de las Instrucciones del Santo Oficio de la Santa Inquisición. Madrid: Alonso Gómez, 1576.

Diccionario de Derecho Canónico arreglado a la jurisprudencia eclesiástica Española antigua y moderna. Paris: Librería de Rosa y Bouret, 1853.

Dugdale, Richard. *Narrative of Unheard of Popish Cruelties towards Protestants beyond Seas; or, A New Account of the Bloody Spanish Inquisition. Published as a Caveat to Protestants.* London: Printed for John Hancock at the Three Bibles in Popes-Head-Alley over against the Royal Exchange in Cornbil, 1680.

García, Pablo. *Orden que comúnmente se guarda en el Santo Oficio de la Inquisición acerca del procesar en las causas que en él se tratan conforme a lo que está proveído por las instrucciones antiguas y nuevas.* Madrid, 1622.

Índice general de Decretos Reales y consultas originales sobre diversos negocios que se contienen en los 20 libros formados de ellos y pertenecen a la Secretaría de Castilla, del Real y Supremo Consejo de la Santa y General Inquisición, sobre competencias de jurisdicción entre el Consejo de la Inquisición y otras Justicias Reales (1535–1738). Archivo Histórico Nacional, Madrid, Inquisición, libros 3 y 4.

Libro primero de votos de la Inquisición de México, 1573–1600. Introducción de Edmundo O'Gorman. México, D.F.: Imprenta Universitaria (Archivo General de la Nación y Universidad Nacional Autónoma de México), 1949.

López de Ayala, Ignacio. *El Sacrosanto y Ecuménico Concilio de Trento Traducida al idioma Castellano.* México: Librería de Garnier Hermanos, 1855.

Manual de Inquisidores: Directorium Inquisitorum de Fray Nicolas Eymeric. With translation, notes, and introduction by José Antoinio Fortea. Madrid: La Esfera de los Libros, 2006.

Nómina del Tribunal de la Inquisición de Nueva España, 1571–1646. Boletín del Archivo General de la Nación, Secretaría de Gobernación. México, D.F., México., 27, no. 3 (1956): 495–559 (part 1); 27, no. 4 (1956): 703–48 (part 2).

Paramo, Ludovicus de. *De origine et progressu officii Santae Inquisitionis.* Madriti: Typographia regia, 1598.

"Proceso contra Miles Philips." *Boletín del Archivo General de la Nación* 20, no. 3 (1949): 467–517 (part 1); 20, no. 4 (1949): 615–63 (part 2).

Proceso criminal del Santo Oficio de la Inquisición y del fiscal en su nombre contra Don Carlos, Indio principal de Tetzcoco. 1539. Edición facsímile. México, D.F.: Edmundo Aviña Levy, 1968.

Proceso Inquisitorial del Cacique de Texcoco. Vol. 1 of the *Publicaciones del Archivo General de la Nación.* México, 1910.

Reglas y Constituciones, que han de guardar los Señores Inquisidores, fiscales, secretarios, oficiales, calificadores, consultores, abogados, comisarios, notarios, honestas personas, capellanes familiares, y otros qualesquier ministros del Tribunal del Santo Officio de la Inquisición de esta ciudad de México, como cofrades de la Nobilísima, y santa cofradía de Señor San Pedro Mártyr; principal patrono, y fundador del Santo Oficio de la Inquisición. México: Viuda de Bernardo Calderón, 1659.

Secondary Sources

Abreu, C. Maqueda. "El auto de fe como manifestación Inquisitorial." In *Perfiles jurídicos de la Inquisición española,* edited by José Antonio Escudero López, 407–14. Madrid: Universidad Complutense, 1986.

Acevedo-Field, Rafaela. "Let the Dead Rest: The Inquisition Case of Gaspar Méndez de Pineiro, Deceased Crypto-Jew in New Spain, 1642–1649." Master's thesis, University of California, Santa Barbara, 2000.

Adams, Eleanor B. "The Franciscan Inquisition in Yucatán: French Seamen, 1560." *The Americas* 25 (1969): 331–60.

Águeda Méndez, María. "Una relación conflictiva: La Inquisición novohispana y el chocolate." *Caravelle: Cahiers du monde hispanique et luso-brésilien* 71 (1998): 9–21.

Aguirre Beltrán, Gonzalo. *Medicina y magia: El proceso de aculturación en la estructura colonial.* México, D.F.: Universidad Veracruzana, Instituto Nacional Indigenista, 1992.

Alberro, Solange. *La actividad del Santo Oficio de la Inquisición en Nueva España, 1571–1700.* México, D.F.: Instituto Nacional de Antropología e Historia, Departamento de Investigaciones Históricas, Seminario de Historia de las Mentalidades y Religión en el México Colonial, 1981.

———. "El discurso inquisitorial sobre los delitos de bigamia, poligamia y de solicitación." In *Seis ensayos sobre el discurso colonial relativo a la comunidad doméstica: Matrimonio, familia y sexualidad a través de los cronistas del siglo XVI, el Nuevo Testamento y el Santo Oficio de la Inquisición,* edited by Solange Alberro et al., 215–26. México, D.F.: Departamento de Investigaciones Históricas, [Cuadernos de trabajo; 35], Instituto Nacional de Antropología e Historia, 1980.

————. "Herejes, brujas y beatas: Mujeres ante el tribunal del Santo Oficio de la Inquisición en la Nueva Espana." In *Presencia y transparencias. La mujer en la historia de México,* edited by François Giraud, 90–91. México, D.F.: El Colegio de México. 1987.

————. *Inquisición y sociedad en México, 1571–1700.* México, D.F.: Fondo de Cultura Económica, 1988.

————. *Inquisition et societé au Mexique, 1571–1700.* México, D.F.: Centro de Estudios Mexicanos y Centroamericanos, 1988.

————. "Negros y Mulatos en los Documentos Inquisitoriales: Rechazo e integración." In *El Trabajo y los Trabajadores en la Historia de México,* 132–61. México, D.F.: Colegio de México, 1979.

————. "Políticas de le iglesia frente a las manifestaciones idolátricas durante la colonia." In *Religión en Mesoamérica: XII Mesa Redonda,* edited by Jaime Litvak King and Noemí Castillo Tejero, 485–94. México, D.F.: Sociedad Mexicana de Antropología, 1972.

Alfassa, Shelomo. "The Origin and Stigma of the Iberian Garment of Shame, the *San Benito.*" *International Sephardic Journal* 1 (September 2004): 1–13.

Araya Espinoza, Alejandra. "De espirituales a histéricas: Las beatas del siglo XVIII en la Nueva España." *Historia* 37, no. 1 (2004): 5–32.

Archivo General de la Nación. *Catálogo de textos marginados novohispanos: Inquisición, siglos XVIII y XIX.* México, D.F.: Archivo General de la Nación, 1992.

Atienza, Juan G. *Guía de la Inquisición en España.* Barcelona: Editorial Arin, Colección Guías de la Espan~a insólita, 1988.

Atondo Rodríguez, Ana María. *El amor venal y la condición femenina en el México colonial.* México, D.F.: Instituto Nacional de Antropología e Historia, 1992.

"Un Auto de Fe en el siglo XVII (Algunos datos desconocidos sobre este célebre suceso)." *Boletín del Archivo General de la Nación,* no. 14 (1943): 215–17.

Ávila Hernández, Rosa. "El tribunal de la inquisición y su estructura administrativa." *Novahispania/México* 1 (1995): 45–109.

Avilés, Miguel. "The Auto de Fe and the Social Model of Counter-Reformation Spain." In *The Spanish Inquisition and the Inquisitorial Mind,* edited by Ángel Alcalá, 249–64. New York: Columbia University Press, 1987.

Barth, Karl. *Church Dogmatics: The Doctrine of the Word of God.* Edited and translated by Geoffrey William Bromiley and Thomas Forsyth Torrance. London: T & T Clark International, 2004.

Baudot, Georges. "La population des villes du Mexique en 1595 selon une enquête de l'Inquisition." *Caravelle: Cahiers du monde hispanique et luso-brésilien* 37 (1981): 5–18.

Baudot, Georges, and María Agueda Méndez. "La Revolución Francesa y la Inquisición Mexicana: Textos y pretextos." *Caravelle: Cahiers du monde hispanique et luso-brésilien* 54 (1990): 89–105.

Behar, Ruth. "Sex and Sin, Witchcraft and the Devil in Late-Colonial Mexico." *American Ethnologist* 14 (Feb. 1987): 34–54.

————. "Sexual Witchcraft, Colonialism and Women's Powers: Views from the Mexican Inquisition." In *Sexuality and Marriage in Colonial Latin America,* edited by Asunción Lavrin, 178–206. Lincoln: University of Nebraska Press, 1989.

Benassar, Bartolomé. *Inquisición española: Poder político y control social.* Barcelona: Editorial Crítica, 1984.

Berco, Christian. *Sexual Hierarchies, Public Status: Men, Sodomy, and Society in Spain's Golden Age.* Toronto: University of Toronto Press, 2006.

Bethencourt, Francisco. "The Auto da Fé: Ritual and Imagery." *Journal of the Warburg and Courtauld Institutes* 55 (1992): 15–168.

Blanchard, Vicki Kay. "The Indians and the Inquisition in Mexico, 1536–1563." B.A. thesis, Newcomb College, Tulane University, 1969.

Bodian, M. "In the Cross-Currents of the Reformation: Crypto-Jewish Martyrs of the Inquisition, 1570–1670." *Past and Present*, no. 176 (2002): 66–104.

Boeglin, Michel. "Moral y control social: El tribunal de la Inquisición de Sevilla (1560–1700)." *Hispania Sacra* 55, no. 112 (2003): 501–34.

Bolaños Mejías, Carmen. "La literatura jurídica como fuente del derecho inquisitorial." *Revista de la Inquisición* 9 (2000): 191–220.

Borah, Woodrow. "An Instruction of the Inquisition to Its Commissioner in Acapulco, 1582." In *Homenaje al Doctor Ceferino Garzón Maceda*, edited with introduction by Carlos Luque Colombres, 27–34. Córdoba: Instituto de Estudios Americanistas Doctor Enrique Martínez Paz, 1973.

Borja Gómez, Jaime Humberto. "El Control Sobre la Sexualidad: Negros e Indios (1550- 1650)." In *Inquisición, muerte y sexualidad en la Nueva Granada*, edited by Jaime Humberto Borja Gómez, 171–98. Santafé de Bogotá: Editorial Ariel, S.A., 1996.

Boyer, Richard. "Juan Vázquez, Muleteer of Seventeenth-Century Mexico." *The Americas* 37, no. 4 (1981): 421–43.

———. *Lives of the Bigamists: Marriage, Family, and Community in Colonial Mexico*. Albuquerque: University of New Mexico Press, 1995.

———. "Women, *La Mala Vida*, and the Politics of Marriage." In *Sexuality and Marriage in Colonial Latin America*, edited by Asunción Lavrin, 252–86. Lincoln: University of Nebraska Press, 1989.

Brading, David A. "La devoción católica y la heterodoxia en el México borbónico." In *Manifestaciones religiosas en el mundo colonial americano. Espiritualidad barroca colonial. Santos y demonios en América*, edited by Clara García Ayluardo and Manuel Ramos Medina, 25–49. México, D.F.: Universidad Iberoamericana, Instituto Nacional de Antropología e Historia, Centro de Estudios de Historia de México, CONDUMEX, 1993.

Bravo, Dolores. *Ana Rodríguez de Castro y Aramburu, ilusa, afectadora de santos, falsos milagros, y revelaciones divinas. Proceso inquisitorial en la Nueva España. Siglos XVIII y XIX*. México, D.F.: Universidad Nacional Autónoma de México, 1984.

Calvo, Thomas. "Concubinato y mestizaje en el medio urbano: El caso de Guadalajara en el siglo XVII." *Revista de Indias* 14, no. 173 (1984): 203–12.

Campos Moreno, Araceli. *Oraciones, ensalmos, y conjuros mágicos del Archivo Inquisitorial de la Nueva España*. México, D.F.: El Colegio de México, 2001.

Cañeque, Alejandro. "Theater of Power: Writing and Representing the Auto de Fe in Colonial Mexico." *The Americas* 52, no. 3 (1996): 321–43.

Cárdenas, Alejandra. *Hechicería, saber y transgresión: Afro-mestizas en Acapulco, 1621*. México, D.F.: Gobierno del Estado de Guerrero, 1997.

Caro López, Ceferino. "Censura Gubernativa, Iglesia e Inquisición en el siglo XVIII." *Hispania Sacra* 56, no. 114 (2004): 479–51.

Castanien, Donald G. "The Mexican Inquisition Censors a Private Library." *Hispanic American Historical Review* 34, no. 3 (1954): 374–92.

Castañeda Delgado, Paulino, Pilar Hernández Aparicio, René Millar, et al. *La Inquisición de Lima*. Vols. 1–3. Lima: Editorial Deimos, 1989–95.

Cavallero, Ricardo Juan. *Justicia inquisitorial: El sistema de justicia criminal de la Inquisición española*. Buenos Aires: Ariel Historia, 2003.

Cervantes, Fernando. "Christianity and the Indians in Early Modern Mexico: The Native Response to the Devil." *Historical Research* 66, no. 160 (1993): 177–96.

———. *The Devil in the New World: The Impact of Diabolism in New Spain*. New Haven: Yale University Press, 1994.

———. "The Devils of Queretaro: Skepticism and Credulity in Late Seventeenth-Century Mexico." *Past and Present* 130 (1991): 51–69.

Chuchiak, John F. "Fr. Juan de Zumárraga: First Bishop and Archbishop of New Spain." In *Oxford Encyclopedia of Mesoamerican Cultures,* edited by David Carrasco, 3:380–81. Oxford: Oxford University Press, 2001.

———. *Guide and Inventory to the Richard E. Greenleaf Ecclesiastical Mexican Collection.* New Orleans: Latin American Library, Tulane University, 1996.

———. "The Holy Office of the Inquisition." In *Oxford Encyclopedia of Mesoamerican Cultures,* edited by David Carrasco, 2:46–48. Oxford: Oxford University Press, 2001.

———. "The Indian Inquisition and the Extirpation of Idolatry: The Process of Punishment in the *Provisorato de Indios* of the Diocese of Yucatan, 1563–1812." Ph.D. dissertation, Tulane University, 2000.

———. "La inquisición Indiana y la extirpación de idolatrías: El castigo y la Reprensión en el Provisorato de Indios en Yucatán, 1570–1690." In *Nuevas Perspectivas Sobre el Castigo de la Heterodoxia Indígena en la Nueva España, siglos XVI–XVIII,* edited by Ana de Zaballa Beascoechea, 79–94. Bilbao: Universidad del País Vasco, Spain, 2005.

———. "The Inquisition in New Spain." In *Encyclopedia of the History of Mexico,* edited by Michael Werner, 704–8. New York: Fitzroy Dearborn Publishers, 1997.

———. "'It Is Their Drinking That Hinders Them': Balché and the Use of Ritual Intoxicants among the Colonial Yucatec Maya, 1550–1780." *Estudios de Cultura Maya* 34 (2004): 137–71.

———. "The Medicinal Practices of the Yucatec Maya and Their Influence on Colonial Medicine in Yucatán, 1580–1780." In *Change and Continuity in Mesoamerican Medicinal Practice,* edited by John F. Chuchiak and Bodil Liljefors Persson. Special edition, *Acta Americana* 10, nos. 1–2 (2006): 5–19.

———. "El regreso de los autos de fe: Fray Diego de Landa y la extirpación de idolatrías en Yucatán." *Península: Revista semestral de la Coordinación de Humanidades* 1, no. 0 (2006): 29–47.

———. "The Secrets behind the Screen: *Solicitantes* in the Colonial Diocese of Yucatán, 1570–1770." In *Religion in New Spain,* edited by Susan Schroeder and Stafford Poole, 83–109. Albuquerque: New Mexico University Press, 2007.

———. "*In Servitio Dei*: Fray Diego de Landa, the Franciscan Order, and the Return of the Extirpation of Idolatry in the Colonial Diocese of Yucatán, 1573–1579." *The Americas* 61, no. 4 (2005): 611–46.

———. "The Sins of the Fathers: Franciscan Missionaries, Parish Priests and the Sexual Conquest of the Yucatec Maya, 1545–1785." *Ethnohistory* 54, no. 1 (2007): 71–129.

———. "Toward a Regional Definition of Idolatry: Reexamining Idolatry Trials in the *Relaciones de Méritos* and Their role in Defining the Concept of *Idolatría* en Colonial Yucatán, 1570–1780." *Journal of Early Modern History* 6, no. 2 (2002): 1–29.

Clendinnen, Inga. "Disciplining the Indians: Franciscan Ideology and Missionary Violence in Sixteenth-Century Yucatan." *Past and Present* 94 (1984): 27–49.

———. "Reading the Inquisitorial Record in Yucatan: Fact or Fantasy?" *The Americas* 28, no. 3 (1982): 327–47.

Cohen, Martin. *The Martyr: The Story of a Secret Jew and the Mexican Inquisition.* Philadelphia: Jewish Publication Society, 1973.

Conway, G. R. G. *An Englishmen and the Mexican Inquisition.* Mexico: privately printed, 1927.

Contreras, Jaime. *Historia de la Inquisición Española, 1478–1834.* Madrid: Arcos Libros, 1997.

———. "The Impact of Protestantism in Spain, 1520–1600." In *Inquisition and Society in Early Modern Europe,* edited by Stephen Haliczer, 47–63. London: Croom Helm, 1987.

———. "The Social Infrastructure of the Inquisition: Familiars and Commissioners." In *The Spanish Inquisition and the Inquisitorial Mind*, edited by Ángel Alcalá, 133–58. New York: Columbia University Press, 1987.

Contreras, Jaime, and Jean-Pierre Dedieu. "Geografía de la Inquisición Española: La formación de los distritos, 1470–1820." *Hispania* 40 (1980): 37–93.

Cortés López, José Luis."Los esclavos y la Inquisición (siglo XVI)." *Studia Historica* 20 (1999): 217–40.

Croft, Pauline. "Englishmen and the Spanish Inquisition, 1558–1625." *English Historical Review* 87, no. 343 (1972): 249–68.

Dedieu, Jean Pierre. "The Archives of the Holy Office of Toledo as a Source for Historical Anthropology." In *The Inquisition in Early Modern Europe: Studies on Sources and Methods*, edited by Gustav Henningsen and John Tedeschi, in association with Charles Amiel, 158–89. DeKalb: Northern Illinois University Press, 1986.

———. "Denunciar—denunciarse. La delación inquisitorial en Castilla la Nueva en los siglos XVI y XVII." *Revista de la Inquisición* 2 (1992): 95–108.

———."Limpieza, poder y riqueza: Requisitos para ser ministro de la Inquisición, Tribunal de Toledo, siglos XVI–XVII." *Cuadernos de Historia Moderna*, no. 14 (1993): 29–44.

Défourneaux, Marcelin. *Inquisición y censura de libros en la España del siglo XVIII*. Translataed by J. Ignacio Tellechea Idígoras. Madrid: Taurus, 1973.

de Micheli, Serra A. "The Inquisition and Physicians in New Spain." *Prensa Médica Mexicana* 44, nos. 11–12 (1979): 273–77.

———. "Physicians and Surgeons during the Inquisition in New Spain." *Gaceta Médica Mexicana* 139, no. 1 (2003) : 77–81.

Domínguez Ortiz, Antonio. *Los Judeoconversos en España y América*. Madrid: Ediciones Istmo, 1971.

Dunigan, Vincent J. "The Establishment of the Monastic Inquisition: An Historical Study of the Coercive Power of the Church against Heretics." Master's thesis, Niagara University, 1948.

Edwards, John. "Review: Was the Spanish Inquisition Truthful?" *Jewish Quarterly Review* 87 (1997): 351–66.

———. *The Spanish Inquisition*. Stroud: Tempus, 1999.

Ernst Powell, Jessica, and Erin M. Rebhan. "Manuscripts of the Mexican Inquisition: The Witchcraft Case against Catalina de Miranda (1650–67)." *eHumanista* 4 (2004): 217–39.

Escudero, José Antonio. "Notas sobre la carrera del inquisidor general Diego de Espinosa." *Revista de la Inquisición* 10 (2001): 7–16.

Esquivel Otea, María Teresa. *Índice del ramo edictos de la santa y general Inquisición*. México, D.F.: Archivo General de la Nación México, 1977.

Farriss, Nancy. *Crown and Clergy in Colonial Mexico, 1759–1821: The Crisis of Ecclesiastical Privilege*. London: Athlone Press, 1968.

Fernández, André. "The Repression of Sexual Behavior by the Aragonese Inquisition between 1560 and 1700." *Journal of the History of Sexuality* 7, no. 4 (1997): 469–501.

Fernández del Castillo, Francisco. *Libros y libreros en el siglo XVI*. México, D.F.: Publicaciones del Archivo General de la Nación, 1914.

Few, Martha. *Women Who Live Evil Lives: Gender, Religion, and the Politics of Power in Colonial Guatemala*. Austin: University of Texas Press, 2002.

Figueras Vallés, Estrella. "Pervirtiendo el orden del Santo Matrimonio: Bigamías en México, siglos XVI–XVII." Ph.D. dissertation, University of Barcelona, 1998.

Flynn, Maureen. "Mimesis of the Last Judgement: The Spanish Auto de Fe." *Sixteenth Century Journal* 22, no. 2 (1991): 281–97.

Friede, Juan. "The *Catálogo de Pasajeros* and Spanish Emigration to America to 1550." *Hispanic American Historical Review* 31, no. 2 (1951): 333–48.

Fuchs, Barbara. "An English Pícaro in New Spain: Miles Philips and the Framing of National Identity." *New Centennial Review* 2, no. 1 (2002): 55–68.

Gacto, Enrique. "El Arte vigilado (sobre la censura estética de la Inquisición española en el siglo XVIII)." *Revista de la Inquisición* 9 (2000): 7–68.

Galende Díaz, Juan Carlos, and Bárbara Santiago Medina. "Las visitas de Navíos durante los siglos XVI y XVII: Historia y documentación de una práctica inquisitorial." *Documenta y Instrumenta* 5 (2007): 51–76.

Galván Rivera, Mariano. *Concilio III Provincial Mexicano celebrado en México el año de 1585*. México: Eugenio Mallefert y Compañía, Editores, 1859.

García, Genaro. "Autos de Fe de la Inquisición de México con extractos de sus causas, 1646–1648." In *Documentos Inéditos o Muy Raros para la historia de México*, edited by Genaro García and Carlos Pereyra, 133–259. 2nd ed. México, D.F.: Editorial Porrúa, 1974.

García, Juan Ramon. "Miguel Hidalgo and the Inquisition." Master's thesis, DePaul University, 1979.

García Marín, José María. "Proceso inquisitorial-proceso regio: Las garantías del procesado." *Revista de la Inquisición*, no. 7 (1998): 137–49.

García-Molina Riquelme, Antonio M. "El Auto de Fe de México de 1659: El Saludador Loco, López de Aponte." *Revista de la Inquisición* 3 (1994): 183–204.

———. "Fernando Rodríguez de Castro, celebrante de Sacramentos sin ordenes: Un caso Relajado Singular." *Revista de la Inquisición* 9 (2000): 221–40.

———. "Instrucciones para procesar a Solicitantes en el Tribunal de la Inquisición de México." *Revista de la Inquisición* 8 (1999): 85–100.

———. "Una propuesta del Tribunal de México: El Sambenito de Media Aspa." *Revista de la Inquisición* 9 (2000): 241–49.

———. *El regimen de penas y penitencias en el Tribunal de la Inquisición de México*. México, D.F.: Universidad Nacional Autónoma de México, 1999.

Gargallo García, Oliva. *La Comisaría Inquisitorial de Valladolid de Michoacán, siglo XVIII*. Morelia, Michoacán, México: Universidad Michoacana de San Nicolás de Hidalgo, Instituto de Investigaciones Históricas, 1999.

Garza Carvajal, Federico. *Butterflies Will Burn: Prosecuting Sodomites in Early Modern Spain and Mexico*. Austin: University of Texas Press, 2003.

Giles, Mary E, ed. *Women in the Inquisition: Spain and the New World*. Baltimore: Johns Hopkins University Press, 1998.

González de Caldas, M. V. "El auto de fe: Modalidades de un ritual." In *Images et representations de la justice du XVIe au XIXe siècle*, edited by G. L. Lamoine, 41–59. Toulouse: University of Toulose-Le Mirail, 1983.

———. "Nuevas imágenes del Santo Oficio en Sevilla, el auto de fe." In *Inquisición española y mentalidad señorial*, edited by Ángel Alcalá et al., 227–65. Barcelona: Ariel, 1984.

González Marmolejo, Jorge René. "El delito de solicitación en los edictos del tribunal del Santo Oficio, 1576–1819." In *Seis ensayos sobre el discursos colonial relativo a la comunidad doméstica: Matrimonio, familia y sexualidad a través de los cronistas del siglo XVI, el Nuevo Testamento y el Santo Oficio de la Inquisición*, edited by Solange Alberro et al., 169–201. México, D.F.: Departamento de Investigaciones Históricas, INAH, 1980.

———. *Sexo y confesión: La Iglesia y la penitencia en los siglos XVIII y XIX en la Nueva España*. México, D.F.: Conaculta-INAH / Plaza y Valdés Editores, 2002.

González Marmolejo, Jorge René, and José Abel Ramos Soriano. "Discurso de la Inquisición sobre el matrimonio, la familia y la sexualidad a través de los edictos promulgados por el tribunal del Santo Oficio, 1576–1819." In *Seis ensayos sobre el discurso colonial relativo a la comunidad doméstica: Matrimonio, familia y sexualidad a través de los cronistas del siglo XVI, el Nuevo Testamento y el Santo Oficio de la Inquisición*, edited by Solange Alberro et al., 105–65. México, D.F.: Departamento de Investigaciones Históricos, INAH, 1980.

González Novalín, José Luis. "Clérigos solicitantes, perversos de la confesión." In *De la santidad a la perversión, o de por qué no se cumplia la ley de Dios en la sociedad novohispana*, edited by Sergio Ortega, 239–52. México, D.F.: Grijalbo, 1985.

———. *El Inquisidor General Fernando de Valdés, 1483–1568.* 2 vols. Oviedo: Universidad de Oviedo, 1968–71.

Green, Otis H., and Irving A. Leonard. "On the Mexican book Trade in 1600: A Chapter in Cultural History." *Hispanic Review* 9 (1941): 1–40.

Greenleaf, Richard E. "Francisco Millán before the Mexican Inquisition: 1538–1539." *The Americas* 21, no. 2 (1964): 184–95.

———. "From Medieval to Modern Inquisition: The Posture of Orthodoxy." Paper presented to the International Congress on the History of the Inquisition, Rome-Naples, 1981.

———. *Gonzalo Gómez, primer poblador español de Guayangareo, Morelia: Proceso inquisitorial.* Morelia, México, D.F.: Fimax Publicistas, 1991.

———. "The Great Visitas of the Mexican Holy Office, 1654–1669." *The Americas* 44, no. 4 (1988): 399–420.

———. "Historiography of the Mexican Inquisition: Evolution of Interpretations and Methodologies." In *Cultural Encounters: The Impact of the Inquisition in Spain and the New World*, edited by Mary Elizabeth Perry and Anne J. Cruz, 248–76. Berkeley: University of California Press, 1991.

———. *La Inquisición en Nueva España. Siglo XVI.* Translated by Carlos Valdés. México, D.F.: Fondo de Cultura Económica, 1981.

———. *Inquisición y sociedad en el México colonial.* Colección Chimalistac de libros y documentos acerca de la Nueva España, 44. Madrid: J. Porrúa Turanzas, 1985.

———. "The Inquisition and the Indians of New Spain: A Study in Jurisdictional Confusion." *The Americas* 22, no. 2 (1965): 138–66.

———. "The Inquisition Brotherhood: Cofradía de San Pedro Mártir of Colonial México." *The Americas* 40 (1983–84): 171–207.

———. "The Inquisition in Eighteenth-Century New Mexico." *New Mexico Historical Review* 60, no. 1 (1985): 29–60.

———. "The Inquisition in Spanish Louisiana: 1762–1800." *New Mexico Historical Review* 50, no. 1 (1975): 45–72.

———. "The Mexican Inquisition and the Enlightenment, 1763–1805." *New Mexico Historical Review* 41, no. 3 (1966): 181–96.

———. "The Mexican Inquisition and the Indians: Sources for the Ethnohistorian." *The Americas* 34, no. 2 (1978): 315–44.

———. "The Mexican Inquisition and the Masonic Movement, 1751–1820." *New Mexico Historical Review* 44, no. 2 (1969): 93–117.

———. *The Mexican Inquisition of the Sixteenth Century.* Albuquerque: University of New Mexico Press, 1969.

———. "Mexican Inquisition Materials in Spanish Archives." *The Americas* 20, no. 2 (1964): 416–20.

———. "Missions, Presidios and the Inquisition in the Spanish Borderlands." In *The Spanish Missionary Heritage of the United States: Selected Papers and Commentaries from November 1990*

Quincentenary Symposium, edited by Howard Benoist, 5–13. Washington, D.C.: National Park Service, 1992.

———. "North American Protestants and the Mexican Inquisition, 1765–1820." *Journal of Church and State* 8, no. 2 (1966): 186–99.

———. "The Persistence of Native Values: The Inquisition and the Indians of Colonial Mexico." *The Americas* 50, no. 3 (1994): 351–76.

———. *Zumárraga and the Mexican Inquisition, 1536–1543*. Washington, D.C.: Academy of American Franciscan History, 1962.

Gringoire, Pedro. "Protestantes enjuiciados por la Inquisición." *Historia Mexicana* 11, no. 2 (1961): 161–79.

Guitton, Jean. *Great Heresies and Church Councils*. New York: Harper & Row, 1965.

Hair, P. E. H. "An Irishman before the Mexican Inquisition: 1574–1575." *Irish Historical Studies* 17, no. 67 (1971): 297–319.

Hale, Michael S. "Behold these English Dogs! Englishmen in the Atlantic World before the Holy Office of the Inquisition, 1560–1630." Master's thesis, Missouri State University, 2005.

Haliczer, Stephen. *Sexuality in the Confessional: A Sacrament Profaned*. New York: Oxford University Press, 1996.

Henningsen, Gustav. "El 'banco de datos' del Santo Oficio: las relaciones de causas de la Inquisición española, 1550–1700." *Boletín de la Real Academia de la Historia* 174 (1977): 547–70.

Henningsen, Gustav, John Tedeschi, and Charles Amiel, eds. *The Inquisition in Early Modern Europe: Studies on Sources and Methods*. Dekalb: Northern Illinois University Press, 1986.

Herrera Sotillo, María Asunción. *Ortodoxia y control social en México en el siglo XVII: El Tribunal del Santo Oficio*. Madrid: Universidad Complutense de Madrid, Departamento de Historia de América, 1982.

Holler, Jacqueline. *Escogidas Plantas: Nuns and Beatas in Mexico City, 1531–1601*. New York: Columbia University Press, 2005.

———. "I, Elena De La Cruz: Heresy and Gender in Mexico City, 1568." *Journal of the Canadian Historical Association* 4 (1993): 143–60.

———. "More Sins Than the Queen of England: Marina de San Miguel before the Mexican Inquisition." In *Women in the Inquisition, Spain and the New World*, edited by Mary Giles, 209–28. Baltimore, Johns Hopkins University Press, 1997.

———. "The Spiritual and Physical Ecstasies of a Sixteenth-Century Beata: Marina de San Miguel Confesses before the Mexican Inquisition." In *Colonial Lives: Documents on Latin American History, 1550–1850*, edited by Richard Boyer and Geoffrey Spurling, 77–100. New York: Oxford University Press, 2000.

Homza, Lu Ann. "Erasmus as Hero or Heretic? Spanish Humanism and the Valladolid Conference of 1527." *Renaissance Quarterly* 50 (1997): 78–118.

———. "How to Harass an Inquisitor General: The Polyphonic Law of Friar Francisco Ortiz." In *A Renaissance of Conflicts: Visions and Revisions of Law and Society in Early Modern Italy and Spain*, edited by John A Marino and Thomas Kuehn, 299–336. Essays and Studies, 3. Toronto: Center for Reformation and Renaissance Studies, 2004.

———. *Religious Authority in the Spanish Renaissance*. Baltimore: Johns Hopkins University Press, 2000.

———. Review of Stuart Schwartz, *All Can Be Saved: Tolerance and Salvation in the Iberian Atlantic World*. *William and Mary Quarterly*, 3rd ser., 66, no. 2 (2009): 409–11.

———. *The Spanish Inquisition, 1478–1614: An Anthology of Sources*. Indianapolis: Hackett, 2006.

Hordes, Stanley M. "Historiographical Problems in the Study of the Inquisition and the Mexican Crypto-Jews in the Seventeenth Century." *American Jewish Archives* 34, no. 2 (1982): 138–52.

———. "The Inquisition and the Crypto-Jewish Community in Colonial New Spain and New Mexico." *Western States Jewish History* 29, no. 1 (1996): 689–701.

———. "The Inquisition as Economic and Political Agent: The Campaign of the Mexican Holy Office against the Crypto-Jews in the Mid Seventeenth-Century." *The Americas* 39, no. 1 (1982): 23–38.

———. *To the End of the Earth: A History of the Crypto-Jews of New Mexico.* New York: Columbia University Press, 2005.

Hossain, Kimberly Lynn. "Arbiters of Faith, Agents of Empire: Spanish Inquisitors and Their Careers, 1550–1650." Ph.D. dissertation, Johns Hopkins University, 2006.

———. "Unraveling the Spanish Inquisition: Inquisitorial Studies in the Twenty-first Century." *History Compass* 5, no. 4 (2007): 1280–93.

Hubbard, Alice Philena. "The Bible of Vatable." *Journal of Biblical Literature* 66, no. 2 (1947): 197–209.

Huerga, Álvaro. *Historia de los alumbrados.* Vol. 3: *Los alumbrados de Hispanoamérica 1570–1605.* Madrid: Fundación Universitaria Española, 1986.

Huertas, Pilar, Jesús de Miguel, and Antonio Sánchez. *La Inquisición: Tribunal contra los delitos de fe.* Madrid: Editorial Libsa, 2003.

Ibsen, Kristine. "The High Places of My Power: Sebastiana Josefa de la Santísima Trinidad and the Hagiographic Representation of the Body in Colonial Spanish America." *Colonial Latin American Review* 7, no. 21 (1998): 251–70.

———. *Women's Spiritual Autobiography in Colonial Spanish America.* Gainesville: University Press of Florida, 1999.

Izquierdo, Ana Luisa. "Un documento novohispano del siglo XVII como fuente para el estudio de la religión maya." *Estudios de Cultura Maya* 19 (1992): 321–35.

———. "Documentos de la división del beneficio de Yaxcaba: El castigo de una idolatría." *Estudios de Cultura Maya* 17 (1988): 158–95.

Jaffary, Nora E. *False Mystics: Deviant Orthodoxy in Colonial Mexico.* Lincoln: University of Nebraska Press, 2004.

———. "Virtue and Transgression: The Certification of Authentic Mysticism in the Mexican Inquisition." *Catholic Southwest: A Journal of History and Culture* 10 (1999): 9–28.

Jiménez Monterserín, Miguel. *Introducción a la Inquisición Española: Documentos básicos para el estudio del Santo Oficio.* Madrid: Editora Nacional, 1980.

Jiménez Rueda, Julio, ed. *Corsarios franceses e ingleses en la Inquisición de la Nueva España, siglo XVI.* México, D.F.: Imp. Universitaria, Archivo General de la Nación, 1945.

———. *Don Pedro Moya de Contreras, primer Inquisidor de México.* México, D.F.: Ediciones Xochitl, 1944.

———. *Herejías y Supersticiones en la Nueva España.* México, D.F.: Universidad Autónoma de México, Imprenta Universitaria, 1944.

Johnson, Lyman L., and Sonya Lipsett-Rivera, eds. *The Faces of Honor: Sex, Shame and Violence in Colonial Latin America.* Albuquerque: University of New Mexico Press, 1998.

Jones, William. *The History of the Christian Church from the Birth of Christ to the XVIII Century.* London: R. W. Pomeroy, 1832.

Kagan, Richard L., and Abigail Dyer, eds. *Inquisitorial Inquiries: Brief Lives of Secret Jews and Other Heretics.* Baltimore: Johns Hopkins University Press, 2004.

Kamen, Henry Arthur Francis. "Confiscations in the Economy of the Spanish Inquisition." *Economic History Review* 18, no. 3 (1965): 511–25.

———. "Galley Service and Crime in Sixteenth Century Spain." *Economic History Review,* n.s., 22, no. 2 (1969): 304–5.

———. *Inquisition and Society in Spain in the Sixteenth and Seventeenth Centuries*. London: Weidenfeld & Nicolson, 1985.

———. *The Spanish Inquisition: A Historical Revision*. New Haven: Yale University Press, 1998.

———. "Toleration and Dissent in Sixteenth-Century Spain: The Alternative Tradition." *Sixteenth Century Journal* 19, no. 1 (1988): 3–23.

Keitt, Andrew. *Inventing the Sacred: Imposture, Inquisition, and the Boundaries of the Supernatural in Golden Age Spain*. Leiden: Brill, 2005.

———. "The Miraculous Body of Evidence: Visionary Experience, Medical Discourse, and the Inquisition in 17th Century New Spain." *Sixteenth Century Journal* 36, no. 1 (2005): 77–96.

Klor de Alva, J. Jorge. "Aztec Spirituality and Nahuatized Christianity." In *South and Meso-American Native Spirituality: From the Cult of the Feathered Serpent to the Theology of Liberation*, edited by Gary H. Gossen, 173–97. New York: Crossroad, 1993.

———. "Colonizing Souls: The Failure of the Indian Inquisition and the Rise of Penitential Discipline." In *Cultural Encounters*, edited by Mary Elizabeth Perry and Anne J. Cruz, 3–23. Berkeley: University of California Press, 1991.

———. "Spiritual Conflict and Accommodation in New Spain: Toward a Typology of Aztec Responses to Christianity." In *The Inca and Aztec States, 1400–1800: Anthropology and History*, edited by George A. Collier, Renato I. Rosaldo, and John D. Wirth, 345–66. New York: Academic Press, 1982.

Koeninger, Frieda. "Pope Bashing by Papists? A Curious Censoring of Alexander Pope's Letters by the Mexican Inquisition." *Eighteenth-Century Life* 26, no. 2 (Spring 2002): 45–52.

Kuehn, Thomas. "Reading Microhistory: The Example of Giovanni and Lusanna." *Journal of Modern History* 61, no. 3 (1989): 512–34.

Kurtz, Lester R. "The Politics of Heresy." *American Journal of Sociology* 88, no. 6 (1983): 1085–1115.

Lahoz Finestres, José María. "Una perspectiva de los funcionarios del Santo Oficio." *Revista de la Inquisición* 9 (2000): 113–80.

Lavrin, Asunción. "Aproximación al tema de la sexualidad en el México colonial." *Encuentro* 2, no. 1 (1984): 23–40.

———. "Ecclesiastical Reform of Nunneries in New Spain in the Eighteenth Century." *The Americas* 22, no. 2 (1965): 182–203.

———. "La escritura desde un mundo oculto: Espiritualidad y anonimidad en el Convento de San Juan de la Penitencia." *Estudios de Historia Novohispana* 22 (2000): 49–76.

———. "Espiritualidad en el claustro novohispano del siglo XVII." *Colonial Latin American Review* 4, no. 2 (1995): 155–79.

———. "In Search of the Colonial Woman in Mexico: The Seventeenth and Eighteenth Centuries." In *Latin American Women: Historical Perspectives*, edited by Asunción Lavrin, 23–59. Westport, Conn.: Greenwood Press, 1978.

———. "The Role of the Nunneries in the Economy of New Spain in the Eighteenth Century." *Hispanic American Historical Review* 46, no. 4 (1966): 371–93.

———. "Sexuality in Colonial Mexico: A Church Dilemma." In *Sexuality and Marriage in Colonial Latin America*, edited by Asunción Lavrin, 47–95. Lincoln: University of Nebraska Press, 1989.

———. "Sor Juana Inés de la Cruz: obediencia y autoridad en su entorno religioso." *Revista Iberoamericana* 61, nos. 172–73 (1995): 605–22.

———. "Unlike Sor Juana? The Model Nun in the Religious Literature of Colonial Mexico." *University of Dayton Review* 16, no. 2 (1983): 75–92.

———. "Values and Meaning of Monastic Life for Nuns in Colonial Mexico." *Catholic Historical Review* 63, no. 3 (1972): 367–87.

———. "Women and Religion in Spanish America." In *Women and Religion in America*, vol. 2: *The Colonial and Revolutionary Periods*, edited by Rosemary Radford Ruether and Rosemary Skinner Keller, 42–78. San Francisco: Harper & Row, 1983.

———. "Women in Convents: Their Economic and Social Role in Colonial Mexico." In *Liberating Women's History: Theoretical and Critical Essays*, edited by Berenice A. Carroll, 250–71. Urbana: University of Illinois Press, 1976.

Lea, Henry Charles. *Chapters from the Religious History of Spain Connected with the Inquisition.* New York: Lea Brothers, 1890.

———. "An Essay on Torture." In *Superstition and Force: Essays on the Wager of Law, the Wager of Battle, the Ordeal, Torture*, 371–511. Philadelphia: Collins Printers, 1878.

———. *A History of the Inquisition of Spain.* 4 vols. New York: Macmillan, 1906.

———. *The Inquisition in the Spanish dependencies.* New York, 1908.

Leonard, Irving A. "Conquerors and Amazons in Mexico." *Hispanic American Historical Review* 24 (1944): 561–79.

———. "One Man's Library, Manila, 1583." *Hispanic Review* 15 (1947): 84–100.

———. "Peyote and the Mexican Inquisition, 1620." *American Anthropologist* 44, no. 2 (1942): 324–26.

———. *Romances of Chivalry in the Spanish Indies with Some Registros of Shipments of Books to the Spanish Colonies.* Berkeley: University of California Press, 1933.

———. "Spanish Shipboard Reading in the Sixteenth Century." *Hispania* 32, no. 1 (1949): 53–58.

Lewin, Boleslao. " '*Las confidencias*' of Two Crypto-Jews in the Holy Office Prison of Mexico: 1654–1655." *Jewish Social Studies* 30, no. 1 (1968): 3–22.

Liebman, Seymour B. "The Abecedario and a Check-List of Mexican Inquisition Documents at the Henry E. Huntington Library." *Hispanic American Historical Review* 44, no. 4 (1964): 554–67.

———. *The Enlightened: The Writings of Luis de Carvajal, El Mozo.* Coral Gables, Fla.: University of Miami Press, 1967.

———. *A Guide to Jewish References in the Mexican Colonial Era, 1521–1821.* Selected, compiled, and translated by Seymour B. Liebman. Philadelphia: University of Pennsylvania Press, 1964.

———. "Hernando Alonso, First Jew on the North America Continent." *Journal of Inter-American Studies* 5 (1963): 291–96.

———. *The Inquisitors and the Jews in the New World: Summaries of Procesos, 1500–1810, and Bibliographical Guide.* Coral Gables, Fla: University of Miami Press, 1974.

———. *The Jews in New Spain: Faith, Flame, and the Inquisition.* Coral Gables, Fla.: University of Miami Press, 1970.

———. *New World Jewry, 1493–1825: Requiem for the Forgotten.* New York: Ktav Publishing House, 1982.

———. "Tomás Treviño de Sobremonte: A Jewish Martyr." *Jewish Social Studies* 42, no. 1 (1980): 63–74.

Llorente, Juan Antonio. *Historia Crítica de la Inquisición en España.* Vols. 1–4. Madrid: Hiperión, 1980.

Longhurst, John Edward. *Erasmus and the Spanish Inquisition: The Case of Juan de Valdés.* Albuquerque: University of New Mexico Press, 1950.

———. *Luther and the Spanish Inquisition: The Case of Diego de Uceda, 1528–1529.* Albuquerque: University of New Mexico Press, 1953.

Maqueda, Consuelo. "Mundo indígena e Inquisición: Conflicto de fe en Nueva España." In *Intolerancia e Inquisición*, edited by José Antonio Escudero, 47–96. Madrid: Sociedad Estatal de Conmemoraciones Culturas, 2006.

Mariel de Ibáñez, Yolanda. *El tribunal de la Inquisición en México (siglo XVI).* México, D.F.: Universidad Nacional Autónoma de México, Instituto de Investigaciones Jurídicas, 1979.

Márquez, Antonio. *Literatura e Inquisición en España (1478–1834).* Madrid: Taurus, 1980.

Martínez Millán, José. "Estructura de la hacienda de la Inquisición." In *Historia de la Inquisición en España y América*, vol. 2: Las estructuras del Santo Oficio, edited by Bartolomé Escandell Bonet and Joaquín Pérez Villanueva, 885–1076. Madrid: Biblioteca de Autores Cristianos, 1993.

———. "Structures of Inquisition Finance." In *The Spanish Inquisition and the Inquisitorial Mind*, edited by Ángel Alcalá, 159–76. New York: Columbia University Press, 1987.

Mathes, W. Michael. "Humanism in Sixteenth and Seventeenth Century Libraries of New Spain." In *Catholic Historical Review* 82, no. 3 (1996): 412–35.

Medina, José Toribio. *El Tribunal del Santo Oficio de la Inquisición en Lima*. Santiago: Imprenta Gutenburg, 1887.

———. *El Tribunal del Santo Oficio de la Inquisición en México*. Santiago: Imprenta Elzeveriana, 1903.

Mejía González, Alma Leticia, ed. *Relación de la causa de Juana María, mulata: Esclava, mulata y hechicera. Historia inquisitorial de una mujer novohispana del siglo XVIII*. México, D.F.: El Colegio de México, 1996.

Méndez, María Agueda, coord. *Catálogo de textos marginados novohispanos. Inquisición: siglos XVIII y XIX*. México, D.F.: Archivo General de la Nación, 1992.

———. "Los 'Mandamientos de Amor' en la Inquisición Novohispana." *Caravelle: Cahiers du monde hispanique et luso-brésilien* 49 (1987): 105–12.

———. "La oración pervertida en la Inquisición novohispana." In *Anales de literatura latinoamericana* 20 (1991): 65–70.

Millar Carvacho, René. "Falsa santidad e Inquisición. Los procesos a las visionarias limeñas." *Boletín de la Academia Chilena de la Historia*, nos. 108–9 (2000): 277–305.

Miralles de Imperial y Gómez, Claudio. "Censura de publicaciones en Nueva España, 1576–1591. Anotaciones documentales." *Revista de Indias* 10, no. 42 (1950): 817–46.

Moffett, Elizabeth Jean. "A Glossary of the Spanish Inquisition." Ph.D. dissertation, University of Illinois, 1966.

Monteiro de Barros Carollo, Denise Helena. "Auto da Fe: A Ceremony More Than Just Words." *Revista de la Inquisición* 8 (1999): 113–20.

Monter, E. William. *Frontiers of Heresy: The Spanish Inquisition from the Basque Lands to Sicily*. Cambridge: Cambridge University Press, 1990.

———. "The New Social History and the Spanish Inquisition." *Journal of Social History* 17, no. 4 (1984): 705–13.

Moreno de los Arcos, Roberto. "Autos seguidos por el provisor de naturales del Arzobispado de México contra el ídolo del Gran Nayar, 1722–1723." *Tlalocan* 10 (1985): 377–477.

———. "La inquisición para indios en la Nueva España, siglos XVI a XIX." *Chicomostoc: Boletín del Seminario de Estudios Prehispánicos para la Descolonización de México*, no. 2 (March 1989): 7–21.

———. "New Spain's Inquisition for Indians from the Sixteenth to the Nineteenth Century." In *Cultural Encounters: The Impact of the Inquisition in Spain and the New World*, edited by Mary Elizabeth Perry and Anne J. Cruz, 23–37. Berkeley: University of California Press, 1991.

Mott, Margaret. "Leonor De Cáceres and the Mexican Inquisition." *Journal of the History of Ideas* 62, no. 1 (2001): 81–98.

———. "The Rule of Faith over Reason: The Role of the Inquisition in Iberia and New Spain." *Journal of Church and State* 40, no. 1 (1998): 57–81.

Muñoz Delaunoy, Ignacio. "Solicitación *in loco confessionis*: Un estudio de caso, 1650–1666." *Historia* 32 (1999): 177–264.

Muñoz García, María José. "Erotismo y celo inquisitorial: Expedientes de escritos obscenos censurados por la inquisición en el siglo xviii y principios del xix." *Cuadernos de Historia del Derecho* 10 (2003): 157–207.

Muñoz Mendoza, Joaquín. "El indio americano y los santos tribunales: La lógica de la locura." *Ibero-Amerikanisches Archiv* 14, no. 4 (1988): 437–52.

Nalle, Sara. *God in La Mancha: Religious Reform and the People of Cuenca, 1500–1650*. Baltimore: Johns Hopkins University Press, 1992.

———. "Inquisitors, Priests and People during the Catholic Reformation in Spain." *Sixteenth Century Journal* 18 (1987): 557–87.

Nesvig, Martin. "Heterodoxia popular e Inquisición diocesana en Michoacán, siglo XVI." *Tzintzun* 39 (2004): 9–38.

———. *Ideology and Inquisition: The World of the Censors in Early Mexico*. New Haven: Yale University Press, 2009.

———. *Local Religion in Colonial Mexico*. Albuquerque: University of New Mexico Press, 2006.

Nunemaker, J. Horace, ed. *Inquisition Papers of Mexico. I. The Trial of Simón de León, 1647*. Pullman, Wash.: Research Studies of the State College of Washington, 1946.

Núñez B., Fernanda. "Doña Bárbara de Echagaray, Beata y Pecadora Jalapeña de fines del siglo XVIII." *Relaciones* 22, no. 88 (2001): 209–42.

Palacios, Vegazo. *El Auto General de Fé de 1680*. Malaga: Editorial Algazara, 1995.

Pelikan, Jaroslav. *The Christian Tradition: A History of the Development of Doctrine*. Vol. 4: *The Reformation of Church and Dogma (1300–1700)*. Chicago: University of Chicago Press, 1985.

Peña, Margarita, ed. *La palabra amordazada: Literatura censurada por la Inquisición*. México, D.F.: Facultad de Filosofía y Letras, UNAM, 2000.

Pérez, Joseph. *The Spanish Inquisition: A History*. New Haven: Yale University Press, 2006.

Pérez de Colosia, M. I., and J. Gil San Juan. "Inspección inquisitorial a los navíos y control de libros." *Jábega* 25 (1979): 25–36.

Pérez Marcos, Regina María. "Derechos humanos e Inquisición, ¿Conceptos contrapuestos?" *Revista de la Inquisición* 9 (2000): 181–90.

Pérez Villanueva, Joaquín, and Bartolomé Escandell Bonet, eds. *Historia de la Inquisición en España y América*. Vol. 1: *El conocimiento científico y el proceso histórico de la Institución (1478–1834)*. Madrid: Biblioteca de Autores Cristianos, Centro de Estudios Inquisitoriales, 1984.

———. *Historia de la Inquisición en España y América*. Vol. 2: *Las Estructuras del Santo Oficio*. Madrid: Biblioteca de Autores Cristianos, Centro de Estudios Inquisitoriales, 1993.

Perry, Mary Elizabeth, and Anne J. Cruz, eds. *Cultural Encounters: The Impact of the Inquisition in Spain and the New World*. Berkeley: University of California Press, 1991.

Peters, Edward. "Editing Inquisitors' Manuals in the Sixteenth Century: Francisco Peña and the Directorium Inquisitorum of Nicholas Eymeric." In *Bibliographical Studies in Honor of Rudolf Hirsch*, edited by William E. Miller and Thomas G. Waldman, with Natalie D. Terrell. *Library Chronicle* 60 (1974): 95–107.

———. *Inquisition*. Berkeley: University of California Press, 1989.

———. *Torture*. Philadelphia: University of Pennsylvania Press, 1996.

Piña y Palacios, Javier. *La Cárcel Perpetua de la Inquisición y la Real Cárcel de Corte de la Nueva España*. México, D.F.: Ediciones Botas, 1971.

Pinto Crespo, Virgilio. "La censura: Sistemas de control e instrumentos de acción." In *Inquisición española y mentalidad inquisitorial*, edited by Ángel Alcalá. Barcelona: Ariel, 1984.

———. "Los Indices de libros prohibidos." *Hispania Sacra* 34, no. 71 (1983): 161–91.

———. *Inquisición y control ideológico en la España del siglo XVI*. Madrid: Taurus, 1983.

———. "Institucionalización inquisitorial y censura de libros." In *La Inquisición Española: Nueva visión, nuevos horizontes*, edited by Joaquín Pérez Villanueva, 513–36. Madrid: Siglo XXI de España Editores, S.A. ,1980.

Pizzigoni, Caterina. "Amid Idealization and Practice: Archbishops, Local Clergy, and Nahuas in the Toluca Valley, 1712–1765." *Swedish Missiological Themes* 91, no. 2 (2003): 249–73.

———. "Between Assimilation and Resistance: The Role Played by Nahua Women in the Communities of the Valley of Toluca, Eighteenth Century." Ph.D. dissertation, University of London, 2002.

———. "'Como frágil y miserable mujer': Vida cotidiana de las mujeres nahuas del Valle de Toluca." In *Historia de la vida cotidiana en México*, edited by Pilar Gonzalbo Aizpuru, 501–30. México, D.F.: El Colegio de México and Editorial Planeta, 2003.

———. "'Para que le sirva de castigo y al pueblo de ejemplo.' El pecado de poligamía y la mujer indígena en el valle de Toluca (siglo XVIII)." In *Las mujeres en la construcción de las sociedades iberoamericanas*, edited by Berta Ares and Pilar Gonzalbo Aizpuru, 193–217. Seville and México: Consejo Superior de Investigaciones Científicas, Escuela de Estudios Hispano-Americanos, and Centro de Estudios Históricos, El Colegio de México, 2004.

Pompa y Pompa, Antonio. *Procesos inquisitorial y militar seguidos a D. Miguel Hidalgo y Costilla.* México, D.F.: Instituto Nacional de Antropología e Historia, 1960.

Poole, Stafford. *Pedro Moya de Contreras: Catholic Reform and Royal Power in New Spain, 1571–1591.* Berkeley: University of California Press, 1987.

Quezada, Noemí. "The Inquisition's Repression of *curanderos*." In *Cultural Encounters: The Impact of the Inquistion in Spain and the New World*, edited by Mary Elizabeth Perry and Anne J. Cruz, 37–57. Berkeley: University of California Press, 1991.

———. "Sexualidad y magia en la mujer novohispana, siglo XVIII." *Anuario de Antropología* 26 (1989): 261–95.

Quezada, Noemí, Martha Eugenia Rodríguez, and Marcela Suárez. *Inquisición Novohispana.* Vols. 1–2. México, D.F.: UNAM, Instituto de Investigaciones Antropológicas, Universidad Autónoma Metropolitana, 2000.

Ramírez Montes, Guillermina, ed. *Catálogo del ramo de Inquisición.* México, D.F.: Archivo General de la Nación, 1979.

Ramos Medina, Manuel. *Imagen de santidad en un mundo profano.* México, D.F.: Universidad Iberoamericana, 1990.

———. "Isabel de la Encarnación, monja posesa del siglo XVII." In *Manifestaciones religiosas en el mundo colonial americano*, edited by Clara García Ayluardo y Manuel Ramos Medina, 1:41–51. México, D.F.: Condumex / INAH / Universidad Iberoamericana, 1993.

Ramos Soriano, José Abel. "Libros prohibidos sobre matrimonio, familia y sexualidad en los edictos promulgados por la Inquisición, 1575–1819." In *Seis ensayos sobre el discurso colonial relativo a la comunidad doméstica: Matrimonio, familia y sexualidad a través de los cronistas del siglo XVI, el Nuevo Testamento y el Santo Oficio de la Inquisición*, edited by Solange Alberro et al., 185–211. México, D.F.: Departamento de Investigaciones Históricas, INAH, 1980.

Rawlings, Helen. *Church, Religion and Society in Early Modern Spain.* Hampshire: Palgrave, 2002.

———. *The Spanish Inquisition.* London: Blackwell, 2006.

Reyes Garza, Juan Carlos. "Del de amores y de otros males: Curanderismo y hechicería en la villa de Colima del siglo XVIII." *Estudios de Historia Novohispana* 16 (1996): 83–99.

Ricard, Robert. *The Spiritual Conquest of Mexico.* Berkeley: University of California Press, 1982.

Rico Medina, Samuel. *Los predicamentos de la fe: La Inquisición en Tabasco, 1567–1811.* Villahermosa, México: Gobierno del Estado de Tabasco, 1990.

Rodríguez Baquero, Luis Enrique. "Sentencia y penitencia: Caminos hacia la reconciliación en la sociedad colonial." *Fronteras* 1, no. 1 (1997): 151–72.

Roman y Zamora, Jerónimo de. *Repúblicas de Indias: Idolatrías en México y Perú antes de la conquista.* Edited by Victoriano Sérez . 2 vols. Colección de libros raros o curiosos que tratan de América, XIV y XV. Madrid, 1897.

Rosas Navarro, Ruth Magali. "El Tribunal de la Santa Inquisición y los negros esclavos en America." *Hispania Sacra* 55, no. 112 (2003): 535–67.

Rubial García, Antonio. "Las santitas del barrio: 'Beatas' laicas y religiosidad cotidiana en la ciudad de México en el siglo XVII." *Anuario de Estudios Americanos* 59, no. 1 (2002): 13–37.

Ruff, Julius Ralph. *Violence in Early Modern Europe, 1500–1800.* Cambridge: Cambridge University Press, 2001.

Ruiz Islas, Alfredo. "Ingresos e egresos del tribunal del Santo Oficio de la Nueva España en el siglo XVIII." *Revista de Indias* 65, no. 234 (2005): 511–34.

———. "El Real Fisco de la Inquisición durante la primera mitad del siglo XVIII en Nueva España." *Secuencia* 56 (2003): 126–71.

Sánchez Ortega, María Helena. *La Inquisición y los gitanos.* Madrid: Taurus, 1988.

———. *La Mujer y la sexualidad en el antiguo régimen: La perspectiva inquisitorial.* Madrid: Akal, 1992.

———. "Women as the Source of Evil in Counter-Reformation Spain." In *Culture and Control in Counter-Reformation Spain,* edited by Anne J. Cruz and Mary Elizabeth Perry, 196–215. Minneapolis: University of Minnesota Press, 1992.

Sanchiz, Javier. "Funcionarios inquisitoriales en el tribunal, siglo XVI." In *Inquisición Novohispana,* vols. 1–2, edited by Noemí Quezada, Martha Eugenia Rodríguez, and Marcela Suárez. 1:165–95 México, D.F.: Universidad Nacional Autónoma de México, 2000.

Santos Zertuche, Francisco José. *Señorío, dinero y arquitectura: El Palacio de la Inquisición de México, 1571–1820.* México, D.F.: El Colegio de México, Centro de Estudios Históricos, Universidad Autónoma Metropolitana-Azcapotzalco, 2000.

Scholes, France V. "The First Decade of the Inquisition in New Mexico." *New Mexico Historical Review* 10 (1935): 195–241.

Scholes, France V., and Eleanor B Adams, eds. *Don Diego Quijada, Alcalde Mayor de Yucatán, 1561–1565.* 2 vols. México: Editorial Porrua, 1938.

Scholes, France V., and Ralph Roys. *Fray Diego de Landa and the Problem of Idolatry in Yucatán.* Washington, D.C.: Carnegie Institution, 1938.

Schons, Dorothy. *Book Censorship in New Spain.* Austin: New World Studies, Book 2, 1949.

Schwaller, John F. "The Cathedral Chapter of Mexico in the Sixteenth Century." *Hispanic American Historical Review* 61 (1981): 651–74.

———. *The Church and Clergy in Sixteenth-Century Mexico.* Albuquerque: University of New Mexico Press, 1987.

———. *Origins of Church Wealth: Ecclesiastical Revenues and Church Finances, 1523–1600.* Albuquerque: University of New Mexico Press, 1985.

Seed, Patricia. "The Church and the Patriarchal Family: Marriage Conflicts in Sixteenth- and Seventeenth-Century New Spain." *Journal of Family History* 10, no. 3 (1985): 284–93.

Sepúlveda y Herrera, María Teresa. *Procesos por idolatría al cacique, gobernadores y sacerdotes de Yanhuitlán, 1544–1546.* México, D.F.: Instituto Nacional de Antropología e Historia, 1999.

Sierra Corella, Antonio. *La censura de libros y papeles en España y los índices y catálogos españoles de los prohibidos y expurgados.* Madrid: Cuerpo facultativo de archiveros, bibliotecarios y arqueólogos, 1947.

Sodi Miranda, Federica, and David Aceves Romero. "El uso y abuso del chocolate en la Nueva España." In *Inquisición Novohispana,* edited by Noemí Quezada, Martha Eugenia Rodríguez, and Marcela Suárez, 1:313–22. México, D.F.: Universidad Nacional Autónoma de México, 2000.

Sousa, Lisa. "The Devil and Deviance in Native Criminal Narratives from Early Mexico." *The Americas* 59, no. 2 (2002): 161–79.

Spach, Robert C. "Juan Gil and the Sixteenth-Century Spanish Protestantism." *Sixteenth Century Journal* 26, no. 4 (1995): 857–79.

Starr-LeBeau, Gretchen D. *In the Shadow of the Virgin: Inquisitors, Friars, and Conversos in Guadalupe, Spain.* Princeton: Princeton University Press, 2003.

Tambs, Lewis A. "The Inquisition in Eighteenth-Century Mexico." *The Americas* 22, no. 2 (1965): 167–81.

Tavárez, David. "Autonomy, Honor, and the Ancestors: Confrontations over Local Devotions in Colonial Oaxaca." In *Local Religion in Colonial Mexico,* edited by Martin Nesvig, 119–44. Albuquerque: University of New Mexico Press, 2006.

———. "Ciclos punitivos, economías del castigo, y estrategias indígenas ante la extirpación de idolatrías en Oaxaca y México." In *Nuevas perspectivas sobre el castigo de la heterodoxia en la Nueva España,* edited by Ana de Zaballa, 37–56. Bilbao: Universidad del País Vasco, 2005.

———. "Escritura y disensión: Resistencia y cosmologías alternas en el México colonial." *Revista de Indias* 69, no. 247 (2009): 81–104.

———. "Idolatry as an Ontological Question: Native Consciousness and Juridical Proof in Colonial Mexico." *Journal of Early Modern History* 6, no. 2 (2002): 114–39.

———. "Legally Indian: Inquisitorial Readings of Indigenous Identities in New Spain." In *Imperial Subjects: Race and Identity in Colonial Latin America,* edited by Andrew B. Fisher and Matthew D. O'Hara, 81–100. Durham: Duke University Press, 2009.

Tomás y Valiente, Francisco. "El crimen y el pecado contra natura." In *Sexo barroco y otras transgresiones premodernas,* edited by Francisco Tomás y Valiente et al., 33–55. Madrid: Alianza Editorial S.A., 1990.

———. "El Santo Oficio de la Inquisición: Entre el secreto y el espectáculo." *Anuario de Historia del Derecho Español* 65 (1995): 1071–78.

———. *La tortura judicial en España.* Barcelona: Editorial Crítica, Biblioteca de Bolsillo, 2000.

Torres Aguilar, Manuel. "Algunos aspectos del delito de bigamía en la Inquisición de Indias." *Revista de la Inquisición* 6 (1997): 117–38.

Torres Puga, Gabriel. *Los últimos años de la inquisición en la Nueva España.* México, D.F.: Miguel Ángel Porrúa, CONACULTA-INAH, 2004.

Tortorici, Zeb. "'Heran todos Putos': Sodomitical Subcultures and Disordered Desire in Early Colonial Mexico." *Ethnohistory* 54 (2007): 35–67.

———. "Masturbation, Salvation, and Desire: Connecting Sexuality and Religiosity in Colonial Mexico." *Journal of the History of Sexuality* 16, no. 3 (2007): 355–72.

Tovar González, María Elena. *Juicios inquisitoriales en Chiapas durante el siglo XVIII.* [Tuxtla Gutiérrez, México]: Instituto Chiapaneco de Cultura, 1988.

Traslosheros, Jorge E. *Iglesia, justicia y sociedad en la Nueva España: La Audiencia del Arzobispado de México, 1528–1668.* México, D.F.: Editorial Porrúa y Universidad Iberoamericana, 1994.

———. "El Tribunal Eclesiástico y los Indios en el arzobispado de México hasta 1630." *Historia Mexicana* 51, no. 3 (2002): 485–516.

Twinam, Ann. *Public Lives, Private Secrets: Gender, Honor, Sexuality, and Illegitimacy in Colonial Spanish America.* Stanford, Calif.: Stanford University Press, 2004.

Uchmany de de la Peña, Eva A. "Cuatro casos de idolatria en la región Maya ante el Tribunal de la Inquisición." *Estudios de Cultura Maya* 6 (1967): 267–300.

———. "Interacción entre las formas religiosas practicadas por algunos cripto-judios y formas religiosas indígenas." In *Religión en Mesoamérica: XII Mesa Redonda,* edited by Jaime Litvak

King and Noemí Castillo Tejero, 503–8. México, D.F.: Sociedad Mexicana de Antropología, 1972.

———. *La vida entre el Judaísmo y el Cristianismo en la Nueva España, 1580–1606*. México, D.F.: Archivo General de la Nación, 1992.

Vekene, Emil Van der. *Bibliotheca Bibliographica Historiae Sanctae Inquisitionis. Bibliographisches Verzeichnis des Gedruckten Schrifttums zur Geschichte und Literatur der Inquisition*. Vol. 1. Vaduz, Liechtenstein: Topos Verlag, 1982.

Villa-Flores, Javier. *Dangerous Speech: A Social History of Blasphemy in Colonial Mexico*. Albuquerque: University of Arizona Press, 2006.

———. "On Divine Persecution: Blasphemy and Gambling in New Spain." In *Religion in New Spain*, edited by Susan Schroeder and Stafford Poole, 238–62. Albuquerque: New Mexico University Press, 2007.

———. "Talking through the Chest: Ventriloquism and Divination among African Slave Women in Colonial Mexico." *Colonial Latin American Review* 14, no. 2 (2005): 299–321.

———. "To Lose One's Soul: Blasphemy and Slavery in New Spain, 1596–1669." *Hispanic American Historical Review* 82, no. 3 (2002): 435–68.

———. "Wandering Swindlers: Imposture, Style, and the Inquisition's Pedagogy of Fear in Peripheral New Spain." *Colonial Latin American Review* 17, no. 2 (2008): 251–72.

Vogeley, Nancy. "Actitudes en México hacia la Inquisición: El pro y el contra (1814, 1824)." *Revista de la Inquisición* 11 (2005): 223–43.

Wiesner, Merry E. *Christianity and Sexuality in the Early Modern World: Regulating Desire, Reforming Practice*. London: Routledge, 2000.

Wobeser, Gisela von. "La Inquisición como Institución creditícia en el Siglo XVIII." *Historia Mexicana* 39, no. 4 (1990): 849–79.

INDEX

The letter "t" after a page reference indicates a table.

Abad, Juan Nicolás, 178, 182–184, 325, 329–330

Abad y Queipo, Manuel, 323–325, 393n144, 393n150

abjurations: as act of contrition, 47, 70, 78, 152, 241–256 passim, 371n276, 382n84; of convicted heretics, 31, 47; *de formali*, 47–48, 153; *de levi*, 47–48, 49t, 71–73, 153–154, 166–170 passim, 219, 255, 275, 371n279; *de vehementi*, 47–48, 49t, 70–73, 148–154, 170–174 passim, 246, 250

abolition: of Mexican Inquisition, 11; of officials, 27; of Spanish Inquisition, xviii

accusations, 7, 15–16, 41–46, 116, 154, 206–211, 224, 230–237 passim, 292, 300; anonymous, 25, 30, 35; denial of, 174–175; false or fabricated, xv, 1, 53; formal, 36, 46, 379n38, 387n56; qualification of, 20; rules about, 63, 68–71, 76–78. *See also* heretics, accused

Acosta, Francisco de, 246

Acosta, Manuel de, 252

acquittals, 45–46, 250, 371n267

Adel y Piñarosa, Vicente, 310

Africans, xviii, xx, 8, 11, 17, 22, 293

African slaves: as accused, 165–166, 246; as assistants in Tribunal, 17; and blasphemy, 206, 214–217, 385n10; harsher punishments for, 382n85; testimony of, 214–217; as witnesses, 214–217

Aguascalientes, 284–291; commissariat of, 23, 258

Agustín, Juana, 169

Alameda, 52, 341

Alarcón, Alonso de, 220–221

Alberro, Solange, 13, 26, 206

Albertus (ship), 268

Alcalá, Agustín, 339

Alcalá, Lucía de, 168

Alcalá de Henares, 323; University of, 392n142

alguacil mayor. See chief constable

Altamirano y Castilla, Juan de, 17

alumbrados (illuminists), 393n142; cases against, 134t, 274–291; philosophy of, 274–275, 389nn86–87, 392n142; relaxation or execution of, 275. *See also* illuminism; mysticism

Álvarez, Catalina, 228–229

Álvarez, Jorge, 173

Álvarez, Leonora, 228–229

Álvarez, Pedro, 260

Álvarez de Arellano, Manuel, 251

Amézquita Sarmiento, Luis de, 248

Amparador, Cristóbal, 309

Anglicans, 257, 264–266, 272, 389nn84–85

Antonio, Marco, 172

Antunes, Clara, 246

Antunez, Manuel, 251

apostasy, 6t, 12, 59, 82–83, 111–120 passim, 138, 240, 300

Arce, Ramón Josef de, 336

archive of the secret, 88

archives, xviii, 187, 293; of New Spain, xviii, xix, 11, 12, 36, 86, 88, 187, 192, 366n170, 379n34; of Peru, xviii, xix, 364n140, 377n10; of Spain, 293; in Toledo, 373n315

Archivo General de la Nación, Mexico City, xviii, xxii, 7t, 9t, 10t, 29t, 59, 82, 91, 108–125 passim; documents from, 144–165 passim, 177–198 passim, 206–219 passim, 227–259 passim, 264–275 passim, 284–313 passim, 320–337 passim, 360n40, 360n47, 370n260

Archivo Histórico Nacional (Madrid), xvii, xxii, 29t, 107, 135, 249, 360n56, 362n75

Arias Río Frío, Felipe, 315

Armenta, María de: arrest of, 293; confession of, 295; denunciation against, 294; formal accusation against, 296–297; order of exile and banishment against, 299; rebellion of, 298–299; sentence against, 297

Armesto y Ron, Juan de, 275, 280, 282, 288, 310

arrests: and chief constable (*alguacil mayor*), 16–17, 26; and defense attorney (*abogado defensor*), 18; and familiars (*familiares*), 21, 26; and imprisonment, 15, 25, 284; of Indians, 309–312; and initial hearing, 38; orders for, 1, 21, 33–36, 59–60, 82, 90–93, 138, 169; of Portuguese New Christians, 28; procedures for, 59–61, 78, 90–95, 123, 208, 220, 231, 259, 368n214, 385n5; and sequestration, 16, 36–37, 61, 186–187; warrants for, 16, 20, 36–37, 60–62, 138–139, 217, 275, 305, 379n39, 386n29, 286n31

Arriarán, Pedro de, 17

Arroyo, Manual, 326, 330–331

astrology, 101, 108, 110–112

audiencia, 21, 79, 162; of Guadalajara (New Galicia), 79, 375n17; of Guatemala, 375n17; judge (*oidor*) of, 140, 148, 160–161, 199, 241, 375nn17–18; lawyer of, 187; of Mexico, 79, 83–84, 87, 156–158, 164, 364n123, 375n17; secretary of, 300

autos da fé (also *autos de fé*): and abjurations, 153; celebrations of, 157, 382n80; compared to day of final judgment, 150; construction of staging for, 158–159, 381n63; executions following, 51–52; expenses for, 184–185, 187; internal regulations of, 155–164; preparations for, 150–151, 180; processions at beginning of, 153, 160, 181–182; protocol for seating in, 155, 160–163; publication of, 158; and public sentencing of heretics, 153, 165–177, 245–249; rules and regulations about, 155–164, 381n77; and *sanbenitos*, 150–151, 154–155, 160, 180–181; sentences read at, 30, 384n99; swearing of oath of loyalty in, 151–152

autos de fé. See autos da fé

Ave Maria (prayer), 38, 209, 239, 273, 295, 298, 368n212, 374n11

Ávila, Francisco de, 231, 234

Ávila, Gonzalo de, 219

Báez, Ana, 170

Báez, Francisco, 177

Báeza de Herrera, Juan, 300–301

baptism, 3, 268, 272

Bárcena, María de: denunciation against, 302; testimony against, 303

Barreda, Miguel de la, 302–303

Battle of Calderón, 339, 341

Bautista, Juan, 125

Bay of Honduras, 272

Beata (pious woman), 251, 284–291, 390nn88–89

Becerra, Pedro, 263–264

Belmonte, Manuel Francisco del, 173

Benavente, Cristóbal de, 206–207

Benavides, Francisco de, 245

Benítez, Daniel, 174

Benítez, Miguel, 341

Bergosa y Jordán, Antonio, 118, 178–179, 183–185, 325, 335; career of, 393n144; letter to, 324

Bermúdez, Catalina, 168

Bernal, Alonso, 245

bestiality, 6t, 109

Betanzos, Domingo de, 9

bibles: Vatable edition, 99, 376n39; Vulgate translation of, 89, 99–100, 321, 327, 329, 376n38, 380nn47–48

bigamy: xx, 155, 380n41, 385n12, 385n14; edict of faith against, 109; involving mainly men, 292; minor or lesser crime of, 5, 6t, 9t, 10t, 47, 219; proof of, 371n272; punishment for, 386n25; and torture, 134t, 374n15; trials about, 218–227

Blanco, Hernán, 154

blasphemy, xx, 5, 7, 9, 9t, 10t, 47, 384n1, 385n10; edicts of faith and, 109; heretical, 6t, 88, 178, 180–181, 205; people convicted for, 154, 166, 209, 212–214, 379n39; punishments for, 382n83, 385n6; qualification of, 78; simple, 6t, 205; torture and, 374n15, 380n40; trials for, 205–217

blood purity. See *limpieza de sangre*

Bonilla, Juan de, 322, 392n142

Book of Martyrs (Foxe), 32

books: burning of, 321; censorship of, 20, 89, 318–320, 363n117, 392n128, 392n130; edicts of faith about, 108–109, 110, 112–113, 114–115; inspections of ships for, 94–96, 319–320; instructions about, 32, 94–95; maintained by Tribunal, 84–86, 108, 187, 188–192 passim; prohibited, 7, 98–104, 155, 176, 239, 300–301; purging of passages from, 115, 321, 324, 392n141; role of Inquisition in censorship and publication of, 82, 318–320; suspicious, 143; trials and documents about, 318–342; visitation of ships for, 94–95. *See also* Index of Prohibited Books

Bouquet of Spiritual Flowers, A, 323

Bravo, Miguel, 311

Budía, Juan de, 245

Bueno, Alonso: self-denunciation of, 213; sentence against, 213–214; trial of, 213–214

Burgos, Agustin de, 331, 332

Cabello, Manuel, 311

Calapiz, Ignacio, 199

Calvin, John, 99, 257, 259, 319

Calvinism, 257, 265–267, 379n37; confusion of, with Lutheranism, 388n68; tenets of, 393n145; trials for, 257–264

Calvo de la Cantera, Lucio, 121

Camacho, Bartolomé, 313–317

Camacho, Joseph, 315–317

Caminos, José María, 129

Campa Coz, Félix de la, 338

Campeche, 23, 258, 305, 307; number of familiars in, 26t

Campos, Gerónimo de, 323

Campos, Martín de, 206–209, 228

Cañego, Cristóbal de, 220, 224

Cano, Antonio, 199

Canon Law, 13–14, 32, 36, 57, 359n28, 361n69, 378n12, 382n79

Cano y Moctezuma, José Ignacio, 195–197

Cantero, Antonio Joseph, 314–315

Caracho, Sebastián, 167

Cardoso, Juan, 247

Carrasco, Juan, 166

Carrasco, Manuel, 248

Carrillo y Alderete, Martín, 26

Carrión, Juan Pablo de, 155

Cartagena de Indias, Colombia, 235, 248; administrative center of Tribunal, xviii; Inquisition Tribunal in, 12, 14, 364n123, 388n61

cartas acordadas (circulars or letters of instruction from the *Suprema*), 18, 31, 108, 363n107, 380n57; on *limpieza de sangre* of ministers, 363n121; on peyote, 391n118; on rules and regulations, 362n81, 366n171; on secrecy, 366n161, 366n163, 366n165

Carvajal, Francisca Núñez de, 175, 240

Carvajal, Juan Antonio, 199

Carvajal, Léonor de, 176

Carvajal, Luis de, "El Mozo" (alias Joseph Lumbroso), xvii, 176–177, 387nn51–52, 387n55; proceedings against, 240–244

castas, xvi, 292–293, 308

Castillo, Josef Lázaro del, 178

Castro, Cristóbal de, 248

Castro, Diego de, 193

Castro, Juan de, 220–226 passim

Castro y Salgado, Antonio, 131, 380n49

Catholic doctrine, 3, 63, 81–103 passim, 167, 205, 314, 358nn14–15, 374n11, 376n36; instruction in, 167, 265–268, 321–324; and knowledge of prayers, 38, 63, 374n11; sacraments, 30, 154, 232, 241, 252, 268, 376n36; Ten Commandments, 5, 273

censorship: of books and ideas, 20, 89, 318–320, 363n117, 392n128, 392n130; Inquisition's role in, 82, 318–320; of politics and ideas, xiv, xviii, xix, 11, 119, 217, 259, 318, 327–330, 378n18. *See also* Index of Prohibited Books

Cerendieta, María, 340

Cervantes, Juan de, 145, 148, 241–243

Cervantes, Rafael de, 297

Cervantes de Salazar, Francisco, 140

Cervera, Pedro, 304

Chab, Diego, 306

chamber of the secret (*cámara del secreto*), 15–16, 83, 86, 126–128, 156–159, 179–181, 192–194, 250, 314, 327–329

Chan, Pablo, 233

Chapultepec, 268

character witnesses (*testigos de abono*), 42–43, 46, 53

Charles V, King of Spain (1517–1556), 4, 374n10, 391n110

Chavarría, Casiano, 200

Chiapas, 83, 186; commissariat of, 23, 24t, 258

chief constable (*alguacil mayor*): and arrest of suspected heretics, 16–17, 25–26, 36–37, 60–62, 90–93, 385n5, 386n29; and celebration of *auto da fé*, 153, 157, 159–163; definition of, 16–17; and execution of torture, 132–133; and prisons, 17, 60–62; salary of, 29t; as witness for execution of sentences, 245

chiromancy, 101, 110–111; definition of, 376n45, 390n96

chocolate, 286; and sorcery, 303

Christianity, xiii, 3, 64

Cires, Ángel de, 331, 332

Cisneros, Ignacio, 339

clergy, 3, 9, 20, 25, 107, 109; crimes of, 6t, 9t, 10t, 218, 333, 336; and solicitation in confession, 116–117

Colima: commissariat of, 24t; map of, 23, 258

commissariats, 368n198: maps of, 23, 258; in New Spain, 20, 22, 24t, 25–26, 230, 326, 334

commissaries (*comisarios*), 8, 25–26, 84; and *autos da fé*, 161; commissions of, 22, 24, 287; duties of, 24–25; and edicts of faith, 107, 115; geographical distribution of, 22, 24, 24t, 88–89, 364nn125–129; instructions and manual for, 91–98, 287–288, 368nn201–202, 390n95; map of regional districts of, 23, 258; oath of office of, 81; powers of, 24, 36; and prohibited books, 103, 109, 318–323 passim; and prohibited herbs, 313; rules and regulations for, 24, 31, 57–58, 84–86, 90–98; and taking of denunciations and testimonies, 303–307. *See also* commissariats

commissioners, 22. *See also* commissariats; commissaries

composition (*composición*), 50

compurgation, 46, 71, 371n271

confession, in trials: as goal of interrogation, 5, 30, 88; and need for full proof, 32–33, 38, 43–44, 47, 132–134, 367n183, 369n217; need to ensure validity of, 144; rules and regulations about, 63–78 passim, 88, 93; sacrament of, 5, 116–119, 154, 159–160, 216, 375n16; suspects' formulation of, 19, 38, 170–177 passim, 208, 209–213, 223–224, 228–231, 238, 295–297, 317; and torture, 44, 54, 134t, 138, 367n181, 370nn246–247, 374n15; to uncover hidden heretics, 63–65

confessors: edict of faith about, 116–118; instructions about, 63, 77–79, 159–160; and prisoners, 122, 375n16; and prohibited books, 99

confiscations, 26–28, 91, 382n85; of goods, 3, 27, 39, 47–50, 86–90, 170–177 passim, 194, 223–224, 243; of moneys, 18, 28t, 365n141, 365n148; procedures in, 37, 69–70, 78; of prohibited books, 101–102, 115, 186, 320; of prohibited herbs, 310–312 passim, 313; of property, 3, 18, 27, 236; as punishment, 382n85, 387n48

constables, xix, 13, 16–17, 21–26, 36–38 passim, 133, 153–163 passim, 220, 227, 245; and arrest of suspects, 299, 309–312; chief, 132, 29t, 385n5, 386n29; and confiscations in Veracruz, 325–331; instructions about, 59–62, 90–93

consultas de fé, 45, 84, 87, 140, 148, 157, 241–242, 298, 370n260

Contreras Estrada y Silva, Santiago Pantaleón, 178

conversos (converts), from Judaism to Christianity, 12, 235–236. *See also* crypto-Jews; New Christians

Coronel, Manuel, 251, 254

corozas (dunce or fool's caps/miters), 48, 51, 372n290; as punishment, 152, 155, 167–169, 174–176, 297–298; as symbols of shame, 48, 51, 167–169; used by convicted heretics in *autos da fé*, 152, 180

Cosamaluapan, 331

Cosío, Manuel Martínez de, 195–197, 200

Council of the Indies, 83

Council of the Inquisition (*La Suprema*), xvii, 7, 12, 14; correspondence with, 15–18, 31–33, 218; and decisions about peyote, 308, 377n6, 377n10; and decisions about procedures, 15–17, 26, 43, 123, 135, 359n31, 366n163, 381n73; definition of, 360n56, 374n7; on edicts of faith, 107–108, 391n119; on licenses to read prohibited books, 319, 333; on tribunal finances, 186–187

Council of Trent, 98, 376n36

Couoh, Pedro, 233

Coustos, John, 43, 132, 380n50

Creed, The (*Credo*), 38, 273, 295, 298, 374n11

Cristo, Ángela de, 283–284

Cruz, Ana, 340

Cruz, Francisco de la, 215–216

Cruz, Marcos de la, 218

crypto-Jews, 27–28, 145, 237, 240, 245, 365n142, 379n34, 384n100, 386n35; practices of, 235–236, 387n40, 387n51; sample trials and testimonies against, 235–256. *See also conversos*; Jews; *judaizantes*/judaizers

Cubas, Ignacio, 340

Cuello, Domingo, 172

Cuquio (village), 285–287, 289–290

curador (guardian or trustee), 65, 374n12

Dedieu, Jean Pierre, 53, 373n315

demons, 51, 111, 152; invoking of, 295, 300–302, 312

denunciations, xix, xx, 11, 22; anonymous, 30; for bigamy, 220–223; for blasphemy, 206–207, 210, 214; for Calvinism, 259–260; and commissaries, 24–25; and edicts of faith, 108, 110, 116, 118, 389n78; false, 54; for illuminism, 275, 286–287; for Jewish practices, 237–238, 250–255 passim; and oath of secrecy and procedures, 33–42 passim; rules and regulations about, 34, 59–64 passim, 386n31; self-denunciations, 213, 264, 267, 270, 337; for sexual immorality, 227–228, 230–231; for sorcery, 293–294, 296, 300, 302, 303–307; for using prohibited herbs, 309–317. *See also* accusations

devil, 51, 113, 118, 377n9; influence of and pact with, 111, 292–293, 308, 377n10

Deza y Ulloa, Francisco de, 15, 214, 280, 286, 310, 362n85

Díaz, Fructuoso, 261–262

Díaz, Hernando, 222

Díaz, Léonor, 170

Díaz, Manual, 170, 174

Díaz Calvillo, Juan Bautista, 337, 342

Díaz de Castilla, Manuel, 248, 254

Díaz de Montoya, Francisco, 246

Díaz Nieto, Diego, 171

Dios, Juan de, 216

Directorium inquisitorum (Handbook for Inquisitors), 14, 32–33, 58, 205, 319, 366n172, 370n264. *See also* Eimeric (or Eymeric), Nicolas

doctrines, false, 3, 38, 81–82, 89, 324; of the *alumbrados*, 392n142

documents, xvii, xix, xxiii, 38, 53; as historical evidence, 52–53; study of, 52–54

Domingo (African slave), 165

Dominican order, 32, 360n42, 391n110

Dominicans: and abuse of inquisitorial powers, 10; in control of Mexican Inquisition, 9–10; as inquisitors, 9, 9t

Donado, Joseph de la Concepción, 312
Donato, Leonardo, 30
Donís, Rodrigo, 303
Drake, Francis, 143

Ecclesiastical History, 324
Echevarría, Pedro de, 309–313
edict of faith (*edicto de fé*): against *alumbrados*,
    108–110; against diverse heresies, 108–109; impact
    of, on subsequent denunciations, 261–264, 286,
    313, 389n78; in Mexican Inquisition, 34, 107–108,
    108–121; against peyote and other prohibited herbs,
    113–114, 308, 377n10, 391n119; procedures about,
    83–84; against prohibited books, 114–116; against
    solicitation of sex in confessional, 116–118
edict of grace (*edicto de gracia*), 84
effigy: and absent heretics, 160, 176–177; and *autos
    da fé*, 152–153, 160, 236; and deceased heretics,
    160, 176–177; relaxation in, as punishment,
    49t, 120, 236, 254
Eimeric (Eymeric/Eymerich), Nicolas, 14, 32–33, 45,
    58, 205, 319, 366nn172–173, 370n264
Ek, Clemente, 230–231, 232
Ek, Francisco, 230–231
emigration, 236, 392n129
Encarnación, María de la, 255
Encarnación, Teresa de la, 276–278
Enchiridion Piarum Precationum, 323
England, 143, 268, 270–272
English, xvii, 265, 268–269, 329; interpretation of,
    326, 271; translation of, 326–327
Englishmen, 138, 271
Enríquez, Beatriz, 246, 249
Enríquez, Catalina, 171
Enríquez, Clara, 170
Enríquez, Diego, 175
Enríquez, Martín de, 156
Enríquez, Pedro, 172
Enríquez Lapavía, Beatríz, 171, 174–175
Episcopal Inquisition, in New Spain, xix, 7, 10–11,
    360n49; abuses of, 11, 385n6, 386n29; beginning of,
    8, 10, 385n4; end of, 11; and heresy, 2; and Indians,
    10–11, 259n37, 360n54, 391n120; trials of, 206–209,
    209–212, 213–214. *See also* Zumárraga, Juan de
Erasmus, 320
Esparza y Escobar, Josef María de, 178
Espejo, Antonio de, 138–139
Espinosa, Ignacio, 339
Espinosa, Maríana, 339
Espinosa, Sebastiana de, 287
Espinosa y Arévalo, Diego de, 7, 22, 82; career of,
    82–83, 375n24; and Instructions to Mexican

Inquisition, 7, 29, 57–58, 91; and procedures and
    rules, 82–91, 156
excommunication: for breaking oath of secrecy, 92,
    97–98, 107, 131, 136; and edicts of faith, 15, 114, 120,
    341; for failure to report heresy, 34, 114, 228; for
    heresy, 109, 224, 243, 338; for non-compliance,
    226, 229–230, 288, 299, 374n9; for reading
    prohibited books, 102, 104; for removing edicts
    of faith, 118, 121; for using prohibited herbs, 311
executions: and *autos da fé*, 51, 52, 179; burning at the
    stake, 4, 9, 11, 52, 153, 236; by secular authorities,
    52; and torture, 191; witnessing of, 384n99
Expugatorio, 115, 329; definition of, 378n14
"Exurge, Domine, judica causam tuam," 130, 151,
    380n46

familiars (*familiares*), 16, 138–139; and *autos da fé*,
    150–153, 159–163, 165, 178–185 passim; distribution
    of, in regional commissariats, 26t; as inquisitorial
    spies and informers, 24–25; as lay officials of
    Inquisition, 21–22; oath of, 81; powers, duties, and
    privileges of, 21–22, 90–94, 97–98, 334–335,
    363nn121–122; rules and regulations about, 79,
    84–90 passim
Farfán, Pedro, 140
Ferdinand II (king), 2, 5, 235
Ferdinand VII (king), 120
Fernández, Ignacio, 338
Fernández Correa, Rodrigo, 249
Fernández de Bonilla, Alonso, 27, 162, 321
Fernández de Torres, Simón, 249
Ferris, Felipe, 341
Ferrón, Juan, 141
Figerora, Nuño Suárez de (alias Don Nuño Perea),
    248, 255
fines, monetary, 50, 50t
flogging, 47–48, 50. *See also* whipping
Fonseca, Pedro de, 145
Fonseca, Tomás de, 124
fornication, 119, 167, 229–230, 250; edicts of faith
    against, 109, 119
Fors, Jacob, 267–270
Foxe, John, 32
Franciscans: and control of Mexican Inquisition,
    9–10, 359n40; and punishment of Indians, 8–10,
    9t; as witnesses, 275, 309–313
Franco Taváres, Rodrigo, 144; sentence of torture
    against, 145; torture session of, 145–149
Fuentes, Bernarbé de, 305, 307

Galán, Bernabé, 169
Galante y Saavedra, Nicolás, 330

Gallegos de Velasco, Joseph, 281, 283–284

Gálvez, Bernardo de, 383n98

Gálvez, Matías de, 182, 383n97

Gama, Juan Antonio de, 215

gambling: blasphemy during, 205–206; edicts and
    rules against, 109; trials about, 206–209

García, Isabel, 155

García, Juan, 215

García Armenteros, Josef, 336–337

García Bravo, Joseph, 326–327, 329

García de la Mora, Javier, 315

garrucha, for torture, 133

Garzarón, Francisco de, 264

geomancy, 101, 110–111; definition of, 376n40, 390n96

Gil Rodríguez, Rafael Crisanto, 131

Gómez, Antonio, 124

Gómez, María, 253

Gómez de Mier, Juan, 15, 281–282, 288, 362n75

Gómez Navarro, Manuel, 173

Gómez Silbeyral, Manuel, 124

González, Laureano, 178

González, Thomasa: decision of Prosecutor about,
    286; denunciation against, 284–286; investigation
    against, 287–288; testimony against, 289–291

González de Benavides, Gil, 300–301

González de Espinosa, Sebastián, 285–287

Granada, Gabriel de, 247

Granada, Rafael de, 249

Granados, Fabián, 177

Granero Dávalos, Alonso, 16, 362n78

Greenleaf, Richard E., xix, xxi, 206, 309, 357n7,
    367n189, 368n210, 372n308; on Episcopal
    inquisition, 385n4; on Inquisition and Indians,
    359n37, 359n39, 360n43, 360n50, 360n52, 376n34,
    391n122; on Mexican Inquisition, 359nn34–35,
    360n41, 360n48, 361n57, 361n61, 380n56, 385n2,
    388n68; on visitations of Mexican Tribunal, 379n3,
    388nn60–61, 388n64

Gregory IX (pope), 2

Guadalajara, 248, 249, 285–288, 317, 340–341,
    379n39; audiencia of, 375n17; bishop of, 262n78;
    bishopric of, 169; commissariat of, 23, 24t, 258;
    number of familiars in, 26t

Guanajuato, 292, 341; commissariat of, 23, 24t, 258

Guatemala, 11, 83, 111–119 passim, 131–138 passim, 154,
    172, 186, 257, 303, 308, 375n17, 383n97; commis-
    sariat of, 23, 24t, 258; number of familiars in, 26t

Guerrero, Marcos de, 148–149

guilt, 1–3, 11, 29, 43–52 passim, 65, 145, 160, 272, 293;
    absolution from, 224; admission of, 43, 70–71, 229,
    236; assumption of, 3, 31, 76; confession of, 38–40,
    43, 71–77, 89, 102, 107–109, 123, 133, 135; decisions

about, 45; denial or rejection of, 70, 303; discovery
    of, 40; gravity of, 103; presumption of, 37, 365n156;
    proof of, 1; suspicion of, 38, 46; validity of, 20;
    verdict of, 46, 167, 169, 181, 186, 219, 244

Guinea, 268

Guipúzcoa, 154

Gutiérrez, Juan, 178

Gutiérrez, Teresa, 303

Gutiérrez Dávila, Julián, 265

Gutiérrez de Páramo, Tomás, 304

Gutiérrez Flores, Juan, 127

hallucinogens: edicts against, 108, 113–114; Mexican
    Inquisition on, 391nn116–118; Suprema decision on,
    391n119; trials for use of, 308–317. *See also* peyote

Havana, 331–332, 393; commissariat of, 23, 258;
    governor of, 272

Henningsen, Gustav, 7, 219

Henríquez, Micaela, 254

Heras Serrano, Vicente de las, 179, 185

Heredia, Diego de, 165

heresy: acts of, 1, 42, 275; authors of, 100; beliefs of, 4,
    8, 270, 325, 376n36, 377n7, 381n70; blasphemy, 6t,
    78, 88, 178; in blood, 208; in books, 82, 103, 115;
    crimes of, 24, 144, 318; and depravity, 5, 9, 82–83,
    108, 111–116, 119, 138, 240, 298, 300; and error, 4,
    325; intentions of, 5; and judaizers, 175; movements
    of, 2, 376n37; and passages, 392n141; practices of, 5,
    9t, 10t, 154, 178–181, 205–210, 243, 292; proposi-
    tions of, 6t, 7, 11–12, 20, 42, 109, 133t, 255, 318;
    revelations of, 251, 255, 275–291, 388n63, 390n89;
    sects of, 250; statements of, 43, 109, 325

heretics: Anglicans, 257, 264–266, 272, 389nn84–85;
    blasphemers, 154, 166, 209, 212–214, 379n39;
    bodies of exhumed, 253; burned in effigy, 153, 176;
    Calvinists, 257, 259, 260–267; crypto-Jews, 235–256;
    crypto-Muslims, 108, 134t; illuminists, 274–276,
    389n86, 393n142; judaizantes, xx, 123, 134t, 144,
    365n148, 387–388n56; Lutherans, 10t, 12, 52, 108,
    134t, 139, 143, 150, 257, 267–269; procession of,
    in *autos da fé,* 150–154, 160; Quakers, 270–273.
    See also alumbrados; bigamy; heresy; illuminism;
    judaizantes/judaizers; Protestantism; sorcery;
    witchcraft

heretics, accused, 1, 2, 15, 19–20, 25, 32–36 passim,
    131–139; defense and rights of, 365n152, 367n188,
    369n224, 371n271, 388n64; evidence against, 30;
    formally, by *fiscal,* 15, 16, 299; goods confiscated
    from, 27; oath of secrecy from, 31; rules and
    regulations on, 60–80 passim, 85–94 passim;
    and torture, 374n15

Hernández, Diego, 322

Hernández, Gonzalo, 227–228

Hernández, Magdalena, 167

Hernández, Pablo, 166

Herrera, Ana de, 169

Herrera, Bernarbé de (alias Barracillo), 305

Herrera, Gabriel de, 175

Herrera, Jurado de, 189, 191

Herrera, Miguel Francisco de, 331–333

Herrera, Petrona de, 315–317

Herrera Sotillo, María Asunción, 219, 236, 362nn77–78; on acquittals, 271n270, 271n272; on Inquisition finances, 365n148; on punishments, 257; on sentences, 372n296; on torture, 370n251; on witchcraft, 293

Herrera y Arteaga, Diego de, 25, 364n133

heterodoxy, 2, 8, 11, 52

Hidalgo y Costilla, Miguel, 118–119, 318, 337–341; edict of faith against, 118–121; revolt led by, 323, 360n55, 378n20; trial for support given to revolt of, 337–342

Hocaba, 230–234

Hoctun, 233

Holy Office. See Inquisition; Inquisition Tribunal in New Spain

Homza, Lu Ann, xviii, xix, 3, 53, 357n1, 357n8, 358n18, 367n189, 373n314

Honduras, 83, 111–116 passim, 119, 270, 272; commissariat of, 23, 24t, 258

Hordes, Stanley M., 28, 365n142, 384n100, 386n35, 387n40

Horta y Barroso, Antonio de, 304–307

Huchim, Alonso, 232

Huerta, Miguel Núñez de, 253

Huidobro, Marcos Alonso de, 250, 256, 388n60

Huiquinaqui (hacienda), 289

Hurtado, Gaspar, 220–226 passim

illuminism, 274, 389n86; men accused of, 275–284; women accused of, 284–291. See also alumbrados; mysticism

imprisonment: cost of, paid by prisoners' goods, 37, 125; cruel conditions of, 122–123; and hunger and food, 123, 124–128; and isolation, 123; permanent, 383n93; temporary, 26. See also prisons

incest, 6t, 109, 227

Index of Prohibited Books (index librorum prohibitorum), 98, 112, 114, 318–320, 321–323, 325, 329, 378n15, 392n142; and catalogue of prohibited books, 112, 114–115, 321–323; edicts of faith and, 113–115, 329; rules about, 98–104

Indians, 11; bibles owned by, 321; cases against, 8–9, 10–11; false accusations of, 233–234; removal of, from jurisdiction of Inquisition, 11, 58, 82, 89; servants and porters of Tribunal, 188–193; torture of, 10; use of peyote and other hallucinogens of, 113–114, 302, 305–307, 309–313, 316; as witnesses or accomplices, 210–212, 237–239, 285, 289, 294–296, 299, 340

Inquisition: and colonial authority and power, xiv, xv, 8, 12, 52, 206; and heresy in New Spain, 2–5; in Spain, 4–5. See also Inquisition Tribunal in New Spain

Inquisition Tribunal in New Spain: compared with Spain, 4–9; creation of, 4, 8–10; crimes prosecuted by, 6t; defense strategies of accused, 18, 39–43; finances of, 26–29; geographical territory of, 22–26; and Indians, 11, 58, 82, 89; ministers, officials, and privileges, 12–27; and punishments, 46–52; role of gossip and rumor in, 25, 36; subordinate personnel of, 18–21, 22–26; torture in, 57–58, 64–66, 71–74, 84, 132–149. See also Inquisition; inquisitors; procedures

inquisitors (inquisidores): as chief ministers of tribunals, 12–13, 14–15; expenses and salaries of, 26–29; goals of, 3–5; jurisdiction of, 4–5, 6t; and manuals and instructions, 57–104; multiple roles of, 1–2; privileges of, 14–15; procedures and rules for, 29–30, 31–52 passim; represented by commissaries (comisarios) in distant regions, 22–25

Irishmen, 272, 273

Isabella I (queen), 2, 235

jail (cárcel). See prisons

jailers (alcaides), xix, 13, 199; activities and duties of, 17–18, 37, 124–127, 131, 138–139, 187–194; role of, in autos da fé, 151–164 passim; role of, in torture, 145; rules and regulations about, 61–67, 74–79, 83–90 passim; salaries of, 29t

Jansenists, 324, 393n145

Jasso, Francisco, 167

Jesuits, 25, 232, 281, 324–325, 366n176; expulsion of, from New World, 393n145

Jews, xiv, 80, 235; burning and execution of, 9, 236, 245; confiscations from, 186; converts, and anti-Semitism, 12, 208; crypto-Jews, 27–28, 145, 237; expulsion of, 4; false accusations against, 235; persecution of, 235–236; Portuguese, 131, 170–174, 235–236; punishment of, 170–177; trials and testimonies against, 235–256. See also conversos; crypto-Jews; judaizantes/judaizers

Jiménez Casarín, José, 340

Jiménez de Cisneros, Francisco, 9

Jorge, Francisco, 176–177

Juárez, Sebastián, 166
judaizantes/judaizers, xx, 123, 134t, 144, 365n148,
    387–388n56; accused and convicted, 175, 235–236;
    and heresy, 9t, 10t; trials of, 237–245. *See also*
    crypto-Jews; Jews
judge of confiscated goods, 86, 158, 161

Kagan, Richard L., 1, 30, 357n4, 365n154,
    368n211
Kamen, Henry, 5, 52–53, 373n310; on finances,
    363n108; on prisoners' defense, 369nn223–225,
    369n236; on procedures, 365n155, 366n159,
    366n169, 367n177, 368n203, 369n221, 372n288,
    372n295; on proof in trials, 367n183, 367nn189–92;
    on Spanish Inquisition, 358n26, 359n29; on use
    of torture, 370n249, 370n253, 370n255

Laís, Jorge, 172
Landa, Diego de: and *auto da fé*, 10, 152–153, 161; as
    monastic inquisitor, 8, 10, 359n35; and *sermón de fe*,
    152–153, 161; and torture, 10; and usurpation of
    Inquisitorial jurisdiction, 10, 359n35, 360n45
Lara, Gertrúdis de, 304
Larrea, Francisco, 329
lashes, 136; as punishment, 31, 47–48, 148, 152,
    154–155, 165–175 passim, 181, 219, 226, 380n40.
    See also flogging; whipping
Law of Moses, 169–177, 240–242, 246–248, 250
Laws of the Indies (*Leyes de Indias*), 57, 359n28,
    386n19
Lea, Henry Charles, xvii, 20, 31, 357n1, 358n13,
    359n30, 367n189, 374n9
León, Gerónimo, 302
León Plaza, Juan de, 125–127, 145, 187–192
León y de la Cueva, Catalina de, 175–176
Lima, administrative center of Peruvian Inquisition
    Tribunal, xviii, xix, 12–14, 254, 361n61, 362n78,
    364n123, 364n140, 365n140, 368n200
limpieza de sangre (purity of blood), 18, 89, 236,
    375n29; as perquisite for service in tribunal,
    89–91, 363n121; proof of, 86–90, 97
Lisbon, 155, 166, 245–248, 265, 268
Llop, Pedro, 129, 131
Llorente, Juan Antonio, xii, 357nn2–3, 361n61
Lobo Guerrero, Bartolomé, 241–243, 362n78,
    362n85
London, 264, 265, 270–272, 393n147
London Company, 268
Loperena, Félix, 199
López, Ana, 170
López, Antonio, 177
López, Diego, 173

López, Francisca, 169
López, José Antonio, 199
López, Pedro, 126–127, 379n38
López Barba, Andrés, 180–181
López Correa, Francisco, 246
López de Legaspi, Miguel, 210–214, 237–239, 300
López de Lizardi, Juan, 289–291
López de Morales, Antonio, 177
López de Vivero, Vasco, 148, 241–244
López de Zárate, Juan, 294
López Monforte, Tomás, 249
López Núñez, Manuel, 254
López Sanz, Francisco, 18, 363n101
López Torrecilla, Matías, 118
López Xardon, Hernán, 260–262
love magic, 167, 382n86, 390n107. *See also* sexual
    magic; sexual witchcraft
Lucena, Manuel de, 175
Luguí, Gerónimo de, 141
Luis (African slave), 166
Luis, Ricardo, 307
Luna, Juan Eusebio de, 178
Luther, Martin, 4, 80, 140–142, 174, 257, 319
Lutheranism, 10t, 12, 52, 108, 134t, 139, 143, 150;
    confusion of, with Calvinism, 257, 388n68;
    identified with Protestantism, 257, 259; trials for,
    257, 267–269

Machado, Lorenzo, 124
Madrid, María Josefa de, 383n98
Maldonado, María, 222
Mangado y Clavijo, Diego, 130
Mañozca, Pedro de, 127, 149, 242–243, 260–264
Manrique de Lara, Alonso, 31, 366n160
Manual of Prayers, 323
Marengo, Salvador, 339, 340, 341
María (mulatta): denunciation of, 313; review of case
    against, 317; testimony against, 315–316
Marín, Diego, 281–282
Márquez, Lorenza, 305–306
marriage, 112, 155; cases about, 219–227. *See also*
    bigamy
Martín, Diego, 281
Martínez, Josef de Jesús María, 178
Martínez, María Gertrudis ("La Mocha"), 178
Martínez Rincón, Santiago, 179–184
Martos de Bohórques, Gonzalo, 145, 240, 259–260
Matías, Nicolás, 310, 311–313
May, Juan, 232
Mayo, Alberto, 124
Mayorga, Diego de, 229–230
Mazo, José del, 341

Medina, García de, 221

Medina Rico, Pedro de, 128–129, 249–250, 365n141, 379n35, 388nn60–61

Medinilla, Pedro de, 299

Meléndez Carreño, Joseph, 285–286

Mella, Manuel de, 253

Méndez, Justa, 171

Méndez, Manuel, 254

Méndez, Nuño: arrest and confession of, 228; denunciation of, 227–228; punishment of, 230; sentence for, 229–230; trial of, 227–230

Méndez, Tomés, 249

Méndez Bilón, Antonio, 245

Méndez de Silva, Diego, 246

Méndez de Villa Viciosa, Juan, 248

Merida, 23, 230–231, 258, 303–307, 320–321; number of familiars in, 26t

messenger (nuncio), 13, 19, 90; activities of, 178–184; salary of, 29t

Mexía Salmerón, Baltazar, 245

Mexican Inquisition. See Inquisition Tribunal in New Spain

Mexico City: as administrative center of Mexican Tribunal, xviii, xix, xx, 22, 23, 26, 36; autos da fé in, 150–185; centrality of, 14; edicts of faith proclaimed in, 107–121; Inquisition palace in, 121–123, 128–131, 186–192, 194–198; number of familiars in, 21–22, 26t

Michoacán, 25, 83, 119, 155, 187, 323–324, 380n41, 393n150; commissariat of, 23, 24t, 258

Mier y Villar, Juan de, 118, 178–179, 183–185, 325, 335, 362n75

Miguel, Cristóbal, 125, 259–264, 389n79; arrest of, 260; denunciation against, 259; prison rations of, 125; testimonies against, 260–264; trial of, 259–264

Miguel, Gregorio, 125

Miranda, Lope de, 140

Miranda, Manuel, 339

Mohammedanism, 6t, 102

Molina, Alonso de, 320–321

Molina y Salazar, Antonio Sebastián de Toledo, 8

Monastic Inquisition in New Spain, xix, 8–10; abuses of, 10; and Dominicans, 9–10; end of, 10–11; and Franciscans, 9–10. See also Landa, Diego de

Montalvo, Enrique, 124

Montes, Juan, 166

Moors, 2, 18, 59, 80, 102, 167, 238, 303, 375n29

Mora, Gerardo, 271, 273

Morales, Juan de, 309–311

Moreira, Doña Mariquita, 254

Morelos, José María, 318

Morgan, Michael, 138–144, 380n51; arrest warrant for, 138; ratification of confession by, 144; torture session of, 140–144

Morton, Joshua, 264–266, 270

Mota, Marina de la, 251

Moya de Conteras, Pedro, 108–110, 138–144, 154–157, 162–164, 302, 319–321, 361n61, 382n79

mulattos, 22, 127, 167, 206, 215–217, 304, 379n39. See also castas

Muñetones, Joseph, 315

Muñoz, Diego, 25

Murillo Ordóñez, Sebastián, 288

mysticism, 274–275, 389–390nn86–89; false, 6t, 274–275, 389nn86–87, 390nn88–89. See also alumbrados; illuminism

Nájera, Matías de, 199

Navarro de Isla, Pedro, 130

necromancy, 101, 110–111; definition of, 376n46; trial for, 299–301

New Christians, 27–28, 90, 170–175, 236, 240, 245. See also conversos; crypto-Jews

New England, 268

Nicaragua, 11, 22, 83, 111–119 passim, 138; commissariat of, 23, 24t, 258

Nicolás, Domingo, 167

Núñez de Rojas, Gerónimo, 247

Núñez de Rumbos, Benito, 288

Núñez Navarro, Francisco, 246

nuns, 117–118, 275–281, 373, 383

oath of secrecy, 30–35, 74, 342; in Inquisition commissions, 287; taken by witnesses, 41, 94, 207–212, 215–220, 228, 260–264, 271, 286–291, 314–316, 331–332

Oaxaca, 10, 83, 154, 165, 186, 294, 300, 338, 391n112, 393n144; commissariat of, 23, 24t, 258

Ocampo, Diego de, 303

Ometochtzin, Don Carlos, 11

Omnimoda, 9

Ordóñez, Juan de, 285, 287–290

Ordóñez Marañon, Juana de, 290, 390n97

Orozco, Cristóbal, 340

Ortíz, Catalina, 168

Ortíz, Pedro de, 275, 278–279

Ortíz de Saavedra, Diego, 25

Orvé, Manuel, 200

Our Father (prayer), 38, 273, 374n11

Pacheco, Brigida, 304

Padilla, Pedro de, 323

palace of the Inquisition, 128–129, 151–158 passim, 160, 164, 183, 187, 271; and *autos da fé*, 382n80; inventory of assets of, 194–198; location of, 383n96; prisons in, 121–123; repairs to, 384n107

Palma, Diego de la, 207

Parián (marketplace), 338–341, 393n151

Pascuala (mulatta slave): denunciation of, 214–215; testimonies against, 215–217; trial of, 214–217

Paul, Saint, 119, 168, 274, 378n19

Payés y Mora, Manuel, 178

Peace of the Soul, 322

Peña, Francisco, 14, 20, 32–33, 45, 58, 319, 361n65, 366nn172–176

Peña, Sebastián de la, 171

penalties: and edicts of faith, 117–118, 121, 131; for reading prohibited books, 103, 115; for using prohibited herbs, 114

penance (sentence and punishment), 26–27, 30, 45–49, 274, 372n291; in *auto da fé*, 150–156; as punishment, 50t, 51–52, 64–65, 76, 80, 85–90, 220–225, 230, 245, 255–259

Peñas, Eugenio de las, 265–269, 270–273, 317

Peralta, Alonso de, 17, 145, 148–149, 241–243, 260–263

Peréz, Juana, 302

Pérez, Isabel, 177

Pérez, Juana, 168

Pérez Camelo, Gonzalo, 234

Pérez de Carrión, Hernán, 207–208

perjury (*testigo falso*), 31, 34–35, 109, 295, 365n163

Peters, Edward, 2, 35; on Eimeric's manual, 366n172; on heresy, 358n11; on procedures, 357n2, 365n153, 367nn178–180, 369n219; on proof in trials, 370n246, 370nn248–249; on torture, 357n6, 367n184, 367n195, 374n15, 380n52

peyote: as divinatory plant, 113, 377n11, 391n120; edict of faith against, 108, 113–114, 391n119; in healing and curing practices, 113; Inquisition opinion on, 377n6, 377n10, 391n115; trials for use of, 308–309, 313–317; used by non-Indians, 113, 313, 391nn117–118. *See also* hallucinogens; pipiltzintzintli

Philip II (king), 4, 235, 259; death of, 257; and establishment of Inquisition in New Spain, 8, 11–12, 81–82; and monetary subventions, 27; and *Suprema*, 31

Philip III (king), 14; and Treaty of London, 257

Philip IV (king), 98, 130

Philosophes, 119, 378n18

pipiltzintzintli: definition of, 308; denunciations against use of, 309–310; as divinatory plant, 309; and sentence and decision in Xochimilco case, 312; used by Indians in Xochimilco, 310–312; used by

non-Indians in healing and curing, 309. *See also* hallucinogens; peyote

pirates, 257

Plata, Gaspar de los Reyes, 165

polygamy, 6t, 10, 178, 218–219, 220–227. *See also* bigamy

Ponce, Antonio, 41

Pontifical History, 323

poor person's ration, 85, 375n28

Pórras, Gonzalo de, 208

Pórras, Juan de: arrest and confession of, 208; denunciation and initial testimony against, 206–208; sentence of, 209; violation of procedures in trial of, 385n5

Portillo, Esteban del, 140–141

Prado y Ovejero, Bernardo de, 121, 325; chamber of, in Inquisition palace, 197

Prayers and Spiritual Exercises of the Christian Soul, 323

Prestes, Marcos, 155

prisons: communication in, 123–174, 379n34; conditions in, 122–123; daily life in, 122–123, 124–129, 187–192, 378n22, 384n108; escape from, 122, 172, 379n28; imprisonment in, 250–256, 259, 388n58; location of, 122, 129–130; oath of secrecy about, 31, 382n81; officials in charge of, 16–17, 19, 21; perpetual, 383n93; rules and regulations about, 85; secret, 30, 37, 123, 165, 174, 178, 187, 212, 250; transportation to, 16; visitation at, 122. *See also* imprisonment

Proano, Diego de, 296

procedures: dual role of inquisitor, 1–2; instructions for Tribunal in New Spain, 82–91; limits of and regulations about, 40, 57–58, 63; manuals published for, 59–82, 91–98; origins of, 1–2, 8–12; use of torture in, 132–134, 135–149

prosecutor (*fiscal*), 1, 12–18, 35, 119–120, 128, 214, 240, 251–252, 260; formal accusations of, 279, 286, 297, 315–317; naming of, 361n62, 361n73; role of, in *auto da fé*, 159–162; rules and regulations about, 39–40, 44, 60, 63–69, 74–77, 84–86, 88, 362n79, 369n217; salary of, 26

Protestantism, 6t, 316, 318. *See also* Anglicans; Calvinism; Lutheranism; Quakers

Protestant Reformation, 4, 376n36

Protestants, xiv, xx, 3–4, 6t, 12, 41, 132, 134t, 145, 376n36; and torture, 133–134, 134t, 376, 389n84; trials and testimonies against, 257–273. *See also* Anglicans; Calvinism; Lutheranism

Provisorato de Indios (Indian Inquisition), 11; discussion of, 359n37, 360n54; jurisdiction of, 360n50, 376n34, 391n122

Puerto, Sancho del, 304

Puerto Caballos, Honduras, 270

Pulo, Hierónimo, 154

purity of blood. See *limpieza de sangre*

pyromancy, 101, 292; definition of, 376n43

Quakers, 270–272

qualifiers (*calificadores*), 13–14, 20, 36, 59–60, 115, 140, 281, 329; instructions about, 59–60, 76–78, 363n115; protocol and place of, in *autos da fé*, 161–162

Quemadero, 372n305

Quiroz, Gutierre Bernardo de, 127, 145, 148, 260, 263

Racine, Bonaventure, 324–325, 393n145

rack (*potro*), 4, 132–133, 135–138, 142–148 passim, 242, 380n51

Ramírez, Hernán, 322

Ramírez, Marco Antonio, 322

Ramírez, Miguel, 217

Ramírez de Montilla, Manuel, 254

Rawlings, Helen, 44; on prisoners' need to recite prayers, 368n212; on procedures, 367n189, 367n193, 370nn249–250, 370n261, 372n288, 372n295, 372n308, 380n53, 381n65

Rebollo, Juan, 212, 221–222

reconciliation (sentence and punishment), 45–48, 49t, 69, 152, 176, 236–241, 252, 382n84; rules and regulations about, 70–80 passim, 87; voluntary, 264–270

reconquest: and expulsion of Jews from Spain, 235; influence of, on orthodoxy in Spain, 2

Regueron, Francisco, 200

Rejón, María, 305

relaxation (sentence and punishment), 33, 45–48, 152, 236, 257, 372n292; appeals about, 87; in effigy, 49t, 120; in person, 49, 49t, 372n296; rules and regulations about, 71, 73–74, 87

Rengel, Rodrigo, 205

Reyes, Antón de los, 126–127, 379n39; probable torture of, 379n40

Riego, Santiago del, 148, 241

Ríos, Esperanza, 246

Ríos, Pedro de los, 132, 139–140, 144, 296, 321, 323, 382nn77–78; instructions from, about *autos da fé*, 156–164

Rivera, Diego de la, 192

Rivera, Margarita de, 253

Rivera, María de, 252

Rivera, Pedro Cabrillo de, 260–261

Rivet, Edward, 270–273

Roa, Juan Simón de, 214–217

Robayna, Francisca de, 295

Rodríguez, Anacleto: letter from commissary about, 334; order from inquisition about, 334–335; petition for license to read prohibited books from, 333–334; response from commissary about, 335

Rodríguez, Andrés, 174

Rodríguez, Antonio, 176

Rodríguez, Constanza, 170

Rodríguez, Domingo, 176

Rodríguez, Duarte, 174

Rodríguez, Francisco, 169

Rodríguez, Gerónimo, 169–170

Rodríguez, Hernando, 246

Rodríguez, Isabel, 170

Rodríguez, Jorge, 124

Rodríguez, Manuel, 172

Rodríguez, Pedro, 171–172

Rodríguez, Sebastián, 171

Rodríguez, Vicente, 338

Rodríguez, Violante, 170

Rodríguez de Andrade, Isabel, 175

Rodríguez de Huerta, Melchor, 251

Rodríguez del Bosque, Isabel, 247

Rodríguez del Bosque, Juana, 248

Rodríguez del Bosque, María, 248, 251

Rodríguez de Ledesma, Francisco, 125

Rodríguez de Matos, Francisco, 175, 177, 240

Rodríguez de Matos, Manuel, 177

Rodríguez de Olvera, Mathías, 252

Rodríguez López, Melchor, 250

Rodríguez Núñez, Manuel (alias Caraballo), 248, 252

Rodríguez Suárez, Juan, 247

Rodríguez Tristán, Marcos, 256

Romero Villalón, Tomás, 286

Rosado, Juana de, 303–305

rosary: beads of, 210, 226, 227; and prayer, 38, 212

Rosas, José Gil de, 338

Rosas, José María, 199

Rueda, Gabriel de, 321

Ruiz, José María, 199

Ruiz Calderón, Pedro: denunciation of, 299–300; testimony against, 300–302

Ruiz de Vallejo, Manuel, 330

Saavedra, Juan de, 309–311

sacraments, 30, 154, 231–232, 241, 252–253, 268; Council of Trent and, 376n36. *See also* confession: sacrament of; marriage

Sainz de Alfaro y Beaumont, Isidoro, 121

Salamanca, Juan de: confession of, 238–239; denunciation of, 237–238; testimony of wife against, 239–240

Salazar, Felipe, 215

Salazar, Gonzalo de, 165

San Antonio, Nicolasa de, 275, 277–278

sanbenitos (penitential garments): and *autos da fé*, 154–186 passim, 372n302; descriptions of, 47–48, 51, 372n290; as garment of shame, 47, 51, 375n19; making of, 180; as punishment, 80, 152, 167–176 passim, 219, 383n94; rules and regulations about, 69, 80; symbolism of, 80, 152

Sánchez, Fernando, 339

Sánchez, Francisco, 341

Sánchez, Gregoria, 340

Sánchez, Josefa, 340

Sánchez, José Ignacio, 337, 342

Sánchez, Magdalena, 339

Sánchez, Matías, 337

Sánchez, Pascuala, 339

Sánchez, Pedro, 312

Sánchez de Tagle, Pedro Anselmo, 130

Sande, Francisco de, 140

Sandre, Pascual, 125

San Joseph, Petronilla de, 276, 279

San Juan de Ulúa (prison), 270

Santa Ana, Juan de: arrest of, 220; denunciations and initial testimony against, 275–277, 278–279; final decision of case of, 284; letter from, 277–278; testimony against, 280–284

Santiago, Simón de, 125

Santo Domingo (church and convent of), 151, 177, 179, 183, 261, 263; and Tribunal, 382n80, 383n96

Santo Domingo, Nicolasa de, 255

Santos García, Francisco, 16, 27, 362n78

Sarmiento, Manuel, 341

Sayavedra, María Josefa, 178

science, 334

secrecy, 1, 2; of burial of prisoners, 77; as cause of complications in prisoners' defense, 42; in collecting witness testimony, 36; and defense attorney, 75; importance of, in trials, 30–33, 53; oath of, 31, 33, 35, 65; punishment for violation of, 366n163, 382n81; requirement for, after acquittal, 46; in withholding names of witnesses, 2

secretaries (*secretarios*), 12–13, 16–17; instructions and rules about, 90–91, 158–162 passim, 361n73; for reading of sentences, 182; as witnesses to executions, 52, 153

self-denunciations, 213, 264, 267, 270, 337

sentences, suspended, 40t, 46, 86, 250, 371n272

sequestration of goods, 16, 30, 40, 170, 200, 220, 223; and Inquisition finances, 27–29, 365n150; inventory

of, 226; officials in charge of, 16–19, 25, 90, 138, 374nn8–9; and prisons, 122–124; procedures in, 36–37; rules and regulations about, 60–62, 75, 79, 85–86, 93–95

Serda, Manuel de la, 250

Sermón de fe (Sermon of Faith), 108; and *autos da fé*, 152–153, 161, 163

sexual crimes. *See* bestiality; bigamy; fornication; incest; love magic; polygamy; sexual magic; sexual witchcraft; sodomy; solicitation

sexual magic, 302, 303, 305, 377n8, 382nn86–87, 390n102

sexual witchcraft, xv, 302, 303, 390n102

Sigüenza, 82–83, 91

Sobresilla, Juan de, 283

sodomy, 6t, 109, 167, 306; prosecution of, 377n7

solicitation, of sex in confessional: denunciations for, 230–234; edict of faith against, 117–118

Solórzano, Josef Ortiz de, 337

Sopuerta, Hernando de, 322

sorcery (*hechicería*): and female body parts and fluids, 294–299, 303–307; in marital conflicts, 167–169; practices of, 292–293; and prohibited books, 101; ritual items used in, 168–169; in sexual witchcraft and love magic, 295–299, 302–307; trials and denunciations for, 292–299, 302–303, 303–307; women's use of, 167–169. *See also* love magic; sexual magic; witchcraft

Sosa, Agustín, 306

Sotelo, Alonso de, 263

Soto, Juan de, 285–287, 289

Sotomayor, Carlos de Andrade, 289–291

Sotomayor, Maria de: arrest of, 220; denunciation and initial testimony against, 220–222; exile of, 224–226; inventory of sequestered goods of, 226–227; letter and petition from, 225; marriage to Juan de Castro, 220–226 passim; marriage to Gaspar Hurtado 220–226 passim; sentence of, 224; testimony against, 220–224

Sotuta, 307

St. Andrew's Cross, 47–48, 51, 152

strappado. See *garrucha*

Sugastí, Francisco de, 306–307

Sugastí, Iñigo de, 306–307

Suprema, La. See Council of the Inquisition

Tacotlan, 287, 289–290

Taváres, María de la Encarnación, 178

Tavárez, Manuel, 124

Téllez Girón, Francisco, 178

Tepepan, 309–312

testimony. *See* witnesses

Texcoco, 10, 138, 143, 174, 313–317, 360

Tinoco, Miguel, 255

Tinoco, Rodrigo, 231

Tirado y Priego, José Antonio, 337, 342

Tlacomulco, 214–216

Tlaxcala, 83, 155, 161, 169, 296, 391n110; commissariat of, 23, 24t, 258

Tocano, Miguel de, 331

toca torture, 133–134, 147–148

Toledo, Francisca de, 208

Tolosa, Juan de, 304

Tomson, Robert, 51–52, 150, 372n301

Toribio, Leonora de, 304

Torquemada, Tomás de, 32, 57, 59, 362n74

Torre, Manuel de la, 340

Torres, Cristóbal, 222–224

Torres, Domingo de, 154

torture: abuses of, 9–10; and confessions, 32–33, 43–45, 374nn14–15; and crypto-Jews/judaizers, 144–149, 253–256, 388n65; frequency of, 44; manual for, 135–138; methods of, 43–45, 132, 135; permitted types of, 132–135; in prisons, 191; and Protestants, 134t, 138–144, 257, 259; role of physicians in, 13; rules for application of, 57–58, 64–74, 84, 367nn181–182, 370n247, 370nn251–252. *See also* rack

torture chamber (*sala de tormento*), 44, 132–135, 140–141, 144, 146, 148, 242, 252

Treasury of Devotions, 322

Treaty of London, 257

Trejo, Pedro de, 155

Tremblers. *See* Quakers

Tribunal of the Holy Office of the Inquisition. *See* Inquisition Tribunal in New Spain

Trinidad, Josef Antonio, 178

Troncoso, Nicolás, 329

Urban VIII (pope), 28

Urisar, Ventura, 331–332

Valderrama, Juan de, 154

Valdés, Fernando de: career of, 59, 82, 368n206, 369n217, 369n227, 369n233, 369n235, 370n245; *Instructions of the Holy Office*, xix, 20, 32, 42, 57–80, 366n170, 370n259, 370nn262–263, 371nn268–269, 388n60

Valencia, Cristóbal de: arrest of, 231; confession of, 231–233; Maya testimony against, 230–231

Valencia, Martín de, 9

Vargas, Catalina de, 307

Vázquez, Juan, 126–127, 380n41

Vázquez, Pedro, 305

Vega, José Miguel, 200

Vega, Pedro de, 194

Velasco y Oviedo, Francisco Xavier de, 276, 279–280, 282–284

Veracruz, 138, 167–169, 226, 245–249, 265, 272, 325–326, 330, 331–333; commissariat of, 24t, 331–334; map of commissariat of, 23, 258; port of, 169, 226, 268, 318–320, 335, 389n81

verdicts, 20, 45–49, 150, 219, 236, 251–252

Verdugo, Cristóbal, 190–191, 384n109

Vergara, Agustín de, 187

Vergara, Diego de, 277, 282–284

Verrepeo, Simón, 323, 392n143

Vicuña, Andrés de, 314

Villa-Flores, Javier, 384n1, 385n10

Villafranca, Gaspar de, 166

Villagra, Francisco Alonso de, 148, 241, 242

Villagran, Josefa, 339

Villalobos, Inés de, 168

Villate, Juan de: arrest of, 211; denunciation of, 210; sentence of, 212; trial of, 209–213

violations: of edicts of faith, 117; of Inquisition procedures, 249–256; of oath of secrecy, 31, 366n163; of rules and regulations, 249, 370–380n40, 386n29, 388nn62–67; of sumptuary prohibitions, 389n78; in trials of Jews, 249–256

Virginia, 268

visitations: district, 85, 88; by inquisitors, 25, 35, 51, 59, 88, 235, 319; to jails and prisons, 80, 85, 122, 191; rules about, 78, 85, 88; of ships (*visitas de naos*), 25, 94–95, 319–320; by visiting judge, 249–256, 379n35, 388n60

Voltaire, 35, 367n194

warrants. *See* arrests

whipping, 166, 216. *See also* flogging; lashes

White Island, 272

witchcraft (*brujería*), 5, 6t, 7t; edicts of faith against, 109, 111–113; gender and, 167–169; Inquisition stance on, 292–293; trials for, 293–307; types of, 88. *See also* sorcery

witches, 250, 292–294, 304, 306

witnesses, 1–2, 12; character, 43, 46, 53, 371n271; defense against prosecution's, 40–43; oaths of secrecy taken by, 30–31; qualification of testimonies of, 20–21; reliability of, 33–35, 368n203, 381n67; rules about, 36–37, 61–78, 88, 92–94, 96. *See also* denunciations; oath of secrecy

women, xiv, 25; and bigamy, 218–219; and fornication, 119; lighter punishments for, 47–48; rules and regulations about, 79; solicitation of sex in confessional from, 116–118; and sorcery, 112, 167–169; and superstitions, 112; and torture, 44; trials and denunciations against, 219–227, 284–291, 293–299, 302–308, 313–317

Ximénez, Ygnacio José, 334–335
Ximénez Cubero, Francisco, 215–217
Xochimilco, 309–312

Yaxcaba, 306
Yllescas, Gerónimo de, 323
Yucatan: bishop of, 152, 161; bishopric of, 83, 186, 231, 359n35, 359n37, 360nn44–45, 360n54, 378n16, 381n64, 386n32; commissariat of, 8, 10, 24t, 83, 230, 303, 320–322; map of commissariat of, 23, 258; peninsula of, 153; province of, 8–10, 111–116, 119, 230, 303–307 passim, 320–322, 391n116

Zacatecas: commissariat of, 23, 24t, 25, 258; number of familiars in, 26t
Zamora, 339
Zapata y Cisneros, Antonio de, 98
Zarasúa, Josef Anastasio, 178
Zárate, Juan Javier, 294, 296
Zelaya, 285, 290
Zenón, Roque, 130
Zumárraga, Juan de: as apostolic inquisitor, 385nn4–5; as episcopal inquisitor, 9–11; trials conducted by, 206–209, 210–212, 213–214, 224–229, 294–299; types of cases tried by, 10t
Zúñiga, José Antonio, 199